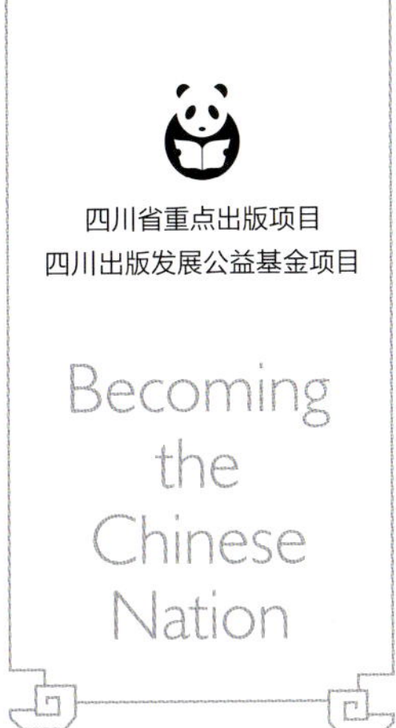

100

一百件文物中的
中华民族共同体历史记忆

The Historical Memories
of the Multi-ethnic Chinese Nation in
100 Cultural Relics

中国民族博物馆　编纂｜郑　茜　主编｜迟剑锋　英译

四川民族出版社

图书在版编目（CIP）数据

何以中华：一百件文物中的中华民族共同体历史记忆：汉文、英文 / 中国民族博物馆编纂；郑茜主编. —成都：四川民族出版社，2023. 8

ISBN 978-7-5733-0861-0

Ⅰ. ①何… Ⅱ. ①中… ②郑… Ⅲ. ①历史文物—研究—中国—汉、英 ②中华民族—民族意识—研究—汉、英 Ⅳ. ①K870.4②C955.2

中国版本图书馆CIP数据核字（2022）第202335号

何以中华：一百件文物中的中华民族共同体历史记忆

Becoming the Chinese Nation: The Historical Memories of the Multi-ethnic Chinese Nation in 100 Cultural Relics

中国民族博物馆 / 编纂　郑茜 / 主编　迟剑锋 / 英译

出 版 人	泽仁扎西
总 策 划	唐　怡
责任编辑	赵正梅　董　冰
特约编辑	迟剑锋
装帧设计	李　庆
责任印制	温祥宇
出版发行	四川民族出版社（四川省成都市青羊区敬业路108号）
成品尺寸	250mm × 305mm
印　　张	60
字　　数	638千
制　　作	成都华桐美术设计有限公司
印　　刷	雅昌文化（集团）有限公司
版　　次	2023年8月第1版
印　　次	2023年8月第1次印刷
书　　号	ISBN 978-7-5733-0861-0
定　　价	598.00元

何以中华

一百件文物中的中华民族共同体历史记忆

Becoming the Chinese Nation:
The Historical Memories of the Multi-ethnic Chinese
Nation in 100 Cultural Relics

著作人员

统　纂

郑　茜

编　著

唐兰冬　　邱先鹏　　周玉州

序言

壹

“中华民族”概念的提出与确立，是近现代中国的一件大事。

20世纪初，梁启超首次提出“中华民族”的概念，进而阐释“中华民族由多数民族混合而成”的观点。李大钊则提出以各民族融合为基础的“新中华民族主义”，热烈呼唤“中华民族之伟大复活”。当时，西方国家试图制造和加深中国边疆危机，利用各民族单一的民族意识分裂中国这个历史悠久的统一多民族国家。

此时，“中华民族”的概念从苍茫厚重的历史巨幕中浮现出来并愈加凸显。这是一个古老的文明国家对她所遭受的西方殖民劫难的历史回应，是中国人在面临亡国灭种之危时对自我身份认同的形塑和强化，是中华民族在历经几千年的自在发展历程后，最终演进为一个自觉民族实体的显著标志。

贰

中华文明依靠考古学重构自身历史，同样是近现代中国的一件大事。

20世纪初，随着近代西方考古学的建立，人类认识历史的方式发生了一次重大转折。此后，仅仅依靠文献史料讲述历史的传统被怀疑，人类历史叙事体系面临着一次重构——将传统的文本叙述转变为以物质文化为核心的考古学叙事。

事实上，中国是世界上唯一拥有数千年连续历史记录的国家。但是，随着历史话语权向考古学漂移，中华历史的可信度受到质疑，不仅上古史变得破碎，关于三皇五帝的历史信仰也被解构。一时间，我们需要重新思考“我们从哪里来”“我们是谁”等问题。思想家梁启超，也是“新史学”的奠基人，紧迫地想要重建新的民族和国家史。中国“考古学之父”李济，立志“寻绎中国人的原始出来”。中国第一代考古学家苏秉琦，则认定中国考古的直接目标就是要回答“中国文化的起源、中华民族的形成、统一多民族国家的形成和发展”。

叁

实现中华文明和中华民族形成发展史的“物”“史”互证，是贯穿20世纪的理想。

一百年来，中国考古学经过艰辛掘进，将历史地层深处的物像一一揭露出来，渐次还原中华文明多元一体的起源和发展演进轨迹。显然，我们无比幸运，因为我们比历史上任何一个时期的中国人，都更加真切地看见了中华文化溯源至一万年前的时间深度，看见了那些鲜活的先民形象和生动的场景细节。与此同时，我们也前所未有地坚定了历史自信：中华文明是世界上唯一绵延不断且以国家形态发展至今的伟大文明。

关于“中华民族”的考古学形象，也一步一步显现。事实上，一个世纪以来，关于中华民族形成发展的历史阐释和表达，经历了民族史研究和考古发掘的互证，不断走向纵深。尽管如此，我们对中华民族历史发展脉络的阐释，主要还是依靠文本来完成的；从“物”“史”互证的角度，对中华民族多元一体历史格局的成因加以系统揭示，对古代民族通过交往交流交融汇聚成一个命运共同体的演进历程加以真切还原，进而构建关于中华民族形成发展源流的完整物像叙事体系，依然还是一个理想。

有鉴于此，2015年，我们启动“中华民族形成发展史实物表征体系研究”课题，并持续开展这项研究工作。这是因为，我们深刻地认识到：构建一个权威的阐释、表达、展示正确的中华民族历史观的收藏和展示体系，应当是中国民族博物馆的重要使命和任务。

在认真研究的基础上，我们分阶段、分步骤完成这样一个严肃的文化使命：用考古文物和民族文物作为主要载体，以“物”“史”互证为核心，着力构建一个能够承载中华民族形成发展历史过程的文物谱系，完成基于“物”的中华民族共同体历史叙事，解码共同体的历史基因，深化对中华民族历史发展规律的科学认识，为铸牢中华民族共同体意识提供有力的理论支撑。

肆

当然，这是一项非常艰苦、充满挑战的工作。

艰苦何在？在于中华文物数量极多，如何在科学构建中华民族形成发展史阐释文本的前提条件下，寻找那些对各民族共同缔造、发展、巩固统一多民族国家具有高度表征力的历史物证，遴选那些对各民族交融汇聚成多元一体的中华民族具有准确叙事力的物化见证？

挑战又何在？在于在考古学与民族学/人类学的双重视野下，构建中华民族形成发展史的实物表征体系。我们不仅需要探寻、梳理、分析那些对理解我国古代民族起源、迁徙、分化、融汇、共生的历史进程具有潜在实证价值的考古文物，凭借其蕴涵的集体记忆和象征意义，来系统还原和深刻再现中华民族共同体形成发展的历史轨迹和演进场景，还需要借鉴民族学/人类学关于夷、蛮、狄、戎等古代族系融入中华民族历史过程的研究成果，系统梳理出承载中央与边疆、华夏与夷狄、农耕与游牧互动交融史实的民族学/人类学器物见证，揭示并阐释背后的商贸互市、婚姻盟誓、战争迁徙、文化传播等族际交往史，最后完成关于“中华民族”历史叙事的物性话语链条。

只有这样，基于“物”的中华民族形成发展史才具有科学的内在逻辑。

伍

在策划一个面对大众的展示体系时，我们选择了“一百件文物”的承载形式，用一个具有意义的数字去完成一次象征性的宏大历史叙事。

一百件文物，既可以理解为一部微缩版的中华民族形成发展史，也可以理解为一个具有高度象征意义的叙事框架。

如何阐释和讲述这一百件文物，也让我们探索良久。文物是点状的，而历史叙事需要绵密与连贯的形式。我们遴选一百件文物的真正目的，不是去孤立地呈现这些文物，而是要通过这些文物爬梳中华民族形成发展史的宏大叙事。所以，这些文物就像一个个演员，演员本身可以有A角、B角的替换，但不可替换的是剧本，是故事。

事实上，要通过一百件文物实现中华民族共同体历史记忆的叙事功能，每件文物需要“扮演”三个角色——或者说，我们需要在每件文物之上，发掘出三层意义：第一层，着眼于文物本体，揭示这件文物本身的来龙去脉及其独特魅力；第二层，揭示这件文物在其时代所牵涉的历史背景、人物事件及其所代表的时代性文化意义；第三层，揭示这件文物辐照和映射的中华民族形成发展的宏大历史脉络，显示其在话语链条上的象征性意义。

比如，河姆渡骨耜。骨耜具有上古时代用于翻土的农耕器具的本体功能，这是第一层意义；骨耜作为七千年前河姆渡文化的代表性文物，关涉河姆渡文化最重要的特征——发达的耜耕稻作农业，这是第二层意义；骨耜作为世界上最早的稻作农业的见证物，辐照了“中华民族的先民是世界稻作文化的发明者”的史实，这是第三层意义。只有抵达第三层意义，河姆渡骨耜才最终完成它在中华民族形成发展历史脉络中的意义表征，才成为“何以中华”宏大叙事的必要性物化语汇。

总之，我们试图通过这些文物的信息总和，描绘出一部中华民族形成发展的历史；我们试图让当今中国56个民族的历史起源及其交往交流交融的脉络轨迹，能够在这一部文物谱系中呈现；我们还试图让中华民族的一系列重要文化符号，也能在一百件文物中找到源头。当然，中华民族作为一个庞大的人口群体，是怎样通过历史上一场又一场波澜壮阔的大交融汇聚而成，也蕴含在这部文物谱系中。

所以，更有可能的是，这一百件文物就是一百个密码，它们蕴含着中华文明的根性基因，我们一一敲击这些密码，借以探索一个人类历史上独一无二的现象——中华文明何以能够历经一代代王朝更迭，却从未割断其文化传统？统一多民族中国何以经历几度南北对峙和分裂，却总能再度聚合，一次又一次重新走向更高水平的统一和更加紧密的交融聚合？“大一统”价值观何以能深深植根于中华民族的血脉，使得各民族即使面对历史上的各种分裂力量仍能凝聚不散，最终发展成为休戚与共、荣辱与共、生死与共、命运与共的共同体？

陆

因此，中华民族形成发展史的文物表述，应当是具有重要象征意义的文化事件。一方面，构筑一部实物实证的中华民族共同体历史，对培育和塑造56个民族共同的历史文化认同，将产生重要影响；另一方面，在全球化时代，我们要向世界说明“中华民族”不是一个“想象的共同体”，而是客观的自觉历史实体，这也需要突破“中华民族”的历史书写方式，以物的实景呈现中华民族共同体形成发展的内在机制和演进路径。

总之，中国民族博物馆通过持续性开展“中华民族形成发展史实物表征体系研究”，构筑了一部实物实证的中华民族共同体历史记忆展示传播文本体系。这是一个具有突破性价值的工作，将推动中华民族共同体理论体系、史料体系、话语体系的创新和发展。

柒

最后，我要致敬我们的团队。

上述工作需要一个团队来完成，需要付出漫长而艰苦的历时性努力。通过不断的积累和不懈的坚持，我们最终呈现出展览展示、出版传播的一体化成果。

2015年，我们成立“中华民族形成发展史实物表征体系研究”课题组，成员主要由中国民族博物馆研究部工作人员组成。我们还邀请历史学、民族史学、民族学/人类学等学科的专家加入课题组。其中，长期在文博机构工作、对中华民族形成发展史作过深入研究的首都博物馆原副馆长高凯军，对本课题研究做出了突出贡献。他全面梳理了涉及中华民族形成发展史的数千件代表性文物，为我们推进本课题研究打下了重要基础。

此后，我与课题组成员唐兰冬、邱先鹏、周玉州花费近两年时间，围绕更加准确的“物”“史”互证目标，构建出“何以中华——一百件文物中的中华民族共同体历史记忆”文物谱系。为检验这一成果的科学性，我们特别邀请中国社会科学院学部委员、著名考古学家王巍，中国人民大学历史学院考古学及博物馆学专业教授魏坚，中国文化遗产研究院总工程师曹兵武，中国社会科学院学部委员、中国人类学会会长郝时远，北京大学教授、著名人类学家王铭铭，中国社会科学院民族学与人类学研究所研究员易华，对已形成的文本进行评审。在及时采纳各位专家的意见基础上，我们进一步完善了对文物的遴选与阐释。

这一百件文物涉及全国各地近60家博物馆的珍贵藏品。课题组成员不辞辛劳，分别与这些博物馆取得联系，得到了它们的大力支持，取得了相关文物图像信息的使用权。此外，“何以中华——一百件文物中的中华民族共同体历史记忆”展分别在北京、广西、甘肃等地推出，取得了良好的社会反响。

了解到“何以中华——一百件文物中的中华民族共同体历史记忆”展的相关情况后，四川民族出版社副社长、副总编辑唐怡提出将一百件文物的信息挖掘整理出版的建议。博物馆展览本乃依托空间叙事进行大众传播的文化媒介，因此我们热烈响应这个进一步增强中华民族共同体意识与理念的出版机会。为此，课题组成员又投入近一年时间，完成内容整理与写作。其中，唐兰冬主要负责秦汉、魏晋南北朝至隋唐时期文物的内容编撰；邱先鹏主要负责宋、辽、金、元、明、清时期文物的内容编撰；周玉州主要负责涉及中华文明多元一体起源、华夏形成、华夷五方格局等文物的内容编撰。我则致力于通篇布局以及对所有文稿的修润改写，以期更加符合精品出版物的质量要求。

借此机会，我还想表达对四川民族出版社诸位同仁的感谢。四川民族出版社副社长、副总编辑唐怡既是出版项目的策划人，也是项目资金申请的执行人。她顺利申请到四川省重点出版项目、四川出版发展公益基金项目资助，使得本书出版有了扎实的资金支持。她协调各方工作，积极与各方沟通，实现了无缝衔接，保证了本书的顺利出版。四川民族出版社编辑赵江梅，她不仅对书稿做了严谨细致的编辑加工，还做了大量的出版业务对接工作。四川民族出版社编辑董冰，承担了后期的编辑工作。此外，本书英文译者、特约编辑迟剑锋，贡献了高质量的英译文本，总体把控书稿的编辑规范和设计方案，提出了诸多宝贵意见。

正是有了一个基于共同理想和追求而建立起来的团队，我们才能向社会和读者献出这样一部作品。

郑　茜

（第十四届全国政协委员，中国民族博物馆副馆长，

《何以中华——一百件文物中的中华民族共同体历史记忆》策展人）

目录 CONTENTS

第二章　中华民族的自在发展
Chapter Two　The Ontological Development of the Chinese Nation

第三章　中华民族自觉实体的形成
Chapter Three　The Chinese Nation: From Self-Being to Self-Making

Prologue

The Roots of Human Life in over One Million Years

Let's ponder the question: What can epitomize the remotest history of the Chinese nation?

General Secretary Xi Jinping points out that: "The great achievements made in archaeological discovery evidence that China has a one-million-year history of human traces, a 10,000-year history of human culture and a more-than-5,000-year history of human civilization."

Su Bingqi, a celebrated archaeologist in the 20th century, sums up the history of the Chinese nation as follows: "China boasts over-one-million-year cultural roots, forges 10,000-year civilization, owns 5,000-year written history, and exists as a unified nation-state in more than 2,000 years."

As the case stands, the long history signals a "collective autobiography" of the Chinese nation and its ancestors in the universe. Simultaneously, Chinese civilization continues to evolve and develop since the ancient times. In a way, no other nations or countries have left such a legacy to human society today.

Now, we will start from the roots of human life in over one million years and trace the origin of the Chinese nation.

序章

超过百万年的人类生命根系

如果用一句话概括中华民族从远古走来的历史，那会是什么？

习近平总书记说："我国考古发现的重大成就实证了我国百万年的人类史、一万年的文化史、五千多年的文明史……"

20世纪著名的考古学家苏秉琦，也曾这样总结中国历史："超百万年的文化根系，上万年的文明起步，五千年的古国，两千年的中华一统实体。"

事实上，这就是中华民族及其先民在这颗星球上书写的一份独一无二的履历，因为中华文明是世界上唯一没有中断过的文明，几乎没有其他任何一个民族和国家，能够向今天的人类社会交出这样一份履历。

那么，就让我们从超过百万年的人类生命根系开始，来追溯中华民族的起源。

为什么说中华大地有超过百万年的人类生命史?

中国古人类连续进化论

元谋人上门齿化石

01

The Fossils of the Upper Incisors of *Homo erectus yuanmouensis*

文物简读

这两颗典型的铲形门齿实证了中华大地超过百万年的人类生命史和古人类连续发展的特征。

“元谋人”腾空出世

1965年，钱方、浦余庆等学者在云南省楚雄彝族自治州元谋县上那蚌村开展地质考察工作。在一位放牛老人的指引下，他们来到距村西约一公里处的山沟里，在一个土包下发现了云南马的化石，同时出土的还有两颗人类上门齿化石。考察队将这批化石标本带回北京，两颗人类上门齿化石引起诸多学者的重视。1976年春，多家科研单位经过多次测定，测出这两颗牙齿化石的绝对地质年代为距今170万±10万年。这一结果震惊中外。

因门齿的发现地点在云南省元谋县，化石主人被命名为“元谋人”。元谋人的发现将中国古人类历史向前推了一百多万年。

中国古人类连续发展的物证

这两颗人类上门齿化石呈浅灰白色，石化程度很高，属于同一个成年个体。两颗牙齿的一个显著特点是齿冠舌面有一个凹面，两边缘翻卷成棱，如同铲子形状，是典型的铲形门齿。

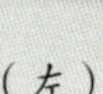

（左）　（右）

名称：元谋人上门齿化石

年代：距今约170万年

规格：长2厘米，宽1.13厘米（左）；长2.1厘米，宽1.14厘米（右）

出土地点：云南省楚雄彝族自治州元谋县上那蚌村

收藏单位：中国地质博物馆

Name: The Fossils of the Upper Incisors of *Homo erectus yuanmouensis*

Historical Period: *c.* 1.7 million years ago

Length: 2 cm, Width: 1.13 cm (The Left)

Length: 2.1 cm, Width: 1.14 cm (The Right)

Excavation Site: Upper Nabeng Village, Yuanmou County, Chuxiong Yi Autonomous Prefecture, Yunnan Province

Housed in: The Geological Museum of China

比起170万年的古老程度，两颗门齿的铲形特征才是更让人震惊的发现！这是因为，今天绝大多数中国人都有铲形门齿！如在中国汉族人口中，有铲形门齿者，男性占89.6%，女性占95.2%；在中国蒙古族人口中，有铲形门齿者，男女均占91.5%；在东亚化石人群和现代人群中，铲形门齿均具有较高的出现率。相反，在世界其他人种中，具有铲形门齿特征者，或者比例为零，或者最高不超过5%，只有在黑人中，男性占9.0%，女性占7.8%。

这是否表明元谋人与现代蒙古人种之间有着某种源流关系？

迄今为止，中华大地上陆续发掘出了不同时期的古人类骨骼遗存，如陕西蓝田人、湖北郧县人、北京房山北京人、安徽和县人、辽宁金牛山人，再如山西丁村人、广东马坝人、内蒙古河套人、黑龙江哈尔滨人、吉林安图人、广西柳江人、贵州兴义人、福建东山人、台湾左镇人等，此外，山东、河南、西藏、新疆等地区也发现了古人类的化石及活动遗迹。从人类发展阶段来看，这些古人类遗址涵盖了直立人、早期智人、晚期智人等人类发展的各个时期；从地域范围来看，它们基本涵盖了中华大地的各个区域。而在上述所有遗址中，凡发现了上门齿的，其铲形特征均十分明显！美国人类学家赫德利希卡因此指出，铲形门齿是蒙古人种的特质。

蒙古人种是对亚洲人种的泛称，其主要特征是有黄色的皮肤、较低的鼻梁、较高的颧骨、铲形门齿、发达的上眼睑褶等。随着中国古人类化石的不断发现，除铲形门齿成为中国古人类体质的重要特征外，还有越来越多的体质特征也被发现在现代蒙古人种身上得到延续。

这又表明，远古先民不仅与现代蒙古人种之间有着某种源流关系，而且呈现出了连续发展的特征。古人类学家由此提出了中国古人类连续进化论。

中华古人类的基因交流

当然，人类在活动的过程中必然会与周边人群发生交流和融合。在中国古人类化石中也发现了一些具有其他人种体质特征的遗存，如南京汤山人鼻梁高耸，具有欧洲人的体质特征。因此，中国古人类在连续进化的过程中与其他人种发生了基因交流，这也是现在各人种之间没有形成生殖隔离的原因。因为从生物学的角度来说，一个物种的不同群体相互隔离百万年以上，便会演变成两个物种，形成生殖隔离。

考古发现客观揭示了这一结果：中华民族的起源具有本土性特征，中华民族是在中华大地独特的地理环境中经过百万年的连续发展、进化形成的群体，其发展过程表现为以本土连续进化为主，以与周边古人类基因交流的镶嵌进化为辅的综合进化模式。

因此，我们可以相信：中华大地是蒙古人种的故乡；中华民族的祖先应是自远古洪荒时期就繁衍生息于这片大地之上，并且继续在这里创造着历史与文化的人们；中华民族在后世的发展中不断吸收外来的文化与族群成分，并使自身变得更加强大。

The two typical shovel-shaped incisors demonstrate the over-one-million-year history of human life and the continuous development of human life in China.

In 1965, Qian Fang, Pu Yuqing and other scholars carried out geological survey at Upper Nabeng Village, Yuanmou County, Chuxiong Yi Autonomous Prefecture, Yunnan Province. Guided by an old cattle herder, they came to a mountain gully *c.* one kilometer west of the village and discovered the fossils of Yunnan Pony under an earth mound, as well as two fossils of human upper incisors. In the spring of 1976, the absolute geochronology of the two teeth fossils was determined to be 1,700,000 ± 100,000 years ago by several research institutions. The discovery rocked both Chinese and foreign academia.

Since the incisors were unearthed in Yuanmou County, Yunnan Province, the owner of the fossils was termed *Homo erectus yuanmouensis*. The discovery of *Homo erectus yuanmouensis* proved that the history *Hominin* in China appeared more than one million years earlier.

The two fossils of human upper incisors look grayish white. Highly fossilized, they belong to the same adult man. Noticeably, the two teeth feature concave surfaces on *corona dentis*, and the marginal parts roll into edges, looking like two shovels in shape. They typify shovel-shaped incisors.

Mongoloid signifies a general term for Asian race. *Mongoloid* has yellow skin, lower bridge of nose, higher cheekbones, shovel-shaped incisors and developed upper eyelid wrinkles. As the fossils of *Hominin* have been successively discovered in China, more physical features have been evinced in modern *Mongoloid* in addition to shovel-shaped incisors.

This indicates incontestably that ancient ancestors shared the same origin with modern *Mongoloid* in continuous development. On this basis, paleoanthropologists put forward the theory of continuous evolution of *Hominin* in China.

Chapter One

The Formation and Origin of the Chinese Nation

To discuss the formation and origin of the Chinese nation, we survey our land first.

China faces the sea in the east, adjoins the Mongolian Plateau in the north, and leans on the Pamirs Plateau in the west. The Qinghai-Tibet Plateau stands majestically in the southwest, and the Yunnan-Guizhou Plateau features rugged cliffs. The terrain forms a four-side natural barrier and safeguards a relatively-independent geographical space.

In the geographical space line up three regions, i.e. high plateaus in the west, mountains in the middle and low plains in the east. Accordingly, three types of modes of production came to rise: nomadism on western and northern grasslands, crop farming on central dry land, and rice farming in the east and south. Three different economic forms, on the one hand, justified an imbalanced and diversified development pattern and produced differences in economy, culture and customs; on the other hand, established an interdependent and complementary relationship among various regions. For example, long-term economic exchanges were carried out between nomadic areas in the west & north and agricultural areas in the central, east & south. Close cultural exchanges arouse therefrom, which forged deep emotional tie or sibship.

As a result, a diversified and complementary geographical space spurred a historical trend, in which ancient residents enhanced unity and cohesion, converging into the surging historical river from all quarters. This laid natural and geographical foundations for the widely dissemination of the idea "grand unification". Diasporic and isolated ancient ethnic groups were propelled to contact, reconcile and assimilate. In the rise and fall, they became a unified ensemble and eventually fused into a community with a shared future.

In brief, the Chinese nation took shape under such natural circumstances.

第一章

中华民族的孕育与起源

中华民族的孕育与起源，应当从我们的国土说起。

中华大地东濒大海，北揽蒙古高原，西据帕米尔高原。西南的青藏高原横空出世，南部的云贵高原崎岖陡峭——环列的自然屏障，拱卫出一个相对独立的地理单元。

在这个地理单元内部，西高东低地排列着三大区域——西部的高原，中部的山地，东部的平原；三大区域内各自发展出了相应的经济形态——西部和北部的草原游牧带，中部的旱地种植带，东部和南部的稻作农业带。而三种不同的经济形态，一方面形成了不平衡的多元发展格局，带来经济、文化、风俗的多样性差异；另一方面却又结成了相互依赖、难以分割的互补依存关系。比如，北部西部的游牧区与中部东部南部的农业区之间，产生长期的经济交往关系，在此基础上交织出密切的文化交流，熔铸出深厚的情感交融乃至血缘交融关系。

这样，一个多元互补的地理格局，就使生活在其间的古代居民形成了一股内向汇聚的历史趋势，他们从不同方向汇进同一条浩荡澎湃的历史大流。这构成了使“大一统”思想深入人心的自然地理基础——它驱动着分散孤立的古代民族，不断地接触、碰撞、混杂、融合，你来我去，我来你去，我中有你，你中有我，此兴彼替，最终融汇成一个有着深刻关联的命运共同体。

中华民族就是在这一自然环境里形成的。

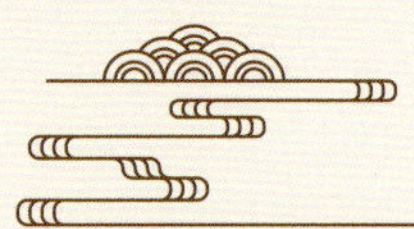

中华文明的多元一体起源

——中华民族多元一体历史格局的起点

The Origin of the Pluralistic and Integrated Chinese Civilization, or the Beginning of the Historical Pattern of the Multi-ethnic Chinese Nation

新石器时期中华文明的多元一体起源，是我们认识中华民族形成发展史的起点。

在过去一百年里，中国考古学取得的重大成就之一，就是深刻地揭示了中华文明在起源阶段的多元一体格局。对于早期中华文明呈现出的多元格局，苏秉琦做了一个形象的比喻：在中华大地上，文明的起源呈“满天星斗”之势，璀璨闪耀。另一位考古学家严文明，也打了一个比喻：中华文明的多元起源，就像是中华大地上开出了一朵“重瓣花朵”——不同区系的文化如同缤纷的花瓣，共同组成了一个大花朵。

多姿多彩的史前文化区系在沿着各自的脉络递进发展时，也在频繁地交流互动，并逐渐形成了历史学家张光直所称的“中国相互作用圈”：“到了约公元前4000年，我们就看见了一个会持续一千多年的有力的程序的开始，那就是这些文化彼此密切联系起来……”

以此为起点，满天星斗的光芒开始交相辉映，交织汇聚——不同区系的文化建立方国，步入文明；它们结成一个个巨大的文化丛体，相互竞争又交流互鉴，呈现出越来越一体化的趋势，使“最初的中国”喷薄而出。

The pluralistic and integrated pattern of Chinese civilization in the Neolithic Period facilitates our understanding of the formation and development of the Chinese nation.

In the last century, one of the great achievements of Chinese archaeology was to insightfully theorize the pluralistic and integrated pattern of Chinese civilization in the early stage. In this regard, Su Bingqi makes a vivid metaphor. Multiple civilizations dotted the "starry sky" (i.e. the land of China) and shone brilliantly. Yan Wenming, an archaeologist, compares Chinese civilization to a "double flower". Diverse regional cultures look like colorful petals and form a flower together.

While progressing independently in history, these colorful prehistoric cultural regions frequently communicated and interacted with each other. This bolstered the birth of "Sphere of Interaction in China", a term from historian Zhang Guangzhi. As he views, "In around 4,000 B.C., a dynamic process started and lasted for more than 1,000 years. To put it in another way, these cultures were closely linked..."

The light of the "starry sky" whereafter sparkled and interwove. In line with various regional cultures, tribe-states appeared and civilizations commenced. Tribe-states forged an extensive cultural alliance in which they competed with and learnt from each other. As the trend of unification intensified, the idea of "the Earliest China" emerged.

名称：河姆渡骨耜

年代：距今约7000年（河姆渡文化早期）

规格：长18.2厘米，刃宽9.8厘米，上部宽5厘米，上部厚4.2厘米

出土地点：浙江省余姚市河姆渡村

收藏单位：浙江省博物馆

Name: Hemudu Bone *Si* (耜, Shovel-Shaped Farming Tool in the Ancient Times)

Historical Period: *c.* 7,000 years ago (The Early Stage of the Hemudu Culture)

Length: 18.2 cm, Width (Blade): 9.8 cm, Width (The Upper Part): 5 cm, Thickness (The Upper Part): 4.2 cm

Excavation Site: Hemudu Village, Yuyao City, Zhejiang Province

Housed in: Zhejiang Provincial Museum

世界上最早的水稻是谁培育出来的呢?

世界稻作农业的发明者

河姆渡骨耜

02

Hemudu Bone *Si* (耜, Shovel-Shaped Farming Tool in the Ancient Times)

文物简读

这件骨制农具反映了七千多年前长江下游地区稻作农业的发展水平，它与同时出土的大量稻谷遗存一道，证实了中华先民是世界稻作农业文明的先驱。

河姆渡的稻作农业

这是1973年。在浙江余姚河姆渡遗址，黑褐色的土层中，突然闪出了一些黄灿灿的金色小颗粒。与空气接触后，它们很快变成了泥土的颜色。考古工作者捡起褐色颗粒仔细辨认，几乎无法相信自己的眼睛——它们居然是碳化了的稻谷!

据碳14测定，这些碳化谷物的年代为距今6950 ± 130年。也就是说，它们已在地下埋藏了约7000年!

河姆渡遗址的发现，成为中国考古史上的一件大事。遗址内发现了大量谷物遗存——稻谷、稻壳、茎叶等交互混杂，形成 0.2—0.5米厚的堆积层，最厚处超过1米。其堆积数量之多，保存程度之完好，为考古史所罕见。

如此多的谷物是怎样生产出来的？河姆渡遗址出土了170余件骨耜农具，其中两件骨耜的柄，竟然是用藤条绑扎着的木棒。这些农具展现出七千年前的耕作情景。此外，河姆渡遗址还出土了大量遗存：大规模的干栏式建筑，最早的木构水井，陶器、骨器、编织物、石制农具，以及窖藏的橡子、南酸枣、菱角等果实；其中，仅骨镞就有一千余件。这些丰富的遗存把一个沉睡了七千年的稻米聚落的形象赫然呈现在今人眼前，也把江南饭稻羹鱼的传统回溯到历史长河的上游——新石器时代。

中国是世界稻作农业的起源地

河姆渡遗址发现后，考古学界曾一度认为它是世界上最早的农耕文化遗存。但事实远非如此。中国南方地区的一次次考古发现，一再改写了稻作农业起源的历史纪录。

1993年，江西万年县仙人洞遗址，发现了1.2万年前的野生稻植硅石和一万年前的栽培稻植硅石；1995年，湖南道县玉蟾岩遗址，发现了距今1.8万—1.4万年的人工栽培稻标本，再度刷新了人类最早栽培水稻的历史纪录。

进入21世纪，栽培水稻考古一再取得突破。2000年，浙江浦江县的上山遗址惊现于世。这里陆续出土了一万多年前的栽培水稻以及镰形石器、石刀、石磨盘、石磨棒等工具，还发现了最早的定居村落遗迹和大量彩陶遗存。目前，学术界一致认为，上山遗址是已发现的世界上最早的稻作农业遗存，是世界稻作文化的起源地。2020年，袁隆平为上山遗址题词："万年上山，世界稻源"。

此后，杭州茅山遗址和余姚施岙遗址等距今约五千年的大规模古稻田遗址也被发现。中国长江中下游地区是世界稻作农业的起源地，成为举世公认的事实。

中华先民如何驯化野生稻?

作为世界稻作农业的发明者，中华先民到底是怎样从事耕作的？这件柄上绑扎着条缕分明的藤条，藤条下残存着一块木棒的骨耜，把古籍中"耒耜"的古老形象清晰地展示在我们面前。透过这件骨耜，在遥想先民"执耜而耕"的同时，我们也可追忆远古祖先驯化野生稻的那条漫长、艰辛的道路。

如果要真切地理解中华先民驯化野生稻的历程，我们就需要将野生稻与其他栽培农作物做比较。比如，驯化于黄河流域的粟和黍，起源于西亚地区的大麦和小麦，发源于中美洲的玉米，这些农作物的野生祖本都生存在旱地。人类早期定居时，很容易与这些植物相遇，并观察到它们开花结籽、自落自生的特性，进而利用和驯化它们。但野生稻却不同，它是远古时代被人类驯化的唯一的湿地植物。确切地说，长江中下游先民驯化的水稻，其野生祖本是典型的水生草本植物，它们生长在池塘、沼泽中，有很强的宿根性和发达的地下茎，可从倒伏茎的高节根中发芽。而我们的祖先能够观察到这种湿地草本植物的食用价值，并最终把这种多年生的植物驯化改造成一年生的农作物，需要多少智慧、探索和辛劳！此后，中华民族还一步一步地把它变成了今天世界上产量最高的农作物，这又是何其了不起的奇迹！

野生稻的驯化、稻作农业的起源与发展，直接影响了早期中国的文明进程，稻作农业的传播也对整个亚洲乃至全世界的文明发展及其格局产生了深远的影响。现在，我们可以清晰地看到一条历史轨迹：稻作农业经由朝鲜半岛向日本传播，直接促成了这些地区的社会复杂化和国家化进程，成为汉字文化圈（东亚文化圈）形成的经济基础；同时，稻作农业的传播也是南岛语系诸民族起源、形成和扩散过程中的标志性特征。

今天，全世界将近一半的人口以稻米为主食，这不能不让我们缅怀中华先民对人类做出的伟大贡献！

The bone farming tool testified to the development level of rice farming in the lower reaches of the Yangtze River more than 7,000 years ago. Together with a large number of rice remains unearthed simultaneously, the bone *Si* verifies the fact that Chinese ancestors play a pioneering role in the rice-farming civilization in the world.

In 1973, at the Hemudu Site in Yuyao, Zhejiang Province, a few yellow golden grains appeared in the dark brown soil layer. When they came into contact with the air, the grains quickly became the color of soil. Archaeologists picked up the brown grains and carefully identified them. They could hardly believe their eyes; the brown grains were actually carbonized rice!

According to the determination with Carbon-14, these carbonized grains dated back to 6,950 ± 130 years ago. In other words, they have been buried underground for 7,000 years!

The discovery of the Hemudu Site signaled a major event in the archaeological history of China. A substantial number of grain remains, e.g. rice, rice husks, stems and leaves, were mixed together, forming a 0.2–0.5m-thick layer. The thickest layer was more than one meter. In terms of the number of accumulation and the level of preservation, grain remains at the Hemudu Site were rarely seen in archaeological history.

As the inventor of rice farming in the world, how did Chinese ancestors labor? The handle of the *Si* was strapped with clearly-seen rattans, under which was a short wood, which vividly showed an image of *Lei Si* (耒耜, plough-shaped farming tool) recorded in ancient books. While visualizing the ancestors “holding *Si* and ploughing”, we can also revisit the long and arduous journey of their domestication of wild rice.

The domestication of wild rice and the origin & development of rice farming had a direct impact on the civilization of early China. The spread of rice farming deeply affected the development and pattern of Asian civilization and even world civilization. Now, we can outline the travel of rice. Rice farming spread to Japan via the Korean Peninsula, which directly contributed to social advancement and national progress and laid economic foundation for the formation of “Sino-sphere” (the East Asia Cultural Circle). Simultaneously, the spread of rice farming meant a landmark in the origin and dissemination of the peoples of the Austronesian family.

花、华山、华夏，这三者之间有关系吗？
中华民族的称谓来自何处？

中华民族为何以“华”为名？

人头形器口彩陶瓶

Female-Head-Shaped-Mouth Painted Pottery Bottle

03

文物简读

在著名考古学家苏秉琦看来，仰韶彩陶上的玫瑰花图案有可能是中华民族以“华”为名的根源。

一个圆雕人头像，披着整齐的短发，耳垂有穿孔，瓶身绘制着抽象的玫瑰花图案。瓶口头像发式，为古羌族的披发样式。这件出土于1973年甘肃秦安邵店大地湾遗址的庙底沟类型彩陶瓶，蕴含的远古信息复杂幽深：它既向我们展示了仰韶文化盛开在华山脚下的玫瑰花的形象——它们有可能是中华民族以“华”为名的来源，又向我们提供了华夏文化和古羌文化相互交流、融合的见证。

华山脚下的玫瑰花

华山脚下、黄河岸边，距今6000—5000年前。这里的人们建筑村落，垒造属于家族的房屋；他们的房屋为方形，系半地穴式，墙壁用木棍做骨架，然后用草拌泥填充；他们在屋内建造火塘，火塘为圆形。最重要的是，他们大量烧制彩陶，作为最日常的生活用具，包括深腹曲壁的碗、盆，还有小口尖底瓶等等。

这群生活在华山脚下的人充满了浪漫的艺术细胞，这从他们对花的情有独钟可以看出——他们在彩陶上绘制大量花的图案。这些图案主要有两种，一种是覆瓦状花冠，一种是合瓣花冠。五六千年后，当考古学家仔细辨识这些图案时，他们认为覆瓦状花冠代表的是玫瑰花，而合瓣花冠代表的则是

名称：人头形器口彩陶瓶

年代：距今约6000年（仰韶文化庙底沟类型早期）

规格：高31.8厘米，口径4.5厘米，底径6.8厘米

出土地点：甘肃省秦安县大地湾遗址

收藏单位：甘肃省博物馆

Name: Female-Head-Shaped-Mouth Painted Pottery Bottle

Historical Period: *c.* 6,000 years ago (The Early Stage of Miaodigou Style of the Yangshao Culture)

Height: 31.8 cm, Mouth Diameter: 4.5 cm, Bottom Diameter: 6.8 cm

Excavation Site: Dadiwan Site, Qin'an County, Gansu Province

Housed in: Gansu Provincial Museum

菊花。而且，他们还相信，正是这群喜欢用玫瑰花图案装饰彩陶的先民，用“花”来命名矗立在自己身边的那座奇伟大山，称它为“华（花）山”。

苏秉琦在对植物学细加考证后，证实了一个重要的源流：玫瑰最早发源于中国，而其原产地就在华山、华县一带。

苏秉琦在仰韶文化众多特征中，紧紧抓住了这一个标志性纹样——抽象化的玫瑰花。他认为这个图案在这一时期的仰韶文化中演变有序，有头有尾，更影响了大半个中国，是仰韶文化中最具生命力的一种因素，与中华文化的起源息息相关。他还认为，“华山”就是以活动在其山脚下的以玫瑰花图案为标志的原始人群命名的，而今天我们自称“华人”，也应源自于此。

一场史前文化大交流

苏秉琦说，庙底沟文化是新石器时代文化“满天星斗”中最璀璨的一颗，它后来发展成为“中国文化总根系中一个重要直根系”，“从某种意义上讲，它影响了当时中华历史的全过程”。

显然，我们可以从庙底沟那些花瓣之上，看出中华文明的一个特质，那就是文化的流动与交融。作为一个光彩夺目的文化中心，仰韶文化庙底沟类型带动了一场史前文化的大交流，在一个“中国相互作用圈”中，逐渐呈现出一个“最早的中国”。苏秉琦清晰地揭示出这条文化交流的轨迹：“仰韶文化庙底沟类型，通过一条呈‘S’形的西南—东北向通道，沿黄河、汾河和太行山麓上溯，至山西、河北北部桑干河上游至内蒙古河曲地带，同源于燕山北侧的大凌河的红山文化碰撞，实现了花与龙的结合，又同河曲地区古文化结合产生三袋足器，这一系列新文化因素在距今5000—4000年前又沿汾河南下，在晋南同来自四方（主要是东方、东南方）的其他文化再次结合，这就是陶寺。”正是陶寺文化，开启了此后夏商周三代的文明化进程。

“从中原到北方再折返到中原这样一条文化连接带，……在中国文化史上曾是一个最活跃的民族大熔炉。”苏秉琦说。作为这个民族大熔炉最重要的成果，以“玫瑰花”为标志的仰韶文化同燕山地区以“龙”为图腾的北方红山文化相遇，并拉开了中华五千年文明的帷幕，这就是以华为名、以龙为徽的“华夏”的前身。我们在“华夏”之上，分明可以看到一个史前文化共同体的形象。

According to Su Bingqi, a well-known archaeologist, the rose image on the painted pottery of the Yangshao Culture probably explains the origin of the Chinese nation (华, *Hua*).

A sculpture of round human head, with neat short hair, holes at earlobes, and nonrepresentational rose image painted on the bottle surface. The hairstyle on the bottle mouth reminds us of that of the ancient Qiang people. Unearthed at Dadiwan Site, Shaodian, Qin'an, Gansu Province in 1973, the painted pottery bottle belonged to the Miaodigou Style. It shows us the rose image in the Yangshao Culture, constitutes the source of the Chinese nation, evidences the mutual exchange and integration of *Hua Xia* (华夏) culture and ancient Qiang (羌) culture.

5,000–6,000 years ago, at the foot of Mount Hua and on the bank of the Yellow River, people formed villages and built houses. Their houses looked square and took the form of semi-pit. The walls were framed with wooden sticks and then filled with grass and mud. They also constructed round fireplaces. Most significantly, they fired a large number of painted pottery, which served as their mostly-used tools in daily life, including bowl and basin with deep belly and curved wall, as well as bottle with small mouth and pointed bottom.

Denizens at the foot of Mount Hua embodied romantic artistic color and had a penchant for flowers. They painted a lot of flower images on painted pottery. There were mainly two types: imbricate corolla and gamopetalous corolla. Five or six thousand years later, when archaeologists carefully identified these images, they speculated that the former represented rose, and the latter chrysanthemum. Besides, archaeologists viewed that these denizens who liked to decorate painted pottery with rose image named the magnificent mountain after *Hua* (花, flower), i.e. Mount Hua (花山 or 华山).

Su Bingqi focused on the iconic image in the Yangshao Culture, the nonrepresentational rose. To him, the rose image continually evolved in the Yangshao Culture and extensively impacted on Chinese civilization. Therefore, Su Bingqi believed that the rose image played a decisive role in the Yangshao Culture and closely related to the rise of Chinese civilization.

如何认识丝绸的文化起源和发展历程?

六千多年的丝绸文化传承

石雕蚕蛹

Stone Carvings of Silkworm Chrysalises

04

文物简读

山西省夏县师村遗址出土的石雕蚕蛹表明，早在六千多年前的仰韶文化早期，生活在晋南地区的远古先民便已经开始养蚕。这让我们看见了中华先民发明丝绸的生动一幕。

在夏县的两次发现

1926年10月，沿着汾河行走的李济来到山西南部考古。在夏县西阴村，他发现了半枚六千年前被人工切割的蚕茧。半枚蚕茧的现世，让“嫘祖养蚕”的传说走到了我们面前，也让中华先民创造丝绸文化的历史有了可以触摸的蛛丝马迹。

2019年，在夏县的另一个仰韶文化早期聚落遗址——师村遗址，数枚石雕蚕蛹被发现。这些蚕蛹整体呈黄褐色，带有天然黑褐斑点，表面有螺旋状的横向弦纹，简洁地勾勒出了蛹的头和尾，酷似现代家桑蚕蛹。这些石雕蚕蛹的出土，呼应了93年前李济的发现，证实了地处黄河中游的晋南先民，早在距今六千多年前就已经了解、喜爱并崇尚桑蚕，这暗示着此地仰韶文化的早期先民很可能已掌握了养蚕缫丝技术。

养蚕、取丝、织绸的中华先民

《史记·五帝本纪》记载了嫘祖的故事：“黄帝居于轩辕之丘，而娶于西陵之女，是为嫘祖，为黄帝正妃，生二子，其后皆有天下。”然而嫘祖之所以流芳百世，并不仅仅因为她的黄帝正妻的身

份，更因为她为中华民族留下了一份辉映古今的伟大文化遗产。《通鉴续编》云：“（嫘祖）治丝茧以供衣服。”与这一记载相应，嫘祖养蚕、取丝、织绸的神话传说，在中华大地上广泛流传。就在发现石雕蚕蛹的晋南地区，流传着这样一则民间传说：远古时代，西陵（夏县一带）有位美丽的姑娘叫嫘祖，嫘祖采集野果时在桑树上发现了能够吐丝作茧的桑蚕，于是把桑蚕带回家饲养，又用茧丝织成布，代替了树叶和兽皮，从此便有了丝绸。文献的记载、传说的呼应、考古的印证，充分表明中原地区具有悠久的人工养蚕历史，是中国丝绸文化的发源地。

而20世纪下半叶以来，中华大地上相继发现的史前丝绸考古资料，则为我们绘出了一幅清晰的丝绸文化传播图：

名称：石雕蚕蛹
年代：距今约6000年（仰韶文化早期）
规格：长约3厘米，宽约1.3厘米
出土地点：山西省夏县师村遗址
收藏单位：吉林大学考古学院

Name: Stone Carvings of Silkworm Chrysalises
Historical Period: *c.* 6,000 years ago (The Early Stage of the Yangshao Culture)
Length: *c.* 3 cm, Width: *c.* 1.3 cm
Excavation Site: Shicun Site, Xiaxian County, Shanxi Province
Housed in: School of Archaeology, Jilin University

河南荥阳汪沟遗址出土的距今5500多年的织物残存，成为迄今为止发现的最早的丝织品实物。专家认为，这些丝织品制作技术已经相当成熟，其孕育发展阶段应该更早，从侧面证实了丝绸技艺在晋南一带孕育出现之后，随着族群流动而沿黄河传播到河南荥阳的文化传播路线。此外，浙江良渚文化钱山漾遗址出土的距今4400年左右的绢片、丝带、丝线等丝织品，应是丝绸制作工艺在中原地区成熟之后，逐渐向南方地区传播的实物见证。

丝绸开启最早的"全球化"商品流通

中华先民发明的丝绸制作技艺，对于整个世界历史而言意味着什么？

20世纪40年代，南西伯利亚阿尔泰山北侧的巴泽雷克墓地出土了刺绣和织锦，墓地的时代在公元前500年至公元前100年之间；克里米亚曾出土汉绮，其时代约在公元1世纪；罗马帝国东方行省巴尔米拉（在今叙利亚境内）和其本土意大利也发现了汉绮。这表明，在战国至汉代，中国的丝绸已经走向世界。

我们在很多西方读物里，都能读到丝绸传播到欧洲的神奇故事。公元前53年，古罗马执政官克拉苏率军与安息人在卡尔莱大战，战斗正酣时，安息人突然展开了一面丝绸军旗。这面军旗在正午的阳光下炫目得令人窒息，让疲于应战的罗马军团顿时阵脚大乱，最终惨败。安息是位于伊朗地区的古代帝国。一些西方学者认为，这面丝绸军旗就是罗马人见到的最早的丝绸。后来，当丝绸传到罗马，便有了另一则更加有名的故事：凯撒大帝穿着丝绸长袍去剧场看戏，引起在场大臣们的惊呼和骚动，他们认为自己看到了世上最豪华的衣服，贵族们因此掀起了追逐中国丝绸的狂潮。一时间，丝绸在罗马与黄金等价，最高的时候一磅丝绸相当于12两黄金。罗马作家培利埃盖提斯这样称羡："中国制造的名贵彩色丝绸，就像田野里盛开的美丽的花朵，它的纤细简直可以和蜘蛛织网相媲美。"而罗马的博物学家老普林尼，则在《自然史》一书中这样猜想丝绸的织造与传播："（赛里斯国）林中产丝，驰名宇内。丝生于树叶上，取出，湿之以水，理之成丝。后织成锦绣文绮，贩运到罗马。富豪贵族之妇女，裁成衣服，光辉夺目。"

老普林尼所说的"赛里斯国"，就是罗马人对中国的第一个称谓，意即"丝国"。可见，西方对于中国的第一印象来自华美的丝绸。而丝绸的魅力，足以令两千多年前的亚欧大陆东西两端之间开启一场最早的"全球化"商品流通。

晚清之际，德国地理学家斐迪南·冯·李希霍芬来到中国考察，回国后他写出了五卷本皇皇巨著《中国》。在书中，他描述了一条古老的道路："从公元前114年到公元127年间，连接中国与河中（指中亚阿姆河与锡尔河之间）以及中国与印度，以丝绸之路贸易为媒介的西域交通路线。"

从此，"丝绸之路"就成为描述历史上古老的东西方文明交流的特殊词汇，映照着人类的历史记忆。

Stone carvings of silkworm chrysalises were unearthed from Shicun Site in Xiaxian County, Shanxi Province. They confirm that in the early stage of the Yangshao Culture (more than 6,000 years ago), ancient ancestors, who dwelled in the south of present-day Shanxi Province, began to raise silkworms. They also vividly present the scene that Chinese ancestors firstly developed the silk culture.

In October 1926, Li Ji, who conducted archaeological work along the Fen River, came to the south of Shanxi Province. At Xiyin Village, Xiaxian County, an epoch-making achievement was the half silkworm cocoon that were manually cut 6,000 years ago. The existence of the half silkworm cocoon supported the legend of "Lei Zu's discovery of sericulture" with historical evidence, and gave scholars a clue to trace the origin of the wonderful silk culture created by ancient Chinese people.

In 2019, another early settlement site of the Yangshao Culture was discovered at Shicun, Xiaxian County. Several stone carvings of silkworm chrysalises were unearthed. These chrysalises looked yellowish brown, with natural black and brown spots and horizontal spiral string-shaped patterns, which roughly outlined the head and tail of the chrysalis and reminded us of modern silkworm chrysalis. The excavation of these chrysalises supplemented Li Ji's discovery 93 years ago, verifying that ancestors in the south of present-day Shanxi Province or the middle reaches of the Yellow River, had known, liked and worshiped silkworm as early as 6,000 years ago, and that they had probably mastered the technologies of sericulture and silk reeling.

In "The Imperial Annals of the Five Emperors" of *Records of the Grand Historian* (《史记・五帝本纪》), the story of Lei Zu said: "The Yellow Emperor lived on the Mountain of Xuanyuan. Lei Zu, daughter of the Lord of Xiling, was the main consort of the Yellow Emperor. Lei Zu gave birth to two sons, who were later enfeoffed with land." Noticeably, Lei Zu's immortality lied not only in the identity of the first wife of the Yellow Emperor, but also in the great cultural heritage for the Chinese nation. In *Tongjian Xubian* (《通鉴续编》, *An Supplement to Comprehensive Mirror in Aid of Governance*), it was stated that: "(Lei Zu) taught people to raise silkworms, made silk cocoons and provide themselves with clothes."

In the 1940s, embroidery and brocade were unearthed from Pazyryk Cemetery in the north side of the Altai Mountains in the South Siberia, dating back to the period from 500 BC to 100 BC. Additionally, the Han-Dynasty *Qi* (绮, figured woven silk material) unearthed in Crimea dates back to the 1st century AD. The Han-Dynasty *Qi* was also unearthed in Palmyra (in present-day Syria), the eastern province of the Roman Empire, as well as Italy. This indicated that Chinese silk spread in the world as early as in the Han Dynasty.

Dionysius Periegetes, a Roman writer, admired Chinese silk: "The precious colored silk made in China looks like beautiful flowers blooming in the field, and its fineness rivals the cobwebs woven by spiders." Pliny the Elder, a Roman naturalist, imagined the weaving and dissemination of silk in *Historia Naturalis*: "In Serica, silk was produced in the tree and was famous in the world. Silk grew on leaves. Taking it out and wetting it with water, the silk can be obtained. Silk was then woven into brocades and other silk materials which were sold to Rome. Women from wealthy or noble families cut silk to make clothes, which looked dazzlingly beautiful."

"Serica" was how Pliny the Elder called China, meaning "the state of silk". Evidently, China's first impression on Western countries was the gorgeous silk. More than 2,000 years ago, silk triggered the earliest global commodity circulation between the eastern and western ends of the Eurasia.

In the late Qing Dynasty, Ferdinand von Richthofen, a German geographer, came to China for an investigation. After returning home, he wrote the five-volume masterpiece *Tagebücher Aus China*. In particular, he described an ancient road: "From 114 BC to 127 AD, a transportation route in the Western Regions connected China and Transoxiana (between Amu Darya and Syr Darya) as well as China and India, with the Silk Road trade as the medium."

Terminologically, the Silk Road gave an account the oldest exchanges between eastern and western civilizations and cast light on the historical memory of mankind.

中华儿女自称“龙的传人”，龙最初是什么样子的？
我们的祖先又是从什么时候开始有“龙”这个概念的？

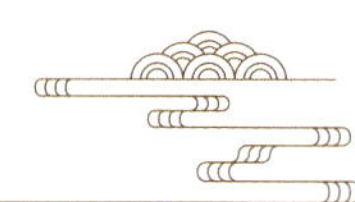

“龙的传人”身份起源

红山玉龙

Jade Dragon of the Hongshan Culture

05

文物简读

这件被考古界誉为“中华第一龙”的红山玉龙，不仅揭示了龙的源头，充分印证了中华民族“龙的传人”身份，而且对探究中华龙文化的发展序列有重要意义。

曲折现世的“中华第一龙”

“中华第一龙”红山玉龙的现世过程，充满了坎坷和离奇。

1971年10月16日，家住内蒙古赤峰市翁牛特旗三星塔拉村的17岁村民张凤祥在田地里劳作，突然“咔”的一声，铁锹好像碰到一块坚硬的石头，震得他手臂发麻。他扒开土，发现一块石板，掀开石板，底下是一个方方正正的坑。他看不清里面有什么，便伸手进去摸，拉出来一个生满锈的“铁钩”，他用铁锹铲了几下，没有把锈铲掉，便随手扔到一边。晚上回家后，张凤祥突然想起这个东西，心想把“铁钩”拿到废品收购站也许能换成钱，于是便回到田地里把它带回了家。张凤祥正值童年的弟弟看到这件“铁钩”后，便找了根绳子从中间小孔中穿过，当作玩具在院子里拉着到处跑。几天后，张凤祥无意中发现“铁钩”的锈居然被磨掉了一部分，露出了晶莹剔透的墨绿色，在阳光下看更像一块玉。晚饭时，张凤祥跟父亲张金贵说了这件事。第二天，张金贵拿着它去了公社文化站。但文化站的人以为这就是块普通的石头，没有重视。

一个多月后，石头表面的锈被打磨得干干净净，露出了墨绿通透的“真身”。张金贵越来越觉得这不是一块普通的石头，便又带着它走了几十里路，到了翁牛特旗文化馆。旗文化馆的领导仔细鉴定后，认为这确实是一件文物，便用30块钱收购了回去。但旗文化馆将其作为一件普通文物，在库房里一搁就是十多年。

名称：红山玉龙

年代：距今6000—5000年（红山文化时期）

规格：高26厘米

出土地点：内蒙古自治区赤峰市翁牛特旗

收藏单位：中国国家博物馆

Name: Jade Dragon of the Hongshan Culture

Historical Period: 5,000–6,000 years ago (The Stage of the Hongshan Culture)

Height: 26 cm

Excavation Site: Ongniud Banner, Chifeng City, Inner Mongolia

Housed in: National Museum of China

直到1983年，辽宁牛河梁遗址出土了一对玉猪龙，成为红山文化的重要代表，翁牛特旗文化馆负责人贾鸿恩越来越觉得库房里那块花30块钱买来的玉不简单。1984年，他带着这块玉坐火车到了北京，找到时任中国考古学会理事长苏秉琦。苏秉琦和故宫博物院相关专家鉴定后，一致认为这是五千多年前红山文化时期的墨玉龙，是中国发现的最早的龙形玉器。专家们还认为，这件墨玉龙雕工精细，选材优良，神态栩栩如生，形体酷似甲骨文中的“龙”字（），背部的孔设计巧妙，用绳子吊起来，龙头和龙尾正好处在一条水平线上，堪称“中华第一龙”。

红山玉龙的发现，使考古学中关于“龙”的许多疑问找到了答案。虽然此后又发现了更早的龙文化遗存，但红山玉龙的典型意义仍不容置疑。

中华民族的龙崇拜

随着中国考古事业的不断发展，中华民族孕育起源阶段的龙文化考古材料不断问世，中华民族“龙的传人”身份意识的来源及其丰富内涵被揭示出来……

1987年，河南濮阳西水坡仰韶文化遗址出土了距今约6400年的龙虎图案，该图案由蚌壳精心摆塑，其中虎形图案居左，龙形图案居右，龙头北面东向，昂首弓背，四足长尾，尾巴作摇摆状，好似正遨游苍穹。

安徽凌家滩出土的阴刻龙形玉器，距今5500—5300年；山西陶寺遗址出土的陶盘彩绘龙图案，距今4300—3900年……

由此可见，早在远古时代，龙已经成为中华先民精神生活的重要内容。

根据考古资料以及文献记载看，中国龙文化的起源具有多元性特征。从原型来看，主要有云、闪电、龙卷风、松树、蛇、鳄、蜥蜴、鱼、鲵、马、牛、猪、鹿、熊、虎、蚕、蛴螬等等，这不仅仅表达了龙的神性变化无常，也反映出龙的地域性差异，显示出中华文明的多元起源特点，以及与中华民族多元一体格局相一致的特征。

龙的形象也有一个逐步演化的过程。夏、商、西周时期，龙形仍存在多种面貌，直到战国、秦汉才逐渐趋于统一。东汉思想家王符总结当时龙的造型：“角似鹿，头似驼，眼似兔，项似蛇，腹似蜃，鳞似鱼，爪似鹰，掌似虎，耳似牛。”至此，中国龙的整体形态基本确定下来。

中华龙文化经历了漫长而连续的发展过程，这个过程与中华民族和中华文明的起源发展过程高度一致。龙的形象从多元走向一体，最终成为中华大一统的高度象征，成为中华民族的象征！

Hailed as the "the first dragon in China" by archaeologists, Jade Dragon of the Hongshan Culture empirically authenticated the source of dragon, fully verified the identity of the Chinese nation as "descendants of the dragon", and tremendously advanced the studies of the development sequence of Chinese dragon culture.

In 1984, Jia Hong'en, a leader of Ongniud Banner Cultural Center, took seriously the jade ware that he bought with 30 *yuan*. He took the jade to Beijing by train and sought help from Su Bingqi, then chairman of Society for Chinese Archaeology. After identification, Su and relevant experts from the Palace Museum agreed that Jia's jade was ink-color jade dragon of the Hongshan Culture more than 5,000 years ago and the earliest dragon-shaped jade ware unearthed in China at that time. The ink-color jade dragon was elaborately carved and made of top-quality materials. With lifelike appearance, its shape resembled Chinese character *Long* (龙) in oracle bone inscriptions (⾋). The hole on the dragon back was ingeniously designed. Hung with a rope, the dragon head remained in alignment with the tail. In a way, the jade dragon boasted "the first dragon relic in China".

Jade Dragon of the Hongshan Culture typified the cultural relics of dragon, and its discovery unlocked some of the secrets of dragon in archaeology.

As more achievements were attained in Chinese archaeology, more archaeological materials on the origin of dragon culture were continuously discovered, expatiating on the identity and recognition of the Chinese nation as "descendants of the dragon".

In 1987, a relic with dragon-tiger pattern was unearthed at a Yangshao-Culture Site, Xishuipo, Puyang, Henan Province, dating back to around 6,400 years ago. It was meticulously shaped with mussel shells. The tiger pattern stood on the left, and the dragon pattern flied on the right, with the dragon head facing the east. The dragon raised the head and bent the back, with four feet and a long tail. The tail wagging, the dragon freely soared in the sky.

The dragon-shaped jade ware with concave inscriptions unearthed at Lingjiatan, Anhui Province, dating back to 5,300–5,500 years ago; painted dragon-pattern pottery plate unearthed at Taosi Site, Shanxi Province, dating back to 3,900–4,300 years ago…

Therefore, dragon played an important part in the spiritual life of Chinese ancestors as early as the ancient times.

The image of dragon kept evolving. In the Xia, Shang and Western Zhou Dynasties, the image of dragon varied. It was not until the Warring States Period and the Qin & Han Dynasties that the image of dragon remained unvaried. With regard to the shapes of dragon, Wang Fu, a thinker in the Eastern Han Dynasty, commented: "The horn looks like deer, the head like camel, the eyes like rabbit, the neck like snake, the belly like flood dragon, the scale like fish, the claw like eagle, the palm like tiger, and the ear like cattle." This basically determined the overall shape of Chinese dragon.

In the long and continued development, Chinese dragon culture was highly consistent with the origin of the Chinese nation and Chinese civilization. No matter in diverse forms or in single form, dragon became a symbol of the grand unification of China and the Chinese nation.

名称：八角星纹玉版

年代：距今约5300年（新石器时代晚期）

规格：长11.4厘米，高8.3厘米，最厚1厘米

出土地点：安徽省含山县凌家滩遗址

收藏单位：故宫博物院

Name: Jade Plate with Octagonal-Star Pattern

Historical Period: *c*. 5,300 years ago (The Late Stage of the Neolithic Period)

Length: 11.4 cm, Height: 8.3 cm, The Maximum Thickness: 1 cm

Excavation Site: Lingjiatan Site, Hanshan County, Anhui Province

Housed in: The Palace Museum

八卦图起源于何时？

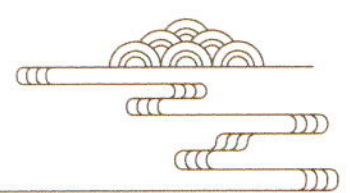

最早的城市和先民的哲学思想

八角星纹玉版

Jade Plate with Octagonal-Star Pattern

06

文物简读

这块凌家滩玉版有可能承载着五千多年前中华先民的原始哲学思想；而文献记载中始创八卦的伏羲留存在南方民族中的神奇传说，又隐现着远古中华大地上各族群文化交流的深度和广度。

神奇的玉版

这块玉版出土时，并非孤零零地躺在墓葬中，而是夹在一只玉龟之中。玉版上刻绘了复杂而精妙的纹饰：主体为两个同心圆，圆中心雕刻着一个十字形的八角星纹，大小圆之间刻绘八个“圭”形，在大圆之外、玉版四角，又分别刻绘着一个“圭”形纹。

如此复杂的图纹代表着什么？

有学者分析，玉版最中心的八角星纹有可能代表太阳，两圆之间的八个“圭”形纹代表八个方位，玉版四角的“圭”形纹表示四维。四维和八方，即《史记·龟策列传》中记载的“四维已定，八卦相望”。学者们由此推断，凌家滩遗址的玉版的纹饰有可能是表示四时历法的原始“八卦图”。

中国最早的城市之一

中国最早的城市在哪里？凌家滩遗址给出了一个参考答案。

位于安徽省含山县的凌家滩遗址（距今5800—5300年），是目前长江中下游巢湖流域发现的面积最大、保存最完整的新石器时代聚落遗址，被认为是中华五千年文明的重要源头之一。随着考古发掘，它清晰而深厚的城市内涵逐渐显现出来。

凌家滩遗址显示出了初步的城市规划格局：第一区域是部落居住区，房屋带有明显的规划和布局设计痕迹，此区域还出土了大量陶片等生活遗物。第二区域是广场祭祀区，用于举行部落会盟、祭祀、集会等活动，也是部落首领的宫殿所在地。广场中心出土了一口红陶土块砌成的水井，据地质专家考证，这口水井应是具有祭祀意义的“圣水”井。由此可见，这片广场区域是凌家滩古城的政治、军事、文化中心。第三区域为大型墓葬区，中心设有祭坛，区域内出土了大量玉器、石器、陶器等陪葬品，还发现了石墙等建筑遗迹。

凌家滩遗址还出土了三千多件玉礼器、石器、陶器等，尤以精美玉石器闻名于世，如玉人、玉龟、玉鹰、玉龙、玉版等，其精湛的工艺水平令人叹为观止。其中的浮雕玉人，展示了当时人类完整的外貌特征；玉人帽饰、配饰等，说明了当时人们已掌握了较为先进的纺织技术，形成了较为时尚的服饰文化。2022年北京冬奥会的奖牌“同心”，其背面就采用了凌家滩遗址出土的双联玉璧元素。

考古专家认为，凌家滩遗址与周边数个小聚落群体构成了众星拱月式的社会结构，中心与周边的等级分化十分明显。这座古城手工业发达，具备了城市文化内涵，是迄今考古发现的中国最早的城市之一。

伏羲与八卦

凌家滩文化与辽宁红山文化、浙江良渚文化并称为中国史前三大玉文化。凌家滩玉礼器反映了五千多年前中华先民的思想与智慧。这块夹在玉龟之中的玉版，尤其能代表凌家滩玉器承载的幽深哲理。

根据上古传说，《周易》和《洪范》来源于河图、洛书。传说伏羲时代，有龙马从黄河中出现，背负河图；夏禹时代，有神龟从洛水中出现，背负洛书。《周易》载：“易有太极，是生两仪，两仪生四象，四象生八卦。”凌家滩玉版的四角和八圭图形，让人联想到四象和八卦。因此，玉版图形有可能表现的是远古的洛书和最早的八卦。

在中华大地上，伏羲创造八卦的故事被广为传颂。约成书于战国时期的《易传》作了最早的记载：“古者包牺氏之王天下也，仰则观象于天，俯则观法于地，观鸟兽之文，与地之宜，近取诸身，远取诸物，于是始作八卦，以通神明之德，以类万物之情。”作为中华民族的人文始祖，伏羲的形象也留存在我国南方地区许多民族的远古记忆中。有意思的是，伏羲女娲兄妹成婚并在大洪水中生存下来繁衍人类的传说，成为西南地区各民族的一个重要神话母题，在不同的民族中被置换成各自的祖先，以不同的版本广泛流传。

由此，从凌家滩的玉版玉龟，到伏羲始作八卦的记载，再到伏羲女娲兄妹成婚的各民族传说，这一条轨迹体现了中华民族在形成发展初期，各地区各族群文化交往交流交融的深度和广度。

The jade plate unearthed at Lingjiatan embodied the simple philosophy of Chinese ancestors more than 5,000 years ago. The mysterious legend of Fu Xi, who invented Eight Diagrams (*Ba Gua*, 八卦) in historical literature, was disseminated among southern tribes, which mirrored the profundity of cultural exchanges among ethnic groups in ancient China.

When the jade plate was unearthed, it was contained in a jade turtle, with intricate and exquisite patterns. In the central part, there were two concentric circles, with a cross-shaped octagonal pattern carved in the center of the circle. Between the big and small circles were eight *Gui* (圭)-shaped patterns. At the four corners of the plate were carved four *Gui* (圭)-shaped patterns.

What did such complicated patterns represent?

As some scholars analyzed, the innermost octagonal pattern probably stood for the sun, the eight *Gui* (圭)-shaped patterns between two circles stood for eight directions, and the *Gui* (圭)-shaped patterns at the four corners stood for four dimensions. In "Collective Biography of Divination-Makers" of *Records of the Grand Historian* (《史记・龟策列传》), it was stated: "Since four directions are determined, eight trigrams are arranged in position." Scholars therefore deduced that the jade plate unearthed at Lingjiatan Site may be the original eight diagrams representing the four-season calendar.

Located in Hanshan County, Anhui Province, Lingjiatan Site dates back to 5,300–5,800 years ago. As the largest and most complete Neolithic settlement site discovered near the Chaohu Lake in the middle & lower reaches of the Yangtze River, Lingjiatan Site boasts one of the important sources of 5,000-year Chinese civilization. With archaeological excavation increased, the town form of Lingjiatan Site became visible.

Archaeologists noticed that Lingjiatan Site, as well as several small settlements around it, constituted a center-periphery social structure, with prominent hierarchical differentiation. People that resided in the ancient town developed handicraft industry and town culture, making Lingjiatan Site one of the earliest towns in Chinese archaeology.

Lingjiatan Culture, the Hongshan Culture in Liaoning and the Liangzhu Culture in Zhejiang are collectively called three prehistoric jade cultures in China. Jade ritual utensils at Lingjiatan Site reflect the thoughts and wisdom of Chinese ancestors more than 5,000 years ago. The jade plate contained in the jade turtle typically represents the profound philosophical ideas implied in jade objects in Lingjiatan.

The jade plate and jade turtle in Lingjiatan, the records of Fu Xi's invention of eight diagrams, and the legends of the sibling marriage of Fu Xi and Nü Wa formed a cultural landscape and concretized deep cultural exchanges among various ethnic groups in the early stage of the formation and development of the Chinese nation.

中华民族崇拜凤鸟的文化根源，来自何处？

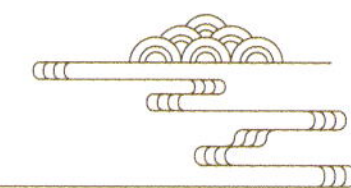

中华凤鸟文化之源

双錾三足白陶鬶

Double-*Pan* (錾, Handle) Three-Legged Unglazed Pottery *Gui* (鬶, Cooking Utensil)

07

文物简读

这件白陶鬶所体现的凤鸟图腾崇拜，是中华民族崇尚凤文化的基因在器物上的体现。

一场大洪水冲出的史前文明

1957年的一场大洪水，冲出了东夷人创造的陵阳河史前文化遗址。这个距今大约五千年的大汶口文化中晚期遗存，标志着五千年中华文明发展史的开端。

在组织第二次考古发掘时，这里出土了一件十分有趣的陶器：鸟喙形流口上翘，颈部细而高，腹部微鼓，三袋足，背部有双带式錾，状如双翅，腹中部饰一圈绳纹，后部饰一条极具装饰意义的短尾——总体看上去，它酷似一只昂首振翅欲飞的鸟。考古学家将其命名为“双錾三足白陶鬶”。

《说文》曰：鬶为“三足釜也，有柄可持，有喙可写（泻）物”。喙，即鸟嘴。也就是说，鬶是一种陶制炊具，可用于炖煮羹汤温酒，其最主要的特点就是有一个鸟嘴形状的流口。

陵阳河出土的双錾三足白陶鬶，不仅有典型的鸟嘴形流口，而且整体被精心塑造成一只翩翩欲翔的鸟。这说明，五千多年前生活在这里的人们对鸟格外钟情。

东夷是谁？

这一群对鸟怀有崇尚之情的先民，就是东夷。

陶鬶是山东龙山文化的典型器物之一，起源于大汶口文化中期。而根据考古发掘与文献记载的互证，东夷正是北辛文化、大汶口文化、龙山文化和岳石文化的创造者。

名称：双鋬三足白陶鬶
年代：距今约5000年（大汶口文化中晚期）
规格：高34.1厘米
出土地点：山东省莒县陵阳河遗址
收藏单位：莒州博物馆

Name: Double-*Pan* (鋬, Handle) Three-Legged Unglazed Pottery *Gui* (鬶, Cooking Utensil)
Historical Period: *c.* 5,000 years ago (The Middle-Late Stage of the Dawenkou Culture)
Height: 34.1 cm
Excavation Site: Lingyang River Site, Juxian County, Shandong Province
Housed in: Juxian County Museum

《礼记·王制》曰："东方曰夷。"《说文》也称："（夷）东方之人也。"从字形来看，"夷"是一个持弓之人的形象。《竹书纪年》和《后汉书·东夷列传》又说："夷有九种。""九"者，极言其多也。东夷并非一支，而是众多人群的联盟，有莱夷、岛夷、嵎夷、鸟夷、淮夷、牟夷等；太昊、蚩尤、少昊、舜等，被认为是东夷在不同发展阶段的重要部落首领。

东夷崇拜鸟，这是其有别于其他族群集团的重要特征之一。《汉书》中说："少阳者，东方。东，动也，阳气动物，于时为春。"东夷人崇拜鸟的原因也许与其所居的东方有关，与东方作为日出之地有关。在人类的原初思维中，太阳便是天空中飞翔的一只火鸟。事实上，在中华民族的精神世界中，太阳神话总是与鸟的意象紧密相关，东夷人对于鸟的崇尚本质上可追溯到太阳崇拜。

鸟崇拜体现在东夷文化的很多方面。少昊是东夷部落集团首领，其名为挚，挚通"鸷"，即鸷鸟。东夷以鸟作为氏族部落的象征，不同的鸟代表不同的部落，甚至东夷的官职也以鸟为名。

东夷融入华夏

东夷的鸟崇拜最终演化为凤崇拜，而中华民族关于凤的文化意识就根源于东夷。

考古发现，东夷曾创造了一个相对独立而完整的文化谱系，以大汶口文化和龙山文化为主要代表，并以强大的力量辐射到周边地区——西至豫东、皖北，南至太湖，北至燕辽文化区及辽东半岛。在这样的文化传播过程中，凤鸟崇拜被中原吸收，渐渐演化为华夏集团的凤文化。

史载，商人、秦人都与东夷一脉相系，都有"鸟生"始祖传说。《诗经·商颂·玄鸟》有"天命玄鸟，降而生商"的记载。商人将东夷文化的鸟崇拜作为重要的文化符号，镌刻在青铜器物上，如商早期出土的提梁卣，多刻有凤鸟纹饰；殷墟妇好墓则出土了玉凤、凤鸟纹偶方彝等。根据清华大学藏战国简《系年》的记载，西周初年，嬴秦西迁。许慎《说文解字》则称："嬴，少昊氏之姓也。"对东夷凤鸟崇拜的继承，使秦人创造出了人面鸟身的神人形象，进而发展出具有中原文化特征的神人体系。

相传，著名的后益（伯益）、皋陶、蚩尤、后羿等神话人物都是少昊的后裔。尤其是蚩尤，相传是三苗部落的祖先。这使作为三苗后裔的苗族，在其文化传统中始终保留着大量凤鸟文化的遗迹，传承至今。今天，在苗族最盛大的祭祀仪式"鼓藏节"中，祭师所穿着的百鸟衣，应当就是这一文化脉络的遗存。

东夷逐渐融入华夏。春秋战国时期，作为东夷故地的齐、鲁两国，早已华夏化；到秦统一六国时，"其淮泗夷皆散为民户"，东夷已完全融入华夏，成为华夏的重要来源和组成部分。

The unglazed pottery *Gui* (鬶) materialized the totem worship of phoenix of the Chinese nation.

In 1957, a flood hit Juxian County. A prehistoric site near the Lingyang River was discovered. The remains belongs to the middle-late stage of the Dawenkou Culture and dates back to around 5,000 years ago and tells the beginning of the 5,000-year history of Chinese civilization.

In the second-time archaeological excavation, archaeologists unearthed an interesting pottery ware. The beak-shaped part curls up, the neck looks thin and high, and the belly slightly bulges, with three bag-shaped legs. On the back are two *Pan* (Handle), looking like two wings. The middle part of the belly is decorated with a circle of rope-shaped pattern, and the back part of the belly with a short tail. On the whole, it resembles a bird raising the head high and flapping the wings. Archaeologists named it Double-*Pan* (鋬, Handle) Three-Legged Unglazed Pottery *Gui* (鬶, Cooking Utensil).

Gui (鬶) was clearly explained in the Han Dynasty. In *Shuowen Jiezi* (《说文解字》, *The Dictionary of Explaining & Parsing Ancient Chinese Characters*), it was stated that: "*Gui* means a three-legged *Fu* (釜, cauldron), with handles for human to hold and a beak-shaped part for things to flow." In other words, *Gui* (鬶) was used as a cooking utensil to make soup or warm up wine. A prominent feature of *Gui* (鬶) was the beak-shaped part.

East-*Yi* (东夷) people worshipped bird, which distinguished them from other ethnic groups. In *Book of Han* (《汉书》), it was mentioned that: "*Shaoyang* (少阳, Lesser *Yang*) relates to the east. The east signifies *Yang* and causes the movements of things. In terms of season, it stands for the spring." This indicates that East *Yi* people worshipped birds because they lived in the east, where the sun rises. To human, the sun was originally seen as a firebird flying in the sky. As a matter of fact, in the spiritual world of the Chinese nation, the myth of the sun was closely associated with the image of bird. Essentially, East-*Yi* people's worship of bird can be traced back to the worship of the sun.

Archaeological findings reveal that East-*Yi* people fashioned relatively independent and complete cultural pedigree (mainly represented by the Dawenkou Culture and the Longshan Culture), which spread to present-day eastern Henan and northern Anhui in the west, Taihu Lake in the south, and Yan-Liao cultural area and Liaodong Peninsula in the north. Accordingly, the worship of phoenix carved a place in the Central Plains and developed into the phoenix culture of *Hua Xia* (华夏).

马家窑彩陶为什么会不断出现神秘莫测的旋涡纹?

黄河上游的绚丽文明

旋涡纹尖底彩陶瓶

Painted Pottery Bottle with Whirlpool-Shaped Pattern and Pointed Bottom

08

文物简读

这件以旋涡纹为主要装饰纹样的马家窑类型陶瓶，是连续发展了五千年的中华彩陶文化在黄河上游的甘青地区再一次走上巅峰的见证；马家窑先民对奔腾的黄河水极具概括力和想象力的描绘，代表了中国史前彩陶文化的最高水平，是新石器时代晚期黄河文明形成与发展的重要见证。

绚烂多彩的彩陶文化

虽然马家窑类型彩陶文物数量巨大，常有纹饰精美的器物出土，但这件旋涡纹尖底彩陶瓶的出现，还是让考古工作者大为折服，赞叹不已：流畅的旋涡纹，带动点与线，有韵律地交错流动，热烈而奔放……这样的图案是在描绘湍急涌动的黄河之水吗?

这件旋涡纹尖底彩陶瓶在器型上也实现了审美与实用的高度和谐：这是一个可系绳的汲水瓶，因其底尖，容易入水；入水后由于浮力和重心的关系，能自动横起灌水；又由于口小，搬运时水不易溢出。正因如此，这件旋涡纹尖底彩陶瓶成为马家窑文化马家窑类型彩陶的代表作。

在中华文明史上，彩陶文化是一个极其显著的存在，它的延续时间如此之长——从距今8000年前一直持续到距今3000年前左右，连续发展五千余年，跨越老官台、仰韶、马家窑、大汶口、屈家岭、大溪、红山、齐家、辛店等文化类型；它的地理范围又如此之广，遍及中华大地每个角落。可以说，彩陶文化对中华文明起到了奠基作用。

而主要分布在距今5000多年前黄河上游的马家窑文化，在这一部宏大绵延的彩陶史中，占据了什么位置呢?

名称：旋涡纹尖底彩陶瓶
年代：距今约5000年（马家窑文化马家窑类型）
规格：高26.8厘米，口径7.1厘米
出土地点：甘肃省陇西县吕家坪
收藏单位：甘肃省博物馆

Name: Painted Pottery Bottle with Whirlpool-Shaped Pattern and Pointed Bottom
Historical Period: *c*. 5,000 years ago (Majiayao Style of the Majiayao Culture)
Height: 26.8 cm, Mouth Diameter: 7.1 cm
Excavation Site: Lüjiaping, Longxi County, Gansu Province
Housed in: Gansu Provincial Museum

被誉为“彩陶之冠”的马家窑文化

在中华文明多元起源的满天星斗中，马家窑文化是黄河上游地区最亮的那一颗。

马家窑文化得名于1923年。这一年，甘肃省临洮县马家窑村新石器文化遗址惊现于世。它是中原仰韶文化庙底沟类型向西北传播和影响的产物，在适应甘肃、青海等地自然地理条件的基础上，马家窑文化形成了鲜明的特色，曾一度被称为“甘肃的仰韶文化”。它出现于距今约5700多年前的新石器时代晚期，前后延续了一千多年。

高度发达的制陶技术是马家窑文化的主要特色。在仰韶文化庙底沟类型彩陶文化的基础上，马家窑彩陶更加精细化，风格绚丽而典雅，堪称中国史前彩陶艺术的巅峰。

而在一步步走向巅峰的过程中，马家窑彩陶文化经历了初步形成—早期发展—成熟—尾声的发展过程，分别表现为石岭下类型—马家窑类型—半山类型—马厂类型。

石岭下类型阶段是承上启下的一个重要阶段，是仰韶文化发展演化为马家窑文化的过渡阶段，清晰地呈现出与仰韶文化庙底沟类型的渊源关系。这一阶段的典型纹饰皆由变体鸟纹演变而来，由圆圈和起伏变化的弧线灵活组合，是马家窑文化的先声。

马家窑类型是马家窑文化的早期发展阶段，距今5300—4900年。彩陶制作工艺从泥条盘筑法和捏塑法逐渐发展为慢轮制陶法，器表打磨得极为光滑，纹饰以旋涡纹、曲线波浪纹为特征，图案繁缛工整，疏密有致；线条奔放流畅，富有节奏感。

半山类型距今4700—4300年。由于农业加速发展，人们对储藏粮食的大型陶器的需求增加。此时彩陶器型逐渐变大，以壶、瓮等大型储藏器为主；纹饰由单一的黑色变为黑红搭配，对比鲜明，更显层次感；装饰纹样除了传统的旋涡纹，还出现了锯齿纹、网格纹、葫芦纹等。造型与图案浑然天成，把中华彩陶文化推向新的高度。

马厂类型距今4300—4000年，分布范围更加广泛，数量极多。目前出土的完整彩陶已经超过一万件；器型更加丰富，风格趋于简练、豪放，主要有四大圆圈纹、变体神人纹、网格纹、回形纹等；颜色变为单一的黑色，但由于纯度不高而呈现为灰黑色；造型、质地及装饰均远不及以前，显示出随着生产力水平不断提高，青铜器开始出现，彩陶逐渐衰落的趋势。

神秘莫测的旋涡纹

黄河中上游地区的文明起源，经历了距今约8000年的大地湾文化、距今约7000年的仰韶文化和距今约5000年的马家窑文化，完成了漫长的文明演进。

马家窑文化出现和形成的一个重要原因，是随着仰韶庙底沟文化生产力水平的不断提高，人口压力不断增大，一部分人离开家园，向西迁徙，到达并逐渐适应黄河上游地区的地理环境。经过一千多年的发展，他们创造了辉煌灿烂的旱作农业文化，把黄河文明的发展进程向前推进了一大步。

当我们注视马家窑彩陶时，一个疑问可能会从脑海中浮起：马家窑彩陶为什么如此反复使用旋涡纹，以至于成为它的重要特征之一？

对于奔腾的黄河之水进行极富想象力的描绘——这是一个可能的答案。马家窑彩陶上的旋涡纹，酷似激流涌动而形成的涡卷。设想，集中在黄河上游及其支流沿岸的马家窑先民，受到河水的滋养，他们升起膜拜之心与神圣感；而面对水流咆哮冲击而成的巨大旋涡，他们又升起敬畏之心与神秘感。于是，他们在彩陶之上反复描摹黄河留在他们心中的形象——神秘莫测又极具动感的旋涡。几千年之后，当我们看到这些图纹时，似乎可以看到一条奔涌不停的大河曾带给中华先民的同样奔腾不息的艺术创造力。

The pottery bottle decorated with whirlpool-shaped pattern belonged to Majiayao Style and bore witness to the peak of the 5,000-year Chinese painted pottery culture in the upper reaches of the Yellow River (e.g. Gansu and Qinghai). Ancestors at Majiayao imaginatively represented the surging Yellow River, which displayed the highest level of Chinese painted pottery culture and saw the formation and development of the Yellow River civilization in the late stage of the Neolithic Period.

Archaeologists were amazed at the painted pottery bottle: smooth whirlpool-shaped patterns, unrestrained and forceful flow of lines, etc. Did the patterns describe the swift current of the Yellow River?

Additionally, the bottle well combined aesthetics and practicality. It can be roped from the two holes. With the pointed bottom, water easily flew into the bottle. Owing to the buoyancy and the adjustment of center of gravity, the bottle would automatically tilt to one side. The small mouth prevented water from overflowing. In brief, the bottle became a *magnum opus* of painted pottery of the Majiayao Culture.

Painted pottery was widely distributed in China. In the history of Chinese civilization, painted pottery culture lasted for more than 5,000 years and played a prominent role, covering such styles as Laoguantai, Yangshao, Majiayao, Dawenkou, Qujialing, Daxi, Hongshan, Qijia and Xindian. In a way, painted pottery culture laid a solid foundation for the Chinese civilization.

The Majiayao Culture emerged in 1923, when a Neolithic cultural site was discovered at Majiayao Village, Lintao County, Gansu Province. Miaodigou Style of the Yangshao Culture in the Central Plains spread to the northwestern region. Under its influence, the Majiayao Culture came into being. With local color, it was viewed as “the Yangshao Culture in Gansu Province”. The Majiayao Culture appeared in the late stage of the Neolithic Period more than 5,700 years ago and lasted for more than 1,000 years.

The Majiayao Culture was characterized with highly-developed pottery-making technology. Painted pottery at Majiayao inherited and advanced the achievements of that at Miaodigou. With colorful and elegant style, it represented the highest artistic level of prehistoric Chinese painted pottery.

Population factor played an important role in the rise of the Majiayao Culture. As the productivity of the Yangshao Culture continuously increased, population pressure intensified. This sparked a wave of westward migration. The immigrant arrived at the middle and upper reaches of the Yellow River and accommodated to new geographical environment. In more than 1,000 years, they created a brilliant dry farming culture and furthered the development of the Yellow River civilization.

名称：蛋壳黑陶杯

年代：距今约5000年（屈家岭文化）

规格：高18.9厘米，口径9.9厘米

出土地点：河南省淅川县黄楝树村

收藏单位：河南博物院

Name: Eggshell-Thick Black Pottery Cup

Historical Period: *c*. 5,000 years ago (The Qujialing Culture)

Height: 18.9 cm, Mouth Diameter: 9.9 cm

Excavation Site: Huanglianshu Village, Xichuan County, Henan Province

Housed in: Henan Museum

中华先民是怎样创造出“薄如纸、硬如瓷”的蛋壳黑陶杯的？

五千多年前的手工业革命

蛋壳黑陶杯

Eggshell-Thick Black Pottery Cup

09

文物简读

这只陶杯薄如蛋壳，所采用的快轮制陶技术是距今5000多年前手工业领域一次重要的新技术革命。这项技术不仅成就了中华文明史制陶艺术的巅峰时刻，也成为整个人类新石器时代手工业技术领域的一个“神话”。

距今5000年前人类手工艺的千古绝唱

一只薄如蛋壳的陶杯！薄，薄到什么程度？

“0.2毫米的精致！”中央电视台《如果国宝会说话》节目在介绍龙山文化时期的蛋壳黑陶杯时，发出这样的惊叹。“距今4000年前地球文明的最精致之制作！”这是世界考古界对龙山时期黑陶杯的赞誉。

但事实上，考古成果很快便刷新了关于中国蛋壳黑陶的历史上限。在屈家岭文化遗址中发掘出来的蛋壳黑陶杯，将这种独步千古的工艺又向前推了一千年左右。

这只造型质朴但工艺精美的蛋壳黑陶杯，正是距今5000年左右的屈家岭文化的代表作，它比龙山文化时期的蛋壳黑陶器更早达到新石器时代人类手工艺的巅峰，留下了那个时代的千古绝唱。

陶器的发明，意味着人类第一次按照自己的意志，在大自然中创造出一种崭新的器物，这种器物的出现开启了人类一个新的时代，即新石器时代。旧石器时代是一个只能直接利用天然物的时代，如石头、骨头、木头；而新石器时代到来之后，人类开始按照自己的主观意志去创造。

在目前世界范围的考古发现中，最早的陶容器发现于中国江西仙人洞遗址，当地出土陶片年代为距今约2万年前。到距今5000多年前，当新石器时代进入晚期，在中国长江中游江汉平原的屈家岭，当时世界上最先进的手工艺发展成形，一种胎壁极薄的陶器被创造出来。这种让人惊叹的技术，无疑宣告了一场手工业领域新技术革命的到来。

屈家岭文化是20世纪50年代发现于湖北省荆门市京山屈家岭地区的新石器时代文化，距今5300—4600年。根据考古发现，这种以胎薄、对称为特征的蛋壳黑陶器在屈家岭文化早期遗址中便已经出现，到屈家岭文化晚期时得到普遍使用。屈家岭所留存的这场手工业新技术革命的遗址，使江汉地区在中华文明多元起源的璀璨星空中，发出了异常夺目的光芒。这只蛋壳黑陶杯发现于河南省淅川县（屈家岭晚期文化遗址），正是屈家岭新技术革命的成果之一。

“神话”是怎样创造出来的?

“黑如漆，亮如镜，薄如纸，硬如瓷。”这是最早发现龙山蛋壳黑陶杯的考古学家的赞叹和总结。屈家岭遗址出土的精美蛋壳黑陶杯，其胎仅厚0.1厘米至0.2厘米。而到龙山文化时期，最轻的蛋壳陶仅重十克左右。即便今天的工艺技术，要达到这样极致的薄度和轻度，也并不容易。那么，距今5000年前的中华先民是怎样做到的呢?

考古鉴定表明，蛋壳陶工艺的实现缘于快轮制陶技术的发明使用。快轮制陶技术是一种利用物体快速旋转而产生的离心力和惯性力来塑造形体的制陶工艺。其大致操作方法为：将泥胎置于轮盘的中央位置，快速旋转轮盘，利用其产生的离心力和惯性力，用手提拉出各种不同的造型。但在高速的旋转中，如此纤薄的陶胎非常容易破碎。薄胎成型堪称当时世界快轮制陶的典范。

屈家岭的快轮制陶技术显然并非一时或一人之功，而是深刻体现出中华文明在多元起源过程中，不同区系文化间相互作用、交互影响的轨迹。据考古发掘显示，位于长江中游地区的新石器时代大溪文化，其年代为距今6400—5300年，是一个以红陶文化为特征的古人类遗存，在其晚期遗址出土的陶器中，便已经出现使用快轮制陶技术的痕迹。屈家岭文化很好地继承了大溪文化的先进制陶技术，并将它逐渐发展成熟；到屈家岭文化晚期阶段，臻于完善的快轮制陶技术得到大力推广和普遍应用，影响范围不断扩大，进而传播到长江下游以及黄河中下游地区，在距今4000多年前的龙山文化中得到进一步发展，并被推向新的高潮。快轮制陶技术不仅成就了中华文明史上制陶艺术的巅峰时刻，也成为整个人类新石器时代手工业技术领域的一个“神话”。

As thin as eggshell, the pottery cup was made when the base was rotating rapidly. The technology signified a major technological revolution in the handicraft industry more than 5,000 years ago. It not only saw the peak of pottery-making art in the history of Chinese civilization, but also created a miracle in handicraft technology in the Neolithic Period.

Eggshell-thick black pottery cup looks simple in shape and embodies exquisite craftsmanship. It was a typical example of the Qujialing Culture about 5,000 years ago, and was earlier than eggshell-thick pottery ware in the Longshan Culture in the Neolithic Period, with everlasting charm in human history.

The invention of pottery meant that human beings created a new kind of artifact from nature at will for the first time and that the Neolithic Period started. That's to say, in the Paleolithic Period, human beings just directly used natural materials like stone, bone and wood, whilst in the Neolithic Period, they transformed natural materials with their cleverness and deftness.

Globally, the earliest pottery container was discovered at Xianren Cave, Jiangxi Province, China. The unearthed pottery pieces dated back to 20,000 years ago. More than 5,000 years ago, or the late stage of the Neolithic Period, at Qujialing, the Jianghan Plain (the middle reaches of the Yangtze River), archaeologists unlocked the most advanced handicraft in the world. A kind of pottery with extremely-thin inner wall was produced. The amazing technology undoubtedly announced a new technological revolution in the handicraft industry.

On the excavation site, archaeologists gasped at eggshell-thick black pottery cup: "Black as paint, bright as mirror, thin as paper, and hard as ceramic".

Archaeological identification confirmed that the realization of eggshell thick pottery technology depended on the invention and use of rapidly-rotating-base technology. It was a technology that used the centrifugal force and inertial force generated by the rapid rotation of objects to shape the body. In general, unfired pottery was firstly placed in the center of the base. Then the base was quickly rotated, which generated centrifugal force and inertial force and formed various shapes. However, in the rapid rotation of objects, the inner wall of pottery was very easy to break. Eggshell-thick black pottery cup epitomized the use of the technology for the first time in the world.

这件有明显凿齿现象的台湾卑南人头骨，与东南沿海地区百越先民的凿齿风俗有内在关联吗?

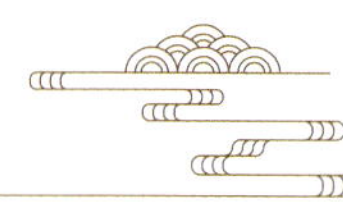

台湾与百越先民共同的文化基因

卑南人头骨

The Skull of the Puyuma

10

文物简读

这件台湾卑南人头骨上的凿齿现象，揭示了台湾地区古代先民与大陆东南百越先民具有相同的文化基因，表明台湾新石器文化是中华文明多元起源的满天星斗中的闪亮一颗。

备受瞩目的卑南遗址

总面积20余万平方米的卑南遗址，是台湾地区最具代表性的新石器时代人类聚落遗址，位于台东市西北卑南山附近。考古人员曾先后进行过13次考古发掘。据碳14测定，卑南遗址的年代为距今5300—2300年，其中又以距今3500—2300年最为兴盛。

卑南遗址出土的陶器和玉器数量巨大，共计两万余件。陶器多为橙色，为露天烧制，烧制温度不高，质地较软，以素面为主，极少纹饰。玉器则极为精美，主要有头饰、耳饰、颈饰、胸饰、腕饰、臂饰等，在造型上以玦形耳饰最富于变化，其中双立人玦形耳饰尤具特色，已成为台湾史前文化博物馆的标志。

卑南遗址还出土了大量石器，包括石锄、石斧、石刀、石镰、石杵等农业生产工具，可见其农业生产已达到较高水平。此外，遗址还出土了石箭镞、石核等狩猎工具，又可见其社会生产方式为农猎兼营。

卑南遗址之所以引人瞩目，是因为发掘出了千余座石板棺墓葬。这些墓葬成群分布，形式多样，结构复杂，甚至出现扣榫结构。其入葬形制绝大多数为单体葬，个别为多人葬。陪葬品丰富，不仅有陶器，而且有玉耳饰等玉器。从墓主人的形态看，有的死者面部盖有被打破的陶罐，有些死者上颌侧门齿被拔除。

为何出现门齿被拔除的现象？这与3500多年前卑南人的文化习俗有关吗？

名称：卑南人头骨

年代：距今5300—2300年（新石器时代晚期）

出土地点：台湾省台东市卑南遗址

收藏单位：台湾史前文化博物馆

Name: The Skull of the Puyuma

Historical Period: *c*. 2,300–5,300 years ago (The Late Stage of the Neolithic Period)

Excavation Site: Beinan Site, Taidong City, Taiwan Province

Housed in: Taiwan Prehistoric Culture Museum

神秘的凿齿风俗

头骨上颌一对侧门齿被人为拔除，这是典型的凿齿风俗。

随着中国史前考古成果的不断积累，越来越多与凿齿风俗相关的史前证据现世。最早发现凿齿现象的是大汶口文化，如山东泰安大汶口遗址、曲阜西夏侯遗址、兖州王因遗址、胶县三里河遗址以及苏北的邳县大墩子遗址等，其年代可追溯到距今6500年左右。这些遗址相继出土过十分丰富的凿齿头骨资料，可见凿齿风俗曾一度在这些地区盛行。但是，这种盛极一时的习俗却在大汶口文化之后的龙山文化中突然消失中断。然而奇怪的是，在远离大汶口的长江下游马家浜文化中却出现了丰富的凿齿遗证，如常州圩墩遗址（距今约6000年）；在长江中游，屈家岭文化的河南淅川遗址（距今约4500年）、湖北房县七里河遗址（距今约4900年）等也发现了凿齿现象；此外，上海崧泽遗址（距今约4000年）、福建闽侯昙石山遗址（距今约3300年），珠江流域的广东佛山河宕遗址（距今约4000年）、增城金兰寺遗址（距今约4500年）等也都有凿齿遗证出土。

这样，一幅新石器时代凿齿风俗的流衍图便被清晰地勾勒出来：凿齿风俗起源于6500多年前山东、苏北一带的大汶口文化早期，继而向南传入长江下游地区的马家浜文化区，而后又进一步传入长江中游的屈家岭文化地区及岭南地区、台湾地区。大汶口文化被新兴的龙山文化取代之后，凿齿风俗在黄河下游地区彻底消失，但在南方地区继续广泛流行和传播。

大汶口文化属东夷文化系统，而马家浜文化属百越文化体系。仅从凿齿风俗的流变，我们便可看出东夷文化与百越文化的密切联系。事实上，一些考古资料已经证明，百越族群的形成和发展很可能与东夷先民的南迁有关。

凿齿遗风在百越诸族中绵延久远。历史文献中有大量关于我国西南地区的僚、仡佬、濮、黎等民族凿齿的记载，如清朝的《百苗图》就描绘过“打牙部落”的形象。事实上，直到近代，西南、岭南及台湾等地区的世居民族还依然延续着凿齿风俗。

一脉相承的海峡两岸文化

古老而神秘的凿齿风俗流变传播图，正是中华民族史前文化传播与交融的真实体现。

台湾地区属于百越民族分布范围，该地区的史前文明与百越文化有诸多联系。这件有着凿齿特征的人头骨，客观上证实了台湾先民与大陆东南百越先民具有共同的文化基因。

最后，为什么凿齿？学者们发现，因实施凿齿的年龄段一般在14—15岁，恰好处于生理上的性成熟时期，所以凿齿风俗可能具有成年礼的性质。此外，也有学者认为凿齿与原始婚姻形态相关，有可能是新石器时代族外婚制度的产物。

On the skull of the Puyuma, the extracted teeth reveal that ancestors of Taiwan Province share the same cultural gene with ancestors of Baiyue tribes in the southeastern China. The Neolithic culture in Taiwan played an important part in the multiple origins of Chinese civilization.

With a total area of more than 200,000 square meters, Beinan Site boasts the most representative Neolithic human settlement site in Taiwan and adjoins the Beinan Mountain in the northwest of Taidong City, where archaeologists have carried out 13 times of excavations. According to the determination of Carbon-14, Beinan Site dates back to 2,300–5,300 years ago and thrived 2,300–3,500 years ago.

At Beinan Site were excavated more than 1,000 tombs with slate coffin. These tombs were distributed in groups, with various forms and complex structures (even the buckled-tenon-structure coffin). In burial form, most tombs had one person, and only several tombs had more than two persons. There were plenty of funerary objects, such as pottery and jade articles (earrings). In terms of the appearance of tomb owners, some were covered with broken pottery pots, and others had incisors in the upper jaw removed.

Why were the incisors extracted? Did it relate to cultural customs of the Puyuma more than 3,500 years ago?

The custom of extracting teeth emerged more than 6,500 years ago in the early stage of the Dawenkou Culture in northern Jiangsu Province and Shandong Province, spread southward to the Majiabang Culture in the lower reaches of the Yangtze River, and arrived at the Qujialing Culture in the middle reaches of the Yangtze River, the Lingnan Region and Taiwan. After the Dawenkou Culture was replaced by the Longshan Culture, the custom of extracting teeth completely disappeared in the lower reaches of the Yellow River, yet continued to prevail and expand in southern China.

The road map of the ancient and mysterious custom truthfully illustrated the dissemination and integration of the prehistoric cultures of the Chinese nation.

Baiyue tribes once lived in Taiwan. The prehistoric civilization in Taiwan was bound up with the Baiyue culture. The skull of the Puyuma with extracted teeth objectively demonstrates the common cultural genes of Taiwan and Baiyue tribes.

Scholars found that a person aged 14 or 15, a period of physiologically sexual maturity, would have his or her teeth extracted to finish traditional coming-of-age ceremony. Meanwhile, scholars viewed that the custom of extracting teeth involved the original marriage form, which probably arose from the exogamy system in the Neolithic Period.

名称：楔形双肩大石铲

年代：距今5000—4000年（新石器时代晚期）

规格：长66.7厘米，宽27.2厘米，厚1.9厘米

出土地点：广西壮族自治区南宁市隆安县大龙潭遗址

收藏单位：广西壮族自治区博物馆

Name: Wedge-Shaped Double-Shouldered Large Stone Shovel

Historical Period: 4,000–5,000 years ago (The Late Stage of the Neolithic Period)

Length: 66.7 cm, Width: 27.2 cm, Thickness: 1.9 cm

Excavation Site: Dalongtan Site, Long'an County, Guangxi Zhuang Autonomous Region

Housed in: Museum of Guangxi Zhuang Autonomous Region

四五千年前，是谁发明了这体形硕大、光滑精巧、用于耕作的石铲？

百越先民的史前稻作文明

楔形双肩大石铲

Wedge-Shaped Double-Shouldered Large Stone Shovel

11

文物简读

大石铲是新石器时代“大石铲文化圈”的重要标志物，在岭南地区随处可见。我们穿过岁月尘埃，依稀看见了百越的古老形象——一群创造了辉煌稻作农业文明的伟大先民。

桂南大石铲文化

1952年，民工们在广西崇左市大新县修筑道路时，无意中挖出一件造型奇特的有肩大石铲。这件文物在当时并没有引起人们的重视，文物部门仅将它归为“有肩石器”之列。几年后，崇左市扶绥县国营金光农场在开垦种植时，发现了大批类似石铲，其分布范围延及周围两公里左右。此时，当地文物部门才加以重视，并在南宁地区开展大规模普查，发现有石铲散布的史前文化遗址有30多处。此外，在南宁市郊，相继出土的石铲遗址之广，数量之丰富，超乎人们的想象。其中，隆安县几乎每一个村庄都发现了大石铲，一些村庄甚至出现整坑整坑的石铲。

自此，广西大石铲文化一鸣惊人。

“大石铲文化圈”

大石铲文化是岭南地区最具地域特色的一种新石器时代晚期的文化形态，以体形硕大、棱角对称、打磨光滑的有肩石铲为文化特征，分布地点主要集中在桂南左江、右江和邕江交汇处的三角地带，因此被称为“桂南大石铲文化”。历史上，大石铲文化以桂南为中心，传播范围遍及广东、海南以及越南北部等地区。学术界将这个以大石铲为主要文化特征的文化区域称为“大石铲文化圈”。

桂南大石铲主要分为三种类型。第一种为直腰型石铲，即铲身两侧边缘为直线，实用性较强；第二种为束腰型石铲，即铲身两侧边缘自肩以下开始收缩，至中腰后外展，然后呈弧状收缩为圆弧铲刃，这种石铲集实用性和装饰性为一体；第三种为短袖型石铲，即石铲双肩突出，造型类似人们夏季穿的短袖上衣，此类石铲体形硕大，装饰性极强，基本丧失了实用功能。

大石铲为何会出现从实用到非实用功能的演变？

学者揭示，在稻作生产过程中，人们越来越感受到大石铲作为生产工具的重要性，认为它是人们与上天进行沟通的媒介，通过特殊的仪式可把人的愿望上达于天，因此大石铲逐渐成为人们崇拜的对象。也正因此，大石铲体形逐渐变大，造型趋于装饰化，并从农业生产工具逐渐演化为礼器和祭器，进一步延伸出更多的宗教意义，如祈求人口繁衍、部落兴旺，作为盟誓见证等。如隆安大龙潭遗址出土的大石铲，以圆圈形或“门”形两种方式排列组合，有学者认为这是天圆地方观念的体现；也有学者认为它可能是男女生殖器的象征，其祭祀的对象是掌控生殖能力的大地之神。

那么，大石铲的使用者是谁？

他们是生活在这一带的百越先民。有肩石器正是百越文化的典型特征之一。

富于开拓精神的百越先民

百越，即古代的越人，是中国古代长江以南最大的族群，支系众多，主要包括吴越、扬越、东瓯、闽越、南越、西瓯、骆越等分支，它们在先秦文献中被统称为“百越”“百粤”“诸越”。百越分布极广，在东南分布于苏、浙、闽、赣、台等沿海地区，在岭南广布于粤、桂各地，在西南则分布于云、贵地区。此外，百越在皖、湘、鄂等地也有一定数量的分布。

百越先民主要生活于气候湿润、土地肥沃、水源充足的东南地区，形成了以农业与渔猎采集为主的生产方式。发达的稻作农业、渔猎文化、干栏式建筑、几何印纹陶器、断发文身凿齿习俗、悬棺葬俗、精湛的青铜冶炼技术、精美的岩画艺术等等，都是百越留下的鲜明的历史文化标记。近年来考古发现的我国最早的稻作农业遗迹湖南道县玉蟾岩遗址距今1.8万年—1.4万年的人工栽培稻标本，浙江浦江县上山遗址距今一万多年的栽培水稻遗迹，浙江余姚河姆渡遗址距今7000多年的大规模稻作农业遗迹，都位于百越的分布地区。其中，河姆渡出土的干栏式建筑，与百越后裔诸民族传承至今的干栏式民居遥相呼应。由此可以推断，百越先民是中国乃至世界上最早发明人工栽培水稻的人群之一。他们极富开拓精神，为中华民族的形成做出了伟大贡献。

Widely distributed in the Lingnan Region, large stone shovel meant an important symbol of "the Stone Shovel Culture Circle" in the Neolithic Period. It enables us to envision the old image of Baiyue tribes in history, a group of great ancestors who created brilliant rice farming civilization.

In 1952, when migrant workers were building roads at Daxin County, Chongzuo City, Guangxi, they unexpectedly dug out a large shouldered shovel with rarely-seen shape. Relevant departments of cultural relics just saw it as a shouldered stone ware and did not pay close attention to it. A few years later, when the state-owned Jinguang Farm at Fusui County, Chongzuo City was reclaimed, a large number of stone shovels were discovered in an area with a circumference of two kilometers. Therefore, competent departments started to conduct large-scale survey in Nanning. As proved, stone shovels dotted more than 30 prehistoric cultural sites. In particular, large stone shovels were discovered in most villages of Long'an County. Later, more stone shovels were unearthed in the suburbs of Nanning.

Large-stone-shovel culture embodied regional characteristics of the Lingnan Region in the late stage of the Neolithic Period. The stone shovel featured large shape, symmetrical edge and polished shoulder. "Southern Guangxi Large-Stone-Shovel Culture" was mainly distributed in the delta in southern Guangxi where the Zuojiang River, Youjiang River and Yongjiang River converged. Historically, large-stone-shovel culture spread from southern Guangxi to Guangdong and Hainan of China as well as northern Vietnam, which formed "Large-Stone-Shovel Culture Circle" in academic terms.

As scholars unmasked, in rice production, people increasingly recognized the importance of large stone shovel as a production tool and considered it a medium for them to communicate with the heaven or tell their wishes to the heaven via special rites. Therefore, they worshipped large stone shovel and enlarged or decorated it. Large stone shovel was then transformed from agricultural production tool into ritual or sacrificial vessel, with more religious color, such as praying for population multiplication, tribal prosperity and testimony of vows. For example, the large stone shovel unearthed at Dalongtan Site in Long'an County combined a circle-shaped structure with a *Jiong* (冂)-shaped structure. Some scholars believed that the shovel embodied the idea of "round sky and square earth". Some scholars regarded the shovel as symbols of male and female genitalia in the sacrificial ceremony for the god of the earth that determined the fertility of land. With a pioneering spirit, Baiyue tribes made outstanding contributions to the formation of the Chinese nation.

距今3000多年前，雪域高原为什么发生了由农而牧的文化突变?

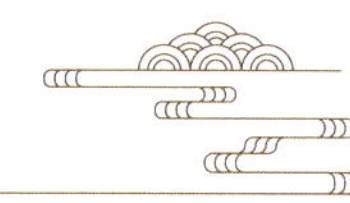

西藏地区史前农业文明之光

双体陶罐

Double-Body Pottery Pot

12

文物简读

这件双体陶罐是新石器时代卡若文化彩陶技艺的代表作，是一件充满宗教仪式感的礼器，体现了西藏地区在距今5000—4000年前高度发达的农业文明。

青藏高原上的文明星光

1978—1979年，考古工作者在西藏昌都地区发掘了一处具有重大意义的高原史前人类文化遗址，这就是大名鼎鼎的卡若文化遗址，它被考古界和古人类学界公认为西藏地区三大原始文化遗址之一。当这件双体陶罐在遗址中显露出来时，考古队员对它产生了极大的兴趣：夹细砂黄陶，腹部为袋形双体，中裆相连，表面饰有双勾三角折线纹和双勾菱形纹。这件连体彩陶罐的造型极为独特，在整个遗址中，类似造型的陶器仅出土一件。它是一件普通的生活用具，还是一件举行祭祀或庆典活动时使用的礼器?

作为目前西藏地区最早的新石器时代人类文化遗址，卡若遗址激发了整个考古界对于青藏高原早期文明起源的巨大探究欲——在中华文明多元一体起源格局中，居于高原独特地理气候环境中的卡若文化有什么特点?卡若文化从早期发达的农耕经济突变为晚期的畜牧经济，表明了什么?卡若文化与周边的新石器文化遗址又有什么关联?

名称：双体陶罐

年代：距今5000—4000年（卡若文化）

规格：高18.7厘米，长31厘米，宽15厘米

出土地点：西藏自治区昌都市卡若村

收藏单位：西藏博物馆

Name: Double-Body Pottery Pot

Historical Period: *c.* 4,000–5,000 years ago (The Karuo Culture)

Height: 18.7 cm, Length: 31 cm, Width: 15 cm

Excavation Site: Karuo Village, Changdu City, Tibet Autonomous Region

Housed in: Tibet Museum

雪域高原上的史前农业文明

这个距今5000—4000年的史前人类文化遗址，因位于昌都市东南澜沧江西岸的卡若村而得名，海拔3100多米，占地面积1万多平方米。遗址分为早、晚两期，古文化堆积层丰富，发现房屋基址遗迹31座，以及数量巨大的打制石器、磨制石器、细石器、骨器、陶片、装饰品；出土14种动物骨骼，其中包括驯养的家猪；还出土了保存较好并且尚未碳化的人工栽培农作物粟。卡若文化遗址有力地证明了早在四五千年前，便有先民在雪域高原上克服重重困难，开创了灿烂的农业文明。

卡若文化所处年代正是甘肃、青海地区马家窑文化高度繁荣时期。卡若文化在很多方面显示出与马家窑文化极深的渊源关系，比如半地穴式的建筑形式，切割器、锥状石核、柱状石核等打制石器以及条形石斧、条形石锛等磨制石器的样式和制作工艺，人工栽培农作物粟，彩陶制作工艺等等，都表现出了与马家窑文化的相似性。

但卡若文化也表现出了强烈的地方特色。如卡若文化遗址出土的陶器均为小平底，没有出现中原仰韶文化和甘青地区马家窑文化中的三足器和圆底器，而且其器型多为罐、钵、盆等，纹饰以刻画和手绘三角折线纹为特色。这些文化特点应当是先民适应高原的特殊地理环境而形成的。

以这件器型独特的双体陶罐而言，研究者认为，它是卡若文化地方特色的集中体现。卡若文化尚处于母系氏族社会阶段，女性具有很高的社会地位。这件连体陶器从造型特征来看，与母亲哺育生命的乳房十分相似，具有生殖崇拜的文化内涵。

卡若文化形态的突变

卡若文化晚期，文化形态呈现出一种突变现象，表现为：磨制石器骤然减少，打制石器和细石器逐渐增多；陶器纹饰突然变得简单化，彩绘纹饰不见了，仅剩简单的刻画纹，单耳罐、带流罐等早期典型器型也都突然消失了；早期的半地穴式房屋逐渐减少，大量石砌建筑取而代之，甚至出现了石砌楼屋，呈现出一派新建筑文化面貌。

是什么导致了这样的文化突变？

考古学家寻找到的答案是卡若先民放弃了农业经济，转而选择了畜牧经济。正是经济形态的转变，带来了文化面貌的巨大变化。

那么，又是什么导致了由农而牧的变化？

自然气候之变是一个决定性因素。根据近年来对远古气候的研究，距今7500—5000年前是全球性气候转暖期，青藏高原地区明显转向温暖湿润的气候。此时正是卡若文化的形成和发展时期，温暖湿润的气候环境为农业生产活动提供了必要条件；距今3000多年前，全新世小冰期到来，全球气候变得寒冷干燥，西藏卡若地区发展农业经济的自然地理优势逐渐消失，为适应外部环境的巨大变化，卡若先民放弃农耕，选择以畜牧业作为主要生计。

主动适应畜牧经济的卡若先民赢得了一片更广大的生存天地，他们从以往仅适合农业生产的河谷地段中解放出来，走出峡谷，在高原上更宽阔的空间中创造了丰富的物质文化和精神文化。

卡若文化晚期大量石砌围墙、石围圈的出现，正是为了满足畜牧生产的需要；尤其是下层圈养牲畜、上层居住的石墙楼屋的出现，更是畜牧业发展的体现。这种建筑形式至今仍广泛流行于西藏地区，并成为独具特色的传统碉房样式。

对复杂多变的自然地理环境的主动适应与积极挑战，使中华先民在不同的地理条件下开创出灿烂的文明，卡若文化遗址就是最好的证明。

Double-body pottery pot is a typical example of painted pottery in the Karuo Culture in the Neolithic Period. As a symbol of religious ceremony, it represents highly-developed agricultural civilization in Tibet around 4,000–5,000 years ago.

From 1978 to 1979, China organized scientific excavation at Karuo Site, a prehistoric cultural site in Changdu, Tibet. Acknowledged as one of the three major primitive cultural sites in Tibet by archaeologists and paleoanthropologists, Karuo Site enjoys a great reputation. Upon excavation, double-body pottery pot aroused archaeologists' interest. Made of yellow pottery mixed with fine sand, it had two large bag-shaped bodies in the belly, connected at the crotch in the middle. The surface was decorated with double-line triangular-broken-line patterns and double-line rhombic patterns. With unique shape, it was *the one and only* at Karuo Site.

Karo Site incontrovertibly proves that as early as 5,000 years ago, ancestors surmounted innumerable difficulties and forged brilliant agricultural civilization on the Qinghai-Tibet Plateau.

Researchers hold the view that double-body pottery pot epitomizes the local color of the Karuo Culture. The Karuo Culture developed in the stage of matriarchal clan society in which women enjoyed a high social status. In shape, double-body pottery pot resembles woman's breasts (for suckling) and culturally typifies the reproduction worship.

According to the research on ancient climate in recent years, about 5,000–7,500 years ago, global warming happened, and the Qinghai-Tibet Plateau became warm and humid. Simultaneously, the Karuo Culture budded and grew. The warm and humid climate or environment provided *sine qua non* for agricultural production. More than 3,000 years ago, with the arrival of the Holocene Little Ice Age, global climate became cold and dry. Karuo Region in Tibet lost natural and geographical advantages for developing agricultural economy. In order to find their feet, Karuo ancestors abandoned farming and chose stockbreeding as a means of livelihood.

In the late stage of the Karuo Culture, many stone walls and stone enclosures were constructed to suit the needs of stock raising. Stone-walled house was also built. The ground floor was used to raise livestock and the first floor was used as a living space. This accorded with the development of stockbreeding. Today, the architectural style remains popular in Tibet and becomes *tnkhar*, a special Tibetan house style.

In the face of ever-changing natural & geographical environment as well as various challenges, Tibetan ancestors created brilliant civilization. Karuo Site is the most convincing evidence.

距今4000多年前的陶器上，赫然写着一个醒目的“文”字。它标识着汉字的源头吗？

四千多年一脉相承的“文”字

朱书扁陶壶

Flat Pottery Pot with Characters Written with Cinnabar

13

文物简读

这件距今4000多年的扁陶壶上的朱书汉字“文”，与当代汉字“文”相比，无论字形还是结构都完全一致，这不仅表明中国文字一脉相承，更体现了中华文明不曾中断、连续发展的特征。

一个四千多年前的“文”字

1982年，山西襄汾陶寺遗址，考古队员在陆续发掘出规模空前的城址、世界最早的观象台、气势恢宏的宫殿之后，竟有了一个小小的但也许更石破天惊的发现：一个残破的陶壶！在扁壶的正面鼓腹部，考古队员们似乎发现了最早的文字！

这是两个用朱砂书写的字符，其中一个能被清晰识读，它酷似甲骨文和金文中的“文”字！

陶寺文化大约兴起于4300多年前，拥有庞大的城市，其都城面积达到惊人的280万平方米。这里不仅建有宫殿、宫城以及贵族居住区，还设立有专门的平民居住区。以王城为中心，陶寺方国的面积大约有1740平方公里。古载“王者居百里之地”，陶寺方国的面积正好与此吻合。专家们指出，陶寺遗址极有可能就是“尧都平阳”的所在。

对于朱书扁陶壶上的另一个字，考古学家何驽对它做了一个大胆推测，认为它是“尧”——两字合为“文尧”。“文”，乃“文德”之意；而尧帝，即为“文德”之君。从时间上推算，朱书扁陶壶的制造时期应为夏朝，早已不是尧帝的时代。因此，朱书扁陶壶有可能代表着对圣君尧帝光荣时代的追忆。

名称：朱书扁陶壶

年代：距今约4000年（中原龙山文化晚期）

规格：口长径20.8厘米，短径9.2厘米，残高27.4厘米

出土地点：山西省襄汾县陶寺遗址

收藏单位：中国社科院考古所

Name: Flat Pottery Pot with Characters Written with Cinnabar

Historical Period: *c.* 4,000 years ago (The Late Stage of the Longshan Culture in the Central Plains)

Mouth Diameter (Long): 20.8 cm, Mouth Diameter (Short): 9.2 cm, Height (Residual Part): 27.4 cm

Excavation Site: Taosi Site, Xiangfen County, Shanxi Province

Housed in: The Institute of Archaeology, CASS

汉字的产生

今天的中国人从古代文物上能清晰识读的最早文字，正是这一个“文”字。这怎么不令中华子孙感到无比骄傲和自豪！四千多年间一脉相承的“文”字，就是一部不曾中断、连续发展的中华文明史的高度象征！

作为世界上最古老的文字之一，汉字的出现并非一蹴而就，而是经历了一个漫长的孕育过程。其中，具有记事功能的刻画符号，尤其是出现在陶器上的符号，就是文字孕育过程的主要表现形式。考古学家在中国多处史前文化遗址中都发现了带有刻画符号的陶器或陶片，如西安半坡仰韶文化遗址，出土了一百余件带有刻画符号的陶器，这些符号大多刻画在陶器的口沿部位，有专家认为它们是汉字的雏形。

山东莒县陵阳河大汶口文化晚期遗址出土的距今约4500年的大口陶尊，其表面也出现了大量的刻画符号，共计十余种类型，其中以“日火山”的组合最为典型。据专家推断，这个符号是对当地日出场景的描绘，而这种大口尊则是用于祭祀太阳的祭器。

河南登封王城岗龙山文化晚期遗址的陶器上也发现了距今4000多年的刻画符号，如在一件薄胎黑陶平底器的外底上刻画着一个符号，由左右两部分组成，与甲骨文和金文中的“共”字极为相似。专家推测王城岗遗址很可能是禹都阳城的遗存，在这里出土的陶器上的“[illegible]”字，与陶寺朱书“文”字互为佐证，表明至少在四千多年前，汉字完成了由记事符号到文字的蜕变。伴随着夏王朝的出现，真正意义上的汉字开始走向成熟。

谁创造了汉字?

传承使用了几千年的汉字，是怎样创造出来的?

中国自古就有仓颉造字的传说。相传，仓颉是黄帝时期的史官，天生睿德。他通过观察星宿的变化规律和鸟兽的足迹创制了文字，被尊奉为“文祖”。那么真如传说所言，汉字是仓颉创造的吗?

汉字的前身刻画符号是广大人民群众集体智慧的结晶，而具有高度概括和抽象特征的文字，则是对大量的刻画符号进行系统的归纳整理、去粗取精后，才形成的固定的形、音、义符号。这是一个十分严密、细致的工程，只有专门从事脑力劳动的人们，如巫史，才有可能完成这项任务。从这个角度来看，仓颉作为“黄帝之史”，的确有可能是汉字的创造者。仓颉生活于距今4600年左右的黄帝时期，而发现最早文字的陶寺遗址和王城岗遗址所处的年代为距今4000多年。由此看来，仓颉造字的传说故事是有根据的。

虽然我们不能武断地说汉字就是仓颉所造，但有一点可以肯定，正是那个时代的“仓颉”们，用智慧对世代使用的刻画符号进行归纳整理、有机组合，经过不懈努力，终于形成一套具有象形、指事、会意、形声四大特点和功能的语言符号体系。

殷商时期，汉字已发展成为成熟的文字体系，甲骨文便是有力的证明。周朝，出现了钟鼎文。秦朝对汉字进行了一次全面、系统的规范，将全国的文字统一为小篆字形。此后，汉字又不断发展演变，出现了隶书、草书、行书、楷书等不同的书体。

四千多年前的“文”字竟与当代简体汉字“文”如此一致，这让我们明白：文字的连续性，就是文明的连续性；文明的连续性，让中华民族的思维逻辑高度统一，这正是中华文明强大凝聚力的体现。

On the flat pottery pot was written a striking Chinese character *Wen* (文) with cinnabar more than 4,000 years ago. The character exactly matches up with its contemporary counterpart in both form and structure. This demonstrates not only the origin of Chinese characters but also the continued development of Chinese civilization.

In 1982, when archeologists successively excavated the unheard-of city site, the earliest observatory in the world and the magnificent palace at Taosi Village, Xiangfen County, Shanxi Province, they saw an inconspicuous broken flat pottery pot that would rock the world. In the front belly of the flat pot, archaeologists probably discovered the earliest characters.

In the two characters, one can be clearly read. It looks like *Wen* (文) in oracle bone inscriptions and bronze inscriptions.

With respect to the other character, He Nu, an archaeologist, conjectured that it was *Yao* (尧) and that the two words read *Wen Yao*. As he explained, *Wen* meant the education of rite-music culture, and *Yao* meant the ancient emperor-sage Yao. From a historical perspective, the flat pottery pot was made in the Xia Dynasty, when Taosi was no longer the center of various states. Therefore, the flat pottery pot may represent the admiration for the glorious age of the Emperor Yao.

Chinese characters developed from carved symbols, which crystallized the collective wisdom of Chinese ancestors. When ancestors used these symbols to express general or abstract meanings, they must systematically re-organize them and choose the expressive symbols, so as to create symbols with fixed form, pronunciation and meaning. It was an arduous task that *Wu Shi* (巫史, those in charge of divination and annals) can assume. Noticeably, Cang Jie, the official historian of the Yellow Emperor, was credited with inventing the Chinese writing system. Cang Jie lived about 4,600 years ago. The earliest characters discovered at Taosi Site and Wangchenggang Site date back to more than 4,000 years ago. Therefore, the legend of Cang Jie was well-founded.

The case of *Wen* on the flat pottery pot illuminates that the continuity of characters means the continuity of civilization. And the continuity of civilization fosters the way of thinking of the Chinese nation and enhances the cohesion of Chinese civilization.

一枚小小的簧片，在中华大地上历经四千余年的发展，仍长盛不衰，是什么让它拥有如此强大的生命力？

贯通古今4000年的神性乐器

骨制口簧

Bone *Kou Huang* (口簧, Stringed Musical Instrument Played with Mouth)

14

文物简读

这件骨制口簧是目前发现的世界上最早的弦乐器。作为至今仍在中国许多民族中传承的乐器，它贯通古今、绵延传承的特性，是中华文明亘古绵长的生命力的象征，也是中华民族历史上深层文化交流的见证。

石峁的发现

石峁，一座四千多年前的古城，面积超过四百万平方米。在中国历史上第一个王朝夏建立的前夜，它就已矗立在陕北沟壑纵横的高山台塬之上。如今，考古发掘已经揭示出它恢宏磅礴的立体城池——金字塔状的皇城台固若金汤，石峁的“王”和贵族们，就生活在台顶近八万平方米的空间；宫室建筑周边，镶嵌着体量巨大、题材丰富的石雕，类似图腾柱的石柱至今仍矗立在四千年前的地面上……

据已有的研究成果，石峁人群的根就在中国北方，他们从距今5000年左右的仰韶晚期文化延续而来，与晋南地区的陶寺古人群具有密切的遗传联系。

石峁的许多发现石破天惊，在石峁考古队队长孙周勇看来，石峁弥漫着浓厚的“圣城”氛围，比如埋藏在城墙石缝之间的玉琮薄片，以及数百片之多的卜骨；而从21件骨制口簧——这种在传说中有“通天”功能、代表着人类初音的乐器之上——更可以感知石峁的神圣一面。

“人类拥有的第一件乐器”

当石峁的骨制口簧刚被发现时，没有人知道它是什么东西。当时的湖北省博物馆馆长、考古学家

名称：骨制口簧

年代：距今约4000年

规格：长8—9厘米，宽逾1厘米，厚仅1—2毫米

出土地点：陕西省榆林市神木市高家堡镇石峁村

收藏单位：陕西省考古研究院

Name: Bone *Kou Huang* (口簧, Stringed Musical Instrument Played with Mouth)

Historical Period: *c*. 4,000 years ago

Length: 8–9 cm, Width: More than 1 cm, Thickness: 1–2 mm

Excavation Site: Shimao Village, Gaojiabao Town, Shenmu, Yulin City, Shaanxi Province

Housed in: Shaanxi Academy of Archaeology

方勤来到石峁后，却一眼辨识了出来："这不就是口簧嘛！"他毫不犹豫地做出如此肯定的判断，源于此前在湖北省博物馆举办的一场名为《初音》的展览。这场精彩的展览由中国民族博物馆举办，展示了来自中国少数民族地区以及世界各地的数百件代表性口簧。摆在方勤眼前的这些四千多年前的口簧，竟与《初音》中展示的我国民族地区的口簧毫无二致！

口簧是一种具有"胚胎"意义、音乐"活化石"价值的原始乐器。"女娲作笙簧"的记载，把簧的发明者直溯于创世始祖女娲。《世本》引《唐乐志》称："女娲作笙，列管于匏上，纳簧其中。"口簧因此被称为"人类拥有的第一件乐器"，曾经被赋予通神的功能。至今，在我国西南一些民族的文化记忆中，口簧仍具有与神灵相通的属性。

在发现石峁骨制口簧的现场，还发现了制作口簧的骨片以及半成品，这使考古学家大致复原出四千多年前的口簧制作过程：选取黄牛肋骨或动物长骨等骨料，经过切磨骨片、剔刻簧舌、簧尾钻孔、精细加工等四个步骤，完成制作。孙周勇认为，石峁骨制口簧有可能被赋予了沟通人神的功能，与骨笛等音乐遗物一起，被运用于石峁上层的祭祀场景中。由此，口簧在某种程度上成为石峁上层控制周边、维系区域政体稳定的重要非物质手段。

一张浩大繁复的口簧传播图

经过细致的研究，孙周勇发现，石峁骨制口簧的框首圆孔外缘，保存了绳子拉振留下的痕迹，表明这件乐器是通过绳拉实现簧舌振动发声，即所谓"绳振簧"。

这是世界上最早的自体绳振簧！孙周勇得出了这个重要的结论。

口簧文化是如何向周围地区传播和扩散的？孙周勇推测，应在夏商时期，不晚于距今3500年前，石峁口簧向周边传播，并影响到夏家店下层文化人群。

事实上，在漫长的传播史中，口簧绘成了浩大繁复的文化版图，融入了各区域、各民族之间复杂而深远的文化交往交流交融中……

《诗经》曾吟唱："我有嘉宾，鼓瑟吹笙，吹笙鼓簧，承筐是将。"今天，口簧在我国汉族地区已很少传承，但它却广泛流行于民族地区，成为纵贯北方与南方乃至台湾地区少数民族的共同文化现象，并获得了不同的称谓：赫哲族称"悲琴"，满族称"莫库尼"，哈萨克族称"阿吾孜考姆兹"，傣族称"拜"，景颇族称"掌共"，佤族称"合朗"，拉祜族称"阿沓"，羌族称"阿珠"，锡伯族称"玛肯"，独龙族称"芒锅"，彝族称"洪洪"或"弄果"，傈僳族称"玛哥"，白族称"毕协"，黎族称"口弓"，高山族称"嘴琴"或"嘎洛波"……在这些民族中，口簧既有沟通人神的神性功能，也有传递爱情的诗性功能。

由此可见，口簧成了一种生生不息、由古衍今的文化现象。其延续传承之久，正是中华文化亘古绵长、不曾中断的象征；其传播辐射之广，又是中华民族文化交融深厚、互动频繁的见证。

The bone *Kou Huang* is the earliest reed instrument in the world. As a musical instrument that is widely played in ethnic minorities in China, *Kou Huang* emblematizes the long history of Chinese civilization and embodies deep cultural exchanges among various ethnic groups.

As an ancient musical instrument, *Kou Huang* (口簧) functions as a living fossil or an evidence of evolution of primitive music. *Sheng* and *Huang* were said to be created by the first female ancestor Nü Wa. In *Records of Music in the Tang Dynasty* (《唐乐志》), it was mentioned that: "When Nü Wa was making *Sheng* (笙), she arranged the tube-shaped instruments on a gourd, after which she put in the reed." Hailed as "the first musical instrument of human beings", *Kou Huang* was deemed as a medium to divine soul, which continues in the cultural memory of ethnic groups in southwestern China.

At Shimao Site, bone pieces and semi-finished products were also discovered, which allowed archaeologists to roughly restore the process of making *Kou Huang* more than 4,000 years ago. Firstly, high-density bone materials, such as cattle ribs or other animal's long bones were selected. After four steps, i.e. cutting & grinding the bone pieces, engraving the mouth part of *Kou Huang*, drilling holes at the end of *Kou Huang* and polishing, *Kou Huang* was completed. According to Sun Zhouyong, the bone *Kou Huang* at Shimao Site, together with bone flute and other musical relics, displayed musical development in the palace-architecture area at Shimao Site. Used in the sacrificial scenes of the upper class, *Kou Huang* functioned as an important non-material means for the upper class at Shimao to harness the surrounding areas and maintain the stability of regional political system to some extent.

Sun Zhouyong speculated that *Kou Huang* at Shimao Site spread to the surrounding areas and had an influence on the masses at Xiajiadian in the Xia and Shang Dynasties, or at least 3,500 years ago.

In *Book of Songs* (《诗经》), ancestors chanted: "I have here admirable guests; /The lutes are struck and the organ is blown for them; / The organ is blown till its tongues are all moving. / The baskets of offerings are presented to them." (The English translation by Xu Yuanchong) Today, *Kou Huang* is widely popular among ethnic groups. It both connects people and gods and expresses love.

In a word, *Kou Huang* forms a cultural phenomenon in the long history of Chinese culture. It takes on new appearance, spreads to the whole country, and witnesses deep cultural integration and interaction of all Chinese ethnic groups.

神秘奇谲而令人惊叹的三星堆文化，其主人是谁？铸造技术如此高超的青铜文明又来自哪里？

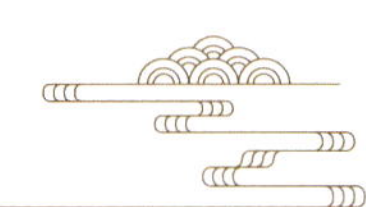

震撼世界的三星堆文化

青铜纵目面具

Bronze Mask with Protruding Eyes

15

文物简读

这件有“千里眼”“顺风耳”之誉的青铜面具，不仅承载了三星堆文化辉煌的青铜文明，而且揭示了三星堆文化与中原夏商文明的内在关联。

震惊世界的发现

1929年春天的一个早晨，一个叫燕道诚的四川广汉农民，像往常一样带着儿子在地里干活。无意中他发现了一个石洞，里面保存着三百多件大大小小的玉器。从此，一个沉睡数千年的文明渐渐醒来。

1931年春，在广汉传教的英国传教士董笃宜（V. H. Donnithorne）敏锐地发现这些玉器不同寻常，并告知了时任华西协合大学博物馆馆长葛维汉（David C. Graham）。1934年春，葛维汉组建考古队，在广汉县县长罗雨苍的主持下，开展了对三星堆遗址的第一次考古发掘。这次发掘成果极为丰硕，出土了大量造型奇特的物品，但现场的考古学家们却完全无法理解他们所看到的东西。此后，全面抗战爆发，三星堆考古工作长期停滞。

中华人民共和国成立后，三星堆考古工作重启。20世纪80年代，三星堆发掘取得重大进展，上千件珍贵文物出土，其中有世界上最早、体形最大的青铜神树；有世界上最早的象征王权与神权的金杖；有被称为“铜像之王”的青铜大立人像……这些文物一经现世，便震惊了世界。

2020年以来，三星堆遗址新一轮考古发掘再启，再度取得重大突破，六个祭祀坑共出土文物近1.3万件，其中有黄金面具、神树纹玉琮、龟背形网格状器、铜顶璋龙形饰、铜神坛、铜巨型神兽等。一个个奇特的发现，一次次轰动了全国。

名称：青铜纵目面具
年代：距今约3200年
规格：两耳间距138厘米，通高66厘米
出土地点：四川省广汉市三星堆遗址
收藏单位：三星堆博物馆

Name: Bronze Mask with Protruding Eyes
Historical Period: *c.* 3,200 years ago
Width (Between Two Ears): 138 cm, Total Height: 66 cm
Excavation Site: Sanxingdui Site, Guanghan, Sichuan Province
Housed in: Sanxingdui Museum

三星堆的出土文物表明，这是一个生产力高度发达的文明。但令人不解的是，浩如烟海的中华史料文献，为何未曾记载这个长江流域高度发达的青铜文明？

三星堆的主人是谁？

这件青铜面具形体硕大，被人们形象地称为“千里眼”“顺风耳”。它带着神秘微笑的面孔上，有两只柱状的、向外凸出的眼球。

面对这件奇怪的青铜面具，人们猛然意识到：三星堆不是没有记载，而是以往的历史学家们往往没有把那些记载当作正史，而只是当作了志怪传说。比如，东晋史学家常璩所著《华阳国志·蜀志》载：“有蜀侯蚕丛，其目纵，始称王。”这件青铜面具不就是“纵目”之相吗？

三星堆的发现让考古学家们开始重新审视那些记录在文献中的传说故事。那么，三星堆文化的主人就是以蚕丛为代表的古蜀国吗？古蜀国从何而来？究竟存在了多久？它与中原王朝是什么关系？

三星堆考古发掘的过程，就是一个探索与解谜的过程。事实上，近30年来持续积累的考古成果，让举世瞩目的三星堆之谜已经初步得到了破解。

从年代来看，三星堆遗址可以划分为四期：

三星堆一期文化，距今4800—4000年，属宝墩文化范畴，为本地文化类型。

三星堆二期文化，距今4000—3600年，大致与夏朝年代相始终，有明显的外来文化因素传入，如陶盉、高柄豆以及铜牌饰等，包含了二里头文化因素。

三星堆三期文化，距今3600—3200年，对应中原的商朝时期，开始大量出现青铜器，明显受商代青铜器制作技艺的影响。

三星堆四期文化，距今3200—2600年，属十二桥文化，与金沙遗址时间相近，文化特征类似。

关于三星堆与中原文化的关系，已经有了较为清晰的揭示。比如，三星堆发现了大量牙璋。作为中原礼器最重要的一个类别，牙璋随着中原文化的发展、礼制礼器的变化而逐渐消失，但它却在古蜀文化中继承并保留了下来。

三星堆青铜器中还出现了尊、罍，这些器物也是中原地区殷商时代的典型礼器，它们异常清晰地显示出三星堆文化对中原文化因素的吸纳。

2012年，中国科学技术大学考古实验室在分析三星堆青铜器皿时，发现其内含一种不同寻常的元素——具有放射性的铅的同位素，学者称之为“异常铅”。经过比对，邻近的金沙遗址、汉中遗址出土的青铜器中，没有发现这种元素；然而江西吴城出土的青铜器中，却发现了这种元素。有意思的是，就在吴城遗址旁，考古工作者还发现了一座规模巨大、设施齐全的古代铜矿遗址；在矿藏的炼渣中，考古工作者同样发现了“异常铅”。

种种研究成果逐渐揭示出三星堆与当时不同区域文化之间的交流联系。

震惊世界的三星堆之谜，仍在探索与解答之中。显然，三星堆的发现，再次有力地证明了中华文明起源的多元一体格局，而三星堆文明正是此格局下富有特色的次级文明。在中华文明的孕育发展过程中，这一极其奇谲瑰丽的华彩篇章最后也融进了中华文明的宏大交响中。

With protruding eyes and winglike ears, the bronze mask not only epitomizes the splendid bronze civilization of Sanxingdui, but also evidences the correlation of the Sanxingdui Culture with the Xia and Shang civilizations in the Central Plains.

The spring, 1929, Yan Daocheng, a farmer in Guanghan, Sichuan, took his son to work in the field as usual in a morning. He accidentally discovered a large stash of jade artifacts (more than 300). This was the first clue that eventually led to the discovery of a mysterious ancient kingdom.

In the 1980s, great progress was made in the excavation of Sanxingdui Site, and thousands of precious cultural relics were unearthed, including the oldest and largest bronze holy tree in the world, the earliest gold scepter symbolizing kingship and divinity in the world, the colossal bronze figure, etc.

Archaeological findings continue to emerge to this day. From 2020 to 2022, nearly 13,000 cultural relics were unearthed at six sacrificial pits, including gold mask, jade *cong* (琮) with holy-tree patterns, tortoise-back-shaped grid-structure bronze artifact (with an oval jade), dragon-shaped bronze ornament with jade *zhang* (璋) on the top, bronze altar, bronze giant divine animal, etc. All these fantastic discoveries caused a sensation across the country.

The bronze mask with protruding eyes and winglike ears could be a depiction of Can Cong, founder of the Shu Kingdom. In "Records of Shu" of *Records of the Lands South of Mt. Hua* (《华阳国志・蜀志》), Chang Qu, a historian of the Eastern Jin Dynasty, stated that: "Can Cong, chief of Shu, has protruding eyes and establishes the Shu Kingdom."

A large number of *Ya Zhang* (牙璋) were discovered at Sanxingdui Site. With the development of the culture and the change of ancient sacrificial vessel, *Ya Zhang* disappeared in the Central Plains yet continued in the ancient Shu culture.

Wine vessels like *Zun* (尊) and *Lei* (罍) were also discovered among bronze artifacts at Sanxingdui, which were typical sacrificial vessels in the Shang Dynasty in the Central Plains. These relics fully proved how the Sanxingdui Culture absorbed the cultural elements of the Central Plains.

In 2012, while analyzing the bronze vessels at Sanxingdui, Archaeometry Laboratory of University of Science and Technology of China detected an unusual element, a radioactive isotope of lead, which was termed anomalous lead. Archaeologists also discovered an ancient bronze-mine site with large scale and complete equipment near Wucheng Site, Jiangxi Province. In the slag smelting of the bronze mine, they found anomalous lead too. As evinced, the Sanxingdui Culture interacted and communicated with different regional cultures at that time.

The discovery of Sanxingdui Site corroborates the multiple origins of Chinese civilization and constitutes a brilliant section in the symphony of Chinese civilization.

作为资深牧羊人的古羌人，对中华民族的形成和发展做出了哪些贡献?

延续三千年的古羌文化符号

骨笛

Eagle Bone Flute

16

文物简读

作为羌笛的前身，这截残存的骨笛不仅是卡约文化农、牧、猎多种生产方式并存的体现，也是羌笛作为中华民族延续至今的文化符号的证明。

传承古今的羌笛

羌笛，一个古老的文化符号。每当我们吟诵起“羌笛何须怨杨柳，春风不度玉门关”的诗句时，心中就会升起幽幽古意，不禁想象那一支在中华历史上轻轻吹起的古笛。

这一支古老的“羌人之笛”用鹰骨制成，出土于青海省西宁市西郊朱家寨青铜时代的卡约文化墓地，笛身有八孔。学术界普遍认为这就是三千多年前的古羌人使用过的笛。

鹰骨笛是古羌先民的传统乐器。研究表明，古羌人有崇拜鹰的习俗。在古羌人的原始宗教中，鹰被认为具有沟通天地的灵性。古羌人用鹰骨制作成笛子，就是希望借鹰的灵性与天地相通。今天，新疆、甘肃、云南、西藏等地的民族中仍有鹰骨笛流传，其形制和吹奏方式与卡约文化的鹰骨笛基本相同，极有可能与古羌人的迁徙密切相关。

古羌人留在历史上的身影

仰望中华文明多元起源的满天星斗，在青藏高原与黄土高原的交界地带，我们会看到哪些闪耀的星光?

名称：骨笛
年代：距今约3000年（卡约文化）
规格：残长15.4厘米，直径约1.1厘米
出土地点：青海省西宁市西郊朱家寨
收藏单位：青海省博物馆

Name: Eagle Bone Flute
Historical Period: *c.* 3,000 years ago (The Kayue Culture)
Length (Residual Part): 15.4 cm, Diameter: *c.* 1.1 cm
Excavation Site: Zhujiazhai, West Suburb of Xining, Qinghai Province
Housed in: Qinghai Provincial Museum

这里曾出现过高度发达的新石器文化，先后有大地湾、马家窑、齐家、卡约、辛店、诺木洪等文化类型，从距今8000多年前一直延续到距今约3000年前，对周人的崛起以及华夏族群的孕育和起源都起到了重要的推动作用。而创造这些文化的先民们，在适应地理气候变化的过程中，逐渐分化出了一支以畜牧业为主要经济形态的后裔，即古羌人。

羌，中华民族大家庭中最古老的族群之一，分布范围极其广泛，支系极其众多，对中华民族的形成和发展产生过广泛而深远的影响。羌与炎帝有着幽深的关联。《国语·晋语》称“炎帝以姜水成”，“故……炎帝为姜”。在甲骨文中，“羌”从“羊”从“人”，“姜”从“羊”从“女”，两字相通。当表示族类和地望时，用“羌”；表示女性和姓氏时，用“姜”。这就显示出炎帝与羌的内在关系。羌还与大禹关系甚深。《史记》称：“禹兴于西羌。”南朝宋裴骃《史记集解》曰：“孟子称禹生石纽，西夷人也，传曰‘禹生西羌’是也。”今天我国的羌族地区仍存有“禹穴”“石纽山”等遗迹。羌还与周人有着深刻的血缘关系。史载，周人来源于西北游牧部落，奉后稷为始祖，后稷母为姜嫄。而姜嫄之姜姓，就表明先周将自身的母系血缘追认为西羌的史实。

中华畜牧文化的起源

发现鹰骨笛的卡约文化遗址，被考古专家认为是古羌人的文化遗存之一。作为青铜时代中国西北地区的一种文化形态，卡约文化与齐家文化具有承继关系，因发现于青海湟中卡约村而得名，是青海地区分布面积最广、遗址数量最多的文化类型，目前所发现的遗址数量已有1700多处。卡约文化遗址出土了大量动物骨骼与畜牧生产工具，出土陶器数量明显减少，质量明显降低，取而代之的是大量木制品和小型青铜制品。因此，卡约文化显示了古羌人以畜牧为主体的经济特征。

与卡若文化由农而牧的突变类似，卡约文化也在三千多年前全球冰期到来时，选择了更加适应干燥少雨气候的畜牧业。

从历史的大视野看，古羌的畜牧业文化以其强大的包容性和适应能力，为中华民族的形成和发展源源不断地输送着新鲜血液，加速了中华文明的发展进程。虞夏时期，一部分羌人因辅助大禹治水有功，迁居黄河以南。西周初期，羌人与周人联系密切，帮助周武王推翻殷商的统治，建立起周王朝，并逐渐吸收、融入周文化，使自己的族群不断壮大。周幽王时期，羌之西戎攻入镐京，杀死周幽王，部分关中地区的羌人东迁至洛阳附近，后融入华夏。此后，羌人的迁徙更加频繁和广泛，大量内迁和南移。内迁的羌人充分吸收中原文化，最终成为华夏的组成部分；而南移的羌人，则经由藏彝通道，与当地族群充分交融，演变成今天的羌族、藏族、彝族、哈尼族、纳西族、白族、拉祜族、傈僳族、景颇族、怒族等汉藏语系藏缅语族诸民族，成为中华民族的重要组成部分。

As the original form of ancient *Qiang* (羌) flute, the remnants of bone flute not only saw the coexistence of agriculture, stockbreeding and hunting in the Kayue Culture, but also exhibited the continuity of *Qiang* flute as a cultural symbol of the Chinese nation.

Qiang flute signified an ancient cultural symbol. The poetic lines, "Why should the Mongol flute complain no willows grow? / Beyond the Gate of Jade no vernal wind will blow" (the English translation by Xu Yuchong), remind us of the sound of the olden flute lingering on in Chinese history.

The eagle bone flute was considered the oldest *Qiang* flute (more than 3,000 years ago). It was unearthed in a tomb of the Kayue Culture in the Bronze Age, at Zhujiazhai, western suburb of Xining City, with eight holes.

Eagle bone flute served as a traditional musical instrument of ancient *Qiang* ancestors. Researchers reveal that eagle worship was a custom of ancient *Qiang* people. In the primitive religions, eagle was believed to have the spirituality that connected the heaven and the earth. Ancient *Qiang* people made flutes from eagle bones, hoping to communicate with the world by virtue of eagle's spirituality. Today, eagle bone flute remains popular among ethnic groups in Xinjiang, Gansu, Yunnan and Tibet, whose shape and playing are basically the same as that in the Kayue Culture. This possibly involves the migration of ancient *Qiang* people and presents us the continuity of ancient *Qiang* culture.

Kayue Site was regarded by archaeologists as cultural remains of ancient *Qiang* people. As a cultural type in northwestern China in the Bronze Age, the Kayue Culture inherited the Qijia Culture. The Kayue Culture was discovered at Kayue Village, Huangzhong, Qinghai Province, with the most extensive distribution and the largest number of site in Qinghai. Presently, more than 1,700 sites have been excavated. The numbers of animal bone and tool for stockbreeding shoot up, yet the number or quality of pottery ware decreases significantly. Simultaneously, a substantial number of woodwork and small bronze wares are unearthed. This suggests ancient *Qiang* people mainly developed stockbreeding in economic structure.

With great inclusiveness and high adaptability, ancient *Qiang* people continuously injected new momentum for the formation and development of the Chinese nation and accelerated the development of Chinese civilization.

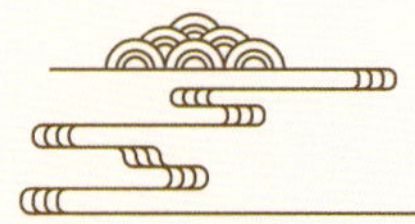

华夏的崛起

——诸夏大认同与“最初的中国”

The Rise of *Hua Xia* (华夏): The Great Recognition of *Zhu Xia* (诸夏) & The Idea of “the Earliest China”

四千多年前，中华文明从“满天星斗”变成了“月明星稀”。

这一时期，中原地区变成一个兼收并蓄的核心，在吸纳周边文化先进因素的基础上，相继出现了夏、商、周王朝。而有可能来自东南的夷夏集团，与来自东夷的殷商集团，以及来自西北的周人，最终融合成“华夏”——这一在中华民族早期形成过程中起着凝聚核心作用的集团。

何谓“华”？苏秉琦指出，仰韶文化庙底沟类型的标志性纹样——抽象化的玫瑰图案，是仰韶文化中最具生命力的一种因素，它以一条清晰的脉络影响到大半个中国。他由“花”引申出“华”，认为“华山”就是由活动在山脚下以玫瑰花图案为标志的人群命名的，这或者就是“华族”“华人”的渊源。

何谓“夏”？“夏”源于夏朝国号。夏朝统治时期，先商居东方，称为“东夏”；先周居西方，称为“西夏”。商、周统治者都以夏朝的继承者自居，自称“中夏”。西周封邦建国，诸侯林立，故又称“诸夏”。西周成王时期，周公迁都洛阳，因为此地居于“天下”之中，始创“中国”之称。

所谓“华夏”，唐大儒孔颖达曾谓：“中国有礼仪之大，故谓夏；有服章之美，故谓华。”费孝通指出，夏商周三代正是汉族前身华夏这个民族集团从多元走向一体的历史过程。

夏商周所孕育的有文字记载的文化，尤其是西周的典章制度和礼乐文化，逐渐被奉为华夏的主导性文化。春秋时期，齐、鲁、晋、郑、陈、蔡等中原诸侯被称为“华夏”“诸华”，而秦、楚等仍是“夷狄”。然而到战国，七雄皆并称“诸夏”，同列“中国”，这就显示出诸夏大认同的历史进程。由此可见，“华夏”在中华民族形成发展过程中起到了中心与主体的作用。

More than 4,000 years ago, the landscape of Chinese civilization changed from "starry sky" to "bright moon & dim stars".

It was in the period that the Central Plains eclectically absorbed advanced cultural factors of the surrounding areas, and that the Xia, Shang and Zhou Dynasties successively came to rise. One view holds that *Yi-Xia* (夷夏) Group from the southeast, Yin-Shang Group from *Yi* in the east, and Zhou from the northwest ultimately amalgamated into *Hua Xia*, a group that played a central role in the early formation of the Chinese nation.

Su Bingqi observes that nonrepresentational rose image, the typical pattern of Miaodigou Style of the Yangshao Culture, played a vital role in the Yangshao Culture, and widely affected Chinese culture in the long history. He deduces *Hua* (华) from *Hua* (花, rose-image), arguing that Mount Hua was named by the people who dwelled at the foot of the mountain and took rose image as their totem. This may explain the origin of the Chinese nation and the Chinese people.

Xia (夏) originates from the Xia Dynasty. In the reign of the Xia Dynasty, before Cheng Tang overthrew the Xia Dynasty and founded the Shang Dynasty, the Shang tribe lived in the east, called *Dong Xia* (East *Xia*). Before it moved to Zhouyuan, the Zhou tribe lived in the west, called *Xi Xia* (West *Xia*). The rulers of the Shang Dynasty and the Zhou Dynasty claimed to be the heirs of the Xia Dynasty, or *Zhong Xia* (Middle *Xia*). The Western Zhou Dynasty adopted the system of enfeoffment and established numerous vassal states, historically called *Zhu Xia*. In the reign of King Cheng of the Western Zhou Dynasty, Duke of Zhou transferred the capital to Luoyang, because Luoyang stood in the center of *Tian Xia* (天下, the whole China under the heaven). The term *Zhong Guo* or the idea of "the Earliest China" took shape.

According to Confucianist Kong Yingda, "*Xia* signified the greatness in the ceremonial etiquettes of the central states, while *Hua* denoted the beauty in the clothing that those states' denizens wore." Fei Xiaotong draws the conclusion that "The Xia, Shang and Zhou Dynasties saw the historical evolution in which *Hua Xia*, an ethnic group as ancestor of the Han people, developed from diversification to integration."

The cultures with written records that matured in the Xia, Shang and Zhou Dynasties, institutional systems and rite-music culture of the Western Zhou Dynasty in particular, were revered as orthodox culture of *Hua Xia*. In the Spring and Autumn Period, vassal states in the Central Plains such as Qi, Lu, Jin, Zheng, Chen and Cai were roughly equated with *Hua Xia* or the central states, whilst Qin and Chu were esteemed *Yi Di* (夷狄). In the Warring States Period, however, Seven Powerful States were collectively termed as *Zhu Xia* or the central states. This substantiated the historical process of the great recognition of *Zhu Xia*, supporting the view that *Hua Xia* played a central and principal role in the formation and development of the Chinese nation.

名称：龙形牙璋

年代：夏

规格：长48.1厘米，中宽11.4厘米，重900克

出土地点：河南省洛阳市偃师区二里头遗址

收藏单位：二里头夏都遗址博物馆

Name: Dragon-Shaped *Ya Zhang* (牙璋, Archaic Jade Blade)

Historical Period: The Xia Dynasty

Length: 48.1 cm, Width (The Middle Part): 11.4 cm, Weight: 900 g

Excavation Site: Erlitou Site, Yanshi District, Luoyang City, Henan Province

Housed in: Erlitou Site Museum of the Xia Capital

在牙璋之上，我们可以看见一个什么样的“华夏”以及“最早的中国”？

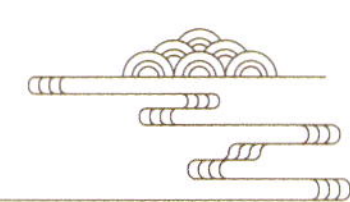

华夏族群的起源

龙形牙璋

17

Dragon-Shaped *Ya Zhang* (牙璋, Archaic Jade Blade)

文物简读

发现于二里头遗址的牙璋是夏王朝的核心礼器，它与二里头时期的青铜礼容器群、青铜礼兵器群、玉器礼器群等，一道呈现出一个王朝的气象，证实了夏王朝国家政治制度的形成，揭示出一个“最早的中国”形象。

牙璋：夏朝的背影

大约在公元前2070年，中华大地迎来了一个转折性的历史事件：禹之子启，首创世袭制王朝，建立了将延续四百多年的夏朝。这一事件前所未有地推动了中华历史的发展，使“满天星斗”式的多个文化区域及政治实体并存的历史格局，进入“月明星稀”式的广域王权国家时期，加速了中华文明从“多元”向“一体”迈进的历程。

夏文化通过商、周王朝的继承和发展，绵延成三代，持续近两千年，进而成为华夏文明的主流。在这一漫长的历史进程中，华夏族群得以孕育，最终发展成一个具有巨大凝聚力的核心群体，在中华民族的形成发展过程中发挥出引领作用。

由此可见，夏王朝的建立是中华历史进程中一个惊天动地的大事件。

对于这样一个王朝，我们能够找到一件什么样的文物，来跨越遥远的历史距离，清晰地看见它的形象？

牙璋！

何为牙璋?

在考古学家看来，牙璋是探索夏史迹最为重要的信物之一。

夏商周是中华文明以“礼”为核心的精神秩序与文化制度的初步形成时期。在这一时期，玉被深刻地注入了“礼”的灵魂，成为祭祀、朝会、交聘等场合的核心器物。“璋，祭祀之礼玉。”为了构筑一个既能与天地神灵相沟通，又能象征王权威严的礼仪世界，夏人选择了牙璋。

牙璋的原型有可能是新石器时代用于翻土的农具耒耜，也有可能是类似戈的兵器。从考古资料看，牙璋最早发现于大汶口文化晚期至龙山文化早期的海岱地区，在漫长的历史中，它完成了由实用器具到礼仪用器的功能转变，成为人们祈求丰收的礼器。就在牙璋功能转型之时，大汶口文化强势崛起，向西辐射和传播。距今约3900年前，牙璋随迁徙的大汶口人群进入黄河中游地区，出现在陕北石峁遗址、陕西商洛东龙山遗址、河南淅川下王岗遗址、河南巩义花地嘴遗址等地。

牙璋升级为国家级礼器，则是在夏朝二里头文化崛起之后。此时，它的工艺更加精美，体形更大，最长达50厘米，有的镶嵌了绿松石。就在它完成这样的功能转变时，牙璋在周边地区迅速消失，这表明它已被夏王室所垄断，成为王朝国家的权力象征。

商朝建立后，青铜冶炼技术得到显著发展，礼器的材质逐渐由玉变为青铜，牙璋被青铜鼎所取代。然而对于夏王朝具有精神象征意义的牙璋，却跟随着夏遗民的步伐，从中原向西、向南迁徙，最远到达岭南地区。有意思的是，三星堆遗址也发现了数量众多、形制多样的牙璋遗存，甚至出现了组合装饰的牙璋形金箔，把牙璋的形制发展到了另一个顶峰。牙璋在遥远的古蜀国延续了生命力，成为三星堆承继中原文化的重要信物之一。

华夏与“最早的中国”

这件牙璋出土于洛阳偃师二里头遗址。它接近五十厘米长，是夏朝牙璋的典型代表。透过它，我们仿佛可以看见夏朝，看见中华历史上第一个世袭制王朝的遥远背影。

历史上，夏人的起源多被追溯到颛顼。《史记·夏本纪》与《大戴礼记 · 帝系》均称鲧为颛顼之子，禹为鲧之子，启为禹之子。《汉书·律历志》载：“颛顼五世而生鲧。”无论世系如何，这些记述表明，夏人很可能是颛顼部落的一支后裔。《史记》载：“禹兴于西羌。”关于禹出自西羌的传说，流衍广泛，涉及古今。今天我国羌族地区仍保留着大量的禹迹，并传承着对禹的崇拜。历史学家徐中舒曾肯定地认为，根据由汉至晋五百年间长期流传的羌人传说，没有理由否定夏来源于羌。事实上，以禹为代表的西羌（姜）戎文化与晋南豫北的中原文化相结合，构成华夏文化的主干，这已成为很多历史学家的共识。而关于夏人来源的追溯，也让我们更加清晰地理解中华民族多元一体发展进程的复杂性。

大禹因带领民众治水成功的丰功伟绩，被奉为“天下共主”，其统辖的区域被称为“夏”。为何以“夏”相称呢?《尔雅·释诂》曰：“夏，大也。”《尚书孔氏传》云：“冕服采章曰华，大国曰夏。”因此，将“华夏”并称，即指有冕服采章之美的大国——“华夏，谓中国也”。

由此可见，夏朝的建立具有划时代的重大意义，它是中国乃至东亚地区最早的核心文化和最早的王权国家，是中华文明总进程的核心和引领者。

21世纪以来，中华文明探源工程对于夏文化的考古发掘已取得重大进展，偃师二里头遗址、登封王城岗遗址考古成果已基本揭开了夏都的神秘面纱。二里头遗址发现了迄今为止可确认的最早的宫城，其纵横交错的道路网和具有中轴线规划的建筑基址群，说明二里头是具有明确规划的都城遗址。后世中国都城的营建规划与其一脉相承，表明二里头开创了中国古代都城规划制度的先河。这也说明，当夏出现在历史舞台上时，一个名副其实的"最早的中国"便已出现在世界的东方。

Discovered at Erlitou Site, *Ya Zhang* was an essential sacrificial vessel in the Xia Dynasty. *Ya Zhang* demonstrated the formation of national political system of the Xia Dynasty and forged the image of "the earliest China".

To archaeologists, *Ya Zhang* means the most credible evidence for exploring the historical relics of Xia.

In the Xia, Shang and Zhou Dynasties, spiritual order and cultural system of Chinese civilization with rite at the core took initial shape. Jade played a core role in sacrificial rites, court meetings and diplomatic relations. "*Zhang*, ritual jade for sacrifice". As the parlance suggested, the Xia people used *Ya Zhang* to construct a realm of rite that allowed them to communicate with gods and symbolized the power of kingship.

Prototypically, *Ya Zhang* probably developed from *Lei Si* (耒耜), a plough-shaped farming tool used to dig earth in the Neolithic Period, or a *Ge* (戈, dagger-axe)-shaped weapon. As archaeological materials reveal, *Ya Zhang* was firstly discovered at Hai-Dai (a historical region extending from the Bohai Sea to Mt. Tai in Shandong), culturally lasting from the late Dawenkou Culture to the early Longshan Culture. In the long history, *Ya Zhang* was functionally transformed from a practical tool to a ritual vessel. And ancestors used it to pray for harvest. As *Ya Zhang* performed its ritual role, the Dawenkou Culture robustly rose and spread westward. Around 3,900 years ago, *Ya Zhang* travelled to the middle reaches of the Yellow River with the migration of Dawenkou people.

It was not until the rise of the Erlitou Culture in the Xia Dynasty that *Ya Zhang* attained its status as national sacrificial vessel, with more exquisite craftsmanship and larger size, up to *c*. 50 cm in length. Some were inlaid with turquoise. Under such circumstances, however, *Ya Zhang* quickly disappeared in the peripheral areas of Erlitou. This indicated that the use of *Ya Zhang* had been cornered by the Xia royal family, symbolizing the power of the state.

Erlitou dragon-shaped *Ya Zhang* was unearthed at Erlitou Site, Yanshi, Luoyang. Nearly 50 cm long, it typifies *Ya Zhang* in the Xia Dynasty, and unfolds before us the dust-laden glory of the Xia Dynasty, the first hereditary dynasty in Chinese history.

Since the 21st century, in "Project to Trace the Origins of Chinese Civilization", great progress has been made in the archaeological excavation of Xia-culture sites. The archaeological achievements of Erlitou Site in Yanshi and Wangchenggang Site in Dengfeng have basically unveiled the mystery of the Xia capital. So far, the earliest acknowledged palace city was discovered at Erlitou Site. The complex road network and building-base group featured central axis and embodied distinct capital planning. In the construction of Chinese capital cities, Erlitou set a precedent for the planning of capital city in ancient China. As the case stood, when the Xia Dynasty was established, the earliest China *per se* appeared in the east of the world.

商朝创造了一个怎样的青铜时代？

商代早期青铜文明的见证

杜岭方鼎

Duling Square *Ding* (鼎, Tripod)

18

文物简读

这口方鼎证实了中国迄今发现的商代早期规模最大、年代最早的一座王都“郑州商城”的存在，见证了“莫敢不来享，莫敢不来王”的商朝辉煌的青铜文明。

王者之都的代言

商的建立，意味着一个辉煌的青铜时代到来了。

使用青铜器来象征统一华夏，是从大禹铸造九鼎开始的。但将这一象征意义发扬光大的，却是商朝。随着商朝走向繁荣鼎盛，青铜鼎成为国之重器，并且一步步走向宏伟。其巅峰便是震惊后世的后母戊大方鼎——已知中国古代最大、最重的青铜器。此时的鼎，高踞于威严神圣的殿堂之上，散发着让人崇拜和敬畏的气质，成为一个王朝制度和精神的代言者。

杜岭方鼎发现于郑州商城遗址一个名叫杜岭的地方。在它出现之前，郑州商城遗址一直被考古学界怀疑为商代的王城之一，但却没有找到能有力印证这一推测的重要文物。1974年，当两尊方鼎从历史厚重的尘埃之中显露出来时，它们对于3500多年前的一座王者之都的佐证力量，马上传递给了考古工作者。若干年后，时任河南省文物考古研究所所长杨育彬回忆起他第一眼看见两尊杜岭方鼎时的感受：“就一眼，直刺心底……两尊青铜大鼎，破土欲出，峥嵘乍现，这种不言自威，这种冲天霸气，非王莫属！”眼前的青铜大鼎，让他真真切切地看见、摸着了一座王者之都。

在杜岭方鼎之后，郑州商城遗址陆续出土了数量众多、形制巨大、铸造精美、纹饰精致的青铜礼器，充分证明了它是商王朝前期的都邑遗址。有学者认为它是“汤始居亳”的亳都，作为中国历史上最早的都城遗址之一，它是那个时期世界上规模最大、最繁华的城市。

名称：杜岭方鼎
年代：商代早期
规格：通高87厘米，口长61厘米，口宽61厘米，重64.25千克
出土地点：河南省郑州杜岭张寨前街
收藏单位：河南博物院

Name: Duling Square *Ding* (鼎, Tripod)
Historical Period: The Early Shang Dynasty
Total Height: 87 cm, Mouth Length: 61 cm
Mouth Width: 61 cm, Weight: 64.25 kg
Excavation Site: Front Zhangzhai Street, Duling, Zhengzhou, Henan Province
Housed in: Henan Museum

以东夷入主华夏的商人

今天，我们可以从规模宏大的王城遗址、雄健厚重的青铜重器之上看见商的形象，更可以从迄今发现的中国最早的系统化的文字甲骨文和金文之上，直接读到商的故事。作为中华历史上第二个王权制朝代，第一个有同时期文字记载的王朝，商朝推动华夏文明走向成熟与稳定，进一步奠定了中华文明的发展基础。

那么，商人从何而来？

商人源出于东夷，根据《史记·殷本纪》记载，有娀氏之女名简狄，吞玄鸟之卵而生契。商人因此以玄鸟为崇拜对象。这一传说印证了商人是东夷后裔的推断，因为东夷有着悠久的凤鸟崇拜传统。从考古资料看，商文化遗址中出土了很多与凤鸟相关的器物，如妇好墓的玉凤，与甲骨文“凤”字极为相似，有“天下第一凤”之称。

商人的祖先契是舜时代的人，因辅佐大禹治水有功，被帝舜命为司徒，封地于商邑，此后以“商”为族名。经过漫长的发展，契的第14代子孙汤联合天下诸侯，推翻了夏的末代君王桀，建立了商王朝。商汤吸取夏朝灭亡的教训，“以宽治民”，追求“有功于民，勤力乃事”；他以仁对待夏朝的遗民，不仅允许保留“夏社”，而且册封大禹后人。汤的一系列仁政，推动商的国力日益强盛。商开创了辉煌的青铜文明，扩展了统治区域，影响远至黄河上游，氐、羌部落纷纷纳贡归服。《诗经》为此吟唱道：“昔有成汤，自彼氐羌，莫敢不来享，莫敢不来王。”

商起于东夷，却能由夷而入主华夏，这表明了中华文明的包容性。

辉煌的青铜文明

青铜因其贵重，曾一度被称为“金”，代表着财富和权力。中国最早的青铜器始见于龙山文化时期，至商而达到鼎盛。商人具有深厚的崇祖敬神观念，因此十分重视祭祀和占卜。青铜器的铸造在一定程度上是祭祀仪礼等重大活动的制度性需求。

商代青铜器的铸造主要采用模范法，形体较大的器物则采用多种形式的合范分铸法，因此能铸造出造型复杂、形制宏大的铸件，如著名的四羊方尊和后母戊大方鼎等。商朝以后，周人又发明了“失蜡法”“分铸法”“错金银”技术，把青铜铸造技术推向了又一个高峰，留下了一系列繁复精致、惊艳绝伦的代表作。

回到禹铸九鼎的故事。太史公司马迁在《史记》中记述了九鼎的传承轮替：“遭圣则兴，鼎迁于夏商；周德衰，宋之社亡，鼎乃沦没，伏而不见。”这就是九鼎与国家命运紧密相连的故事。鼎成为国家兴亡的象征：失鼎代表国亡；夺鼎代表开天辟地；定鼎代表王朝开国。

今天，鼎仍然是一种重要的国家礼器。我们依旧将鼎作为团结、统一、昌盛、吉祥的象征；我们依旧像华夏祖先那样，追求国家民族的鼎新、鼎立、鼎盛。关于鼎的观念传承至今，这正是中华文化绵延恒久、生生不息的表现。

Duling Square *Ding* testifies to the existence of Zhengzhou Shang City, the largest and oldest capital of the early Shang Dynasty. The founding of the Shang Dynasty forecast the coming of the glorious Bronze Age.

Duling Square *Ding* was unearthed at Duling, Zhengzhou Shang City Site. In 1974, no sooner had archaeologists seen two square tripods than they realized the existence of the capital of the Shang Dynasty more than 3,500 years ago.

In the Shang Dynasty, bronze wares were mainly cast by using *Mofan Fa* (模范法, the model-casting technology). Larger artifacts were cast by using *Hefan & Fenzhu Fa* (合范分铸法, making models first and pouring bronze fluid later) in various forms. Therefore, castings with complex shape and grand structure, e.g. the well-known Bronze Square *Zun* Decorated with Four Rams (四羊方尊) and Houmuwu Rectangular Tripod (后母戊大方鼎), were cast. Bronze technology continued to evolve in the Shang Dynasty, and fully developed in the Western Zhou Dynasty and the Spring and Autumn Period. In the Western Zhou Dynasty, craftsmen invented such technologies as *Shila Fa* (失蜡法, beeswax-model casting), *Fezhu Fa* (分铸法, the main body and accessories of a bronze ware separately cast and then integrated) and *Cuojinyin* (错金银, decorating a bronze ware with gold or silver). These marked the historical peak of the bronze-casting technology and created a series of exquisite and unparalleled masterpieces.

In *Records of the Grand Historian* (《史记》), Sima Qian, also known as *Taishigong*, recounted what the nine tripods (cast by Yu the Great) had experienced in the Pre-Qin Period: "The nine tripods appeared when sagacious kings ruled. They were successively inherited in the Xia, Shang and Zhou Dynasties. (However), owing to the wrongdoings of the rulers, the Zhou Dynasty eventually declined and perished. The nine tripods fell into the Wei River and disappeared since then." In a way, the nine tripods symbolized the destiny of a state: to lose them meant its ruination; to vie for them meant its ambition for kingship, and to obtain them meant its founding.

Today, tripod still serves as an important national ritual vessel, and emblematizes solidarity, unity, power and auspiciousness. Like their ancestors, the Chinese people pursue national reformation, stability and prosperity. The idea of tripod comes down the ages, materializing the enduring and everlasting Chinese culture.

三千多年前，一位名叫“墙”的西周史官书写的“青铜史书”，隐含着周朝的什么秘密?

礼乐文明与协和万邦的理想

史墙盘

19

Shi Qiang Pan (史墙盘, Bronze Plate Made by the Historian Qiang)

文物简读

这件青铜盘证实了司马迁在《史记·周本纪》中的记载，是周人起源、发展并建立周王朝统一政体的重要见证。

“青铜史书”

在青铜器上铸造铭文的传统起源于商。当周人接过青铜文化的接力棒时，他们把这个风尚推向了一个新的高潮。学者们认为三千多年前人们在青铜器上刻写文字的热情，来源于商周青铜器作为祭天礼器的功能——通过祭祀的仪式，青铜器上的信息得以隐秘地传递给祖先和神灵。

我们常在西周青铜器上读到笔力浑厚、首尾出锋、波磔转折的铭文，它们所提供的信息让西周这部宏大浩瀚的历史巨著，在某些细部变得清晰可触。

位于陕西省宝鸡市扶风、岐山一带的周原，是周文化的发祥地和周人灭商之前的聚居地，也是周人祭祀天地、祖宗和神祇的圣地。周原遗址出土的青铜器大多铸有纪实铭文。正是在这里，被称为“青铜史书”的史墙盘破土而出。

这是西周中期微氏家族一位名叫“墙”的人铸造的铜盘，因为墙在周朝担任史官，所以这件铜盘被考古学家命名为“史墙盘”。也许正是因为史官的身份，墙带着浓厚的历史记录意识，刻铸了这一篇共计18行、284字的“青铜史书”。铭文的前半部分，颂扬西周文王、武王、成王、康王、昭王、穆王、共（恭）王等七代周王开创伟业的功绩；铭文的后半部分，叙述自己祖先的功德，即微氏家族迁入周原地区并在此地兴旺昌盛的事迹。墙所记述的七位周王的政绩，与司马迁在《史记·周本纪》中

名称：史墙盘
年代：西周中期
规格：通高16.2厘米，口径47.3厘米，深8.6厘米
出土地点：陕西省宝鸡市扶风县庄白村
收藏单位：宝鸡周原博物院

Name: *Shi Qiang Pan* (史墙盘, Bronze Plate Made by the Historian Qiang)
Historical Period: The Middle Western Zhou Dynasty
Total Height: 16.2 cm, Mouth Diameter: 47.3 cm, Depth: 8.6 cm
Excavation Site: Zhuangbai Village, Fufeng County, Baoji City, Shaanxi Province
Housed in: Baoji Zhouyuan Museum

记载的内容吻合；而关于微氏家族在周原地区的发家史，则填补了西周史的空白。所以，铭文可谓从宏观与微观的双重视野，留下了一份珍贵的历史资料。

事实上，史墙盘的价值不止于此。这件铜盘还具有极高的艺术价值：它的腹部装饰着凤鸟纹，有华丽的鸟冠，逶迤的鸟尾；圈足部位则装饰着同样精美的变形凤鸟纹。它代表了那个时代周人充实而华美的精神世界。

创造中华民族独特精神标识的周朝

孔子的祖先是商人。作为商的后裔，孔子并未因周灭商而对周产生反感和敌意。相反，他热爱周的文化，对周公创制的礼乐典章制度发出深深的赞叹。在深入研究夏、商、周三代文化制度后，孔子认为周借鉴了夏、商两代千余年的文化成果，又通过改革和创新，开创了完备的礼制法度。所以，他鲜明地表达了自己的文化立场："周监于二代，郁郁乎文哉！吾从周。"

在中华文明的发展历程中，周朝是一个极其重要的历史时期。它锐意革新，开创了一系列成熟的思想文化和制度体系，影响了此后近三千年的中华文明史。周朝先后创建和完善的分封制、宗法制、礼乐制、井田制、国野制等制度，构成了中华古代社会体系的基础，此后的各个朝代或多或少都继承了周朝的制度体系。更加重要的是，周朝在制礼作乐的实践中，开创了具有长久生命力的思想文化体系，成为中华文化一系列精神追求和道德观念的源头，形成了中华民族独特的精神标识，深深影响了后世中国人的精神气质和心理结构。

起于羌戎而入主中原的周人

为中华文明的发展做出伟大贡献的周人，并非起于中原华夏，其祖先源自羌戎。周人融入华夏并成为华夏核心的历史，生动地说明了历史上各个不同地域的族群通过深刻复杂的交融，共同创造出中华文明的历史逻辑。

周人奉后稷为始祖，后稷的母亲为姜嫄。古籍中频繁记载了一则关于后稷降生的传说：姜嫄在野外发现了一个巨人脚印，她因好奇而踏足其上，因此怀孕生产。她以为不祥，三番五次把生下的婴儿抛弃在陋巷之中、树林之间、寒冰之上，但总有神迹示现，婴儿安然无恙。姜嫄将孩子抱回，取名为"弃"。长大后的弃善于稼穑，教民耕作，成为司农之神，被子孙尊为"后稷"，即稷王。这则故事隐含着后稷时代只知其母、不知其父的母系氏族社会信息。而"姜嫄"的姓氏，表明了周起源于羌。周虽来源于西北游牧部落，但在构筑自己的始祖记忆时，却追溯到农业之神后稷。这就表明，当周人从游牧的西羌集团中分化出来时，正是其完成由游牧经济向农耕经济转型之时。

后稷的子孙公刘率族人迁居至豳，建立起城邑；后经九世相传，到古公亶父时，周人受北方薰育戎的侵袭，不得不南迁至渭河流域岐山以南的周原。他们在这里造田营舍，建邑筑城，又经历了若干代，到姬昌时已拥有了强盛的势力。为反抗商末的暴政，姬昌次子姬发与天下诸侯会盟于孟津，经牧野大战，大败商朝军队，从而建立了周朝。

周起于羌戎而最终入主中原，经西周、东周而延续790年，创造了辉煌灿烂的文化，成为华夏族群的核心组成部分。这一历史生动地显示了中华民族多元一体的发展轨迹，有力地说明了中华文明亘古不息的生命力来源于其包容开放的文明根性。

Shi Qiang Pan authenticates the records in "Chronicles of Zhou" of *Records of the Grand Historian* (《史记·周本纪》) by Sima Qian. It saw the origin and development of Zhou tribe as well as the founding of the Zhou Dynasty, a unified state.

Zhouyuan adjoins Fufeng and Qishan, Baoji City, Shaanxi Province. As the cradle of Zhou culture and the settlement of the Zhou tribe, Zhouyuan was a sacred place where Zhou people worshipped the heaven and the earth, ancestors and gods, before they crusaded against the Shang Dynasty. At Zhouyuan Site, a large number of bronze wares were unearthed, which had documentary inscriptions. It was also at Zhouyuan Site that *Shi Qiang Pan* was excavated.

The bronze plate was cast by a man named Qiang, who came from the Wei family in the middle Western Zhou Dynasty. Qiang served as a historian in the Zhou Dynasty, so archaeologists benamed the bronze plate *Shi Qiang Pan*. The identity of a historian endowed Qiang with a strong sense of history, who carved the bronze plate, with 18 lines and 284 characters totally. The first half of the inscriptions celebrated the tremendous achievements of the seven kings of the Western Zhou Dynasty, i.e. King Wen, King Wu, King Cheng, King Kang, King Zhao, King Mu and King Gong. The second half of the inscriptions narrated the merits and virtues of Qiang's ancestors, or how the Wei family migrated to Zhouyuan and thrived there. Qiang's narration tallied with the records in "Chronicles of Zhou" of *Records of the Grand Historian* by Sima Qian, and filled the gap in the history of the Western Zhou Dynasty. At the macro and micro levels, Qiang's inscriptions left us valuable historical materials and boasted "a historical book on bronze ware".

Zhou tribe took origin of *Qiang* & *Rong* (羌戎), and ultimately ruled the Central Plains. In 790 years, the Zhou Dynasty created a splendid culture and played a core part in the formation of the Chinese nation. The history of Zhou vividly demonstrates the development trajectory of the multi-ethnic Chinese nation, and incontrovertibly proves the eternal vitality of Chinese civilization, owing to the inclusiveness and openness of Chinese culture.

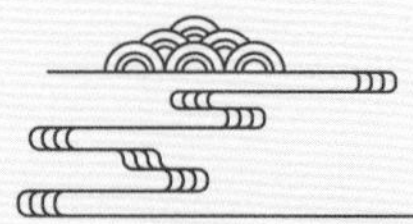

华夷五方格局

——“天下主义”观念的形成

The Five-Direction Pattern of *Hua* (华)-*Yi* (夷, Four Neighboring Ethnic Groups): The Formation of the Idea of *Tian Xia* (天下, the Whole China under the Heaven)

历史向前发展，中华文明从“月明星稀”向着“众星拱月”的格局进一步演进。

春秋战国时期，华夏与东夷、西戎、南蛮、北狄共同组成“五方之民”，他们共居“四海”，同为“天下”。这一由华夷五方格局生成的天下主义，既是中国古代传统地理观念的体现，也是古代处理夷夏关系的重要依据，为统一多民族国家的形成奠定了思想基础。天下主义观念认为华夷之间并无绝对的族群界限，族类区分的基本标准是礼乐教化而非血缘世系，即“华夷之辨”的首要标准在于文化，而非以血缘划分的族类。

华夷五方格局包容了多族群、多文化、多种经济类型，在中华民族孕育之初就具有包容力极强的开阖性，也形成了构建大一统格局的和合思想机制。天下主义既承认各族群之间存在语言、习俗的差异，也强调不同群体在基本伦理和互动规则方面存在共性并能和睦相处。正是凭借这种巨大的包容性，“夷”“夏”得以在漫长岁月中，跨越彼此间的界限隔阂，完成一次次民族大融合，最终实现“华夷一家”的理想；也正是凭借这一种可互易其位的“夷夏观”，无论历史上哪一个民族建立王朝，都自觉地接过了中华文化的火炬，最终使中华文明成为世界上唯一不曾中断的悠久文明。

大一统是一个“修文德以来之”的文化机制，是一个“四海一家，协和万邦”的文明理想。中国用自身历史表明，大一统国家形成的条件不在于民族成分的单一，而在于对共同文化的认同。这是多元一体的中华民族不断发展并走向强大的基因密码。

As the history progressed, the landscape of Chinese civilization changed from "bright moon & dim stars" to "stars twinkling around the bright moon".

In the Spring and Autumn Period and the Warring States Period, *Hua Xia* (华夏), with *Yi* (夷) in the east, *Man* (蛮) in the south, *Rong* (戎) in the west and *Di* (狄) in the north, formed the Five-Direction Pattern. People lived together in *Tian Xia* or the whole China under the heaven. As a traditional geographical idea in ancient China, *Tian Xia* not only provided the groundwork for addressing the *Hua-Yi* relationship in the ancient times, but also laid an ideological foundation for the formation of a unified multi-ethnic country.

The Five-Direction Pattern of *Hua-Yi* covered diverse ethnic groups, cultures and economies. In the early stage of the Chinese nation, the pattern established an ideological mechanism for grand unification, with immense openness and inclusiveness. The idea of *Tian Xia* acknowledged the differences in languages and customs among ethnic groups and emphasized the commonalities in basic ethics and interactive rules among ethnic groups as well as their harmonious coexistence. It was precisely because of the great inclusiveness that *Hua* (*Xia*) and *Yi* ended estrangement and actualized assimilation in the long years, with the realization of the unity of *Hua* and *Yi*. It was precisely because of the transposition of *Hua* (*Xia*) and *Yi* that any nationalities that established dynasties in history would voluntarily take over the torch of Chinese culture, making Chinese civilization to be the only continued civilization in the world.

Grand unification signaled a cultural mechanism in which "all the influences of civil culture and virtue were to be cultivated to attract the remoter people to be submissive", and an ideal that "all nations lived in harmony under the heaven". Chinese history indubitably demonstrated that national unification relied on cultural recognition rather than ethnic uniformity. This generated a genetic code that enabled the Chinese nation to continuously develop and expand.

"中国"这一称谓最早出现于何时？关于"中国"的观念经历了怎样的发展过程？

"中国"观念的产生

何尊

He Zun (何尊)

20

文物简读

据目前的考古资料来看，何尊上有着"中国"一词最早的文字记载，体现了"中国"观念的产生以及中华文明独特的天下主义哲学观。

国宝重器

1963年，陕西省宝鸡市宝鸡县（今陈仓区）贾村镇的一名村民，无意中在房后的土崖下发现了一个"铜罐"。他清理掉上面的泥土后，便拿回家用于储存粮食。两年后，这位村民把"铜罐"卖给了废品收购站。值得庆幸的是，宝鸡市博物馆的一名工作人员在收购站及时发现了这件造型凝重雄奇、表面刻绘饕餮纹高浮雕的器物，断定它是一件珍贵文物。随后，博物馆以30元的价格买下它，这件文物成为成立不久的宝鸡市博物馆的第一件青铜器藏品。又过了十年，为支持国家文物局组织的全国新出土文物精品出国展，宝鸡市博物馆将这件饕餮纹铜尊送去参展。

作为展览负责人，著名青铜器专家、时任上海市博物馆馆长马承源特别注意到了这件纹饰精美的器物，决定把它送到故宫博物院做除锈处理。当除锈工作完成后，幽深的尊内底部，一篇清晰的铭文赫然显现！

惟王初迁，宅于成周，复禀武王，礼福自天。在四月丙戌，王诰宗小子于京室。曰："昔在尔考公氏，克弼文王。肆文王受兹天命；惟武王既克大邑商，则廷告于天。曰：'余其宅兹中或（国），自之乂民。'呜呼，尔有唯小子，亡识视于公氏，有爵于天，彻命。敬享哉！"叀王恭德裕天，顺我不敏。王咸诰何，锡贝卅朋，用作叀公宝尊彝。惟王五祀。

名称：何尊

年代：西周早期

规格：高38.8厘米，口径28.8厘米，重14.6千克

出土地点：陕西省宝鸡市宝鸡县贾村镇

收藏单位：宝鸡青铜器博物院

Name: *He Zun* (何尊)

Historical Period: The Early Western Zhou Dynasty

Height: 38.8 cm, Mouth Diameter: 28.8 cm, Weight: 14.6 kg

Excavation Site: Jiacun Town, Baoji County, Baoji City, Shaanxi Province

Housed in: Baoji Bronze Ware Museum

铭文解开了铜尊的身份之谜：这是一个名叫“何”的西周宗室贵族，为纪念其先祖叀公而铸造的礼器。铭文首先记述了周成王继承周武王遗志，营建洛邑、建筑新都等一系列重要历史事件；紧接着记述了周成王在宗族大会上公开赞扬叀公追随文王、武王的事迹及其做出的贡献，并因此赏赐给“何”三十朋贝，“何”便用周成王赏赐的朋贝铸造了这件铜尊。

对于铭文的解读，让饕餮纹铜尊获得了一个新的命名——“何尊”。

何尊铭文

“宅兹中国”

何尊不是一件普通的青铜尊。当“余其宅兹中或（国）”的词句从漫漶斑驳的尊底显露出来时，何尊在中国文化史上便具有了特殊的地位和意义，它成为当之无愧的国宝和国之重器。这是因为，“宅兹中国”是迄今为止关于“中国”一词最早的文献记录。

在何尊铭文中，“中”字如同旗杆，上下有旌旗飘舞，旗杆正中竖立；“或”是“国”的本字，它由城池和干戈构成，表示“执干戈以卫社稷”，意味着当时的人们已经意识到，一个国家不仅要有属于自己的城池，而且要有军队来保护疆土和臣民，这才叫“国”。后来，“或”外加“口”，以为国界，演变成“国”，属于文字的自然演变。

在铭文中，“中国”一词并非国家政权的概念。“宅兹中国”大意为“住在天下中央地区”。《尚书·梓材》中有周成王所谓“皇天既付中国民越厥疆土于先王”的记载。史书与铭文相互印证，说明周王统治的地域即为“中国”。

“中国”的边界在哪里？

那么，周成王所说的“中国”，它的边界在哪里？

事实上，当“中国”概念在西周形成时，一个与之相应的文化观念，也在西周至春秋之间逐渐形成，并成为影响深远的价值理念。这就是“天下主义”观念。

天下主义观念基于华夷五方格局的空间观念而形成。在五方格局中，四夷拱卫“中国”，其间有着一个“化内”与“化外”的模糊边界。它不是一道固定不变的界限，而是在文明教化的影响下可超越种族、宗族、地域的可移动边界——只要接受了发源于中原的礼乐教化典章制度，就可成为“中国”的一部分。著名历史学家许倬云曾说，在中国文化之中，没有绝对的“他者”，只有相对的“我者”；“天下”是普世的、绝对的，而夷夏却是相对的、历史性的。钱穆则指出，中华帝国与罗马帝国是不同的，罗马帝国是以军事为后盾向外扩张，但中华帝国却是以文化为中心将四边向内凝聚。“中国人常把民族消融在人类观念里面，也常把国家观念消融在天下或世界的观念里。”

正是基于这样独特的天下主义观念，“华”与“夷”在漫长的历史岁月中通过迁徙、通婚和文化融合，实现了“华夷一家”的历史大融合，使中华文明在一次次王朝更迭中从未中断，也使历史上各民族沿着多元一体的格局，一步步走向中华民族共同体。

As the existing archaeological materials suggest, *He Zun* contains the earliest written record of *Zhong Guo* (中国, the central state), corroborates the rise of the idea of *Zhong Guo*, and embodies unique philosophy of *Tian Xia* (天下, the whole China under the heaven) in Chinese civilization.

The inscriptions unravel the story of the bronze *Zun*. In the Western Zhou Dynasty, an aristocrat surnamed He cast the bronze *Zun*, a ritual vessel, to commemorate his ancestor Zhuan Gong. As the inscriptions suggest, King Cheng of Zhou carried out the behest of King Wu of Zhou, constructed Luoyi (present-day Luoyang), and sited new capital. Later, King Cheng of Zhou lavished praise on He's ancestor Zhuan Gong, who served King Wen and King Wu wholeheartedly and attained outstanding achievements, at the clan assembly. King Cheng bestowed 30 *Peng Bei* (coins made from ancient shells strung together) on He, with which He cast the bronze *Zun*.

Among the inscriptions, the character *Zhong* (中) looks like a flagpole, with banners fluttering above and below, and the flagpole stands upright in the center. The character *Huo* (或) was originally *Guo* (state). Pictographically, *Huo* means “taking up arms to protect the state”. In other words, people came to realize the fact that a state comprised both cities and armies to safeguard its territory and people. Afterwards, the character *Huo* was encircled by the part 囗, meaning the boundary of states. This formed the character *Guo* (國).

The four characters *Zhai Zi Zhong Guo* (宅兹中国) were the earliest written record of *Zhong Guo* (中国) to date, which signified “living in the central region of the world”. In “On Governing the State” (“Zi Cai”) of *Book of Documents* (《尚书・梓材》), it was said that: “The heaven commended the subjects and territories of the central state (中国) to King Wu of Zhou.” To rulers of Western Zhou, their territories were the central state, and their subjects were *Hua Xia*. *Hua Xia*, alongside East *Yi* (夷), South *Man* (蛮), West *Rong* (戎) and North *Di* (狄), constituted “people in the five directions”. Geographically, *Tian Xia* concretized the imagination of the world that centered on the Central Plains.

中华民族对“龙凤呈祥”这一美好寓意的向往来自哪里?

“龙凤呈祥”的历史起点

青铜䢼

Bronze *Ling* (䢼, Cooking Vessel)

21

文物简读

这件青铜器是春秋时期莒国的传统尚鸟习俗与华夏龙图腾文化相融合的物质见证，呈现出东夷凤鸟文化和华夏龙文化最初的交融。

龙凤相遇

春秋时期，山东南部地区的东夷古国莒国，依旧承袭着东夷遗风。“莒虽小国，东夷之雄者也。”莒国之侧，是代表华夏文化的齐、鲁二国。在群雄纷争的时代，三国之间虽不可避免地发生争斗，但文化的交流与交融才是历史的主旋律。

因此，当莒国贵族在铸造这只高规格的青铜䢼时，他们把纽盖铸为凤鸟——这是东夷的古老崇拜，把双耳铸为龙首——这是华夏的神圣敬畏。这样，2500多年后，我们就在沂水之畔出土的一只青铜䢼上，看见了龙与凤的相遇。这是东夷与华夏相遇时的一个文化表情。

龙凤相融

黄河下游地区是殷商的发源地。商人立国后，将之作为自身疆域的重要组成部分，东夷文化也在此地得到传承和发展。发源于泰沂山区的东夷文化，有着清晰的发展序列，历经后李文化、北辛文化、大汶口文化、龙山文化、岳石文化，涵盖了传说中的包羲、太昊、少昊、蚩尤、伯益、皋陶等，自新石器时代到西周中期，在中华文明起源与发展过程中一直处于重要地位。

名称：青铜酃

年代：春秋早期

规格：通高53.4厘米，口径25.1厘米

出土地点：山东省沂水县

收藏单位：山东博物馆

Name: Bronze *Ling* (酃, Cooking Vessel)

Historical Period: The Early Spring and Autumn Period

Total Height: 53.4 cm, Mouth Diameter: 25.1 cm

Excavation Site: Yishui County, Shandong Province

Housed in: Shandong Museum

西周时期，山东地区作为东夷故地、殷商东土，被统治者高度重视。统治者特别将此地分封给两位为建立周朝立下汗马功劳的人——周公旦和姜子牙。两人的后代来到这里，分别建立了姬姓鲁国和姜姓齐国。此时，周边地区的莒国、郯国、莱国等东夷小国依旧存留。作为华夏政权的代表，鲁国试图对东夷人实行“变其俗，革其礼”的政策，齐国则对东夷人实行更为包容的“因其俗，简其礼”策略。到春秋之时，东夷文化与中原华夏文化完成了深度交融。

战国中期，莒国传三十世后，被楚国所灭。后来，这个东夷古国曾经顽强复国，但最终灭于齐。从此，东夷成为华夏的组成部分，而东夷文化带着凤鸟的精灵，融入华夏文明，为中华文化带来了一份浪漫的文化基因。

龙凤呈祥

对于凤鸟的崇拜，是东夷文化最重要的标识性特征。正是在东夷族群的文化传承中，凤鸟最终演化为中华文化最吉祥的凤凰形象。至少在商周时期，凤凰已经成形，《尚书·虞书·益稷》载：“箫韶九成，凤皇来仪。”孔颖达释：“雄曰凤，雌曰皇。”

中华龙文化在辽河畔的红山文化中初显其形，经龙山时代的传承发展，到夏商时期则协和融通，包容更多物象，最终在中华文化的天空中风掣雷动，孕育成形。中华龙是撷取纷繁动物表象交融而成的神物，正是华夏文化包容开放、兼收并蓄而成就其大的象征，也是中华文明由多元向一体演进格局的典型表达。

东夷居于华夏“中国”之东。在华夏与四夷同居“四海”的“天下”格局中，东夷是极其重要的部分。它曾创造出灿烂辉煌的文化，孕育出经天纬地的中华人文始祖，作为一个重要角色参与华夏文明的缔建进程。在历史大流的推动下，东夷作为一个独立族群的意识不断淡化，到春秋战国时期融入华夏族群，成为华夏的主要成员。

东夷与华夏的交融，带来了龙与凤的相遇，也激发出中华文明最吉祥的一个表情，那就是“龙凤呈祥”。

几千年来，“龙凤呈祥”演变为中华民族最为独特的文化符号和精神标识，是中华民族对美好世界的最生动表达。

Bronze *Ling* provides material evidence to the fusion of traditional phoenix worship in the State of Ju and the dragon totem in the Central Plains in the Spring and Autumn Period, and presents the early meeting of phoenix culture in East *Yi* (夷) and the dragon culture in the Central Plains.

When the nobles of the state of Ju were casting the bronze *Ling* for solemn and sacred rite-music culture, they cast the button cover into the shape of phoenix (the ancient worship of East *Yi*) and the two ears into the shape of dragon head (the sacred reverence in the Central Plains). As a result, more than 2,500 years later, we see the cultural meeting of dragon and phoenix on the bronze *Ling* unearthed by the banks of the Yishui River.

East-*Yi* culture features the worship of phoenix. In the cultural inheritance of East *Yi*, the worship of phoenix ultimately evolved into an auspicious image in Chinese culture. In the Shang and Zhou Dynasties, the words *Feng* and *Huang* (凤凰) emerged. In "Officials Yi and Ji", "Book of Yu" of *Book of Documents* (《尚书・虞书・益稷》), it was stated that: "When the music *Xiao Shao* (箫韶) draws to a close, *Feng* and *Huang* dance trippingly with the music." As Kong Yingda explained, "*Feng* stands for the male phoenix, and *Huang* for the female phoenix."

Chinese dragon culture took initial shape in the Hongshan Culture along the Liaohe River. Inherited and developed in the Longshan Era, dragon culture became mature and diverse in the Xia and Shang Dynasties. Chinese dragon, as a divine object, combined various auspicious animal images and embodied the inclusiveness and eclecticism of Chinese civilization.

For thousands of years, the idea of "prosperity brought by dragon and phoenix" has evolved into the most unique cultural and spiritual symbol of the Chinese nation, which vividly expresses the pursuit of the Chinese nation of a better world.

名称：大角羊形金车舆饰

年代：战国晚期

规格：长7.5厘米，高6.7厘米，重4.57克

出土地点：甘肃省天水市张家川回族自治县马家塬

收藏单位：甘肃省文物考古研究所

Name: Bighorn Sheep-Shaped Gold Foil Chariot Decoration

Historical Period: The Late Warring States Period

Length: 7.5 cm, Height: 6.7 cm, Weight: 4.57 g

Excavation Site: Majiayuan, Zhangjiachuan Hui Autonomous County, Tianshui City, Gansu Province

Housed in: Gansu Provincial Institute of Cultural Relics and Archaeology

西戎曾在中原的历史进程中扮演过什么角色？

中原历史进程中的西戎身影

大角羊形金车舆饰

Bighorn Sheep-Shaped Gold Foil Chariot Decoration

22

文物简读

这件大角羊形金车舆饰，见证了西戎作为一个古老而庞大的游牧族群，对中国西北边疆的早期开发，以及农牧过渡带多元文化交融的历史情态。

西戎的形象

马家塬墓葬深藏在甘肃省张家川的大地之下。2006年，当考古工作者将它一点点揭开时，一个2500多年前的草原文化世界在人们眼前展开，关于西戎的隐性形象也浮出水面。

除了1600件随葬器物，两座墓葬中的十辆二轮马车震惊了考古工作者。位于墓室内的马车，饰以一系列富丽奢华的配件：车轮和车厢侧面镶嵌金、银、铜、错金铁等金属花饰，以及玛瑙、串珠、贝壳等纹饰；车厢侧板布满铜质大角羊、银箔大角羊、金箔大角羊、金箔虎等动物形装饰。这些饰物数量之多，做工之精美复杂，令人叹为观止。

这一件金箔大角羊用锤揲工艺将金料锤成薄片，再镂空刻绘成精细的纹样，显示出游牧族群对金银装饰的极度喜爱；而大角羊形象的塑造，则充分体现了崇尚羊的游牧群体，对自身文化的张扬。

华夷五方格局中的西戎

在华夷五方格局中，戎居西方，称为“西戎”。事实上，在历史文献中，西戎有狭义和广义之分，狭义指氐羌诸部，广义则指中国西部与华夏、东夷、南蛮、北狄共同构成华夷五方格局的游牧族群。

将“戎”作为族称，始于西周。周人把周原以西、以游牧为主要生产方式的各部落统称为“西

戎”，包括氐羌、姜戎（羌戎）、犬戎、骊戎、义渠戎等族群。从西周至春秋，戎不仅出现在西方，在北方、东方，甚至是南方也都有关于戎的记载。可见，当时的戎还没有成为一个独立的群体，而是周人对四方游牧族群的泛称。战国时期，“西戎”一词开始频繁出现在历史文献中，这表明西戎逐渐发展成为一个轮廓相对清晰的群体。

中国西北地区历史悠久的游牧文明，是游牧部族在农业文明基础上为适应自然生态环境而逐渐发展起来的文明形态。在考古视野中，西北地区诸多以游牧经济为特征的考古遗址，显示出游牧人群所创造的丰富物质文化成果，如寺洼文化、卡约文化、辛店文化、沙井文化等，西戎与这些考古文化密切相关。到商周时期，西戎与华夏的交往交流日益频繁，畜牧文化与农业文化产生深层次交融，西戎形成了辉煌而独具特色的文明成果。马家塬遗址就充分显示出这一时期农牧过渡地带多元文化交融的历史信息。

参与中原历史进程的西戎

作为中华文明发展进程的一个重要参与者，西戎与中原华夏的关系悠久而紧密，甚至在一些重大的历史节点，也都有西戎的身影。

商朝末年，“披发左衽”的西戎曾参与周人领导的反商联盟，帮助周人建立了政权。西周时期，西戎与中原保持密切联系，尤其是与关中地区的诸侯国秦国缔结了政治、经济、文化方面的密切关系。西戎通过秦国学习中原的礼乐文化、秦国也通过吸收西戎的游牧文化因素得以壮大自身，为此后参与诸侯争霸积蓄了实力。

西周末年，昏聩的周幽王上演了荒诞的“烽火戏诸侯”闹剧。公元前772年，秦国申侯联合缯国和西戎支系犬戎，举兵攻破西周镐京，周朝的历史翻开了新的一页。

至春秋战国时期，群雄争霸，逐鹿中原。此时在历史舞台上的主要角色，不仅有春秋五霸、战国七雄，也有异常活跃的西戎，他们与中原诸侯国或战或和，从经济、文化乃至婚姻等多方面与华夏互动交接，从而上演了一出出历史大剧。如晋献公曾娶犬戎女子狐姬为妻，狐姬生下晋文公重耳；成年后的重耳为避难而逃奔母亲的故国狄，在那里得到养精蓄锐的机会，最后他回到晋国，励精图治，成就了一番霸业。

这样一些历史往事，正是西戎以各种方式参与中华文明缔造与发展的表现，在中华民族多元一体形成演进的舞台上，它是重要的主角之一。

战国之后，众多西戎部落融入秦、晋，成为华夏一员。

It reflects the early development of West *Rong* (戎), an ancient and large nomadic group, in the northwest border of China, as well as the historical integration of diverse cultures in the transitional zone between agriculture and stockbreeding.

The chariot decoration was made with *Chuidie* (锤揲, hammering and extending) technology. Gold foils were firstly hammered into thin pieces, and then carved into exquisite patterns. This demonstrated that West *Rong* ardently loved golden or silver decoration and enthusiastically idolized sheep in their nomadic culture.

In the five-direction pattern of *Hua Xia* & *Yi*, *Rong*, *Man* and *Di*, *Rong*, or West *Rong*, occupied the west. As a matter of fact, *Rong* can be understood in two ways in historical literature. In a narrow sense, West *Rong* included various tribes of *Di* & *Qiang* (氐羌); in a broad sense, West *Rong* covered nomadic ethnic groups in western China, which contributed to the five-direction pattern.

Nomadic civilization enjoyed a long history in northwestern China. Grounded in agricultural civilization, nomadic tribes developed nomadic civilization to adapt to natural and ecological environment. Archaeological sites in northwestern China saw the development of nomadic economy, as well as advanced material and cultural achievements attained by nomadic groups, such as the Siwa Culture, the Kayue Culture, the Xindian Culture and the Shajing Culture, in which West *Rong* played an indispensable role. In the Shang and Zhou Dynasties, the communication and exchanges between West *Rong* and *Hua Xia* became increasingly frequent, and the integration of stockbreeding and agriculture deepened, forming brilliant and unique civilization of West *Rong*. Majiayuan Site fully displayed the historical integration of diverse cultures in the transitional zone between agriculture and stockbreeding.

楚对华夏族群的形成发挥了什么作用?

作为文化大熔炉的楚

《龙凤仕女图》帛画

Dragon, Phoenix and Witch (Silk Painting)

23

文物简读

这幅中国最早的帛画所绘制的龙凤合体引领灵魂飞升的图像，在体现楚民族的宇宙观、生命观和信仰世界的同时，也充分呈现出战国时期南蛮文化与华夏文化深度交融的景象。

一只振翅腾空、夭矫起舞的凤鸟，一条弯曲细长、扶摇直上的龙，同时引领着一个人的灵魂飞升……距今2500多年的陈家大山战国楚墓出土的《龙凤仕女图》，是迄今为止我国发现的最早的帛画之一。此时，在楚人的信仰世界里，除了有被认为与祖先祝融融为一体的神圣凤鸟，龙也开始占据一席之地。

这是楚人凤文化与华夏龙文化深度融合后，楚人在信仰层面所形成的新图景。此时是战国中晚期，楚国已经从居丹阳之隅、不足百里的蕞尔小国，发展壮大为问鼎中原、饮马黄河的战国七雄之一。

一条独特的华夏化道路

楚是南蛮的代表。

“南蛮”的称呼出现于战国，是对分布于伏牛山脉以南汉水流域、淮河中上游、长江流域、珠江流域以及云贵高原的复杂族系的统称：长江中上游有濮、巴、蜀；长江中游有三苗、楚、群蛮；长江下游及珠江流域有百越；云贵高原上有西南夷……

名称：《龙凤仕女图》帛画

年代：战国中晚期

规格：纵31.2厘米，横23.2厘米

出土地点：湖南省长沙市陈家大山楚墓

收藏单位：湖南博物院

Name: *Dragon, Phoenix and Witch* (Silk Painting)

Historical Period: The Middle and Late Warring States Period

The Vertical: 31.2 cm, The Horizontal: 23.2 cm

Excavation Site: Chu Tomb, Chenjiashan Hill, Changsha City, Hunan Province

Housed in: Hunan Museum

虽然楚的国民是由长江中下游一带各具地方特色的多族群交融而成的，但楚王室却是正宗的炎黄后裔。史载，楚人的祖先出自颛顼，楚王族的“芈”姓出自祝融八姓，祝融八姓正是颛顼集团吸收部分炎、黄、三苗形成的。对于这一身份，屈原在《离骚》中说：“帝高阳之苗裔兮，朕皇考曰伯庸。”“高阳”指的就是颛顼。至夏商更替时，为躲避战火，楚人辗转迁徙到了荆楚地区，成为中原王朝与诸侯心中的“南蛮”之一。

商周更替之际，楚人祖先鬻熊主动率部翻山越岭来到中原，积极参与武王伐纣之战，为周灭商做出了贡献。楚人由此获得了“子爵”封号，封地五十里，虽然国土狭小，但却成为周朝礼乐体系中的一员。这一年是公元前1042年。

楚国由此开启了八百年立国之路。楚国后来成就大国气象，是以祖先熊绎“筚路蓝缕，以启山林”的决心为精神源头的。周成王盟会诸侯，熊绎出使受到冷遇，回楚后告知群臣，要立志发奋图强。此后，楚国从五十里小国发展成“车毂击，民肩摩，市路相排突，号曰朝衣鲜而暮衣敝”的泱泱大国，创造了先秦发展史上的奇迹。

“我蛮夷也。”这是公元前706年，楚武王在渡江伐随之时对自身身份的宣称。然而在此后发展壮大的历程中，楚国却一直心向中原，不仅自身完成了华夏化的历程，而且实现了对南方诸族群的整合，为中华民族多元一体的进程做出了巨大的历史贡献。楚还创造出令中原华夏折服的文化成果，如青铜冶铸、漆器、楚辞、艺术等。

“夷夏之辨”中的楚

孔子对楚的态度，鲜明地体现了儒家思想的天下主义哲学。

引起孔子对楚国政治极大关注的，是楚国的一代明君楚庄王。楚庄王韬光养晦，一鸣惊人。公元前597年，楚国与晋国发生邲之战，楚大获全胜，声威大振，但楚庄王却以尊重生命为由，拒绝建造用以炫耀武功的“京观”；楚国打败了陈国，但却没有把陈灭掉，而是把流亡在外的陈国公子迎回即位；在郑国穷途末路之际，楚庄王赦免了郑襄公，并与郑国议和……楚国的这一系列仁义之举被中原政权刮目相看，得到华夏中国的称颂。楚庄王还曾经就“止戈为武”提出自己的见解：“武”由“止”“戈”组成，止戈为武，才是真正的武功。

《史记》记载，当孔子读到楚庄王的事迹时，他对楚庄王的美德赞赏有加：“贤哉楚庄王！轻千乘之国而重一言。”楚庄王表现出的政治智慧，与孔子坚持的儒家道德高度吻合，这标志着楚国的政治文化已经走在了华夏文化的前列。

在治国理政方面，楚人最早在今湖北荆门设立县制，将其列为一级行政区划，改变了贵族分封制度，进而引发了军事、土地、赋税改革。县制改革加速了楚国之内的南蛮诸族跟随楚的步伐逐渐华夏化的历程。

公元前223年，秦灭楚，楚人及南蛮诸族群一同成为秦汉郡县属民，共同构成“华夏—汉”的重要组成部分，其丰富多彩的文化也随之融入中华文明。

由此可见，楚国用八百年历史，生动地表达了“夷夏之辨”的标准与本质，成为中华文明独特的天下主义文化传统的生动诠释。

Dragon, Phoenix and Witch was one of the earliest silk paintings in China. With the images of dragon and phoenix juxtaposed, the witch was praying that the soul of the dead would ascend to the heaven. The painting not only mirrored the outlooks on the universe and life of Chu people, as well as their religious faith, but also represented the deep integration of the cultures of South *Man* (蛮) and *Hua Xia* (华夏) in the Warring States Period. Chu people iconized phoenix, an incarnation of their ancestor Zhurong, and embraced dragon, an image in *Hua Xia* culture. This formed new faith of Chu people.

The State of Chu, a statelet whose first capital was Danyang, came to rise in hundreds of years. As one of the powerful states in the Warring States Period, Chu coveted the throne. Besides, it amazed the world with unique technologies for casting bronze and lacquer wares, romantic *Ci* and *Fu* (辞赋), and eccentric art.

Confucius lauded King Zhuang of Chu, regarding him as a rarely-seen Confucianist monarch in the Spring and Autumn Period. To Confucius, the political wisdom of King Zhuang ideally agreed with Confucianist morality. This indicated that in terms of politics and culture, Chu was in the van, *vis-à-vis* the Central Plains.

作为南蛮重要组成部分的巴人为何以虎为标识?

以虎为标识的巴人

虎纽錞于

Chun Yu (錞于, Percussion Instrument in the Battle) with Tiger-Shaped Button

24

文物简读

此“錞于王”是战国时期长江中游以虎为图腾的巴人的典型标识物，充分体现了巴文化的悠久历史。

巴师与錞于

巴人第一次出现在中原历史的聚光灯下，是在武王伐纣的战争中。《华阳国志·巴志》记载了巴人这次浓墨重彩的历史亮相：

周武王伐纣，实得巴蜀之师……巴师勇锐，歌舞以凌，殷前徒倒戈，故世称之曰：“武王伐纣，前歌后舞也。”

巴人在战场上上演了一种什么样的歌舞，竟能令纣王的军队纷纷倒戈？有研究者推测，巴师“前歌后舞”之所以势如雷霆，是因为他们捶响了一种乐器，这种乐器或许便是錞于。

巴人的錞于起初是一种打击军乐器，后来发展成为祭祀用的礼乐器。史载，錞于“声震如雷”“清响良久”，能很好地传递军令。这件战国晚期的虎纽錞于，出土于重庆市万州区，形体特大，有“錞于王”之誉，代表着巴人高超的青铜铸造水平；其顶部的虎纽栩栩如生，是巴人虎崇拜的象征。

透过这件“錞于王”，我们似乎能够看到2500多年前牧野之战中骁勇善战的巴人形象。

名称：虎纽錞于

年代：战国晚期

规格：高68厘米，上径36厘米，底径28厘米，重30千克

出土地点：重庆市万州区甘宁镇

收藏单位：重庆中国三峡博物馆

Name: *Chun Yu* (錞于, Percussion Instrument in the Battle) with Tiger-Shaped Button

Historical Period: The Late Warring States Period

Height: 68 cm, Upper Diameter: 36 cm, Bottom Diameter: 28 cm, Weight: 30 kg

Excavation Site: Ganning Town, Wanzhou District, Chongqing

Housed in: Chongqing China Three Gorges Museum

巴人之源

作为南蛮的主要成员之一，巴人有悠久的历史。据《山海经》载："西南有巴国。大皞生咸鸟，咸鸟生乘厘，乘厘生后照，后照是始为巴人。"学术界普遍认为"大皞"即为太皞、太昊，是东夷部落的重要首领。据此可以大致推断，巴人的族源与东夷人的迁徙有关。

巴在先秦时期有狭义和广义之分。狭义即以长江支流清江流域的廪君蛮为核心的古代民族，也包括嘉陵江支流渠江流域的板楯蛮；广义包括巴人所建方国内的所有族群，主要有濮、苴、獽、共、奴、蜑等。

据《尚书·牧誓》记载，巴人作为"西土之人"参加了周人领导的牧野誓师，在灭除商纣政权的战争中发挥了重要作用，为建立西周王朝立下了汗马功劳。正因如此，周朝建立后，巴人首领被周王封为子爵，正式成为一方诸侯。巴人在建国之初，并无固定的疆域，也无固定的政治、经济、军事中心。春秋时期，随着楚国崛起，巴国被迫向鄂西和川东地区迁徙，最终形成"川东巴国，川西蜀国"的格局。据《华阳国志·巴志》记载，至战国初期，巴人主要活动在川东、鄂西及陕西汉中一带，其地域范围大致为：东到鱼复（今奉节），西至僰道（今宜宾），北接汉中（今陕南一带），南及黔（今湘西、黔东相连地带）、涪（彭水县），与楚、蜀、秦为邻。战国中后期，在巴楚之间的战争中，巴国节节败退，甚至都城江州都沦丧于楚。巴国最终沦为楚国的附庸，偏安于阆中一带，至公元前316年，被秦所灭。

巴人的虎崇拜

巴人是一个崇拜虎的族群。作为巴人主体的廪君蛮和板楯蛮，都有关于虎崇拜的记载和传说。以廪君为祖先和首领的廪君蛮，世代流传着"廪君死，魂魄世为白虎"的传说。这是廪君蛮尊白虎为祖先，从而形成白虎崇拜习俗的体现。而在板楯蛮中，白虎同样占据重要的位置，他们有"专以射白虎为事"的习俗，实质上是对白虎的敬畏。总之，白虎是巴人的文化标志。

秦灭巴后，巴人与巴国境内的众多族群接受中央集权的统治，融入统一多民族国家中，成为华夏的成员。同时，也有相当多的巴人及巴国内部族群在西南、中南地区继续发展，如巴人的一支迁徙到今鄂东，东汉时成为江夏蛮的重要组成部分，西晋、南北朝时则发展为五水蛮；另一支迁至今天的湘西、鄂西南地区，构成武陵蛮的一部分，成为土家族的先民。

今天，鄂西、湘西、川东一带的土家族中仍流传着崇拜白虎的习俗，这揭示出远古巴人与今日土家族之间的源流关系。

As a clan of South *Man* (蛮), Ba people lived in the middle reaches of the Yangtze River in the Warring States Period. The largest *Chun Yu* typified their totem of tiger and fully reflected the long history of the Ba culture.

Ba people firstly appeared in the punitive expedition of King Wu against King Zhou, as dramatically described in "Records of Ba" of *Records of the Lands South of Mt. Hua* (《华阳国志・巴志》):

When King Wu crusaded against King Zhou, Ba soldiers joined... They put all to rout wherever they went. Ba soldiers danced to attack Yin armies who turned their coat at the front. The high morale of King Wu's soldiers was perspicaciously observed.

Some scholars hold the view that Ba soldiers played a kind of war drum, or what we call *Chun Yu*.

Originally, Ba people used *Chun Yu* with war drums. Later, *Chun Yu*, a percussion instrument in the battle, was used as a ritual vessel in sacrifice. As historical records suggested, *Chun Yu* made sounds as loud as thunder, and the crisp sound lasted for a long time. Therefore, *Chun Yu* effectively delivered military orders. *Chun Yu* with tiger-shaped button was made in the late Warring States Period and unearthed in Wanzhou District, Chongqing. It represented high bronze-casting technology of Ba people. The tiger-shaped button on the top looks lifelike and symbolizes the worship of tiger among Ba people.

Ba tribe enjoyed a long history. In *Shan Hai Jing* (《山海经》, *The Classic of Mountains and Seas*), it was asserted that: "The State of Ba stood in the southwest. Dahao gave birth to Xianniao, Xianniao gave birth to Chengli, and Chengli gave birth to Houzhao. Houzhao was the ancestor of Ba people." Dahao was widely acknowledged as Taihao, an important head of East *Yi*. Accordingly, the origin of Ba tribe involved the migration of people from East *Yi*.

In Linjun *Man* (廪君蛮) and Bandun *Man* (板楯蛮), two major clans of Ba tribe, there were records and legends on the worship of tiger. Legend has it that after Linjun, ancestor and chief of Linjun *Man*, died, his soul was reincarnated in a white tiger. This explained why Linjun *Man* venerated white tiger as their ancestor and inherited the worship of white tiger. For Bandun *Man*, white tiger also played a prominent role. Bandun *Man* had the custom of "shooting white tiger", which essentially showed their reverence for white tiger. In brief, white tiger was a cultural symbol of Ba people.

名称：太阳神鸟金饰

年代：春秋

规格：直径12.53厘米，厚度0.02厘米，重20克

出土地点：四川省成都市青羊区金沙遗址

收藏单位：金沙遗址博物馆

Name: Sun and Immortal Birds Gold Ornament

Historical Period: The Spring and Autumn Period

Diameter: 12.53 cm, Thickness: 0.02 cm, Weight: 20 g

Excavation Site: Jinsha Site, Qingyang District, Chengdu, Sichuan Province

Housed in: Jinsha Site Museum

金沙遗址所凸显的古蜀文明太阳崇拜，是如何形成的？

令人惊叹的古蜀文明

太阳神鸟金饰

Sun and Immortal Birds Gold Ornament

25

文物简读

这枚金饰是古蜀文明的巅峰之作，其令人惊叹的工艺既体现了古蜀文明的辉煌灿烂，也证实了以金乌之形承载太阳崇拜的古蜀文明与以凤鸟崇拜为特征的东夷文明之间隐秘而幽深的关联。

古蜀的演进

春秋中叶以前，长江中上游的小国、部落不计其数，而以蜀为大。《蜀王本纪》载，古蜀国历经了蚕丛、柏灌、鱼凫、开明四个王朝。这些王朝的统治者分别来自不同的族属，如蚕丛有可能是来自西北地区的氐羌，在岷江上游带领古蜀族群发展壮大；鱼凫则有可能来自东方，带领古蜀部落南下成都平原，创造了辉煌的三星堆文明。

在考古发掘的成果中，古蜀文明也清晰地呈现出四个发展演进阶段：成都平原史前城址群（宝墩遗址）、三星堆遗址、金沙遗址、战国船棺墓葬遗址。其中三星堆文明是古蜀国的鼎盛时期，创造了辉煌的青铜文明；金沙文明承继了三星堆文明的知识体系和价值理念，在三星堆文明的繁荣鼎盛之后，将古蜀文明推向了又一个高峰。

这件金沙遗址出土的太阳神鸟金饰，就体现着金沙遗址与三星堆遗址之间深刻的继承关系。

古蜀的太阳崇拜

金沙太阳神鸟金饰的工艺达到了令人惊叹的水平。在极薄的金箔之上，镂空雕刻着内外两层图案：内层等距分布着12条旋转的齿状光芒，酷似空中旋转不停的太阳；外层为四只逆时针飞行的神鸟。这些

图案承载着与三星堆青铜神树相同的文化母题——“金乌负日”。

“金乌负日”的神话传说始载于《山海经》。《山海经》中有三段相关记载：

大荒之中，有山名曰孽摇頵羝。上有扶木，柱三百里，其叶如芥。有谷曰温源谷。汤谷上有扶木，一日方至，一日方出，皆载于乌。

东南海之外，甘水之间，有羲和之国，有女子名曰羲和，方日浴于甘渊。羲和者，帝俊之妻，生十日。

汤谷上有扶桑，十日所浴，在黑齿北。居水中，有大木，九日居下枝，一日居上枝。

这就是《山海经》中关于“金乌负日”的故事：名为羲和的女神生下十个太阳，栖于扶桑神树之上，九个停留在下方树枝，只有一个留在最顶端枝头。当一只金乌背负着一个太阳慢慢爬上枝头，太阳便慢慢升起来，阳光普照大地……

三星堆遗址出土的青铜神树，其树枝分为三层，每层每枝上均站立一只鸟，共计九鸟；据文物出土情况看，树顶应还有一段树枝，可惜已残；据此推测，树顶应该还有一只鸟，代表升起的太阳。由此看来，这件青铜神树应是《山海经》中“金乌负日”传说的实物体现。而金沙遗址出土的太阳神鸟金饰，是对“金乌负日”传说的发展和延伸——在太阳神鸟金饰上，纹饰更加抽象化，四只神鸟首尾相接，围绕着中间有12条光芒、呈顺时针旋转的太阳，增加了动态的视觉感受，同时突出了太阳崇拜的文化寓意。

有研究者认为：太阳神鸟金饰还体现了古蜀文明中对天文历法的理解和感悟，四只神鸟代表四时，12条太阳光芒代表一年中的12个月，顺时针和逆时针旋转所营造出的动态视觉效果，是对时光流逝、四时轮回、周而复始的表现。

金沙遗址所代表的古蜀文明，为什么反映了如此强烈的太阳崇拜意识？这种意识与东夷文化的鸟崇拜和太阳崇拜是否具有某种内在关联？三星堆和金沙的先民是否曾与迁徙中的东夷部落发生过深刻的文化交流和融合？

这些上古文化之谜虽未完全解开，但都指向一个清晰的事实：在中华文明的形成和发展过程中，多元起源的文化曾经发生过广泛而深刻的交融。

古蜀与中原文化融合

金沙遗址位于成都城西，距离三星堆遗址50公里，距今3200—2600年，相当于商晚期至春秋中期。金沙遗址出土了大型建筑基址，规模宏大，布局严谨，祭祀区、居住区以及墓葬区分区明确。此外，金沙遗址还出土了金器、青铜器、玉器、漆器等珍贵文物五千余件，还有数以万计的陶片和数以

吨计的象牙等文化遗存。考古学家推断此地极有可能是古蜀国晚期的都邑所在，约等于三星堆文明的最后一期，代表了古蜀的一次政治中心转移。

战国中叶，古蜀文明以联姻、货赂等方式与秦等诸侯国相交往，与中原文化的联系日益密切，蜀国的政治、经济、文化因此加速汇入中华民族形成发展的整体进程。当秦惠文王并灭巴蜀之后，蜀国诸族群最终成为西南华夏的重要来源；而散布于西南其他地域的蜀民，则融入了当地民族。

Considered the acme of ancient Shu civilization, Sun and Immortal Birds Gold Ornament captivates the world. Its exquisite workmanship testifies to brilliant ancient Shu civilization. More importantly, it unveils the cultural connection between the worship of *Jin Wu* (金乌, golden crow) in ancient Shu and the worship of phoenix in East *Yi*.

In *Shu Wang Ben Ji* (《蜀王本纪》, *Biographies of the Kings of Shu*), ancient Shu Kingdom saw the existence of four regimes, i.e. Cancong, Baiguan, Yufu and Kaiming, which were established by four tribes respectively. As archaeological excavation suggests, ancient Shu civilization underwent four stages of development or evolution: the Chengdu Plain Prehistoric City Site Group (Baodun Site), the Sanxingdui Site, the Jinsha Site, and the Warring States Boat Coffin Burial Site.

On extremely thin gold foil were carved two-circle hollowed-out patterns. Twelve tooth-like rotating rays were evenly distributed in the inner circle, resembling the sun spinning incessantly in the sky. Four immortal birds flew counterclockwise in the outer circle. These patterns shared the same cultural motif with the Bronze Divine Tree at Sanxingdui, or "Golden Crow Bearing the Sun". The myth and legend of golden crow were firstly recorded in *Shan Hai Jing* (《山海经》, *The Classic of Mountains and Seas*).

Some scholars observe that Sun and Immortal Birds Gold Ornament also justifies the understanding of astronomy and calendar of ancient Shu people. Four immortal birds signify four seasons, and twelve solar rays represent twelve months. The counterclockwise rotation forms a dynamic visual effect and materializes the ideas of time and cycle of nature.

The Jinsha Site is located in the west of Chengdu, 50 kilometers away from the Sanxingdui Site, dating back to *c*. 2,600—3,200 years ago (the late Shang Dynasty to the middle Spring and Autumn Period). More than 5,000 valuable cultural relics, such as gold, bronze, jade and lacquer wares, as well as tens of thousands of pottery pieces and tons of ivory, have been unearthed at the Jinsha Site. Archaeologists infer that Jinsha probably served as the capital of ancient Shu Kingdom when the Sanxingdui civilization came to an end. This meant the transfer of political center for ancient Shu Kingdom.

被世人取笑了两千多年的夜郎在面对汉使的时候为何敢于尊大?

"西南夷之最大"的夜郎

立虎辫索纹耳大铜釜 26

Large Bronze Cauldron with Standing-Tiger Decoration and *Bian Suo* (辫索, Braid Rope-Shaped)-Pattern Ear

文物简读

夜郎，作为战国时期"南蛮"之一，因"道不通"，直到西汉时期才被中央王朝了解并载入史册。作为具有标识性的夜郎文化形态，"套头葬"直到西汉中晚期才因中原文化的逐渐融入而发生变化，最终消失。这件"套头葬"铜釜，见证了夜郎在与中原的不断交往交流中逐渐融入华夏的过程。

"夜郎自大"?

司马迁在《史记》中，记载了一个有名的故事：

汉武帝元狩元年（前122），为探寻通往身毒（今印度）的道路，派汉使来到古滇国和夜郎国。"滇王与汉使者言曰：'汉孰与我大？'及夜郎侯亦然，以道不通故，各自以为一州主，不知汉广大。"

"汉孰与我大？"面对汉使，滇王与夜郎侯提了一个相同的问题，且滇王提问在前，但不公平的是，却是夜郎落得了个"自大"的名声，被世人取笑两千多年。

那么，当时的夜郎侯究竟有没有"自大"的资本呢?

史载，夜郎是西南地区古老的地方政权，辖区内族群繁多，以百越系的僚人、南蛮系的濮人为主体。也有部分学者认为，夜郎政权的统治阶层及主体成员是彝族先民，因为现存的众多彝文文献都有关于夜郎历史的记载。

夜郎国大致兴起于战国时期，其起源与竹崇拜有关。《后汉书》载："夜郎者，初，有女子浣于遁水，有三节大竹流入足间，闻其中有号声，剖竹视之，得一男儿，归而养之。及长，有才武，自立

名称：立虎辫索纹耳大铜釜

年代：战国至秦汉

规格：通高32.8厘米，口径44.3厘米

出土地点：贵州省毕节市赫章县可乐遗址

收藏单位：贵州省博物馆

Name: Large Bronze Cauldron with Standing-Tiger Decoration and *Bian Suo* (辫索, Braid Rope-Shaped)-Pattern Ear

Historical Period: From the Warring States Period to the Qin and Han Dynasties

Total Height: 32.8 cm, Mouth Diameter: 44.3 cm

Excavation Site: Kele Site, Hezhang County, Bijie City, Guizhou Province

Housed in: Guizhou Provincial Museum

为夜郎侯，以竹为姓。”夜郎国王因此也被称为竹王。据彝文史料记载，夜郎主要经历了四个王朝，分别为武米夜郎、洛举夜郎、撒骂夜郎和金竹夜郎。

相关研究表明，夜郎国的核心区域主要集中在北盘江流域，到西汉金竹夜郎统治时期夜郎国达到鼎盛阶段。《后汉书》载：“西南夷者，有蜀徼外，有夜郎国，东接交趾，西有滇国，北有邛都国，各立君长，其人皆椎髻左衽，邑聚而居。”根据汉朝曾在夜郎设置的犍为郡和牂牁郡的版图，大致可以推断出夜郎国的统治范围：西到朱提，与滇国接壤；东到且兰（沅江上游），与黔中郡（武陵郡）相接；北到大娄山，和巴蜀接壤；南到交趾，与南越相邻。夜郎国总面积达40万平方公里，在西南地区可谓大国。

此时的夜郎政权，类似于夏商时期的方国联盟，其治下的方国达到22个之多，拥兵十万，足以威慑整个西南夷地区。因此，《史记》称：“西南夷君长以什数，夜郎最大。”此外，夜郎王与滇王是西南夷地区仅有的两个被汉朝赐予金印封王的首领，可见夜郎当时在西南地区的重要地位。

由此可见，夜郎在西南夷中确有“自大”的资本。当然，若与中原政权相比，自是相差甚远。可惜，因为“道不通”，当时的夜郎王并没有意识到这一点，竟在西汉成帝河平年间（前27—前25）带领22小国叛离汉朝，被牂牁郡太守陈立平复，随之灭国。夜郎终因“自大”而付出了代价。

夜郎的套头葬习俗

考古发现，贵州赫章可乐墓葬遗址的年代从战国一直持续到西汉晚期，与夜郎政权相对应，应是夜郎政权统治的核心区域。

在可乐遗址中，考古工作者发现了一个独具特色的夜郎习俗——套头葬。

套头葬是一种用铜洗、铜釜或铜鼓等器物套于死者头部的下葬方式，其中绝大多数为铜釜。套头葬分为三种类型：一是仅在墓主人头部套一件器物；二是在墓主人头部套一件器物的同时，脚部也套一件器物；三是在墓主人头部套一件器物的同时，脚部垫一件铜洗。

为什么要实行套头葬？学术界普遍认为，使用套头葬的墓主人，通常为类似巫师的神职人员，用于套头的器物便是其身份象征。在宗教仪式中，“巫师”将铜釜戴在头顶，作为沟通神灵的法器；他们去世后，人们仍然希望他们能够与神灵世界沟通，以达到护佑族群的目的。也有专家根据套头葬墓葬中普遍出土了具有使用痕迹的兵器随葬品，认为墓主人可能为军事长官或有一定地位的武士。

考古发现，可乐遗址中的套头葬经历了一个清晰的发展演变过程：战国中期以前未出现套头葬现象；战国晚期，始现铜洗垫头或盖头现象；战国晚期至西汉早期，始现铜釜套头现象；西汉前期，铜釜类型和数量增多，套头葬现象达到鼎盛阶段；西汉中期以后，套头葬中开始出现汉式铁釜，并不断增多；至西汉晚期及东汉早期，夜郎墓葬形式及随葬品与中原基本无异，套头葬习俗完全消失。

独特的套头葬习俗及其演变，揭示出古夜郎文化的发展演变以及接受中原文化影响的过程。

这件立虎辫索纹耳大铜釜，出土于可乐遗址中一座规模最大、规格最高的套头葬墓，其与可乐遗址前期造型风格简单粗糙的铜釜截然不同，极具装饰意义，是套头葬铜釜中制作工艺最精美的一件：其肩腹部装饰一对圆雕立虎，两虎昂首长啸，威武不凡；两虎颈部装饰一条海贝纹项圈，与徐州狮子山西汉楚王陵出土的玉豹颈部项圈十分相似。此外，墓主人颈部还有一枚铜印，印文为隶书“敬事”，属典型汉式印，应与西汉王朝开发西南夷后，汉廷对夜郎地区的管辖有关。牂牁郡设立后，大量汉人迁入夜郎，不仅带来了先进的物质文化，对当地的精神文化也产生了很大影响。

The bronze cauldron typified the unique custom of *Taotou Zang* (套头葬, burying the dead with a bronze ware on the head), and witnessed the cultural exchanges and integration between Southwestern *Yi* (夷) and the Central Plains.

Historically, Yelang was an ancient state in the southwest. Archaeological discoveries showed that Kele Tomb Site, located in Hezhang, Guizhou, existed from the Warring States Period to the late Western Han Dynasty, which coincided with the rule of Yelang. Therefore, Kele constituted the core area of Yelang. At Kele Tomb Site, archaeologists noticed the unique custom of Yelang: *Taotou Zang*.

Generally speaking, *Taotou Zang* referred to the practice that the dead was buried with a bronze ware on the head, e.g. bronze *Fu* (釜, cauldron), bronze *Xi* (洗, washing vessel) and bronze drum. Bronze cauldron was used in most cases. Scholars commonly agree that the owners of *Taotou Zang* tombs were sorcerers who took charge of religious affairs, and that their identities were clarified by bronze wares. Noteworthily, a great quantity of weapons (as burial objects) were unearthed in these tombs. Some scholars argued that the owners of these tombs were military officers or warriors with high status.

The bronze cauldron with standing-tiger decoration was unearthed in the largest and highest-ranking *Taotou Zang* tomb in Kele Tomb Site in Hezhang, Guizhou. Totally different from bronze cauldrons that were shoddily made, it was elaborately designed with the most exquisite skills.

Its shoulder and belly were decorated with a pair of round-carved standing tigers, which raised their heads and roared, looking grand and imposing. The necks of the two tigers were adorned with two seashell-pattern necklets, with a striking similarity to the necklet of the jade leopard unearthed from the Tomb of King of Chu (the Western Han Dynasty) at Lion Mountain, Xuzhou. Additionally, a bronze seal was unearthed around the neck of the tomb owner, with the inscriptions of *Jing Shi* (敬事, respectfully serving the god) in clerical script. As a typical Han-style seal, it proved the jurisdiction of the Han court over Yelang after the Western Han Dynasty developed the Southwestern *Yi* region.

名称：立牛铜葫芦笙

年代：战国

规格：高28.2厘米

出土地点：云南省玉溪市江川区李家山24号墓

收藏单位：云南省博物馆

Name: Bronze Gourd-Shaped *Sheng* (笙) with a Standing-Ox Design

Historical Period: The Warring States Period

Height: 28.2 cm

Excavation Site: No. 24 Tomb, Lijiashan, Jiangchuan District, Yuxi City, Yunnan Province

Housed in: Yunnan Provincial Museum

中国古代“八音”之一的“匏”为什么会出现在神秘的古滇国墓葬中?

“华化”与“夷化”双向变奏中的古滇国

立牛铜葫芦笙

Bronze Gourd-Shaped *Sheng* (笙) with a Standing-Ox Design

27

文物简读

这件工艺精湛的铜葫芦笙是古滇国的传统吹奏乐器。它以铜作为材质，逼真地再现了作为中国古代“八音”之一、以葫芦为主要材料的“匏”，从而彰显了古滇国作为中华文化参与者的身份。

一件独特的古滇国乐器

1972年，云南江川李家山古墓群遗址24号墓出土了一件十分特别的随葬品——立牛铜葫芦笙。这件铜笙整体为葫芦形，上半部分为曲管，顶端铸造一头栩栩如生的立牛；下半部分呈圆球状，正面有五孔，出土时有腐断的竹管痕迹。由此可见，这是一件五管芦笙，是中国古代“八音”（八种不同材质的乐器）之一的“匏”，作为古滇人重要的吹奏乐器而成为随葬品。

这件铜葫芦笙上的立牛造型是古滇国文化中颇具标识性的文化因素，表现的是亚洲南部特有的“印度瘤牛”，即《山海经》中所记载的“留牛”。其普遍出现于古滇国器物中，充分体现了古滇国牛崇拜的文化习俗以及高超的手工艺制作水平；仿葫芦笙的造型，则充分体现了古滇文化与中原文明的深度融合。

庄蹻与古滇国的故事

江川李家山古墓群被认为是古滇国的贵族墓地，出土了大量规格极高的墓葬。参照碳14测定以及相关研究，该墓群年代上限可以追溯到战国中晚期，下限至东汉初期。学术界普遍认为，这个时间段基本覆盖了古滇国的始终。

司马迁在《史记·西南夷列传》中，记载了古滇国的故事：

将军庄蹻将兵循江上，略巴、黔中以西。蹻至滇池……以兵威定属楚。欲归报，会秦击夺楚巴、黔中郡，道塞不通，因还，以其众王滇，变服，从其俗，以长之。

战国时期，楚国派遣将领庄蹻率领军队向西南进攻，一直打到滇池一带。庄蹻凭借强大的军事实力征服了当地。然而公元前277年，秦夺取楚国的黔中郡，断了庄蹻的归路。于是，庄蹻带领其属下，改变了自己的服饰，依从了当地的习俗，成为第一代滇王。

由此可见，古滇国年代的上限可以追溯到公元前277年，这与考古发掘资料得到的信息基本吻合。

然而，从古滇墓葬考古发掘来看，早在“庄蹻入滇”以前，古滇文化已经达到相当高的水平，尤其是其极具创造力和想象力的青铜文明，成为先秦晚期中华文明的突出代表。因此，古滇文化的起源绝非从庄蹻入滇开始，而是此前就已经历了漫长的发展历程。

云南地区自远古时期开始就有人类的足迹，中华民族百万年的人类生命史便在此肇始。新石器时代晚期，滇池地区涌现出诸多人类文化遗迹。古滇文化是在滇池地区史前文化的基础上，吸收周边劳浸、靡莫、叟、僰等部族文化成果以及中原文化、楚文化等文明因素，逐渐形成的极具地方特色的文化形态。由此可见，古滇文化并非单一民族文化形态，而是由多民族文化相互吸收融合而成的。

“女娲作笙簧”：滇人的创造性发展与传承

“庄蹻王滇”的故事表明了在中华民族形成发展的过程中，各民族间相互渗透、吸收与融合，存在着“华夏化”与“夷化”的双向过程，其中充满了多层次、多面向的复杂因素。立牛铜葫芦笙就生动地呈现出古滇文化与华夏文化之间互相融合、互为印证的关系。

笙属中华古“八音”中的“匏”，匏即葫芦。相传“女娲作笙簧”，笙簧是中原地区传统的古乐器之一，在陕西榆林石峁遗址曾出土距今约4000年的骨质口簧。《旧唐书·音乐志》载：“匏，瓠也，女娲氏造。列管于匏上，内（纳）簧其中。”由此可见，女娲所作的笙是用多根竹管插在匏上，并将簧片纳入其中以发出声响。这跟古滇国墓葬出土的铜葫芦笙的形制如出一辙。古滇人用铜材仿制匏，这一材质的变化隐现着边地民族对中原文化的创造性发展。

事实上，女娲所作之笙簧有着深刻的象征意义——将竹簧之管插入葫芦，使之发声，这样的形象隐喻性地表达了先民对两性交合方能生育的认识。因此，笙簧便具有一种乞生巫仪的意义。《博雅》引《世本》云：“女娲作笙簧。笙，生也，象物贯地而生……”这一记载揭示了女娲作笙簧与女娲造人、创制婚姻、繁衍人类之间的深刻关联。

笙簧所蕴含的这一内涵，在我国西南少数民族中间递相传承，绵延不绝，苗、瑶、傈僳、侗、彝、佤、怒、拉祜、傣、纳西、德昂等民族一直挚爱着葫芦笙、芦笙、口弦，并将之演化为青年之间求爱与乞婚的媒介。直到20世纪中叶，这些民族中仍可见这样的情景：每当节日来临，山林溪畔，竹影月下，便响起笙簧声声，青年男女以乐传情，表达爱意……

The exquisitely-crafted bronze gourd-shaped *Sheng* was a traditional wind instrument in the ancient Kingdom of Dian. *Pao* (gourd) was one of eight materials for making musical instruments in ancient Chinese music. The gourd-shaped *Sheng* attested to the contribution of Dian to Chinese culture.

In 1972, an unusual burial object, bronze gourd-shaped *Sheng*, was unearthed from No. 24 Tomb at Lijiashan Ancient Tomb Group Site, Jiangchuan, Yunnan, with the vestiges of rotted bamboo pipe. The overall shape of the *Sheng* looks like a gourd. On the upper part is a curved pipe, where a standing ox was cast in a true-to-life way. The lower part forms a globe, with five holes on the front. As archaeologists judged, the five-hole *Sheng* was made from gourd, also known as gourd musical instrument. As a wind instrument, the *Sheng* was buried with the tomb owner in Dian.

The standing-ox design, as a cultural icon in Dian, visualized *Bos indicus* (瘤牛), a species exclusive to southern Asia, which was also recorded in *Shan Hai Jing* (《山海经》, *The Classic of Mountains and Seas*), with a different spelling in Chinese (留牛). The widespread use of ox image fully represented the cultural custom of ox idolization and the marvelous craftsmanship of ox artifacts in Dian, and the gourd shape convincingly proved the deep cultural integration between Dian and the Central Plains.

Legend goes that Nü Wa fashioned *Sheng Huang* (笙簧). A bone harmonica was unearthed at Shimao Site in Yulin, Shaanxi, dating back to about 4,000 years ago. This ran in the same groove with the bronze gourd-shaped *Sheng* in Dian and justified how remote ethnic groups developed the culture of the Central Plains in an innovative way.

春秋战国时期，作为北狄政权的中山国为什么能够在诸侯争霸的中原地区立足并开创辉煌灿烂的中山文明呢?

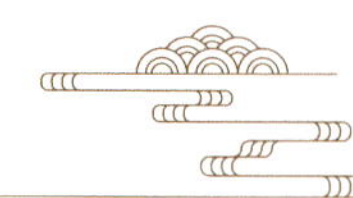

掀动历史风云的中山国

错金银四龙四凤铜方案座

28

Square Bronze Table-Seat with Four-Dragon & Four-Phoenix Design Inlaid with Gold and Silver（*Cuojinyin*, 错金银）

文物简读

这件铜方案座是中山国第五代国王的心爱之物，它见证了白狄鲜虞部建立中山国的历史风云，充分反映了北方游牧文明与中原农耕文明的高度融合。

中山国的遗物

这件于1977年在河北省平山县一座战国墓葬中出土的青铜方案，采用了错金银的工艺装饰。龙的鳞片、凤鸟的翎毛、梅花鹿的皮毛斑纹等，均用不同材质的金属勾勒和填充，色彩炫目斑斓。四只跪卧的梅花鹿，两雄两雌，作为四足支撑着方案的圆环形底座；四龙四凤，穿插组合，设计复杂，视觉华丽，构成方案的中层，起到连接底座和承托桌案的作用；放置案板的方形框架构成最上层，木制案板已腐朽。考古学家证实，这件结构复杂、工艺精湛的随葬品是战国时期中山国的遗物，它见证了中山国跌宕起伏的发展历程。

名称：错金银四龙四凤铜方案座

年代：战国中期

规格：通高36.2厘米，边长47.5厘米，重18.65千克

出土地点：河北省平山县中山王墓

收藏单位：河北博物院

Name: Square Bronze Table-Seat with Four-Dragon & Four-Phoenix Design Inlaid with Gold and Silver（*Cuojinyin*, 错金银）

Historical Period: The Middle Warring States Period

Total Height: 36.2 cm, Side Length: 47.5 cm, Weight: 18.65 kg

Excavation Site: The Tomb of King of the State of Zhongshan, Pingshan County, Hebei Province

Housed in: Hebei Museum

中山国的传奇

中山国的创立者是北狄的一支，称为白狄鲜虞部。《左传》记载了关于中山国的传奇史：

春秋末期，东迁至河北中部的白狄鲜虞部屡遭晋国的攻击，但它最终在公元前507年的平中战役中击败晋国，并于第二年迁居中山城，建立中山国。中山城位于今河北省唐县境内，因“城中有山，故曰中山”。中山国依据险要的地形，有效抵挡了晋国此后的屡次讨伐和围攻，顽强地生存了下来。直到公元前414年，中山武公以当时诸侯的最高爵位自立，迁居于顾（今河北省定县）。但好景不长，武公初立后，中山国被晋国的赵氏打败，虽未亡国，但已风雨飘摇。后继者中山桓公被迫迁都灵寿（今河北省平山县境），其统治中心进入太行山域。公元前408年，魏国派大将乐羊进攻中山国，中山桓公利用险要的地形顽强抵抗了三年，于公元前406年最终战败，导致亡国，中山故地被魏国占有。公元前381年，中山桓公趁魏国与赵楚联军作战失败之机，率领部众起义，成功复国。公元前327年，年仅16岁的措成为中山国国君。措是一位富有魄力和胆识的君主。首先，他将自己的封号由“公”改为“王”，成为名副其实的国王；其次，他征战四方，北迎燕，南击赵，一时间小小的中山国竟与三晋、燕比肩争雄。至此，中山国达到了辉煌的顶峰。中山国的极盛之期维持了30多年，到公元前295年时，中山国最终灭于赵。

中山国在诸侯争霸的环境中，尤其是在魏、赵、燕三大强国的夹缝中，顽强生存，一度成为与“战国七雄”争辉的强大诸侯国，掀动了历史风云，推动了先秦时期中华文明的发展进程。

北狄

春秋时期，在秦、晋、郑、卫、邢等诸侯国以北，即今陕西北部以及山西、河北等地区的中部和北部，生活着许多强悍的游牧部落，因位于北方，他们被统称为“北狄”，主要包括赤狄、白狄、长狄等诸多支系。史载，北狄曾与炎黄集团有密切关系，其源出于商周时期的鬼方、猃狁，属羌戎族系。他们南面与诸夏往来，彼此之间存在着复杂的经济、文化、军事及联姻关系。北狄甚至吸收了部分诸夏人口，既对中原诸夏构成威胁，又深刻地受到华夏文化的影响，促进了其华化的进程。

此外，北狄在北面又与山戎、阴山以北的胡人以及东胡也存在彼此吸收和交融的关系。战国时期，随着胡人南下，赤狄、白狄等北狄部落有很大部分融入胡人部落。因此，到战国中晚期至秦汉时期，北狄成为北方胡人、东胡族系各民族的统称。随着胡人的兴起、匈奴的强大，北狄与中原的联系与交往也更加密切和深入。

中山国的文明成果

中山国何以能在诸侯环伺、群雄争霸的春秋战国时期表现出如此强大的生命力和创造力？其根本原因在于，白狄鲜虞部进入中原后，以开放的姿态促成了农牧文化交融，与燕、赵、魏等政权发生了深度的政治与文化交往，并在此基础上创造出了辉煌灿烂的文明成果。

考古发掘及相关研究表明，河北省平山县战国古城就是中山国都城灵寿，此地发现的战国墓葬群就是中山国国王措以及贵族王公的墓葬群。对墓葬的形制以及出土陶器、青铜器、铁器等随葬品的研究表明，该墓葬与同时期中原地区的王公墓葬形制及规格基本一致，充分体现了中山国的华夏化程度之高。同时，中山国又保留了部分游牧文化传统。这件错金银四龙四凤铜方案座受商周青铜文化的影响而又独具游牧民族的文化特征：游牧者所热爱的鹿与华夏文化所崇尚的龙凤集于一身，多种工艺聚于一体，复杂精巧，具有独特的中山风格。

As a treasure of the fifth king of the State of Zhongshan, the bronze table-seat saw the rise of Baidi Xianyu (白狄鲜虞) tribe. Its shape fully reflects the deep fusion of nomadic and farming civilizations.

The bronze table-seat was unearthed in a Warring States tomb at Pingshan County, Hebei Province, in 1977. It is decorated with inlaid gold and silver. The dragon scales, phoenix feathers, and the spotted skin patterns of sika deer are all outlined and filled with various metal materials, with dazzling colors. Four kneeling sika deer, two males and two females, serve as a circular base for supporting the table-seat, like four legs. Four dragons and four phoenixes interlace, with intricate design and flamboyant appearance. Located in the middle part of the table-seat, they connect to the base and support the table-seat. The square frame stands in the upper part, with rot on the wooden table-seat. Archaeologists confirm that the exquisitely-designed bronze table-seat was a burial object in the State of Zhongshan in the Warring States Period.

The State of Zhongshan was established by Baidi Xianyu, a clan of North *Di* (狄). In the late Spring and Autumn Period, Baidi Xianyu, which had migrated eastward to the central part of present-day Hebei Province, was continuously harried by the State of Jin. Ultimately, it vanquished the latter in the Pingzhong Battle in 507 BC. In 506 BC, Baidi Xianyu transferred to Zhongshan, present-day Tangxian County, Hebei Province. The heyday of Zhongshan lasted for more than 30 years. In 295 BC, it was swallowed up by Zhao.

Archaeological excavations and studies elucidate that the Warring States Ancient City Site lied in Lingshou, the capital city of Zhongshan, and the tomb group belonged to Cuo, King of Zhongshan, and the Xianyu nobles. As evinced, the shapes and burial objects (e.g. unearthed pottery, bronze and iron wares) of the tombs basically coincide with their counterparts in the Central Plains, deeply influenced by the *Hua Xia* style.

赵武灵王大力推行的“胡服骑射”给中华民族的发展带来哪些影响?

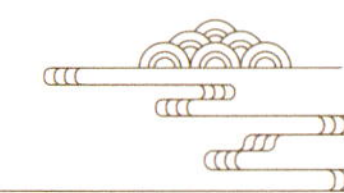

胡服骑射的故事

鎏金鸭形铜带钩

Gilded Duck-Shaped Bronze Girdle Hook

29

文物简读

这件体现战国时期游牧民族服饰特点的铜带钩，反映出华夏族与北狄之间的文化互鉴关系，隐现着“胡服骑射”及其背后波澜壮阔的历史故事。

赵武灵王为何推行“胡服骑射”?

战国中期，赵国曾一度国势衰落。公元前325年，15岁的少年赵雍从父亲赵肃侯手中接过了赵国的最高权力，成为赵国第六代君主赵武灵王。

此前，赵国曾频繁地与魏、楚、秦、燕、齐等国发生战争，尤其是与魏国之间连年征战。赵国采用合纵攻势打击魏国，使魏国的百年基业受到严重削弱，但赵国自身也因此内耗严重，国势日渐衰弱。赵肃侯去世后，魏惠王便立即联合楚、秦、燕、齐四国，以吊唁之名，各派万人精锐之师，趁赵国新君年幼之际，欲俟机灭赵。年幼的赵武灵王在托孤重臣肥义的辅佐下，采取强硬措施，以举国之力，破灭了五国联军的图谋，经受住了严峻的考验。

虽然渡过一劫，但赵国仍面临着三大严峻危机。一是来自西边秦国的威胁，自公元前328年魏国把河西割让给秦国后，秦便与赵接壤，成为秦攻赵的便利通道。二是来自东边的齐国和中山国的侵扰，此时的齐国是实力强大的“战国七雄”之一，赵国的东南部与齐为邻，齐国一直觊觎赵国的领土，存有蚕食赵国的企图；而中山国西靠太行山，三面与赵国为邻，曾在齐国的大力支持下多次侵犯赵国，充当了齐国的“打手”。三是来自胡人的威胁，东胡、林胡、楼烦是北方三个实力强大的游牧族群，精于骑射，行动迅速，合称为“三胡”，他们经常趁火打劫，使赵国苦不堪言。《史记》载，赵武灵

名称：鎏金鸭形铜带钩

年代：战国

规格：通长4厘米，通宽2厘米，通高2.6厘米，重28克

出土地点：山西省晋中市榆次区猫儿岭

收藏单位：晋中市榆次区文物所

Name: Gilded Duck-Shaped Bronze Girdle Hook

Historical Period: The Warring States Period

Total Length: 4 cm, Total Width: 2 cm

Total Height: 2.6 cm, Weight: 28 g

Excavation Site: Mao'erling, Yuci District, Jinzhong City, Shanxi Province

Housed in: Institute of Cultural Relics of Yuci District, Jinzhong City

王十九年，这位胸怀壮志的赵国君主曾忧心忡忡地对自己的臣子说：“今中山在我腹心，北有燕，东有胡，西有林胡、楼烦、秦、韩之边，而无强兵之救，是亡社稷，奈何？”可见，赵武灵王怀着强烈的忧患意识。

为摆脱赵国所处的困境，赵武灵王积极寻求强国之道。赵武灵王观察到，匈奴、东胡、林胡、楼烦等游牧族群身穿窄袖短衣，长裤革靴，乘骑射箭，行动十分便捷利索，与中原的兵车、长矛相比具有更大灵活性。他感叹道：“北方游牧的骑兵来如飞鸟，去如绝弦，带着这样的部队驰骋疆场，哪有不取胜的道理？”在经过认真的思考后，赵武灵王提出了“着胡服”“习骑射”的主张，下令在全国范围内进行声势浩大的服饰改革，即着短装，束皮带，用带钩，穿皮靴；同时淘汰战车，改为骑马射箭。

借助于“胡服骑射”，赵国一举建立起一支以骑兵为主体的强大军队，此后国势大盛，成为战国后期唯一可与强秦抗衡的诸侯国。

“胡服骑射”的意义

“胡服骑射”在中国历史上的意义是多方面的——

从中国古代的军事史来说，它构成了一个具有划时代影响的事件，标志着华夏历史上第一支独立骑兵部队的诞生。

从中国古代的服饰史来说，它促成了华夏衣饰从“上衣下裳”逐渐向 “上衣下裤”的演变，裤子、靴子及使用带钩的腰带慢慢进入中原人的生活。

从中华民族多元一体的历史进程来说，它使得“华贵夷贱”的观念产生了动摇，拉近了华夷之间的距离，激发出华夷之间的互鉴、互参、互化，引发了“华化”与“夷化”的双重变奏，从而塑造了中华文明内部的包容心态，为后世奠定了一个悠久而牢固的思想文化传统，那就是兼容并蓄、互鉴融通。

“胡服骑射”的见证物

如果我们要为当年的“胡服骑射”找到一件相关的历史见证物，那有可能是什么呢？

带钩！

带钩是服饰之上用于系挂革带的衣物部件，学界普遍认为带钩是游牧民族为方便骑射而发明的衣饰。在推行“胡服骑射”之前，赵国作为中原华夏的主要诸侯国，崇尚带有礼法规范的服饰制度，其服饰为上衣下裳、宽袍大袖的“深衣”。所谓“深衣”，其形制为将上衣和下裳连在一起，包住身体，“被体深邃”，使身体深藏不露，雍容典雅。而胡服则为窄袖短衣、长裤和革靴，衣身紧窄；腰束郭洛带，使用带钩，便于骑射。

这件战国时期的鎏金鸭形铜带钩，整体造型如鸭凫水，曲颈回首，颈弯如钩，通体鎏金，造型生动，工艺精湛，体现出浓郁的北方游牧民族崇尚动物的文化特征。这件带钩的出土地晋中市，正是战国时期的赵国的领地。所以我们有理由相信，它正是赵武灵王大力推行“胡服骑射”的历史见证。

In overall shape, the bronze girdle hook looks like a duck swimming in water. Looking back, the duck bends the neck, forming a hook. The entire body is gilded, with lifelike style and consummate workmanship. Culturally, it reflects the worship of animals among northern nomads. It was unearthed in present-day Jinzhong City, which belonged to the territory of the State of Zhao in the Warring States Period.

In 325 BC, Zhao Yong, a 15-year-old boy, succeeded to the throne upon the death of his father Zhao Yu (Marquis Su), and became the sixth king of Zhao, known as King Wuling of Zhao. Owing to years of warfare, the power of Zhao waned. To make his country rich and build up military power, King Wuling racked his brains.

As he observed, nomadic tribes like Xiongnu, Donghu, Linhu and Loufan wore narrow-sleeves short clothes, long pants and leather boots, rode on horses and performed archery easily and agilely, which proved much swifter than chariots and spears in the Central Plains. Later, King Wuling initiated a large-scale reform on military force and dress, ordering people to wear short clothes, girdle hooks and leather boots, and soldiers to practice equitation and archery. After the reform, or “wearing Hu dress and shooting on horse”, the State of Zhao forged a valorous army of cavalry and gained great power, boasting the only state that threw down the gauntlet to Qin, a western power, in the late Warring States Period.

King Wuling’s reform signaled an epoch-making event in the histories of Chinese army and dress. It bred the formation of the first cavalry in the Han states and catalyzed the fundamental change of dressing style in the Central Plains. More significantly, the reform re-shaped the idea of “*Hua Xia* (华夏) superior to *Yi* (夷)”, and honed the inclusiveness of Chinese civilization.

曾经叱咤中国北方草原的匈奴人从哪里来，最终又去了哪里?

匈奴崛起的见证

鹰顶金冠饰

Eagle-Top Gold Crown Ornament

30

文物简读

这是目前所发现的唯一的匈奴首领金冠，它不仅见证了匈奴崛起及其高度发达的游牧文化，更体现了推动北方统一的匈奴人对中华大一统格局的巨大贡献。

匈奴王的黄金冠饰

一只展翅欲飞的雄鹰，傲然立于穹庐状的冠顶中央，仿佛俯瞰着大地；它的头和颈以绿松石打造，展现着雄鹰特有的神采与威严。鹰的脚下，是四狼四羊咬斗相缠之景，以浮雕形式描绘于冠盖之上；狼作卧伏状，盘角羊前肢弯曲，后肢被狼咬住，作反转态。额圈则以两条绳索式的金带巧妙并合而成，上条呈半圆形，两端为卧虎造型；下条呈完整的圆形，两侧对称装饰马、盘羊造型。

这是中国迄今为止发现的唯一的匈奴贵族金冠饰，它通体用纯金打造，总重约1.5千克，代表了战国时期我国北方贵金属工艺的最高水平，体现了匈奴游牧文化在极盛期的创造力。金冠于1972年出土于内蒙古自治区鄂尔多斯市杭锦旗，是内蒙古博物院的镇馆之宝。

专家们认为，因为鹰在匈奴人心中是草原王者的象征，这只金冠很可能是匈奴王的所有物。

匈奴

匈奴是中国历史上第一个在北方草原游牧区建立起统一政权的族群，其诞生的摇篮在今内蒙古自治区大青山一带。匈奴的称谓最早见于战国时期。据考证，“匈奴”的原意为“天帝之子”，可直译为“人”或“居民”“土民”等。王国维认为，“匈奴”二字急读为“胡”；而“胡”一词在匈奴

名称：鹰顶金冠饰

年代：战国

规格：通高7.3厘米，带长30厘米，重1394克

出土地点：内蒙古自治区鄂尔多斯市杭锦旗匈奴墓地

收藏单位：内蒙古博物院

Name: Eagle-Top Gold Crown Ornament

Historical Period: The Warring States Period

Total Height: 7.3 cm, Belt Length: 30 cm, Weight: 1,394 g

Excavation Site: A Xiongnu Tomb, Hangjin Banner, Ordos City, Inner Mongolia Autonomous Region

Housed in: Inner Mongolia Museum

人心目中，即为“天之骄子”。匈奴的族源，与殷商以来的鬼方、猃狁、荤粥、胡有着密切的渊源关系；历史学家认为，匈奴是在上述族群的基础上，吸收周边的戎、狄、东胡等不同族群，逐渐发展起来的联合体。

考古成果表明，早在春秋早期，即公元前8—前7世纪时，匈奴便已在内蒙古大青山地区建立起氏族部落联盟。而在后世发展过程中，匈奴的政治、经济中心逐渐转移至漠北。至公元前4世纪末，匈奴部落联盟逐渐发展壮大，具备了强大的军事实力，开始与强悍的以骑射著称的楼烦部落相对抗，并将势力范围逐步扩展至秦、赵、燕边境，对中原产生了极大的威胁。

公元前3世纪，匈奴进入铁器时代，其社会经济得到极大发展，氏族制度全面瓦解。战国末年，在头曼单于的带领下，匈奴部落联盟融合了周边大量不同族系的族群，逐渐形成了一个新的联合体。随着社会经济文化的发展，匈奴从氏族联盟转变为匈奴政权，从而实现了北方草原的第一次统一。其时，匈奴的势力范围东起大兴安岭，西到祁连山和天山，北面囊括了贝加尔湖，南达长城。

当秦汉在中原地区实现统一的时候，匈奴则在部落林立的北方游牧区实现了统一，形成了“南有大汉，北有强胡”的局面。这一格局在中华历史上意义重大。费孝通说：“南北两个统一体的汇合才是中华民族作为一个民族实体进一步的完成。” 匈奴建立的北方游牧统一体，以局部统一为中华大一统格局的形成奠定了基础，是中华民族多元一体历史进程的重要环节；而匈奴的历史，也成为中华民族形成发展史上极其重要的组成部分。

匈奴去了哪里？

由于游牧文化的流动性，匈奴在向南方移动的过程中，构成了对中原王朝的长期威胁和侵扰。因此，汉匈之间发生了漫长的历史互动，汉武帝所发动的几次击溃匈奴的战争，对于匈奴的走向产生了决定性的影响。

西汉末年，匈奴分裂为南北两部分。其中，南匈奴内附汉朝，北匈奴则留居漠北草原。东汉初年，北匈奴再次分裂。而内迁的南匈奴在中原地区政治、经济的影响下，在与当地各民族的交融中，先后分化出屠各胡、卢水胡、铁弗匈奴等不同分支，并在魏晋南北朝时期，先后建立汉—前赵、北凉、大夏等地方政权。这几个匈奴政权灭亡后，匈奴民众便与汉、鲜卑、氐、羌等族群共同生活，并逐渐融合为其中的一部分。从此，显赫一时的匈奴便在中华历史舞台上消失了。而留居草原的北匈奴在汉军的强大威慑之下，大部分远走他乡，西迁西域。

An eagle expands its wings, standing proudly in the center of the dome-shaped crown, as if overlooking the earth. The eagle's head and neck are made of turquoise, exuding the unique dignity of the eagle. The golden crown is the only ornament of the Xiongnu nobility discovered in China to date. Entirely made of pure gold, it weighs approximately 1.5 kilograms, representing the highest level of precious-metal craftsmanship in northern China in the Warring States Period, as well as the creativity of the nomadic culture of the Xiongnu in its heyday. Unearthed in Hangjin Banner, Ordos City, Inner Mongolia Autonomous Region, in 1972, the golden crown is the treasure of Inner Mongolia Museum. Given that eagle emblematizes the kingship for the Xiongnu people, the golden crown is credited to the Xiongnu king.

The Xiongnu firstly appeared in the Warring States Period. Archaeological findings affirm that in the 8th century BC, the Xiongnu had established a tribal alliance at the present-day Daqingshan Mountain, Inner Mongolia. Afterwards, the Xiongnu moved its political and economic centers to the Northern Desert. In the end of the 4th century BC, the tribal alliance of Xiongnu grew rapidly, and began to challenge the powerful Loufan, a tribe skilled at horsemanship and archery, and covet the States of Qin, Zhao and Yan, posing a great threat to the Central Plains.

In the 3rd century BC, the Xiongnu made enormous strides socially and economically owing to the use of iron. In the late Warring States Period, under the leadership of Touman Chanyu, the Xiongnu conquered other tribes and unified the northern grasslands for the first time. The Xiongnu regime dominated the vast territories that started from the Greater Khingan Mountains in the east, arrived at the Qilian Mountains and Tianshan Mountains in the west, extended to the Lake Baikal in the north, and leant on the Great Wall in the south.

Chapter Two

The Ontological Development of the Chinese Nation

The Qin Dynasty unified the agricultural areas in the south of the Great Wall and established the first unified multi-ethnic country in Chinese history. As an epoch-making event, Qin's unification ushered in a new historical stage: the ontological development of the Chinese nation.

The ontological development of the Chinese nation meant that with the formation and development of the unified multi-ethnic country, ancient nationalities in China came to stage of deep-degree reconciliation of fundamental interests. From the Qin & Han Dynasties to the Qing Dynasty, in the historical evolution of "local unification, regional multi-ethnic unification and national unification", diasporic and isolated ethnic groups intermingled into a unitary state, via exchanges, communication and blending which consolidated national unity.

Admittedly, various ethnic groups wrestled with each other. Yet, they deeply recognized Chinee culture and firmly forged a consensus on the ideal of grand unification. Rulers from the Han nationality and other nationalities all assumed their responsibilities of unifying China, regarded themselves as the legitimate successors of Chinese culture, and picked up the baton of developing Chinese civilization. Therefore, albeit the stalemate between the southern Han emperors and the north khans, ancient China did not split. Instead, China enjoyed higher-degree unification and became a unified multi-ethnic country.

"State Institutions" of *Book of Rites* (《礼记・王制》) proposed the governance model that "rulers were advised to focus on enhancing the education of rites among citizens rather than changing their customs, on making uniform rules rather than changing their habits". In the long history, the model was commonly embraced and observed by all the dynasties. While safeguarding national unity, various ethnic groups can maintain their traditional systems, religions, rites and customs. With the practice of "ruling in accordance with ethnic customs", the farming civilization that advocated etiquette and benevolence continuously interacted with the nomadic civilization that admired valour and robustness. In philosophical terms, the movement of *unity of the opposites* bred the Chinese spirit of eclecticism and inclusiveness, and saw the peak of Chinese civilization among ancient world civilization.

As a unified multi-ethnic country, China valued peace under the heaven, harmony among nations and harmony without uniformity, which voiced the ideal, goal and pursuit of the Chinese people and became the genes of the Chinese nation.

第二章

中华民族的自在发展

秦朝统一了长城以内的农业区，建立了中国历史上第一个统一的多民族国家。这是一件划时代的大事，它为中华民族的形成发展开启了一个新的阶段——中华民族自在发展的历史时期。

中华民族的自在发展，是指随着统一多民族国家的形成和发展，中华大地上的古代民族进入了相互之间根本利益的深层交接时期。从秦汉到清朝，经过“局部性统一—地区性的多民族统一—全国性统一”的层层历史演进，许许多多分散孤立的族群单位，相互接触、混杂、联结和融合，逐渐扭结成一个不可分割的整体，一体性不断得到发展和增强。

在这一过程中，不同族群之间虽然互有争夺，但却对文化意义上的“中国”执有深切的认同，对大一统理想怀有牢固的共识。无论哪一个族群入主中原，都以统一天下为己任，又以中华文化的正统继承者自居，更以高度的自觉接过中华文明的接力棒。所以，在经历两次“南北朝”对峙以及诸王、诸汗分庭抗礼以后，古代中国不但没有分裂，反而一次次重新走向更加高度的统一，最终确立为统一的多民族国家。

在这一漫长的历史时期里，《礼记·王制》中提出的“修其教不易其俗，齐其政不易其宜”的治理模式，被历代王朝共同崇奉和遵循：在维护国家统一的前提下，各民族可保持其固有的制度、宗教、礼俗，实行“因俗而治”。这也使得崇礼亲仁的农耕文明和勇猛刚健的游牧文明始终处于不断汇聚和相互辐射之中，进行着复杂的矛盾统一运动，并在反复碰撞中凝聚起兼收并蓄、海纳百川的中华精神，使中华文明一次次跃上世界古代文明的巅峰。

这样一种以“天下大同”为理想，以“协和万邦”为旨归，以“和而不同”为追求的统一多民族国家，与西方古代帝国有着显著不同，它是中华民族创造的独特历史传统。

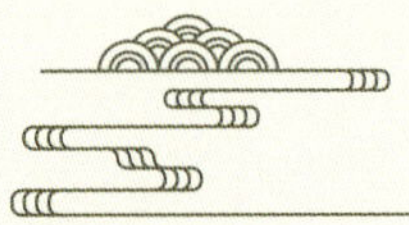

统一多民族国家的开端

The Beginning of a Unified Multi-ethnic Country

自秦以后，统一成为中国历史发展的主流。

秦朝实行了一系列“整齐”制度——车同轨、书同文、立郡县、统一度量衡标准等，结束了各区域间“田畴异亩，车途异轨，律令异法，衣服异制，语言异声，文字异形”的状态，为统一体确立了制度化规范，从而促进了各民族间共同经济和文化的形成，有力地推动了古代民族的一体化进程。

在秦朝迈开强有力的统一步伐时，周边许多民族集团也在分区域地向着由分而合的道路迈进。在北方游牧区，匈奴冒顿单于统一了长城以外的游牧区，结束了诸部落联盟并立纷争的局面，这在中华民族的形成发展史上同样是一件具有重要意义的大事。农业文明与游牧文明两大统一政权的先后出现，为此后长城内外的统一创造了基础性条件。事实上，统一多民族中国的疆域，正是沿着由局部统一向全国大一统的轨迹逐步确立的。

汉朝在打破农牧界限、混同南北的进程中做出了更加富有历史意义的成就。此前，战国至秦留下了一条横亘在农牧两大统一体之间的长城，表现出牧攻农守的态势；而当农耕文明的统一体逐渐壮大后，汉武帝采取反守为攻的战略，改变了农业区长期以来的防御性姿态，打通了河西走廊，设置河西四郡和西域都护府，加强了农业区与游牧区在经济、文化上的联系，促进了农业经济与游牧经济的结合，强化了中国古代经济的整体结构，并最终推动了南北两个统一体的汇合，这使中华民族向着一个民族实体的形成之路大大迈进。

After the Qin Dynasty, unification became the main trend of Chinese history.

The Qin Dynasty implemented a series of "centralized systems". It standardized the wheelbase of axles and the characters of writing, invented the prefecture-county system, and specified measures for length, volume and weight, which ended the state of "different calculation methods of field sizes, wheelbase of axles, laws & regulations, styles of clothing, pronunciations of languages and forms of writings" among regions. Qin's policies established institutional norms for national unity, promoted the formation of economic and cultural communities among all ethnic groups, and effectively boosted national integration.

As the Qin Dynasty stepped up efforts to unify the Central Plains, its neighboring ethnic groups mended their pace in regional unity. Modu Chanyu, founder of the empire of the Xiongnu, unified the nomadic areas outside the Great Wall and ended the stalemate of various tribal alliances, which represented a milestone in the history of the formation and development of the Chinese nation. The emergence of two unified empires for agricultural and nomadic civilizations created basic conditions for the unification of China. The territory of a unified multi-ethnic China *de facto* took shape in the trajectory from regional unification to national unification.

The Han Dynasty made greater historical achievements in breaking the boundary between agricultural civilization (in the south) and nomadic civilization (in the north). From the Warring States Period to the Qin Dynasty, the Great Wall spanned agricultural area and nomadic area, withstanding the military attacks from the north. When the Western Han Dynasty became powerful, Emperor Wu of Han abandoned the long-standing defensive strategies and waged wars against the Xiongnu. He unclogged the Hexi Corridor, established four prefectures in Hexi and dispatched officials to the Protectorate of the Western Regions. This augmented the economic and cultural ties between agricultural area and nomadic area, deepened the interation of agricultural economy and nomadic economy, and improved overall structure of ancient Chinese economy. In brief, the unity of the south and the north accelerated, marking a big step toward the formation of the Chinese nation as a nation-state.

度量衡，这个看似再平常不过的标准器，对于统一多民族国家的发展进程有什么重要意义？

统一度量衡背后的大变革

铜诏铁权

Iron Weight Inlaid with a Bronze Plate (Imperial Edict)

31

文物简读

作为度量衡中测度重量的标准器，这件铁权反映的是秦帝国结束了春秋战国以来中华大地上五百多年的诸侯割据混战局面，建立起了中国历史上第一个中央集权制国家，奠定了延续两千多年的中华大一统的基本政治格局。

统一度量衡如何影响中国历史的发展？

权，即秤锤；衡，即秤杆。它们是中国古代最重要的测重工具。“权衡”一词就来源于此。这件铁权呈馒头状，上部有鼻形提梁，提梁一侧镶嵌铜诏版，其上阴刻篆书40字，共六行，内容为秦始皇统一度量衡的昭告：

廿六年，皇帝尽并兼天下诸侯，黔首大安，立号为皇帝。乃诏丞相状、绾，法度量则不壹、歉疑者，皆明壹之。

大意为：秦王政二十六年（嬴政于公元前247年继位，于公元前221年统一六国，所以称“廿六年”），皇帝全部兼并了天下诸侯，百姓非常安定，因此确立了“皇帝”之号。现在诏令丞相隗状、王绾统一度量衡制度，凡不统一、疑惑难明的，都要使之明确、统一。

要注意的是，这一段发自中央政权的诏令，虽然铸刻在铁权之上，却不仅仅是关于重量的规范诏告，而是涉及所有的“法、度、量”。也就是说，这条诏令，是当时的秦朝政府发布天下的一则“公

名称：铜诏铁权

年代：秦

规格：高19厘米，底径25厘米，重31.6千克

出土地点：甘肃省天水市秦安县上袁家村秦墓

收藏单位：甘肃省博物馆

Name: Iron Weight Inlaid with a Bronze Plate (Imperial Edict)

Historical Period: The Qin Dynasty

Height: 19 cm, Bottom Diameter: 25 cm, Weight: 31.6 kg

Excavation Site: The Qin-Dynasty Tomb in Upper Yuanjia Village, Qin'an County, Tianshui City, Gansu Province

Housed in: Gansu Provincial Museum

告”，意在通过铁权这样一种在全国范围内发放和流通的测重标准器，把统一全国度量衡制度的重要信息散播到秦朝疆域内的每一个角落。

设想一下：两千多年前，当一个统一多民族国家首次在中华大地上建立起来时，普通民众对于大一统格局的最强烈感受，除了战乱结束，生活终于得以安宁和平，还会是什么呢？而这些要求全社会统一执行和严格遵守的制度规范，一定会给黎民百姓带来一个强烈的心理感受：九州一统，天下从此一家！

“一法度衡石丈尺”

“六王毕，四海一”——这是中国历史上一件开天辟地的伟大事件。秦朝开辟了中华民族走向大一统的历史道路，奠定了绵亘两千多年的统一多民族国家的基础。自称“始皇帝”的嬴政实施了一系列建立中央集权制度的根本性变革：在中央设立三公九卿，管理国家大事；在地方废除分封制，实行郡县制。为了尽可能消除长期分裂割据造成的地区差异，秦始皇又迅速推行了一系列以原秦国制度为标准，统一全国政治、经济、文化的法度措施——这就是《史记·秦始皇本纪》记载的：“一法度衡石丈尺，车同轨，书同文。”

统一度量衡包括三个方面的内容，一是长度，二是量制，三是重量，每一方面又涉及计量单位、进位制和量值标准三个指标。而只有度量衡的一致、可靠，才能保证货币、车轨、田亩等的规格、尺寸和重量是按照同一口径测算，全社会的生产生活才能有序开展。

秦始皇的“整齐”制度

当然，除了度量衡的统一，秦始皇推行的更重要的“壹之”政策，是“书同文”“车同轨”以及货币统一。其中，文字的统一对于中华文化的历史延续性以及中华民族多元一体历史格局的形成，更是产生了无可估量的影响。

战国时期，各诸侯国“言语异声，文字异形”，客观上阻碍了政令的畅通，妨碍了经济发展和文化传播。秦始皇命令丞相李斯等人整理七国文字，“罢其不与秦文合者”，把原来的大篆简化为小篆，并写成范本，在全国推行。这一举措，有力地弥合了广袤国土里的文化差异，使分布在遥远地域的人们能够彼此无障碍交流。因此，统一文字成为跨越时空的一种凝聚性力量，为中华民族的历史发展织就了一条充满柔韧性的文化脉络。

这正是秦始皇实行一系列“壹之”政策而给中国历史带来深远影响的原因，它们成为维系中华文化历史延续性、推动中华民族多元一体发展的重要因素。

这件铁权重达31.6千克，器型之大，实属罕见——即便是在今天，我们也很少见到如此巨大的秤砣。现在，它就静静地躺在博物馆里，隐现着那段震撼历史的大变革。

As a standard of measurement for weight in Length-Volume-Weight System, the iron weight betokened that the Qin Empire laid the foundation for political unity in China, which lasted for more than 2,000 years. Qin ended the over-500-year wars among vassals and established the first centralized country in Chinese history.

The iron weight looks like a steamed bread in shape, with a nose-shaped handle on the upper part. A bronze plate with imperial edict is inlaid on one side. The plate totally contains 40 incised seal-script characters in six lines. It tells Qin Shi Huang's order on standardizing the measures of length, volume and weight:

Ying Zheng succeeded to the throne in 247 BC. In 221 BC (26 years later), he unified China and became the first emperor of China. (Therefore), all citizens enjoyed a peaceful life. (Under such circumstance), Qin Shi Huang issued an edict, ordering two prime ministers Wei Zhuang and Wang Wan to "clarify or uniformize any laws and regulations related to weights and measures that remained ambiguous and chaotic".

In general, *Du*, *Liang* and *Heng* (度量衡) signified length, volume and weight, which included measurement, numeration and standard. The standardization of *Du*, *Liang* and *Heng* facilitated the calculation of currency, wheelbase and farmland and ensured social and economic order among citizens.

The Qin Dynasty paved the path for the grand unification of the Chinese nation and laid the foundation for a unified multi-ethnic country. Simultaneously, Qi Shi Huang implemented a series of fundamental reforms and established the centralized system. At the central level, he appointed *San Gong* and *Jiu Qing* (三公九卿, Three Excellencies and Nine Ministers) to manage national affairs. At the local level, he abolished the enfeoffment system and promoted the prefecture-county system. In order to bridge various regional differences, he evened up national political, economic and cultural systems based on original Qin systems, as recorded in "Biography of Qin Shi Huang" of *Records of the Grand Historian* (《史记·秦始皇本纪》): "(Qin) uniformized the regulations on weights and measures, and standardized the wheelbase of axles and the characters of writing."

名称："文帝行玺"金印

年代：西汉武帝时期

规格：长3.1厘米，宽3厘米，通高1.8厘米，重148.5克

出土地点：广东省广州市象岗山西汉南越王墓

收藏单位：南越王博物院

Name: Gold Seal with Characters *Wen Di Xing Xi* (文帝行玺)

Historical Period: In the reign of Emperor Wu of the Western Han Dynasty

Length: 3.1 cm, Width: 3 cm, Total Height: 1.8 cm, Weight: 148.5 g

Excavation Site: The Tomb of King of Nanyue (The Western Han Dynasty), Xianggang Mountain, Guangzhou, Guangdong Province

Housed in: Nanyue King Museum

中国考古发现的最大的西汉金印，为什么出现在偏居一隅的南越国?

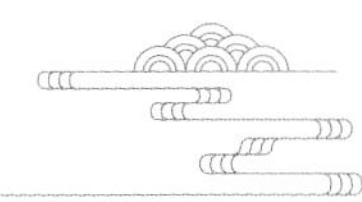

统一南越的历史印记

“文帝行玺”金印

Gold Seal with Characters *Wen Di Xing Xi*（文帝行玺）

文物简读

此枚金印龙形纽，龙昂首而体盘曲成“S”形，鳞爪俱全，形态生动。印面有田字界格，印文阴刻小篆“文帝行玺”四字，书体工整，刚健有力。这枚目前中国考古发现的最大的西汉金印，是秦汉两朝统一南越，岭南百越汇入中华民族多元一体历史进程的重要见证。

寻找金印之主

位于广州象岗山的南越王墓，除了“文帝行玺”金印，还出土了大量珍贵物品。墓主腰两侧佩戴着十把铁剑，足箱中有一罕见的银盒，上有“私宫”铭刻；墓主有14个殉人，包括妃妾三四人，随之出土了“泰子”“右夫人玺”金印以及“赵眜”“帝印”“左夫人印”等印鉴；另有高浮雕玉剑饰、透雕龙凤纹圆形玉饰等玉器以及青铜礼器、乐器、漆木器，共一千余件（套）。考古学家因此判断，此墓主拥有至高无上的权力，生活奢华，结合“文帝行玺”金印，墓主可能为南越文王赵眜。

赵眜，南越武王赵佗之孙。公元前137年赵佗去世，因赵眜的父亲赵始较早亡故，所以赵眜继承王位，史称“南越文王”。

虽然考古学家判断墓主为赵眜，但金印上的“文帝行玺”却一度让人疑惑：在中原王朝，“文帝”往往是帝王离世后，后世依其过往行迹而为之确立的谥号；而此印的沟槽和四壁都有碰撞和划伤的痕迹，应是主人生前使用过的证据。那么，赵眜生前就自称“文帝”吗？这似乎与惯例不符。对此，考古学家做出了解释：有可能因为当时南越对谥号规制还未做严格和清晰的界定。这种情况也出现在赵眜祖父赵佗身上，他在生前就曾自称“南越武帝”。

赵眜死后，赵婴齐继承王位。《汉书》里的记载更加证实了这枚金印的主人是赵眜："婴齐嗣立，即藏其先武帝、文帝玺。"历史记载与考古成果达成了高度的互证。

赵佗——开发岭南第一人

被称为"第一代南越王"的赵佗，是秦始皇为征发南越而派遣的50万大军的副统帅，后来成为经略岭南的一位政治家。

秦朝甫一建立，就一方面向北派出蒙恬征伐匈奴，收复河套；另一方面向南派出屠睢，征服百越。到公元前214年，秦军终于彻底征服南越，而屠睢在战场上中箭身亡，秦始皇又派任嚣担任主将。任嚣与赵佗继续进攻西瓯、骆越，最终完成平定岭南的大业。秦始皇在岭南地区设置了桂林郡、象郡、南海郡三个郡，完成了统一帝国在岭南的首次行政规制，并征发众多戍卒、工匠、楚人和罪民移居南越。而南征幸存的数十万秦军，也再未回到北方，全部留在了南越。这些来自北方的人和越人杂居，成为今天岭南汉族的祖先。

此后，秦末农民战争爆发，秦帝国分崩离析，赵佗以武力实现了岭南地区的统一，于公元前204年创立了南越国。

汉朝建立后，在汉高祖刘邦的感召下，赵佗决定归汉，接收印绶。但高祖逝世后，吕后禁止南越与内地的关市，区别对待蛮夷。于是赵佗反汉，自称"南越武帝"，汉越关系中断。汉文帝即位后，派遣陆贾出使南越，向赵佗晓以利害，说服他再度归汉。赵佗离世后，其后代续任了四代南越王，到公元前111年，南越国被汉朝所灭。从此，岭南正式列入汉朝统一版图，百越诸部也由此踏入了融汇于中华民族的历史进程之中。

赵佗的"和辑百越"政策

赵佗是一个值得历史大书特书的开拓者。他和南迁的中原官民，把中原先进的耕作、打井灌溉以及冶金技术，传播到岭南地区，极大地促进了岭南的开发进程。赵佗还"以诗书而化国俗"，在岭南推行汉文字，使越人"习汉字，学礼仪"，迅速推动了岭南文化的发展。他实行"和辑百越"的政策，吸收当地有威望的越人首领参与政权管理，任用颇具威望的越人首领吕嘉为丞相。吕嘉此后连相三王。他提倡中原人与岭南人通婚，南越王室带头与越人通婚，如明王赵婴齐就娶越女为妻，生子建德；他还十分尊重岭南风俗，他称自己为"蛮夷大氏老"，脱掉中原官服，穿戴越人服饰，体现出高超的政治智慧。

当然，历史的发展何其曲折坎坷！此印玺的独特之处就在于隐含着这样的信息：秦汉时期，天子用玺以白玉为材料，以螭虎为印纽；而此玺用黄金铸成，且是实用器非陪葬品，成为中国考古发现的唯一的汉代龙纽帝玺。有专家认为，金印所刻“文帝行玺”的称谓颇具特色，表现出南越国对汉王朝的礼制文化既认同又僭越的态度，其中隐蕴着汉越关系的对立和统一。

The gold seal has a dragon-shaped button. The dragon raises its head and coils its body. With scales and claws, the dragon looks true to life. Four characters *Wen Di Xing Xi* in small seal script are incised in the *Tian* (田)-shaped area. The gold seal evidenced how the Qin and Han Dynasties administered Nanyue and how Baiyue in the Lingnan Region partook in the formation of multi-ethnic Chinese nation.

In the Qin and Han Dynasties, the seals of emperors were usually made of white jade, with the images of dragon and tiger on the seal button. *Wen Di Xing Xi* was made of gold, boasting the only Han-Dynasty dragon-button imperial seal. To some scholars, the gold seal implied the two-edged attitudes of Nanyue toward the Han court: recognition and transgression.

On the basis of the inscriptions, archaeologists have confirmed that the gold seal belonged to Zhao Mie, the second ruler of Nanyue. Zhao Mie was the grandson of Zhao Tuo, King Wu of Nanyue, who died in 137 BC. As Zhao Shi, father of Zhao Mie, died early, Zhao Mie succeeded to the throne and became King Wen of Nanyue.

In the reign of Zhao Tuo, officials and citizens who came to Nanyue took advanced technologies in farming, digging well, irrigation and metallurgy in the Central Plains to Lingnan. This tremendously boosted the development of Lingnan. Zhao Tuo popularized the characters and rites of Han people, which rapidly promoted the development of Lingnan culture. He practiced the policy of "maintaining the harmony and unity with Baiyue", and invited local reputable leaders to undertake official posts. He also advocated the intermarriage between local people and immigrants from the Central Plains. Notably, he respected Lingnan customs and embraced the dressing style of Yue people, demonstrating his political wisdom.

In 111 BC, the Western Han Dynasty annexed Nanyue, which reshaped the domain of China. Baiyue in the Lingnan Region had contributed to the formation of the multi-ethnic Chinese nation ever since.

名称："马踏匈奴"石雕
年代：西汉武帝时期
规格：长1.9米，高1.68米
出土地点：陕西省兴平市道常村西北霍去病墓
收藏单位：茂陵博物馆

Name: *Mata Xiongnu* (马踏匈奴, Horse Treading on a Xiongnu Soldier) Stone Carving
Historical Period: In the reign of Emperor Wu of the Western Han Dynasty
Length: 1.9 m, Height: 1.68 m
Excavation Site: Huo Qubing's Tomb, Northwest of Daochang Village, Xingping City, Shaanxi Province
Housed in: Maoling Museum

"封狼居胥"为什么被古代武将视为最高荣耀?

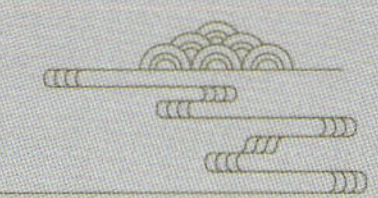

农耕文明与游牧文明的正面交汇

"马踏匈奴"石雕 33

Mata Xiongnu (马踏匈奴, Horse Treading on a Xiongnu Soldier) Stone Carving

文物简读

"马踏匈奴"堪称霍去病墓石刻作品的杰出代表，学术界大多数认为该石雕是汉武帝时期北击匈奴历史事件的重要纪念和象征。在北击匈奴的数次决定性战役中，"西汉第一战神"霍去病所展露的卓越军事才能和建功立业的豪情，书写了统一多民族国家历史发展进程的重要一章；在他所驰骋的疆场和所向披靡的战役背后，奏响的是农耕文明与游牧文明发生正面交汇与历史碰撞的宏大交响乐章。

秦汉之际的北疆格局

著名学者蒙文通、竺可桢曾揭示古代游牧民族的活动与气候变化之间的关系：游牧经济对自然环境的依赖性极大，畜群饲养和繁殖需要适宜的气候和丰美的水草，所以历史上北方草原移民运动的方向总是与气候冷暖变迁表现出大体一致的趋势。秦汉之际，北方气温由暖变冷，这正是此一时期匈奴多次南下侵占"河南地"，双方展开漫长的拉锯战的自然动因。

秦朝初立，蒙恬北筑长城而守藩篱，匈奴试图冲破长城，争夺今鄂尔多斯地区。公元前215年，匈奴头曼单于战败，北退七百余里。但秦末中原混战，匈奴趁楚汉相争、无暇北顾之机再度崛起，夺走了河套以南地区，重新控制了大漠南北和河西、河湟等广阔地带。公元前209年，冒顿鸣镝弑父，自立为匈奴单于。作为草原民族的一代雄奇首领，他严格治军，励精图治，带领匈奴军队"破东胡，走月氏，威震百蛮，臣服诸羌"，构成对中原的持续侵扰，"汉兴以来，胡虏数入边地，小入则小利，大入则大利"。汉初，高祖刘邦率军攻打匈奴，却经历了“白登之围”的挫败。之后，汉朝廷便只能采取消极防卫策略，被动承受汉弱匈强的局面。

这一格局在西汉王朝休养生息五代之后，悄然发生了变化。文、景时期，朝廷轻徭薄赋，与民休息，国家经济实力不断上升，呈现出“文景之治”的强盛和富庶，拥有了可与匈奴抗衡的物质基础。汉武帝刘彻即位后，一改汉初的战略收缩和防御政策，立志解除匈奴对汉朝的强大威胁，力图实现“王者无外”的大一统理想。为此，他首先派遣张骞出使西域；在时机成熟后，果断提拔卫青、霍去病，做出北击匈奴的战略决策。

从公元前127年开始，汉武帝对匈奴展开了三场重大反击战役，大破匈奴，迫其远遁，从此漠南无王庭，从根本上解决了匈奴的南下袭扰问题；又设置张掖、武威、酒泉、敦煌等河西四郡，为凿通西域和丝绸之路奠定了基础，从而决定性地改变了西北边疆的历史格局。

“封狼居胥”的荣耀奇勋

如果用最简洁的方式描绘霍去病的盖世奇功，那么以下三个片段至为关键：

霍去病18岁为剽姚校尉，跟随卫青出击漠南，史载他率领八百骑兵长途奔袭，斩敌两千余人，汉武帝刘彻赞其勇冠三军，从而封其为“冠军侯”。

二十岁时，霍去病两次指挥河西之战，在千里大漠中利用闪电奔袭以及大迂回战术，歼灭和招降匈奴近十万人，给匈奴以沉重打击，使匈奴不得不放弃祁连山，从此汉朝打通了河西走廊。“失我焉支山，令我妇女无颜色。失我祁连山，使我六畜不蕃息。”这是匈奴离开祁连山时，用一首歌唱出的无奈和悲凉。

公元前119年，卫青、霍去病奉命各领五万骑兵出击匈奴，其中霍去病率部奔驰两千余里，深入漠北，大破匈奴左部主力七万余人，并在追击匈奴军至狼居胥山（现乌兰巴托以东，今蒙古肯特山）时，在狼居胥山举行了祭天封礼，在姑衍山（今蒙古肯特山以北）举行了祭地禅礼，临瀚海而还。由此，“封狼居胥”成为后世武将的最高荣耀，成为军人们一生奋斗的终极梦想。

两年后，年仅24岁的霍去病病逝，留下了“匈奴未灭，何以家为”的千古豪言。

为表彰霍去病的显赫战功，汉武帝在茂陵东侧为他修筑了一座形如祁连山的巨大墓冢。墓前雕刻一组浑厚深沉的石雕，代表作品即此“马踏匈奴”。此马表现的是与霍去病生死相依的战马，它的形象凝重庄严，蕴含着高昂饱满的刚毅气概，传神地表现出霍去病以国为先、建功立业的豪迈气概和伟大精神。

霍去病短短的一生如此震古烁今，是因为他的荣耀功勋与统一多民族国家的历史发展进程紧紧相连。

Mata Xiongnu is regarded as a representative stone carving in Huo Qubing's Tomb. Scholars generally agree that *Mata Xiongnu* was carved to memorialize Han's attack on the Xiongnu in the reign of Emperor Wu of Han. In several decisive battles against the Xiongnu, Huo Qubing displayed outstanding talent and heroic spirit, making tremendous contributions to the historical development of unified multi-ethnic country. Beneath military conflicts was grand symphony of the communication between agricultural and nomadic civilizations.

Renowned scholars Meng Wentong and Zhu Kezhen brilliantly expound the relationship between the activities of ancient nomads and the changes of climate. Nomadic economy relied heavily on natural environment, and the breeding and reproduction of livestock need favorable climate and lush pasture. Historically, the migration direction of northern nomads basically corresponded to the trend of climate change. In the Qin and Han Dynasties, the temperature dropped dramatically in the north. Owing to the natural factor, the Xiongnu constantly invaded and occupied the land in the south of Hetao, starting seesaw battles with Qin and Han.

In 127 BC, Emperor Wu of Han started three significant counterattacks against the Xiongnu, forcing them to flee to *Mobei* (漠北, the vast areas north of the deserts and Gobi in northern China). The loss inflicted by Huo Qubing was felt hard by the Xiongnu, who sang: "Losing my Qilian Mountains, made my cattle unthriving; Losing my Yanzhi Mountains, made my women colorless." Besides, Emperor Wu of Han set up the "Four Prefectures in Hexi", i.e. Zhangye, Wuwei, Jiuquan and Dunhuang, which established diplomatic relations with the Western Regions and opened up the Silk Road, fundamentally reshaping the historical pattern of the northwest frontier of China.

In 119 BC, Emperor Wu of Han planned a massive expeditionary campaign. Han forces were deployed in two separate columns, each consisting of 50,000 cavalry, with Wei Qing and Huo Qubing serving as the supreme commander for each. In particular, Huo Qubing advanced over 2,000 *li* and directly engaged the Left Worthy Prince in a swift and decisive battle, quickly encircled and overran the Xiongnu, killing more than 70,000 men. He then went on to conduct a series of rituals upon arrival at the Khentii Mountains to symbolize the historical Han victory, then continued his pursuit as far as the Lake Baikal, effectively annihilating the Xiongnu clan.

中原王朝在西域行使国家主权始于何时？“五星出东方利中国”的星占之辞预示着什么？

设置西域都护的尘封往事

“五星出东方利中国”织锦护膊

34

Brocade Bracer with Seal-Script Characters *Wu Xing Chu Dong Fang Li Zhong Guo* (五星出东方利中国, Five Planets Gather in the Eastern Sky, an Auspicious Omen for the Central Plains)

文物简读

这片织锦，见证了丝绸之路上两千年来的民族交融，隐现着西域在汉代正式成为统一多民族国家组成部分的历史，它因此被誉为20世纪中国考古学最伟大的发现之一。

一个神奇的发现

1995年10月，中国日本联合科考队在尼雅遗址进行学术考察，中方队长为北京大学教授齐东方，日方队长为日本佛教大学客座教授小岛康誉。据说在科考队进入尼雅古城的前一天，和田县政府官员为科考队送行，特意赠送了一面国旗。到达营地之后，齐东方教授就将五星红旗高高升了起来。之后，科考队发现了这片“五星出东方利中国”织锦护膊 。

一串尘封的历史事件

假如进入有“死亡之海”之称的塔克拉玛干大沙漠，很难想象两千年前这里散发着勃勃生机。当越来越多的考古发现，特别是“五星出东方利中国”织锦护膊重见天日之时，我们的目光才有可能穿透千年尘沙去拼凑起历史的碎片：雪山融水潺潺，商道驼铃阵阵，人们往来不息，一个个古国——楼兰、精绝、于阗、龟兹等映入眼帘，而西域首次融入统一多民族国家的那段尘封历史，也慢慢清晰起来……

名称：“五星出东方利中国”织锦护膊

年代：汉

规格：长18.5厘米，宽12.5厘米

出土地点：新疆维吾尔自治区和田地区民丰县尼雅遗址

收藏单位：新疆维吾尔自治区博物馆

Name: Brocade Bracer with Seal-Script Characters *Wu Xing Chu Dong Fang Li Zhong Guo* (五星出东方利中国, Five Planets Gather in the Eastern Sky, an Auspicious Omen for the Central Plains)

Historical Period: The Han Dynasty

Length: 18.5 cm, Width: 12.5 cm

Excavation Site: Niya Site, Minfeng County, Hotan, Xinjiang Uygur Autonomous Region

Housed in: Xinjiang Uyghur Autonomous Region Museum

织锦护膊发现于西域三十六国之一的精绝国遗址。

精绝位于尼雅河畔，接受汉朝西域都护府统辖，是丝绸之路的必经之地，曾经商贾云集，富庶繁华。两千多年前，在这片织锦护膊戴上墓主人手臂之前，西域的历史舞台上已经上演了一系列重大历史事件——

汉武帝两次遣张骞出使西域，与三十六国中的乌孙、大宛、大月氏等国取得了联络。卫青、霍去病北击匈奴取得成功，汉朝在据有河西走廊设置河西四郡后，汉武帝正式展开对西域诸国的经略：下嫁细君与解忧公主，与乌孙国结成联姻关系；派遣使者厚赠财帛于西域诸国；对联合匈奴抗汉的车师、楼兰、轮台、大宛等国进行武力平定，驻兵屯田，设置西汉在西域的最早行政机构“使者校尉”。

公元前60年，匈奴发生内讧，驻守西域的匈奴王率部归服西汉，西域诸国由此一并归附西汉王朝。此后，汉宣帝在轮台设置西域都护，统领西域诸国，葱岭以东的西域地区正式纳入汉朝版图，中原王朝开始在此地行使国家主权。

一段星占卜辞

与这块色彩绚烂、纹样诡秘、意蕴神奇的织锦同时出土的，还有一片残损的“讨南羌”锦，其组织结构和图案风格与“五星出东方利中国”基本相同。考古学家据此认为，两块织锦应是从同一片锦料上裁剪下来的，整片织锦上的织文应为“五星出东方利中国讨南羌……”。

“五星出东方利中国”，还见于太史公司马迁在《史记·天官书》中记载的一段星占之辞：

五星分天之中，积于东方，中国利；积于西方，外国用（兵）者利。五星皆从辰星而聚于一舍，其所舍之国可以法致天下。

“五星”即太阳系的五颗行星，古称辰星、太白、荧惑、岁星、填星（镇星）。《史记·天官书》记载：“天有五星，地有五行。”因此以地上的五行元素金、木、水、火、土与五星相配，称为水星、火星、木星、金星、土星。“五星出东方”是一种特殊的天象，指五颗行星同时出现于东方天空，即“五星连珠”或“五星聚会”。中国古代星占家认为“五星出东方利中国”，即出现五星共现东方之天象，则于中国的军国大事有利。而汉代的星相家们尤为关注“五星聚会”，将“汉之兴”附会于这一天象的出现，“汉之兴，五星聚东井”是汉代社会的一种普遍思想观念。

“五星出东方利中国”护膊采用青、赤、黄、白、绿（代替黑）五色，正好与金、木、水、火、土五星相对应，考古学家因此推断它是以天象占辞预示“讨南羌”的祥瑞。史载，汉宣帝时，羌人曾与汉朝反复争夺湟水流域牧地，76岁的名将赵充国毛遂自荐率兵六万西征羌人。在战争之初，赵充国

对羌人保持威慑而不出击，静待其内部分化。而汉宣帝想速战速决，借天象催促其发兵，下诏曰："今五星出东方，中国大利，蛮夷大败。太白出高，用兵深入敢战者吉，弗敢战者凶……"后赵充国按照既定策略，平定西羌，将羌人迁往金城（今兰州）等地与汉人杂居。这有可能便是织锦护膊所书"讨南羌"之由来。

那么，载有这段历史的织锦，为何会出现在遥远的西域精绝古国墓葬中呢？据专家推测，此墓的主人应为精绝国的贵族阶层，很有可能曾参与帮助汉王朝征讨南羌，此织锦或是一种嘉奖，作为墓主人生前的荣耀伴随他长眠地下。显然，这也反映了以精绝国为代表的西域民众对中央王朝的认同。

可见，这片织锦背后隐现着西域首次融入统一多民族国家的诸多历史往事。

The brocade bracer evinced the history in which the Western Regions became a part of the unified multi-ethnic country in the Han Dynasty, boasting one of the greatest archaeological discoveries of the 20th century in China.

In October 1995, a Sino-Japanese joint archaeological team conducted academic investigation at Niya Site and unearthed the original brocade bracer inscribed with the phrase *Wu Xing Chu Dong Fang Li Zhong Guo*, which means "it is a favorable time for the Central Plains when Venus, Jupiter, Mercury, Mars and Saturn appear in the eastern sky at the same time".

The five stars refer to five planets in the solar system, formerly known as *Chenxing* (辰星), *Taibai* (太白), *Yinghuo* (荧惑), *Suixing* (岁星) and *Tianxing* (填星, *aka Zhenxing*, 镇星). In "Book of Celestial Phenomena" of *Records of the Grand Historian* (《史记・天官书》), it was stated that: "There are five stars in the heaven and five elements in the earth." Therefore, the five elements of gold, wood, water, fire and earth on the earth are paired with the five stars of Mercury, Mars, Jupiter, Venus and Saturn. That five stars appear in the eastern sky signals a special celestial phenomenon, known as the gathering of five stars. Ancient Chinese astrologers observed the celestial phenomenon, believing that the appearance of the five stars in the eastern sky meant an auspicious omen for military activities. In the Han Dynasty, astrologers connected the rise of Han with the gathering of five stars in a far-fetched way, as suggested in the common idea that "Five stars gather at the Jing constellation, and the Han Dynasty comes to rise".

Why did the brocade bracer appear in the tomb of Jingjue Ancient Kingdom (精绝古国) in the Western Regions? Scholars reckon that the owner of the tomb once helped the Han Dynasty to conquer South *Qiang* (羌) people. The brocade bracer, as a largess from Han emperor, was buried with its owner.

中央王朝对西南之地的开发始于何时?

经略西南夷的珍贵史迹

"滇王之印"金印

35

Golden Seal of *Dian Wang Zhi Yin* (滇王之印, The Seal of the King of Dian)

文物简读

这枚用纯金铸成的印，蛇纽，蛇首昂起，身躯盘曲，背有鳞纹，印面凿刻篆体白文"滇王之印"。1956年，此印一出土就引起了轰动——这件文物高度印证了司马迁在《史记》中对西南夷纳入汉朝统一多民族国家疆域历史过程的记述。

一碗枸酱引发的边疆经略潮

对西南夷的经略始于秦，秦亡后西南夷又陷入了割据状态。而新的转折则起源于一个看似偶然的历史机遇。

汉武帝建元六年（前135）八月，闽越王郢自以为军力强盛，从冶南（今福建漳州地区）发兵，进犯它的邻居南越国。南越王赵眜自知难御强邻，因此上书朝廷请求支援。汉武帝立即命令大军出兵，征讨闽越。闽越王不战自溃。汉武帝又派遣唐蒙作为使者前往南越国，告知其胜利的消息。

南越国款待汉朝使者时，用了一种独特的枸酱。唐蒙对此十分留意，打听道："这枸酱是从哪里来的呢？"主人回答："枸酱产自蜀地，是经由夜郎国一条名叫牂柯的大江，运输到南越国都的。"对于汉使而言，这真是让人惊喜的重大"情报"！要知道，两千多年前，人类社会发展面临的重大困境，就是地理险阻、交通障碍。此刻，一碗枸酱让唐蒙同时获知了两大重要信息：一是蜀地与南越之间，有一条可供行船往来的大江，名曰牂柯江；二是牂柯江畔，有一个名叫夜郎的地方政权。

名称："滇王之印"金印

年代：西汉武帝时期

规格：边长2.3厘米，高1.8厘米，重89.5克

出土地点：云南省昆明市晋宁区石寨山

收藏单位：中国国家博物馆

Name: Golden Seal of *Dian Wang Zhi Yin* (滇王之印, The Seal of the King of Dian)

Historical Period: In the reign of Emperor Wu of the Western Han Dynasty

Side Length: 2.3 cm, Height: 1.8 cm, Weight: 89.5 g

Excavation Site: Shizhai Mountain, Jinning District, Kunming, Yunnan Province

Housed in: National Museum of China

回到长安，唐蒙在进一步打听和证实之后，立即上书汉武帝，提出了“以汉之强，巴蜀之饶，通夜郎道，为置吏”的建议。汉武帝欣然赞同，当即拜唐蒙为中郎将，让其率领千余人的队伍，从巴蜀筰关进入夜郎。唐蒙把丰盛的缯帛等礼物厚赐予夜郎，并与夜郎侯做出了如下约定：设置郡县，以其子为夜郎县令，将其地划入犍为郡。

此后，汉武帝又任命当时著名的文学家司马相如为中郎将，派遣他出使巴蜀，“略定西南夷，邛、筰、冉、駹、斯榆之君皆请内附，边关日益开广。”

西汉王朝经略西南夷迈开了重要一步。

西南夷变国为郡

唐蒙在南越见到蜀国枸酱的13年后，张骞又在大夏国见到了蜀国的布帛和邛都的竹杖。这成为汉朝经略西南夷的又一个历史机缘。

汉武帝元狩元年（前122），张骞出使大夏国归来，向汉武帝报告：汉朝西南方的大夏国竟然有蜀布和邛杖，是经由身毒国而来的，假若能开通蜀地向身毒国的道路，对汉朝有利无害。汉武帝于是派人前往西南寻找身毒国，这些寻路的使者来到了滇国。滇王见到汉朝使者后，便提出了一个著名的问题：“汉孰与我大？”

据文献记载，滇国曾经存在过五百年，其疆域主要在滇池中心的云南中部及东部地区。滇的开国者庄蹻是史料记载的内陆开发云南边疆第一人，他把楚国的先进文化和生产技术带到了云南，加速了当地的经济和社会发展，为秦汉时期在云南设置郡县创造了条件。

汉武帝元鼎六年（前111），汉武帝统一南越后，又乘胜攻灭了对抗汉朝的且兰、邛都、筰都等西南夷，使夜郎、冉駹内附，两年后又攻灭劳浸、靡莫等部。此时，滇王做出了一个深明大义的决定：举国称降汉朝。这使汉武帝对滇国之君充满赞许。汉朝在滇国设置了益州郡，并赐滇王王印，对滇民特别加以优抚和封赏。司马迁在《史记》中感叹道：“西南夷君长以百数，独夜郎、滇受王印。滇小邑，最宠焉。”

太史公的记述在这枚金印上得到了印证：滇王属于列侯，但滇王印却是王侯的形制与规格。这表明滇王国同西汉中央王朝有着密切的政治关系，是一个有特殊地位的内臣。

夜郎、滇等先后归附汉王朝，变国为郡，设官置吏，这一过程揭示了不同地域、不同民族最终汇入统一多民族国家的历史进程。而这枚金印的出土，不但确证了古滇国的存在，也证明了《史记》记载的真实可信。

The seal is made of pure gold, with a snake-shaped button. The snake raises its head and coils its body, with scale pattern on the back. Four characters *Dian Wang Zhi Yin* are incised in seal script. The seal was unearthed in 1956, which immediately caused a sensation. It corroborates how Southwest *Yi* joined the formation of unified multi-ethnic country in the Western Han Dynasty, as recorded in Sima Qian's *Records of the Grand Historian*.

The governance of Southwest *Yi* started in the Qin Dynasty. After the fall of Qin, Southwest *Yi* fell into a state of disunity again.

According to historical records, the Kingdom of Dian existed for 500 years, whose territory roughly covered present-day central and eastern regions of Yunnan. Zhuang Qiao played a pioneering role in the development of the frontier of Yunnan. He brought advanced culture and technology to Yunnan, which accelerated local economic and social development, and created conditions for setting up prefectures and counties in Yunnan in the Qin and Han Dynasties.

In 111 BC, after Emperor Wu of Han unified Nanyue, he overran Southwest *Yi* tribes like Julan, Qiongdu and Zuodu that opposed the Han Dynasty, and in 109 BC, vanquished Laojin and Mimo. Yelang and Ranmang also surrendered to Han. Against such backdrop, the King of Dian wisely paid allegiance to Han. Emperor Wu of Han spoke highly of him. The Han Dynasty established Yizhou Prefecture in Dian and bestowed the seal on the king, giving special preferential treatment and rewards to the Dian people.

The excavation of the gold seal indicates a close political tie between the Kingdom of Dian and the Western Han Dynasty. It not only verifies the existence of the ancient Kingdom of Dian, but also authenticates the records in *Records of the Grand Historian*.

回望数千年的椰风海韵，海南岛是从何时起隶属于中央王朝的？

开发海南的千古物证

“朱庐执刲”银印

Silver Seal with Characters *Zhu Lu Zhi Kui* (朱庐执刲)

文物简读

被誉为“海南第一古印”的“朱庐执刲”银印，通体银质，以一条兽首小蛇为纽，蛇身弯曲饰鳞纹，中部拱起为穿，鱼形尾鳍回摆，印面铸刻阴文篆体白文“朱庐执刲”四字。以蛇、鱼为原型糅合造型的印式，在现存的秦、汉官印中仅此一例。此印证实了海南岛在两千多年前隶属于汉朝中央政府的历史，是西汉王朝治理开发海南岛的物证。

海南是怎么纳入西汉王朝管辖范围的？

汉朝经略海南始于汉武帝。而这一历史过程又与南越国的叛乱和灭亡有关。

吕嘉是岭南的越人，深受第一代南越王赵佗的信赖。赵佗奉行“和辑百越”政策，拜德高望重的当地越人吕嘉为相。此后，吕嘉接连辅佐了三位南越王，位高权重，亲信众多。当第四代南越王赵兴试图加强与汉朝的联系时，吕嘉却屡次建议赵兴放弃这一想法，但赵兴不接受，于是吕嘉最终发动了叛乱，杀害了赵兴，并立术阳侯赵建德为南越王。南越之乱惊动了中央王朝。汉元鼎五年（前112）秋，汉武帝命卫尉路博德为伏波将军，几路出击，直捣南越王都番禺，俘获了吕嘉和赵建德。至此，传国93年的南越国灭亡。

此后，汉武帝将南越国故地分置为九郡，其中珠崖、儋耳两郡即设置于海南岛上。《汉书》对在海南设置郡县的过程做了这样的描述：“自合浦、徐闻南入海，得大州，东西南北方千里，武帝元封元年略以为儋耳、珠崖郡。”

名称："朱庐执封"银印

年代：西汉武帝时期

规格：边长2.4厘米，通高1.9厘米

出土地点：海南省乐东黎族自治县志仲镇谭培村

收藏单位：海南省博物馆

Name: Silver Seal with Characters *Zhu Lu Zhi Kui* (朱庐执刲)

Historical Period: In the reign of Emperor Wu of the Western Han Dynasty

Side Length: 2.4 cm, Total Height: 1.9 cm

Excavation Site: Tanpei Village, Zhizhong Town, Ledong Li Autonomous County, Hainan Province

Housed in: Hainan Museum

在上述记载中，汉武帝派遣使者“略得”海南岛的过程并没有提及战争或其他武力征服。有学者认为，这一次历史性的渡海略地，有可能是一次和平招抚。

汉武帝在海南岛设置珠崖、儋耳二郡，这是海南历史上划时代的大事件，是其正式并入中国版图的起始。开郡之初，汉朝在岛上设置16县，辖2.3万余户，这是关于海南岛人口最早的记载。郡县制的建立，不仅宣告了中央王朝对海南管治的开始，也在海南建制史上具有开创性的历史影响，成为后世中央王朝在海南建置的范例和治理开发的依据。

朱庐在哪里？何为执刲？

朱庐到底在哪里？专家们对“朱卢（朱庐）”与“珠崖”郡的关系及其位置问题进行了一些探讨。由于考古资料与相关史料缺乏，专家们的看法也莫衷一是。孙慰祖依据银印的形制、历史年代、当时官制，又结合西汉罢郡置县历史事件，认为“朱卢”“朱崖”“珠崖”实本于“朱庐”无疑。汉代开边所置郡县多用本地旧名，取其音而不取其义。加上郡经废置，地处僻远，当时簿籍又据当地口音载记，早期文献音近字异，后来渐次衍生出不同的解读。因此，他的结论为：“‘朱庐’即武帝开郡之正名，冠于‘执刲’前之地名属之于郡，或指‘朱庐地’……朱庐先郡后县，与珠崖本为一事。”

执刲，原为楚国爵位名称，汉初沿袭以封功臣，其行政地位应相当于郡守、都尉一级的官吏。西汉“执刲”印目前全国仅发现两枚，另一枚印1975年出土于广西合浦县的西汉墓葬，该印文暂释作“劳邑执刲”。

“朱庐执刲”印从何而来呢？学术界主要有楚国颁赐、南越自镌、汉朝颁赐三种不同意见。孙慰祖认为，西汉中期击西南夷，对归降的蛮夷首领授给蛇纽官印，其后沿袭至魏晋，蛇纽和驼纽、马纽、羊纽一样，成为中原王朝赐给周边民族官印的族属标志之一。“朱庐执刲”银印即是汉武帝开郡之际赐给朱庐当地内附汉朝的主要部族首领的印绶。

以上所述，可能还无法揭示“朱庐执刲”的真实信息，有赖于进一步的考古证据辅助和深入研究。不管如何，此印的发现实证了海南岛在两千多年前隶属于汉朝中央政府的史实，也是西汉王朝治理开发海南岛的物证。

The silver seal is hailed as the "first ancient seal of Hainan". Made of silver, it has a button with beast head and snake body. The snake coils its body, decorated with scale pattern. The central arch is a hole. The fish-shaped tail swings back. The four characters *Zhu Lu Zhi Kui* are incised in seal script. The seal is the only one with the snake-fish style in the existing official seals of the Qin and Han Dynasties. It affirms the historical fact that the Hainan Island belonged to the central government over 2,000 years ago, and provides material evidence for the governance and development of the Hainan Island by the Western Han Dynasty.

The governance of the Hainan Island started in the reign of Emperor Wu of Han, in which the rebellion of Lü Jia was put down.

Lü Jia came from *Yue* in the Lingnan Region. Deeply trusted by Zhao Tuo, the first king of Nanyue, he took up the post of prime minister. Having successively assisted three kings of Nanyue, Lü Jia arrogated all authority to himself and fostered his cohorts. Zhao Xing, the fourth king of Nanyue, attempted to strengthen ties with the Western Han Dynasty, and turned a deaf ear to Lü Jia's disagreement. Lü Jia finally rebelled against Zhao Xing and killed him, choosing Zhao Jiande, Marquis of Shuyang, as the new king. This rocked the Han court. In the autumn of 112 BC, Emperor Wu of Han appointed Lu Bode, a minister in charge of guarding the palace, as Fubo General (伏波, *Fubo* literally means quelling the unrest). Han army occupied Panyu, capital of Nanyue, and captured Lü Jia and Zhao Jiande. Consequently, the kingdom of Nanyue, with a history of 93 years, came to an end.

Afterwards, Emperor Wu of Han divided Nanyue into nine prefectures, of which Zhuya and Dan'er lied in the Hainan Island. This was an epoch-making event in the history of Hainan, because it officially became a part of China. Demographically, there were 16 counties and more than 23,000 households in Hainan Island. The establishment of the prefecture-county system signaled the legitimate governance and development of Hainan and set an example for later dynasties.

一方残碑蕴藏了汉代儒学的什么历史信息？

儒学作为统一思想观念的传播

熹平石经（《周易》残碑）

Xiping Shijing, or Stone Carvings of Confucianist Classics in the Reign of Emperor Xiping (The Remaining Stele of *Book of Changes*)

文物简读

这块东汉《周易》残碑，是中国古代官方刊刻的最早石质儒经“熹平石经”遍历颠沛与劫难的幸存之物，是汉朝时期思想文化实现大一统以及儒家思想上升为国家意志的直接物证。儒家思想成为诸多统治者的治世圭臬，深刻影响了中国古代历史的进程以及中华民族的形成发展。

中国式石刻书籍林的先河

《后汉书》中记载了东汉时期洛阳城南一个壮观震撼的场景：

公元183年，在官办最高学府洛阳太学的讲堂前，整齐地竖立起了46块巨大的石碑。每块石碑高三米多，宽一米多，其上用结体方正、规矩敦厚的隶书刻写儒家七经——《鲁诗》《尚书》《周易》《春秋》《公羊传》《仪礼》《论语》。这些石经由当时著名的史学家、书法家蔡邕等人亲自书写，一共花费了八年时间，碑上所镌文字共20多万字。当气势恢宏的“石刻书籍林”出现在太学门前时，顿时轰动了洛阳城，甚至轰动了全国。前来参观和摹写的人络绎不绝，太学门前车乘每日竟达千余辆，街头巷尾交通堵塞的热闹场景持续了很长一段时间。

这是中国历史上刻在石碑上的最早的官定儒家经本，因为刻写于汉灵帝熹平年间，所以被称为“熹平石经”。一些学者认为，“熹平石经”从某种意义上可以理解为印刷术发明前的一种图书编辑出版活动，它开创了中国历代刻写石经的最早范例。以“熹平石经”为先河，此后将经典文献雕成水火难侵、不腐不朽的石质文本成为一种“出版”模式，历朝历代刻写了诸多儒、释、道石经，形成了

名称：熹平石经（《周易》残碑）

年代：东汉

规格：高31.5厘米，宽66厘米

出土地点：河南省洛阳市

收藏单位：西安碑林博物馆

Name: *Xiping Shijing*, or Stone Carvings of Confucianist Classics in the Reign of Emperor Xiping (The Remaining Stele of *Book of Changes*)

Historical Period: The Eastern Han Dynasty

Height: 31.5 cm, Width: 66 cm

Excavation Site: Luoyang, Henan Province

Housed in: Xi’an Beilin Museum

世界上独有的中国式石刻书籍林。

历史上第一部官方校刻的经学教科书

“熹平石经”的意义并不止于首创刻石形式的图书出版活动，它更为本质的意义，是标志着儒学作为统一思想观念在中国古代历史上的进一步确立。

西汉时期，汉武帝采纳董仲舒“罢黜百家，独尊儒术”的建议，将儒学定为官学，建立起了中国最早的官办高等学府太学，在其中设立《诗》《书》《礼》《易》《春秋》五经博士，统一讲授和传播儒学。儒家从此成为中国社会的正统思想，中国历史上首次实现了思想意识的大一统。东汉时期，儒学得到进一步尊崇，思想一统成为政治一统的强大基础，儒家思想在统一多民族国家的主流思想地位得到了稳固。这是“熹平石经”得以出现的历史背景。

当然，蔡邕等人提出将儒家经典刻写于石的大胆创意，还有着特定的历史机缘。

东汉时，太学儒生在考试中名列前茅者，可以为官。为了统一考试标准，朝廷对各种儒家经典都设置了一部标准读本，每部读本用不易腐朽的漆书书写，藏于兰台，称为“兰台漆书”。由于儒生们手中的经书在传抄过程中常发生讹谬，文字上时有误差，为了在应试中胜出，就出现了儒生贿赂兰台掌管漆书的官吏，暗改漆书文字，以与自己的应试之文相符的现象。这样的事情一再发生，导致儒家典籍变得真伪莫辨。正是因此，为了使经文从此不再轻易遭到篡改，蔡邕联络一批经学家，向汉灵帝提出了校正标准经书并刊刻于石的设想。

事实上，西汉虽然确立了儒家思想的主导地位，但儒家经典却存在着“今文古文之争，官学私学之别，齐学鲁学之异，师法家法之分”等亟待解决的问题。汉朝廷曾多次召集儒家学者讨论经学文本，如著名的“石渠阁议经”和“白虎观议经”等，目的就是在认识上达成一致。然而，这种方式多流于形式，问题未得到根本的解决，到东汉桓、灵二帝时期，不同经学流派之间的纷争愈发激烈。通过刻经校正儒典文本，解决长期遗留的学术争端，这是汉灵帝欣然批准刻写“熹平石经”的原因之一。

“熹平石经”作为国家最高学府太学的权威教材、中国历史上第一部官方校订推行的经学教科书，在中国古代教育史上无疑是一座里程碑，极大地促进了儒家思想的传播和儒家经学教育的发展。自东汉之后，历代王朝又进行了六次儒经校勘刻石行动，将这些石经作为官定儒经标准，供儒生士子观览摹写。

历经浩劫的“熹平石经”

“熹平石经”刻立六年后，权臣董卓为避袁绍攻击，挟持汉献帝退往长安，临走时烧毁洛阳宫庙，导致太学荒废，“熹平石经”由此首次遭到破坏。南北朝时期，北齐统治者高澄将石经从洛阳迁往邺都，石经掉进水中，运至邺都时只余不到一半。隋朝开皇年间，剩余石经再度从邺都运往长安，过程中损毁严重。到唐朝贞观年间，大臣魏征去收集残存的石经时，石经几乎已毁坏殆尽。

这一块《周易》残碑，是“熹平石经”历经近两千年颠沛与劫难后的幸存之物。直到近现代进入西安碑林之前，它还遭遇了一番惊心动魄的历险。

1931年，对中国古代文化颇有研究的于右任在洛阳古玩市场偶然发现了一块汉代残碑，他辨识

出此碑的重要价值，便以四千块大洋的天价，从古董商手里将其买下。但当时于右任手中没有足够的钱，只付了两千块大洋作为定金，并未马上带走残碑。两年后，于右任委托因公路过洛阳的杨虎城将军将两千块大洋补交给古董商，残碑才被带回南京。

1936年，于右任秉持“天下为公”的理念，将这块残碑与三百多方大名鼎鼎的鸳鸯七志斋藏石（多数为北朝墓志）一并捐予西安碑林。此后，全面抗战爆发，为避战祸，西安碑林管理委员会主任张扶万将残碑带回老家陕西富平，藏于枯井之中。抗战胜利后，残碑又被秘密转运至陕西省三原县于右任资助的民治小学校，不久又转运到于右任的侄子于期家中保存。直到1952年，陕西文管会专门派人从三原县将残碑运回，重新安置于碑林之中。

至今，“熹平石经”所有存世残石共计8800多字，除西安碑林博物馆外，中国国家博物馆、洛阳博物馆等也有收藏。

凝视这件汉代遗珍，尽管它没有挽救东汉王朝的倾颓于危难之间，也未能阻挡南北朝分裂局面的到来，但它所完成的历史使命——调和今、古文经学之争，统一世人的思想观念，实现社会权力在文化与现实政治的多向融通与互动等——都对后世产生了重大的影响。这或许就是南北朝之后中国能够重新回归统一多民族国家的深层逻辑所在。

Xiping Shijing were the earliest stone carvings of Confucianist classics that the Eastern Han court sponsored. The remaining stele of *Book of Changes* saw the disasters of *Xiping Shijing* in the long history, and evidenced the grand unification of ideology in which Confucianism was elevated to state will. Since the Han Dynasty, Confucianism had been the guiding ideology for feudal rulers, which had a profound impact on the development of ancient China and the formation of the Chinese nation.

In *Book of Later Han* (《后汉书》), a spectacular scene appeared in the southern part of Luoyang in the Eastern Han Dynasty. In 183, 46 huge steles were neatly erected in front of the lecture hall of Luoyang Imperial Academy, the highest governmentally-run educational organization. Each stele was over three meters high and over one meter wide. On these steles were inscribed seven Confucianist classics, i.e. *The Lu-School Version of Book of Songs* (《鲁诗》), *Book of Documents* (《尚书》), *Book of Changes* (《周易》), *Spring and Autumn Annals* (《春秋》), *The Gongyang Commentary on Spring and Autumn Annals* (《公羊传》), *The Norms of Etiquette* (《仪礼》) and *The Analects* (《论语》), in square and formal official script. Cai Yong, a famous historian and calligrapher, alongside others, spent eight years on completing the work, in a total of approximately 200,000 words.

The stone-carving activity happened in the reign of Emperor Ling or Xiping; therefore, the earliest authorized Confucianist texts on the steles were called *Xiping Shijing*. In a way, *Xiping Shijing* were regarded as an editing & publishing event prior to the invention of printing, setting an example for the stone carvings in later generations. More essentially, Confucianist doctrines were ideologicalized in the Han Dynasty, which was the underlying reason for the Chinese nation to be unified after the long-term division in the Northern and Southern Dynasties.

In 1931, Yu Youren purchased the remaining stele of *Book of Changes* at Luoyang Antique Market. In 1936, he donated it to Xi'an Beilin Museum. There are now nearly 8,800 words on the remaining stele. *Xiping Shijing* are also housed in National Museum of China and Luoyang Museum.

在浩如烟海的中华古代文物中，这匹马何以被选作“中国旅游标志”？

丝绸之路上的文明交流

铜奔马

Bronze Galloping Horse (Bronze Horse Treading on a Flying Swallow)

38

文物简读

作为一件国宝级文物，这匹体形健硕、昂首嘶鸣、对侧步奔走的铜奔马已经成为中国旅游的标志。它疾足奔驰、一往无前的形象，仿佛让我们看见汉朝开通丝绸之路后，在亚欧大陆两端之间为贸易、文化、思想的交往交流而不畏险阻、奔驰不息的车马人流。这匹显露着豪情壮志的铜奔马，当之无愧地成为丝绸之路的象征。

马踏飞燕

1700多年前，一匹铜奔马跟随一支阵容强大的青铜仪仗队，一同被放入古墓之中，守护主人的安宁。当墓穴被打开时，它从未想过自己会名满天下：体形不算伟岸，比它高大的马俑还有很多；身份不算高贵，只是青铜仪仗队的随从。然而，20世纪著名文学家、历史学家郭沫若与它相遇的一刹那，却被它倾倒：

躯干壮实，腿蹄轻捷，三足腾空，一足轻踏飞燕；飞燕回首惊顾间，更加映衬出骏马凌空飞腾、奔跑疾速的姿态。而奔马全身的着力点集于踏掠飞燕的一足之上，雕铸者准确地掌握了力学平衡原理，显示出卓越的工艺技术水平。

名称：铜奔马

年代：东汉晚期

规格：高34.5厘米，身长45厘米，宽13厘米，重7.3千克

出土地点：甘肃省武威市雷台汉墓

收藏单位：甘肃省博物馆

Name: Bronze Galloping Horse (Bronze Horse Treading on a Flying Swallow)

Historical Period: The Late Eastern Han Dynasty

Height: 34.5 cm, Total Length: 45 cm, Width: 13 cm, Weight: 7.3 kg

Excavation Site: Leitai Tomb of the Han Dynasty, Wuwei City, Gansu Province

Housed in: Gansu Provincial Museum

此后，这件铜奔马便成为中华“马”文物中的“巨星”，其地位从未被撼动。

丝绸之路

这件铜奔马出土于丝绸之路上的文化名城——河西走廊东端的武威。根据铭文、墓制、出土的钱币以及墓葬规格，专家们推断墓主人应为前凉第四位国主张骏。前凉是魏晋南北朝十六国之一，张骏作为雄踞河西的一代霸主，曾经在丝绸之路上驰骋奔突。跟随着这样的主人，铜奔马显然见证过彼时丝路上的人声鼎沸，当然也应见证过河西走廊的历史风云……

丝绸之路始辟于西汉中期。汉武帝先后两次派遣张骞出使西域，开启了被太史公司马迁称为“凿空”西域的壮行。同时，汉武帝发动北击匈奴的军事行动，在取得河西走廊后，设置河西四郡，不仅彻底畅通了西汉与西域间的联系，也使得以长安为起点，经中国甘肃、新疆，到中亚、西亚，并连接地中海各国的陆上通道为之一通。这条伟大的道路开创性地打通了东西方的联系，首次形成了一个世界性的交通网络，极大地促进了古代世界的商品大流通，率先实现了东西方商贸互通和经济往来。数千年来，游牧者、商人、外交家、学者、思想家、修行者，沿着丝绸之路往复行走；中国的四大发明——造纸术、印刷术、火药、指南针，逐步传到西方；西方的数学、天文学、地理学、化学以及宗教艺术等也随着商人和文化交流的队伍来到中国。这条道路是联结古代东西方文明的交汇之路，它深刻地影响和推动了古代世界的社会变革与人类进步。

两千年后，当我们回望丝绸之路，它不仅仅是一条道路，更是不同国家、不同文明相互浸染、相互包容的珍贵纽带，是人类社会开放和包容精神的历史象征。

文明交流

当这件铜奔马被精心铸造出来时，丝绸之路的起点已经延伸到了东汉都城洛阳。史载，东汉永元十二年（100），古罗马属下的马其顿地区，曾“遣使内附”，汉和帝“赐其王金印紫绶”。此后，延熹九年（166），罗马皇帝安敦又曾派使者至洛阳，朝见汉桓帝。

可以想象的是，在绵延数个世纪的丝绸之路上，马是重要的交通使者之一。马载着中国的丝绸、瓷器、茶叶向西而行；又驮着西方的毛皮、石榴、葡萄、芝麻乘风东来；跟随着马队的，是中国的冶铁、凿井等技术相继西传，古印度的佛教、音乐、舞蹈、雕塑一路东往……

据甘肃农业大学崔堉溪教授考证，此件铜奔马在造型上有粗脖、阔胸等杂交马的特征，应是汉武帝以来引进西域马杂交改良的结果。在两汉之际开拓疆域、凿通西域的行动中，马发挥了独特的作用，因此两汉时期有着浓厚的尚马习俗。“初，天子发书《易》，云‘神马当从西北来’。”这一记载反映了汉武帝用卜卦的瑞应说，谋求良马、扩建骑兵的急切心情。得知在敦煌渥洼水获“太一天马”时，汉武帝作《天马歌》，并三次派人到西域求取乌孙宝马。汉朝甚至给马立“口籍”，马在各种场合被神化和歌颂……经此种种，从西域而来的“天马”有了崇高的政治象征意义和历史含义。

这匹铜奔马带着“天马”的血脉与气质，从那一条连接亚欧大陆、宣告人类文明交融新时代到来的丝绸之路上，远远地奔来；它见证着中华文明兼收并蓄、互鉴融通的博大性、包容性的形成和发展，见证着东西方文化的交流如何在丝绸之路上达到前所未有的程度，从而大大推进了人类文明的发展进程。

As a national treasure, Bronze Galloping Horse becomes a symbol of Chinese tourism. With strong muscles, the horse raises its head and neighs. It runs with both legs on the same side of the body. Its image of galloping swiftly and advancing courageously reminds us of incessant stream of horses and carriages along the Silk Road, a bridge for Asian-European commercial, cultural and ideological exchanges in the Han Dynasty. Obviously, Bronze Galloping Horse is a sign of the Silk Road.

Bronze Galloping Horse was unearthed in Wuwei, a famous cultural city along the Silk Road, in the eastern end of the Hexi Corridor. On the basis of the inscriptions, tomb shape, unearthed coins and tomb size, scholars infer that the tomb owner was Zhang Jun, the fourth emperor of the Former Liang Dynasty. Zhang Jun, an overlord, ruled the roost in the Hexi Corridor.

According to Professor Cui Yuxi at Gansu Agricultural University, Bronze Galloping Horse features thick neck and wide chest. It is a cross-bred horse with Western Regions horses, which were introduced by Emperor Wu of Han. Horse played a vital role in expanding territories and establishing diplomatic relations with the Western Regions. In the Han Dynasty, horse was deeply worshipped. “Initially, the emperor opened *Book of Changes* for divination, saying that the divine horse should come from the northwest.” This reflected Emperor Wu of Han was eager to obtain excellent horses and expand cavalry, in accordance with auspicious signs. Upon learning that the heavenly horse or *Tai Yi Tian Ma* appeared near the Wowa River in Dunhuang, Emperor Wu of Han wrote *Song of the Heavenly Horse* (《天马歌》), and sent people to the Western Regions three times to seek Wusun horses. Han government even established “household registers” for horses. Horses were deified and eulogized in a lot of literature. The heavenly horse from the Western Regions was politically and culturally elevated.

Bronze Galloping Horse embodied the eclecticism and inclusiveness of Chinese civilization, and witnessed far-reaching cultural exchanges between the East and the West along the Silk Road, thus tremendously promoting the development of human civilization.

名称：北流型云雷纹大铜鼓

年代：西汉

规格：面径165厘米，高67.5厘米，重约300千克

出土地点：广西壮族自治区北流市六靖镇水冲庵

收藏单位：广西民族博物馆

Name: Beiliu-Style Bronze Drum with Cloud-Thunder Pattern

Historical Period: The Western Han Dynasty

Surface Diameter: 165 cm, Height: 67.5 cm, Weight: *c.* 300 kg

Excavation Site: Shuichong Nunnery, Liujing Town, Beiliu City, Guangxi Zhuang Autonomous Region

Housed in: Anthropology Museum of Guangxi

古代铜鼓是我国众多文化遗产中的一个重要类别，现存于世最大的铜鼓在哪里？

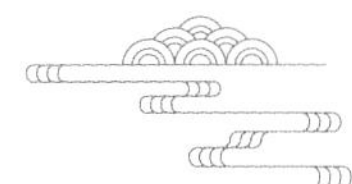

南岭走廊上的文化共享

北流型云雷纹大铜鼓

Beiliu-Style Bronze Drum with Cloud-Thunder Pattern

文物简读

这面被称为“铜鼓王”的西汉北流型云雷纹大铜鼓，是世界上迄今为止发现的最大的古代铜鼓。作为我国南方少数民族最广泛拥有的共同文化遗产，铜鼓见证着濮越、汉族、氐羌及苗瑶民族集团在南岭走廊上的流动迁徙、深刻交融等共同历史记忆。

南岭走廊

秦汉时期，当岭南和云贵高原被纳入多民族国家的统一体时，生活在这一地带的众多族群，就不可避免地进入了加速流动和相互交往的大潮。他们从北向南移动，从东向西迁徙，形成了一条人口流动的通道，费孝通称之为“南岭走廊”。

南岭走廊是由南岭群山的峡谷隘道以及诸多河流水系构成的一条天然通道，历史上诸多族群在这里迁徙、流动、融合。其中，百越集团在这条走廊上发生了大规模从东向西的迁徙，苗瑶族群在秦汉以后循南岭走廊而渐入西南、东南，大量中原人从北向南渗入走廊内部……这里形成了今天中华大地上堪称文化多样性缤纷绚丽的一条人文地理带——除汉族外，这里还有百越的后裔，如壮族、布依族、水族、侗族、毛南族；有苗瑶的后裔，如苗族、瑶族、畲族……

随着不同族群的交融共居，铜鼓逐渐成为南方民族最具共享性的文化符号。今天，南岭走廊上几乎所有的少数民族都将铜鼓作为本民族的神圣文化遗产。

“铜鼓王”

铜鼓是我国古代具有特殊意义的一种礼器，最早出现于公元前7世纪。铜鼓的起源与南方稻作文化有密切关系。有研究者认为它起源于铜釜，并从日常炊具演化成礼器，成为沟通人神的媒介，广泛运用于祭祀、战争、集会、丧仪、庆典等神圣场合中。在许多南方民族心中，铜鼓是有神性的，其声具有上达天听、下抵人心的力量，拥有联结人神两界的功能。

在我国，考古发现的铜鼓年代横跨春秋战国至明清，其中汉代铜鼓最为精美，式样最多。这面收藏于广西民族博物馆的西汉北流型云雷纹大铜鼓，鼓面中心饰八芒太阳纹，三弦分晕，晕圈间满布粗犷古朴的云雷纹，面径165厘米，高67.5厘米，重约三百千克，是迄今为止世界上发现的最大、最重的古代铜鼓，因此被称为“铜鼓王”。

“铜鼓王”原存于广西北流县六靖乡（今北流市六靖镇）水冲庵，于1955年由广西壮族自治区博物馆征集收藏。关于其出土的时间和经过，铜鼓研究专家万辅彬和姚舜安曾专程到广西北流考察调研。他们从水冲庵附近一位名叫陈德初的老人处了解到相关情况。那是清朝末期，北流石窝乡（今石窝镇）的农民在山上挖地时，锄头碰到了一件硬物，挖出来发现是一面大型铜鼓。铜鼓庄重古朴，气势逼人，泥锈斑驳却掩饰不住其照人的光彩。附近的人们闻讯前来观看，一致认为这是一件神物，应该送到六靖圩头冼夫人庙供起来。但没想到，当“铜鼓王”被抬到水冲庵附近时，原本结实的绳子突然断了，于是大家打卦向神灵祈问：究竟是抬到冼夫人庙还是放在水冲庵？结果是水冲庵。此后，这面谜一般的“铜鼓王”就被供奉在水冲庵。

复杂的文化载体

铜鼓存在了近三千年，直到今天它仍绵延不息。而与其漫长历史相联系的，是它在广大地域中的流动和传播——从中国的云南、广西，再到东南亚，南岭走廊所延伸和辐射的广袤区域，形成了一条广阔的铜鼓文化传播带。在这条跨越许多国家的文化带上，中国是铸造和使用铜鼓历史最长、保存铜鼓数量最多的国家。

20世纪80年代，铜鼓文化研究成为我国考古文化的“显学”之一。中国古代铜鼓研究会在前人对铜鼓分类研究的基础上进行了修正、完善，最后采用以标准器出土地命名的八型法进行分类，将铜鼓分为万家坝、石寨山、冷水冲、北流、灵山、遵义、西盟、麻江八个类型。其中，麻江型铜鼓由于体形较小且轻，容易携带，存世数量最多，至今仍在众多南方民族如壮、布依、苗、瑶、侗、水、彝等民族的节日祭祀仪式中扮演神圣角色。

著名铜鼓研究专家蒋廷瑜曾这样说道："铜鼓是一个复杂的文化载体，面对它们那庞大的身躯和精美的图纹，谁不为之动情？"我们在这样一种器物之上，看到了各民族交往交流交融而形成的共同文化意识，看到了中华民族多元一体的具体形象。

It is the largest ancient bronze drum discovered to date in the world. As the cultural heritage of ethnic minorities in southern China, the bronze drum saw the migration, integration and memory of ethnic groups like Han, Baiyue, Baipu, Di & Qiang and Miao & Yao in the Nanling Corridor.

The Nanling Corridor signifies a natural passage that comprises deep canyons and narrow roads as well as numerous river systems around the Nanling Mountains. In history, many ethnic groups migrated and communicated there. As a result, a geographical belt with the most diverse and splendid culture took shape in the Nanling Corridor. There were various ethnic groups, including descendants of Baiyue (e.g. Zhuang, Buyi, Shui, Dong and Maonan) and Miao & Yao (e.g. Miao, Yao and She).

As a significant ritual vessel in ancient China, bronze drum firstly appeared in the 7th century BC. Its origin was associated with rice culture in southern China. Some scholars consider that bronze drum originated from bronze cauldron, evolved from a daily cooking utensil to a ritual vessel, and became a medium for the communication between humans and gods. It was widely used in sacred ceremonies such as sacrifice, war, gathering, funeral and celebration. In many ethnic groups in southern China, bronze drum was divinized, whose sound had primitive power and connected humans and gods.

The bronze drum was made in the Western Han Dynasty, with eight-ray sun pattern and three-circle halo. The surface of the drum is decorated with simple and elegant cloud-thunder pattern. With a surface diameter of 165 cm, a height of 67.5 cm and a weight of *c*. 300 kg, it boasts the largest and heaviest ancient bronze drum discovered in the world, known as the "king of bronze drum".

Jiang Tingyu, a famous scholar in the studies of bronze drum, says: "The bronze drum is a complex cultural form. We cannot help being awestruck by its gigantic body and exquisite pattern." It crystallizes the common cultural consciousness forged in the communication and integration of various ethnic groups and the formation of the multi-ethnic Chinese nation.

古滇国青铜扣饰中出现了异域民族的形象，他们为何高鼻深目，穿着与古滇人迥异的服装？

藏彝走廊上的民族迁徙

鎏金双人盘舞扣饰

Gilded Buckle Decoration with Two Men Dancing with Round Plates in Hands

文物简读

这件西汉时期的鎏金双人盘舞扣饰上，两名男子脑后挽成小髻，着左衽紧身长袖衣，腰间配长剑，跣足，手中各持一盘，踏于一蜿蜒长蛇身上，边歌边舞。迥异于古滇国风俗的人物形象和装束，映射出秦汉时期藏彝走廊上浩大而持久的民族迁徙运动，隐现着中华民族大家庭成员所内蕴的丰富而复杂的基因构成。

来自西域的宾客？

20世纪50年代以来，伴随着古滇国上万件青铜器的出土，古滇文化的文明之光愈发闪耀，让世人对偏居一隅的西南边陲刮目相看。这些青铜器种类多样，器型丰富，造型独特，其中可供系戴、悬挂与装饰的青铜扣饰，存放财富的贮贝器，代表权力与财富的铜鼓等，铸造工艺精美，具有吸纳、融合异文化的特征，向世人展示出一个不同凡响的古代方国形象。由于其鲜明的地域特征，滇青铜艺术成为与中原青铜文化、北方青铜文化齐名的三大青铜文化之一。

在古滇国的青铜器艺术中，扣饰堪称一朵奇葩。它是背面有矩形齿扣可供系戴、悬挂的一种青铜装饰品，主要流行于战国至西汉时期的滇池区域，是滇青铜文化的重要组成部分。

在众多的出土扣饰中，这件鎏金双人盘舞扣饰上的人物形象显得尤其特别，引起考古学家们的重重疑窦：两位男子显然与古滇人大不相同——他们为何高鼻深目？他们所佩之剑为何比古滇人所用之剑长得多？他们为何没有佩戴古滇人的耳饰？他们为何穿着长裤而非古滇人的短裤或短裙？

名称：鎏金双人盘舞扣饰

年代：西汉

规格：高12厘米，宽18.5厘米

出土地点：云南省昆明市晋宁区石寨山13号墓

收藏单位：云南省博物馆

Name: Gilded Buckle Decoration with Two Men Dancing with Round Plates in Hands

Historical Period: The Western Han Dynasty

Height: 12 cm, Width: 18.5 cm

Excavation Site: No. 13 Tomb, Shizhai Mountain, Jinning District, Kunming, Yunnan Province

Housed in: Yunnan Provincial Museum

事实上，考古学家还发现，在同一墓葬出土的另一件贮贝器盖上，也有两个同样奇异的人物形象，“混”在一群滇人之中：那是一组四人一牛的雕像，其中两位高鼻深目、多须髯的贵族人物，上身穿着窄袖过手的上衣，下身穿着长及脚背的长裤，同样佩戴着长剑。这说明，鎏金双人盘舞扣饰上的人物并非偶然和个别。

专家学者通过文献研究和深入分析，最后把疑问指向一个推测：这是一个通过迁徙来到古滇国的异域族群的形象，他们有可能是来自新疆伊犁河流域的西域游牧者——塞人的一支。

这个推测来自《汉书》记录过的一场多米诺骨牌式的迁徙运动：匈奴打败大月氏，大月氏向西征服塞人，塞人的一支被迫南迁。根据这一记载，有研究者认为，双人盘舞扣饰上的人物有可能是经由藏彝走廊而南迁的一支塞人。公元前160年前后，塞人受大月氏驱赶，向南迁徙。这支塞人后来成为滇国属民，最后融入西南族群之中。

一条民族走廊的缩影

“藏彝走廊”是费孝通提出的一个学术概念，指四川、云南、西藏三省区毗邻地区由一系列南北走向的山系和河流所构成的高山峡谷区。自古以来，这个区域就是藏缅语族诸民族先民南下、壮侗苗瑶语族诸民族先民北上，众多民族交汇融合的天然地理通道。今天，这个通道里既居住着藏缅语族的藏、羌、彝、傈僳、白、普米、纳西、景颇、怒、独龙、哈尼、拉祜等民族，也居住着壮侗语族中的傣族和壮族，还居住着苗瑶语族中的苗族、瑶族，以及汉族、回族、孟—高棉语族中的一些民族。

藏彝走廊之所以被称作“走廊”，乃因其山脉、河流均为南北走向，地理上呈典型的走廊形态。在走廊中，北部有大片游牧区，中部为农牧混合区，南部为山地农耕地区，所以藏彝走廊处于北部游牧区向南部山地农耕地区过渡的地理带。这正是历史上北方游牧族群从藏彝走廊南下并与南方农耕民族发生密切关系的地理原因。藏彝走廊在沟通西南与西北之间以及游牧民族与农耕民族之间发挥了重要的历史作用。有学者甚至指出，藏彝走廊是一条沟通南北丝绸之路的国际走廊，是一条具有国际性和国际意义的历史、地理、民族和文化的走廊。历史上，游牧民族沿着这条走廊南下的动因，既有气候变化的自然因素，也有族群互动的人文因素。而南下的迁徙是通过不同的渠道，在多时空范围内进行的，在时间上甚至有可能远至新石器时代。

到秦汉时期，藏彝走廊进入了历史活跃期——因秦国向西拓展，迫使西北河湟一带的西羌族群向西、向南迁移，其中一些族群通过藏彝走廊北端和西北端入口，先后进入走廊，南迁者最远至雅砻江及安宁河中下游。汉武帝统一西南夷，又促使滇国的濮越系民族向西、向北拓展，在走廊南端一带与藏缅语族群发生接触、冲突、交流和融合。

扣饰人物的形象，隐现着藏彝走廊上曾经发生过的民族交往交流交融的频繁性和深广性。沿着这条连接中国南北丝绸之路的通道，众多游牧人群从西北高原的河湟地带一路南下，与自东向西进入这条通道的百越民族，以及在秦汉以后循南岭走廊进入通道的部分苗瑶民族，相互碰撞、交融，演化出今天分布在这里的众多民族以及丰富多彩的民族文化。今天的云南，是中国世居少数民族最多的省份，也是民族文化最为缤纷斑斓的地区。这使藏彝通道典型地展现出了各民族因不断迁徙和互动，而形成的“你来我去，我来你去，你中有我，我中有你”的历史演化格局。

It was made in the Western Han Dynasty. Two men are dancing, having their hair in a bun. They wear tight long sleeved garment with a left lapel, with a long sword at the waist, barefoot, holding a plate in each hand, treading on a coiling snake while singing and dancing. The images and costumes are totally different from these of ancient Kingdom of Dian. This implies the far-reaching migration of ethnic groups in the Tibetan-Yi Corridor in the Qin and Han Dynasties, as well as the complex gene of the Chinese nation.

In the bronze art of ancient Kingdom of Dian, buckle decoration displays unique charm. It is a type of bronze decoration with rectangular tooth-like buckle on the back for wearing and hanging. It mainly prevailed in Dian from the Warring States Period to the Western Han Dynasty and constituted an important part of Dian bronze culture.

Among numerous unearthed buckles, the image of the two men in the present gilded buckle decoration seems quite unusual. Archaeologists are bemused. The two men look different from ancient Dian people. What do their tall noses and deep eyes suggest? Why is the long sword they wear much longer than the swords used by ancient Dian people? Why don't they wear earrings as ancient Dian people did? Why do they wear long trousers instead of the shorts or skirts of ancient Dian people?

Based on the existing literature and in-depth analysis, scholars draw the conclusion that the two men were probably Scythians, a nomadic tribe along the Ili River Basin in the Western Regions.

In *Book of Han* (《汉书》), there was a domino-like migration movement. The Xiongnu defeated Great Yuezhi, and Great Yuezhi conquered Scythian in the west. A clan of Scythian was compelled to move southward. Therefore, some scholars view that the two men in gilded buckle decoration were Scythians who migrated south along the Tibetan-Yi Corridor. Around 160 BC, a clan of Scythian was expelled by Great Yuezhi to the south, which was later ruled by ancient Kingdom of Dian and eventually integrated into ethnic groups in the southwest.

当秦汉时期的塞外草原上出现了代表定居生活的典型器具——灶，这意味着什么？

塞外草原上的多民族杂居

龙首青铜灶

Bronze Cooking Stove with Dragon-Shaped Head

41

文物简读

这件在内蒙古地区出土，目前考古发现体量最大的龙首青铜灶，具有典型的中原风格，是秦汉时期农耕族群定居生活场景出现在长城之外的见证，反映了当时游牧族群与农耕族群之间不断加深交融互动的历史趋势，呈现了多民族聚居情景不断扩大的历史景象。

马蹄声声与炊烟袅袅的交替

这是一件外表极其美观、功能极其完备的龙首青铜灶。即便用今天的眼光看，它的科学设计也让人大为惊讶——

这是一只三眼灶，主体部件由甑锅、釜、灶门和烟筒等组成；整体造型为龙头船形，船身上分布着三釜，一大二小，大釜上有甑，釜均为敛口，折腹，圜底；正面留有长方形灶门；灶两侧各装饰着一只铺首衔环，灶底有四只相互对称的兽蹄足。最妙的是，灶的烟筒设计成一只昂首嘶吼的龙头，龙头与船形灶身浑然一体，让整只灶看起来就像一条精美的龙船。而且，高耸的龙形烟囱除了代表吉祥，还有吸风拔火的功能，所以堪称设计精巧。

如果设计如此巧妙的铜灶出现在中原农耕区，想必考古学家不会大为惊讶，但它却发现于长城以北的蒙古草原——在想象中，逐水草而居的游牧者应当不会与这种代表着定居生活的器具发生关联。尤其它还是一只多眼灶——多眼灶使同一时间进行多项烹饪活动成为可能，这不仅是饮食的丰富程度达到一定阶段的客观需求，也是烹饪技巧达到一定高度的反映。

名称：龙首青铜灶

年代：汉

规格：高40厘米，长40.5厘米，宽28.5厘米

出土地点：内蒙古自治区呼和浩特市金河镇格尔图村

收藏单位：内蒙古博物院

Name: Bronze Cooking Stove with Dragon-Shaped Head

Historical Period: The Han Dynasty

Height: 40 cm, Length: 40.5 cm, Width: 28.5 cm

Excavation Site: Ge'ertu Village, Jinhe Town, Hohhot, Inner Mongolia

Housed in: Inner Mongolia Museum

沿着阴山山脉一路往西，从呼和浩特到巴彦淖尔，这里曾经水草丰美、宜牧宜耕，是游牧经济和农耕经济的连接地点，因此自古便是草原民族与农耕民族、草原文化与农耕文化交流、碰撞的主要场所之一。今天，我们凝望着这只昂首怒吼的龙首青铜灶，仿佛穿越时空，看见了这里轮回交替于马蹄声声与炊烟袅袅之间的历史岁月……

塞外的土地上人来人往

当史前的那一簇火苗被自由掌控，我们的先民开始迈入“熟食时代”。最早的灶可能是由挖地成穴保存火种演化出来的，这从金文中“灶”的字形以及《说文解字》中对“灶”的释义可见一斑。到新石器时代，伴随着陶器的发明，灶也经历了从篝火式到锅台式的漫长演化，与之配套的炊具形态也发生了变化。商代，灶基本定型；汉代，灶成为庖厨的重要设施，与人们的生活息息相关，《汉书·五行志》称：“灶者，生养之本。”

秦汉时期，由于受“鬼犹求食”和“事死如事生”观念的影响，灶被作为模拟日常生活用品的冥器，陪葬到地下。这只龙首青铜灶，实际上就是一件冥器。所以，作为与中原农耕文明紧密相连、代表着定居生活的灶，出现在草原墓葬之中，说明秦汉时期多民族杂居局面已出现雏形，游牧文化和农耕文化的交融力度在逐渐加深。只有经历了一次次规模宏大的民族交往和相契相融，灶具才会进入塞外草原上的生活日常，甚至进入人们的信仰世界，寄寓着墓主人对在另一个世界也有美好生活的企盼和向往。

秦汉时期，随着统一多民族国家的发端，中原与边疆地区之间的经济、文化联系进入一个新的历史阶段。据记载，南匈奴呼韩邪单于率众内附后，在此后90年间，陆续内迁的南匈奴人达到60万，他们与当地汉族交错杂居，其中近20万人融入了汉族。汉朝在内蒙古地区实行郡县制管理，营建了40余座边疆城镇并屯垦开发，其时的呼和浩特地区就属云中郡管辖。

“它不仅让我们领略到先民的智慧，更让我们体会到文化互融所带来的祥和与美好。”作为龙首青铜灶的收藏单位，内蒙古博物院这样评价。

Unearthed in Inner Mongolia, it is the largest bronze cooking stove in archaeological discoveries. With the typical style of the Central Plains, it demonstrated the existence of the farming civilization or settled life in the north of the Great Wall in the Qin and Han Dynasties, reflected the historical trend of continuous interaction between nomadic and agricultural groups, and verified the expansion of the harmony among ethnic groups in Chinese history.

It is a three-kettle stove, containing steamer, kettle, stove door and chimney. In shape, it looks like a boat with dragon-shaped head. There are three kettles (one big and two small), with a steamer on the big one. Their mouths of the three kettles narrow towards the top, and their bellies bend in the middle, with round bottom. A rectangular stove door is opened on the front. Both sides of the stove are decorated with animal-head knocker-holder, with four symmetrical hooves attached to the bottom of the stove. The most striking feature is that the chimney of the stove is designed as a dragon raising the head and roaring, which is perfectly integrated with the delicate boat-shaped stove. The dragon-shaped chimney expresses an auspicious sign. Besides, it can absorb the wind well and enhance fire, which uses the law of thermodynamics in a creative way.

For archaeologists, it is a big surprise to discover the elaborately-designed bronze cooking stove in the Mongolian grassland north of the Great Wall. In particular, it is a multi-kettle stove, which facilitates several cooking activities at the same time, enriches the diet of nomads and embodies their high cooking skills.

The bronze cooking stove is a burial object. As a symbol of agricultural civilization or settled life in the Central Plains, it indicates that the coexistence of various ethnic groups took initial shape in the Qin and Han Dynasties, and that the integration of nomadic and agricultural civilizations deepened.

"It allows us to appreciate the wisdom of our ancestors and understand the peace and happiness of cultural integration," says a staff of Inner Mongolia Museum.

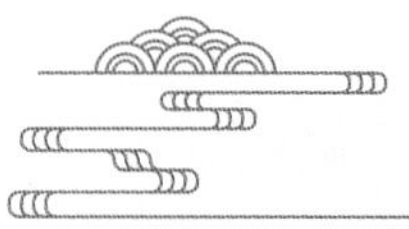

对峙与依存

——魏晋南北朝时期的民族大融合

Confrontation and Coexistence: National Integration in the Wei, Jin, Southern and Northern Dynasties

这是一场跨越近三个世纪的南北对峙——魏晋南北朝时期，中国历史迎来了一次严峻的考验。在这个历史岔路口上徘徊近三百年后，中华历史最终从分裂、混乱，从多族群的矛盾对峙中走了出来，重新归于融合依存，迎来了更高度的统一，开启了又一个强大的大一统秩序。中国历史为何总能从战争与动荡中愈合，再造统一？这一古老的历史密码，就藏在魏晋南北朝的故事中。

魏晋以来，匈奴、羯、氐、羌、鲜卑等北方游牧民族，在社会发展和自然环境变化等因素的驱动下，发动了一场场大规模迁移，跨越了因自然生态而形成的农牧地理线，进入了中原历史舞台，拉开了“五胡入华”的大幕，开启了南北朝的对峙。但这一场大分裂的背后，却演绎着另一条故事线——在卷入这场数百年的混杂、碰撞后，五胡纷纷自觉或不自觉地完成了文化转型，实现了定居化、农耕化，接受了中原文化传统，并最终大部分融入了华夏。

这不仅表现为五胡曾以各种方式认定自身的炎黄裔胄身份，比如建立北魏的鲜卑拓跋氏，将祖先追溯至黄帝轩辕氏；也表现为五胡以中国分裂为变态，追求大一统的理想，比如建立前秦的氐人苻坚发出了“混六合为一家”的历史强音。此外，五胡均以秦汉制度为基础建立王朝，又以农业经济为立国之本，力图使自己的王朝成为“中华正统”，并皆自称“中国人”。这就使“中国人”从原先仅限于“华夏—汉”的自称，变而为各民族共有的称号。

正是因此，这些由北方游牧民族所建立的王朝成为中国历史不可缺少的一环。中华文明的传统并不因为少数民族成为统治者而被割断；相反，农耕者与游牧者经由这些大动荡而逐渐融入同一部历史之中，成为中华史册的共同书写者，又在同一束历史追光灯下，成为中华史诗大剧的共同出演者。

In the Wei, Jin and Southern and Northern Dynasties, the north-south confrontation lasted for three centuries, which put China into the grip of crisis. Plunged into the 300-year division and war, China eventually marched toward unification and order. For ethnic groups, assimilation and coexistence replaced conflict and confrontation, ushering in extensive unification and stable order. Why did China always recover from turbulence and re-forge unity? The secret of ancient China's resilience lied in the history of the Wei, Jin, Southern and Northern Dynasties.

Since the Wei and Jin Dynasties, the five *Hu* (胡, nomadic tribes in the north, e.g. Xiongnu, Jie, Di, Qiang and Xianbei) started a large-scale migration, owing to the requirements of social development and the changes in natural environment. They crossed the geographical boundary of farming and nomadic civilizations (determined by natural and ecological conditions) and appeared in the history of the Central Plains. This signaled the confrontation between the Southern and Northern Dynasties. Simultaneously, beneath national split was an upsurge of cultural transformation. In hundreds of years of reconciliation, the five nomadic tribes ended nomadic life, took up farming, and embraced cultural tradition of the Central Plains, consciously or unconsciously. Finally they assimilated into *Hua Xia* (华夏).

Specifically, the five *Hu* recognized their identity as "descendants of the Yan Emperor and the Yellow Emperor" in various ways. For instance, the Tuoba Xianbei that established the Northern Wei Dynasty traced its ancestor back to the Yellow Emperor (the Xuanyuan). The five *Hu* longed for unification in the long-term division. Fu Jian (Di), who founded the Former Qin Dynasty, aspired to unite the whole country. Additionally, the five *Hu* adopted the institutions of the Qin and Han Dynasties and took agricultural economy as political foundation, in a bid to legitimize their regimes. They viewed themselves as peoples of the Central Plains. In this way, the Chinese people, originally used as an appellation of *Hua Xia* or the Han nationality, extended to all ethnic groups in China.

To conclude, nomadic tribes in the north as well as their dynasties played a vital role in Chinese history. Nomadic emperors admired the Han traditions and advanced Chinese civilization. Amidst political turbulence, the Han people and nomads constituted the *one* history of the Chinese nation and performed their roles in the historical stage.

石勒，这个从奴隶成为皇帝的羯人首领，为什么有些历史学家认为他带来了“中古政治文化的新变局”？

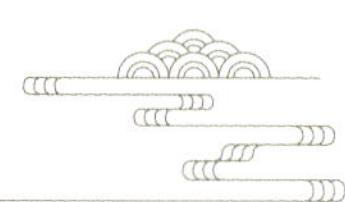

“胡头汉舌”：羯人的故事

“大赵万岁”瓦当

Eaves Tile with Characters *Da Zhao Wan Sui* (大赵万岁)

42

文物简读

这件用近于隶楷的优美汉字书写着“大赵万岁”的瓦当，出自五胡之一的羯人所建立的后赵国城邑，它见证了魏晋南北朝时期羯人入华所经历的纷争与动荡，以及胡汉血缘交融的历史场景，映射出后赵政权自觉融入中华历史序列的民族记忆。

羯人石勒

深目、高鼻、多须髯，操粟特语，有人说他们是西域小月氏的后裔，也有人说他们是南匈奴的一支，还有人说他们是羌胡，等等。公元4世纪初，他们在杰出首领石勒的带领下，不仅形成一个强大的族群，而且还成为中原地区的“国人”——他们就是建立了后赵政权的羯人。

羯人的来源及形成，是学术界一个长期论而未定的议题。目前所知道的是，他们的先民被认为是匈奴别部，跟随匈奴入塞。到3世纪中期至4世纪初（西晋末年），经历了几次迁徙、分化和聚合，羯人逐渐形成一个人口众多的群体，主要分布在山西、河北、陕西、甘肃一带。他们备受压迫和歧视，生活艰辛困苦。正是这样的土壤，孕育出了英勇的羯人领袖石勒。

石勒是上党郡武乡县（今山西武乡）人，年轻时当过佃农、做过买卖，最后被贩卖到山东为奴。由于气宇轩昂，谈吐不凡，石勒在山东主人家很快获得自由之身，可是后来却落入乱军之手，充当军卒。经历了生与死的考验，石勒最后率领同为胡人的“十八骑”参加汲桑率领的农民起义军，之后成为南匈奴刘渊手下的一员骁勇战将。公元319年，石勒与汉—前赵政权决裂，建立后赵。公元329年，石勒攻灭前赵。至此，除了辽东、辽西和凉州，中国的北方地区在西晋灭亡后第一次实现了统一。石勒于公元330年称帝，完成了从奴隶到将军再到皇帝的惊天逆转。

名称："大赵万岁"瓦当

年代：后赵

规格：宽58厘米，高62.2厘米，厚8.8—10厘米

出土地点：河北省邯郸市临漳县邺城遗址

收藏单位：邺城考古队

Name: Eaves Tile with Characters *Da Zhao Wan Sui* (大赵万岁)

Historical Period: The Later Zhao Kingdom

Width: 58 cm, Height 62.2 cm, Thickness: 8.8–10 cm

Excavation Site: Yecheng Site, Linzhang County, Handan City, Hebei Province

Housed in: Yecheng Archaeological Team

不识字的“雅好文学”者

佃农、奴隶出身的石勒，大字不识几个，却“雅好文学”。据史书记载，他常在军旅之中命儒生为他念《汉书》。据说有一次，当听到书生郦食其劝说汉高祖刘邦恢复分封制的时候，石勒大为惊慌地说：“这种做法太不妥当，最终怎能得到天下呢？”在听到留侯张良劝阻刘邦时，石勒就说：“幸亏有这个人呀！”由此可以看出，他在听人读书的过程中不仅身心投入，而且能根据局势做出准确的分析和判断。

石勒建立后赵政权之后，在一次接待外宾的宴会中，大臣徐光吹捧石勒的宏谋伟略超过了汉高祖刘邦和魏武帝曹操，仅次于黄帝。石勒没有虚荣地接受，而是说大臣吹捧太过，自己对汉高祖心悦诚服。这番自我评价体现出他对汉文化的推崇和对中华历史的高度认知，也展示了他的智慧自明。史书记载，他的话音刚落，群臣立即顿首，齐称万岁。

“夷狄不足为君论”的破局者

两晋王朝为了维护自身的正统地位以及应对内迁的胡人首领们跃跃欲试建立政权的压力，便提出“夷狄不足为君”，宣称胡人为臣则有先例，为君自古未有，“夷狄”不具备称帝的资格。这个理论给成汉政权的氐族首领李雄、前赵政权的匈奴首领刘渊以及前燕政权的鲜卑首领慕容廆等都带来了合法性的困扰。

事实上，“五胡入华”的过程，正是这些北方民族以各种方式确立自身是中原政权合法继承者身份的过程。刘渊作为南匈奴单于之孙，自认为是汉高祖刘邦的后代，在建立政权时，打的是“汉”的旗号。另一位南匈奴贵族后裔赫连勃勃，则根据《史记》的记载，把自己追认为夏后氏的后代，将自己建立的政权命名为“大夏”。

但不论是刘渊还是赫连勃勃，都没有从本质上破解“夷狄不足为君论”。而作为羯人的石勒，却在这个问题上实现了历史性突破。

石勒称帝后，以“赵”为国号。他要求羯人改用汉姓，采用汉语，以致羯人一时间被称为“胡头汉舌”；他严禁呼羯为“胡”，模糊血统和族类差异……这一系列政策，使后赵政权在本质上实践了西周以来的天下主义传统，以文化认同取消华夷区隔，为夷狄继承华夏正统带来了一个重要的历史转折，也消解了对五胡政权合法性的质疑，因此有学者认为这是中古政治文化的新变局。可惜后来石勒的继任者石虎暴虐凶残，激发了极大的民族矛盾。后赵于公元351年灭亡后，羯人也就在第一次民族大融合的洪流当中，成为其中的一朵浪花。

但石勒建立的后赵深刻表明，南北朝虽然陷入混战与分裂，但来到中原的北方民族却将自身纳入中华文化之中，自觉地维护着中华历史的延续。

There are four Chinese characters on the eaves tile, *Da Zhao Wan Sui*, written in official script and regular script. The eaves tile was unearthed from the city of the Later Zhao Kingdom established by the Jie (羯) people, one of the five *Hu* (胡) ethnic groups. It saw the troublous history of Jie who came to the Central Plains in the Wei, Jin, Southern and Northern Dynasties, as well as the historical scene of national integration between *Hu* and Han. As evinced, the Later Zhao Kingdom voluntarily contributed to the history of *Hua Xia* (华夏).

The Jie people had deep eyes, high nose and bushy beard. They spoke the Sogdian language. They were said to be descendants of Minor Yuezhi, Southern Xiongnu or Qiang *Hu*. In the early 4th century, under the leadership of Shi Le, the Jie people formed a powerful ethnic group and established the Later Zhao Kingdom.

The origin and formation of Jie remain a controversial issue in the academic circle. Jie ancestors were believed to be a clan of Xiongnu. From the middle 3rd century to the early 4th century (the late Western Jin Dynasty), after migration and evolution, Jie formed an ethnic group with a large population, roughly distributed in the areas of present-day Shanxi, Hebei, Shaanxi and Gansu.

In 330, Shi Le became the king of the Later Zhao Kingdom. He requested the Jie people to use the surnames and languages of the Han people, strictly prohibited calling Jie as *Hu*, and minimized the differences of blood lineage and ethnicity. Through these policies, the Later Zhao Kingdom essentially practiced the idea of *Tian Xia* (天下), a tradition since the Western Zhou Dynasty, and counteracted the formal barrier between *Hua Xia* and *Yi* with cultural identity. The establishment of the Later Zhao Kingdom meant a significant turn for *Yi* to inherit the tradition of *Hua Xia* and dispelled the doubt about the legitimacy of the five *Hu* regimes, signaling a new change in the 4th-century Chinese politics and culture.

一个在《三国演义》里出演过轰轰烈烈大戏的古代族群，为何最终消失在历史长河中？

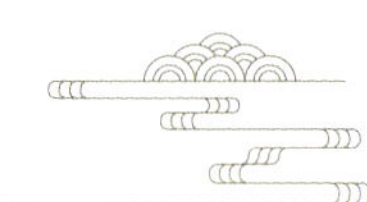

兴起与消失：乌桓的故事

“晋乌丸归义侯”金印

43

Gold Seal with Characters *Jin Wu Wan Gui Yi Hou* (晋乌丸归义侯)

文物简读

这枚西晋王朝赐给乌桓首领的金印，诉说着一个英勇善战的古代民族兴起与消失的故事，勾勒出一件北方民族在历史舞台上活跃一时又融入中华民族血脉之中的往事。

《三国演义》中的活跃角色

作为最早内迁中原的游牧族群之一，乌桓是《三国演义》中一个十分活跃的角色——曾担任过西汉王朝的侦察兵，还曾充当汉朝皇宫的警卫；曹操在击败乌桓军队后，仍然十分赏识其骁勇善战，特别组建了“天下名骑”征战四方……然而三国之后，这个名噪天下的群体却融入历史大潮，了无痕迹。

今天，我们能从何处寻迹乌桓呢？一枚“晋乌丸归义侯”金印，是乌桓留给历史的一个信物。这枚用纯金制成的印玺出土于内蒙古自治区乌兰察布市凉城县小坝子滩村，印玺呈扁方体，印上方为蹲踞式骆驼纽，正面印文阴刻篆书“晋乌丸归义侯”。虽然它印迹斑驳，却让我们似乎触摸到了一个曾经热血激荡的群体留在岁月深处的体温。

一个消失的族群

战国末年，北方草原兴起两大部落，一为匈奴，二为东胡。东胡因“在匈奴东，故曰东胡”。到了西汉初，东胡部落首领借匈奴冒顿单于弑父自立而兴师问罪，接二连三索要千里马、美女等。冒顿

名称："晋乌丸归义侯"金印

年代：西晋

规格：长2.3厘米，宽2.3厘米，高2.25厘米

出土地点：内蒙古自治区乌兰察布市凉城县小坝子滩村

收藏单位：内蒙古博物院

Name: Gold Seal with Characters *Jin Wu Wan Gui Yi Hou* (晋乌丸归义侯)

Historical Period: The Western Jin Dynasty

Length: 2.3 cm, Width: 2.3 cm, Height: 2.25 cm

Excavation Site: Xiaobazitan Village, Liangcheng County, Ulanqab City, Inner Mongolia Autonomous Region

Housed in: Inner Mongolia Museum

单于使用"扮猪吃老虎"的计策，一一应允，麻痹东胡。等到东胡再次贪得无厌索要土地的时候，冒顿单于率领部众奇袭毫无防备的东胡部落。匈奴成为草原上唯一的霸主，东胡部落则溃散为两支：一支逃往乌桓山，发展成为乌桓；另一支逃往鲜卑山，发展成为鲜卑。乌丸者，乌桓之别称。

此后一百多年间，乌桓和鲜卑不仅无法重新聚合起来与匈奴抗衡，而且乌桓邻近匈奴，一直受到匈奴的奴役和驱使。匈奴每年向乌桓征收牲畜、皮革，若逾时不交，或数量不够，便没收其妻子和子女为奴婢。

到了汉武帝时期，就在少年战神霍去病大破匈奴之时，为防止乌桓向匈奴提供人力物力，汉武帝迁乌桓于上谷、渔阳、右北平、辽西、辽东五郡，断了匈奴左臂，并首次设置校尉府管理乌桓事务。校尉府作为管理东北西部民族事务的机构，经两汉到魏晋，前后存在四百多年。此一时期，乌桓成为西汉王朝在北部的缓冲，在汉朝与匈奴之间又摇摆了近一百年。东汉光武帝时期，辽西乌桓首领到洛阳朝贡，请求内迁，得到光武帝允许，大量乌桓人得以迁入长城以内。

内迁的乌桓人入乡随俗，将原来以游牧为主的生产方式转变为农耕。乌桓人虽然成为农民，却没有改变英勇善战的特性。东汉末年，内迁到辽东、辽西、右北平三郡的乌桓曾一度统一，特别是蹋顿总领三郡乌桓时期，他们又形成了一支不可忽视的军事力量，干成了一系列惊天动地的大事：与袁绍结盟，派军队帮助袁绍打败公孙瓒，使袁绍得以成为东汉末年最强大的诸侯。此后，曹操为统一北方，讨伐袁绍，不得不集结强大兵力击破乌桓。乌桓虽破，但剩勇犹在，被曹操整编成骑兵部队，因英勇善战而号称"天下名骑"，并享有在战时免除租赋的待遇。

然而，魏晋时期，乌桓悄然融入汉、鲜卑等民族中，从此退出各种历史文献，成为一个消失了的古代族群。

中华民族血脉中的深层记忆

在"晋乌丸归义侯"金印出土之时，考古工作者在同一墓中，还发现了"晋鲜卑归义侯"金印、"猗㐌金"四兽形金牌饰、"晋鲜卑率善中郎将"银印等珍贵文物。

它们为何会出现在同一墓中呢？其中，"猗㐌金"四兽形金牌饰被认为是拓跋鲜卑最具代表性的物证之一。有专家推测，"晋乌丸归义侯"金印的主人为拓跋部东部大人禄官，其中东部所辖部众以乌丸为主。据此是否可以推断乌桓与拓跋鲜卑已经有了近百年的共生和互动？当然，从地理位置上来看，乌桓的内迁也为鲜卑的南下腾出了发展壮大的空间，并为两部的重新聚合提供了契机。

然而不论怎样，这个与鲜卑重聚的族群，最终消失在历史深处，成为中华民族血脉中的深层记忆。这枚"晋乌丸归义侯"金印，就代表着多元一体的中华民族在形成发展过程中所融合的多民族基因。

The gold seal was bestowed by the Western Jin Dynasty on the leader of Wuhuan. It tells the history of Wuhuan, a brave ancient tribe that came to rise in northern China and contributed to the formation of the Chinese nation.

Made of pure gold, the seal was unearthed at Xiaobazitan Village, Liangcheng County, Ulanqab City, Inner Mongolia. In the shape of flat square, the seal has an crouching camel-shaped button on the top, with incised inscriptions of *Jin Wu Wan Gui Yi Hou* at the bottom.

In the late Warring States Period, two major tribes emerged on the northern grasslands, the Xiongnu and the Donghu. The Donghu dwelled in the east of the Xiongnu. In the early Western Han Dynasty, Modu Chanyu routed the Donghu and dominated the grasslands. The Donghu fell into *sauve qui peut*. One clan fled to the Wuhuan Mountain and developed into Wuhuan or Wuwan. The other clan rushed to the Xianbei Mountain and developed into Xianbei.

In the reign of Emperor Guangwu of the Eastern Han Dynasty, the leader of Wuhuan in west of the Liao River went to Luoyang to pay tribute to Han. Emperor Guangwu allowed the Wuhuan people to immigrate to the south. Wuhuan observed the customs of the Han people and transformed traditional nomadic life into agricultural life. In the late Eastern Han Dynasty, the Wuhuan tribes that moved to Liaodong, Liaoxi and Youbeiping prefectures were unified. Under the leadership of Tadun, Wuhuan became an important military force.

Scholars surmise that the owner of the seal was Tuoba Luguan, who undertook the post of *Dongbu Daren* (东部大人, a title of tribal leader) and ruled the Wuhuan people in the east. Does the seal prove the 100-year coexistence and interaction between Wuhuan and Tuoba Xianbei? Geographically, the southward immigration of Wuhuan provided a space for the development and growth of Xianbei and an opportunity for the integration with Xianbei.

名称：马头鹿角形金步摇

年代：北朝

规格：高16.2厘米，重约70克

出土地点：内蒙古自治区包头市达尔罕茂明安联合旗

收藏单位：中国国家博物馆

Name: Horse-Head Deer-Horn Gold *Buyao* (步摇, a Kind of Headdress)

Historical Period: The Northern Dynasties

Height: 16.2 cm, Weight: *c.* 70 g

Excavation Site: Damao Banner, Baotou, Inner Mongolia Autonomous Region

Housed in: National Museum of China

中原人的头饰步摇为什么会成为鲜卑人的服饰特征？

金步摇之爱：慕容鲜卑的故事

马头鹿角形金步摇

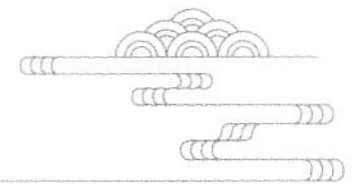

Horse-Head Deer-Horn Gold *Buyao* (步摇, a Kind of Headdress)

文物简读

这件精美绝伦的金步摇，让我们想起那个有趣的历史传闻：大名鼎鼎的慕容鲜卑，因喜爱中原汉朝的步摇，而将步摇变为自身的民族特征，并进而由“步摇”之谐音得名为“慕容”。

“步摇”与“慕容”

在金庸笔下，慕容复在《天龙八部》中初次出场之时，他还是风度翩翩、武功超群的佳公子，后来才知他是燕国王族后裔。慕容氏的复国之梦从未间断，而曾经的故国在何处？在遥远的梦境中，我们仿佛看见公元4世纪最负盛名的慕容鲜卑登上历史舞台，诉说着他们曾有的光荣与骄傲。

在博物馆追寻慕容鲜卑的遗迹，最让人心动的莫过于一件比一件精美的金步摇。这些珠玉点缀、玲珑有致的饰物，让我们看见了慕容鲜卑对美的热烈追求。

步摇原是两汉时期汉族妇女的头饰，因其随着人的步伐而颤动撞击，一步一摇，给人以视觉和听觉的美感，故名“步摇”。步摇在汉代是宫廷贵族妇女的首饰，是身份地位的象征。鲜卑南迁之后，在与汉人的混居中，他们接触到了步摇，进而狂热地喜爱上这种装饰物。此后，这一部分鲜卑人不仅改变了自身的装饰习惯，不分老少皆佩戴步摇，而且连男子也戴上了步摇冠。如此，步摇便成为这一部分鲜卑人的鲜明特征，并发展成为区别于其他鲜卑部落的标志，被人们作为这部分鲜卑人的族称。又因为音讹，“步摇”变成“慕容”之音，所以有了慕容鲜卑之称。

尽管上述说法并未有确切的历史记载，但大量精美的鲜卑步摇冠的出土，却显示出南迁鲜卑人的审美意识一步步与中原趋同的史实。事实上，鲜卑人在将中原步摇变成自身装饰物的同时，还吸收了经匈奴传入北方游牧地区的中亚摇叶装饰元素。他们创造出独具特色的树状步摇，继而随着慕容鲜卑的上层逐渐接受中原舆服制度，又创造了别具一格的慕容鲜卑式步摇，对隋唐以后的妇女冠饰产生了深远影响。

风光无限的慕容家族

慕容鲜卑是南北朝时期对中国历史产生重大影响的游牧族群鲜卑的一支。秦汉之际，东胡被匈奴打败，其中一部退居鲜卑山，以山名为族名，形成鲜卑族群。发展壮大的鲜卑按所居方位，分为东部鲜卑（包括慕容、段和宇文三部）、西部鲜卑（包括乞伏部和秃发部）、北部鲜卑（拓跋部）。三国时期，慕容鲜卑部首领莫护跋随同司马懿参与征讨辽东公孙氏政权有功，被封为“率义王”。从莫护跋到木延、涉归、慕容廆、慕容皝，经过百年的经营与征战，慕容部统一东部鲜卑。十六国时期，慕容鲜卑挺进辽东和中原，先后建立与前秦、东晋鼎立的前燕，与北魏号称北方双雄的后燕，以及西燕、南燕等政权。这些政权均是以鲜卑为主导、以汉族为多数居民的多民族混合政权。

4世纪的慕容家族风光无限，上天似乎把所有的好运都给予了慕容皝和他的儿子们。首先是慕容皝统一了东部鲜卑，自称“燕王”；继而年轻有为的次子慕容儁成为前燕皇帝；四子慕容恪是十六国时期的第一名将，年轻时就以战功威震四方；五子慕容垂，文韬武略，曾被前秦国主苻坚引为知音，后成为复兴燕国之人（史称后燕），当盛之时最有希望统一北方；幼子慕容德，南燕开国国主。然而物盛则衰，辉煌的时光却逐渐被家族之间的猜忌、残杀所损耗，先辈披荆斩棘奠定的基业终究被荒唐的后人毁于一旦，慕容鲜卑建立的各个政权都先后湮灭在北魏、东晋等的攻伐之下。

“慕容”之姓的深层内涵

关于“慕容”姓氏的来源，还有一种说法。慕容鲜卑自称源于远古时的高辛氏，是帝喾后裔；“慕容”之姓取自“慕二仪（日月）之德，继三光（日月星）之容”，意为“虽远离中原，也要发扬光大正统的中华文化”。

将慕容氏的先祖追溯为天下共主黄帝的后裔，这成为慕容鲜卑接受中原文化、融入中原文化的一种合理解释。著名历史学家陈寅恪曾如此评价慕容皝和他叱咤风云的儿子们：“他们都能博览群书，有很高的汉文化水平。他们建立的国家，比匈奴、羯人所建国家，汉文化色彩更浓。”主动吸收中原文化为己所用，立章建制，提升治理国家的水平和能力，这正是慕容鲜卑得以先从鲜卑部崛起的根本原因。

佩戴着金步摇的慕容鲜卑，一步步成为改变南北朝历史走向的重要政治力量，与此同时，他们也一步步走进中华民族共同体的形成与发展这条奔流不息的历史长河当中。

The exquisite gold *Buyao* reminds us of the interesting story. The Xianbei people liked *Buyao* in the Central Plains, and wearing *Buyao* became an ethnic identity of them. More interestingly, the pronunciation of *Buyao* sounds like that of *Murong*. This may be related to the tribe of Murong Xianbei.

Murong Xianbei is a clan of Xianbei, a nomadic ethnic group. In the Qin and Han Dynasties, beaten by the Xiongnu, a tribe of the Donghu was forced to retreat. They arrived at the Xianbei Mountain, where they got the name Xianbei. Geographically, the Xianbei can be divided into East Xianbei (including Murong, Duan and Yuwen tribes), West Xianbei (including Qifu and Tufa tribes) and North Xianbei (Tuoba tribe).

Buyao was originally a headdress of the Han women in the Han Dynasty. The headdresses swayed back and forth when a woman walked, creating a visual and auditory beauty. In the Han Dynasty, only empresses and princesses can wear *Buyao*, indicating that *Buyao* was a symbol of identity and status. After the Xianbei people moved southward and mixed with the Han people, they got to know *Buyao* and became keenly fond of it. Gradually, they changed their original dressing habits. Men also wore *Buyao*. In this way, *Buyao* evolved from an aesthetic sign to an ethnic sign. The Xianbei people who liked *Buyao* formed a new tribe. Additionally, *Buyao* was mispronounced as *Murong*, and the tribe was called Murong Xianbei.

A large number of exquisite Xianbei hats with *Buyao* have been unearthed, demonstrating that the Xianbei people who came to the Central Plains accepted the aesthetic taste of the Han people. Noticeably, the Xianbei people absorbed the element of *Yaoye* (摇叶, leaf-like ornament) in the Central Asian, which was introduced to the northern nomadic areas by the Xiongnu, and formed the unique tree-like *Buyao*. As the rulers of Murong Xianbei gradually embraced the *Yu-Fu* (舆服) System in the Central Plains (*Yu*, chariot and sedan chair; *Fu*, dressing etiquette), Xianbei-style *Buyao* took shape, which had a far-reaching impact on the popular style of women's headdress in the Sui and Tang Dynasties.

一个从慕容鲜卑中负气出走的部落，何以在遥远的西北高原建立起一个强大政权并存续三百多年？他们最终归于何处？

聚合与分散：吐谷浑的故事

吐谷浑公主夫妇合葬墓汉文墓志铭（拓片）

45

The Rubbing of the Chinese Epitaph of Tuyunhun Princess Hui Hua and Her Rouran Husband

文物简读

吐谷浑公主夫妇合葬墓发现于2015年，这通记载着吐谷浑、鲜卑、柔然三个政权间政治联姻关系的墓志铭，把一个充满历史传奇色彩的北朝部族鲜活地呈现了出来。

出走

吐谷浑最初是慕容鲜卑的一支。史载，吐谷浑是慕容廆的庶长兄，麾下有1700余户部众。父亲涉归死后，嫡出的慕容廆继任单于。公元4世纪晚期，慕容部人畜繁盛，牧场承载力不足，部族内部常常出现马斗现象。吐谷浑认为马斗是一种正常的行为，但慕容廆却指责吐谷浑的部众不讲道理。此言激怒了吐谷浑，他负气出走，率众西迁。据说慕容廆对此也极为后悔，派人追回。

使臣追上了吐谷浑的队伍，说服吐谷浑赶着马群向东返回，但只走了几百步，马群就发出悲鸣，固执地转头西行。吐谷浑说：“兄弟俩的别离是因马而起，如今是否回去，也应当根据马的启示来决定。”于是，他率领部众，继续向西迁移。队伍穿过了今天辽宁、内蒙古东部，在河套平原驻扎下来。在这里生活二十多年后，为避开锋芒正盛的拓跋鲜卑部，吐谷浑再次率部西迁，最终抵达了羌人居住的甘肃、青海一带。总计三十年的迁徙，一路的风餐露宿、与狼同行，磨炼了他们隐忍坚毅的品格。

名称：吐谷浑公主夫妇合葬墓汉文墓志铭（拓片）

年代：西魏、北周

出土地点：陕西省西安市长安区吐谷浑公主夫妇合葬墓

收藏单位：陕西省考古研究院

Name: The Rubbing of the Chinese Epitaph of Tuyunhun Princess Hui Hua and Her Rouran Husband

Historical Period: The Western Wei Dynasty and the Northern Zhou Dynasty

Excavation Site: The Tomb of Tuyuhun Princess Hui Hua and Her Ruoran Husband, Chang'an District, Xi'an, Shaanxi Province

Housed in: Shaanxi Academy of Archaeology

后悔不已的慕容廆写下了思念兄长的《阿干之歌》，常常吟唱。而接下来的一百多年间，两兄弟及其后代都名扬天下，各自干出了一番轰轰烈烈的大事业。吐谷浑的后代更是强盛延绵几百年。

崛起与衰落

晋咸和四年（329），吐谷浑之孙叶延用祖父的名字作为族名和国名，建立了吐谷浑国，将都城设在伏俟城（今青海铁卜卡古城），模仿中原的政治制度，在辖地内设置长史、司马等官职。吐谷浑统治的部众除鲜卑外，还有羌人、匈奴后裔等众多族群。这些不同族属的人民在同一个政权之下，逐渐融合为以"吐谷浑"为族名的族群共同体。

自吐谷浑至树洛干，吐谷浑经八位国君，其中多具才略，他们留心吸收儒生为官，其国力一度欣欣向荣，最盛时的疆域东起今甘肃南部、四川西北，南抵青海南部，西至新疆若羌、且末，北隔祁连山与河西走廊相接。当其时，吐谷浑所占据的青海地区成为区域交通中心之一，联系着中原与漠北、西域、青藏高原、印度等地的交往。

吐谷浑奉行睦邻政策，与柔然、东魏、隋、唐皇室相继通婚。吐谷浑公主夫妇合葬墓，墓主为吐谷浑的晖华公主和丈夫柔然骠骑大将军乞伏孝达。这篇墓志铭，记载了吐谷浑编织的复杂的族际婚姻网络：晖华公主是当时吐谷浑国君的第四个女儿，她嫁给了柔然的骠骑大将军；她的姐姐，则嫁给了柔然的可汗，成为柔然国的王后；这位王后的女儿，又嫁给西魏文帝，成为魏文帝的皇后。

事实上，吐谷浑与各个政权之间的姻亲关系远不止于此，比如墓志铭提到的晖华公主的夫婿乞伏孝达，应是西秦的王族后裔。后来，吐谷浑更为世人所熟知的联姻事件，是隋朝宗室光化公主和吐谷浑世伏可汗的和亲，唐朝弘化公主和吐谷浑诺曷钵可汗的和亲等。

联姻与和亲，在吐谷浑的历史上成为异常引人瞩目的事件，这大概是一个在夹缝中求发展的游牧政权的一种生存策略。

史载，吐谷浑政权存续了三百多年，最终于公元663年被吐蕃消灭。其后，吐谷浑部众一部分加入吐蕃；另有约十万人内迁，被唐朝安置在凉州等地，融入当地汉人；遗留在青海的部众，成为今天土族的核心成分；进入宁夏、陕西的部众，则逐渐与当地的回、汉融合。

青海骢

吐谷浑创造了灿烂的游牧文化，其所培育出来的青海骢远近闻名，号为"龙种"，是波斯马与当地土著马杂交而生的品种，能日行千里。此外，吐谷浑还训练出了一种独特的"舞马"，因为不断进贡至中原而闻名遐迩。史载这种具有舞蹈能力的马"有奇貌绝足"，动作协调能力强，能解人语，善知音节。

吐谷浑与马之间建立了深切的联系。当初，是马群指示他们的祖先一路西行，找到了一片适宜他们生存的土地；而后，他们又将马文化发展到一个如此耀眼的高度！

从慕容鲜卑的一支，到融合众多西北民族生成一个名为“吐谷浑”的部族，最终又分散进不同的民族之中——这个过程，生动体现出古代族群在分散与融合的多重复杂运动中，最终凝聚成多元一体的中华民族共同体的历程。

The tomb was discovered in 2015. The epitaph records the intermarriage or political relationship between Tuyuhun, Xianbei and Rouran Kingdoms, and vividly tells the story of Tuyuhun in the Northern Dynasties.

In 329, Ye Yan, the grandson of Tuyuhun, established the Kingdom of Tuyuhun (the namesake of the grandfather) and chose the city of Fu'ai (present-day Tiebuka Ancient City in Qinghai) as the capital. He followed the political system of the Central Plains, and appointed such officials as *Zhangshi* (长史, adjutant in charge of administrative work) and *Sima* (司马, high-ranking military officer). In the Kingdom of Tuyuhun, there were various tribes, such as Xianbei, Qiang and Xiongnu. In the long history, Tuyuhun, as an ethnic group, emerged.

From Tuyuhun to Shuluogan, eight kings reigned over the Kingdom of Tuyuhun. In its heyday, the territory of Tuyuhun extended from present-day southern Gansu and northwestern Sichuan in the east to southern Qinghai in the south, to Ruoqiang and Qiemo in Xinjiang in the west, and to the Qilian Mountains and the Hexi Corridor in the north. At that time, Qinghai became a traffic hub, facilitating the exchanges between the Central Plains and Mobei, the Western Regions, the Qinghai-Tibet Plateau, India and other areas.

Tuyuhun pursued the policy of good neighborliness and advocated the intermarriage with the upper classes of Rouran, the Eastern Wei Dynasty, the Sui Dynasty and the Tang Dynasty. The owners of the tomb were Hui Hua, a Tuyuhun princess, and her husband Qifu Xiaoda, a Rouran major general with the title of *Piaoqi* (骠骑). The epitaph suggests a complex inter-ethnic marriage network. Princess Hui Hua was the fourth daughter of the king of Tuyuhun. Her elder sister married the Khan of Rouran and became the queen of Rouran, whose daughter married Emperor Wen of the Western Wei and became his queen.

Political marriage was an eye-catching phenomenon in the history of Tuyuhun, which was a political strategy for a nomadic kingdom in pursuit of development in the midst of powerful tribes.

这个古代族群犹如划破历史长空的流星，曾经如此耀眼，在高光消失之后仍然残存着忽隐忽现的痕迹：他们是谁？他们又从何而来？

迁徙、融合与壮大：拓跋鲜卑的故事

鲜卑山嘎仙洞摩崖石刻祝文（拓片）

46

The Rubbing of Sacrificial Odes Carved on a Stone Tablet at Gaxian Cave, the Xianbei Mountain

文物简读

这块石碑承载了拓跋鲜卑从大兴安岭的莽莽山林中走出，继而尽占匈奴故地，在南北朝时期完成统一北方的大业，又最终悄然融进多元一体中华民族中的故事。

《魏书》中记载，公元443年，完成了统一北方大业的北魏太武帝拓跋焘，为纪念自己的祖先、显其国威，派遣官员长途跋涉到大兴安岭深处的鲜卑山，在传说中祖先曾居住过的山洞石室里祭祀祝祷，并刻石纪念。

此后，这块石碑渐被尘封，只留在文献记载中，也留在子孙的记忆里。后人曾依照历史记录，苦苦寻找，始终未见踪迹……

1979年，内蒙古呼伦贝尔盟文物站站长米文平和他的同事们一起，先后三次对呼伦贝尔盟鄂伦春自治旗阿里河镇西北十公里处的天然山洞嘎仙洞进行探测。在1980年7月30日的第四次探查中，发现了北魏太武帝派使者祝祭后刻于石壁之上的祝文。

一部艰辛的迁徙史和奋斗史

拓跋鲜卑原在今大兴安岭北段密林中过着原始穴居式的渔猎生活。

东汉初年，其第五代远祖带领部族历经九难八阻，向南迁徙到呼伦湖。东汉末年，首领诘汾进一步率部南迁，到达匈奴故地，与留居当地的匈奴融合。此后，诘汾之子力微又历经三十多年的努力，

名称：鲜卑山嘎仙洞摩崖石刻祝文（拓片）

年代：北魏太平真君四年（443）

出土地点：内蒙古自治区呼伦贝尔市鄂伦春旗嘎仙洞遗址

现存地点：嘎仙洞遗址

Name: The Rubbing of Sacrificial Odes Carved on a Stone Tablet at Gaxian Cave, the Xianbei Mountain

Historical Period: The 4 year of Emperor Taiping Zhenjun of the Northern Wei Dynasty (443)

Excavation Site: Gaxian Cave Site, Oroqen Banner, Hulunbuir, Inner Mongolia Autonomous Region

Housed in: Gaxian Cave Site

终于将拓跋部从一个弱小部落发展成“控弦上马二十余万”的强大部落联盟，并再次将部众迁至今内蒙古和林格尔，在迁徙过程中又吸收了氐、羌、乌桓、柔然、丁零、高车、月氏等多族群成分。

西晋末年，拓跋部已达到“控弦骑士四十余万”，再后来“西兼乌孙故地，东吞勿吉以西，控弦上马将有百万”；到公元338年，拓跋什翼犍在今山西省浑源县西南正式建国称王，国号“代”。

此时，中原已进入群雄并起的时代，氐人在其首领苻坚的带领下，建立了前秦，统一了北方。代国在建立38年后，被前秦所灭。

公元383年，盛极一时的前秦由于在淝水之战中失利，什翼犍的嫡孙拓跋珪抓住历史机遇，召集旧部，重新建国，在平城（今山西大同）建立北魏王朝，与慕容垂建立的后燕并称为“北方双雄”。

此后，拓跋珪之孙、16岁登基的北魏第三代皇帝拓跋焘，怀着“廓定四表，混一戎华”的远大志向，先后攻灭十六国中的夏、北燕、北凉等割据政权，又征伐山胡，降伏鄯善、龟兹、粟特等西域诸国，驱逐吐谷浑，终于在公元439年统一了中国北方，结束了中原地区持续一个半世纪纷争混战、民不聊生的局面。

彪炳千秋的拓跋氏

正当北魏繁荣兴盛之际，居住在大兴安岭深山中的小国乌洛侯，派使者千里迢迢来到北魏都城，进献赤貂皮等地方特产，同时向拓跋焘报告说，大兴安岭深山中有一座大石室，是拓跋部祖先们开凿的祖堂，百姓们常去祭祀祈祷，有求必应，十分神奇。

乌洛侯使者的报告引发了拓跋焘对祖先的追思，他立即派人前往石室，告祭天地，并把祝文刻于祖庙石壁上。

在祝文中，拓跋焘歌颂祖先走出大兴安岭森林，一步步南迁到黄河流域的辛劳，颂扬祖先护佑子孙扫平群雄、定鼎中原的恩德，并祈求祖先保佑后代兴旺发达。

从最初逐水草而居的游牧部落，到建立起北朝的第一个王朝，拓跋部经历了多少艰难坎坷才完成了统一北方的伟业！此后，拓跋氏崇汉尊儒，学习中原王朝政治制度，促进北方地区广泛而深刻的民族大融合，为隋唐的大一统奠定了基础。

公元471年，北魏孝文帝拓跋宏即位，他开展了轰轰烈烈的改革，迁都中原腹地洛阳，要求皇室和鲜卑人均改汉姓、着汉服、讲汉语，鼓励与汉人通婚，逐渐使拓跋鲜卑民族融入中华民族多元一体进程的滚滚洪流之中。

今天，当我们回望拓跋鲜卑时，那首让中华儿女传诵千古的北朝民歌又回响在耳际——史载，太武帝拓跋焘接受高车的归降，将他们安置在阴山放牧。高车又名“敕勒”，因此留下了“敕勒川”之名，并留下了这首最初用鲜卑语演唱的《敕勒歌》：

敕勒川，阴山下。天似穹庐，笼盖四野。天苍苍，野茫茫，风吹草低见牛羊。

The stone tablet tells the story of Tuoba Xianbei, who emerged in the wild forests of the Great Khingan Mountains, occupied the land of the Xiongnu, unified the northern China in the Northern and Southern Dynasties, and became a part of the multi-ethnic Chinese nation.

In 1979, Mi Wenping, head of Inner Mongolia Hulunbuir League Cultural Relics Center, in collaboration with his colleagues, successively conducted archeological investigation of Gaxian Cave, a natural cave ten kilometers northwest of Alihe Town in Oroqen Autonomous Banner, Hulunbuir League, for three times. On July 30, 1980, in the fourth-time investigation, they discovered the sacrificial odes carved on the stone wall by the emissaries of Emperor Taiwu of the Northern Wei.

In *Wei Shu* (《魏书》, *Book of Northern Wei*), it was recorded that in 443, Tuoba Tao, also known as Emperor Taiwu of the Northern Wei, who unified the northern China, dispatched officials to the Xianbei Mountain, a range of the Great Khingan Mountains. In the stone chamber of the cave where Tuoba ancestors lived, the officials read sacrificial odes and carved the stone tablet.

Tuoba Xianbei founded the Northern Wei Dynasty, the first dynasty of the Northern Dynasties, unifying northern China. Tuoba emperors revered Han culture and Confucianism, learnt the political systems of the Central Plains, deepened the cultural integration of ethnic groups in northern China, and laid a foundation for the grand unification of the Sui and Tang Dynasties.

According to historical records, the Gaoche people, known as Chile, pledged allegiance to the Northern Wei. Tuoba Tao ordered them to graze at the foot of the Yin Mountains, who left us the popular *Song of Chile* originally written in the Xianbei language:

By the side of the rill,
At the foot of the hill,
The grassland stretches' neath the firmament tranquil.
The boundless grassland lies
Beneath the boundless skies.
When the winds blow
And grass bends low,
My sheep and cattle will emerge before your eyes.
(The English translation by Xu Yuanchong)

历史上最著名的胡服易汉服的改革是由谁发起的？他为什么发起这场改革？

衣冠号令，华夏同风：北魏孝文帝改革

彩绘站立女俑

Standing Colored Female Figurine

文物简读

这件出土于洛阳杨机墓的北魏彩绘站立女俑，其上敛下丰的襦裙式着装，兼容了胡服的灵活方便与汉装的儒雅宽博，正是北魏孝文帝在鲜卑人中推行“改易汉俗”的场景再现。

“礼仪富盛”的长江之北

写成于公元6世纪的《洛阳伽蓝记》记录了一则有趣的故事：

南朝梁武帝萧衍派遣使者陈庆之到北魏都城洛阳。陈庆之本以为一旦渡过长江，便会看到在“夷狄”统治下的北方大地，应为一片文化“荒土”。但当他进入洛阳城后，却见眼前呈现出一片“礼仪富盛，人物殷阜”的景象，这让他大为震惊，不由得赞叹：“始知衣冠士族，并在中原。”

陈庆之在洛阳看到了什么样的“衣冠士族”？

从这件出土于洛阳杨机墓的北魏彩绘站立女俑，或许可见一斑。女俑面饰花钿，颊点红彩，眉眼描墨，口涂朱，梳双髻，发髻施黑彩，身着交领右衽宽袖衫，胸部束带，下着裙褶繁复的长裙。只见她右手轻拽裙摆，左手置于胸前，面露微笑，恬静怡然。这种上敛下丰的襦裙式着装，应是北魏孝文帝实行改革后，洛阳一带妇女们的典型服饰。这儒雅宽博的风格，不就是“衣冠士族”的形象？

一场轰轰烈烈的改革

建立北魏的拓跋珪曾宣称“《春秋》之义，大一统之美”。太武帝拓跋焘即位时，他大量重用汉人士族，把河西学者迁到首都平城，让鲜卑子弟学习儒典，于是出现了“儒林转兴”的情景。

名称：彩绘站立女俑

年代：北魏

规格：高18.4厘米

出土地点：河南省洛阳市宜阳县北魏杨机墓

收藏单位：洛阳博物馆

Name: Standing Colored Female Figurine

Historical Period: The Northern Wei Dynasty

Height: 18.4 cm

Excavation Site: The Tomb of Yang Ji (The Northern Wei Dynasty), Yiyang County, Luoyang, Henan Province

Housed in: Luoyang Museum

当从小深受汉文化熏陶的孝文帝拓跋宏亲政后，立即着手制礼作乐，推行一系列“以夏变夷”式的强制性汉化改革：

迁都洛阳：为便于学习和接受中原的先进文化，进一步加强对黄河流域的统治，孝文帝将国都从平城迁到洛阳。

尊奉孔子：迁都洛阳后，孝文帝下令修建孔庙，设立祭孔制度。

变革官制和律令：参照南朝典章制度变革北魏政治。

推行均田制和户调制：颁布均田令，对不同性别的成年百姓和奴婢、耕牛做出详尽的授田规定；授田有露田、桑田之别；露田种植谷物，不得买卖，70岁时交还国家；桑田种植桑、榆、枣树，不须交还国家，可出卖多余部分；授田时对老少残疾鳏寡给予适当的照顾。

改易汉俗：以汉语代替鲜卑语，以汉服代替鲜卑服，改鲜卑姓为汉姓，鼓励鲜卑贵族与汉人士族联姻。

这一系列轰轰烈烈的改革掀起了民族大交流大融合的一轮高潮。鲜卑人不仅大都穿上了宽袖阔带的汉服，变成了雅歌儒服的“衣冠士族”，而且充满自信地宣示自己是中华文化的正统继承者，将自己的王朝列入中华序列。

关于“拓跋”的释义

在进入中原建立北魏的过程中，鲜卑逐渐加深对中原华夏文化的认同。拓跋氏曾自认为是黄帝后裔——因为黄帝以“土德之瑞”称王，鲜卑族谓“土”为“拓”，谓“后”为“跋”，所以“拓跋氏”意即“黄帝土德的后代”。鲜卑将自己的祖先追认为与汉人同根同源的炎黄裔胄，这反映了中华文明强大的包容力和凝聚力。

当然，文化的融合并不是单方面的，这一时期北方民族上衣下裤的“裤褶服”，不仅在中原地区流行，在南方民间也得到了普及。正是在“汉化”与“胡化”的双重变奏中，中华文明的生命力不断得到滋养而愈发强大。

北魏孝文帝改革对北魏社会政治生活乃至整个中国历史产生了深远的影响。这一时期民族大融合的加速演进，为隋唐王朝结束长期分裂格局、重新走向更高水平的大一统局面，奠定了深厚的基础。

皇室、贵族鲜卑姓改汉姓对照表

鲜卑姓	汉姓
拓跋	元
邱穆陵	穆
步六孤	陆
贺赖	贺
独孤	刘
贺楼	楼
勿忸于	于
纥奚	嵇
尉迟	尉

It was unearthed from the tomb of Yang Ji, an official of the Northern Wei Dynasty. The female figurine wears *Ru* skirt (襦裙, short jacket and long skirt), which fuses the convenience of *Hu* (胡) dress with the elegance of Han dress, and represents the Han style-oriented reform of Emperor Xiaowen of Northern Wei among the Xianbei people.

The female figurine is adorned with flower-shaped pearl ornament, with red cheeks. Her eyebrows and eyes are painted with ink, and her mouth is painted bright red. Her hair is combed in two buns and painted black. She wears a cross-collar right-lapel wide-sleeve jacket (upper garment) and a long skirt with intricate pleats (lower garment), with the sash at her breast. She gently tugs at the hem of her skirt with the right hand and places her left hand on her chest. With a smile on the face, she looks calm and happy. *Ru* skirt was a typical dress of women in Luoyang after the reform of Emperor Xiaowen of Northern Wei.

Tuoba Hong, or Emperor Xiaowen of Northern Wei, became so well acculturated to the Han culture that he initiated a series of reforms upon ascending the throne. In order to learn the advanced culture of the Central Plains and strengthen the rule over the Yellow River Basin, Emperor Xiaowen moved the site of the capital to Luoyang from Pingcheng. He ordered to construct Confucian temples and respect Confucius. He promoted a number of political changes, made Chinese the official language of the court, ordered the nobles to adopt Chinese dress and family names, and advocated the intermarriage with the Han people. Significantly, he instituted the *juntian* (均田, equal-field) system of agriculture, providing the fiscal basis for the formation of the Sui and Tang Dynasties.

The reform of Emperor Xiaowen had a profound impact on the society and politics of the Northern Wei as well as the history of China. It deepened the cultural integration of ethnic groups, and laid a solid foundation for the grand unification of the Sui and Tang Dynasties.

The Family Names of the Xianbei Nobles and Their Han Counterparts

Xianbei	Han
Tuoba 拓跋	Yuan 元
Qiumuling 丘穆陵	Mu 穆
Buliugu 步六孤	Lu 陆
Helai 贺赖	He 贺
Dugu 独孤	Liu 刘
Helou 贺楼	Lou 楼
Wuniuyu 勿忸于	Yu 于
Hexi 纥奚	Ji 嵇
Yuchi 尉迟	Wei 尉

是什么造就了云冈石窟这一恢宏的世界文化遗产?

佛教走向中国化的鸿篇巨制

云冈石窟第20窟

48

The 20th Cave of Yungang Grottoes

文物简读

云冈石窟与敦煌石窟、龙门石窟、麦积山石窟并称中国四大石窟，2001年被联合国教科文组织列入《世界文化遗产名录》。云冈石窟第20窟是著名的“昙曜五窟”之一，其主像双腿呈跏趺坐，双手结禅定印，比例匀称，造型简洁，是北魏拓跋鲜卑大兴佛教的直接体现，也是佛教自此开始走向中国化的体现。

不可思议的佛国世界

石窟依山而凿，东西绵延约一公里，佛龛1100多个，造像5.9万余尊，雕刻面积达1.8万平方米。在层见叠出的石雕群中，雕像最高达17米，最矮仅两厘米，既气魄宏大，又精致细腻，满目庄严，蔚为大观。

公元5世纪，北魏著名地理学家郦道元来到云冈石窟，眼前的壮景变成了他在《水经注》中的赞叹：“凿石开山，因岩结构，真容巨壮，世法所希。”1400多年后，著名作家冰心来到云冈石窟，她也写出了自己的惊叹：“万亿化身，罗刻满山，鬼斧神工，骇人心目。……事后追忆，亦如梦入天宫，醒后心自知而口不能道，此时方知文字之无用了。”

2001年，云冈石窟被联合国教科文组织列入《世界文化遗产名录》，成为中华民族为世界创造的一笔宝贵文化财富。

名称：云冈石窟第20窟
年代：北魏文成帝时期
规格：主佛高13.7米
现存地点：山西省大同市

Name: The 20th Cave of Yungang Grottoes
Historical Period: In the reign of Emperor Wencheng of the Northern Wei Dynasty
Height: 13.7 m (The Big Buddha)
Housed in: Datong, Shanxi Province

这样伟大的世界文化遗产，是谁为我们留下的？

中国石雕艺术发展的一块里程碑

云冈石窟是拓跋鲜卑为中华民族留下的伟大作品。

公元460年，北魏文成帝接受高僧昙曜的建议，修建五处石窟。《魏书·释老志》载："昙曜白帝，于京城西武州塞，凿山石壁，开窟五所，镌建佛像各一。高者七十尺，次六十尺，雕饰奇伟，冠于一世。"这就是著名的昙曜五窟。由此，北魏开启了长达六十年的云冈石窟开凿史，在北魏孝文帝迁都洛阳之前达到顶峰。这一时期，北魏渐至最繁华、最稳定的阶段，佛教在北魏皇室的推崇下，已经具有了一定的普遍性和民众性。正因为如此，云冈石窟的开凿如火如荼。

云冈石窟是中国佛教艺术第一个巅峰时期的经典建筑杰作。在雕造技法上，云冈石窟继承和发展了秦汉时期传统雕刻艺术的优良传统，又吸收和融合犍陀罗艺术的精华，由此创造了中国传统石雕艺术第一次古今中外的大融合，创建出独特的云冈风格，成为中国石雕艺术发展史上的一块里程碑。

胡人政权：弘扬佛教文化的载舟人

佛教在西汉末年传入中国，到南北朝时迎来了一个重要的弘扬期。在此过程中，建立前秦、后凉、北凉、后秦的少数民族政权，都对佛教的传播做出了突出贡献。

一度统一北方的氐族前秦皇帝苻坚，曾万分仰慕西域的佛学家、翻译家和思想家鸠摩罗什，他派大将吕光经略西域之时，就千叮万嘱要迎请鸠摩罗什"入辅中国"。前秦灭亡后，鸠摩罗什又受羌族后秦皇帝姚兴之邀，于公元401年到长安译经弘法。经此种种，鸠摩罗什翻译了大量高水平的佛经，并培养了一批投身佛教事业的杰出人才，对中国佛教的发展产生了重大的影响。

这一时期，出自卢水胡的北凉政权修建了马蹄寺、千佛洞、金塔寺等佛教文化圣地，为佛教文化的兴盛做出了重要贡献。到北魏时期，佛教已成为北方各民族的普遍信仰。

北魏道武帝拓跋珪既好黄老，信奉道教，也阅读佛经，礼敬名僧。他下令在京都平城为沙门建佛塔、佛殿、讲堂和禅室，请赵郡沙门法果统辖僧徒。北魏明元帝拓跋嗣承袭父业，道、佛二教并奉，从京城到各地广设佛像。公元439年，当北魏太武帝拓跋焘攻灭北凉时，塔寺甚多、僧人工匠无数的凉州佛教借机东传，极大地促进了北魏佛教的繁荣兴盛。

佛教的传播直接推动了佛教石窟艺术的极大发展。闻名古今的大同云冈石窟、洛阳龙门石窟，在这一时期由北魏政权主持开凿，显示出空前绝后、非同凡响的宏伟气势。作为北魏在北方的政治、经济中心，平城形成了被称为"平城模式"的佛教艺术形式，对当时中原地区的佛教艺术发展起着指导作用。

北魏后期，尤其是经过孝文帝改革后，拓跋鲜卑与汉族进行了深度的融合，佛教领域亦然，不管云冈石窟晚期还是洛阳龙门石窟，其造像风格都由鲜卑化转变为汉化特征，为佛教实现中国化、融入中华文明奠定了基础。

Yungang Grottoes, Dunhuang Grottoes, Longmen Grottoes and Maijishan Grottoes are collectively called the "Four Major Grottoes in China". In 2001, Yungang Grottoes was included in *The World Heritage Lists* by the UNESCO World Heritage Committee. The 20th Cave is one of the famous "Five Caves Carved by Tan Yao". The big Buddha sits cross-legged, and the hands show a *mudra* of meditation. With a symmetrical proportion and simple shape, the 20th Cave saw the palmy days of Buddhism in the Northern Wei Dynasty and signaled the development of Buddhism in China.

Yungang Grottoes is carved on the mountain, stretching about one kilometer from the east to the west, with over 1,100 Buddhist niches, over 59,000 statues and a carving area of over 18,000 square meters. The highest statue reaches 17 meters and the smallest statue only reaches two centimeters. The statues look both grand and exquisite, presenting a splendid sight.

In "A Brief History of Buddhism and Taoism" of *Book of Northern Wei* (《魏书・释老志》), the birth of "Five Caves Carved by Tan Yao" was recorded as follows: "Monk Tan Yao advised the emperor to construct five caves at rock cliff in the west of Wuzhou Mountain at Western Capital (Now Datong), each with a Buddha statue. The higher stood as high as 70 *chi* (尺, one *chi* equals 1/3 meters) and others 60 *chi*. The carvings were amazingly magnificent with eternal charm." Yungang Grottoes had been carved for 60 years ever since. Before Emperor Xiaowen moved the capital site to Luoyang (494), the Northern Wei Dynasty enjoyed economic prosperity and stable politics. The emperors of the Northern Wei adored Buddhism, and spread Buddhism among the public. These set off an upsurge of the construction of Buddhist caves.

Yungang Grottoes represents a classic architectural masterpiece of Chinese Buddhist art in the first peak. In carving techniques, Yungang Grottoes developed traditional carving arts in the Qin and Han Dynasties and absorbed the essence of the Gandhara art, which created the unique Yungang style and meant a milestone in the development history of Chinese stone carving art.

看似平凡、简单的马镫，为什么在世界历史上产生了巨大的影响？

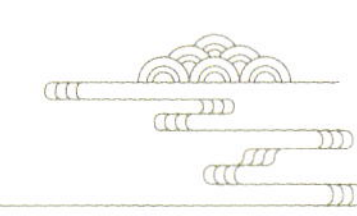

“中国靴子”的千年漫游

铜鎏金木芯马镫

Bronze Gilded Stirrups with Wooden Loops

文物简读

马镫的发明，是中华文明对世界的一项重要贡献。这副出土于辽宁北票冯素弗墓，年代为公元415年的铜鎏金木芯马镫，是迄今为止世界上最早的有绝对年代可考的马镫。它是马镫起源于中国的又一重要物证。

世界上最早的马镫产生于中国

马镫，是指垂悬于马腹两侧供骑马者踏脚的马具，兼备上马和保持身体在马上的稳定、平衡功能。1958年，湖南长沙南郊金盆岭的西晋墓出土了一批陶俑，其中有三件陶马俑的前鞍桥左侧下垂一个三角形的镫，右侧没有。这是目前考古发现最早的具有明确纪年（永宁二年，302）的马镫资料，只不过是单镫。学者认为这种单镫是为了上马蹬踏所用。尽管单镫在功能上无法与双镫相提并论，但是它迈开了真正意义的马镫的第一步。

中国考古发现的马镫实物，还有河南安阳孝民屯154号晋墓出土的单马镫，以及辽宁朝阳袁台子东晋墓出土的双马镫等。其中，辽宁北票冯素弗墓出土的一副铜鎏金木芯马镫，由桑木条揉成木芯，外覆盖有鎏金铜片，墓主为北燕宰相冯素弗，明确纪年为公元415年，是考古所见年代最早的马镫实物。

正是因为这一系列考古证据，英国著名的科学史学家李约瑟以及日本、朝鲜的学者都认为世界上最早的马镫产生于中国。中国社科院考古所研究员杨泓在《冯素弗墓马镫和中国马具装铠的发展》一文中梳理了马镫的考古出土情况，认为在东晋十六国时期，中国各地都已普遍使用马镫。北京大学齐东方教授在《中国早期马镫的有关问题》一文中也指出：“在4世纪之前，马镫已经出现，并且是游牧于中国北方的骑马民族发明的。”

名称：铜鎏金木芯马镫

年代：北燕太平七年（415）

规格：高23厘米

出土地点：辽宁省北票市冯素弗墓

收藏单位：辽宁省博物馆

Name: Bronze Gilded Stirrups with Wooden Loops

Historical Period: The 7th year of Emperor Taiping of the Northern Yan (415)

Height: 23 cm

Excavation Site: The Tomb of Feng Sufu, Beipiao City, Liaoning Province

Housed in: Liaoning Provincial Museum

“中国靴子”

马镫被西方马文化研究界称为“中国靴子”。顾名思义，正如穿上靴子可在砾石遍布的地面自由而快速地行走一样，“中国靴子”为在马上快速行动和全方位施展马术提供了无限的可能。在马镫发明前，骑乘者的双腿只能悬空垂荡，当飞奔或腾越时，一般人难以保持身体的稳定和平衡，必须还得依靠手来辅助。马镫通过固定双脚提供横向稳定性，将人和马结为一个整体，这就解放了双手，使骑射、刺、劈等杀伤技能与马的冲击力融为一体，大大提升了骑兵的战斗力。

北燕冯素弗墓出土的这件铜鎏金木芯马镫，证实了中国古代少数民族鲜卑在发明或者说在改进马镫上的卓越贡献。北燕继承了后燕、前燕在燕山以北以及辽东的疆域，而前燕的创建者慕容皝之所以能统一东部鲜卑，其克敌制胜的法宝就是不断壮大的骑兵力量。鲜卑在普遍使用马铠、马镫和高鞒马鞍后，不仅拥有了完备的马具，而且成立了重甲骑兵，作战能力大为增强，故而能够入主中原、统一北方。

马镫传入欧洲

马镫传入西方后，成为欧洲骑士的重要装备，从而促进了这一欧洲中世纪新的社会阶级的诞生。

那么，马镫是怎样传入欧洲的？

追溯历史，那个曾经在中国北方草原叱咤一时而又悄然消失的游牧族群——柔然，扮演了极为重要的角色。

公元4世纪末，柔然兴起于漠北地区，主要由匈奴、鲜卑、高车等许多民族和部落所组成。“柔然”一名始于部落首领车鹿会的自称，有学者认为是“聪明”“贤明”之意。

柔然政权历经北魏太武帝拓跋焘的重创以及高车族副伏罗部阿伏至罗率十余万部众脱离柔然之变故后，开始由盛转衰。至北魏末期六镇起义之后，柔然可汗阿那瓌乘机中兴，成为中国北部草原最强的军事力量。北魏分裂后，东魏和西魏争相与柔然结好，以获取柔然的支持。公元552年，草原新兴力量突厥首领土门（伊利可汗）因求婚于阿那瓌被拒绝，联合高车击败柔然，阿那瓌兵败自杀。在凄绝的残阳里，一部分柔然部众辗转西走，从此柔然淹没于中国的历史长河中。

Stirrup meant an important contribution of Chinese civilization to the world. The bronze gilded stirrups were unearthed from the tomb of Feng Sufu in Beipiao, Liaoning Province, dating back to 415. As the earliest stirrup in the world, it incontrovertibly proves that stirrup originates in China.

Stirrups are two metal loops which are attached to a horse's saddle by long pieces of leather. One places his feet in the stirrups when riding a horse. Stirrups maintain the stability and balance of body on the horse. The loops are made from mulberry wood and wrapped with gilded bronze.

Joseph Needham, a famous British historian of science, as well as several Japanese and Korean scholars, believes that the first stirrup in the world emerged in China. In the article "The Stirrups Unearthed from the Tomb of Feng Sufu and the Development of Chinese Harness and Armor", Yang Hong, a research fellow at the Institute of Archaeology, CASS, discusses the archaeological discovery of the stirrups, concluding that stirrups were widely used in various regions of China in the Eastern Jin Dynasty & the Sixteen Kingdoms Period. In the article "On the Early Chinese Stirrups", Qi Dongfang at Peking University affirms that "Before the 4th century, stirrups had already appeared and been invented by the nomadic tribes that rode horses in northern China".

The bronze gilded stirrups materialize the outstanding contributions of the Xianbei, an ancient Chinese tribe, to inventing and improving stirrup. The Xianbei people used stirrups and saddles with high bow, which made their harness more complete. Additionally, the use of horse armor triggered the formation of armored cavalry, tremendously enhanced the military strength of the Xianbei soldiers, and helped the Xianbei to unify northern China.

楷书，一个了不起的文化成就，为何是在晋室南渡的动荡背景下完成的？

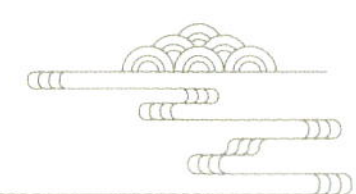

南北交融中的文化高峰

晋人《乐毅论》楷书法帖

Regular-Script Model Book of Wang Xizhi's Calligraphic Work *My Views on Yue Yi* (《乐毅论》)

文物简读

五胡入华，晋室南迁。在历史的大动荡之中，中华文明依然生生不息。在南迁士大夫手中，汉字楷书发展到完善的境地，汉字书法艺术矗立起了第一个历史高峰——以《乐毅论》为代表的王羲之书法，正是分裂格局下中华文明依然生机勃勃、健康发展的象征。

汉字书法走向完善

在汉字书法中，楷书被称为“正书”，又称“真书”，因为“形体方正，笔画平直，可作楷模”，后统称为“楷书”。

楷书的鼻祖是钟繇。东汉末年，汉字书写逐渐发展成为一种专门艺术，即书法。到曹魏时期，钟繇以篆、隶、真、行、草闻名天下，其中最擅长的就是楷书。钟繇的楷书笔法清劲、结体高古、书风纯朴，《宣和书谱》赞其“备尽法度，为正书之祖”。

晋室南迁之际，东晋开国元勋王导把他所珍藏的钟繇的楷书作品《宣示表》缝藏在衣带中，带到江南，送给他的侄子王羲之。王羲之有深厚的家学渊源，其书法启蒙老师正是深得钟繇妙传的著名书法家卫夫人。十四五岁时，他又师从“书画称江左第一”的叔父王廙，得众体之技法。20岁后，王羲之的正书、行书效法钟繇，去其隶意，变其古朴自然为妩媚遒劲，完善了楷书之法，确立了今体楷书的风貌。

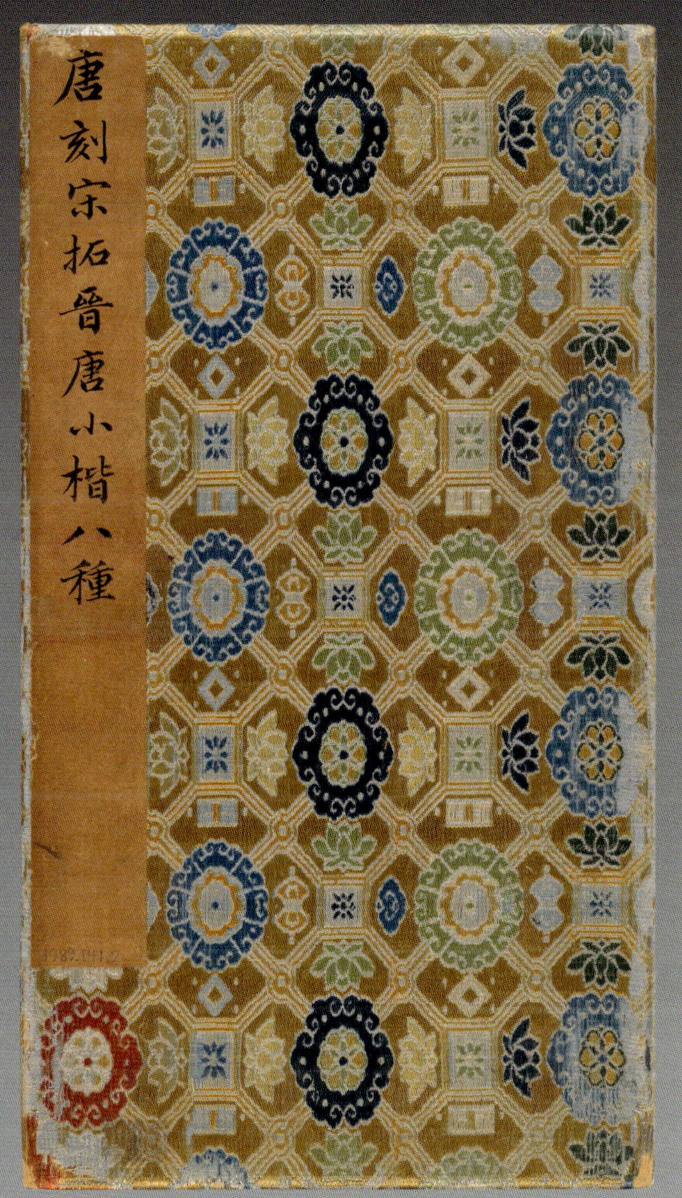

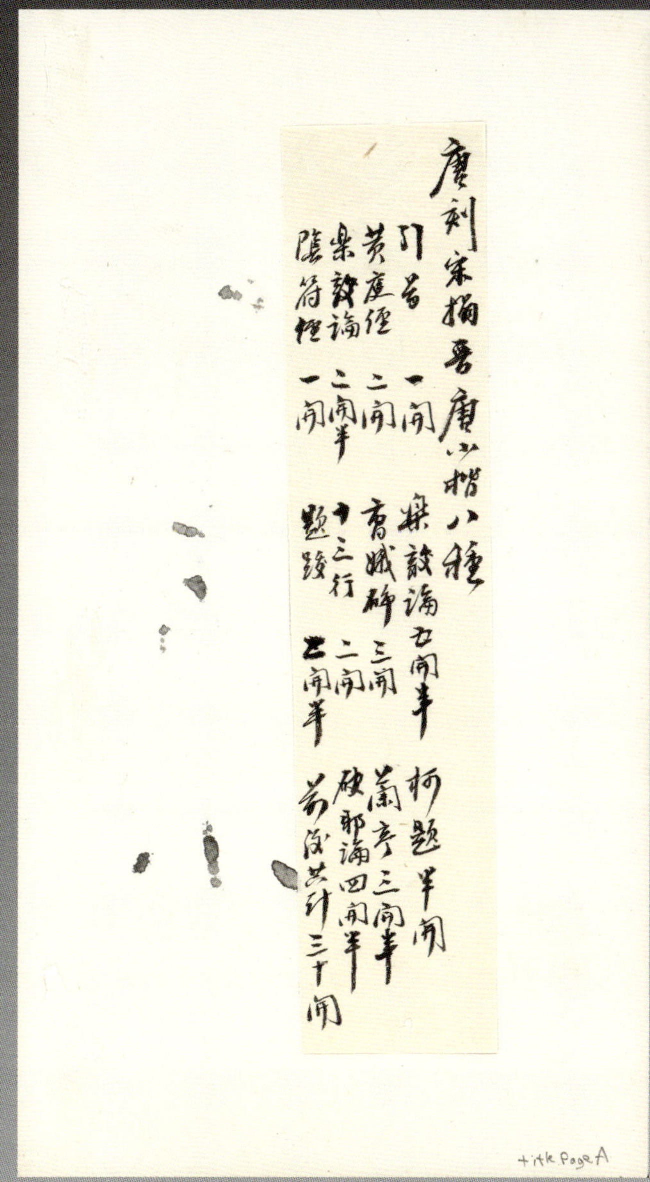

名称：晋人《乐毅论》楷书法帖

年代：唐刻宋拓本

规格：版心高25.1厘米，版心宽9.7厘米

收藏单位：美国纽约大都会艺术博物馆

Name: Regular-Script Model Book of Wang Xizhi's Calligraphic Work *My Views on Yue Yi* (《乐毅论》)

Historical Period: Inscriptions in the Tang Dynasty, Rubbings in the Song Dynasty

Height: 25.1 cm, Width: 9.7 cm (The Type Page)

Housed in: Metropolitan Museum of Art, New York, the USA

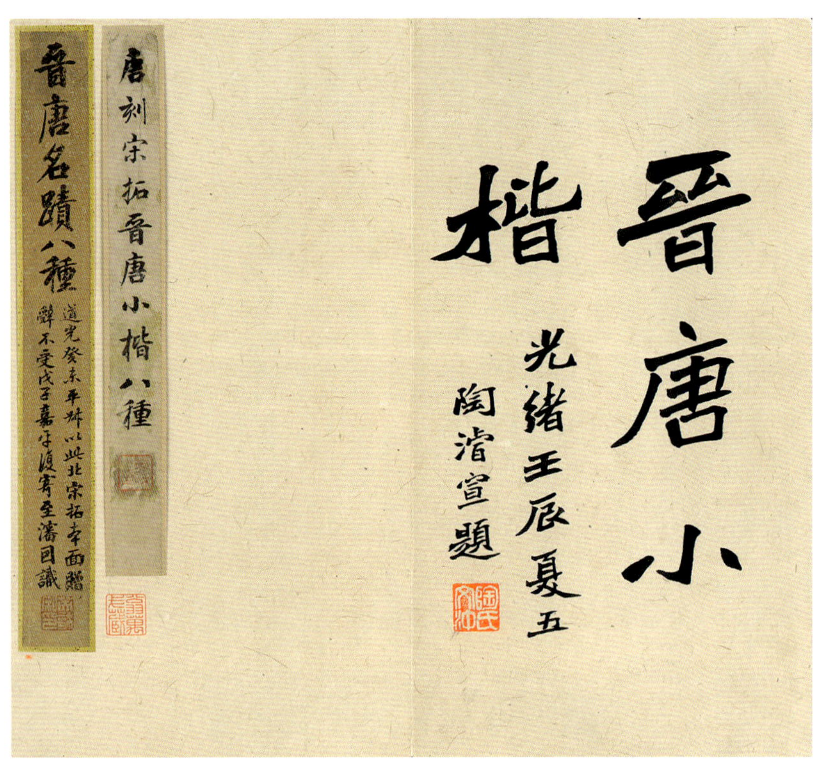

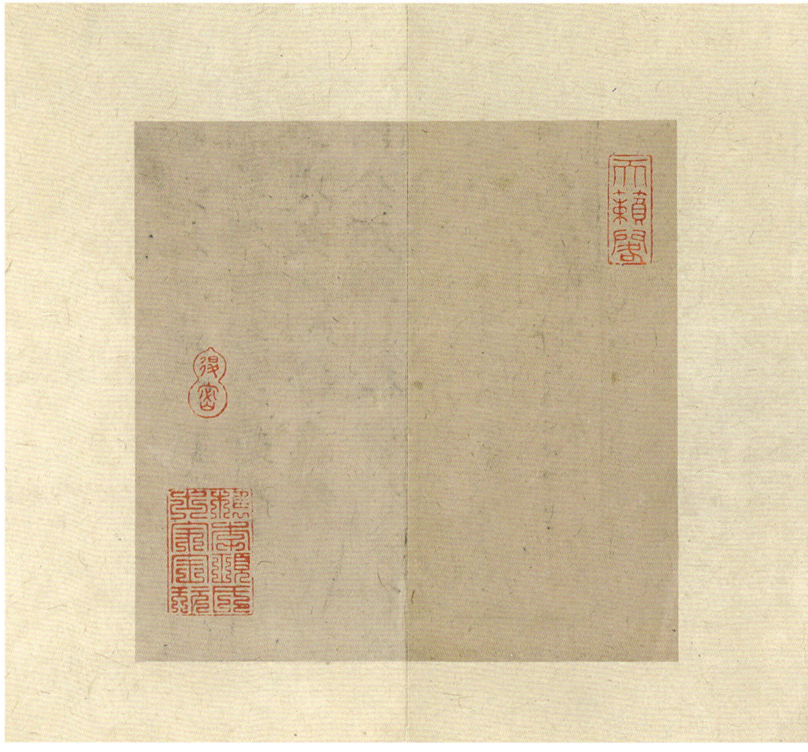

《乐毅论》为三国时期魏国夏侯玄所撰，文章讲述战国时代燕国名将乐毅征讨齐国大胜时却围两城而不攻的故事，赞颂了乐毅仁义、仁慈的美德。王羲之特书之，给儿子王献之临摹。这幅书法作品王羲之自评“有君子之风”；唐代书法家褚遂良赞其“笔势精妙，备尽楷则”，称之为“正书第一”；清朝书法家钱泳赞其“冲融大雅，方圆适中”。王献之、智永、褚遂良、虞世南、欧阳询、赵孟頫、俞和、文征明、董其昌等大书法家，均从中学习用笔的法度及气韵。据说唐太宗珍爱它的程度一点都不逊于昭陵六骏，还把它刻在石上，随葬于昭陵。千余年来，《乐毅论》成为百代之楷则，也是今天人们学习小楷的最佳范本。不过，由于王羲之的原帖已佚，现在我们见到的《乐毅论》多为宋以后的摹刻本。

《乐毅论》楷书法帖标志着中国楷书字体发展成熟。楷书成形，意味着汉字手写正体字走向完善，汉字书写走向规范化和标准化。而中华文明取得的这一新的发展成就，是在晋室南迁、建立起偏安江南的东晋政权后实现的。这表明虽然中国进入南北对峙的历史格局，但中华文明依然生生不息。

南方的文化高峰

南北朝的历史大动荡之中，中华文明依然延续着旺盛的生命力：北朝方面，入主中原的民族政权都尊崇汉学，使中华文明得以延续并注入新鲜血液；南朝方面，渡江避难的世家大族如琅琊王氏、陈郡谢氏、陈郡袁氏、兰陵萧氏等，由于在政治上拥有较高的地位，加上文化底蕴深厚，文化大家辈出，他们将中原文化有力地传播到了南方，促进了南北文化的深层次融合。

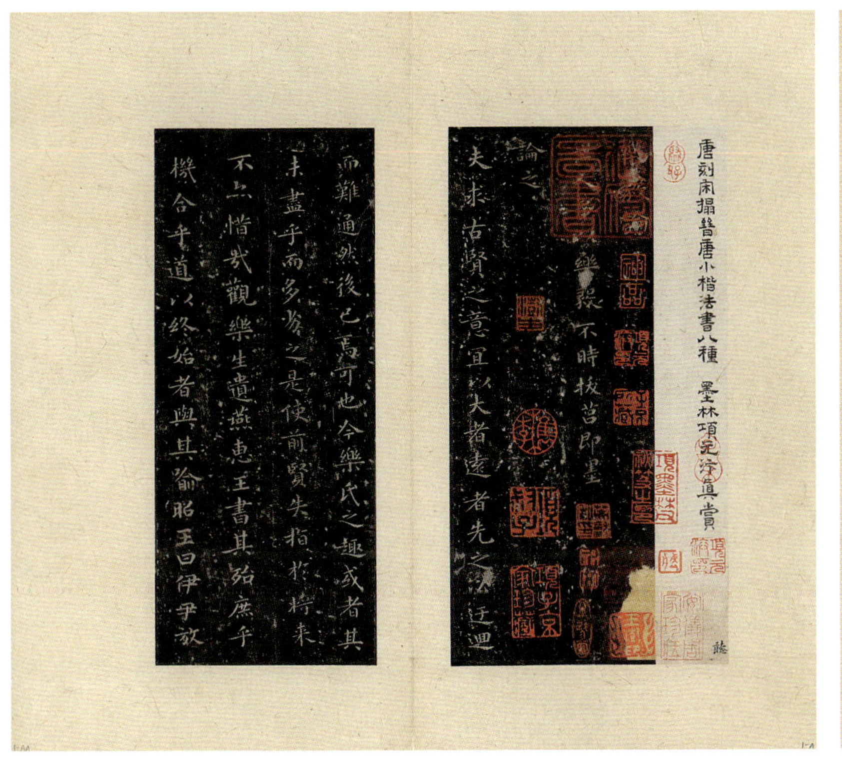

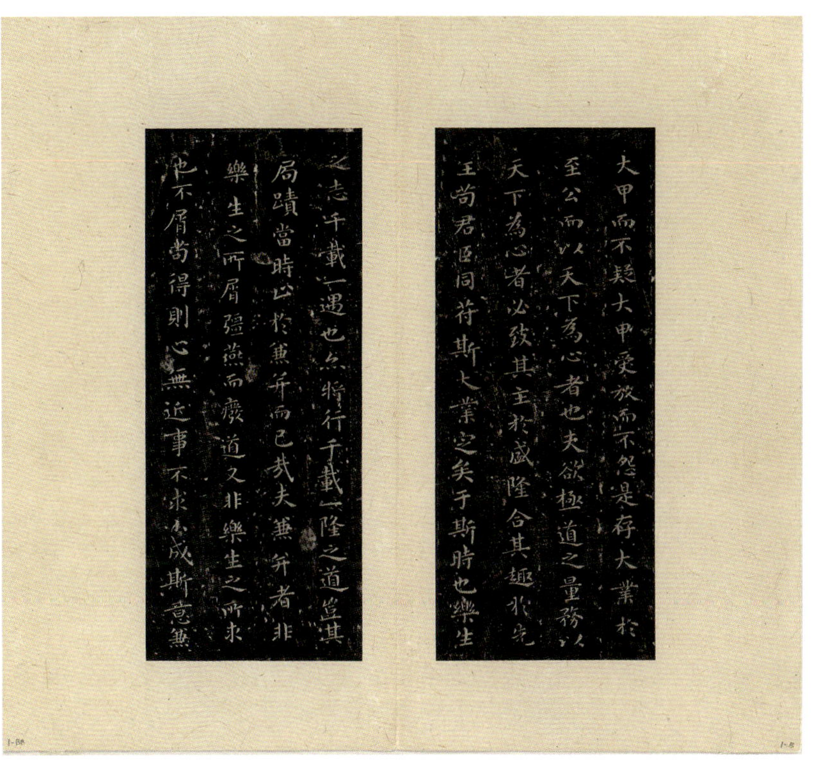

这一时期，北方士民纷纷涌入江南，形成了“衣冠南渡”的潮流。据统计，南迁的北方人口达到90万。这场南渡不仅仅是人口的大迁徙，也是文化的大迁徙，它带来了北方士族文化与江南吴越文化的碰撞、交流，从而成就了中华文明在书法、文学、绘画、雕塑等方面的一个文化高峰。

仰望这一时期群星闪耀的天空，书法上有王羲之高高矗立，其《乐毅论》《兰亭序》千古流传；文学上有开创田园诗派的陶渊明，其《归园田居》亲切有味；有开创山水诗派的谢灵运，其《山居赋》自然灵动；美术上有被誉为“画绝”的顾恺之，其《洛神赋图》《女史箴图》等经典名作和“迁想妙得”“以形写神”的理论，为中国传统绘画的发展奠定了基础。此外，刘义庆的《世说新语》、刘勰的《文心雕龙》、范晔的《后汉书》等影响深远。

与此同时，东晋朝廷将南方少数族群纳入编户，促使以往从事渔猎的南方民族转向农耕。这些民族历经东晋、南朝近三百年同汉族交错杂居的生活，彼此在文化上互相影响，在血缘上互相融合，从而为隋唐时期更高水平的统一和文化一体化准备了条件。

In the 4th century, the Five *Hu* came to the Central Plains and the nobles of the Western Jin moved to the south. Amidst a time of change and turbulence did Chinese civilization continue to advance. Under the efforts of literati and officials, regular script matured, standardizing the writing of Chinese characters. Wang Xizhi's calligraphic work *My Views on Yue Yi* testified to the first peak of the art of Chinese calligraphy as well as the vitality of Chinese civilization in the south-north stalemate.

In Chinese calligraphy, regular script is also termed *Zheng Shu* (正书, model writing), because "its form is square and its strokes are straight". In the late Eastern Han Dynasty, the writing of Chinese characters developed into a unique art, or calligraphy. In the Kingdom of Wei, Zhong Yao was famed for seal script, official script, regular script, running script and cursive script, especially regular script. As stated in *Xuanhe Shupu* (《宣和书谱》, *Calligraphic Works in the Reign of Emperor Xuanhe*), Zhong Yao's writing "matures in rules and standards, and breeds regular script". With clear and vigorous brushwork, archaic structure and simple style, Zhong Yao was regarded as father of regular script.

My Views on Yue Yi was an essay written by Xiahou Xuan in the Kingdom of Wei. Xiahou Xuan told the story of Yue Yi, a famous general of the State of Yan, who besieged two cities of the State of Qi and protected the citizens, and praised the humane conduct of Yue Yi. To Wang

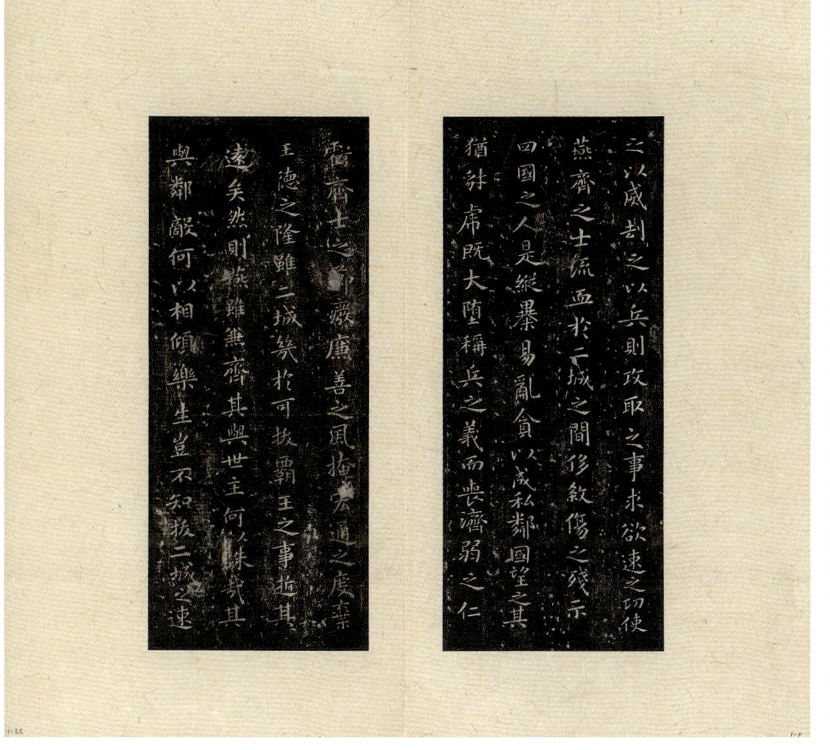

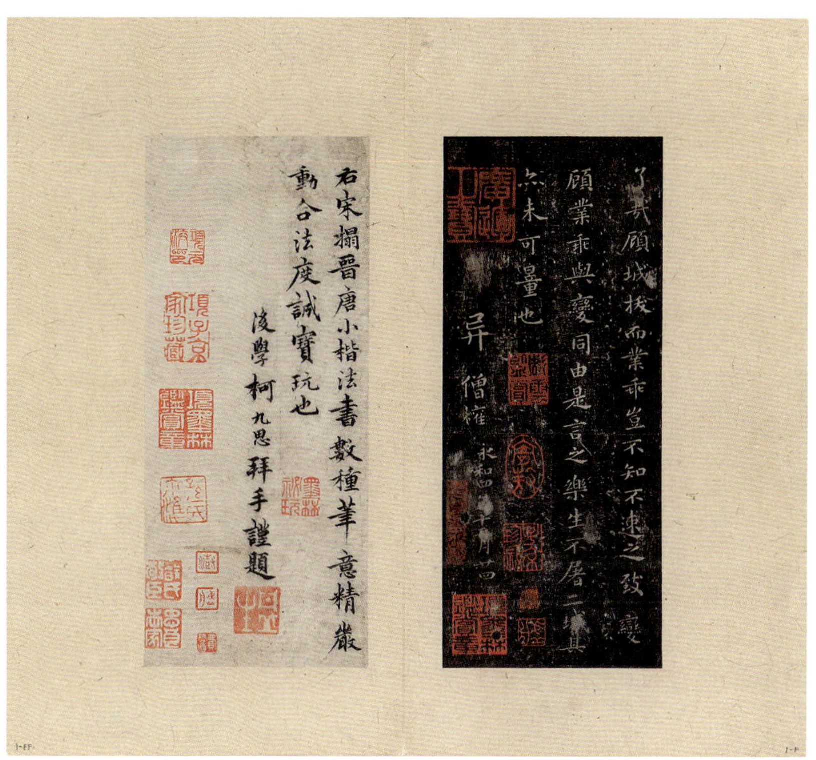

Xizhi, Yue Yi was an ideal *jun zi* or Confucianist gentleman. Wang Xizhi wrote the essay so that his son Wang Xianzhi can copy it. Chu Suiliang, a calligrapher in the Tang Dynasty, extolled Wang Xizhi's writing as "the best regular script work" that embodied "marvelous brush use and perfect rules of regular script". Qian Yong, a critic in the Qing Dynasty, spoke highly of the "harmony, elegance and moderation" in Wang Xizhi's work. Great calligraphers, including Wang Xianzhi, Zhi Yong, Chu Suiliang, Yu Shinan, Ouyang Xun, Zhao Mengfu, Yu He, Wen Zhengming and Dong Qichang, all learnt the brush use and artistic style of Wang Xizhi. Emperor Taizong of Tang treasured Wang Xizhi's *My Views on Yue Yi* as much as *The Stone Carving of Six Steeds of Zhaoling Mausoleum*. He carved it on a stone and buried it in Zhaoling Mausoleum. For more than 1,000 years, Wang Xizhi's *My Views on Yue Yi* has been the best model for people to learn the rules of regular script and regular script in small characters (*Xiao Kai*, 小楷). As Wang Xizhi's original work was lost, the copybooks we use today are generally rubbings in the Song Dynasty.

南北朝有多少古代民族融入了汉族之中?

民族大杂居：碰撞中的民族大融合

徐显秀墓壁画

The Mural Unearthed from the Tomb of Xu Xianxiu

文物简读

视野开阔宏大，色彩斑斓如新，人物栩栩如生，徐显秀墓壁画深刻再现了南北朝时期民族大杂居、大融合的社会面貌。

名称：徐显秀墓壁画
年代：北齐
规格：通高约480厘米，通长1930厘米，人物高140—180厘米
出土地点：山西省太原市王家峰村王墓坡

Name: The Mural Unearthed from the Tomb of Xu Xianxiu
Historical Period: The Northern Qi Dynasty
Total Height: *c.* 480 cm, Total Length: 1,930 cm
Height (Figures): 140–180 cm
Excavation Site: Wangmupo Hillside, Wangjiafeng Village, Taiyuan, Shanxi Province

多民族混杂交融的社会面貌

这是一幅气势恢宏的壁画。我们仿佛看到一支八十多人的胡汉混合仪仗队，从公元5世纪的时光深处缓缓走来。那匹高大神俊的枣红马在队列中特别惹人注目，佩剑武士、旗手和马夫站在马前，捧官印、扛胡床的侍从跟在马后。假如坐在帷幔之中那位身披兽皮大衣、雍容华贵的男主人（北面壁画右）起身上马，必有气宇轩昂、不怒自威的风仪。而那位端庄优雅的女主人（北面壁画左）应当坐在那辆华丽无比的牛车上，后面跟着捧披风、包袱、梳妆盒的侍女……

再仔细看——那辆金黄色车轮的牛车，华盖后有一胡人，他头戴毡帽，浓眉大眼，络腮胡子，身着翻领长衫，脚蹬紫色长靴，正扭头向后，似乎在小心翼翼地等待女主人上车。牛车后的伞盖下，有两个头戴卷曲发套的侍女，这样的发型在中国古代十分罕见，显然透露着复杂的外来文化信息。其中身着红色长裙的侍女走在后面，她的裙上饰有联珠纹，联珠环绕着一个头戴莲花冠的人头像。据学者考证，这种花纹“是伊朗系统的图像进入佛教王国以后，与佛教图像相融合的反映，是伊朗—印度混同文化东渐的结果”。

再看北面壁画，正中帷帐高悬，男女乐伎或弹四弦曲项琵琶、五弦、竖箜篌，或吹笙、横笛，或拍钹——既有来自中原的传统乐器，又有充满异域色彩的陌生乐器……

这幅2002年在山西太原王家峰村王墓坡考古发现的徐显秀墓壁画，从人物形象、装饰图案到吹奏乐器，都带着如此浓烈的多民族交融特点，呈现出南北朝时期民族大杂居、大融合的典型社会面貌。

跌宕起伏的人生

墓主人徐显秀跌宕起伏的人生故事，折射出南北朝时期多民族混杂交融的历史情景。

徐颖，字显秀，一个生长于河北的汉人，祖父和父亲都曾担任北魏的边镇官员。虽出身于汉人家庭，但因自幼成长于多民族杂居的环境，徐显秀深受彪悍民风的熏陶，少年时就显出慷慨任侠之气。在他的人生经历中，有两个对他影响极深的重要人物，一个是胡人出身的尔朱荣，契胡族群的首领；一个是汉人出身的高欢，一位典型的鲜卑化汉人，不仅会说鲜卑话，还拥有一个鲜卑名字——贺六浑。史称高欢“累世北边，故习其俗，遂同鲜卑”。

尔朱荣在镇压北朝六镇起义的过程中，积累起雄厚的军事实力。公元528年，北魏胡太后杀死孝明帝。尔朱荣以替孝明帝报仇的名义进军洛阳，将胡太后、皇帝和大臣王公等两千余人沉入黄河，制造了“河阴之变”的惨案，后因独断专行、把控朝政而被孝庄帝诛杀。

尔朱荣被杀后，侄子尔朱兆掌控了实权。此时高欢闪亮登场，他先是韬光养晦，发展自己的势力，最终铲除尔朱氏集团，北魏分裂成东魏和西魏，高欢成为东魏的实际操控人。

徐显秀先是投奔尔朱荣，后又追随高欢，依靠战功稳步升迁，其为人处世之道，颇得益于这两位乱世枭雄。高欢之子高澄取代东魏建立北齐后，徐显秀再次因战功被封为武安王，成为鲜卑北齐政权中显赫的汉人权贵。

公元571年，徐显秀于晋阳去世，结束了风云变幻的一生，享年70岁。

南北民族大杂居

魏晋南北朝，中华大地上出现了民族大迁徙、大流动、大融合的浪潮。经此一个时代，汉人的血液中融进了复杂多元的新成分。在北方，五胡入华人口达到540万，到北朝结束时，他们均已成为汉人的一员。在南方，随晋室南迁的汉人九十多万，他们在向南方传播中原文化的同时，也带动了南方少数民族融入汉人之中。经东晋和南朝近200年，融入汉人的南方少数民族人口有一百多万。

南北朝的人口大交融情形极为复杂。比如鲜卑，内部就杂糅着很多其他民族成分。拓跋鲜卑初期吸收了大量匈奴人，南迁过程中又吸收了氐、羌、乌桓、柔然、丁零、高车、月氏等。迁都洛阳以后，有很多域外族群前来归附，“自葱岭以西，至于大秦（古罗马），百国千城，莫不款附”，迁入洛阳的西域各国人等“万有余家”。此外，鲜卑与吐谷浑、柔然、突厥等的政治联姻和商贸往来也促使各民族杂居共处。

而在南方，东晋和南朝时期的少数族群主要有蛮、僚、俚。蛮主要有盘瓠蛮和廪君蛮的后裔；僚、俚则分布在今广西、贵州深山，往往“依树积木，以居其上”，过着巢居生活。针对盘瓠蛮和廪君蛮，东晋和南朝设置左郡、左县加以管理，使其从山地走向平原，从渔猎转向农耕；在僚、俚地区，对“熟僚”采取纳入编户的办法，对居住在大山里的“生僚”则采取羁縻怀柔政策，使之与南朝建立起朝贡互市的关系。纳入编户的南方少数民族，历经东晋、南朝近三百年同汉族交错杂居的生活，到隋初已大部分融入汉族。特别是汉中地区的僚族，“富室者，颇参夏人为婚，衣服、居处、言语，殆与华不别”；两广、海南地区的俚族也“渐慕华风……椎跣变为冠带，侏离化为弦诵，才贤辈出，科甲蝉联，彬彬然，不亚于中土”。

南北方族群在文化和血缘上的融合，为多元一体的中华民族迎来下一次大统一和大繁荣准备了充分的条件。

东汉至隋初内迁并融入汉人的北方少数族群人口

族称	迁入时间	迁入人口（万人）
匈奴	东汉	60
羯	东汉	40（其中被冉魏屠杀20万）
氐	东汉、三国	44
羌	两汉	76
乌桓	东汉、三国	40
鲜卑（含杂胡）	西晋至十六国	300
合计 540		

With grand scale and brilliant color, the mural realistically represents the ethnic integration and communication in the Southern and Northern Dynasties.

The mural was about a guard of honor in the 5th century, comprising more than 80 Han and *Hu* (胡) people. The tall and majestic jujube red horse was particularly eye-catching in the queue. The man with sword, the flagman and the groom stood in front of the horse, and attendants holding official seals and carrying *Hu Chuang* (胡床, a foldable and lightweight seat in ancient times) followed the horse. Dressed in a fur coat, the *distingué* male master (right of the northern mural) sat in the curtain hangings. The female master (left of the northern mural) sat on the magnificent ox cart, followed by maids holding the cloak, bundle and dressing box.

Behind the canopy of the ox cart with golden wheels was a man with a *Hu* blood. He wore a felt hat, a lapel shirt and purple boots, with thick eyebrows, big eyes and large whiskers. He was turning his head backwards, as if cautiously waiting for the female master to board the cart. Under the canopy were two maids wearing curly hair wigs. The hairstyle was rarely seen in ancient China, with exotic color. The maid dressed in red long skirt followed the two maids. Her skirt was adorned with beaded pattern, in which there was a portrait of a person wearing a lotus-shaped crown. As scholars reveal, the pattern "reflects the integration of Iranian images with Buddhist images as well as the eastward spread of Iranian-Indian mixed culture".

On the northern mural was a curtain hangs. Male and female musicians played the four-stringed *pi pa* (琵琶), the five-stringed or vertical *kong hou* (箜篌), the *sheng* (笙), the flute and the *yue* (钺, an axe-shaped object), which came from the Central Plains or foreign lands.

The Population of Ethnic Groups in Northern China that Migrated to the Central Plains and Assimilated into the Han People from the Eastern Han Dynasty to the Early Sui Dynasty

Ethnic Groups	Historical Period	Population
Xiongnu	The Eastern Han Dynasty	600,000
Jie	The Eastern Han Dynasty	400,000 (200,000 were massacred by the Kingdom of Ranwei)
Di	The Eastern Han Dynasty, The Three Kingdoms	440,000
Qiang	The Han Dynasty	760,000
Wuhuan	The Eastern Han Dynasty, The Three Kingdoms	400,000
Xianbei (Including *Za Hu*, or Various *Hu* Tribes)	From the Western Jin Dynasty to the Sixteen Kingdoms	Three Million
In Total: 5.4 Million		

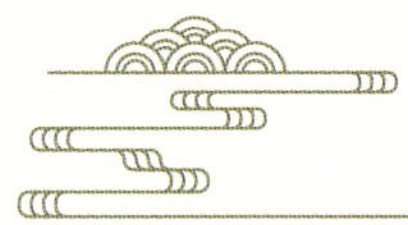

统一多民族国家的发展

The Development of a Unified Multi-ethnic Country

一个具有空前开放视野和恢宏包容气度的大一统时代，在魏晋南北朝三百年民族大融合的基础上，横空出世——生机勃勃的隋唐登上了历史舞台。比起秦汉，这个时代实现了更高水平的统一。此时，中华民族的内涵发生了深刻的变化——以汉族为主体，融合了“五胡”以及边疆羁縻府州和附属国而形成的新族体，构成了“中华”的新形象，显示出中华民族多元一体历史进程的崭新进展。

隋唐皇室具有胡、汉混血的特征。两朝的朝野上下，汉化的鲜卑人和胡人出身的达官显宦、文人学士、能工巧匠比比皆是。据统计，隋唐两朝人口的年均增长率超过12‰，远远高于中国古代人口年均增长1.4‰的水平。显然，这一数值仅仅依靠汉族人口的自然增长是绝不可能的，它包含了内迁列入户籍并逐渐与汉族融合的边疆少数民族人口。

对异彩纷呈的各民族文化的采撷吸收是这个时代的主旋律，胡汉互化为这个时代打上鲜明烙印。社会自上而下“大有胡风”——胡乐、胡舞，左右乐坛，引领时尚；胡骑、胡妆、胡帽、胡食，风靡长安，流行街头；夜光杯、葡萄酒，雍容华贵，流光溢彩。这一切共同造就了辉煌盛唐的宏大气象。今天，我们仍能从敦煌以及吐鲁番文书中，从胡人识宝的唐代传奇小说中，从唐三彩深目高鼻的胡人商旅团队陶俑中，深深感受到“天下一家”“华夷如一”的美好氛围。

古代中国的统一，实际上是农牧两大系统的统一；中华文化的形成，总体上也是农牧两大文化系统的辩证结合。这两条路线在隋唐均得到了里程碑式的推进。在完成开疆拓土的统一大业后，唐太宗偃武修文，以“四夷一家”的理念确立了和谐相处的民族政策，获得了各民族的共同拥护，被北方游牧民族尊为“天可汗”。唐太宗曾说：“自古皆贵中华，贱夷狄，朕独爱之如一。”正是这样一种“中华观”，使唐朝成为当时世界上最强盛的国家之一，声名远播，万国来朝，实现了“中国既安，四夷自服”的古代天下主义的最高理想追求，也把儒家文化描绘的“吾修文德以来远人”的美好图景，化为了真切的现实。

The 300-year national integration in the Wei, Jin, Southern and Northern Dynasties bequeathed China an era of the grand unification that featured political openness, social prosperity and cultural inclusiveness. *Vis-à-vis* the Qin and Han Dynasties, the Sui and Tang Dynasties presented high spirit and deepened national unity. In particular, the Chinese nation took on a totally new form. In a broad sense, China covered the Han nationality (as the majority), ethnic minorities, regions administered under the *Ji-Mi* (羁縻, halter-and-bridle) system and dependent states. This signaled a significant progress in the formation of the pluralistic and integrated pattern of the Chinese nation.

In the Sui and Tang Dynasties, the royal families had both the Han and the *Hu* (胡) blood. There were numerous high-ranking officials, literati & scholars and craftsmen who had *Hu* blood and accepted Han culture. As historical records suggested, demographically, the Sui and Tang Dynasties achieved an average annual growth rate of more than 12‰, much higher than 1.4‰ in ancient China. Apparently, this resulted from the inflow of ethnic minorities who came from border areas, merged into the Han nationality and became registered residents.

The acceptance and absorption of diverse ethnic cultures, or the mutual learning between Han and *Hu* civilizations, became the main trend. In the Tang Dynasty, *Hu* style prevailed among both the court and the masses. *Hu*-style music, dance, horse-riding, cosmetics, hat and food came into vogue in Chang'an the capital and streets. As a poetic line extolled, "Fine vintage in the goblets glows at night". All of them forged the glorious age of the Tang Dynasty. Today, we can deeply comprehend the ethos of the unified Tang from the documents and books unearthed in Dunhuang and Turpan, from *Hu* people's distinguishing treasures in Tang-Dynasty *Chuan Qi* (传奇, legendary short stories) , and from the pottery figurines of *Hu* business travel team (with the technique of Tang Tri-Color Glazed Ceramics) with deep eyes and high noses.

Generally speaking, the political unity of ancient China came with that of farming and nomadic economies; the formation of Chinese culture organically combined farming and nomadic cultures, reaching the peak in the Sui and Tang Dynasties. Emperor Taizong, honored as The Great Khan or *Tian Ke Han* (天可汗), adopted Confucianist statecraft and theorized the national policy of harmonious coexistence, which won widespread support of all ethnic groups. He treated Han and *Hu* subjects equally and actualized the Confucianist highest ideal of *Tian Xia* (天下, the whole China under the heaven), making Tang the most powerful country in the world.

“中国古代第一老丈人”是谁？为什么他的身上集中折射出隋唐王室胡汉融合的血缘信息？

胡汉融合的隋唐王室

独孤信多面体煤精组印

Polyhedral Jet Seal of Dugu Xin

文物简读

这枚拥有8棱26面，包含18个正方形印面和8个角形印面的组印，其主人是被称为“中国古代第一老丈人”的独孤信。这位鲜卑贵族不仅自身有着传奇辉煌的经历，还以其三个女儿的姻亲关系成为隋唐王室胡汉融合的推动者。

印面最多的古代印章

1981年，这枚印信被一名中学生发现于陕西省旬阳县的河滩地中。此后，它又在文化馆内默默无闻地沉睡了十年后，才被专家慧眼识珠，进行了鉴定和研究。从此，它的故事才逐渐清晰起来。

这是我国迄今为止出土的印面最多、正文字数最多的古代印章——它竟拥有8棱26面，包含18个正方形印面、8个角形印面！

根据印文，此印的用途可归纳为三类：

公文用印：大司马印、大都督印、刺史之印、柱国之印、密、令；

上书用印：臣信上疏、臣信上章、臣信上表、臣信启事；

书信用印：信启事、信白笺、独孤信白书、耶勑。

根据印文内容，印章的主人也透露出他的名字——独孤信。这枚印章的发现，将楷书入印的历史

名称：独孤信多面体煤精组印
年代：西魏
规格：高4.5厘米，宽4.35厘米
出土地点：陕西省旬阳县
收藏单位：陕西历史博物馆

Name: Polyhedral Jet Seal of Dugu Xin
Historical Period: The Western Wei Dynasty
Height: 4.5 cm, Width: 4.35 cm
Excavation Site: Xunyang County, Shaanxi Province
Housed in: Shaanxi History Museum

提前了四百多年，同时也成为研究南北朝印玺制度、西魏官制的重要文物资料。一枚印章，折射出的是印章主人的人生及其所处时代的风云变幻。

战功赫赫、治绩超群的全能型人才

独孤信的传奇一生，是秦建立统一多民族国家后，中华大地迎来第二次民族大融合的历史缩影。

独孤信身份显赫。他是一位风度翩翩的鲜卑公子，文韬武略，雄才过人：他精于骑射，善于谋略，战功赫赫；他治绩超群，是闻名遐迩的北周八柱国之一。然而这些似乎都不及后人给他的称号——“中国古代第一老丈人”更让人印象深刻。

据《周书·独孤信传》等文献记载，独孤信乃云中（今山西大同）人，本名“如愿”。独孤氏是鲜卑极为古老的贵族，与拓跋氏一同兴起。独孤信的先祖伏留屯曾是拓跋鲜卑的部落首领之一。北魏文成帝拓跋濬在位时，独孤信的祖父俟尼带着一家人从云中郡来到武川镇担任镇守之职，此后独孤信的父亲独孤库者继任部落酋长。库者为人讲义气、有节操，深受敬重。可惜北魏孝文帝迁都洛阳时，独孤信一家没有一同前往。但独孤信却凭借自己的真本领，先后追随北魏农民起义军首领葛荣、北魏末年权臣尔朱荣、北魏和西魏时期将领贺拔胜，最后加入关陇集团，成为西魏实际掌权者宇文泰的心腹，一步步进入权力中心。西魏沿用东汉的郡县制，保留了刺史和大都督的职位，宇文泰任命独孤信为陇右十州大都督、秦州刺史。在这里他因为政绩卓越、信著遐迩，被赐名为“信”。西魏末年，宇文泰又依照《周礼》设立六官制度，任命独孤信为大司马，即兵马大元帅；创立府兵制，命独孤信为八柱国之一。

至此，独孤信在西魏、北周的权力中心站稳了脚跟。他的这一上升经历充分反映了西魏时期鲜卑族学习、吸收汉族文化，努力向中原政治传统靠拢的历史过程。

慧眼识婿，促进隋唐胡汉交融

隋、唐的统一是在南北方民族大融合的基础上完成的，这一多元融合的特征也鲜明地体现在隋唐皇室身上。独孤信三个女儿的姻亲关系，就集中体现了隋唐王室的胡汉融合特征。

《北史·独孤信传》中记载：“信长女周明敬后，第四女元贞后，第七女隋文献后。”独孤信慧眼识英才，把长女嫁给了北周的明帝宇文毓，成为周明敬后；把七女儿嫁给隋朝开国皇帝杨坚，谥号“文献皇后”，与杨坚并称“二圣”，生下了隋炀帝杨广；又把四女儿嫁给西魏八柱国之一李虎的儿子唐国公李昺，生下了唐朝开国皇帝唐高祖李渊，追封“元贞皇后”。这就是文献记载的“周、隋及皇家，三代皆为外戚，自古以来，未之有也”。

此外，唐高祖李渊的皇后窦氏，原姓纥窦陵氏，也是鲜卑贵族，她生下了李世民；唐太宗李世民的皇后长孙氏也是汉化了的鲜卑贵族。隋唐王室因此具有浓厚的胡、汉混血特征。

胡汉融合的血缘带来了兼容并蓄的开放心态，这为中国历史上迎来一个包容开放、海纳百川、繁荣鼎盛、辉煌宏大的盛唐时代，奠定了文化心理基础。

The seal has eight edges and 26 faces (18 square faces and eight angular faces). Its owner was Dugu Xin, known as the "first father-in-law in ancient China". As a Xianbei nobleman, Dugu Xin not only had legendary experience, but also facilitated the *Hu*-Han integration via the marriage among the royal families of the Sui and Tang Dynasties.

According to "Biography of Dugu Xin" of *Book of Northern Zhou* (《周书・独孤信传》), Dugu Xin was born in Yunzhong (present-day Datong, Shanxi), originally called Dugu Ruyuan. As one of the oldest nobles of the Xianbei, the Dugu family emerged with the Tuoba family. Fu Liutun, ancestor of Dugu Xin, was one of the tribal leaders of Tuoba Xianbei. In the reign of Tuoba Jun, or Emperor Wencheng of Northern Wei, Qi Ni, grandfather of Dugu Xin, led his family to Wuchuan Garrison from Yunzhong Prefecture, serving as military officer. Afterwards, Dugu Kuzhe, father of Dugu Xin, succeeded as tribal leader. In the late Western Wei Dynasty, Yuwen Tai established the Six Ministers System in accordance with *Zhou Li* (《周礼》, *Rites of Zhou*), as well as *Fu Bing* (府兵, Garrison Militia) System, appointing Dugu Xin as *Da Sima* (大司马, Supreme Military Officer) and *Zhu Guo* (柱国, State Pillar) General.

According to "Biography of Dugu Xin" of *The History of the Northern Dynasties* (《北史・独孤信传》), his eldest daughter married Yuwen Yu, Emperor Ming of Northern Zhou, and became Queen Mingjing. His seventh daughter married Yang Jian, the first emperor of the Sui Dynasty, and was posthumously titled Queen of Wenxian. His fourth daughter married Li Bing, Duke of Tang, the son of Li Hu (*Zhu Guo* General in the Western Wei Dynasty), and gave birth to Li Yuan, the first emperor of the Tang Dynasty. She was posthumously conferred the title of Queen Yuanzhen. This accords with the historical record: "The royal families of Northern Zhou, Sui and Tang were kinswomen, which was seldom seen since the ancient times."

The fusion of *Hu* (胡) and Han bloodlines nurtured the inclusive and open mind of the Chinese nation, which laid a psychological foundation for the Tang Dynasty, an era with economic prosperity and cultural confidence.

名称：虞弘墓石椁雕刻
年代：隋开皇十二年（592）
规格：高96厘米，宽100厘米，厚12.5厘米
出土地点：山西省太原市晋源区王郭村南
收藏单位：山西博物院

Name: Carving on the Stone Outer Coffin of the Tomb of Yu Hong
Historical Period: The 12th year of Emperor Kaihuang of the Sui Dynasty (592)
Height: 96 cm, Width: 100 cm, Thickness: 12.5 cm
Excavation Site: South of Wangguo Village, Jinyuan District, Taiyuan, Shanxi Province
Housed in: Shanxi Museum

一个粟特人为什么能成为历经三个朝代、始终深受宠信的外交官?

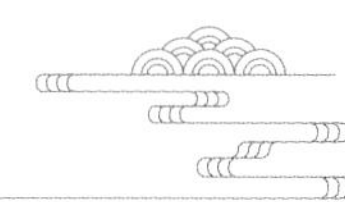

隋唐官僚集团中的胡人

虞弘墓石椁雕刻

Carving on the Stone Outer Coffin of the Tomb of Yu Hong

53

文物简读

这座融合了粟特、波斯、中原风格的虞弘墓，是目前中国发现的反映中亚古国和东西方文化交流最集中、最丰富、最珍贵的墓葬，是北朝至隋唐时期东西方文化交流最有力的见证，充分说明了隋唐政治的开放性和包容性，揭示了推动盛唐走向中国古代历史高峰的内在源泉。

一座异域风格的奇特墓葬

山西是中国文物大省，考古学家在这里常有惊人的发现。然而，1999年在太原市晋源区王郭村南的考古成果，却以另一种方式震惊了中外——在华夏文明的中心区域，竟然出现了如此典型、完整的波斯和中亚人物、乐舞图像资料!

这是一座有明确纪年的隋代墓葬，年代为隋开皇十二年（592）。其汉白玉石椁的四周，布满精美的浅浮雕，由50余幅单体图案组合而成：宴饮图、乐舞图、射猎图、家居图、行旅图等。图中满是波斯和中亚风格的服饰、器皿、乐器、舞蹈；人物形象皆深目、高鼻、黑发、多须髯，是典型的西域人种。石椁正面的浮雕上，有一男子脚踏圆形小地毯，飞快旋转，衣带飘飞——其姿态很容易让人联想起隋唐时期来自西域、风靡中原的胡腾舞。石椁上还有一个情景十分引人瞩目：一座灯台形火坛，上部为三层仰莲形，火焰升腾；火坛左右两边各有一个人头鹰身之人，均上身倾向火坛，一手捂嘴、一手抬着火坛一侧。显然，这象征的是古代波斯帝国国教琐罗亚斯德教的通用礼仪。北魏时期传入中国的琐罗亚斯德教，又称“祆教”，在粟特人的生活中占据了重要的地位。

这是我国迄今为止发现的反映中亚文化图像最丰富、承载古代东西方文化交流信息最集中的墓葬考古成果。正因为如此，它傲视群雄，跻身“1999年度全国十大考古新发现”和“中国20世纪100项考古大发现”。

他是谁?

那么，这座墓的主人是谁？他是一个怎样的人？

墓志铭清晰地揭示了墓主人的身份：虞弘，字莫潘，祖籍在中亚鱼国。他从小随父归附柔然，13岁时就代表柔然出使波斯、吐谷浑等国，表现了突出的外交才能。后来他出使中原，在新建立的北齐政权中崭露头角，并依靠自己的才华扎根中土。此后他又在北周、隋朝为官，曾任“检校萨宝”，长期主管入华外国人事务。历经三个朝代，他始终是深受朝廷宠信的外交官员。

虽然墓志铭提供了许多重要信息，但仍有一些谜团未解，比如：虞弘祖籍所在的中亚鱼国在哪里？虞弘到底来自何处？

考古学家推测，虞弘应是来自中亚的粟特人。北朝以来，大批来自西域的胡人进入中国，这些胡人中以属东伊朗人的粟特人势力最大。粟特人进入中国后聚族而居，首领被称为“萨宝”，在粟特语中是商队首领的意思。由于其人数众多，中原王朝就采取了以“萨宝”统管粟特人事务的方法。《隋书·百官志下》中记载：“诸州胡二百户以上萨宝，为视正九品。”

“鱼”“虞”在中古汉语中本来不同音，但是南北朝时期在北方一些地区，两字却逐渐有混同之势。颜之推在《颜氏家训》中说：“北人以庶为戍，以如为儒。”即是指北人“鱼”韵和“虞”韵的混淆，其范围主要分布在以河南为中心的地区。虽然晋阳（今太原）一带的情况并不十分清楚，但无论如何，来自鱼国的胡人决定采用虞作为自己的汉姓，这似乎合情合理，就如同来自康国（撒马尔罕）的粟特人采用了康姓，来自石国（塔什干）的粟特人采用了石姓那样。

聚天下英才的大国气度

虞弘墓之所以在研究东西方文化交流方面具有重要意义，是因为它不仅有着鲜明的中亚特征和波斯风格，更展现了中原汉人的思维文化和生活场景。虞弘墓所处之地是中原传统观念中的风水宝地，虞弘墓的形制、葬具、随葬品都具有中原丧葬特色。可见，这一时期来自异域的人们早已在中原安居乐业，熟谙中原文化。

而虞弘本人则是胡人在隋唐时期官僚集团中施展才能的一个缩影。许多来自西域的胡人凭借军事或外交才能，在隋唐朝廷中获得厚禄。史载，隋唐朝野上下，汉化了的西域胡人出身的达官显宦、文人学士、能工巧匠比比皆是。据统计，在隋朝中央政府中，身居要职的胡人有27位，在十二卫中任大将军之职的胡人有13位；在唐朝，胡人进入官僚集团的比例进一步增加，担任过宰相的具有匈奴、鲜卑、高车、乌丸、突厥、沙陀、高句丽、龟兹、粟特等胡人血统者竟达33人，占唐朝全部宰相（369人）的9%。不得不说，有容乃大、兼收并蓄的隋唐开明政策为盛唐的出现打下了坚实的社会基础。

The Tomb of Yu Hong combines the styles of Sogdiana, Persia and the Central Plains. It saw the cultural exchanges between the East and the West in the Northern Dynasties and the Sui and Tang Dynasties, fully demonstrating the openness and inclusiveness of the Sui and Tang politics, and brilliantly elucidating the inherent source of the Tang Dynasty, the peak of ancient China.

Archaeologists presume that Yu Hong was Sogdian from the Central Asia. According to the remaining records in the tomb of Yu Hong, Yu Hong was once appointed as *Jianjiao Sabao*① (检校萨宝). Since the Northern Dynasties, a large number of *Hu* people from the Western Regions had flowed to the Central Plains. The most powerful tribe was Sogdian, a clan of Eastern Iranian.

The tomb can be exactly dated (592). Around the white marble outer coffin were exquisite bas reliefs, comprising more than 50 single patterns, e.g. banquet, music & dance, hunting, family life, travel, etc. There were plenty of Persian and Central Asian styles of dress, vessels, musical instruments and dances. The people were of races in the Western Regions, with deep eyes, high noses, black hair and large whiskers. In the front of the stone coffin, the scene was depicted that the male and female hosts were holding a feast and enjoying music and dance in the tent. A man was stepping on a small circular carpet and spinning rapidly, and his clothes was flying. The dance resembles *Huteng* dance (胡腾舞) from the Western Regions in the Sui and Tang Dynasties, which was quite popular in the Central Plains. The lampstand-shaped fire altar was eye-catching. On the top was a three-layer lotus-shaped pattern, with the flames rising from the top. On both sides were two people with human heads and eagle bodies, both leaning towards the fire altar, covering their mouths with one hand and extending their arms to lift one side of the fire altar. Obviously, this was the religious sign of Zoroastrianism in the ancient Persian Empire.

Hitherto, the tomb of Yu Hong has been the most significant achievement in tomb archeology in China. It represents a diverse cultural landscape in the ancient Central Asia and bridges the East-West cultural exchanges, shortlisted for "Top 10 New Archaeological Discoveries in China in 1999" and "Top 100 Archaeological Discoveries in China in the 20th Century".

① The post can be basically understood as an officer in charge of the Sogdian businessmen. The views on the etymology of the Chinese words *Sa Bao* (or 萨宝) vary, such as the Syrian origin *sâbâ*, the Persian origin *šaθ-pāv*, the Sanskrit origin *sārthavāho*, and the Sogdian origin *sārthavāk*. See Rui Chuanming: "The Reconsideration of *Sa Bao*", *Historical Review*, 2000 (3). (芮传明:《"萨宝"的再认识》，《史林》2000年第3期)—Translator's Note

"昭陵六骏"的名字——拳毛騧、什伐赤、白蹄乌、特勒骠、青骓、飒露紫，为何叫起来这么拗口?

唐太宗的中华观

"昭陵六骏"浮雕石刻 54

The Stone Carvings of Six Steeds of Zhaoling Mausoleum (Bas-Relief)

文物简读

将生前爱马刻于墓前是突厥人的风俗习惯。唐太宗以突厥语或突厥官名命名自己心爱的六匹坐骑，并将它们雕刻成像，置于昭陵之中。这从一个侧面反映了他的中华观："自古皆贵中华，贱夷狄，朕独爱之如一。"

以突厥语命名的坐骑

这也许是中国古代最独特的六匹马——它们不仅留下了自己的形象，而且留下了自己的名字：拳毛騧、什伐赤、白蹄乌、特勒骠（又称"特勤骠"）、青骓、飒露紫。

只是，它们的名字叫起来为何如此拗口?

公元7世纪，唐太宗在营建昭陵时，决定把自己从跟随父亲起兵反隋到统一全国的过程中，曾经骑乘的六匹战马雕刻在青石之上，放在陵墓旁一条专门用于记载帝王丰功伟绩的长廊之中。为此，他特地命令当时最著名的画家阎立本及其兄长、工艺家阎立德，分别将六匹战马的形象精心绘制和雕刻出来。这就是名垂青史的"昭陵六骏"。

六骏雕成后，唐太宗亲自作《六马图赞》以记之，于是这六匹马的名字便永远地留在了青石之上。而这些名字之所以叫起来拗口，是因为取自突厥语或者突厥官名。

名称："昭陵六骏"浮雕石刻

年代：唐

规格：长约2米，宽约1.7米

出土地点：陕西省咸阳市礼泉县唐太宗昭陵

收藏单位：西安碑林博物馆、美国宾夕法尼亚大学博物馆

Name: The Stone Carvings of Six Steeds of Zhaoling Mausoleum (Bas-Relief)

Historical Period: The Tang Dynasty

Length: *c.* 2 m, Width: *c* 1.7 m

Excavation Site: Zhaoling Mausoleum, Liquan County, Xianyang, Shaanxi Province

Housed in: Xi'an Beilin Museum, University of Pennsylvania Museum

青骓

战马与战功

马具装备在南北朝时期进一步完备，骑兵的机动性和攻击力愈发得到提升。李渊、李世民父子高瞻远瞩，早在太原起兵时就竭尽全力搜集良马精骑，大力引进突厥良马。此后在征服北方群雄的一系列战役中，李世民更是注重骑兵攻击战术和不断补充马匹供给的重要性，从而为一统天下、开疆拓土奠定了基础。

自武德元年起，李世民南征北战，指挥了三场对统一全国具有决定意义的重大战役：一、解扶风之围，取得与陇西割据势力薛氏父子博弈战的阶段性胜利；以少胜多，在浅水原破薛举之子薛仁杲大军，赢得决定性胜利，彻底铲除了唐王朝来自西北方面的威胁，在关中站稳脚跟。二、大败宋金刚、刘武周，收复并、汾失地，巩固唐王朝的大后方。三、在虎牢关之战和洺水决战中，一举翦灭关东地区两大割据势力——盘踞于东都洛阳的王世充和占据河北地区的窦建德军事集团。特别是在洺水决战中，利用地形优势，水淹窦建德旧将刘黑闼大军，取得了唐王朝统一战争的决定性胜利。

拳毛騧（复制品）

飒露紫（复制品）

在这些重大战役中，李世民正是骑乘着这六匹骏马，身先士卒，冲锋陷阵；也正是在这些战役中，六匹骏马表现出了英勇无畏的雄奇风采，为成就李世民的不世战功，哪怕长途奔袭，哪怕刀光剑影，哪怕身中箭矢，仍然为李世民效劳。

“昭陵六骏”浮雕石刻是古代中国著名的文化遗产。但令人痛心的是：20世纪初叶，六骏中的拳毛騧、飒露紫被以12.5万美元盗卖至国外，现藏于美国宾夕法尼亚大学博物馆。其余四骏虽得以幸存，但在被盗卖的过程中却惨遭破坏，现存于西安碑林博物馆。

什伐赤

“四夷一家”

“昭陵六骏”所承载的记忆，在彰显了唐太宗丰功伟绩的同时，也客观体现了隋唐时期的民族关系，成为盛唐时代博大中华观的隐性表达。

唐太宗敏锐地认识到魏晋南北朝的民族大融合已成为一个必然的历史趋势。唐太宗的祖母元贞皇后、母亲窦皇后、妻子长孙皇后，都有着鲜卑的血统，胡汉混血的唐太宗对“混同华夷”的历史意义感受尤深。他积极采纳魏征提出的“偃武修文，中国既安，四夷自服”的儒家王道思想，在攻灭东突厥和薛延陀，扫除高昌、龟兹和吐谷浑等分裂势力后，设立安西四镇；又在完成统一大业后，积极倡导“四夷一家”的观念，确立了各民族和谐相处的政策，营造了兼收并蓄、包容开放的社会风气，获得了北方游牧民族的共同拥护和爱戴，被尊奉为“天可汗”。

在唐太宗的中华观中，“中华”的概念与北朝时期相比，已经有了新的发展——它是指以汉人为主体、广泛融合了“五胡”等族群乃至相当数量的外国族裔而形成的新族体，同时也涵盖了认同唐朝的边疆羁縻府州和附属国，“中华”因而具备了多元一体中华民族的概念内涵。

特勒骠

It was a custom of the Turks to carve their beloved horses in front of their tombs during their lifetime. Emperor Taizong of Tang addressed the beloved horses as *Quan Mao Gua* (拳毛騧, *Khowar*), *Shi Fa Chi* (什伐赤, *Shad*), *Bai Ti Wu* (白蹄乌, *bo-ta*), *Te Le Biao* (特勒骠, *Tegin*), *Qing Zhui* (青骓, *Cin*) and *Sa Lu Zi* (飒露紫, *isbara*), whose origins were Turkic language or Turkic office. He carved the images of them and placed them in Zhaoling Mausoleum.

In the 7th century, when Emperor Taizong of Tang constructed Zhaoling Mausoleum, he ordered Yan Liben, a celebrated painter, as well as his brother Yan Lide, a craftsman, to carve the six horses on a bluestone, which galloped across the battlefield with him. After *The Stone Carvings of Six Steeds of Zhaoling Mausoleum* was completed, Emperor Taizong wrote *Odes to the Six Horses* (《六马图赞》) to glorify them. *The Stone Carving of Six Steeds of Zhaoling Mausoleum* not only highlighted the great achievements of Emperor Taizong of Tang, but also objectively reflected the ethnic relations in the Sui and Tang Dynasties, becoming a metaphorical expression of the idea *Zhong Hua* that took shape in the prosperous Tang Dynasty.

With *Hu* and Han bloodlines, Emperor Taizong of Tang highly recognized the significance of *Hua Xia-Yi* assimilation. After acceding to the throne, he vigorously practiced the idea "community of Han and non-Han people" and promoted the harmonious coexistence of all ethnic groups, and fostered an inclusive and open social atmosphere. Therefore, Emperor Taizong of Tang, revered as *Tian Ke Han* (天可汗) or the Great Khan, won wide support and respect from all northern nomads.

Emperor Taizong of Tang developed the idea *Zhong Hua*. It signified a new community or multi-ethnic Chinese nation that covered the vast majority of the Han people, the five *Hu*, foreign minorities, as well as remote Ji-Mi (羁縻, halter-and-bridle) prefectures and satellite states subject to Tang.

文献中广泛记载的大唐“胡腾舞”，是什么样子的?

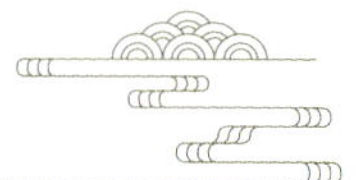

盛唐起舞：恢宏的黄金时代

鎏金铜胡腾舞俑

55

Gilded Bronze Figurine Performing *Huteng* Dance (胡腾舞)

文物简读

唐朝迎来了中国舞蹈史上的黄金时代，胡腾舞作为在唐代盛行一时的舞蹈，不仅形式多样，而且在表现形式、表演内容、艺术技巧和表演风格等方面都达到了一个全新的高度。这件胡腾舞俑仿佛让我们跨越千年，看到了它背后百川入海、宏伟开阔的大唐气象。

风靡长安的胡腾舞

出生于新西兰的路易·艾黎（1897—1987），是20世纪为中国人民的解放事业做出过巨大贡献的国际友人。1982年，他决定把自己平生收藏的3700多件文物全部捐赠给他工作和生活过的“第二故乡”——山丹县，其中，便有一件鎏金铜舞蹈俑。这件舞蹈俑引起了专家学者的高度重视。细细辨识，它不就是在历史文献中一再被提及、在敦煌壁画中一再被描绘、在唐诗中一再被吟咏赞叹的胡腾舞吗?

胡腾舞是一种以急速的腾踏跳跃为主要动作，通过高难度腾跃和大幅度下腰展现刚性之美的男子单人舞，它由粟特人从中亚石国传入唐朝，在大唐的市井坊间曾盛行一时。

山丹县博物馆所藏的这件铜舞俑，把壁画上关于胡腾舞的二维画面立体化了，也把诗歌中关于胡腾舞的文字描述具象化了——

只见这位圆目钩鼻、满面笑容的舞者，头戴尖顶小毡帽，身穿紧身窄袖衫，下着过膝宽裙，足蹬长筒翘头软靴，背系酒葫芦，右手翻飞卷袖，左手轻扬置于胯间，一足挺立于垂瓣莲托之上，另一足斜向踢出，裙摆随舞而动，翻卷飞扬……

唐代诗人们是怎样描绘胡腾舞的?李端的《胡腾儿》写道：

名称：鎏金铜胡腾舞俑

年代：唐

规格：高13.5厘米

收藏单位：甘肃省山丹县博物馆

Name: Gilded Bronze Figurine Performing *Huteng* Dance (胡腾舞)

Historical Period: The Tang Dynasty

Height: 13.5 cm

Housed in: Shandan County Museum, Gansu Province

……

扬眉动目踏花毡，红汗交流珠帽偏。

醉却东倾又西倒，双靴柔弱满灯前。

环行急蹴皆应节，反手叉腰如却月。

刘言史的《王中丞宅夜观舞胡腾》如是吟咏：

石国胡儿人见少，蹲舞尊前急如鸟。

织成蕃帽虚顶尖，细氎胡衫双袖小。

……

跳身转毂宝带鸣，弄脚缤纷锦靴软。

四座无言皆瞪目，横笛琵琶遍头促。

……

在诗人的描绘中，来自中亚的白皮肤、高鼻梁舞者，头带尖顶帽，身着窄袖胡衫，腰束带，足蹬锦靴，以横笛、琵琶为伴奏。但见他痛饮一杯酒后，扬眉转目，在一块花毯上纵情起舞。他一会儿像醉酒似的左右倾倒，长靴不停地在灯下闪动；一会儿腾空跳起，一会儿环行急蹴，一会儿反手叉腰。舞步繁复、变化多端，时而刚毅奔放，时而柔软潇洒，身姿轻盈洒脱，飘扬的裙裾与烛光交相辉映，场面煞是热闹。而观众早已如痴如醉……

胡旋舞

大唐的坊间，跳跃着的不仅有激烈奔放的胡腾舞，还有另一种同样节拍奔腾欢快的西域健舞——胡旋舞。胡旋舞同样经由丝绸之路传入，是中亚康国一带的舞种。胡旋舞以打击乐为伴奏，以连续、轻捷的旋转为主要表演内容。与专属于男子的胡腾舞不同，胡旋舞以女子独舞或群舞为主，但男子也可以跳。白居易曾诗吟："中有太真外禄山，二人最道能胡旋。"这让我们确知当年的杨贵妃和安禄山，均是跳胡旋舞的顶级高手。

胡旋舞在当年有多么流行？白居易和元稹均为它写过长诗。在白居易的诗里，胡旋女的姿态、神情跃然纸上：

胡旋女，胡旋女，心应弦，手应鼓。

弦鼓一声双袖举，回雪飘摇转蓬舞。

左旋右转不知疲，千匝万周无已时。

人间物类无可比，奔车轮缓旋风迟。

曲终再拜谢天子，天子为之微启齿。

……

开放包容的盛唐气象

胡腾舞、胡旋舞风靡长安，成为上至贵族、下至平民的新时尚，尤其深受文人墨客推崇。它们还被宫廷吸收，成为宫廷乐舞。从这两种外来舞蹈的兴盛，我们可以遥想盛唐时期磅礴辉煌的东方大国气象。

繁荣强盛、社会稳定的唐朝，吸引着四周的国家纷纷前来进行经济文化交流。东有日本、高句丽、新罗、百济，南有临邑（今越南）、泥婆罗（今尼泊尔）、骠国（今缅甸）、赤土（今泰国宋卡）、真腊（今柬埔寨）、室利佛逝（今印尼苏门答腊）、诃陵（今印尼爪哇）、天竺（今印度、巴基斯坦、孟加拉）、狮子国（今斯里兰卡）、波斯（今伊朗），西有大食（今阿拉伯）、西域诸国……这些国家的使者来到大唐，流连忘返。而他们所带来的文化，也被唐朝广泛吸取，成为唐朝文化的重要组成部分。

史载，唐朝宫廷乐曲中的“十部乐”吸收了高昌、龟兹、康国、安国等八国的音乐成分，这在历代中原王朝中十分罕见。西域声乐在民间也大受欢迎。来自中亚何国、米国的著名歌唱家何满子、米嘉荣曾受到唐朝著名诗人的热情赞美，元稹写道：“何满能歌能宛转，天宝年中世称罕。”刘禹锡则称赞：“唱得凉州意外声，旧人唯属米嘉荣。”

此外，唐代的汉人还接纳了内迁少数族群的服饰、饮食等文化。一时间，胡服、胡乐、胡舞、胡饼、夜光杯、葡萄酒等，成为雍容华贵的盛唐文化的重要符号。此外，唐朝还采取了宽容的宗教政策，作为外来宗教的袄教和景教都在唐朝得到了传播。

The Tang Dynasty saw the golden age in the history of Chinese dance. *Huteng* dance (胡腾舞) enjoyed great popularity in the Tang Dynasty, with various dancing forms and high artistic level. The figurine performing *Huteng* dance shows us the *zeitgeist* of Tang, or free and romantic spirit, which stemmed from the frequent and deep cultural exchanges between Tang and the Central Asia.

Huteng dance was a solo dance for male that mainly featured rapid leaps and jumps, showcasing the beauty of masculinity through difficult jumps and significant waist movements. *Huteng* dance was spread to the Tang Dynasty by the Sogdians from Tash in the Central Asia, present-day Tashkent of Uzbekistan.

The figurine concretizes *Huteng* dance in murals and carvings as well as in Tang poems and records. The dancer has round eyes and hooked nose, with smile on the face. He wears a small pointed felt hat, a tight narrow-sleeved shirt, a knee-length wide skirt, and long curled soft boots, with a wine gourd tied to the back. He rolls up the sleeves with the right hand, and places the left hand lightly in the crotch. One foot steps on the lotus petal-pattern holder, and the other foot tilts to one side. The hem of the skirt moves with the dance…

Huxuan dance (胡旋舞) was also introduced to Tang via the Silk Road. It was a whirling dance in Kangju, present-day Samarkand of Uzbekistan. *Huxuan* dance was accompanied by percussion music. When a dancer performed, he whirled continuously and quickly. Unlike *Huteng* dance exclusive to male, *Huxuan* dance was solo or group dance for female, and open to male. In the poem “Female *Huxuan* Dancer” (《胡旋女》, *Hu Xuan Nü*), Bai Juyi states: “Taizhen (Yang Guifei) and An Lushan, in and out of the imperial court, performed the best *Huxuan* dance.”

Additionally, the Han people welcomed the dressing style and food of other ethnic groups. *Hu* dress, *Hu* music, *Hu* dance, *Hu* pancake, luminous wine glass and grape wine came into vogue and became important symbols of elegant Tang culture. Tang also upheld religious tolerance. Foreign religions, such as Zoroastrianism and Nestorianism, carved a niche in the Tang land.

这件材质名贵、赏心悦目的镶金兽首玛瑙杯本应是西域之物，为何出现于大唐长安附近？

陆上丝绸之路的黄金时代

镶金兽首玛瑙杯

Agate Cup Inlaid with Gold with Cow-Head Pattern

56

文物简读

迄今为止，这件兽首玛瑙杯仍是考古发现的唯一的唐代俏色玉雕，其典型的“来通”造型，以及产自西域的缠丝玛瑙材质，成为陆上丝绸之路在唐朝迎来黄金时代的珍贵见证物。

丝路黄金时代的到来

公元630年，唐太宗李世民率军击败东突厥贵族政权，扫除高昌、焉耆、龟兹等分裂势力，并在西域地区设立安西大都护府，由此加强了对西部边疆的军事和行政管理，保证了丝路的繁荣畅通。随后，唐朝政府又完成了对漠北地区的统一，在回纥以南开辟“参天可汗道”，沿途设置邮驿，并备驿马、酒肉，为往来官吏和行贾提供便利。此举开辟了西部与北部边疆往来的通道，使西部地区和广大漠北连成一片，丝绸之路向北面获得显著扩展。一些新兴都市和贸易中心出现在丝路北道上，著名的有庭州、弓月、轮台、热海、碎叶、怛罗斯等。

开明宽容、自强自信的大唐王朝，以开放的态度和博大的胸怀迎接着众多文化、人种、身份迥异的域外来客。繁华的长安城是当时世界的中心城市和丝绸之路上的重要枢纽城市。商贾们将中国的丝绸、茶叶等源源不断地运向西方，西方各国的物产也大量输入长安。丝绸之路因此在唐代迎来了继汉代以来的又一个顶峰。这件被称为陕西历史博物馆“镇馆之宝”的镶金兽首玛瑙杯，正是这一时期的见证物。

名称：镶金兽首玛瑙杯

年代：唐

规格：高6.5厘米，长15.6厘米，口径5.9厘米

出土地点：陕西省西安市碑林区何家村

收藏单位：陕西历史博物馆

Name: Agate Cup Inlaid with Gold with Cow-Head Pattern

Historical Period: The Tang Dynasty

Height: 6.5 cm, Length: 15.6 cm, Mouth Diameter: 5.9 cm

Excavation Site: Hejia Village, Beilin District, Xi’an, Shaanxi Province

Housed in: Shaanxi History Museum

丝路遗存的国宝级文物

何家村原本是一个寂寂无名的小村庄，在1970年的城市扩建中，村子里一处不起眼的窖藏里，出土了三个平淡无奇的罐子，打开后却让人大吃一惊！罐子里装着上千件文物，其中既有唐朝的，也有唐朝之前的；既有金银器、玉器，也有许多国内外的钱币。数量之多、器物之奇，瞬间使何家村闻名全国。

其中，一件精美至极的镶金兽首玛瑙杯，更是让考古队员震惊不已。玛瑙杯以牛形兽首为前端，以兽双角为杯柄，嘴部镶金帽作杯塞，眼、耳、鼻皆刻画得精细入微，形神毕肖。杯首的一对兽角呈螺旋状，弯曲着与杯身连接；杯沿恰到好处地装饰两条圆凸弦，线条流畅自然。它的精美还体现在材质上，它用缠丝玛瑙这一名贵、罕见的西域舶来品制作而成。整件玛瑙杯巧用俏色技巧，随形变化，将兽眼刻画得黑白分明，真正达到画龙点睛的效果。

此件兽形玛瑙杯来自何处？它的制作者是谁？

兽形玛瑙杯是典型的“来通”造型。“来通”，是希腊语的译音，有“流出”的意思，大多制作成兽角形。酒杯底部一般有孔，液体可从孔中流出，功能如同漏斗，用来注酒。这种造型的酒具在中亚、西亚，特别是波斯（今伊朗）十分常见。从唐代以前的图像资料看，“来通”常常出现在胡人的宴饮场景中。到了唐朝，随着胡人沿丝绸之路涌入大唐，“来通”这种酒具便有可能出现于长安的酒肆食坊。也有学者认为，并不排除它出自居住在长安的中亚或西亚工匠之手，抑或是唐朝工匠学习外来工艺的杰作。

这样一件用料考究、造型奇巧的酒器，唐朝的贵族会在什么场合用到它呢？据现有资料和专家研究表明，这件器物是唐人宴饮时的罚酒器。唐人宴饮，喜行酒令，行令时输者须受科罚，即被罚喝酒。科罚又称作“飞觥”或“抛觥”，此“觥”即兕觥，与此件玛瑙杯造型十分相似，均为角形器，是唐代专用的罚酒器。其特殊的造型——尖端有流角，不能放置，只能一饮而尽，既体现对违令者的处罚，又十分有雅趣。

“兕觥”最早见于《诗经·卷耳》：“我姑酌彼兕觥”。在当时，兕觥并非专用罚爵，而且底端不开口。《后汉书·郅恽传》有“司正举觥，以君之罪，告谢于天”的记载，说明最迟至东汉时期，已经有了用“觥”罚酒的实例。为什么会有这种改变？中原地区的“觥”与西方的“来通”是否有着千丝万缕的联系呢？

我们不妨大胆猜测一下，两汉时期丝绸之路的开通为东西方文化交流架起一座桥梁，当“来通”从西方传入中原，其与兕觥相似的造型以及与之截然相反的底端开口设计，很可能引起有着猎奇心理的上层贵族的关注和喜爱，遂将之与本土的“兕觥”相融合，演变为宴饮时的专用罚酒器。而在大唐经济繁荣、文化包容的时代氛围里，罚爵兕觥逐渐流传开来，成为市井酒肆的流行物，也是情理之中的事情。

这件镶金兽首玛瑙杯的现世，以及史料文献中关于“兕觥”的记载，无不诉说着漫漫丝路上东西方文化交流互鉴的故事。

透过玛瑙杯，我们仿佛看到了那些络绎不绝、不畏艰险的使者、商人们，奔波不息于黄金时代的丝绸之路，演绎出一场场轰轰烈烈的经济文化交流大戏。

Hitherto, the agate cup has been the only jade carving in the Tang Dynasty that was made with the *Qiaose* (俏色, jade article wrought in a natural way) technique. Made of sardonyx from the Western Regions, it has a typical *Rhyton* (来通) shape.

In the Tang Dynasty, Chang'an was an international city in the Silk Road. Merchants continuously transported Chinese silk, tea and other goods to the West, and brought a great quantity of Western products back to Chang'an. Under such circumstances, the Silk Road reached the pinnacle since the Han Dynasty, as evidenced by the agate cup, the most valuable treasure of Shaanxi History Museum.

The agate cup features a cow-head-pattern front end and a cow-horn-pattern handle. Gold is inlaid in the mouth, forming a cup stopper. The eyes, ears and nose are meticulously carved. A pair of cow horns on the head look like a spiral, connected to the cup body in the form of curve. The rim of the cup is perfectly decorated with two round convex chords, with smooth and natural lines.

Rhyton was the transliteration of the Greek word *ῥυτόν*, meaning a drinking cup in the shape of an animal. Generally, there was a hole at the bottom of the drinking cup, from which liquid flowed out. *Rhyton* functioned as a funnel, and was used for pouring wine. It was commonly discovered in the Central Asia and West Asia, especially in Persia (present-day Iran). As the pictorial records in the Tang Dynasty suggested, *Rhyton* often appeared in the banquets of the Hu people. There was a vogue for exotica among the Tang people. *Rhyton* was used in wine shops frequented by Han people.

To some scholars, the agate cup was made by craftsmen who came from the Central Asia or Western Asia and lived in Chang'an, or by Tang craftsmen who learnt foreign techniques.

名称：柳州罗池庙碑

年代：原碑为唐代，宋代复建

规格：碑高231厘米，宽129厘米

现存地点：广西壮族自治区柳州市

Name: Liuzhou Luochi Temple Stele

Historical Period: Originally Erected in the Tang Dynasty, Rebuilt in the Song Dynasty

Height: 231 cm, Width: 129 cm

Housed in: Liuzhou, Guangxi Zhuang Autonomous Region

唐代政治角力场的谪贬制度，如何意外地促进了岭南地区的思想文化启蒙？

岭南的“汉越一家”

柳州罗池庙碑

Liuzhou Luochi Temple Stele

57

文物简读

柳宗元、韩愈、苏轼——站在中华文化巅峰上的三个巨人，同时会聚于一块碑上，成就了一座“三绝碑”。罗池庙碑集中反映了隋唐时期岭南少数民族加速融入中华民族多元一体的历史进程，折射出其时“汉越一家”的历史情景。

罗池庙里罗池碑

史载，唐长庆二年（822）——柳宗元在柳州去世后的第三年，柳州百姓因感念柳宗元为柳州做出的巨大贡献，为其修建罗池庙以作祠祭。罗池庙建成后，柳宗元的好友韩愈为其撰写悼文《柳州罗池庙碑》，碑文后附有《迎享送神诗》。随后，唐代著名书法家沈传师将诗文用小楷刻写于石碑之上，立于庙中。可惜，此碑在宋代被盗。

北宋年间，大文豪苏轼被贬广东，途经柳州，应邀重书碑文。苏轼以楷书书写了碑文后面的《迎享送神诗》。南宋嘉定十年（1217），苏轼所书被刻于碑上，立于罗池庙中。

至此，这块中国历史上绝无仅有的“韩文、柳事、苏书”的“三绝碑”就诞生了。

柳州城中柳宗元

唐朝平定安史之乱后，一批官僚士大夫为加强中央集权，反对藩镇割据，打击宦官势力，革除政治积弊而发动了“永贞革新”，这场改革历时180多天后宣告失败。参与革新的大文学家柳宗元被贬为

永州司马；十年后，他又被改贬为柳州刺史。

柳州古属百越之地，是西瓯、骆越居地。秦始皇统一岭南后，设置桂林郡、南海郡、象郡，柳州属桂林郡。汉朝平定南越后，柳州又属郁林郡。隋唐之时，柳州仍是社会经济较为落后的“化外之地”。

来到柳州后，柳宗元摒弃“华贵夷贱”的偏见，“不鄙夷其民，动以礼法”，与当地民众建立了亲密的关系，施以一系列善政：禁绝人口买卖，坚决革除恶劣的蓄奴和残奴之风；化民成俗，破除迷信，抑制杀牲祀鬼；修复孔庙、兴办文教、设立学堂、传授儒家思想，为当地青年文士指点文章书法；引进中原地区先进的生产技术，组织民众垦荒，发展地方经济；带领官民在柳江河畔种下柳树，以美化风景，防护河堤；等等。

短短四年，柳宗元将柳州治理得井然有序，“城郭巷道，皆治使端正”，与之前的“宿贼遍野”“越人信祥而易杀，傲化而偭仁”形成鲜明对比。柳州地区文化也逐渐昌明。清代《马平县志》载：“自唐柳侯来守是邦，建学明伦，而都人始翕然向化。”自此之后，柳州“鸿儒硕生，后先相望”，学者和人才辈出。

四年后，柳宗元在柳州刺史任上溘然长辞。而他留在柳州的丰功伟绩，却让柳州人深深怀念。由此，才有了这空前绝后的“三绝碑”。

“并服礼仪，衣服、巾带如中国焉”

隋唐以来，岭南地区加速汇入中华民族多元一体的历史进程。唐朝在岭南设置广州、桂州、容州、安南和邕州五个总管府，史称“五管”。五管之下，又在少数民族地区设置93个羁縻州，由当地民族的首领担任刺史等官职，并实行世袭制。这些政策赢得了当地族群的拥护，建立了岭南民众对唐朝的国家认同，推动了边疆地区主动融入中华文化圈，逐渐出现了“汉越一家”的局面。

这一时期，还有一个特别的因素促进了岭南地区的发展，那就是官员贬谪制度。岭南一带是唐代官员最主要的贬谪之地，而被贬官员多是社会精英、朝中肱股，作为中原文化的优秀传承者和引领者，他们将满腹学识带到了岭南，无论是寄情山水、作诗撰文，还是助民耕种、重教兴学，都极大地影响了岭南民风，促进了中原文化在边疆的传播，推动了当地的社会经济发展。

比如，除柳宗元被贬为柳州刺史外，王义方被贬为儋州吉安县丞，这位著名的忠臣和教育家在此“蛮荒之地”讲经授学，教授礼乐，成为第一个在海南开启儒学教育的人。又如，李德裕被贬为潮州司马，这位杰出的政治家、文学家对“江、岭之间信巫祝，惑鬼怪”的陋习，“谕之以言，绳之以法，数年之间，弊风顿革”。再如，被称为一代循吏的水利专家韦丹，在出任广西容州刺史后，“教民耕织，止惰游……教种茶、麦，仁化大行”。

正是这一批身处江湖之远却心怀天下的文人士大夫，为岭南民众带来了“并服礼仪，衣服、巾带如中国焉”的深刻文化认同，促使这里的文化土壤与社会心理结构悄然发生改变。岭南的儒生、文人与日俱增。这一现象也引起了朝廷的极大重视，进一步采取了积极鼓励和提携的特殊政策，使当地出现了更多儒学造诣颇深的少数民族知识分子。

In 819, Liu Zongyuan died in Liuzhou. Three years later, or the 2nd year of Emperor Changqing (822), the people in Liuzhou decided to build Luochi Temple for Liu Zongyuan to commemorate his great contributions to Liuzhou. After the completion of the temple, Han Yu, a friend of Liu Zongyuan, wrote the eulogy *Liuzhou Luochi Temple Stele*, with an ode to the dead soul. Later, Shen Chuanshi, a famous calligrapher of the Tang Dynasty, was invited to inscribe the eulogy on the stele in small regular script. Unfortunately, the stele was stolen in the Song Dynasty.

Su Shi, a worthy of Northern Song, was exiled to Guangdong by way of Liuzhou, where he was invited to rewrite the inscription. He wrote the ode to the dead soul in regular script. In the 10th year of Emperor Jiading of the Southern Song Dynasty (1217), Su Shi's writings were inscribed on the stele and erected in Luochi Temple.

In the Sui and Tang Dynasties, the political stability or grand unification catalyzed the integration of minorities in Lingnan Region into the multi-ethnic Chinese nation. The Tang court established five General Governor Offices in Lingnan, i.e. Guangzhou, Guizhou, Rongzhou, An'nan and Yongzhou, which administered 93 *Ji-Mi* (羁縻, halter-and-bridle) prefectures. In the *Ji-Mi* System, local tribal leaders were appointed as *Ci Shi* (inspector of a prefecture), which can be passed on through generations. These policies were welcomed by ethnic groups in Lingnan, enhancing political cohesion and enlarging cultural influence of the Tang Dynasty.

The relegation-exile system fully developed in the Tang Dynasty. Officials, as cultural celebrities or political elites, were generally banished to Lingnan. They spread the culture in the Central Plains to Lingnan. Their sighting trips, literary writings, agricultural labors or educational activities all had a deep impact on the ethos in Lingnan, boosting local socio-economic development of Lingnan.

唐朝时期中华民族的人口在其内部发生了怎样的结构性变化?

盛唐时期民族融合推动人口繁荣

三彩骑俑队列

58

Tri-Colored Glazed Han-Hu Figurines on Horseback in Formation

文物简读

总发为髻，冠以巾帻，束着典型的汉式头饰，身上穿的却是对襟翻领的胡式夹袍——这一混搭的装扮来自生活在唐朝境内的胡人。三彩骑俑队列，以群像的形式真实反映了盛唐时期民族融合潮流下的人口大繁荣盛况。

一次爆发式的人口增长

这组具有典型盛唐风格的三彩骑马俑，女骑俑头绾高髻，身穿窄袖圆领或“V”领紧身衣；男骑俑头戴软幞头，身着圆领窄袖紧身衣。其中一俑深目高鼻，长着旋颊及耳的大胡须，身穿翻领胡式大衣，足着长靴，为典型的胡人形象。这一组胡汉混杂的唐三彩骑马俑群像，是甘肃河西走廊出土的大量骑马俑的代表作。与此同时，北方多个地区如陕西、河南、山西、山东等地，也有胡汉混杂的文武将俑、伎乐俑等社会地位高低不一、等级差别明显的三彩人物俑出土，印证了盛唐时期人口构成的多元性，反映了这一时期人口震撼式增长的情景。

曾有学者根据各种古代人口资料，得出了一个统计结果：中国古代人口的年平均增长率为1.4‰。根据葛剑雄《中国人口发展史》一书的研究结果，从贞观十三年（639）到天宝十四年（755）的116年间，唐朝人口从1200多万迅速增长到5300万左右，人口的年平均增长率高达12‰，这远远超出了中国古代人口的年平均增长水平。

盛唐时期的人口增长为什么会如此迅速？学者们认为，如果仅仅依靠中原人口的自然增长，绝不可能达到这一水平。这一增长率应该包含了内迁列入户籍并逐渐与汉人相融合的边疆少数族群的人口。

名称：三彩骑俑队列

年代：唐

规格：俑高36—38厘米，长36厘米，宽12厘米

出土地点：甘肃省秦安县叶家堡

收藏单位：甘肃省博物馆

Name: Tri-Colored Glazed Han-Hu Figurines on Horseback in Formation

Historical Period: The Tang Dynasty

Height: 36–38 cm, Length: 36 cm, Width: 12 cm

Excavation Site: Yejiabao, Qin'an County, Gansu Province

Housed in: Gansu Provincial Museum

当然，盛唐人口增长与唐初统治者采取的一系列轻徭薄赋、恢复社会经济的措施有关，也与唐朝政府提倡嫁娶、鼓励生产的政策有关，同时还得益于唐朝对城市户籍管理制度的科学化调整，使那些由于战乱脱籍、漏籍的人口得以重新登记。但除去这些，大量少数族群从边疆内迁，列入唐朝户籍，也是一个重要的因素。从一组数字可以管窥一二：南北朝时期内迁的南、北方少数族群合计约540万人，到隋唐时，这些人口已稳固地融入中原汉人之中，列入户籍，并占到唐朝在籍人口峰值的10%强。

中华民族人口内涵的变化

这组胡汉混杂的三彩骑马俑是当时民族融合的一个缩影，映射的是这一时期不同族群、不同阶层融入中华民族的生动情景。纵观整个唐朝，这些胡人在拓展大唐疆域、促进经济繁荣、推动文化发展、维护社会稳定方面做出了重要贡献。尤其是骁勇善战的胡人武将，在唐朝开疆拓土、平定四海的功劳簿上，留下了浓墨重彩的一笔，这从唐朝“凌烟阁二十四功臣”可略窥一斑。如长孙无忌和尉迟敬德是鲜卑人，屈突通是奚人。

此外，忠心耿耿、多次为唐朝征战的突厥贵族阿史那·社尔，曾经平高昌、征高句丽，以主将身份率军远征西域，一路击败西突厥、焉耆等国，最后灭掉龟兹，威震西域。率部归唐的契苾何力原本是铁勒可汗，他曾击败吐谷浑，平定高昌、薛延陀，远征龟兹。唐玄宗时期，唐军在西域的主要镇将、安西四镇节度使高仙芝是高句丽人，他赤胆忠心为唐朝守卫和经略西域通道，防御吐蕃和大食军队的入侵。当安史之乱烽烟四起时，远在西域的于阗国王尉迟胜闻讯，立即带领自己的军队入唐驰援，并放弃王位，甘心在唐朝为臣。契丹部落酋长李光弼、王思礼等大批将领，都曾被唐朝重用以平定安史之乱。

在唐朝大一统格局引领下，这些处处可见的胡人武将，带着他们彪悍的体质和能征善战的特性，融入了中华民族多元一体的历史洪流中。

隋唐王朝本是在民族大融合的基础上建立起来的，其中隋唐皇室的母系祖先都是被汉化了的鲜卑人。这样的血缘交融奠定了隋唐王朝开明包容的文化心理。更重要的是，隋唐大一统的政治环境、强盛的经济实力和兼容并蓄的民族政策，吸引着边疆各地的民众受王道感化，主动向中原凝聚、靠拢，由此引发了自北朝以来绵延至盛唐的大规模人口融合，刺激人口迅速增长，使这一时期的人口构成表现出鲜明的多元交融特征。

所以，当历史行至隋唐时，中华民族的人口内涵已经发生了深刻的变化——以传统意义上的“华夏—汉”为主体，广泛融合了北方五胡以及南方蛮夷等族群乃至相当数量的外国族裔，形成了一个充满生机活力的新族体。

The group of tri-colored glazed Han-Hu figurines embodies typical Tang style. The female figurines have their hair in high buns, and wear clothes with narrow sleeves and round collar, or tights with V-shaped collar. The male figurines wear soft caps and tights with round collar and narrow sleeves. One figurine has deep eyes and a prominent nose, with large whirlpool-like whiskers reaching the ears. He wears a Hu-style coat with lapel and long boots. Obviously, he has the blood of Hu. In addition to the Hexi Corridor, similar tri-colored glazed figurines were unearthed in Shaanxi, Henan, Shanxi and Shandong. They were Han-Hu officials, generals or musicians from different hierarchies. These archaeological findings mirror the diversity and proliferation of population in the prosperous Tang Dynasty.

In *The History of Chinese Population Development*, Ge Jianxiong calculates that in 116 years (639—755), or from the 13th year of Zhenguan to the 14th year of Tianbao, the population of Tang shot up from over 12 million to 53 million, with an average annual growth rate of 12‰, much higher than the average level in ancient China.

The group of tri-colored glazed Han-Hu figurines crystallizes the ethnic integration in the Tang Dynasty. The Hu people made outstanding contributions to expanding the Tang's domain, promoting economic prosperity, deepening cultural exchanges and safeguarding social stability. Particularly, the Hu generals were brave and battlewise. Their meritorious services to Tang lied in enlarging the Tang's territory and quelling the unrest, as seen in "Statue of 24 Heroes at Lingyan Pavilion". For example, Zhangsun Wuji and Yuchi Jingde had the origin of Xianbei, and Qutu Tong came from the Xi, a clan of Donghu.

In the Sui and Tang Dynasties, the population structure of the Chinese nation significantly changed. Taking *Hua Xia* or Han as the main part, the Chinese nation included the five Hu tribes in the north as well as a considerable number of foreign ethnic groups, injecting new blood into *Hua Xia*.

当突厥在北部和西北部边疆造成重大安全威胁时，唐朝是如何解决这一边疆危机的？

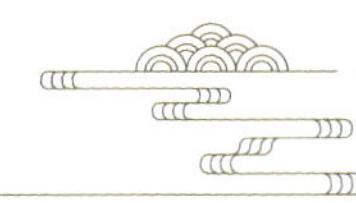

画中窥唐：盛世的边疆武略

陈及之《便桥会盟图》卷

Alliance at Bianqiao Bridge by Chen Jizhi (陈及之)

59

文物简读

246人，180匹马和四头骆驼，人马虽盈寸方，但神情毕肖，尽见风采——长近八米的白描纸本《便桥会盟图》是绘制人马最多的元代传世名作。公元626年，东突厥颉利可汗趁唐太宗李世民初登帝位，局势未稳，率大军南下，兵锋直指长安城。危难之际，李世民只身率房玄龄等六骑，赴渭水便桥，隔河严正斥责颉利可汗毁约之不义，后双方在便桥斩白马结盟，颉利可汗退兵。元代画家陈及之根据这一史实绘制的《便桥会盟图》，把唐朝妥善处理与突厥的关系，从而安定西北边疆的史实带到了我们面前。

突厥：从柔然“锻奴”到草原霸主

突厥是6世纪中叶兴起于阿尔泰山地区的一个游牧部落。公元552年，突厥首领阿史那土门建立了突厥汗国，其子木杅可汗即位后，迅速灭亡柔然，威服塞外，成为北方草原的新兴霸主。在南北朝的后30年间，突厥对北朝政治局势的影响可谓举足轻重。隋朝开皇三年（583），突厥汗国分裂为东西两部，东突厥汗国南下臣服于隋，并与隋朝一道对抗在中亚地区独霸一方的西突厥汗国。隋末战争期间，东突厥脱离隋朝，又逐渐强盛起来，并屡次发兵南下，掠夺边境各州。唐朝建立后，唐高祖李渊与东突厥始毕可汗订立和平约定。但此后，始毕可汗的弟弟颉利可汗继位，撕毁了与唐高祖的和平协议，趁李世民初登帝位，率大军侵犯长安，直抵城外渭水，于是便有唐太宗危急之中与东突厥军隔河对阵的“便桥会盟”。

当其时，唐太宗与侍中高士廉、中书令房玄龄、将军周范等六人驰马出城，到达渭水河畔，与颉

规格：纵36厘米，横774厘米

收藏单位：故宫博物院

Name: *Alliance at Bianqiao Bridge* by Chen Jizhi (陈及之)

Historical Period: The Yuan Dynasty

The Vertical: 36 cm, The Horizontal: 774 cm

Housed in: The Palace Museum

陳及之便橋會盟圖

利可汗隔岸说话。太宗大义凛然，义正词严地斥责他负约。随后，唐朝军队赶到，部队整肃，旌旗猎猎，突厥兵大惊。唐太宗指挥大军退而列阵，单独与颉利可汗按辔交谈。颉利可汗心生畏惧，于是请和。第二天，双方杀白马，在便桥盟誓，颉利可汗引兵退走，并欲献马三千匹、羊万头，但唐太宗没有接受，只让他们把抢掠的中原人口放归。随后，唐太宗诏令部下护送突厥军队。

和则休戚与共，乱则虽远必诛

便桥会盟后，唐王朝与东突厥的形势发生了逆转：突厥政权内部发生了纷争，薛延陀、回纥、拔野古等部相继叛离，颉利可汗与突利可汗发生内斗。这一时期，唐朝在外交方面沿用隋朝“远交近攻、离强合弱”的政策，联合薛延陀、回纥等部，共同抗击东突厥，上演了一场“三英战吕布”的大戏。

贞观三年（629），将军张公瑾上书唐太宗李世民，陈列六条出兵东突厥的理由。唐太宗诏命李靖率大军兵分六路，经过数次战役，东突厥军溃散，被歼万余人，被俘十余万人，颉利可汗被擒获。唐太宗并未处死颉利可汗，不仅释放了他和他的家人，还赐予他房屋和土地，封他为右卫大将军，让他在长安城度过余生。

面对突厥百姓，唐太宗采取了“全其部落，顺其土俗”的开明政策，为他们划出繁衍生息之地，并给予他们与唐朝百姓同等的地位和待遇。同时，东突厥的官员也被委以重任，在唐朝任职。这些政策最终使东突厥融入中原，成为汉人的一部分。

东突厥对中原的袭扰止息后，唐王朝得以腾出手来应对西突厥。

唐武德元年（618），西突厥射匮可汗去世，其弟统叶护可汗继位。统叶护可汗东征西讨，北并铁勒，西拒波斯，南接罽宾，称霸西域，将西突厥汗国推向一个鼎盛时期。

此后，西突厥乙毗咄陆可汗自恃兵势强盛，发兵攻打唐朝管辖的焉耆、伊州（今新疆哈密）。唐朝于贞观十四年（640）派大将侯君集、契苾何力西征，打败进犯的突厥军，设立西州、庭州，建安西都护府。贞观二十三年（649），唐太宗去世，西突厥可汗阿史那贺鲁趁机反叛，侵犯唐朝管辖的庭州轮台县（今乌鲁木齐）、蒲类县（今木垒县）等地。显庆元年（656），唐高宗派遣程知节（即程咬金）为行军大总管，率兵西征，大败西突厥于鹰娑川（今巴音布鲁克草原）。显庆二年（657），唐高宗又派遣苏定方为行军大总管，率领唐军将士与回纥将士，翻越阿尔泰山，由北道进军；同时派遣归附唐朝的西突厥将领阿史那弥射和阿史那布真为流沙道安抚大使，带领突厥将士沿天山北麓向西进军。在两路大军夹击之下，西突厥汗国大败，并就此灭国，阿史那贺鲁成为俘虏。但是就像唐太宗当年赦免颉利可汗那样，唐高宗赦免了阿史那贺鲁，并将他留在长安居住。

和则休戚与共，乱则虽远必诛——这是唐朝中央政权解决边疆问题的基本策略。唐朝完全统一了西域，实现了西北边疆的安宁稳定，为辉煌的大唐盛世创造了重要的条件。

In *Alliance at Bianqiao Bridge*, there are 246 people, 180 horses and four camels. Albeit as small as one *cun* (寸, one *cun* roughly equals 3.33 cm), the people and horses are vividly drawn, displaying unique charm.

In the 3rd year of Emperor Kaihuang of the Sui Dynasty (583), the Turkic Khaganate split. Eastern Turkic Khaganate moved southward and pledged loyalty to Sui, resisting Western Turkic Khaganate, an overlord in the Central Asia. In the late Sui Dynasty, wars swept the Central Plains, and Shibi Khan broke away from Sui and came to rise again. Shibi repeatedly harassed and spoliated the northern border of Sui. In the Tang Dynasty, Li Yuan, Emperor Gaozu, signed a peace agreement with Shibi Khan. However, after Illig Khan, the younger brother of Shibi Khan, succeeded to the throne, he ripped up the peace agreement and mounted a large-scale offensive against Tang. The Turkic troops arrived at the Wei River. At the moment of crisis, Emperor Taizong bravely had a dialogue with Illig Khan at Bianqiao Bridge and forged an alliance with him. This event was called "Alliance at Bianqiao Bridge".

The situations for Tang and Turk went into reverse. Se-Yanto, Uighur and Bayirqu successively betrayed Eastern Turkic Khaganate, and Illig Khan and Tolis Khan engaged in internal strife. Tang, in conjunction with Se-Yanto and Uighur, attacked Eastern Turkic Khaganate. In 629, under the order of Emperor Taizong, Li Jing led the six-column Tang forces and engaged the Eastern Turkic army, killing more than 10,000 men and capturing more than 100,000 men. Illig Khan was also seized.

In 649, Emperor Taizong died. Ishbara Khan (Ashina Helu) of Western Turkic Khaganate rebelled and invaded Tang's Luntai County (present-day Urumqi) and Pulei County (present-day Mulei County) of Tingzhou Prefecture. In 657, Emperor Gaozong commissioned Su Dingfang as Chief Commander. Su led Tang and Uighur soldiers, crossing the Altai Mountains and marching from the north. Ashina Mishe and Ashina Buzhen, two Western Turkic generals that paid allegiance to Tang, were designated as *Liushadao Anfu Dashi* (流沙道安抚大使, military officer), leading the Turkic soldiers and advancing westward along the northern foothills of the Tianshan Mountains. Under pincer movement, Western Turkic Khaganate suffered a crushing defeat, with Ishbara Khan captured.

唐太宗李世民被尊称为“天可汗”，这一巨大的荣耀背后，关联着唐王朝什么样的政治制度安排？

羁縻府州制度

“蒲类州之印”铜印

The Bronze Seal of *Pu Lei Zhou* (Pulei Prefecture)

文物简读

这枚铜印为正方形，桥形纽，印文为篆书“蒲类州之印”。在这枚不起眼的印章背后，关联着唐代对边疆民族地区实施的一项重大政治制度——羁縻府州制度。

揭开一枚铜印之谜

1973年，蒋其祥先生在新疆吉木萨尔县北庭故城进行文物调查时，获得了一枚铜印，经专家鉴定，这枚铜印为新疆首次发现的唐代官印，而且是与唐代实施羁縻府州制度高度吻合的实物。

似乎一切顺理成章的事，在实证当中却遇上了令人困惑的谜团。一是“蒲类州”之名未见于史载，新、旧唐书与唐代的总地志《元和郡县图志》只有“蒲类县”和“蒲类镇”的记载。蒲类州与蒲类县是同一回事吗？蒲类州大概在什么地方？这枚铜印为何出现于北庭故城吉木萨尔？

史载，显庆二年（657），唐朝平定西突厥可汗阿史那贺鲁之乱后，在天山以北设立了都护府、都督府和州。其中设立的昆陵都护府管辖范围包括天山北麓至楚河流域，封阿史那弥射为兴昔亡可汗、昆陵都护，领五咄陆部。据《新唐书·地理志》记载，唐朝政府设置的管理模式是：“即其部落，列置州县，其大者为都督府，以其首领为都督刺史，皆得世袭”，“其役属诸胡皆为州”。昆陵都护府下辖23个都督府，一一都有列载，由于州比较小，所以没有记录在案。显庆四年（659），唐朝政府对所建立的府、州“各给印契，以为征发符信”。

专家们认为，“蒲类州之印”很可能就是显庆四年唐朝政府为刚建立的府州颁发的印契。但是专家们也指出，蒲类州与蒲类县有本质的区别，蒲类县是县制单位，最新的考古成果表明其治所在

名称：“蒲类州之印”铜印

年代：唐

规格：印面边长5.7厘米，通高4厘米

出土地点：新疆维吾尔自治区吉木萨尔县北庭故城遗址

收藏单位：新疆维吾尔自治区博物馆

Name: The Bronze Seal of *Pu Lei Zhou* (Pulei Prefecture)

Historical Period: The Tang Dynasty

Side Length (The Seal Surface): 5.7 cm, Total Height: 4 cm

Excavation Site: Site of Bashbaliq (Beiting) City, Jimsar County, Xinjiang Uyghur Autonomous Region

Housed in: Xinjiang Uyghur Autonomous Region Museum

今昌吉回族自治州奇台县城东的唐朝墩古城；蒲类州是羁縻州，治所有可能在蒲类县，管辖范围应在今新疆东部，东天山北麓奇台、木垒一带。那么，为什么"蒲类州之印"出现于北庭故城？从地理位置上看，由于蒲类州与北庭故城距离较近，常有来往，此枚铜印有可能是因为战乱或者其他原因，遗落于北庭故城。

边疆治理的创新

自秦汉建立统一多民族国家以来，在疆域辽阔、民族众多、习俗各异的形势下，历代统治者多沿用"修其教不易其俗，齐其政不易其宜"的传统来治理边疆民族地区，这种传统最早可以追溯到西周时期所确立的朝贡制度。这种制度明确规定：距离王朝统治中心2500里的"要服"之地，须定期向天子贡献方物；距离王朝统治中心2500里之外的"荒服"之地，则须承认天子的统治地位，并且在其君更替和新天子登基之时，须前来朝拜天子以示臣服。

唐贞观四年（630），东突厥汗国灭亡后，针对突厥降户的安置问题，唐太宗李世民召集大臣进行了商讨，唐太宗综合考虑几种意见后采纳了中书令温彦博建议中的合理部分，决定设置羁縻府州进行管理：突厥首领担任羁縻府州的长官，管理其本部事务。《旧唐书·突厥传》记载："其酋首至者，皆拜为将军、中郎将等官，布列朝廷，五品以上百余人，因而入居长安者数千家。"有学者认为，羁縻府州制度是唐太宗李世民吸取处理东突厥和高昌问题的经验教训，把"因俗而治"与内地州县制度结合起来，在周边少数民族地区推行的一种特殊的州县行政制度。

唐王朝在处置东突厥内附各部特别是击败薛延陀、招附铁勒诸部之后显示出来的明智手段和宽广胸怀，赢得了边疆民族各部的尊重，成就了唐太宗的"天可汗"之名。羁縻府州制度进而愈加受到唐王朝的重视和推广，并逐渐形成了一套相对完备和制度化的模式。羁縻府州派代表前往中央政府进行朝贡、拜谒、求亲、上书等，唐王朝则通过册封、贡赐、互市、和亲、盟誓或委派专人到边疆羁縻府州慰抚、巡视等方式，来维系民族关系，稳固边疆秩序。简而言之，羁縻府州制度是唐王朝以建立府州来对边疆民族地区进行行政管理的制度。在羁縻府州内，由各民族自己的首领担任中央王朝的官职，朝廷对首领册封相应的职官称号，首领"因俗而治"，朝廷不过问其内部事务。

从唐太宗时期到唐玄宗时期，全国设置的羁縻府州达到856个。羁縻府州的管理方式是：任命当地族群首领担任可世袭的都督、刺史，实行高度自治；羁縻府州人口不纳入户部统计，不列入编户，只承担当地政府赋役；受到任命或册封的边疆族群首领有执行中央政府政策和传播唐朝文化的义务；中央政府可根据情况变化对羁縻府州进行调整，如将羁縻府州改为正式府州，或将正式府州改为羁縻府州，将都督府改为都护府等。

大唐盛世的制度保障

唐朝之所以空前强盛，除了军事上的优势以及文化上采取包容开放的政策，还在于特别注重对国家的有效治理，如继承了隋朝的三省六部制、完善了科举制、开创了羁縻府州制度等等。羁縻府

州制度是唐朝承袭“因俗而治”传统对经略边疆民族地区以及安抚内附的民族而做出的制度创新，虽然蕴含着“夷夏有别”的观念，但却把“大一统”的思想、“仁德”思想贯通其中，形成了一套完备的管理体系，保证了边疆地区的相对稳定，促进了边疆与中原的政治、经济、文化交流，使周边民族对中央王朝的向心力和凝聚力不断得到增强。

羁縻府州制度影响深远，宋朝仍在部分地区沿用，元明清时期实行“参用土人为官”的土司制度，本质上仍然是对羁縻府州制度的继承，只不过在土司的设置上更有针对性，管控更有力度。

The bronze seal has a square shape and a bridge-shaped knob, with the seal-script inscriptions of *Pu Lei Zhou Zhi Yin*. In 1973, Jiang Qixiang, an archaeologist, discovered a bronze seal at Site of Bashbaliq (Beiting) City, Jimsar County, Xinjiang Uyghur Autonomous Region. As the first official seal of the Tang Dynasty discovered in Xinjiang, it provided material evidence for the existence of the *Ji-Mi* (羁縻) or halter-bridle prefecture system (a special type of administrative system in remote areas where hereditary tribal rulers received duties from the central court while keeping the high degree of autonomy) in the Tang Dynasty.

However, as a place name, *Pu Lei Zhou* (Pulei Prefecture) was not seen in historical records. In *Old Book of Tang*, *New Book of Tang* and *The Atlas of Prefectures and Counties in the Reign of Emperor Yuanhe* (a general geographical book), only *Pu Lei Xian* (Pulei County) and *Pu Lei Zhen* (Pulei Township) were mentioned. Some scholars argue that the bronze seal of *Pu Lei Zhou* was probably the seal-token issued by the Tang court for the newly-established prefecture in the 4th year of Emperor Xianqing. Other scholars disagree, stressing that *Pu Lei Zhou* and *Pu Lei Xian* are fundamentally different. As the latest archaeological findings suggest, *Pu Lei Xian* was a county, located in Site of Dun City in the Tang Dynasty, in the east of present-day Qitai County, Changji Hui Autonomous Prefecture. *Pu Lei Zhou*, as a *Ji-Mi* prefecture, was probably seated in Pulei County, administering the eastern part of present-day Xinjiang, and Qitai and Mulei at the northern foot of the East Tianshan Mountains. Geographically, Pulei Prefecture was near Site of Bashbaliq City at Jimsar. Owing to the scourge of war, the bronze seal was left at Site of Bashbaliq City.

In brief, the *Ji-Mi* prefecture system signified a way of administrative management in border ethnic areas in the Tang Dynasty. The *Ji-Mi* system came into effect in the reign of Emperor Taizong. In the reign of Emperor Xuanzong, the Tang court had established 856 *Ji-Mi* prefectures. In a *Ji-Mi* prefecture, local tribal rulers, who were appointed as hereditary prefectural governor (e.g. *Dudu* or *Cishi*), enjoyed the high degree of autonomy. Citizens were not involved in the national census of Ministry of Household Registration, and obliged to pay taxes and undertake corvee to local rulers. Local tribal rulers fulfilled the duties of implementing the policies of the Tang court and disseminating the culture of the Central Plains. The status of *Ji-Mi* prefecture can be adjusted to changing circumstances, administrative prefecture or protectorate, for example.

一个东北边疆政权如何因学习中原，而成为影响历史的“海东盛国”？

举国学唐风的渤海国

“天门军之印”铜印

The Bronze Seal with the Inscriptions of *Tian Men Jun Zhi Yin* (天门军之印, The Seal of Imperial Army)

文物简读

这枚国内现存唯一的一方渤海国官印，为青铜质，铜片镶成，呈长方形，印文为汉字篆书“天门军之印”。笔画细挺有力，圆润活泼；印背楷书“天门军之印”，与唐朝官印形制一样。“天门军”是渤海国中类似唐朝中央禁军的军事组织，“天门军之印”出土自渤海国上京皇城内，可作为研究天门军这一军事组织的重要线索，也是渤海国使用汉字的重要例证。这枚印章在一定程度上反映出唐朝在渤海国册封属国的史实，以及渤海国与唐朝之间“车书本一家”的友好关系。

“海东盛国”

公元7世纪，东北地区的肃慎族系分化成两大部落联盟：黑水靺鞨和粟末靺鞨。其中粟末靺鞨居住于南部，位于现吉林省吉林市一带。

公元696年，唐朝对粟末靺鞨采取招抚政策，封其首领乞乞仲象为震国公。713年，唐朝又封乞乞仲象的儿子大祚荣为左骁卫大将军、渤海郡王，并以其所统治区域为忽汗州，为唐朝的羁縻州，加授大祚荣为忽汗州都督。大祚荣随即去“靺鞨”号，以“渤海”为国号。

渤海国在政治体制和典章法律上，“大抵宪象中国制度”。当其第三世国王大钦茂在位时，渤海国对中原文化的吸收进入了高峰阶段。大钦茂大兴文治，模仿唐朝完善中央集权的政治制度，在中央设立三省六部，在地方设置府、州、县。他在位56年，即位第二年就派人入唐抄写《唐礼》《三国志》《晋书》《三十六国春秋》等典籍，又多次派子弟前往唐朝学习，遣使入唐达49次。他曾效仿唐

名称：“天门军之印”铜印

年代：唐

规格：边长5.3厘米，通高4.3厘米

出土地点：黑龙江省宁安市渤海上京龙泉府遗址

收藏单位：黑龙江省博物馆

Name: The Bronze Seal with the Inscriptions of *Tian Men Jun Zhi Yin* (天门军之印, The Seal of Imperial Army)

Historical Period: The Tang Dynasty

Side Length: 5.3 cm, Total Height: 4.3 cm

Excavation Site: Shangjing Longquan Prefecture Site of the Bohai Kingdom, Ning’an City, Heilongjiang Province

Housed in: Heilongjiang Provincial Museum

朝国子监，在渤海国内设置“胄子监”，作为传播儒家文化的重要基地。因为文化日趋繁荣，国力蒸蒸日上，渤海国一时获得了“海东盛国”的美誉，大钦茂去世后也获得了“文王”的谥号。

渤海国生产力水平也大幅度提高。此时渤海国人已经普遍使用铁制工具，畜牧业发达，其饲养的马、牛成为与中原地区进行商业贸易的重要物品，当时的山东半岛地区“货市渤海名马，岁岁不绝”。此外，渤海国的渔猎采集业仍占有一定地位，貂、虎、豹、熊、人参等成为向唐朝纳贡的重要方物。

渤海国内部由众多民族组成——除靺鞨人之外，还有高句丽、契丹、汉人、奚人、九姓杂胡、达姑、回鹘等。从族系来说，靺鞨属于肃慎族系，高句丽属于夫余—濊貊族系，契丹、奚人与达姑属于东胡—鲜卑族系……在渤海国两百多年的历史中，其内部民族交往交融的情形十分和谐融洽。

公元926年，契丹酋长耶律阿保机攻灭传世15王的渤海国，渤海人后来逐渐融于女真人之中，其文化对辽、金两代仍有重要影响。

唐朝的附属国

渤海国一直保持着与唐朝的宗藩关系，在安史之乱期间也未贸然卷入，而是迁都上京，以防止叛军侵入。公元762年，刚刚平定安史之乱的唐代宗，为示褒奖，下诏将渤海从忽汗州升格为国，册封大钦茂为渤海国王，加授正一品检校太尉。渤海的地位由此得到提高。

此后，每任渤海王的继承人均在得到唐王朝认可（即被唐王朝册封）后才获得合法性，否则只能称“权知国务”。唐王朝在册封渤海国新任国王的同时，必任命其为忽汗州都督，即继位者同时接受作为唐王朝地方官的任命。立国后两百多年间，渤海国定期向唐王朝朝贡，共计140余次。

渤海国是唐朝以册封属国的方式统辖边疆地区的一个典型例子。这种治理策略不仅使当地民族建立了对唐朝的国家认同，也将当地纳入了中华文化的影响范围，对中华民族多元一体的发展起到了促进作用。

唐朝册封的属国不少，有的在今天中国版图以外，存在的时间长短也不一样。今天仍在中国境内的有渤海国、回鹘汗国、于阗国、南诏国等。

It boasts the only existing official seal of the Bohai Kingdom in China. It is made of bronze and inlaid with copper sheet, in a rectangular shape. On the seal are Chinese characters *Tian Men Jun Zhi Yin* in seal character. The strokes are robust and balanced. On the back of the seal are regular-script *Tian Men Jun Zhi Yin*, which resembles the form and shape of the Tang-Dynasty official seals. Unearthed in the imperial city of Shangjing, the seal provides important evidence for the studies of the military organization *Tian Men Jun* of the Bohai Kingdom, similar to the imperial army in the Tang Dynasty. It demonstrated the historical facts that Chinese characters were used in the Bohai Kingdom, and that the Bohai Kingdom was the dependent state of the Tang Dynasty, as described in the poetic line "The Tang and Bohai are culturally connected".

In the 7th century, the Sushen clan in northeastern China split into two major tribal alliances: the Heishui Mohe and the Sumo Mohe. The latter dwelled in the southern region, present-day Jilin City, Jilin Province.

In 696, the Tang Dynasty adopted the policy of appeasement and conferred the title of Duke of Zhen on Qiqi Zhongxiang, leader of Sumo Mohe. In 713, the Tang Dynasty appointed Da Zuorong, the son of Qiqi Zhongxiang, as General of Left Brave Guard and Prince of Bohai, in order to administer Huhan Prefecture, a *Ji-Mi* (羁縻) prefecture of Tang. Da Zuorong was bestowed the title of Governor of Huhan Prefecture. He stopped using Mohe and replaced it with Bohai.

In 926, Yelü Abaoji, the chief of Khitan, annexed the Bohai Kingdom, which had a history of 229 years (15 kings). The Bohai people gradually assimilated into Jurchen, and their culture had a significant impact on the Liao and Jin Dynasties.

名称：回鹘王妃供养像

年代：五代十国

现存地点：甘肃省敦煌市莫高窟409窟

Name: The Portrait of Huihu Princess, a Buddhist Patron

Historical Period: The Five Dynasties and Ten Kingdoms

Housed in: Cave 409, Mogao Grottoes, Dunhuang, Gansu Province

2-5

回鹘是当今维吾尔族的先民吗?

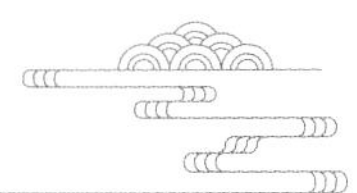

从回纥到回鹘的历史图景

回鹘王妃供养像

The Portrait of Huihu Princess, a Buddhist Patron

文物简读

回纥曾经与唐朝中央政权之间形成一种罕见的亲密信任关系。为了反抗突厥汗国的统治，回纥曾与唐朝军队有力配合，在唐朝对东突厥汗国和后突厥汗国的灭国之战中，扮演了重要角色。回鹘西迁高昌后，遂皈依佛教，并在敦煌创造了精美的壁画遗产。回鹘后来成为今天维吾尔族的先民……寻踪神奇的回鹘人，敦煌莫高窟的许多回鹘供养人壁画，让我们仍能清晰地看见他们的形象。

罕见的亲密互信关系

回鹘，原称回纥。其起源可追溯至贝加尔湖一带的赤狄、丁零。北魏时，铁勒的一个分支袁纥游牧于伊犁河、鄂尔浑河和色楞格河流域，受到突厥汗国的征服和统治。后来，为了反抗突厥的压迫和奴役，袁纥联合铁勒诸部中的仆固、同罗、拔野古等部，趁隋朝与西突厥作战的有利时机，奋起反抗，摆脱了突厥的统治，正式组成了回纥部落联盟。

此后不久，突厥汗国卷土重来。唐贞观三年（629），当唐朝向东突厥发起进攻时，回纥又一次抓住机会，联合薛延陀部，与唐朝军队呼应，大败东突厥；并于第二年与唐军一道乘胜追击，俘获了东突厥可汗，东突厥从此灭国。

十多年后，回纥首领吐迷度率部又一次配合唐朝军队，于贞观二十年（646）攻灭了薛延陀汗国。此战之后，吐迷度遣使入朝，表示归顺。唐朝遂在回纥统辖区设立瀚海都督府，任命吐迷度为瀚海都督、怀化大将军，回纥统辖区成为唐朝的一个边疆羁縻府。唐朝还在回纥地区修筑交通大道，设驿站，抽赋税。同时，回纥军队接受唐朝中央政府的直接征调。

武则天时期，东突厥东山再起，建立后突厥汗国，于8世纪初侵入西域地区，拓地万余里。天宝三载（744），后突厥汗国发生内乱，回纥在唐军的配合下，彻底灭亡后突厥汗国，并建立了回纥汗国。回纥首领骨力裴罗被唐朝册封为怀仁可汗。

此后，回纥还在安史之乱中三次派军帮助唐朝大将郭子仪平叛，为唐朝恢复国家安定立下了汗马功劳。

贞元四年（788），顿莫贺可汗向唐德宗奏请改“回纥”为“回鹘”，取回旋轻捷如鹘之意，得到唐朝批准。

回顾回纥的兴起历程，正是凭借唐王朝强有力的扶持，回纥抓准时机，顺利崛起，成为盘踞漠北的强大势力。也正是因此，回纥和唐朝之间形成了亲密互信关系，双方共同促进了中原与边疆的经济文化发展，巩固了大一统的局面。

唐朝还与回纥建立了密切的姻亲关系。公元758年，唐肃宗的幼女宁国公主嫁给回纥葛勒可汗，这是历史上中原皇帝第一次将亲生女儿嫁给边疆民族首领。此后，唐朝先后又将小宁国公主、咸安公主、太和公主等五位公主，下嫁回纥可汗。而回纥葛勒可汗也以可敦（即王后）之妹嫁予敦煌王李承寀。

回鹘的聚散离合

公元840年，长期受回鹘统治的黠戛斯人进攻回鹘都城，焚毁了回鹘王宫，回鹘汗国由此灭亡。回鹘之民离析为四。一支南下中原，被唐朝收编到卢龙和振武节度使麾下，此后逐渐与当地的汉人融合。另有三支西迁：一支进入河西走廊，被称为河西回鹘或甘州回鹘，他们后来经历了与党项、契丹之间的密集攻伐，逐渐退至瓜、沙二州，与当地诸族交往融合，逐渐演变为今天的裕固族；一支进入吐鲁番盆地和今天的吉木萨尔地区，建立了高昌回鹘王国，这一部分回鹘人相继融合了吐鲁番盆地的汉人以及塔里木盆地的焉耆人、龟兹人、于阗人、疏勒人等，成为元朝时的“畏兀儿”，此后元明时期察合台汗国的蒙古人又和畏兀儿人融为一体，最终演变为今天的维吾尔族；还有一支西越葱岭迁入中亚七河流域，并在那里建立起强盛一时的喀喇汗王朝，其可汗自称为“桃花石汗”或“东方与秦之主”，表明了这一部分回鹘人与中原王朝之间割不断的心理联系。喀喇汗王朝后来被西辽国征服，最后连同建立西辽的契丹人一道，融入了中亚各民族之中。

回鹘在漠北时期信仰摩尼教。9世纪中期，西迁至高昌的回鹘在高昌国居民的影响下，逐渐融入了定居的农耕生活，同时又在高昌国浓厚的佛教信仰氛围中，逐渐舍弃摩尼教而皈依佛教。就是在这一时期，高昌回鹘采用粟特文字母来拼写回鹘语，逐渐演变为回鹘文字。高昌回鹘使用回鹘文书写了许多佛教经典，如《金光明经》《法华经普门品》《弥勒下生经》《尊胜陀罗尼经》等，留下了宝贵的文化遗产。此后，回鹘人还在敦煌石窟里留下了丰富的回鹘文献、回鹘文木活字，又在敦煌和安西榆林开凿了大量的佛教石窟，绘制了众多精美的供养人壁画。今天，我们既能从壁画中直接看到回鹘人的形象，又可从中领悟一个道理：辉煌灿烂的敦煌文化是包括回鹘人在内的各民族共同创造的。

Historically, Huihe had close ties with the Tang court. The Huihe people played an important role in resisting the rule of the Turkic Khaganate and annihilating the Eastern Turkic Khaganate, in tandem with the Tang army. After having settled in Gaochang, the Huihu people converted to Buddhism and created exquisite mural heritage in Dunhuang. In Mogao Grottoes, numerous murals of Huihu Buddhist patrons depicted the historical images of the Huihu people.

Huihu, formerly known as Huihe, originated from Chidi and Dingling in the area of the Lake Baikal. In the Northern Wei Dynasty, Yuanhe, or OnUigur, a clan of Tiele, led a nomadic life in the Ili River, Orkhon River and Selenge River basins, subject to the Turkic Khaganate. Afterwards, in defiance of the Turkic oppression and enslavement, Yuanhe joined forces with various tribes of Tiele, such as Pugu, Tongluo and Bayirqu. The Sui Dynasty launched an attack on the Western Turks. Seizing the chance, Yuanhe cast off the yoke of the Turkic rule and then officially established Huihe tribal alliance. In 788, Dunmohe Khan presented a petition to Emperor Dezong of Tang, asking that the official name of his nation of people be changed from Huihe to Huigu (literally meaning swirling as nimbly as a falcon).

The Huihu people believed in Manichaeism in the Mongolian grasslands. In the middle 9th century, the Huihu people flowed westward and settled in Gaochang, where Buddhism thrived. Gradually, they were acculturated to farming life, and converted from Manichaeism to Buddhism. Henceforth, Gaochang Huihu used the Sogdian script to spell the Uyghur language, which evolved into the Uyghur script. Many Buddhist scriptures were transcribed in the Uyghur language, such as *Suvarṇaprabhāsottama Sūtra* (*Sutra of Supreme Golden Light*), *The Universal Gate* of *The Lotus Sutra*, *Maitreyavyākaraa* (*The Prophecy of the Superior Maitreya*) and *Uṣṇīṣa Vijaya Dhāraṇī* (*Buddha-Crown Superb Victory Dharani*), leaving a valuable cultural legacy to later generations.

From the 9th to the 15th centuries, the Huihu people had professed Buddhism. They handed down abundant Uyghur literature and wooden movable characters in Dunhuang grottoes, carved many Buddhist grottoes in Dunhuang and Yulin, and painted exquisite murals of Buddhist patrons. These murals not only show the images of the Huihu people, but also prove that the brilliant Dunhuang culture was jointly created by various ethnic groups including the Huihu people.

大唐盛世的吸引力有多强？有人为了留在大唐，甘愿舍弃王位！

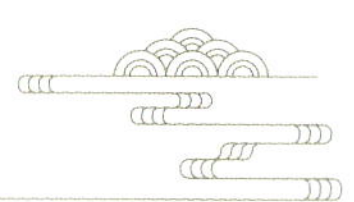

最长寿的地方政权——于阗国

于阗王李圣天礼佛壁画

Li Shengtian, King of Khotan, Worshipping Buddha (Mural)

文物简读

敦煌莫高窟千佛洞的于阗王李圣天礼佛壁画，见证了于阗国对大唐王朝的尊奉和认同。画面上，于阗国王李圣天与王后头戴王冠，一身宽衣博带、雍容华贵的装束几乎与中原人无别。壁画题记“大朝大宝于阗国大圣大明天子”。这里的“大朝”，正是于阗国王对唐朝的尊称。

千年王族尉迟氏

于阗国，一个信仰佛教的古老西域王国，从公元前232年一直延续到公元1006年，也就是从中原的战国时代一直延续到北宋时代，国祚长达1238年，其间始终由王族尉迟氏执政，是中国历史上最长寿的地方政权。唐朝玄奘大师西行取经，路过于阗国，在《大唐西域记》中留下了关于它的明确记载：“自兹以降，奕世相承，传国君临，不失其绪。”

于阗国的先民是操印欧语系的吐火罗人。但有意思的是，西域诸国中，唯独于阗人的形象与华夏人相貌相近。《北史》记载：“自高昌以西诸国人等，深目高鼻，惟此一国，貌不甚胡，颇类华夏。”

于阗国的国力时有消长。《汉书》记载，于阗“户三千三百，口万九千三百，胜兵二千四百人”。但到东汉时期，于阗国兼并了皮山、渠勒、戎卢、扜弥等城郭，于是有了《后汉书》所载：“从精绝西北至疏勒十三国皆服从”，“领户三万二千，人口八万三千，胜兵三万余人”。于阗由于地处丝绸之路要冲，东通且末、鄯善，西达莎车、疏勒，成为中西商旅集散地，曾繁荣一时。

名称：于阗王李圣天礼佛壁画

年代：五代十国

规格：画像高2.82米，宽1米余

现存地点：甘肃省敦煌市莫高窟千佛洞

Name: *Li Shengtian, King of Khotan, Worshipping Buddha* (Mural)

Historical Period: The Five Dynasties and Ten Kingdoms

Height: 2.82 m, Width: More than 1 m

Housed in: Thousand-Buadha Cave, Mogao Grottoes, Dunhuang, Gansu Province

兄弟互禅王位的千古佳话

到了唐代，当吐蕃攻击于阗国时，唐朝庇护了于阗，并对其进行册封。受此恩惠，于阗举国上下对唐朝充满了崇敬。随着唐朝建立安西都护府和安西四镇，于阗国成为唐朝的羁縻府州。

649年，于阗国王尉迟伏阇信来到长安，朝觐唐高宗李治。高宗非常高兴，拜尉迟伏阇信为右骁卫大将军，又授予他的儿子右骁卫将军之衔，并赐予“金带、锦袍、布帛六十段，并宅一区”。天宝年间，于阗国王尉迟胜来到长安，向唐玄宗进献了名马、美玉等于阗特产，唐玄宗对于阗王十分亲善，将宗室女嫁予他，并任命尉迟胜为骠骑大将军、毗沙府都督。

755年，安史之乱爆发。尉迟胜闻讯后，毅然决定把于阗国事交给弟弟尉迟曜代为执掌，自己匆忙率领五千精兵，赶赴大唐支援，协助唐朝平乱。安史之乱终于平息后，尉迟胜决定留在中原。为此，他请求唐代宗准许他把王位传给弟弟尉迟曜。764年，唐代宗正式任命尉迟曜为于阗国王，兼安西四镇节度副使。从此，一代于阗王尉迟胜舍弃王位，举家留在长安，做起了大唐的官员。

尉迟胜历经玄宗、肃宗、代宗、德宗四朝皇帝，始终对唐朝爱得深沉热烈。785年，尉迟胜的弟弟尉迟曜派遣使者，向唐德宗李适奏请返还王位于尉迟胜之子尉迟锐，却被尉迟胜坚决推辞。

这便是于阗王尉迟胜兄弟相互禅让王位的千古佳话。

斩不断的向心力

这幅敦煌莫高窟千佛洞壁画中，庄严奉佛的于阗王，名叫李圣天。

作为千年一系的于阗王，尉迟氏为何突然变成了“李”姓?

根据史料对李圣天样貌和事迹的记载，多数专家推测李圣天应当就是五代初期的于阗王尉迟娑跋（912—966年在位）。此时唐朝已终结，由于吐蕃一度占领了于阗国，切断了于阗与中原地区的联系，故于阗王不知唐朝已亡，仍以唐的属国自处。

912年，于阗王尉迟娑跋即位。因仰慕唐朝王室，也为延续于阗历来与中原王朝的关系，他决定改姓“李”，取汉名“李圣天”。934年，为与中原地区恢复联系，李圣天通过联姻方式，娶了沙州（敦煌）归义军节度使曹议金的次女为妻，又把自己的三女儿嫁予曹议金的孙子曹延禄。由此，于阗进一步加深了在建筑、服饰、民风方面的汉化进程。

为进一步加强与中原的关系，李圣天于938年派遣使者进入中原朝贡，向后晋高祖石敬瑭表示归顺；后晋派遣使者张匡鄴、高居诲前往于阗，册封李圣天为“大宝于阗国王”。“大宝于阗国”成为10世纪中叶于阗国的正式国号。

960年，赵匡胤统一中原，建立宋王朝。此时，于阗仍自认为是中原之宗属，一直渴望国家统一和安定的李圣天向宋太祖表达了祝贺和归顺之意，期望与宋朝重续唐时的“甥舅关系”。

《大唐西域记》记载，于阗国人性温恭，知礼仪。可惜的是，这样一个其国丰乐、人民殷盛的古老王国，却在11世纪初遭遇喀喇汗王朝的攻击。于阗军民顽强地抗击了四十年，最终被征服，延续一千多年的国祚就此终结。

后来，喀喇汗王朝西迁，留在故地的于阗遗民逐渐融入了维吾尔等当地族群中。

It materializes Khotan's respect for and recognition of the Tang Dynasty. Li Shengtian (李圣天), king of Khotan, and his queen are worshipping Buddha. Crown on head, they wear loose garment with large girdle, looking dignified and graceful. Their attire is exactly alike that in the Central Plains. In the inscriptions of *Da Chao Da Bao Yu Tian Guo Da Sheng Da Ming Tian Zi* (大朝大宝于阗国大圣大明天子, Great Empire Great Treasure Great Sagacity King of Khotan), Tang is respectfully addressed as *Da Chao* or Great Empire.

The Khotan people sprang from Tocharians who spoke Indo-European languages. Khotan, an ancient Buddhist Kingdom in the Western Regions, had been ruled by the Yuchi family, enjoying a longevity of 1,238 years (232 BC—1006 AD), spanning from the Warring States Period to the Northern Song Dynasty. Adjacent to Qiemo and Shanshan in the east and Shache and Shule in the west, Khotan controlled travel and trade in the Silk Road, and formed a trade network that connected Europe, India and China.

In the mural, the pious king was Li Shengtian. According to historical records, scholars agree that Li Shengtian ought to be Yuchi Poba, who reigned from 912 to 966, or the Late Tang Dynasty and the Early Five Dynasties. He adored the Tang culture and chose the Han-style name Li Shengtian (literally corresponding to the family name of the Tang emperor). In 934, to resume diplomatic relations with the Central Plains, Li Shengtian married the second daughter of Cao Jinyi, *Jiedushi* (节度使, regional military governor) of the Guiyi Circuit, and married his third daughter to Cao Yanlu, grandson of Cao Yijin. The political and marital alliance between Yuchi and Cao deepened the Han color of Khotan in architecture, dress and folk customs.

In the early 11th century, the Buddhist Khotan was conquered by the Karakhanid, which converted to Islam in 960.

名称：南诏德化碑

年代：唐大历元年（766）

规格：高397厘米，宽227厘米，厚58厘米

现存地点：云南省大理市南诏太和城遗址

Name: Nanzhao *De Hua Bei* (德化碑, Monument in Defense of Nanzhao)

Historical Period: The 1st year of Emperor Dali of the Tang Dynasty (766)

Height: 397 cm, Width: 227 cm, Thickness: 58 cm

Housed in: Nanzhao Taihe City Site, Dali, Yunnan Province

一块用以志功颂德的碑文，字里行间隐藏了哪些复杂难言的苦衷？

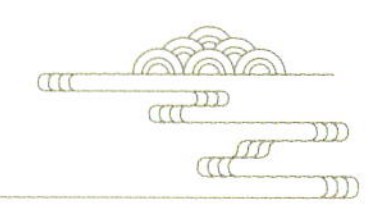

一心归唐的南诏国

南诏德化碑

Nanzhao *De Hua Bei* (德化碑, Monument in Defense of Nanzhao)

64

文物简读

被誉为“云南第一碑”的南诏德化碑是“唐代滇文之杰作”。这篇40行、3800余字的碑文，文辞典雅畅达，陈说慷慨激昂，不仅为南诏统治者志功颂德，也把不得已背叛唐朝的苦衷娓娓道出。作为一个边疆政权，南诏对中央王朝的复杂情感，从世界历史范围来看都是十分特殊的。可以说，南诏德化碑的出现并非偶然，它是多元一体的中华民族特有的内聚情感和认同观念的典型表达。

何以归化？

唐朝初年，分布在云南洱海地区的乌蛮和白蛮等众多族群经过相互兼并，最后形成了六个大的联盟，称为“六诏”。其中，蒙舍诏在巍山县境内，居于其他五诏之南，故称南诏。

六诏之中，南诏尤为亲近唐朝。南诏第一代王细奴逻在653年派儿子出使长安，唐高宗封细奴逻为巍州刺史。南诏第五代王皮逻阁又在713年获唐玄宗赐名“归义”，册授“云南王”。由于南诏始终依附于唐朝，得到唐朝的极大支持，皮逻阁得以在738年兼并了其他五诏，统一了洱海地区。南诏请剑南节度使王昱代向朝廷奏请合六诏为一，得到唐玄宗的允准。皮逻阁将王都从巍山迁至大理，正式成为唐朝属国。

南诏王室因此树立了深固的归化思想，自认为“世为唐臣”，是唐朝版图内的“西南藩屏”。

何以背唐？

748年，皮逻阁去世，其子阁逻凤承袭云南王。其时，唐朝国政被杨国忠把持，杨国忠爪牙鲜于仲通担任剑南节度使，为官不仁的张虔陀担任云南太守。张虔陀向朝廷诬告阁逻凤，阁逻凤在几度申诉无果后，愤然起兵，攻杀张虔陀；又在吐蕃的帮助下，大败鲜于仲通的军队。三年后，剑南留后李宓率兵七万进击南诏国都，却在南诏的有力反击下，惨遭全军覆没。

即便如此，南诏仍有意归唐。此后，中原发生安史之乱，唐朝已无力经略南诏，但阁逻凤仍顾念南诏与唐朝的臣属关系，为表忠心，他派人将唐朝的阵亡将士“祭而葬之，以存旧恩”；又刻碑勒石，题为“大唐天宝战士冢”。大碑落成之日，阁逻凤率军民前往祭奠，亲自致悼词曰：“君不正而朝纲乱，奸佞起而害忠良。生乃祸之始，死乃怨之终。呜呼悲哉！唐师阵亡兄弟！”词情凄惨，催人泪下，表明了他不得已而为之的难言之隐和希望与唐重修旧好的心意。

此后，阁逻凤又在都城中竖立了一块巨碑，名为“德化碑”。他在碑文中表明自己“不得已而叛”的苦衷，称南诏世世臣属唐朝，累受封赏，希望后嗣者“悦归皇化”，“若唐使者至，可指碑澡祓吾罪也”。

阁逻凤王的归化之心在碑文中表达得明明白白。这块南诏德化碑碑文用汉字写成，书法苍劲，辞令工巧，酣畅淋漓，一气呵成，为唐代少有的精品。但除了艺术价值，这块碑更大的意义在于，南诏作为一个边疆政权，对中央王朝所表达的复杂情感从世界历史范围来看都是特殊的，它是多元一体的中华民族特有的内聚情感和认同观念的典型表达。

何以回归？

阁逻凤的愿望仅仅在三十年后就实现了。

由于南诏叛唐后降蕃，吐蕃对南诏课以沉重的赋税徭役，导致南诏与吐蕃之间爆发战争。吐蕃悔怒，南诏恐惧，第八代南诏王异牟寻因此决心重新归附唐朝。

为了将“弃蕃归唐”的决心完好无缺地呈报给唐朝中央，异牟寻派遣了三位使者，兵分三路，携带着朱砂、黄金，前往长安。结果三路使者皆安全到达长安，向唐朝皇帝表达了“牟寻请归大国，永为藩国”的请求，其“所献生金，以喻向北之意如金也；丹砂，示其赤心耳”。另有文献记载，异牟寻还让使者携带了当归，表示“应当归附”“理当回归”之意。

吾心安处向长安

因为仰慕中原文化，南诏王阁逻凤“不读非圣之书”，此后几乎每一代南诏王都认真学习汉文典籍。唐玄宗天宝年间，西泸（今四川西昌）县令郑回精通儒学，他被俘至南诏后，竟被阁逻凤任命为

清平官（宰相），向王室子弟传授儒家经典、中原诗文，对南诏的文化与政治都产生了深远的影响。异牟寻归唐后，每年派数十成百的南诏子弟到成都和长安学习汉文化。于是，南诏“蔼有华风”，成为“馨香礼乐之域”，逐渐成长起一批深通汉文、擅长诗赋的知识分子。异牟寻之子寻阁劝就是一位诗人，其诗被收入《全唐诗》。

南诏曾从成都等地掳走大批汉人工匠，他们对南诏以及后来大理国的手工艺尤其是建筑艺术产生了重要影响，一时间洱海畔“城池郭邑，皆如汉制”，保存至今的大理崇圣寺三塔，在造型风格上就同西安大、小雁塔如出一辙。

史载唐朝时期，有数十万内地人经各种途径来到云南，使汉语在云南广泛传播。从汉晋到唐宋，滇东地区的官方语言和文字是汉语、汉字。今天出土的南诏字瓦上存留的文字，有不少是汉字。南诏还参照汉字创造了记录白族语言的文字，称为“白文”，所谓白文就是用汉字写白语、读白音、解白义。

Hailed as the first monument in Yunnan, it was a masterpiece of Dian literature in the Tang Dynasty. In 40 lines and 3,800 words, it reads eloquently and vehemently. The monument not only records or eulogizes the military achievements of Nanzhao rulers, but also justifies Nanzhao's betrayal of Tang. As evinced, Nanzhao, a local regime in the southwest, bore a complex feeling toward the Tang court.

In the early Tang Dynasty, numerous ethnic groups in the Lake Er, including Wuman and Baiman, eventually formed six alliances, known as the Six *Zhao* (六诏). Among them, the Mengshe *Zhao*, located in present-day Weishan County, stood in the south, thus being called Nanzhao. In 738, Piluoge, leader of Nanzhao, swallowed up five fragmented kingdoms, with the strong support of the Tang Dynasty.

In 748, Piluoge died and his son Geluofeng acceded to the throne. In the Tang court, Yang Guozhong arrogate all powers, appointing his lackeys Xianyu Zhongtong and Zhang Qiantuo as *Jiedushi* (节度使) of Jiannan and viceroy of Yunnan respectively. Zhang Qiantuo lodged a false accusation against Geluofeng. After several unsuccessful appeals, Geluofeng angrily attacked and killed Zhang Qiantuo, and then defeated Xianyu Zhongtong, with the help of Tubo. Three years later, Li Mi, *Liuhou* (留后, deputy *Jiedushi*) of Jiannan, led a force of 70,000 soldiers and attacked the capital of Nanzhao, which was completely annihilated.

Later, Geluofeng erected a huge monument in the capital, as we call Nanzhao *De Hua Bei* today. He justified the rebellion of Nanzhao, and recalled Nanzhao's loyalty to Tang, hoping that his heirs would return to Tang and exonerate him from the crime of treason before the Tang envoy.

Having defected from Tang, Nanzhao surrendered to Tubo. Tubo imposed heavy taxes and corvees on Nanzhao, resulting in a war between them. Yimuxun, the eighth-generation king of Nanzhao swore allegiance to Tang again. Yimuxun also dispatched dozens and hundreds of young people to Chengdu and Chang'an every year, in a bid to learn the Han culture. Gradually, Nanzhao practiced the Han lifestyle and became a land of propriety.

吐蕃与中央王朝的密切关系始于何时?

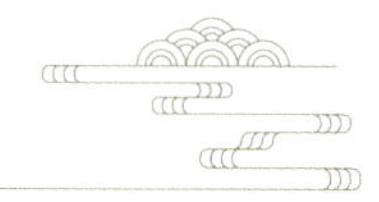

唐蕃和亲的历史瞬间

阎立本《步辇图》卷

Bunian Tu (《步辇图》, *Emperor Taizong of Tang Receiving the Tibetan Envoy*) by Yan Liben

文物简读

唐贞观十五年(641),吐蕃赞普松赞干布派禄东赞来到长安向唐太宗请求和亲。这一历史情景被著名画家阎立本描绘出来,成为中国十大传世名画之一的《步辇图》。画面中,唐太宗面目俊朗,目光深邃,蔼然可亲,展现出盛唐明君的风范与威仪;禄东赞诚挚谦恭、持重有礼……唐蕃和亲,增进了汉藏友好,促进了汉藏文化的交流和交融,推动了中华民族多元一体的历史进程。

名称：阎立本《步辇图》卷
年代：唐贞观年间
规格：纵38.5厘米，横129.6厘米
收藏单位：故宫博物院

Name: *Bunian Tu* (《步辇图》, *Emperor Taizong of Tang Receiving the Tibetan Envoy*) by Yan Liben
Historical Period: In the reign of Emperor Zhenguan of the Tang Dynasty
The Vertical: 38.5 cm, The Horizontal: 129.6 cm
Housed in: The Palace Museum

三次求亲，松赞干布迎娶文成公主

生活在青藏高原的吐蕃人是现代藏族的先民。公元6世纪，青藏高原出现了苏毗、附国、蕃部等分立小国。其中，苏毗和附国曾先后向隋朝进贡。7世纪初，松赞干布统一了青藏高原各部，建立了吐蕃政权，定都逻些（今西藏拉萨），并创制文字，制定法律，发展佛教，逐渐发展成中国西南地区强大的地方政权。

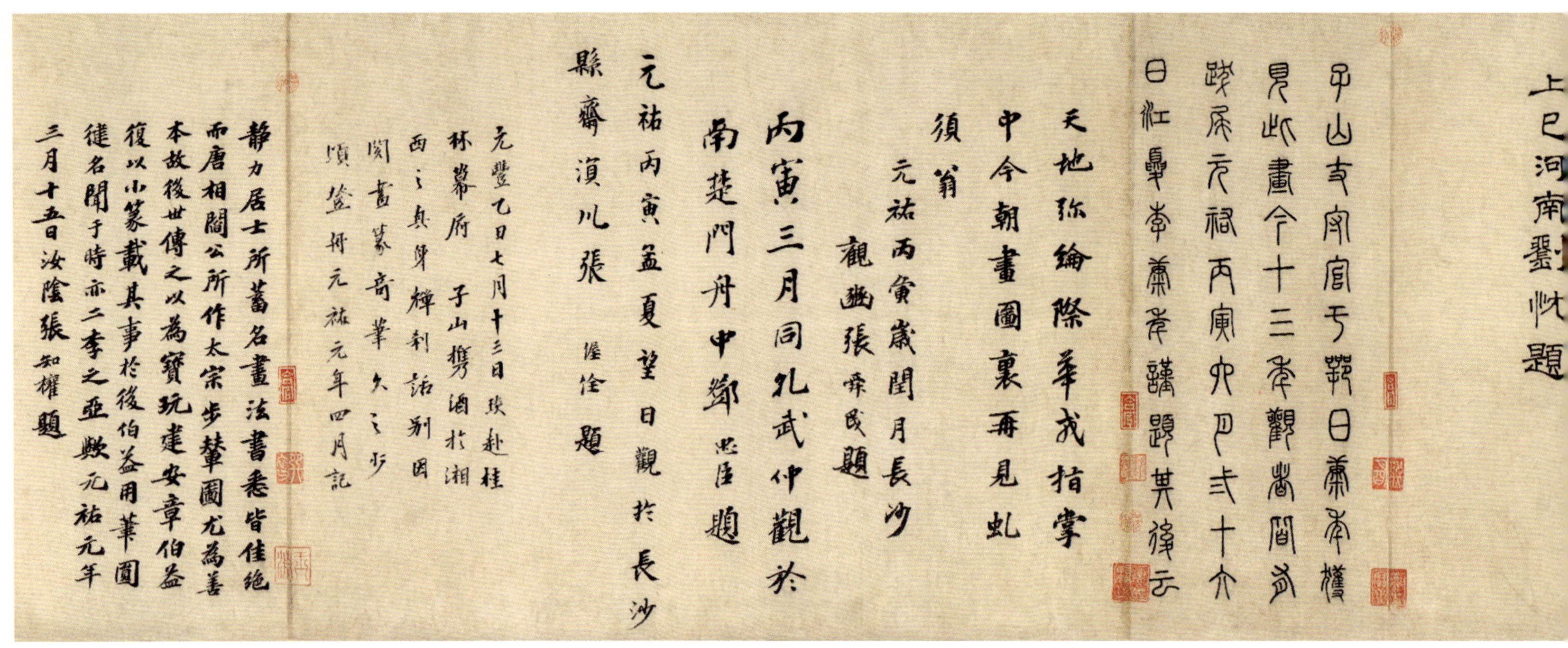

贞观四年（630），唐朝军队攻灭东突厥汗国，俘虏并善待了颉利可汗，威震西域，西域各部尊唐太宗为“天可汗”，纷纷遣使来唐，称臣纳贡，并以与唐宗室联姻为荣。松赞干布也不例外，于贞观十二年（638）派遣使臣入唐，提出要像突厥王、吐谷浑王一样，迎娶大唐公主为妻。

这次求亲没有得到唐太宗的应允。当时恰好吐谷浑王入唐，吐蕃使者认为求亲失败的原因是吐谷浑王从中挑拨。为此松赞干布组织吐蕃军队，发兵攻打吐谷浑，将吐谷浑逼往青海等地；又率大军攻下党项、白兰羌，直逼唐朝松州（今四川松潘）。随后，松赞干布再次派遣使者入唐，扬言如果不答应和亲，便率兵攻打大唐。唐太宗断然拒绝，并派唐朝开国名将侯君集率领五万唐军迎击吐蕃。然而，侯君集的主力部队还没来得及出手，唐朝先锋部队就大败蕃军，表现出大唐军队强大的战斗力。松赞干布立即率部退出党项、白兰羌、吐谷浑等地，并派遣自己最得力的宰相禄东赞前往长安谢罪，进献黄金与珍宝，再次恳请迎娶大唐公主。这一次，唐太宗终于答应了松赞干布的请求。

六试婚使，禄东赞展露聪明才智

禄东赞，本名噶尔·东赞，是吐蕃著名政治家、军事家和外交家。作为吐蕃的迎亲使者，禄东赞充分表现出他的外交才能和智慧。民间有一个流传广泛的“大唐六试婚使”的故事。

禄东赞到达长安后，发现天竺、大食、霍尔等地的国王也派出了使者前来求婚。为了公平合理，唐太宗决定通过组织各国婚使进行公开测试的方式，来决定将大唐公主下嫁给哪个国王。

测试一：绫缎穿九曲明珠。禄东赞找来一根丝线，将丝线的一头系在蚂蚁腰上，另一头缝在绫缎上；又在明珠孔眼的一端抹上蜂蜜，蚂蚁闻到蜂蜜的香味，带线穿过明珠，绫缎也就穿过去了。

测试二：辨认一百匹母马和一百匹马驹的母子关系。禄东赞把所有的母马和马驹分开，一天之中只给马驹投料而不喂水。次日把马驹放出，它们口渴难忍，纷纷找到各自的母亲吃奶。

测试三：一百名随从一日内喝完一百坛酒，吃完一百只羊，还要把羊皮鞣好。禄东赞让一百名随从一面小口咂酒、小块吃肉，一面鞣皮子，边吃边喝边劳动，不到一天的时间，就完成了任务。

测试四：分辨一百根粗细均等的松木的根和梢。禄东赞命人将木头全部投进河中，木头根部密度较大而下沉，梢头密度较小而上浮，轻松分辨了出来。

测试五：夜晚出入皇宫不迷路。一天晚上，唐太宗突然传召使臣进宫，进宫后又命他们独自返回住处。禄东赞因初来长安，为不致迷路，就在关键路口涂上了标记。结果，禄东赞凭借事先做好的标记，顺利通过了测试。

测试六：辨认公主。唐太宗命人组织三百名衣着华丽、相貌相当的宫女站在一起，文成公主便在其中。禄东赞因事先得到了曾经服侍过公主的侍女的指点，知道了公主的容貌特征，经过反复辨认，成功认出了公主。

至今，描绘“六试婚使”故事的壁画仍完好地保存在拉萨大昭寺和布达拉宫。

文成公主入藏的深远影响

贞观十六年（642）正月，文成公主踏上前往吐蕃的道路。

《吐蕃王朝世袭明鉴》记载了文成公主入藏的陪嫁物品：“释迦佛像、珍宝、金玉书橱、360卷经典、各种金玉饰物”，又有各种锦缎垫被，卜筮经典三百种，营造与工技著作六十种，治404种病的医

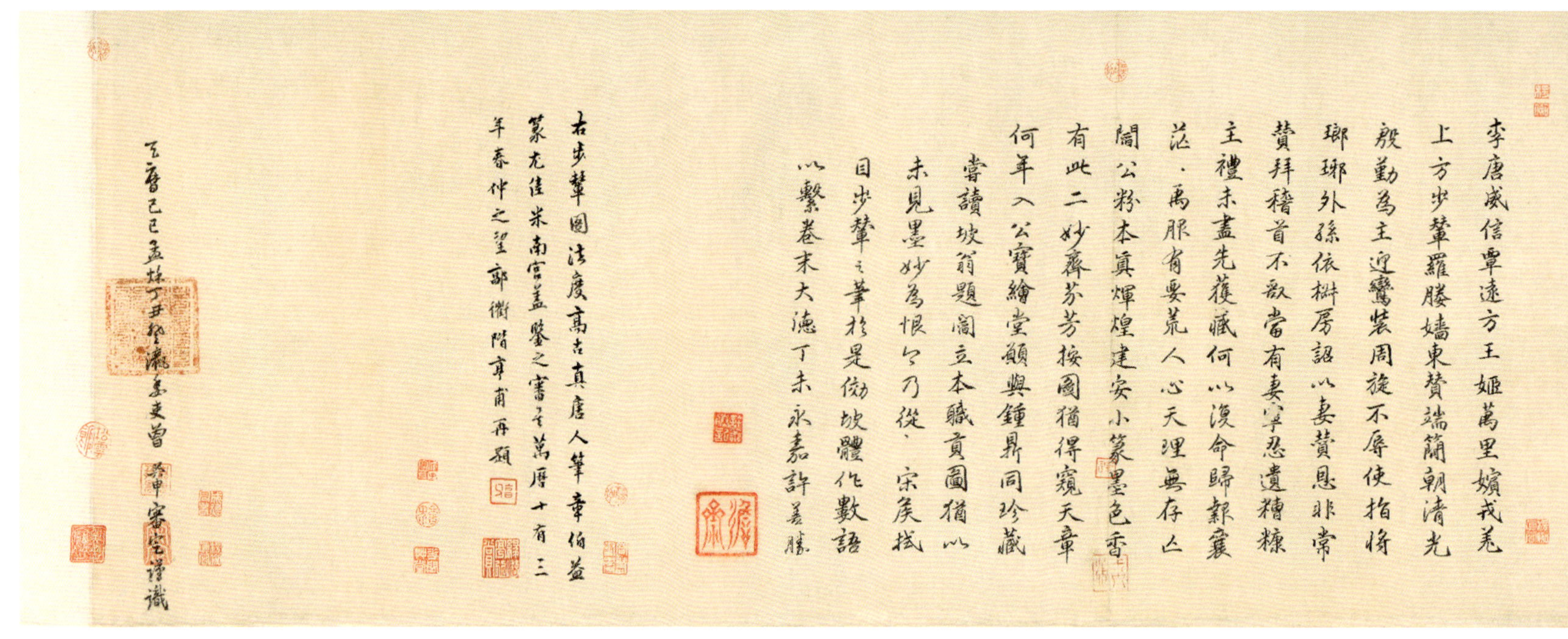

方一百种，医学论著四种，诊断法五种，医疗器械六种。

据《旧唐书》记载，松赞干布见到文成公主后，激动地说："我父祖未有通婚上国者，今我得尚大唐公主，为幸实多。当为公主筑一城，以夸示后代。"而据《新唐书》记载，为迎娶文成公主，松赞干布专门兴建了布达拉宫。由于文成公主笃信佛教，又在拉萨建造小昭寺。

文成公主入藏，为吐蕃带来了先进的农耕、酿酒、造纸、冶金、蚕桑养殖与纺织等技术；唐朝的茶叶、瓷器、乐舞杂技等随之传到吐蕃，茶叶开始成为吐蕃人民不可或缺的饮品。松赞干布"渐慕华风"，脱掉毡裘，改穿绢绸，派遣吐蕃子弟到长安学习，并请唐朝文人为吐蕃掌管表疏。吐蕃学者还参考唐朝历法，创制了吐蕃历法。

In the 15th year of Zhenguan (641), Songtsän Gampo of Tubo sent an envoy (Lu Dongzan) to Chang'an to propose a marriage alliance. Emperor Taizong accepted the proposal and decided to give him his daughter Princess Wencheng in marriage. *Bunian Tu* was created by Yan Liben, an accomplished painter in the Tang Dynasty. Listed in top 10 Chinese paintings, it depicts the historical event. On the right side of the painting, Emperor Taizong sits on a sedan chair surrounded by maidens holding fans and a canopy. He looks composed and peaceful, showing the extraordinary dignity of an emperor of the prosperous Tang Dynasty. On the left side of the painting, three persons stand in a line. The one in red is an official in the royal court, Lu Dongzan (in the middle) stands aside formally looking in awe at the emperor, and the last person is an interpreter. The painting displays a contrasting yet harmonious scene.

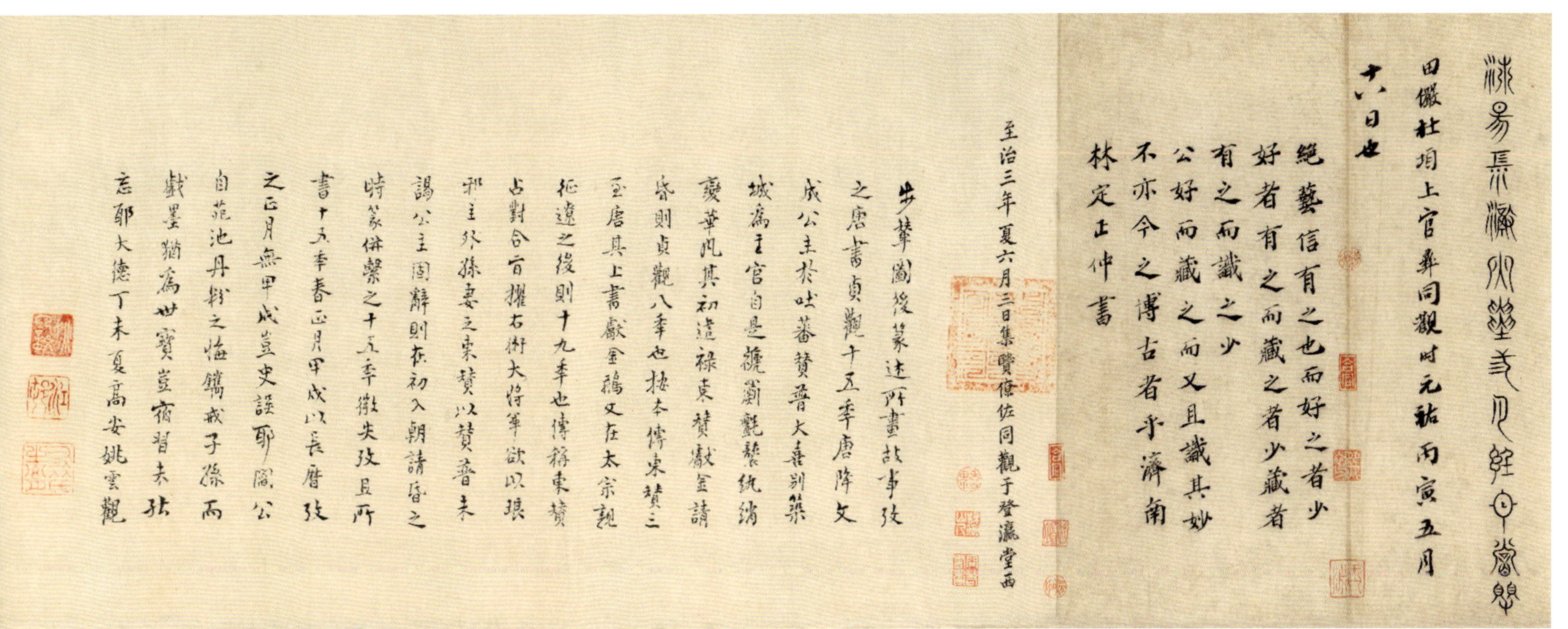

In the early 7th century, Songtsän Gampo, leader of the Tubo tribe, conquered the whole Tibetan region and established his Tubo Kingdom, choosing RaSa (Lhasa) as capital. He improved languages, enacted laws, and popularized Buddhism in Tubo, making Tubo a powerful kingdom.

Lu Dongzan, or Gar Tongtsen Yulsung, was a famous Tibetan politician, strategist and diplomat. As the marriage envoy of Tubo, he fully demonstrated diplomatic talent and wisdom. To this day, the mural *Six Tests for the Marriage Envoy* (《六试婚使》) is housed in Jokhang Temple and Potala Palace in Lhasa.

In the first lunar month of the 16th year of Zhenguan, Princess Wencheng set out. In *Records of the Emperors of the Tubo Dynasty* (《吐蕃王朝世袭明鉴》), the dowries of Princess Wencheng were enumerated as follows: Buddha statues, treasures, gold or jade bookcases, 360 volumes of classics, various gold or jade ornaments, brocade bedding, 300 kinds of divination classics, 60 works on construction and engineering, 100 medical prescriptions for treating 404 diseases, four medical treatises, five diagnostic methods, and six medical equipment.

Princess Wencheng took advanced technologies to Tubo, such as farming, brewing, paper-making, metallurgy, sericulture and textile. Subsequently, tea, porcelain, music & dance and acrobatics of Tang were introduced to Tubo. Tea became an important drink for the Tubo people. Songtsän Gampo admired the Tang culture, and sent young people to study in Chang'an. He also invited Tang literati to conduct state affairs, and invented Tubo calendar based on Tang calendar.

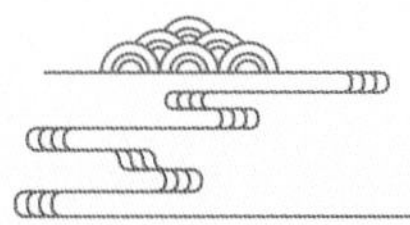

新鲜血液

——宋、辽、金、西夏的民族大融合

New Blood: Ethnic Integration in the Song, Liao, Jin and Western Xia Dynasties

公元907—1271年，中华历史再度进入大变动期，又一次面临南北王朝的对峙与分裂。契丹、女真、党项等民族相继建立地方政权，与北宋、南宋对峙，形成了被史家称为“中国历史上第二个南北朝”的局面。然而历史在这场漫长的盘桓与跌宕后，却再度演绎了由分而合的辩证法——13世纪末，一个新的大一统秩序又一次被孕育了出来，疆域辽阔的元朝赫然面世。回头看，这一场曲折起伏的历史震荡，最终清晰地显现出它在中华历史进程中的真实意义：历史在这里伸出巨手，将一股新鲜血液强力注入中华民族的躯体，同时将中华民族多元一体的历史进程大大向前推进。

宋、辽、金、西夏和一系列边疆王朝，共同组成了10—13世纪一部不可分割的中国史。其中，三个北方民族建立的王朝为中华历史写下了不可忽略的篇章——契丹建立的辽，传承国祚两百多年，在历史上首次实现了中国北方和东北地区的完整统一，有效整合了长期分散的北方少数民族。女真建立的金，迁都燕京，开启了北京在后来一千多年间作为中国政治文化中心的历史；它采用唐宋制度有效治理国家，极盛时期人口达到5600万，超过此前任何一个王朝的北方人口；它的统治者还自认为比南宋更能代表中华，金太祖曾提出“中华一统”“不分夷夏”的主张，响亮地发出了民族大团结的政治呼吁。党项建立的西夏，创造了灿烂的文化，对中原文化大传播的贡献尤为卓著，不仅首创了汉字和西夏文两种文字合璧的雕版印刷，还开创了草书文字印刷；它不仅继承了中原的泥活字印刷，还成功实践了木活字印刷，时间上比中原早了一个多世纪……

In more than 300 years (907–1271), China advanced amidst turbulence. The Khitan, Jurchen and Tangut established the Liao, Jin and Western Xia Dynasties respectively, which rivaled the Northern and Southern Song Dynasties, forming what historians called "the Second Southern and Northern Dynasties in Chinese history". However, beneath the long-year social upheaval was the dialectic of division and unity. In the late 13th century, the Yuan Dynasty achieved the grand unification of China, with unprecedentedly vast territory. In the tempestuous centuries, new blood was infused into the Chinese nation, and the formation of the unified multi-ethnic country was accelerated.

The Song, Liao, Jin and Western Xia Dynasties constituted an important chapter in the three-century Chinese history. The Khitan Liao Dynasty unified the northern and northeastern regions of China for the first time, which tremendously promoted ethnic integration of the tribes in northern China. The Jurchen Jin transferred the capital to Yanjing, present-day Beijing, which serves as the political and cultural center of China for over 1,000 years. Jin inherited the political systems of the Tang and Song Dynasties, with a population of 56 million in its heyday, larger than the previous dynasties. Emperor Taizu of Jin proposed the ideas of "the unity of *Hua Xia*" and "the equality of *Hua* and *Yi*", calling for national solidarity. The Western Xia Dynasty created the brilliant Tangut culture and made an outstanding contribution to the dissemination of the culture of the Central Plains. It pioneered the Han-Tangut woodblock printing and cursive-script printing. The Western Xia adopted clay movable type printing in the Central Plains, and successfully developed wooden movable type printing, which was more than a century earlier than the Central Plains.

轰轰烈烈两百多年后，契丹的血脉都到哪里去了？

契丹的兴起：不同凡响的北方民族

陈国公主金覆面

Gold Mask of Princess of Chen

文物简读

一只依照陈国公主生前形象捶制而成的金覆面，让后世有了可以遥想契丹人形象的依据。契丹，这个建立起强大的辽政权，翻开了公元10世纪后中国北方历史新篇章的古代民族，他们的面孔和形象都值得后人细细品味。

陈国公主及驸马墓

1986年，在内蒙古通辽市奈曼旗青龙山水库的建设工地上，发现了一座规格仅次于帝陵的辽代墓葬。根据墓志铭，这是辽代陈国公主和驸马的合葬墓。墓室开启，考古队员看见了令人震惊的景象：陈国公主和驸马全身穿着银丝网衣，头戴金冠，面覆金面具，脚穿鎏金银靴，并系有腰带。墓中，精美的金银、陶瓷、玻璃、木器、玉器及珍珠、玛瑙、水晶、琥珀制品，总计三千多件。由于辽代帝陵几乎被毁坏殆尽，陈国公主和驸马墓因此成为辽代历史最珍贵的见证物，让人去追怀一个曾经强大无比又悄然消融于历史的古代民族。

陈国公主是辽景宗的孙女，去世时年仅18岁。根据墓志铭，她起初被封为“太平公主”，去世后被追封为“陈国公主”。与她合葬的驸马名叫萧绍矩，也是她的舅舅，去世时只有35岁。

多民族融合的契丹国

契丹来自何处？

名称：陈国公主金覆面

年代：辽

规格：长20.5厘米，宽17.2厘米，厚0.05厘米，重184克

出土地点：内蒙古自治区通辽市斯布格图村陈国公主墓

收藏单位：内蒙古博物院

Name: Gold Mask of Princess of Chen

Historical Period: The Liao Dynasty

Length: 20.5 cm, Width: 17.2 cm, Thickness: 0.05 cm, Weight: 184 g

Excavation Site: The Tomb of Princess of Chen, Sibugetu Village, Tongliao City, Inner Mongolia Autonomous Region

Housed in: Inner Mongolia Museum

契丹兴起于北方游牧民族频繁迁徙和复杂交融的西拉木伦河和老哈河一带。史载，契丹与汉魏时期的宇文鲜卑有着亲缘关系。在鲜卑大量南迁后，西辽河一带的鲜卑分裂为契丹和室韦。《隋书》载："室韦，契丹之类也。其南者为契丹，在北者号室韦。"唐贞观二十年（646），契丹首领窟哥派遣使者向唐朝进贡，并请求"内属"。唐朝因此在其地设置松漠都督府，任命窟哥为都督，赐姓"李"。到公元9世纪时，契丹已深受中原经济文化的影响，开始务农种桑，纺织冶金。

916年，契丹首领耶律阿保机东征西伐，一举统一了契丹各部，又征讨周边的室韦、吐谷浑、奚、党项等民族，建立起多民族融合的契丹国。他仿照中原王朝的体制，建元"神册"，采用"皇帝"称号，自称为"大圣大明天皇帝"。

唐朝末年，契丹曾一度被强大的回鹘汗国控制。但当回鹘汗国被黠戛斯灭亡后，残留的一部分回鹘人就逐渐融入了契丹。其中，回鹘述律氏在契丹开疆拓土的过程中，给予了耶律阿保机强有力的辅佐。所以，耶律阿保机称帝后，就以汉高祖刘邦自居，把自己的回鹘妻子述律平比作名相萧何，赐予述律家族"萧"姓，并规定此后的契丹皇后只能从萧氏一族中产生。此后，辽代（包括西辽和北辽）一共出现过22位萧氏皇后。由此可知，契丹王室是契丹与回鹘融合的后裔。

一段不同凡响的历史印迹

唐朝终结后，中国历史上出现了一段被称为"五代十国"的分裂期——中原地区依次出现了五个短暂存在的王朝，中原之外又相继出现了十多个割据政权。后唐是五个王朝中的第二个，由西突厥存留的一支沙陀人建立。其时，驻守太原的河东节度使石敬瑭以出卖燕云十六州为代价，请求契丹国帮忙推翻后唐，建立起后晋，定都汴梁，当上了契丹国的"儿皇帝"。此举使得契丹国的疆域一举扩展到长城沿线。946年，契丹皇帝耶律德光攻陷开封，灭掉后晋，并在这里改国号为"大辽"。

辽朝对统一多民族中国的疆域进行了划时代的开拓——辽朝全盛之时，东北疆域到达库页岛，北至蒙古国中部，西到阿尔泰山，南抵天津、河北一线，总面积超过489万平方公里，在历史上首次实现了中国北方和东北地区的完整统一，有效整合了长期分散的北方少数民族，对中华民族多元一体的历史进程产生了重大影响，也为元朝缔造多民族统一国家奠定了重要基础。

此外，辽朝对北方民族的融合做出了不可磨灭的贡献。契丹曾先后征服了室韦、奚、乌古、女真、吐谷浑等，又在征伐中与回鹘、新罗、吐蕃、党项、沙陀等不断融合。据统计，唐初时契丹人口仅二十万，到五代时期已经发展到两百万，显示出民族大融合带来的人口繁荣景象。

辽朝共传九帝，享国218年。1125年，辽被金灭。但辽并未就此退出历史舞台。辽德宗耶律大石西迁到中亚楚河流域一带，建立了西辽，存续近一个世纪，虽然在1218年被蒙古所灭，但却把契丹的赫赫名声传播到了中亚以及欧洲。

The gold mask was made according to the real image of Princess of Chen, providing material evidence for the studies of the appearance of the Khitan people.

In 1986, archaeologists in Inner Mongolia discovered a Liao-Dynasty tomb, whose size was smaller than imperial tombs. As the epitaph suggested, the tomb owners were Princess of Chen and her husband. They wore clothes sewn with silver, with golden crowns on the head, gold masks on the face, gilded boots on the feet, and belts fastened around the waist.

Princess of Chen was granddaughter of Emperor Jingzong of Liao, who passed away at the age of 18. According to the epitaph, she was firstly awarded the title of Princess of Taiping and promoted to Princess of Yue. Princess of Chen was a posthumous title for her. Xiao Shaoju, her husband, also her mother's brother, was buried with her, who passed away at the age of 35.

Khitan came to rise near the Xar Moron River and the Laohahe River. According to historical records, Khitan was genetically related to Yuwen Xianbei in the Han and Wei Dynasties. After the large-scale southward migration of the Xianbei people, the Xianbei clan in the West Liaohe River split into Khitan and Shiwei, as stated in *Sui Shu* (*Book of Sui*, 《隋书》), "Shiwei shared the same origin with Khitan. Khitan roamed in the south and Shiwei wandered in the north".

In 916, Yelü Abaoji, leader of Khitan, having unified various Khitan tribes and conquered such ethnic groups such as Shiwei, Tuyuhun, Xi and Dangxiang, established the Khitan Kingdom. In 946, Khitan emperor Yelü Deguang captured Kaifeng and tamed the Later Jin Dynasty, replacing Khitan with Liao.

With nine emperors, the Liao Dynasty enjoyed a history of 218 years. By the early 12th century, Liao's was challenged by the Jurchen, a subject tribespeople in the northeastern part of China. In 1125, Liao finally collapsed. Yelü Dashi, Emperor Dezong of Liao, moved westward to the Chu River Basin in the Central Asia. A new Khitan dynasty, the Khara Khitai (*aka* Xi Liao), was founded, albeit it would not last long and was ultimately swept away by the rise of the Mongols in the early 13th century. Liao firstly unified present-day northern and northeastern regions of China and laid a foundation for Yuan, a unified multi-ethnic empire.

名称：辽三彩印花海棠盘
年代：辽
规格：高2厘米，口径25.5厘米
收藏单位：中国民族博物馆

Name: Floral Dish with Crabapple Pattern (Liao Tri-Color Glazed Ceramics)
Historical Period: The Liao Dynasty
Height: 2 cm, Mouth Diameter: 25.5 cm
Housed in: Chinese National Museum of Ethnology

辽三彩与唐三彩有何关系？

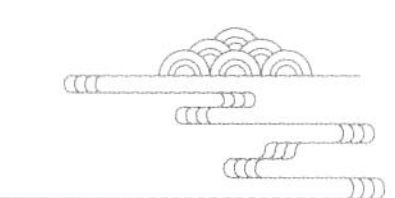

尊孔崇儒的契丹文化

辽三彩印花海棠盘

Floral Dish with Crabapple Pattern
(Liao Tri-Color Glazed Ceramics)

文物简读

契丹人继承唐三彩传统而创造的独具特色的辽三彩，用黄、绿、褐三色釉烧制，又成为辽代陶瓷的重要品种。辽代陶瓷不仅在丰富多彩的中华瓷艺中占据了一席之地，同时也成为博大精深的中华陶瓷文化传承发展链条中的一环。辽三彩映照出古代民族交往交流交融的另一种场景，而契丹也用自身历史展现了“华夷一家”的历史大融合进程和走向。

辽三彩如何诞生

契丹在从“转徙随时，车马为家”的游牧生活转向定居生活的过程中，发生了一系列革命性的变化。这样的变化可以从他们留给历史的一项独特文化遗产辽代陶瓷看出。

瓷器的发明是中华民族对世界的伟大贡献。显然，契丹在对中原地区的征伐过程中，接触到了这项神奇的手工技艺。《辽史》记载契丹人在征战“燕赵之地”时遭遇的两个特殊地点：“天赞初……破磁窑镇”，“天赞二年秋……攻下磁窑务”。这两大战事都发生在辽太祖耶律阿保机的时代。由此，契丹收获了最重要的战利品——大量技艺精湛的汉人制瓷工匠。有了这些匠人，契丹的制瓷业便奠定了基础。

史载，契丹的手工业主要由战争中俘获的汉人和渤海人发展而来。在契丹的手工业中，制瓷业是最可圈可点的。查阅文献，有明确记载的辽代瓷窑就有七处，分布在今黑龙江、吉林、辽宁、内蒙古等地。这些瓷器汲取了唐代、北宋的制瓷工艺。辽代陶瓷是契丹学习中原文化的成果，同时又具有鲜明的地方色彩和独特的民族风格。辽代陶瓷不仅在丰富多彩的中华瓷艺中占据了一席之地，同时也成为博大精深的中华陶瓷文化传承发展链条中的一环。

辽代陶瓷之中，辽三彩最具代表性。这种低温彩釉陶制品是契丹向唐三彩学习的文化成果。辽三彩用黄、绿、褐三色釉烧制，通过运用铁、铜、铅釉的流动性能，烧造过程中各种釉色自然交融，获得了人工无法取得的效果。辽三彩浑然大气、粗犷豪放，却不失精巧；朴拙巧慧、沉着敦厚，却不乏典雅灵秀。

海棠盘的形制常见于辽代墓室壁画。此类海棠盘一般呈八曲海棠花瓣式，红色陶胎；釉色以黄色或白色为基调，其他黄绿两色搭配，象征黄花、绿草、蓝天、白云；其口沿一般压印卷草或蔓叶纹，内底的印花多见折枝牡丹，又有单朵或三朵团菊，辅以流云、流水纹，一派生机盎然的草原景象，表现出深厚的游牧文化情结。

辽三彩以一种独特的陶瓷美学，成为契丹留给中华历史的一个耀眼的文化符号，也映照出古代民族交往交流交融的一个独特情景。

“吾修文物彬彬，不异中华”

契丹有着悠久而深刻的中华文化认同。一方面，契丹人流传着乘坐青牛车的天女和骑白马的神人相遇而生契丹人的始祖传说；另一方面，契丹人也有奉炎帝为祖先的观念。《辽史》载：“辽之先，出自炎帝……”这种“炎帝子孙”的意识影响着契丹人对中原文化的态度。《辽史》记载，辽初，朝廷内部进行过一次先尊儒还是先奉佛的辩论，侍臣们都说应先奉佛，但太子耶律倍说：“孔子大圣，万世所尊，宜先。”太祖耶律阿保机对太子的看法非常赞赏，于是下令建造孔庙，确立了尊崇儒家的文化立场。

辽太子耶律倍是一个汉化程度很深的契丹知识分子。他尊孔尚儒，主张以儒家思想为治国之术。他曾经从中原购得万卷书，收藏在他隐居的医巫闾山的绝顶之上。他博学多才，通晓阴阳、音律，精于医药，工于诗画。作为著名画家，他擅长描绘放牧和骑射的情景，他的15幅经典画作被收录进宋徽宗编撰的宫廷藏画名录《宣和画谱》中。耶律倍后来与其弟耶律德光争夺皇位失败，遂投奔后唐。因为他对中原文化的热爱，后唐皇帝特为他赐名“慕华”，后又赐名“赞华”。

辽道宗耶律洪基是辽朝的第八位皇帝，他也挚爱中原文化，曾下令颁行《五经》传疏、《史记》、《汉书》，又在中京置国子监，定期祭祀先圣先师；他写作的汉诗气象磅礴、意境深远。史载，辽道宗曾以千两白银铸成两尊佛像，在佛像背后刻下“愿后世生中国”的文字，供奉于开泰寺。《契丹国志》还记载了一个有名的故事：一次，辽道宗听汉人儒生讲解《论语》，当讲到“夷狄之有君，不如诸夏之亡也”时，儒生想一带而过。不料辽道宗却说：“上世獯鬻、猃狁，荡无礼法，故谓之夷。吾修文物彬彬，不异中华，何嫌之有！”坦然地让儒生继续讲下去。这个故事表现出辽道宗对自身中华文化修养的充分自信，也说明他早已建立起“夷夏之别并非血缘，而在于文化认同”这样的儒家天下观。

辽道宗的懿德皇后萧观音，是一个契丹化的回鹘人，也具有深厚的汉文化修养，从她写的这首五言律诗可见一斑：

虞廷开盛轨，王会合奇深。
到处承天意，皆同捧日心。
文章通鹿蠡，声教薄鸡林。
大寓看交泰，应知无古今。

因为尊孔崇儒，开科取士，提倡诗赋，契丹整体精神文化得到空前提升。契丹统治者还以汉字为蓝本，创造了契丹大字、契丹小字，促使契丹文化走向辉煌。

The Khitan people inherited traditional *Tangsancai* (Tang Tri-Color Glazed Ceramics) and developed unique *Liaosancai* (辽三彩). Fired with yellow, green and brown glazes, Liao ceramics gained a foothold in colorful Chinese ceramics art. *Liaosancai* reflected how the Khitan people partook in cultural exchanges and witnessed the historical trend of national assimilation between *Hua Xia* and *Yi*.

The Khitan people used to lead a nomadic life. They migrated as seasons changed, taking their horses and carriages. Liao ceramics, a unique cultural heritage, saw their shift to farming life, which played a decisive role in the Khitan history.

According to historical records, there were seven Liao-Dynasty kilns in present-day Heilongjiang, Jilin, Liaoning and Inner Mongolia. Liao ceramics basically adopted the craftsmanship of the Tang Dynasty and shared the same origin with the Song-Dynasty counterparts.

Liaosancai represented the highest level of Liao ceramics. *Liaosancai* was glazed ceramics fired at low temperatures, culturally copied from *Tangsancai*. Using yellow, green and brown glazes, craftsmen utilized the fluidity of iron, copper and lead glazes, which naturally coalesced. The natural change of glaze colors made *Liaosancai* look simple, gorgeous and elegant.

In shape, the floral dish with crabapple pattern was often discovered in the Liao-Dynasty tomb murals. The dish has eight-section crabapple petals, with red pottery roughcast, embellished with yellow and white colors, symbolizing yellow flower, green grass, blue sky and white cloud. The mouth edge is generally embossed with rolled grass or vine-leaf pattern, and the inner bottom is often stamped with *Zhezhi* (折枝)-style (partial branches) peony, as well as single or three clusters of chrysanthemums. Coupled with flowing cloud or water patterns, the dish creates a scene of exuberant grassland and expresses a deep complex of nomadic culture.

Liaosancai, as a special ceramic aesthetics, evolved into a brilliant cultural symbol of the Khitan people and testified to ethnic communication and integration in ancient China.

契丹建立起“信威万里”的辽国后，是怎样管理偌大的疆域与众多的人口的？

“南北面官制”：契丹的制度创举

鎏金双凤纹玛瑙柄刺鹅锥

Gilded Awl with Double-Phoenix Pattern and Agate Handle for Stabbing Gooses

文物简读

这件十分罕见的辽代鎏金双凤纹玛瑙柄刺鹅锥，见证了契丹统治者出于其游牧文化习俗而实行“四时捺钵”的独特历史，闪耀着辽朝秉承“因俗而治”的政治理念而创造一系列特色治理形式的智慧光辉，让我们回头去重温契丹这个古代民族对中国古代制度文化的创造性贡献。

“四时捺钵”

刺鹅锥在契丹文物中十分罕见，而这一件经鎏金装饰，刻有双凤纹，以玛瑙为柄的刺鹅锥就更为罕见了，它是契丹统治者的独特政权运行机制——“四时捺钵”的珍贵见证物。

“捺钵”是契丹语“行宫”“行帐”“行营”一词的音译，后来引申为帝王在一年之中所从事的与游牧习俗相关的营地迁徙和射猎活动。辽帝始终没有抛弃祖先的游牧传统，他们建立了一套居处无常、四时转徙的“行朝”体制。《辽史·营卫志中》说：“辽国尽有大漠，浸包长城之境，因宜为治。秋冬违寒，春夏避暑，随水草就畋渔，岁以为常。四时各有行在之所，谓之‘捺钵’。”“四时捺钵”是辽朝政治生活中的一件大事，捺钵之地成为实际的政治中心，一些重要的行政机关如中书省、枢密院等也随驾而行，重要臣僚都扈从皇帝在野外生活，重大国策通过在大帐中举行会议确定，故称“行朝”。

名称：鎏金双凤纹玛瑙柄刺鹅锥

年代：辽

规格：长23厘米，直径2厘米

出土地点：内蒙古自治区通辽市斯布格图村陈国公主墓

收藏单位：中国民族博物馆

Name: Gilded Awl with Double-Phoenix Pattern and Agate Handle for Stabbing Gooses

Historical Period: The Liao Dynasty

Length: 23 cm, Diameter: 2 cm

Excavation Site: The Tomb of Princess of Chen, Sibugetu Village, Tongliao City, Inner Mongolia Autonomous Region

Housed in: Chinese National Museum of Ethnology

捺钵期间还要举行很多与游牧相关的传统活动。刺鹅锥就是在春捺钵期间，契丹贵族在捕鹅活动中所用的器具。狩猎者用海东青击晕天鹅后，要用刺鹅锥将天鹅正式刺死，取出鹅脑喂海东青，让它补充体力，继续捕鹅；还要将以河蚌为食的天鹅的嗉囊划开，取出珍珠。当然，用金、银、玛瑙等材质制作的刺鹅锥是身份的象征，能参加捺钵捕鹅活动的人，不是皇亲国戚就是股肱重臣。

二元格局的上京城

虽然四时捺钵居无常所，但辽朝也仿照中原设立了固定的政治中心。而且，辽建立了不止一个都城。随着王朝版图的扩大，辽朝花了一百多年时间逐步建立起了上京（在今内蒙古巴林左旗南）、东京（在今辽宁辽阳）、南京（在今北京市西南）、中京（在今内蒙古宁城）、西京（在今山西大同），这就是辽朝的五京制。

辽上京是辽朝的政治中心。虽然辽帝都传承捺钵制度，但当举行某些重要礼仪时，皇帝也须回到上京城居住；此外，辽朝国家机构的大部分臣僚及其下属官吏，也须在上京城处理日常事务。上京城作为辽国皇都，尤其反映了辽在国家治理过程中，既保有浓郁的游牧文化特点，又一步步融汇中原文化传统而形成的二元特征。

上京城在规划设计之初，考虑到契丹传统的拜日习俗，“国俗凡祭皆东向，故曰祭东”，因此皇都面向东方，以东门为正门，又在城内北部留下了大片空白区域，以供契丹贵族搭设毡帐之用。后来，辽太宗耶律德光扩建都城时，又加筑了汉城，以供从事手工业和商业贸易活动的汉、渤海、回鹘等族群居住。这样，上京城就形成了“皇城+汉城”的二元格局。此后，当辽太宗准备盛大典礼，接受后晋奉献的燕云十六州图籍时，他又仿照汉人礼仪，将皇城大门由东门改为南门，城内的主要建筑也都改为南向，并仿照中原王朝的宫门，兴建了承天门。

“南北面官制”

在坚守游牧文化的同时，为了管理族群成分复杂的国家子民，契丹统治者还创立了一套独特的“一国两制”治理体系——“南北面官制”。

契丹因有拜日“祭东”之俗，所以殿帐东向，官衙分置北、南两侧。在牙帐之北，设置契丹枢密院和契丹行宫都总管司，称为“北面官”，是管理契丹和其他游牧民族的政府机构；又在牙帐之南，模仿唐代制度设置三省六部，称为“南面官”，是管理汉人事务的政府机构。

这套“以国制治契丹，以汉制待汉人”的“南北面官制”，是遵照“因俗而治”的政治理念而形成的二元制行政体制，它从制度层面保障了契丹和汉拥有对等的权力，都可参与辽朝的政权建设。同时，这套二元模式不仅体现在中央组织结构上，在地方行政层面也得到了有效贯彻，游牧地区的部族首领、农耕地区的州县官员分别划归各自所属的北面官系统和南面官系统。

实行“南北面官制”使辽朝国力得到了飞跃式发展。辽境内广阔的田地以及来自中原的农耕者使得契丹农业大步向前迈进，农业又带动了畜牧业的升级，手工业、商业等也随之逐步发展起来。可以说，“南北面官制”堪称创举，这种差异化的政治制度既适应了多民族共存的国情，也在统一秩序内促进了民族融合，所以元朝评价契丹“得其宜矣”。

The gilded awl for stabbing gooses was rarely seen in the Khitan cultural relics, with double-phoenix pattern and agate handle. It bore testimony to *Sishi Nabo* (四时捺钵), a unique Khitan political system.

Nabo (捺钵) was a transliteration of the Khitan word, meaning “an imperial palace for short stays away from the capital”. Later, *Nabo* referred to a nomadic emperor’s transfer of campsites in four seasons, where he indulged in *šikār*. Bearing traditional nomadic customs in mind, the Liao Emperors institutionalized the system of *Sishi Nabo*, or the roaming court. In “Records of the Imperial Guards (Two)” of *The History of Liao* (《辽史・营卫志中》), it was mentioned that: “The Liao Dynasty controlled the vast desert in the north and the Great Wall in the south. The Liao emperors sited their courts according to seasons. In autumn and winter, they went to warm regions, whilst in spring and summer, they preferred cool regions. They hunted and fished near rivers and grasslands year after year. In this way, the Liao emperors dwelled in portable palaces in four seasons, *aka Nabo*.” *Nabo* had a far-reaching impact on the Liao politics. As officials of major central organs, such as the Imperial Secretariat (*Zhong Shu Sheng*, 中书省) and the Commission of Military Affairs (*Shu Mi Yuan*, 枢密院), accompanied the emperors, *Nabo de facto* formed a political center, where imperial meetings were held and national policies were determined.

In order to administer the multi-ethnic Liao, the Khitan rulers initiated the North-South Official-Appointment System (南北面官制). The Khitan people traditionally worshiped the sun, and their court faced the east, with government offices standing in the north and south. In the north of the court were the Commission of Military Affairs and General Office of Palace Affairs, and in the south of the court were the Three Departments and Six Ministries, which handled the affairs of non-Han ethnic groups and the Han people, respectively. The North-South Official-Appointment System, as a dual administrative system, tallied with the philosophy of “governing according to ethnic customs”, ensuring that the Khitan and Han people had equal power at the institutional level.

名称：金上京铜坐龙

年代：金

规格：重约2.1千克，高19.6厘米

出土地点：黑龙江省哈尔滨市阿城区金上京遗址

收藏单位：黑龙江省博物馆

Name: Bronze Squatting Dragon Unearthed at the Jin-Dynasty Shangjing Site

Historical Period: The Jin Dynasty

Weight: *c* 2.1 kg, Height: 19.6 cm

Excavation Site: Jin-Dynasty Shangjing Site, Acheng District, Harbin, Heilongjiang Province

Housed in: Heilongjiang Provincial Museum

中华龙的形象一般是腾跃于天的，为何这条龙却采取踞坐式的姿态？

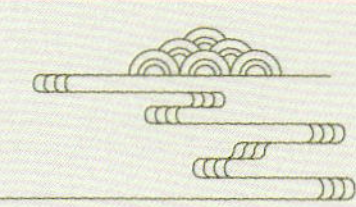

势如破竹——女真的兴起

金上京铜坐龙

69

Bronze Squatting Dragon Unearthed at the Jin-Dynasty Shangjing Site

文物简读

这尊出土于金上京的铜坐龙，集合了龙、麒麟、狮、犬的特点，以独具特色的踞坐式姿态，显示出八百多年前的女真人用自己的文化思维，对中华龙文化所进行的一次独特创造。

铜坐龙

一条蹲坐的龙？它为何与中华大地上的龙都不相同？

1965年的一天，黑龙江省哈尔滨市阿城区金上京皇城古城墙遗址边，一尊铜坐龙从剥落的青砖中显露出来。这是考古学家从未见过的龙形文物。

仔细观察它的形象：龙头、犬身、麒麟背、狮尾；龙首微扬，张口似吟啸，肩微前躬，前左腿翘起，其爪飞踏瑞云，瑞云与后腿相连，前右腿略向前方直立，爪与地面相连，龙尾上翘向外卷曲，龙首、肩部和四肢饰有卷鬣。

因铜坐龙的出土地点东距金上都宫殿遗址不足四百米，西距金太祖完颜阿骨打陵约五百米，考古工作者初步确定它是金代文物。专家又在金代文献中查阅翻检，终于搜寻到了蛛丝马迹——

《金史》记载，金世宗完颜雍于大定六年将皇帝乘坐的马车“轼上坐龙改为凤”。又载：“大辇……顶轮施耀叶，中有银莲花，坐龙。”

据此，答案基本清晰了：铜坐龙应是金代皇室御用马车上的装饰物，它曾用于皇室马车座前扶手的横木上，还曾用于马车的顶轮上。总之，它俨然就是八百年前的坐龙形豪华车标。

有了这样的结论，再回头去看铜坐龙，一切似乎皆可得到合理解释：金上京的铜坐龙，以独具特色的踞坐式姿态，显示出八百多年前的女真人用自己的文化思维，对中华龙所进行的一次独特创造——坐龙头顶三朵卷似流云的鬃毛，原型应取自马鬃，体现了女真人作为游猎者对马的热爱；龙嘴像鹰，则与女真人对海东青的喜爱有关；而将龙身雕塑成犬形，则是因为犬是猎人的好帮手……

从“始雄诸部”到西出天山

女真在先秦文献中被称为“肃慎”或“息慎”；秦汉时期，肃慎被转称为“挹娄”；魏晋后又被称为“勿吉”“靺鞨”；辽、宋时期，回归“肃慎”本名，汉语又译为“女真”。契丹建立辽后，征服并控制了女真各部。其中，以蜿蜒河而得名的完颜部发展得较快，在学会种植五谷、掌握冶铁技能后，完颜部统一了生女真部族。后其首领乌古乃因协助辽政权生擒叛辽之臣有功，被辽道宗任命为生女真部节度使，至此，完颜部“有甲兵千余”，“始雄诸部”。

辽朝晚期，政治走向混乱的契丹对女真各部施以沉重的民族压迫，贪婪地索求贡品，强征珍珠和海东青等土特产，鱼肉女真百姓。1112年，天祚帝赴长春州与女真各部酋长聚会，竟对酋长们肆意侮辱。这一切都引起了女真人的极度愤恨，致使完颜阿骨打决意反辽。1114年，完颜阿骨打率众南下伐辽，攻克宁江州、宾州、祥州之后，于1115年正式称帝，建立大金国，定都上京，即今哈尔滨市阿城区。

金建立后，其军队势如破竹，仅用十年时间，于1125年灭辽，于1127年亡北宋，又使西夏、高丽臣服，在北方建立起一个幅员辽阔的国家。作为一个多民族统一政权，金朝再度稳固了东北及广阔的北方疆域，对确立中国北方版图起到了奠基性的历史作用。

中华一统，不分夷夏

金朝是中国历史上汉化较深的少数民族政权之一。

早在金太宗时期，金朝就已学习辽国的汉官制度。1135年，金熙宗即位，从以往仿照辽国的制度改为直接采取唐制，兼采宋制。同时，金朝统治者也重视使用汉官，《金史》记载金明昌四年的全国官员数量：“官万一千四百九十九，内女真四千七百五员，汉人六千七百九十四员。”海陵王完颜亮在位期间确立了“汉地本位”政策；到金章宗时，他限制女真特权，允许族际通婚，大修孔庙，完善科举，健全法制。研究者认为，金朝的汉化到金章宗这一代已告完成。当我们读到史籍中金章宗与汉儒名士们一起创作书法、绘画、诗词的情景时，感觉他已经和宋朝皇帝没有多大区别了。

因为金朝皇帝在学习中原文化方面毫无顾虑，所以海陵王可以不加改造地直接沿用宋朝帝王的大辇：“七宝辇，制如大辇，饰以玉裙网，七宝，滴子用珍珠。宋钦宗为上皇制，海陵自汴取而用之。”遗憾的是，我们不知道——海陵王的大辇之上，是否安置了那尊独特的铜坐龙？

The squatting dragon conflates the features of dragon, kylin, lion and dog. The unique squat posture demonstrated how the Jurchen tribespeople re-created Chinese dragon culture over 800 years ago.

One day in 1965, near the ruins of the ancient city wall of Jin-Dynasty Shangjing Site, Acheng City, Heilongjiang Province, a bronze squatting dragon heaved into sight from mottled blue bricks. Archaeologists carefully observed its dragon head, dog body, kylin back and lion tail. The dragon slightly raised head and roared, slightly arched its shoulder forward, and curled up the left leg. Its claw trod on cloud forcefully, which was connected to its back leg. Its right leg (in the front) extended forward, with its claw connected to the ground. The dragon's tail curled outward, and its head, shoulder and limbs were adorned with curly manes. Archaeologists confirmed that the squatting dragon was used as a decorative object on the carriage of the Jin nobles. Three curly manes that resembled flowing clouds were inspired by horse mane, which displayed Jurchen hunter's love for horse. The dragon's mouth looked like that of eagle. This involved Jurchen's worship of Jongkhurun. The dragon body was carved into a dog shape, because dogs were good helpers for hunting.

In Pre-Qin historical records, Jurchen was called Sushen or Xishen. In the Qin and Han Dynasties, Sushen was renamed Yilou; and in the Wei and Jin Dynasties, Yilou was changed to Wuji and Mohe. In the Liao and Song Dynasties, the original name of Sushen was used again, translated into Chinese as Jurchen. In 1115, Wanyan Aguda officially mounted the throne and established the Jin Dynasty, siting the capital in Shangjing, present-day Acheng District, Harbin City.

Jin vanquished Liao in 1125 and Northern Song in 1127. Having subdued Western Xia and Goryeo, Jin became a country with a vast territory in northern China. As a unified multi-ethnic state, Jin provided a solid foundation for the formation of the northern territory of China.

是谁首先在燕京城正式建都，从此开启了北京作为中华民族政治文化中心的历程？

北京作为国都的起点

金中都铜坐龙

Bronze Squatting Dragon Unearthed at the Middle Capital of Jin

70

文物简读

这尊铜坐龙出土于北京房山金陵遗址，见证了女真从上京迁都燕京，北京从此成为中华民族政治文化中心的历史。与此同时，从上京铜坐龙到中都铜坐龙的形象变化，也反映了来到中原的女真对中华传统文化的接受和吸收。

迁都

天德三年（1151）的一天，金朝第四代皇帝海陵王完颜亮在上京皇宫中召集众臣宴饮，酒至酣畅时，完颜亮问右丞相梁汉臣："朕在会宁府花园的池塘里，栽了两百株莲花，全都死了，这是怎么回事呢？"梁汉臣回答道："自古橘生江南，枳生江北，这是地理条件决定的。上京地寒，唯有燕京气温地暖，方可栽莲。"梁汉臣声音刚落，完颜亮立即接过话去："依卿所请，择日而迁。"

此言非同寻常，海陵王这不是在宣布将都城从上京迁往燕京吗？

大臣萧玉大惊失色，立刻进谏："上京之地，乃龙兴宝地，国家根本，怎能弃之？"却见兵部侍郎何卜年站起身来，说道："燕京地广土坚，人物蕃息，乃礼义之所，郎主可迁都。北番上都，黄沙之地，非帝居也。"又见梁汉臣马上接过话去："不忙不忙，待臣为君主招集天下民工，在燕京修整好内苑宫殿以后，再迁都不迟！"

迁都之事，惊天动地，竟然就在一个酒宴上确定下来！当然，千年之后，我们回头去读这一段历史时，显然不会怀疑这一幕是蓄谋已久、精心导演的结果。海陵王完颜亮在弑金熙宗自立之后，一心要实现"天下一统"的雄心，早已决意将金朝政治中心迁离偏居一隅的会宁府，南下燕京，实现远大的政治抱负。

名称：金中都铜坐龙

年代：金

规格：高19.6厘米，重2.1千克

出土地点：北京市房山区金陵遗址

收藏单位：首都博物馆

Name: Bronze Squatting Dragon Unearthed at the Middle Capital of Jin

Historical Period: The Jin Dynasty

Height: 19.6 cm, Weight: *c* 2.1 kg

Excavation Site: Fangshan Jin Mausoleum Site, Beijing

Housed in: Capital Museum

海陵王紧接着就颁布了《议迁都燕京诏》，下令在原辽朝南京城的基础上，仿照北宋都城汴京的规制建造皇城和宫城。这可是一项巨大的工程！金朝征集了四十万军队和八十万老百姓共同修建。《顺天府志·金故城考》记载："人置一筐，左右手排立定，自涿州至燕京传递，空筐出，实筐入……"用时两年多，一个富丽堂皇的都城终于竣工。

公元1153年4月21日，意气风发、踌躇满志的海陵王，乘坐豪华铜坐龙大辇，带领皇室成员从上京出发到燕京新都。进入燕京后，海陵王认为"燕"乃六国之名，不当为京师之号，于是"改燕京为中都，府曰大兴"。

能诗善文海陵王

史载，海陵王完颜亮自幼聪明好学，拜汉儒张用直为师，曾"学弈、象戏、点茶、延接儒生，谈论有成人器"。在金熙宗时代，他就通读隋唐的律文，还参考《北齐律》《唐六典》等，为金朝制定了一部真正意义上的成文公法，即《续降制书》。

完颜亮还是一个文学家，"一吟一咏，冠绝当时"。他的诗词雄浑遒劲，气象恢宏，充满雄霸之气，不但影响了金朝的一代文风，也为南宋文学注入了一股刚劲之气。在做藩王时，他为人题写扇面："大柄若在手，清风满天下。"流露出非凡志向。有一日他入妻子居室，见瓶中木樨花溢彩流金，立刻索笔为诗："绿叶枝头金缕装，秋深自有别般香。一朝扬汝名天下，也学君王着赭黄。"显示出一腔鸿鹄大志。

作为一代少数民族君王，海陵王却对统一华夏、兴国百业有着强烈的理想追求。他要求"政教号令，一切不异于中国"。他推行唐宋典章制度，重用汉人官吏，以使金朝成为一个真正的中原王朝。他曾在不同场合说过，"自古帝王混一天下，然后可以为正统"，"天下一家，然后可以为正统"。也曾赋诗言志："自古车书一混同，南人何事费车工？提师百万临江上，立马吴山第一峰。"

公元1160年，为了实现"混一天下"的抱负，海陵王发动六十万大军，欲南征南宋，却在瓜洲渡江作战时死于完颜元宜等人之手，时年40岁。

但是，完颜亮的政策被继承了下来。金世宗完颜雍即位后，依然将燕京作为首都，继续推进汉化政策，使女真继续行进在融入中华民族的历史道路中。

铜坐龙：从上京到中都

对于中华历史而言，金迁都燕京是一个值得铭记的大事件：从此，北京开启了作为国都的历史，成为一千年来中华民族的政治经济文化中心。

在金朝的经营下，金中都成为一座繁华富丽的都市，奠定了今天北京城的基本地理格局，并留下了一系列重要的文化遗产，如北海、香山、钓鱼台、玉泉山、陶然亭、玉渊潭等，这些都是当年金朝皇帝的离宫别苑和休闲娱乐之处。

这一尊铜坐龙，出土于北京房山金陵遗址。当我们端详它时，发现它与金上京铜坐龙有了很大的不同：它更多地融合吸收了宋代中原流行的龙形特点，虽然还是蹲坐态，但龙背鬃毛已经不太像马鬃了，更接近羽翼；嘴部不再近似鹰喙，下颚较长，特别是上颚端肌肉发达，高高突起，呈如意状，更接近龙山文化的猪龙。

显然，从上京来到中都，在女真人的心中，龙的形象悄然变化，表明游牧文化和农耕文化已深深融合。

The squatting dragon was unearthed at Fangshan Jin Mausoleum Site, Beijing. Since the Jin Dynasty, Beijing has been the political and cultural center of China. Noticeably, the squatting dragon differs from its counterpart unearthed at the Jin-Dynasty Shangjing Site. Its hair is not much like a horse's mane, and it resembles the dragon in the Central Plains in shape. This reflects the fact that the Jurchen tribespeople deeply embraced the culture of the Central Plains.

In 1151, Prince of Hailing released *The Imperial Edict on Relocating the Capital to Yanjing*, ordering to construct the imperial city and the palace city at Yanjing (formerly Nanjing of the Liao Dynasty), according to the scale and structure of Bianjing (present-day Kaifeng), capital of the Northern Song Dynasty. It took two years to construct the imposing capital. On April 21, 1153, following the Han etiquette, Wanyan Liang, seated on a jade-decorated imperial carriage, entered Yanjing in a grand manner.

According to historical records, Prince of Hailing was intelligent and studious as a young boy. He formally acknowledged Zhang Yongzhi, a Confucianist scholar, as his master. When he learned to play chess and *Xiangxi* (a kind of throwing-race game), make tea and receive Confucianist scholars, he acted like an adult. His poems embodied a bold and unconstrained style and expressed an imperial atmosphere, which not only influenced the literary trend in the Jin Dynasty, but also injected vitality to the literature of the Southern Song Dynasty. Besides, in the reign of Emperor Xizong, Prince of Hailing carefully read the legal provisions of the Sui and Tang Dynasties. On the basis of *The Laws of the Northern Qi Dynasty* (《北齐律》) and *The Six Statutes of the Tang Dynasty* (《唐六典》), he issued *The Compilation of Various Laws of the Jin Dynasty under the Imperial Order* (《续降制书》), a statutory law for the Jin Dynasty.

Prince of Hailing entertained great ambitions for unifying the whole China and promoting national prosperity. He adopted the institutions of the Tang and Song Dynasties and appointed the Han officials, aiming to build Jin into a Han culture-based dynasty.

在号称“北方马王堆”的金代齐国王墓，一件“左衽”的紫地云鹤金锦棉袍承载着哪些复杂多元的文化交融信息?

对峙与交融：宋金的隔江唱和

紫地云鹤金锦棉袍

Golden Brocade Cotton Robe with Purple Background and Cloud-Crane Pattern

文物简读

作为北方游牧民族典型文化标志的“左衽”与作为中原文化代表性纹饰的“云鹤纹”交织于一衣，草原贵族酷爱的金锦与中原皇家喜爱的紫色融合于一袍——这一件锦袍承载着女真族主动融入多元一体中华民族的历史记忆。

“北方马王堆”

黑龙江阿城——金源故都，有一座金代齐国王墓，墓主人为完颜晏，金景祖之孙，也是金太祖完颜阿骨打的堂弟，生前为太尉开府仪同三司事齐国王，“级别”仅次于皇帝。完颜晏曾在太宗、熙宗、海陵王、世宗四朝为官，崇尚汉文化，通晓汉文、契丹文，他的一生就是女真与汉文化融合的写照。他死后埋葬的习俗与女真葬俗大不相同，有棺有椁，呈现出浓重的中原习俗风尚。齐国王墓出土了33件丝织物，可谓“北方马王堆”。有专家根据出土丝料的特点，推断其为宋代产的浙绢，这说明宋金以丝织业为代表的贸易交流非常繁荣。

这件紫地云鹤金锦棉袍，出土时穿戴在完颜晏身上，保存完整，雍容华贵，堪称国宝。有意思的是，这件金锦棉袍是一件“左衽”袍服。

上古时代，华夏尚右，习惯衣襟右掩，称为“右衽”；而北方游牧民族尚左，衣襟左掩，是为“左衽”。“右衽”与“左衽”因此成为早期华夷之别的典型标志。《大金国志校证》记载：金初，“君臣之服大率与中国相似，止左衽异焉”。也就是说，金入主中原后，基本接受了北宋的冠服制度，唯独保留了“左衽”这一习俗。

名称：紫地云鹤金锦棉袍

年代：金

规格：袍长142厘米，领高5.6厘米，袖口宽21厘米

出土地点：黑龙江省哈尔滨市阿城区巨源镇城子村遗址

收藏单位：黑龙江省博物馆

Name: Golden Brocade Cotton Robe with Purple Background and Cloud-Crane Pattern

Historical Period: The Jin Dynasty

Robe Length: 142 cm, Collar Height: 5.6 cm, Cuffs Width: 21 cm

Excavation Site: Chengzi Village Site, Juyuan Town, Acheng District, Harbin, Heilongjiang Province

Housed in: Heilongjiang Provincial Museum

这件紫地云鹤金锦棉袍就是一件典型的文化交融之物：它将北方游牧民族典型文化标志“左衽”跟中原文化代表性纹饰“云鹤纹”交织于一衣，又将女真贵族酷爱的金锦与中原皇家喜爱的紫色融合于一袍。

民族文化交融具有双向性。翻阅史籍可以发现，金朝统治者不仅把“左衽”习俗保留了下来，而且在一个时期里，中原汉人百姓也广泛接受了女真的“左衽”习俗。南宋名臣、文学家范成大曾经出使金朝，当他来到北宋故都东京时，竟发现当地百姓“衣装之类，其制尽为胡矣”。他所说的这种汉人“胡服”现象，最重要的一个表现大概就是“左衽”与“短衣”。东京作为北宋都城，本是受中原文化影响极深的地区，然而这里的汉人百姓竟穿上了“左衽”短衣！这样的历史情景深刻地反映了民族文化交融的复杂性、多向性。

隔江唱和

绍兴十一年（1141），南宋与金达成“绍兴和议”，形成南北对峙的政治格局。此后宋金之间虽时有交战，但经济文化交流却难以阻断。

史载，建炎南渡后，由于北方儒士对南方文学艺术著作颇有需求，书贾为了谋利，纷纷翻刻南宋的著述，如王十朋编纂的《集注分类东坡先生诗》就在北方广为翻印，反映出金国士人对南方书籍的需求。而南方则对北方的医学著作、释道论著需求旺盛，这些书籍也都在北方经过翻刻刊印，贩运过江。金章宗年间，南宋理学家的著作纷纷传入金国，改变了北方儒学沉寂的局面；南宋繁荣的诗文评论引起了北方学者的关注，南宋诸宫调等通俗文艺作品也广泛传入北方。

元好问是北魏鲜卑皇室后裔，他是宋金对峙时期北方文学的主要代表，享有“北方文雄”的美誉。他的一首《被缴夜赴邓州幕府》中，有“未能免俗私自笑，岂不怀归官有程”之句，与陆游《思子虡》中的“未能免俗予嗟老，岂不怀归汝念亲”何其相似！可知陆放翁的作品肯定流传到了北方，为元好问所激赏，以至于情不自禁套用了放翁的诗句。元好问还曾撰写过一部《续夷坚志》，有研究者认为他是心慕南宋洪迈的《夷坚志》一书，仿而续之，撰成续志。这说明，洪迈的《夷坚志》也曾在北方受到欢迎和传播。与此同时，北方文学以格调雄浑为南宋人所关注，如海陵王的诗词就曾为南方诗坛带来一股恢宏之气。

心有灵犀，隔江唱和，这是在宋金南北对峙的历史背景下，文化艺术交流难以阻断的生动情景。

这说明，虽然族群、身份不同，但来自远方的少数民族却以对中华文化的深刻认同，把自己变成了中华文化的共同继承者和共同创造者。这正是中华文明历经对峙与分裂，却始终生生不息、延续不断的基因密码。也正是因此，各民族沿着多元一体的历史进程，不断汇入中华民族共同体之中。

The robe blended left lapel, a typical cultural symbol of the northern nomads, and cloud-crane pattern, a representative pattern in the Central Plains, as well as golden brocade and purple color favored by Jurchen and Han nobles respectively. It saw the history in which the Jurchen people assimilated into the Chinese nation.

A Jin-Dynasty tomb was discovered in Acheng County, southeast of Harbin. The tomb owner was Wanyan Yan, King of Qi. Wanyan Yan was the grandson of Emperor Jingzu of Jin and the cousin of Wanyan Aguda, Emperor Taizu of Jin. He filled the offices in the reigns of Emperor Taizong, Emperor Xizong, King of Hailing and Emperor Shizong. Well versed in Han and Khitan languages, Wanyan Yan admired Han culture. The burial custom of his tomb remarkably differed from the Jurchen tradition. The coffin and outer coffin showcased the burial custom in the Central Plains.

33 pieces of silk fabrics were unearthed in the tomb of Wanyan Yan. Scholars judged that the silk was produced in Zhejiang in the Song Dynasty, signaling the peak period of Jin-Song trade represented by the silk manufacturing industry. Well preserved, the robe was elegant. Upon close looking, it had a left lapel.

In terms of ancient dress, the Han people respected the right and covered the right side (or the right lapel), whereas the nomads worshipped the left and covered the left side (or the left lapel). In early Chinese civilization, the lapel became a cultural sign that distinguished *Hua Xia* and *Yi*. In *The Collation of The Annals of the Great Jin Dynasty* (*Da Jin Guo Zhi Jiao Zheng*, 《大金国志校证》), it was recorded that "the attire of the early-Jin emperors and officials was almost identical to that in the Central Plains, barring the left lapel".

Ethnic integration meant a two-way process. As historical records suggested, the Han people in the Central Plains also embraced the Jurchen dress with left-lapel style. Fan Chengda, a famous politician and poet, once served as an envoy to Jin on behalf of the Southern Song Dynasty, and came to Dongjing (present-day Kaifeng), former capital of Northern Song. As he observed, the Han citizens were "all dressed in the Hu style". The Hu-style clothes were actually characterized with left lapel and short sleeve. This deeply reflected the complexity of ethnic integration.

为什么中国迄今为止发现的世界上最早的木活字印本出自西夏?

西夏：戈壁草原上的灿烂文化

72 木活字印刷西夏文佛经《吉祥遍至口和本续》

The Tangut Buddhist Scripture *Dpalkun-tukha-sbyorzhes-bya-ba'irgyud* Printed with Wooden Movable Type

文物简读

1991年出土于宁夏贺兰县的西夏文佛经《吉祥遍至口和本续》，是我国迄今为止发现的世界上最早的木活字印本。这一令人震惊的发现，把中国木活字的发明和使用时间提早了一个朝代。它不仅承载着党项所创造的辉煌的西夏文化，也见证了西夏对中华文明做出的重大贡献。

世界上现存最早的木活字印本

1991年，位于贺兰山腹地的拜寺沟方塔出土了西夏文佛经九册，《吉祥遍至口和本续》就是其中之一。在研究过程中，考古学家牛达生发现：这本佛经与同时代的雕版印本有许多不同之处，它的版框栏线交角处缺口很大；同一面同一字笔锋、形态不一；栏线和版心行线有漏排、错排，以及数字倒置等现象……也就是说，这本佛经具有明显的活字版印本特征。

这个判断非同小可——在传统观点中，木活字是元代的王祯首创或发明的；而这本佛经的印行时期早于王祯一个多世纪。

此后，专家小组进行了周密的鉴定，最终得出结论：《吉祥遍至口和本续》不仅是活字印本，而且是木活字印本。这意味着这本西夏文佛经是世界上现存最早的木活字版印本，而元代王祯"排字作行，削成竹片夹之"的技术，其实早在西夏时期就已经出现。这就把中国木活字的发明和使用时间从元代提早到了宋代。

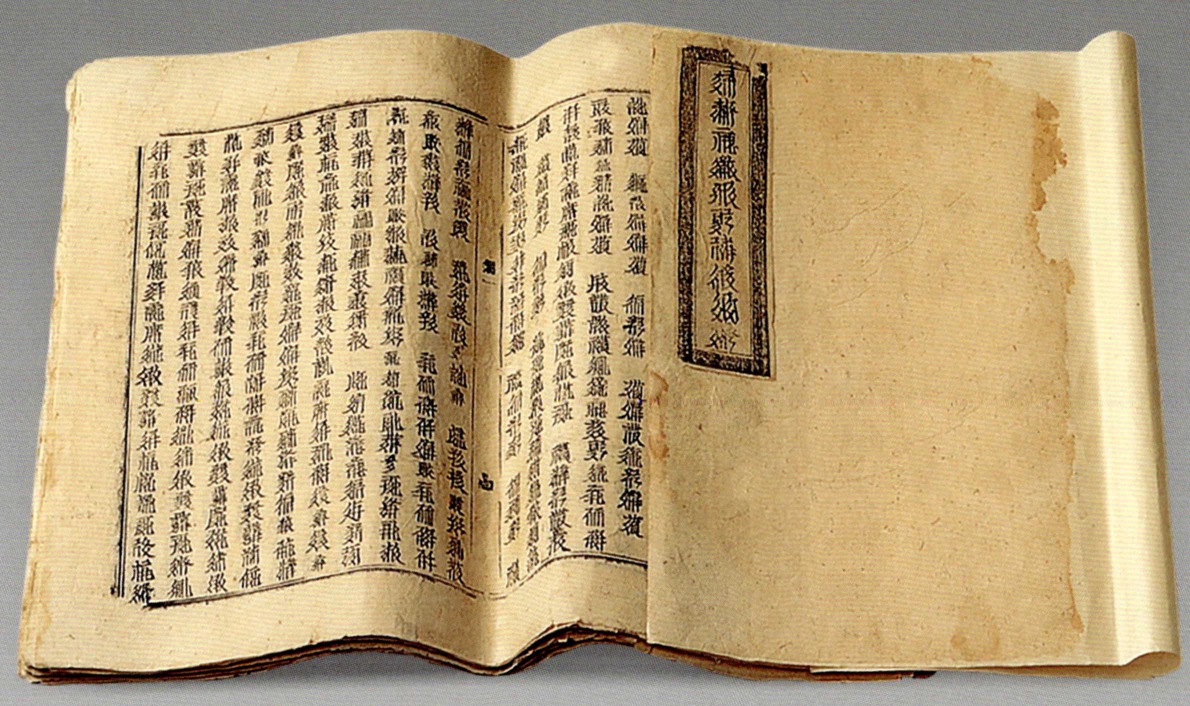

名称：木活字印刷西夏文佛经《吉祥遍至口和本续》

年代：西夏

规格：全页版框高30.5厘米，宽38.8厘米

出土地点：宁夏回族自治区贺兰县拜寺沟方塔

收藏单位：宁夏回族自治区文物考古研究所

宁夏回族自治区博物馆

Name: The Tangut Buddhist Scripture *Dpalkun-tukha-sbyorzhes-bya-ba'irgyud* Printed with Wooden Movable Type

Historical Period: The Western Xia Dynasty

(Full Page Frame) Height: 30.5 cm, Width: 38.8 cm

Excavation Site: Fang Pagoda at Baisi Gully, Helan County, Ningxia Hui Autonomous Region

Housed in: Ningxia Institute of Cultural Relics and Archaeology

Ningxia Museum

《吉祥遍至口和本续》共计九册，其中七册现藏于宁夏回族自治区文物考古研究所，两册现藏于宁夏回族自治区博物馆。

党项与西夏

在宋金对峙的格局之外，还有一个地方政权自成一极，这就是西夏。

西夏的建立者是党项。党项是羌的一支，《旧唐书》载："党项羌……汉西羌之别种也。"唐初，党项羌生活在青藏高原，常和吐谷浑联合起来对抗吐蕃。吐蕃灭掉吐谷浑后，党项羌失去依附，向唐朝请求内附，唐朝将其安置于松州（今四川松潘）。开元年间，党项又遭吐蕃的进攻，再度向唐玄宗求救，唐又将其迁至庆州（今甘肃庆阳）。安史之乱后，唐代宗把党项迁往银州和夏州，这一地区即是南北朝时匈奴人赫连勃勃建立大夏国的地方。唐末党项首领拓跋思恭参与平定黄巢起义有功，就被封为"夏国公"，并被赐姓"李"，其军队被称为"定难军"。李思恭由此成为一股藩镇势力。

宋朝建立后，宋太祖虽然致力于削夺藩镇兵权，但对西北少数民族政权依然宽宥，"许之世袭"。982年，李继捧接任夏州节度使，因为家族内部产生矛盾，就率领族人入京朝见宋朝皇帝，自愿献出银、夏等四州八县。但他的族弟李继迁却集结武装占领了银州，又向辽国请降，被契丹人封为"夏国王"。1038年，李元昊称帝建国，国号"夏"。因处于宋的西北，被称为"西夏"。

西夏的西面有吐蕃、回鹘等，东面和北面有辽、金、蒙古，几方势力在西北地区犬牙交错，这使西夏一直生存在夹缝当中。西夏发展最鼎盛之时，人口不过三百万，面积不过77万平方公里，国力远逊于辽、金。西夏境内，生活着党项、汉、吐蕃、回鹘、契丹、女真等民族，他们长期彼此交融、互相影响，形成了多种文化并存的现象。

其中，儒学是西夏思想文化的支柱。西夏历代帝王莫不学习和模仿汉制，李继迁时"潜设中官，尽异羌人之体，曲延儒士，渐行中国之风"。因深受儒家文化影响，西夏逐渐由番汉二元政治演变为一元化的汉法制度。《西夏记》载："（西夏）尊孔子为文宣帝，彬彬乎质有其文，固未尝不可与辽金比烈！"与此同时，佛教也是西夏立国的支柱之一，吐蕃高僧因此大量进入西夏。甘州回鹘在归附西夏后，河西走廊成为回鹘人和党项人的杂居之地，因此西夏国也留下了许多回鹘文献。

中国印刷史上的"西夏第一"

1036年，李元昊命大臣野利仁荣创制西夏文字，仿照汉字结构，历三年始成，共五千余字。西夏文的创制直接推动了西夏印刷业的发展，西夏由此在中国印刷史上开创了古代少数民族文字印刷的先河。

西夏在政府机构中专设了掌管刻印事务的机构——刻字司，这在历朝历代是绝无仅有的，成为中国出版史上的一个创举。

西夏还首创了两种文字合璧的印刷。《番汉合时掌中珠》是中外历史上最早的一部双语双解词典，它以西夏文和汉文的对照翻译，首次将两种文字雕刊在同一版面上。

活字印刷术的发明，是一个划时代的伟大变革，对世界文明的整体进步起着决定性的推动作用。北宋沈括在《梦溪笔谈》中明确记录了当时毕昇发明活字印刷的事件，但11—13世纪的活字印刷物却未能在中原地区保存下来。考古发现的西夏活字印刷品，为中国发明活字印刷术提供了珍贵的实物证据。这一切有力地向我们揭示出一个真理：灿烂辉煌的中华文化是古往今来的各民族共同创造的。

Unearthed in Helan County, Ningxia, in 1991, the Tangut Buddhist scripture *Dpalkun-tukha-sbyorzhes-bya-ba'irgyud* boasts the earliest Chinese presswork with wooden movable type in the world. The discovery rocked the world, displaying the glorious Tangut culture created by the Tangut people and demonstrating the significant contributions made by the Western Xia to Chinese civilization.

In his long-term research of *Dpalkun-tukha-sbyorzhes-bya-ba'irgyud*, archaeologist Niu Dasheng made a groundbreaking discovery: the Buddhist scripture greatly differed from contemporary woodblock-printing copies. There was a large gap at the corner of the frame and column lines. On the same page, the strokes and shapes of the same characters varied. Besides, omissions, errors and inverted numbers were found in the column lines and type pages. On this basis, scholars finally concluded that *Dpalkun-tukha-sbyorzhes-bya-ba'irgyud* was a wooden movable type print. The conclusion justified that given that the Tangut Buddhist scripture was the earliest wooden-movable-type print, the invention and use of wooden movable type dated back to the Song Dynasty rather than the Yuan Dynasty, as previously acknowledged.

In 1036, Li Yuanhao, founder of the Western Xia, ordered his official Yeli Renrong to create the Tangut patterned on the structure of the Han language. Three years later, Yeli totally coined more than 5,000 characters. The invention of the Tangut directly facilitated the development of the printing industry in the Western Xia. Additionally, the Western Xia specially established *Kezi Si* (刻字司), a department in charge of engraving affairs, and firstly printed bilingual works. *The Han-Tangut Transliteration Palm Pearl* (*Fan Han He Shi Zhang Zhong Zhu*, 《番汉合时掌中珠》) was the earliest bilingual dictionary in the world. The Han and Tangut characters were successfully engraved and printed on the same page. This was an epoch-making event in the publishing history.

The wooden-movable-type printing of the Western Xia indisputably proved that the brilliant Chinese culture was jointly created by various ethnic groups.

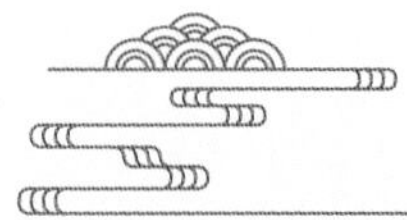

统一多民族国家的巩固

The Consolidation of the Unified Multi-ethnic Country

13世纪初，蒙古人建立了元朝，扫除了东西屏障。中亚、西亚民族大量迁入中国并从此融入中华大地，与汉、蒙古等民族通婚杂居而孕育出回、东乡、保安等新生民族，这使中华民族又完成了一次新的塑造。元末，在农民战争风起云涌的背景下，朱元璋提出了“驱逐胡虏，恢复中华”的口号。但在建立明朝后，朱元璋却以“元以北狄入主中国，……实乃天授”，来承认元朝的历史合法性，消泯民族仇恨。而对于元灭明兴，朱元璋也用“天命归弃”来阐释。朱元璋还特别强调明朝的蒙古、色目之民，“能知礼义愿为臣民者，与中夏之人抚养无异”。明太祖的政治智慧，显然来自多民族共处中华这一悠久传统所积淀的深厚历史经验，是对“天下主义”观念的直接继承与发扬。清朝建立后，彻底废弃了长城这道横亘在农耕与游牧之间的军事防线，将草原文明与农业文明整合进同一国家秩序之中，开启了民族交往交融更加广阔的地理空间。持续134年的康雍乾盛世，迎来爆发式人口增长——从顺治年间约七千万，到道光年间激增至四亿，用了仅一百多年，就使中华民族人口约占到世界总人口三分之一。显然，这与满族统治者实行促进民族交融与生产力发展的政策直接相关。

自元至清，这一时期的历史轨迹，是统一多民族国家最终走向确立和巩固的历程。其中，元朝与清朝对中华疆域的拓展和捍卫，尤其显示出其对中华历史所做出的巨大贡献。元朝将西藏正式纳入统一多民族国家版图；清朝经由康、雍、乾三代，前仆后继，历经七十年，终于彻底平定了准噶尔部和大小和卓叛乱，保卫了国家对新疆的领土主权。此外，在北方，康熙坚决阻止了准噶尔部对漠北的进犯，实现了蒙古高原的统一；在东南，清朝收复了台湾；在西藏，清朝采取一系列制度，有力强化了藏族民众对中央王朝的认同；在东北，清朝同沙俄侵略者进行了长达四十年的斗争，经两度雅克萨之战，终将其击败，坚定地发出了黑龙江流域是中国领土不可分割的一部分的外交宣言……清朝拓展了空前辽阔的疆域，为今日的中国版图奠定了基础。

In the Yuan, Ming and Qing Dynasties, the unified multi-ethnic country was eventually forged and cemented. In the early 13th century, the Mongols founded the Yuan Dynasty and bridged the east and the west. A large number of tribes in the Central Asia and the West Asia immigrated to China, and lived and intermarried with the Han, Mongolian and other people. New ethnic groups, such as Hui, Dongxiang and Bao'an, emerged, which reshaped the landscape of the Chinese nation.

After the founding of the Ming Dynasty, Zhu Yuanzhang recognized the legitimacy of Yuan and dispelled ethnic hatred, as he stated, "The Mongolian rule was ordained by the heaven, so was the fall of Yuan and the rise of Ming". He declared that: "I will treat the Mongolians and *Semuren* (色目人), who learnt the etiquette of Han, equally with the Han subjects." Obviously, the political wisdom of Emperor Taizu of Ming stemmed from the long-standing tradition of multi-ethnic coexistence, inheriting and developing the idea of *Tian Xia* (天下, the whole China under the heaven). The Qing Dynasty completely abandoned the false idea of the Great Wall as a military barrier between the Central Plains and the northern tribes. In combination of the farming and nomadic civilizations, the Qing Dynasty expanded the geographical space for ethnic exchanges and integration. The Great Reign of Kangxi, Yongzheng and Qianlong Emperors, which lasted for 134 years, ushered in an explosive growth in population, jumping from about 70 million (in the reign of Emperor Shunzhi) to 400 million (in the reign of Emperor Daoguang). In just one century, the Chinese nation accounted for about one-third of the world's total population. Evidently, this directly related to the policies of the Manchu rulers who promoted ethnic integration and productivity development.

The Yuan and Qing rulers made significant contributions in enlarging and defending the territory of China. The Yuan Dynasty formally incorporated Tibet into the unified multi-ethnic country. Emperors Kangxi, Yongzheng and Qianlong totally pacified the rebellions of the Junggar and the Altishahr Khojas. Their 70-year anti-separatist struggle protected the Qing's territorial sovereignty over Xinjiang. Emperor Kangxi successfully contained the Junggar invasion of Mobei Mongolia and unified the Mongolian Plateau. In the Reign of Kangxi, the Qing court resumed the exercise of sovereignty over Taiwan. In Tibet, the political and religious systems enhanced the recognition of the central government among the Tibetan monks and seculars. The Qing troops engaged in the 40-year struggle against Tsarist Russian invaders, and achieved a great victory in the Battle of Jaxa, powerfully demonstrating that the Heilongjiang River Basin was an inseparable part of Chinese territory. The Qing Dynasty expanded its domain and drew the map of China today.

什么样的身份证，需要同时使用五种文字？

元朝：延续中原正统王朝

天字拾二号夜巡铜牌

Bronze Token for Night Patrol with the Inscriptions of *Tian Zi Shi Er Hao* (天字拾二号, No. 12 in the *Tian* Sequence)

文物简读

这枚刻有五种文字的铜牌，蕴含的历史信息格外丰富。它不仅见证了元朝管理辽阔疆域的独特方式，也生动地体现了当时民族大融合的盛况，还让我们真切地看到：蒙古人所建立的元朝，不仅推进了中华民族多元一体的历史进程，而且将统一多民族国家进一步推向巩固。

一种独特的元朝文物

在元朝文物中，符牌独具特色——其数量之多、种类之丰、用途之广、影响之大，构成了一种前所未有的文化景观，形成了元朝特有的一种历史文化遗产。

事实上，历朝历代都使用符牌，为何元朝最多？研究者认为，这与元代版图达到了中国古代史的空前规模有关。《元史》称元代疆域“北逾阴山，西极流沙，东尽辽左，南越海表”，汉唐极盛之时不及也。在前所未有的辽阔疆域里，怎样保证中央的信息及时传递到四面八方？元朝在配套建设水陆通道、驿站、递铺等庞大的交通网络的同时，又非常重视符牌作为使者“身份证”的作用，这就使符牌制度在元朝达到了历史的顶峰。

在元朝留存的众多符牌中，这枚“天字拾二号夜巡铜牌”十分独特——在16厘米高的圆牌上，竟铸有汉文、八思巴文、波斯文、藏文、畏兀儿蒙古文五种文字，它是迄今为止发现的蒙元时期各类符牌中使用文字种类最多的一枚。这枚铜牌是元上都卫戍部队夜间巡逻时佩戴的身份牌。而铸刻五种文

名称：天字拾二号夜巡铜牌

年代：元

规格：高16.3厘米，直径11.3厘米，缘厚0.6厘米，重725克

出土地点：内蒙古自治区兴安盟科尔沁右翼中旗

收藏单位：科尔沁右翼中旗博物馆

Name: Bronze Token for Night Patrol with the Inscriptions of *Tian Zi Shi Er Hao* (天字拾二号, No. 12 in the *Tian* Sequence)

Historical Period: The Yuan Dynasty

Height: 16.3 cm, Diameter: 11.3 cm, Edge Thickness: 0.6 cm, Weight: 725 g

Excavation Site: Horqin Right Wing Middle Banner, Xing'an League, Inner Mongolia Autonomous Region

Housed in: Horqin Right Wing Middle Banner Museum

字，显然表明卫队巡视保卫的地方聚集了大量来自各民族的上层人物和官吏，所以铭刻多种文字，以避免语言误会，减少交流麻烦。

因此，这枚铜牌不仅能够见证元朝管理辽阔疆域的独特方式，也能生动地体现当时民族大融合的盛况。

“大哉乾元”

1260年，蒙古国大汗蒙哥去世，忽必烈即位称帝，为自己确立了第一个年号——“中统”。据说，这个年号取自“中华开统”之义。在开国诏书中，忽必烈诏告天下：“建元表岁，示人君万世之传；纪时书王，见天下一家之义。法《春秋》之正始，体大《易》之乾元。”

11年后，忽必烈决定采用《易经》中“大哉乾元”之意，将国号从“大蒙古国”改为“大元”；次年定都大都，即今日的北京，正式开启了元朝的历史。

忽必烈为何改国号为“元”？他说，自古以来，即使汉唐也不如元朝之盛大，“元也者，大也。大不足以尽之，而谓之元者，大之至也”。因此，“大元”国号首先表明了元朝疆域是历代王朝“开辟以来未有也”。

但忽必烈此举显然还包含着更加深刻的意义。元代第一部大型通制类政书《经世大典》，把忽必烈改国号为“大元”之举，与唐虞、商汤一直到秦、汉、唐、宋相提并论。这揭示出元世祖确立新国号的本质意义——忽必烈已经不是蒙古族的大汗，而是中国的大汗；蒙古人所建立的朝代，是中原正统王朝的延续。

“行中国之道”

元朝是我国历史上第一个由北方游牧民族建立的大一统王朝。入主中原的元世祖忽必烈在一批汉儒幕僚的辅助下，积极“行汉法”，制定了一套“行中国之道”的汉化政策，既实现了他欲“大有为于天下”的个人抱负，又延续了中华文化传统。

首先，元世祖以中原王朝体制为框架，建立了元朝的国家机构与职官制度。他废除了蒙古传统的“忽里台”——古代蒙古负责推举部落首长及可汗的政治军事会议；在中央设立中书省，在地方设置行中书省；又实行行政、军事、监察三权分立；整顿地方诸侯在封地内各自为政的现象，以迁转制度代替蒙古地方官世袭制。他依照汉人大臣提出的建议，将皇子真金立为太子，这是元朝首次以中原王朝立储制度来确立皇位继承人。

其次，元世祖积极推动蒙古游牧社会向农耕文明转变的进程——这是统一的多民族国家巩固与发展的重要前提。他制定了以农桑立国的方针，试图改变蒙古人逐水草而居的游牧生活。在中央，他

设立大司农司以考察国家农桑水利，编修农事科学技术书籍等。仅在1270年，他便颁布了14条农桑制度。在地方上，他又选任“劝农官”，负责巡视蝗灾、分配荒地、管理水利、教授农学等。正是在这样的背景下，元朝出现了郭守敬这样杰出的水利学专家。

再回过头来看这枚“天字拾二号夜巡铜牌”，上面的“天字”是什么意思？这源自元世祖在建国之初就做出的一项明确规定：全国的牌符必须统一编号，编号依据《千字文》中“天地玄黄，宇宙洪荒……”的词语顺序编制。

这显然是中华传统文化根深蒂固植入元朝符牌制度的体现。这样，元朝的这种独特文物便让我们更加真切地看到：蒙古人所建立的元朝，不仅推进了中华民族多元一体的历史进程，而且使统一多民族国家进一步得以巩固。

Engraved with five languages, the bronze token possesses great historical significance. It showed how the Yuan Dynasty governed the vast territory in an innovative way. As a symbol of ethnic integration, it truthfully demonstrated that the Yuan Dynasty promoted the formation of the Chinese nation and cemented the unified multi-ethnic country.

Tokens constituted a unique cultural landscape or heritage of the Yuan Dynasty. Interestingly, tokens were most widely used in the Yuan Dynasty. To some scholars, that was because that Yuan ruled the largest territory in ancient China. According to *The History of the Yuan Dynasty* (《元史》), the territory of Yuan crossed the Yinshan Mountains in the north, reached the Taklimakan Desert in the west, extended to the east of present-day Liaoning, and leant on present-day Xisha Islands in the south, overriding the zenith of the Han and Tang Dynasties. While building complex land-water transportation networks, Yuan emperors set up post houses and *Di Pu* (递铺, an office that delivered imperial documents), in which tokens served as an identity card. Gradually, the token system was in full swing in the Yuan Dynasty.

The bronze token looks extraordinary. Round in shape, it has a height of 16 cm, with five languages, i.e. Han, Phags-pa script, Persian, Tibetan and Uyghur Mongolian. It boasts the token with the most diverse languages in the Yuan Dynasties to date. The bronze token was an identity card for soldiers garrisoned in the Xanadu during night patrols. In the garrison, there were many citizens, officials and nobles from various ethnic groups. The use of multiple languages minimized the misunderstandings in daily exchanges.

名称：宣慰使司都元帅府夜行铜牌

年代：元

规格：直径17.2厘米，厚0.7厘米

出土地点：江苏省扬州市元代旧城

收藏单位：扬州博物馆

Name: Bronze Token for the Night Tour of Yangzhou High Pacification Commissioner's Office Military Command

Historical Period: The Yuan Dynasty

Diameter: 17.2 cm, Thickness: 0.7 cm

Excavation Site: The Yuan-Dynasty Old City, Yangzhou, Jiangsu Province

Housed in: Yangzhou Museum

今天中国省级行政管理制度的雏形，可追溯至哪一个朝代？

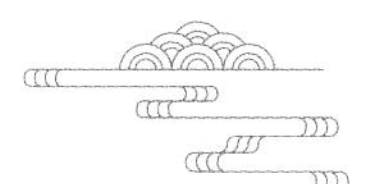

行省制的创立

宣慰使司都元帅府夜行铜牌

74

Bronze Token for the Night Tour of Yangzhou High Pacification Commissioner's Office Military Command

文物简读

此枚铜牌见证了元朝创立行省制以管理空前辽阔的疆域版图，从而为统一多民族国家的地方管理提供一个新制度模式的历史。

又一枚元代夜行铜牌

元朝对统一多民族国家的地方行政管理做出了一个创造性的制度贡献，这就是行省制。我们今天的省级行政管理制，与此有直接关系。对于一个如此重要的历史事件，我们能通过什么文物来观照？

又一枚元代夜行铜牌，出现在我们面前。

“宣慰使司都元帅府夜行铜牌”，牌面为圆形，正面竖铸汉字，从右至左分别为“公务急速”“宣慰使司都元帅府”“持此夜行”“玄字拾号”；背面有波斯文和八思巴文各一行。这枚出土于江苏扬州的铜牌，是元朝扬州“宣慰使司都元帅府”的公务员在夜间执行紧急公务时所持的通行证。宣慰使司，是元朝设在沿海地区和边疆民族地区的军政机关，相当于管理边疆民族事务的机构；而其顶头上司，就是行省。

所以，如果说上一枚“天字拾二号夜巡铜牌”见证了元朝在辽阔疆域里的政令传递情景，那么这一枚“宣慰使司都元帅府夜行铜牌”，则让我们看到元朝是如何管理空前未有的广袤版图的。

犬牙相错的行省

元朝创设行省制，是对辽阔疆域管理难题的一个有效应对。

但行省的设置，首先是蒙古军事征伐过程中的一项政治遗产。随着军事行动的扩大，需要管理的区域越来越广，蒙古统治者就在军事占领地设置临时性的中央派出机构，即“行中书省”，简称“行省”。所谓“行”者，即“中央派出”之意，意为“代表中央行使权力”。忽必烈的大军在进攻南宋时，对于所攻克之地，都以行中书省总其军政。

所以，行省制是在军事推进过程中形成的。但战争平息后，这些临时性的中央派出机构却在持续运行之中，显示出了制度优越性，因而逐渐向常设行政机构转变。此后，元朝便形成了“中书省+行中书省”的行政管理制度：中书省的使命是控驭中央的直辖属地；行中书省的使命是管理中书省直辖区以外的广大国土。

到元朝中期，中央政府一共设置了陕西、四川、云南、江浙、江西、福建、湖广等十数个行省，以及一个管理北京、河北、河南、山东、山西等地的中书省。

有专家认为，元朝的行省制并非简单地将过去的行政区改换名称而已，它其实是中国古代三级行政区的雏形。由于汉朝的州、唐朝的道、宋朝的路，本质上还是中央在地方设立的“监察区”，并无完整的行政权力，因而不能称为正式行政区；而元朝设置的行省，却被赋予了完整的行政权。

元朝的行省面积广阔，即使较小的行省也有数十万平方公里之巨，而且行省长官握有巨大的行政权力，完全有可能出现地方的分裂割据。如何有效防范这一现象？这又是一道管理难题。元世祖忽必烈的对策是：对于行省的划界，不依靠自然的山川地理，而是采用犬牙相错的做法，使得任何一个行省都不能成为完整的形胜之区。

地方治理的新模式

行省制这一创举对后世影响深远。

作为地方行政制度的一大变革，行省制完善了中央和地方的权力结构，适应了大一统行政体制的需要，解决了宋金时代官府分权而治的某些弊端，为“天下一统”的地方治理提供了新模式。

通过设立行省，中央强化了对边疆民族地区的社会管理，保障了国家的统一。在元朝以后的历史进程中，行省所握权力大而不专，极少扮演片面强化地方独立性、凸显地方狭隘利益的角色，起到了拱卫中央政权、维护大一统局面的作用。

此外，行省在南方尤其是西南边陲，如四川、云南等地，得到了更为充分的发展。在行省制下，边疆地区的部落和地方首领变为土官，直隶于行省，有效地加强了中央与边地的联系，促进了民族融合，使多民族国家的统一性得到进一步巩固。

由于吐蕃的自然地理具有独特性，元朝特别在中央设立了相当于一个行省的宣政院，直接管辖吐蕃。

行省制固然是元朝蒙古统治者的一个创造，但其中显然也混合了汉地制度，其本质是自先秦以来中华“天下观”行政理念的一次制度演进，乃是各民族探索统一多民族国家治理的可贵成果和制度遗产。

The bronze token tells us the history of Branch Secretariat, via which the Yuan Dynasty ruled the unprecedentedly vast territory, thus providing a new paradigm for local governance in a unified nation-state.

The bronze token has a circular shape. Chinese characters are inscribed on the obverse. From the right to the left, the top to the bottom, it reads “Urgent Official Affairs”, “High Pacification Commissioner’s Office Military Command”, “For the Night Tour”, and “No. 10 in the *Xuan* (玄) Sequence”. On the back are two lines in Persian and Phags-pa script respectively. Unearthed in Yangzhou, Jiangsu Province, the bronze token was a *laissez-passer* held by civil servants at Yangzhou High Pacification Commissioner’s Office Military Command, who undertook urgent official affairs at night. High Pacification Commissioner’s Office was a military and political organization in coastal and border ethnic areas in the Yuan Dynasty, and its immediate superior was Branch Secretariat.

The political system of Branch Secretariat emerged with the military conquest of the Mongolian troops. As military operations proceeded, the Mongolian possessions expanded, where the Mongolian rulers established *ad hoc* secretariats, or *en-route* secretariats, on behalf of the central government. Gradually, the Yuan court institutionalized the administrative system of “secretariate and branch secretariate”. The former controlled the regions directly under the jurisdiction of the central government, and the latter administrated other vast territories. In the middle Yuan Dynasty, the Yuan empire was divided into eleven branch secretariates in Shaanxi, Sichuan, Yunnan, Jiangzhe, Jiangxi, Fujian and Huguang, as well as a secretariate that administered present-day Beijing, Hebei, Henan, Shandong and Shanxi.

As a significant reform of local administrative system, Branch Secretariat improved the central-local power structure, optimized national governance, rectified the decentralization in the Song and Jin Dynasties, and set an example for local governance in a unified multi-ethnic country.

汉朝以后，历朝正史中关于西南少数民族的记载都以“南蛮传”“西南夷传”等为题，但到元朝却改称为“土司传”，这是怎么回事？

土司制度的形成

75 勐往甸军民官印

The Bronze Seal with the Inscriptions of *Meng Wang Dian Jun Min Guan Yin* (勐往甸军民官印, The Seal for the Military and Administrative Official at Mengwang Dian)

文物简读

这枚元世祖忽必烈在位时期颁发给西双版纳勐往土司的官印，是延续了七百多年的土司制度作为大一统王朝管理民族事务的制度设计并发挥积极作用的见证。

元朝土司制度的罕见见证

今天的勐往是云南省西双版纳傣族自治州勐海县的一个乡，它静伏于澜沧江畔，与繁华喧闹的普洱市和景洪市隔江相望。1958年，在邻近勐往乡的勐遮镇出土了一枚斑驳嶙峋的正方形铜印，上面清晰的“勐往甸军民官印”字样揭示了一个史实：如今平凡而安静的勐往乡，七百多年前曾是土司官衙所在地。

这枚方正的铜印上，正面刻铸着八思巴蒙古文，背面左侧刻铸汉文“中书礼部造，至元三十年二月一日”，表明它是元世祖忽必烈在位时期的物件；右侧刻铸的“勐往甸军民官印”，则表明它来自元朝中央，是最高权力机构直接颁发给这里的土司的印信。

即便是在全国范围内，元朝土司制度初定时期的文物都十分罕见。因此，这枚铜印极其珍贵。

土司制度四问

土司制度是元朝始创的边疆民族地区地方政权组织形式。土司又称“土官”，是由中央王朝任命和分封的地方官，具有“世官、世土、世民”的三重特点：“世官”，即世袭的政治统治权；“世土”，

名称：勐往甸军民官印

年代：元至元三十年（1293）

规格：高7.4厘米，印面边长6.2厘米

出土地点：云南省西双版纳傣族自治州勐海县勐遮镇

收藏单位：西双版纳傣族自治州民族博物馆

Name: The Bronze Seal with the Inscriptions of *Meng Wang Dian Jun Min Guan Yin* (勐往甸军民官印, The Seal for the Military and Administrative Official at Mengwang Dian)

(The Seal for the Military and Administrative Official at Mengwang Dian)

Historical Period: The 30th year of Emperor Zhiyuan of the Yuan Dynasty (1293)

Height: 7.4 cm, Seal Side Length: 6.2 cm

Excavation Site: Mengzhe Town, Menghai County, Sipsongpanna Dai Autonomous Prefecture, Yunnan Province

Housed in: Museum of Ethnology of Sipsongpanna Dai Autonomous Prefecture

即辖区土地的世袭所有权；“世民”，即对附着在土地上的民众的世袭统治权。通过这一“以夷治夷”的制度，朝廷把土司正式纳入了国家的官吏体制之中。

元朝为何要对边疆民族地区实行土司制度？

这是因为在征服云南地区的初期，蒙古统治者曾经推行北方常见的万户制度，但却发生了许多动乱和不安定现象。为此，元朝吸收了南宋在广西设置土官的管理经验，又借鉴委任降附者以继任原职的传统方式，在云南行省实行土司制度，并迅速获得成功。此后，在情况类似的其他西南边疆地区，元朝开始普遍推行土官制度。

土司制度与行省之间有什么关系？

在元朝空前辽阔的疆域上，有些偏远的边疆地区远离行省的首府，成为鞭长莫及之地。于是中央政府在这些边疆地区设置宣慰司、安抚司、宣抚司等，作为土司管理辖地的行政机构，它们介于行省与路、府、州之间，肩负着上传下达的职能；必要之时，这些土司机构还可以代表行省单独处理军政事务。

土司制度跟唐宋的羁縻制度有什么不同？

如果说，唐宋中央王朝对边疆民族地区采用的羁縻制度，是一种间接的、具有象征意义的管理方式，那么元代的土司制度就是基于西南族群的实际情况，通过中央对土司的世袭、考核、奖惩等一系列干预措施，实现的对边疆民族地区的直接管理方式。

实行土司制度的结果如何？

通过土司制度，元朝将西南地区完全纳入中央王朝的版图之中，有效增强了对边疆的治理和控制力度。历史地看，自土司制度实行后，边疆地区再没有出现过如南诏国、大理国、罗氏鬼国、自杞国等地方性独立政权，这大大巩固了多民族国家在政治上的统一。

与此同时，元代以后西南各地土司逐渐归附和内化，客观上增强了土司辖区内的民众对统一多民族国家的认同。他们不再认为自己是“边裔蛮夷”，而将自身认同为“内地编民”，其所纳粮税成为国家可支配的统一资源。因此，土司制度的推行，既尊重了边疆民族地区经济社会发展的独特性和差异性，又将其纳入统一多民族国家的整体发展轨道，有力地推动了边疆的发展。

西南夷融入共同体

元朝开创的土司制度是一次因地制宜的创造，对此后边疆地区的治理产生了深远的影响。明代不仅延续了这一制度，而且将其发展到鼎盛阶段。直到清朝改土归流，土司制度才趋于衰落。

元明清三代实施土司制度的辖区包括了今天我国西南的许多少数民族聚居区。在元代以前的正史中，关于这些地区的记述都题为“南蛮传”“西南夷传”等，但到《明史》和《清史稿》却改为“土司传”。这一演变，不仅反映了统一多民族国家对边疆治理的制度嬗变，也昭示着“西南蛮夷”融入多元一体的中华民族，并成为共同体成员的历史进程。

Kublai Khan, temple name Shizu of the Yuan Dynasty, awarded the seal to *Tusi* (土司) at Mengwang, Sipsongpanna. The seal bore witness to the over-700-year-existence of *Tusi* system, which had a far-reaching impact on the governance of ethnic groups in ancient China.

In 1958, a mottled square bronze seal was unearthed at Mengwang Town, Menghai County, Sipsongpanna Dai Autonomous Prefecture, Yunnan Province. The inscriptions unveiled the historical fact that Mengwang, a remote and quiet town in southern China, was the location of the *Tusi* office more than 700 years ago.

The front side of the square seal was engraved with the Phags-pa script (an alphabet system for the Mongol language), and the left side of the back with Chinese words *Zhong Shu Li Bu Zao, Zhi Yuan San Shi Nian Er Yue Yi Ri* (“中书礼部造，至元三十年二月一日”, Made by the Ministry of Rites of Department of Imperial Secretariats, on February 1st, the 30th Year of Emperor Zhiyuan). This indicated that the seal was engraved in the reign of Kublai Khan. The right side of the square seal was engraved with *Meng Wang Dian Jun Min Guan Yin* (The Seal for the Military and Administrative Official at Mengwang Dian). As suggested, the official seal was conferred upon *Tusi* at Mengwang Dian by the Yuan court, as the symbol of the power of *Tusi*.

The *Tusi* system① signified the form of the governance of ethnic minorities in remote areas in the Yuan Dynasty. *Tusi*, also known as *Tuguan* (土官), was a local official appointed and enfeoffed by the central government. The hereditary system enabled the offspring of *Tusi* to rule the land and people after he died.

Under the *Tusi* system, the southwestern region fell within the orbit of the Yuan Dynasty, and separatist regimes, such as Nanzhao, Dali, Luodian and Ziqi, completely came to an end. Yuan effectively tightened its grip on border areas and consolidated the political unity of the multi-ethnic country.

① Located in the mountainous areas of south-west China, this property (Tusi Sites) encompasses remains of several tribal domains whose chiefs were appointed by the central government as *Tusi*, hereditary rulers from the 13th to the early 20th century. The *Tusi* system arose from the ethnic minorities' dynastic systems of government dating back to the 3rd century BCE. Its purpose was to unify national administration, while allowing ethnic minorities to retain their customs and way of life. See Tusi Sites - UNESCO World Heritage Centre.

崇尚武力的蒙古大军为什么最终以和平方略完成了对西藏的统一?

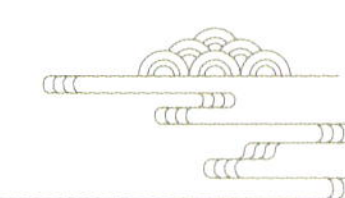

西藏正式纳入中央政府统一管辖范围

《萨班致乌思藏蕃人书》

Letter from Sakya Pandita to the People in Dbus-Gtsang

76

文物简读

公元1247年，被誉为“雪域三大文殊化身”之一的萨迦班智达与成吉思汗之孙阔端举行了“凉州会谈”，他用一封《萨班致乌思藏蕃人书》，化解了战争与杀戮，为西藏带来了和平。这封书函，成为西藏地区正式纳入统一多民族国家行政体系的珍贵历史见证。

来自成吉思汗之孙的邀请

元朝统一中国本土的过程，主要以战争方式推进。蒙古大军扫平了金朝国都，消灭了西夏王国，占据了北方的广大疆域后，为进一步统一西藏，成吉思汗的孙子、凉州王阔端虎视眈眈地陈兵卫藏边境，兵临藏北热振寺，战争一触即发。

然而，笃信武力、战功赫赫的阔端，这一次却选择了和平方略。

1239年秋，阔端派部将多达那波率领一支蒙古军，途经青康多堆、多迈和索曲卡，进入前藏。这支蒙古军在西藏驻留两年多。多达那波在详细调查了解后，向阔端禀告了西藏宗教、军事、经济等方面的情况，并指出后藏的萨迦派是西藏地区实力最强的教派，能够直接影响西藏的宗教、政治、经济走向。阔端由此做出了一个重要决策：邀请萨迦寺寺主萨迦班智达·贡嘎坚赞来凉州，商谈西藏归属问题。

1244年秋，多达那波作为阔端的“金字使者”，携带着邀请书和丰厚的礼品，不远千里，深入后藏萨迦寺，迎请萨迦班智达。

名称：《萨班致乌思藏蕃人书》
年代：元
规格：长45.5厘米，宽7.3厘米
收藏单位：西藏博物馆

Name: *Letter from Sakya Pandita to the People in Dbus-Gtsang*
Historical Period: The Yuan Dynasty
Length: 45.5 cm, Width: 7.3 cm
Housed in: Tibet Museum

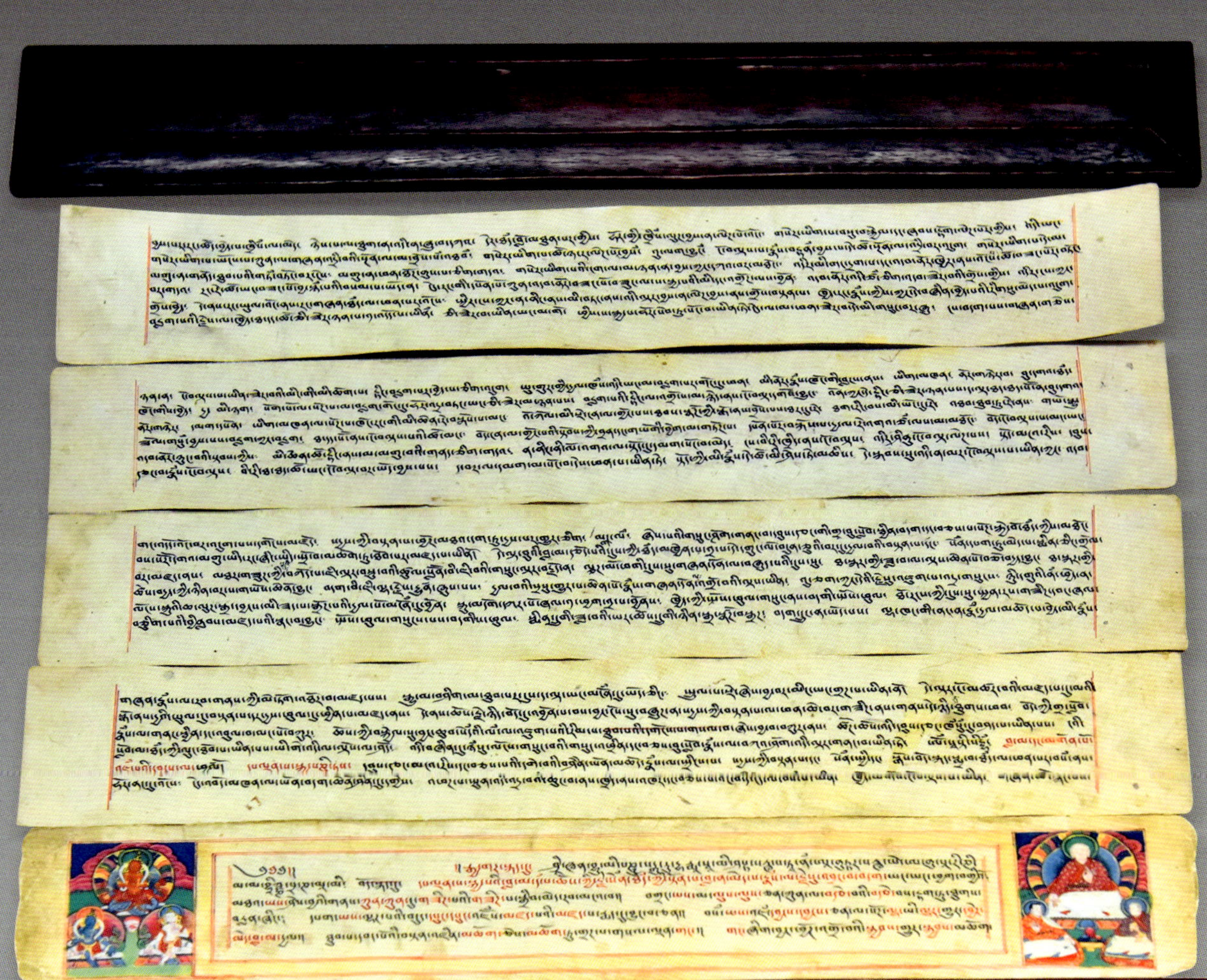

凉州会谈

班智达的称号意为“学识渊博的大学者”。萨迦班智达·贡嘎坚赞是西藏佛教史上第一位被誉为班智达的大师，他精通五明，智慧无比，被称为“雪域三大文殊化身”之一。

在接到阔端的邀请书后，63岁的萨迦班智达经过深思熟虑，带着两个侄子——10岁的八思巴和6岁的恰那朵尔只，从萨迦寺动身前往拉萨，与僧俗各界人士详细商议应对蒙古大军的事宜，充分听取各方面的意见。此后，他毅然启程，风尘仆仆，行向凉州。

萨迦班智达一行经过千辛万苦的跋涉，终于在1246年8月抵达凉州。

此时，阔端正在蒙古和林，参加推举其长兄贵由继承汗位的忽里台大会。

次年，返回凉州的阔端终于与来自西藏的尊贵客人相见，两人举行了具有深远影响的历史性会谈。在会晤中，阔端表明了蒙古大汗要统一四海的决心，西藏也不能例外。萨迦班智达则向阔端介绍了西藏的实际情况，希望蒙古大汗能照顾西藏人的利益和宗教习惯，使西藏人心甘情愿地接受统治。最终双方达成协议，发布了《萨班致乌思藏蕃人书》，宣告西藏正式臣服于蒙古大汗。

这就是历史上著名的“凉州会谈”。

顺应历史潮流的吉祥书函

《萨班致乌思藏蕃人书》（也称《具吉祥萨迦班智达致乌思藏纳里速各地善知识大德及诸施主书》）是一份具有重大历史意义的文件。在这封写给吐蕃僧俗民众的长信中，萨迦班智达表明了自己的心迹：

阔端励精图治，愿有益于天下各部族人民，用意甚善；蒙古军队众多而战术精良，西夏等部先后覆亡，反抗阔端之藏族偏师一败涂地，因而只有归附一途；只要真诚归附纳贡，作一个没有二心的臣属，即可同畏吾儿部族一样得到优待，地方官吏依旧任职，人畜依旧归己；正因为出于上述考虑，为了佛法、众生，造福吐蕃人民，我才亲往阔端驻地接洽归附事宜；也正因为蒙古接受我之归顺，近年蒙古军队才未袭击吐蕃；汝等凡遵从蒙古法令者，必能受福。

在信中，萨迦班智达嘱告西藏僧俗民众：西藏地方的僧俗官员和百姓，都要承认自己是蒙古大汗的臣民；各地僧俗官员及百姓有关行政方面的事务，须由蒙古指派的官员来管理；有关宗教和寺庙僧众的事务，由蒙古委托萨迦派首领管理；等等。

《萨班致乌思藏蕃人书》顺应了历史潮流，反映了当时西藏人民及绝大多数教派势力、地方势力的愿望，为西藏带来了和平。

阔端与萨迦班智达见面后，被他的智慧与学识品德深深折服，邀请他前去蒙古传授佛法。1251年，萨迦班智达圆寂于凉州弘化寺。

1260年，元世祖忽必烈封八思巴为国师，后升号帝师；又封恰那朵尔只为“白兰王”。1264年，元世祖设置管理吐蕃全境军民事务的总制院，后改名为“宣政院”，命八思巴执掌院事；又命恰那朵尔只担任乌思藏三区最高执法官。此后，元朝中央政府实现了对吐蕃全境的统治管辖。

这就是“凉州会谈”最深远的影响——西藏从此成为中国不可分割的领土，统一多民族国家进一步确立和巩固。

Sakya Pandita Künga Gyeltsen was held in the tradition to have been an emanation of Mañjuśrī, the embodiment of the wisdom of all the Buddhas. In 1247, Sakya Pandita had a talk with Godan, the grandson of Genghis Khan, historically known as “Liangzhou Meeting”. With *Letter from Sakya Pandita to the People in Dbus-Gtsang*, Sakya Pandita beat swords into ploughshares. And the letter *per se* became valuable historical evidence for Tibet to be officially governed by the Yuan Dynasty.

Pandita means “a knowledgeable scholar”. Künga Gyeltsen was the first Pandita in the history of Tibetan Buddhism, a title given to him in recognition of his scholarly achievements and knowledge of the five great sciences. After trekking a long way, Sakya Pandita and his entourage finally arrived in Liangzhou (present-day Wuwei, Gansu) in August 1246. The following year, Godan, who returned to Liangzhou, met Sakya Pandita. They reached an agreement and released *Letter from Sakya Pandita to the People in Dbus-Gtsang*, declaring Tibet’s allegiance to the Mongolian Khan. The event was historically called “Liangzhou Meeting”.

Letter from Sakya Pandita to the People in Dbus-Gtsang was of paramount importance in the history of Tibet. In the letter, Sakya Pandita admitted that all Tibetan monks, officials and citizens pledged loyalty to the Mongolian Khan, that all administrative affairs in Tibet were handled by central officials dispatched by the Mongolian Khan, that religious affairs including temples and monks were managed by leader of Sakya Sect authorized by the Mongolian Khan, etc. In alignment with the tide of historical development, the letter reflected the wishes of the Tibetan people and the vast majority of religious and local forces, and brought peace to Tibet.

In 1264, Kublai Khan, temple name Shizu of the Yuan Dynasty, ordered to establish *Zong Zhi Yuan* (总制院, General Administration Commission) to manage military and civil affairs throughout Tibet, which was later renamed *Xuan Zheng Yuan* (宣政院, Buddhist and Tibetan Affairs Commission), appointing Phags-pa, his adviser, as Commissioner, and phyag na rdo rje as Chief Administrative Officer in Dbus-Gtsang. Henceforth, the Yuan Dynasty extended its sphere of influence to the entire territory of Tubo.

为什么波斯语仍将纸币称作"钞"？

元朝纸币制度：世界货币史的首创

中统元宝交钞

77

Yuanbao Jiaochao Issued in the 1st Year of Emperor Zhongtong

文物简读

这张八百多年前的"中统元宝交钞"，实证了中华民族由一个北方游牧民族引领重新回到大一统道路后，所成就的人类货币史上一次重要创举，中国亦因此创举成为世界上第一个全面使用纸币的国家。正是因为马可·波罗在游记中详细记录了元朝纸币的印制和发行流通情况，才使西方开始了解纸币。

让马可·波罗最感惊讶的事

刘秉忠是忽必烈最信任的汉人军师，他对元朝政治体制、典章制度的奠定发挥了重大作用。正是这位兼通释、道、儒的政治家，向元世祖忽必烈提出建议：废除历朝历代以铜币为主的货币制度，发行纸币作为元朝的主体货币。忽必烈接受了这一建议。此后，元朝将纸钞作为法定货币，采用纯纸钞流通体制，为后世开创了以银为后备金的纸钞发行制，也就是银本位制。

当意大利著名旅行家马可·波罗来到中国，看到元朝的纸币时，他感到无比惊奇。在《马可·波罗游记》中，他感慨自己在中国遇到了两件最惊讶之事：一件是中国人烧黑色的石头（煤）；另一件就是中国人使用纸币。事实上，正是因为马可·波罗在游记中详细记录了元朝纸币的印制工艺和发行流通情况，欧洲人才开始了解纸币。美国学者罗伯特·坦普尔认为，欧洲最早的纸币应当是受中国的影响而发行的。

元朝为何发行纸币？

秦、汉以降，以铜铸币作为本位货币，以金银作为辅币的货币制度渐趋成型。在这种传统货币制

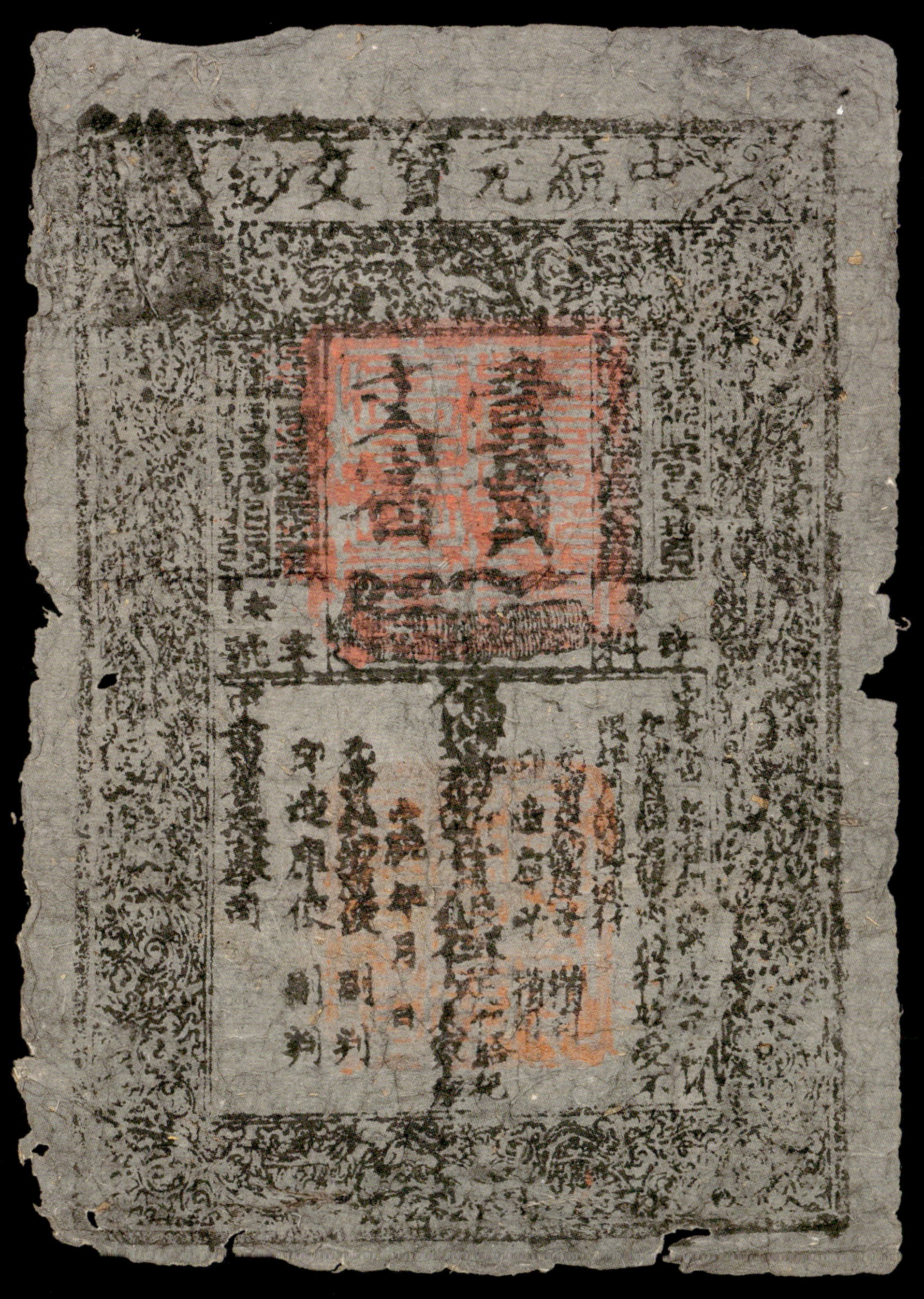

名称：中统元宝交钞

年代：元

规格：长29厘米，宽21厘米

收藏单位：西藏博物馆

Name: *Yuanbao Jiaochao* Issued in the 1st Year of

Historical Period: The Yuan Dynasty

Length: 29 cm, Width: 21 cm

Housed in: Tibet Museum

度之下，铜铸币是最主要的交易货币，金银参与流通较少，主要用于大额交易和作为财富贮藏。随着商贸越来越发达，涉及大额支付时，金属货币运输成本高、交易风险大的弊端逐渐显现，纸币便开始出现。如唐朝有飞钱，宋朝有交子、会子，金朝也有交钞。但是，唐朝的飞钱、宋朝的会子等都只是特殊时期用于特殊目的的权宜纸币，并没有在广大范围内流通，也没有得到广泛的认可。所以，以金银作为储备、在全国范围内推行全面纸币化的货币制度，是由元朝开创的。

有些研究者认为，元朝的货币制度是对金朝遗产的继承。这是因为，金朝末年，因其国内出现了财政窘境，政府为了应对危机开始发行纸币。但因战争失利、军费开支增大，货币无限超发等原因，金朝出现了严重的通货膨胀，致使其纸币体系崩溃。但蒙古人在接管金朝政权后，继续在一些地区试行纸币。比如一位名叫何实的金朝旧臣，就在1227年于山东博州（今聊城）发行可兑换的丝钞，这是蒙古入主中原后在局部地域实行纸币制度的首次尝试。何实在博州发行的地方性纸币成为一次成功的试验，它为元朝中央政府进行统一的纸币制度革新提供了参考。

还有研究者指出，元朝如此重视纸币，跟蒙古人比其他游牧民族更加重视商业有关。1218年，成吉思汗派遣商队和使节出使中亚的花剌子模，希望与其建立和平的通商关系，然而商队却遭遇了不测，随身携带的大量实物财富被花剌子模的讹答剌城官员抢夺，商队成员也惨遭杀害。事实上，花剌子模作为控制东西商路的帝国，其统治阶层无法容忍蒙古人与其分享商业利益；而讹答剌城官员的抢劫行为，最终成为蒙古大军西征的导火索。或许，这也是元朝统治者重视纸币并有意将之用于国际贸易的一个重要心理因素。

人类货币史上的一次创举

元世祖忽必烈对商业非常重视。元朝的大一统，将从波斯湾到中国沿海的海上丝绸之路和草原丝绸之路连接到一起，创造了一条横跨欧亚大陆的商业路线。而纸币的使用，有力地推动了“欧亚贸易圈”的大规模资源流动。

元朝纸币制度实行之初，既有金银储备的基础，又有全面的回收机制和相应的法律规范。这种有些类似于现代货币制度雏形的发行与管理机制，保障了元初货币制度的顺畅运行。马可·波罗在游记中写道：“不管走到哪，都可以用纸币进行支付。也就是说，除珍珠、宝石、金银之外的一切物品都可以用纸币购买；他们可以购买任何想要的东西，支付的时候只要拿出纸币就可以了。”

英国学者菲利克斯·马汀认为，货币的本质是一种信用体系，而这种信用体系须由国家信用作为支撑，它是货币发展的成熟阶段。从这个意义上来说，元钞的出现，堪谓人类货币制度史上的一次早熟。元钞起初是可兑换金银的兑换券，后来转变为无储备的信用货币，这无疑是现代信用货币体系出现之前的一次创举。

此外，元朝在东征西伐和对外商贸中，催生了一个特殊的官商群体——斡脱阶层。“斡脱”一词源于突厥语，实际上就是“国有企业”，指受蒙古统治阶层支持和控制的官商。斡脱的资本往往来自蒙古诸王、驸马和母妃，斡脱的职能是充当外来客商和贵族的中间人，或者用贵族提供的资本从事放贷活动。而纸币的发行，刺激了斡脱的不断壮大，元朝统一之后还专门设立了管理斡脱的官方机构。正是在类似国有商业的推动下，元朝创造了马可·波罗在其游记中描述的繁荣富庶景象。

元朝是中国历史上唯一采用纯纸钞流通体制的朝代，这使中国成为世界上第一个全面使用纸币的国家。纸币制度贯穿整个元朝，并影响了欧亚大陆。据记载，当时印度、高丽、日本等国都曾效仿元朝印造纸币；由元世祖忽必烈的胞弟旭烈兀建立的伊利汗国，也采用元朝钞法，就连纸钞的形制也完全效仿元朝，纸钞上还印有“钞”字。在波斯语中，“钞”这个汉语借词一直保留到今天，可见元朝纸币制度影响之深。

Yuanbao Jiaochao was issued more than 800 years ago. It evidenced the facts that the Chinese nation made outstanding contributions to the history of currency and that China pioneered in the wide use of paper money. In his travels, Marco Polo detailed the printing, issuance and circulation of the paper money in the Yuan Dynasty, which introduced paper money to the West.

Some scholars assert that the Yuan Dynasty inherited the monetary system of the Jin Dynasty, while other scholars insist that the Yuan Dynasty invented *Jiaochao* to meet the commercial needs of the Mongolian merchants. Simultaneously, as the Yuan rulers frequently launched wars and vigorously developed foreign trade, *ortoq* (斡脱), a class of official merchants, emerged. *Ortoq* was originally a Turkic word, referring to official merchants financially supported and controlled by the Mongolian nobles. The business patterners of *ortoq* included Mongolian princes, sons-in-law and princess consorts. *Ortoqs* served as the middleman for foreign merchants and Mongolian nobles, or conducted money-lending with the capital invested by their partners. The circulation of *Jiaochao* fostered the development of *ortoq*.

Kublai Khan or Emperor Shizu of Yuan attached great importance to trade. The grand unification of Yuan facilitated the connection between the maritime silk road (from the Persian Gulf to Chinese coastal areas) and the grassland silk road, and built a business route across Eurasia. The use of *Jiaochao* effectively promoted the large-scale flow of resources in the Eurasian trade circle.

Jiaochao had a far-reaching impact on both Yuan economy and global monetary system, expanding the cultural influence of the Chinese nation on the world. According to historical records, India, Goryeo, Japan and other countries followed suit and printed their paper money. The Ilkhanate, established by Hülegü Khan, the younger brother of Kublai Khan, exactly copied *Jiaochao* of Yuan, with the word *Chao* (钞) on it. In Persian, the loanword *Chao* from Chinese has been retained to this day, indicating the deep influence of *Jiaochao* of Yuan.

在礼教森严的中国古代，谁是主持祭孔的女性第一人？

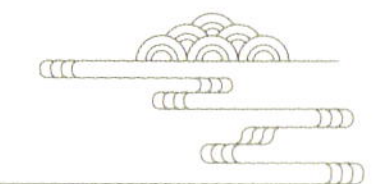

元朝对儒家文化的继承和弘扬

《皇妹大长公主祭孔庙碑》78

The Stele on the Confucius Memorial Ceremony Presided over by Grand Princess of Imperial Sister

文物简读

这块至今仍竖立于曲阜孔庙的《皇妹大长公主祭孔庙碑》，见证了元世祖忽必烈的曾孙女祥哥剌吉公主获得中国历史上“第一女性祭孔人”称号的史实。这位深深服膺于儒家文化、心驰于中华传统艺术的蒙古公主，还曾获得过“中国古代第一女收藏家”的美誉。她所举办的“天庆寺雅集”名垂后世，作为一个鲜活的历史情景，显示出元朝作为少数民族所缔造的朝代，在继承和弘扬中华文化方面所发挥的承上启下的重要作用。

“第一女性祭孔人”

祥哥剌吉（1284—1331）是元世祖忽必烈的曾孙女、元武宗之妹、元仁宗之姐、元文宗之姑，元武宗时被封为“鲁国大长公主”，后又进号“皇妹大长公主”；仁宗即位后，称为“皇姊大长公主”。了解祥哥剌吉，须先从祥哥剌吉的曾祖父忽必烈说起。

1251年，忽必烈的长兄蒙哥继任蒙古大汗，命令忽必烈总领漠南汉地事务。忽必烈由漠北南下，以经营天下的目光，选择了靠近幽燕之地的金莲川作为驻帐地。在这里，他广揽人才，“征天下名士而用之”，形成了一个号称“金莲川幕府”的谋臣侍从集团。这个文武兼备的政治集团，主要由精通治道的汉儒名士组成，其中有智绝天下的刘秉忠，满腹经纶的许衡、姚枢，还有通晓儒家文化的畏兀尔人廉希宪。他们孜孜不倦地向忽必烈讲述治理天下、安邦治国的道理。正是在这些人物的影响下，忽必烈对汉文化有了深刻认识，奠定了他此后开创大元盛世伟业的基础。

名称：《皇妹大长公主祭孔庙碑》

年代：元

规格：碑宽86厘米，碑高227厘米

收藏单位：曲阜孔庙

Name: The Stele on the Confucius Memorial Ceremony Presided over by Grand Princess of Imperial Sister

Historical Period: The Yuan Dynasty

Width: 86 cm, Height: 227 cm

Housed in: The Confucius Temple, Qufu

忽必烈的嫡长子真金正是在金莲川幕府的名士陪伴下成长起来的。忽必烈把真金的教育交给理学家姚枢，姚枢对真金“日以三纲五常、先哲格言熏陶德性”。刘秉忠的弟子王恂作为真金的伴读，也常以历代治乱之理加以课教。这使真金成为元朝皇室中受中原传统文化思想影响最深的一位。

真金之妻阔阔真还聘请汉儒李孟，教导自己的嫡孙海山和寿山，他们正是祥哥剌吉的亲兄弟。在这样的家风熏陶下，公主自幼诵习经史。祥哥剌吉受封于鲁国，孔子故里曲阜成为她的“汤沐之邑”。1307年，当海山即任元朝第三位皇帝时，为树立尊孔崇儒的风气，元武宗海山加封孔子为“大成至圣文宣王”。由于孔庙在鲁王封地之内，祥哥剌吉遂派遣承务郎应昌路同知王谦前往孔庙，代她主持祭孔仪式，在孔庙留下了《皇妹大长公主祭孔庙碑》，该碑另一面刻《皇妹大长公主懿旨释典祝文碑》，祥哥剌吉因此被后世称为“第一女性祭孔人”。二十年后，元泰定帝泰定四年（1327），祥哥剌吉又遣总管府总管赵昌龄来到孔庙举行祭孔活动，并留下了《皇姊大长公主降香碑》。

“中国古代第一女收藏家”

除了第一女性祭孔人，祥哥剌吉还被称为“中国古代第一女收藏家”。据统计，祥哥剌吉保存的古代名人书画（有著录的）有六十多件，特别是唐宋两代名家书画精品，堪称一笔辉煌的古代艺术宝藏。

祥哥剌吉雅好收藏，她于英宗至治三年（1323），在大都南城天庆寺举行了一次全国性的艺文书画鉴赏活动——“天庆寺雅集”。雅集中，公主将她所藏的书画作品提供给参加雅集的人欣赏，并请他们为作品题跋。根据当时负责雅集的秘书监丞李师鲁的记载，藏品包括了黄庭坚的行书代表作《书松风阁诗》、展子虔《游春图》、唐《定武兰亭真本》、元《元世祖出猎图》等，光是宋徽宗的作品就有五幅之多。藏品规格、等级、品味之高，足以见这位蒙古公主受汉文化濡染之深以及对书画收藏的热爱。

1310年，祥哥剌吉公主的丈夫去世。她没有依从蒙古收继婚习俗，再嫁丈夫的弟弟桑哥不剌，而是遵从汉人习俗，秉持守节理念，直到终老。

承上启下的元朝

不论是中华历史上的“第一女性祭孔人”，还是名垂青史的“天庆寺雅集”，这些鲜活的历史情景，都显示出元朝作为少数民族所缔造的朝代，在继承和弘扬中华文化方面所发挥的承上启下的重要作用。

在元朝，儒家文化的社会地位得到进一步提升，不仅孔子、孟子被赐予崇高的封号，元朝还在中国历史上首次专门设立“儒户”阶层，以保护知识分子。儒家文化更深入地传播到边疆民族地区，儒家经典被翻译成蒙古文出版，漠北、云南等偏远地区首次出现了传授儒家文化的学校。元朝还首次出现了由中央政府批准的、全国性的少数民族语言文字教育机构——蒙古国子学和“回回国子学”，蒙古、契丹、女真、色目人中，涌现出一大批汉文著述家。与此同时，西域文化也进一步向中原流传，藏传佛教在更广大范围内传播。在较为宽松的政治文化氛围中，各民族间的交融进入了一个新高潮，多种文化和谐并存，“天下一家”观念深入人心。

Sengge Ragi (1284–1331) was the great-granddaughter of Kublai Khan, Shizu of the Yuan Dynasty, the sister of Khayishan (Wuzong) and Ayurbarwada (Renzong), and the aunt of Tugh Temür (Wenzong). She was granted the titles of Grand Princess of Lu and Princess Supreme of Lu successively.

Known as the first Confucius-Memorial-Ceremony hostess, Sengge Ragi had an appanage at Lu, the hometown of Confucius. In 1307, Khayishan conferred the title “Great Sage and Perfect Teacher King of Wenxuan” on Confucius. Sengge Ragi dispatched Wang Qian, Vice Governor of Yingchang Route, to the Confucius Temple to preside over the Confucius Memorial Ceremony on her behalf. “The Stele on the Confucius Memorial Ceremony Presided over by Grand Princess of Imperial Sister” was erected, and *Memorial Speech Made on Behalf of and under the Order of Grand Princess of Imperial Sister* was inscribed on its back.

Sengge Ragi was also a renowned cultural collector. In 1323, the 3rd year of Emperor Zhizhi (Yingzong), she hosted an elegant gathering at Tianqing Temple in the south of Dadu. Numerous scrolls were brought out to the attendees, who were instructed to add colophons to them. According to Li Shilu, the secretary-general in charge of the gathering, the collections included Huang Tingjian’s representative work *Poem on Pine-Wind Pavilion* (running script), Zhan Ziqian’s *Spring Excursion*, *Dingwu Stone Inscription of Essay on the Orchid Pavilion in the Tang Dynasty (Original Edition)*, Liu Guandao’s *Emperor Shizu of Yuan Going Hunting*, etc. Astonishingly, there were as many as five works by Emperor Huizong of the Norther Song Dynasty. The high taste of Sengge Ragi reflected her admiration of the Han culture and the enthusiasm for the Han art.

The Yuan emperors deeply respected Confucianism. They not merely bestowed honorary titles to Confucius and Mencius, but also firstly provided household register for Confucianist scholars to protect intellectuals. Confucian culture was embraced among border ethnic groups, and Confucianist classics were translated into Mongolian. Academies that taught Confucian culture were founded in remote areas such as Mobei and Yunnan.

名称：青花缠枝牡丹纹罐
年代：元
规格：高28厘米，腹径32厘米
收藏单位：山西博物院

Name: Blue and White Glazed Jar with the Pattern of Interlocking Peony
Historical Period: The Yuan Dynasty
Height: 28 cm, Belly Diameter: 32 cm
Housed in: Shanxi Museum

青花瓷为什么在元代成为中国制造的“全球化商品”？

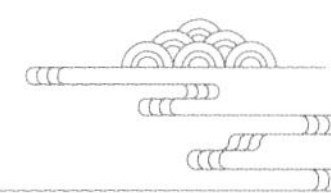

元朝的世界文化景观

青花缠枝牡丹纹罐

Blue and White Glazed Jar with the Pattern of Interlocking Peony

文物简读

这件元青花传世精品是元朝推动中华文化包容性与开放性达到一个全新历史高度的见证，它展现出元朝时期的中华文化在与世界文化的交流融通中，所共同创造出的新的世界文化景观。

世界珍稀的元青花瓷

元青花瓷器因存世量极少而珍贵。2005年，世界著名艺术品拍卖行佳士得拍卖的元青花“鬼谷出山故事纹大罐”，以2.3亿元的高价创下了当时中国艺术品在世界上的最高拍卖纪录，引起了收藏界、文博界的巨大轰动。这使得国内博物馆所收藏的元青花，成为观众争相一睹的明星藏品。

山西博物院收藏的这件青花缠枝牡丹纹罐，造型浑厚敦实，色泽浓艳深沉；器身绘精美的海水、缠枝石榴、缠枝牡丹和莲瓣纹；主题花纹为不同视角的怒放的牡丹；画面饱满而不拥挤，装饰繁而不乱；整体兼具中国本土文化和伊斯兰文化的特点，是难得的元青花精品。

元朝如何创造出了如此珍贵的世界文化艺术精品？

“全球化商品”

元以前，以宋代五大名窑为代表的中国瓷器以素为美，士大夫美学追求可谓登峰造极。但从元青花开始，中国瓷器不再固守极简主义，进入了青花和彩绘竞相绽放的时代。人们把青花瓷比作瓷器舞台上的青衣，素雅、高洁、纯净。蓝色的花纹与洁白的胎体交相映衬，宛若一幅传统的水墨画。

青花瓷起源于何时？一代瓷学宗师陈万里曾将其列为“中国瓷器史上十五大难题之一”。唯一可以下定论的是，元朝是青花开始登上陶瓷艺术顶峰的时期。元青花气势宏大、饱满雄健，从器物造型到装饰都有一种阳刚之美，其独特的品类、造型、纹饰具有浓郁的时代特征，体现了元瓷工艺从原料、制作、绘画到烧成的完美程度。元青花的出现成为我国制瓷工艺划时代的事件，不仅开辟了由素瓷向彩瓷过渡的新时代，也使景德镇一跃成为中世纪世界制瓷业的中心。

瓷器早在汉晋时期就已成为古代世界“中国制造”的标志性产品。在元朝开拓出的空前未有的东西方文化大交流局面下，中国瓷器更加广泛地传播于阿拉伯世界。正是在与伊斯兰文化的交流中，青花瓷这一“全球化商品”被创造出来，并攀上了世界艺术殿堂的巅峰。其间，中国与伊斯兰世界的交流互动，是促成青花瓷艺术走向完美的重要因素。这是因为：

其一，由于伊斯兰世界有着尚蓝、尚白的审美传统，青花瓷的色彩极大地满足了这些地区的文化需求。这一时期的贵族和重臣通常在青花瓷上刻上自己的印记，表明他们将青花瓷视作一种珍贵的财富。

其二，据西北大学教授温睿考证，青花瓷所用的“苏麻离青”颜料来自伊斯兰世界。当阿拉伯商人忙碌地往返于元代的海上丝绸之路时，他们发现阿拉伯地区的“苏麻离青”颜料比青花瓷器的现用颜料更美观，便将其带来中国试用。这一试便使中国青花瓷攀上了辉煌巅峰。

“苏麻离青”在高温中演化出苍翠色，色浓处深入胎骨，闪烁出宝石般的光泽。元朝至正年间，景德镇的陶瓷工匠们成功地将“苏麻离青”应用于陶瓷呈色。以白瓷为地，以“苏麻离青”作料，于釉下彩绘花鸟、灵兽和人物等图纹，精美至极的青花瓷从此大量向海外出口，使世界贸易的舞台上频繁地闪烁着一抹深蓝。

包容性的文化符号

从14世纪中叶开始，青花瓷成为景德镇的主打国际贸易产品。

“苏麻离青”的最大魅力，在于成就了明亮鲜艳的元代“至正青花”。至正（1341—1368）是元朝最后一个皇帝元惠宗的年号。从至正十一年起的二十年间，景德镇虽陷于战争旋涡，但其“瓷都”地位并未削弱，相反还得以逆势增强。景德镇的千年窑火在各方战事的间隙中，奇迹般地保存下来。在这个不稳定的时期，许多抑郁不得志的书生画匠，也用“苏麻离青”抒情宣怀，用不同程度的蓝色表达心境。从近处的墨黑，到遥远的幽蓝，中华文人在青花的世界中找到了承继中华文明的力量，传续着中华文脉。

纵览中国瓷器的发展史，元青花无疑是其中一个亮点，其魅力和价值不仅仅在于收藏，更重要的是它体现了中华文化兼容并蓄、海纳百川的包容性。这种有容乃大的文化特性，在有元一代被浓缩成一个如此精致的文化符号，凝练成一个如此经典的中外文化交流成果。元朝开启了中国古代中西文化交流最繁荣的时代，元青花正是这一个时代所创造的世界文化景观的集中体现。

As a cultural icon, the blue and white glazed jar materialized the open-mindedness of the Chinese nation and represented new landscape of global culture, as honed in the Yuan Dynasty via the exchanges and integration of Chinese and world civilizations.

Housed in Shanxi Museum, the blue and white glazed jar has a round shape and thick colors, with exquisitely-painted patterns of sea water, interlocking pomegranate, interlocking peony and lotus petal. The central pattern is blooming peony in various forms. Complex as they seem, the pictures and decorations are arranged in an orderly way. The jar conflates the artistic elements in Chinese and Islamic cultures and boasts a gem of blue and white porcelains in the Yuan Dynasty.

Chinese porcelain, represented by the five famous kilns in the Song Dynasty (i.e. Guan kiln, Jun kiln, Ru kiln, Ding kiln and Ge kiln), pursued the aesthetics of simplicity and embodied the tastes of scholar-bureaucrats. In the Yuan Dynasty, however, Chinese porcelain abandoned the minimalist style and favored colored painting in an unbridled manner. To craftsmen, blue and white porcelain can be personified as *Qingyi* (青衣, a demure middle-aged or young female role in Chinese operas), looking elegant and pure. The blue patterns contrasted finely with the pure white body, resembling a traditional ink painting.

The blue and white porcelain in the Yuan Dynasty showcased great vigor, whose unique shape and pattern epitomized the *zeitgeist* of Yuan as well as the perfect crafts of design, painting and firing. Blue and white porcelain meant a landmark in Chinese porcelain industry. It ushered in a new era of colored porcelain, in which Jingdezhen became the center of porcelain industry in the world.

Since the Han and Jin Dynasties, porcelain had been a symbolic product of the ancient China. In the Yuan Dynasty, the East-West cultural exchanges advanced considerably, and Chinese porcelain widely spread to the Arab States. Particularly, the exchanges and interaction between Chinese and Islamic civilizations played an important role in perfecting the art of blue and white porcelain.

马可·波罗向欧洲讲述的中国元朝故事，真的重塑了世界历史的发展格局吗?

马可·波罗的中国故事

云肩织金锦辫线袍

Nasich Bianxian (辫线, Braided Thread) Robe with Cloud-Design Shoulders

80

文物简读

这一件用金线与蚕丝交织而成的织金锦袍，正是马可·波罗在其游记中所描绘的蒙古族喜爱异常的“纳石失”——这种集中西文化于一体的代表性物质文化，印刻了超大地域大一统国家推动的多元文化交融景象，见证了一个中西文化直接对话的时代，以及因为前所未有的世界性文化交流所开启的全新的世界历史进程。

马可·波罗讲述的元朝故事

“我所说的，还不及我见到的一半。”马可·波罗这样告诉欧洲人。

1271年，忽必烈定国号为“元”。就在这一年，17岁的马可·波罗跟随父亲和叔叔踏上前往东方的经商旅途。四年后，他们在元上都觐见了元世祖忽必烈，向他奉上威尼斯教会委托波罗家族呈送的礼物和书信。此后，马可·波罗在中国游历十多年，流连于大都、杭州、扬州等几十个城市，他到过西南的四川，甚至连西昌邛海也出现在他的游记中。最后，他从当时世界上最大的对外贸易口岸泉州，踏上返回欧洲的商船。此时，他已届壮年。在疆域广袤、民族众多的元朝土地上畅行无阻、出入自如，给马可·波罗带来了无比震撼的生命体验。

回到家乡的马可·波罗，因参加热那亚战争而被俘。在狱中，由他口述，由他人记录并出版了《马可·波罗游记》。这本“奇书”在欧洲激起了长达一个多世纪的轰动效应，书中那个“东方最富有的国家”成为欧洲人向往的天堂，欧洲由此引发了探寻东方世界的狂热潮流。

名称：云肩织金锦辫线袍

年代：元

规格：袍长126厘米，两袖通长210厘米，下摆宽120厘米

收藏单位：中国民族博物馆

Name: *Nasich Bianxian* (辫线, Braided Thread) Robe with Cloud-Design Shoulders

Historical Period: The Yuan Dynasty

The Length of the Robe: 126 cm, The Total Length of the Sleeves: 210 cm

The Width of the Hem: 120 cm

Housed in: Chinese National Museum of Ethnology

马可·波罗见过的织金锦

那么，马可·波罗在中国到底看到了什么？

如果要找出一件马可·波罗在中国亲眼见过、多次在游记中赞叹过的东西，那么，织金锦无疑是其中之一。

在元世祖诞辰日的纪念会上，马可·波罗看见“大汗于其庆寿之日，衣其最美之金锦衣。同日至少有男爵骑尉一万二千人，衣同色之衣，与大汗同”。他描述元大都城丝织业和金锦业的繁荣：“百物输入之众，有如川流之不息。仅丝一项，每日入城者计有千车。用此丝制作不少金锦绸绢，及其他数种物品。”他还说，一些元朝军队奢华到用织金锦来制作营帐，竟然明晃晃地在他眼前绵延了数里路。

织金锦到底是什么东西呢？

这是一种用金线织出花纹的丝绸。它在阿拉伯语中被称为“纳石失”（*nasich*），意为“金锦”。当年，蒙古军队西进之时，阿拉伯工匠坐在织机前，用一根根金丝织成细密的“纳石失”的情景，曾让他们惊喜万分。蒙古人对黄金的珍爱源远流长。成吉思汗曾站在阿勒泰山上（阿勒泰即为“黄金”之意），发誓要把妻妾媳女“从头到脚用织金衣服打扮起来”。“纳石失”的出现，意味着蒙古人把黄金穿在身上的梦想不再难以实现。

这件云肩织金锦辫线袍，是迄今为止蒙古高原考古发现的最为精致的蒙古贵族织金锦男服之一。远观它，一片片金光交织成辉；细看它，缕成细丝的金线与温软绕指的蚕丝融为一体，精美绝伦。

不可忽视的是，这件织金锦袍最大的特点依然是中西文化的交汇：中亚的织金锦工艺与江南丝织技艺交融；窄袖、束腰、上紧下松、上衣下裳，便于骑射、利于保暖的蒙古袍裙形制；锦袍面上与缠枝纹、卷草纹等中国传统图案交织……

《元史》载：“既而得西域织金绮纹工三百余户。”蒙古人把在征战中俘获的西域织金锦工匠带回了中原。元朝建立后，中央政府专门建立了金锦织造局，一方面从西域全面引进人才，另一方面又不断在全国范围内培养和招纳织金锦工匠，使得“纳石失”完成了本土化生产。

民族文化大交融的中西对话时代

就在中亚“纳石失”流行于中国宫廷时，指南针、火药、造纸术、印刷术，甚至印花布技术，也正沿着陆上丝绸之路和海上丝绸之路传播到西方。在被蒙古人征服的西亚地区，中国的水利工程家甚至受雇于两河灌溉工程。

元朝确立了中国古代史上最大力度的鼓励通商的开放政策，又为国际间、地区间的交往创造了前所未有的便利交通条件。《元史》称：“适千里者，如在户庭；之万里者，如在邻家。”通过海上丝绸之路进行商贸往来的国家和地区，从宋朝的五十多个增加到元朝的140多个。

无数的“马可·波罗”们奔走往来于亚欧之间，带来了一个中西文化直接对话的时代。彼时，中西文化交流信息量之大，传播范围之广，对未来历史影响之大，都是人类历史上空前的。正是这样一个中西方文明成就首次全方位共享的局面，引领世界文明史进入了新时代。

Woven with gold thread and silk, the *Nasich* robe was recorded in the travels of Marco Polo, which remained in vogue among the Mongols. While fusing Chinese and foreign cultures, it testified to the dialogue between Chinese civilization and world civilization in the Yuan Dynasty.

At the commemoration of the birthday of Kublai Khan (Cublay Kaan), Marco Polo saw that: "Now, on his birthday, the Great Kaan dresses in the best of his robes, all wrought with beaten gold; and full 12,000 Barons and Knights on that day come forth dressed in robes of the same colour, and precisely like those of the Great Kaan, except that they are not so costly; but still they are all of the same colour as his, and are also of silk and gold." Marco Polo also described the prosperity of the silk manufacturing industry and the gold brocade industry in the City of Cambaluc (Dadu): "To this city also are brought articles of greater cost and rarity, and in greater abundance of all kinds, than to any other city in the world... As a sample, I tell you, no day in the year passes that there do not enter the city 1,000 car-loads of silk alone, from which are made quantities of cloth of silk and gold, and of other goods."

As Marco Polo mentioned, "In Baudas they weave many different kinds of silk stuffs and gold brocades, such as *nasich*, and *nac*, and cramoisy, and many another beautiful tissue richly wrought with figures of beasts and birds." In the Western Regions, the Mongols captured many *nasich* craftsmen and took them to the Central Plains. After the founding of the Yuan Dynasty, the central government specifically established a *nasich* department, which continuously recruited craftsmen from the Western Regions and trained craftsmen nationwide, realizing the local production of *nasich*.

European travelers like Marco Polo enkindled the direct dialogue between Chinese and Western cultures, which featured multiple fields and various regions and had an everlasting impact on human civilization. The Chinese nation engaged in the multi-dimensional cultural exchanges with the West, marking a new era of global civilization.

明朝是如何有效管理西藏，使之一直倾心内附的？

明朝对西藏的管理

“如来大宝法王之印”玉印

81

The Jade Seal of “Great Treasure Dharma King”

文物简读

此印是明朝对西藏行使有效主权统辖的重要文物见证。明朝对西藏采取了“众建多封、贡市羁縻”等明智而理性的管理策略，使西藏地区一直倾心内附，汉藏关系吉祥和睦，与祖国内地的交往和联系进一步密切。

这枚“如来大宝法王之印”玉印，是明成祖朱棣于永乐五年（1407）颁发给西藏噶玛噶举派黑帽系第五世活佛噶玛巴却贝桑布的印玺，印文为九叠体篆书“如来大宝法王之印”。永乐四年（1406）五世噶玛巴活佛应明朝廷之召，亲赴南京，次年被封赐“如来大宝法王西天大善自在佛”名号，明朝中央政府为之特制印玺。它见证了明朝对西藏采取“众建多封、贡市羁縻”政策，顺乎时局、因势利导，实现对西藏有效统辖的历史事实。

“众建多封、贡市羁縻”

明朝继承了元朝的政治体制，试图将元朝的疆域也全部继承下来。但显然，明朝面对的边疆局势十分复杂。在明军占领元大都后，元朝政权北逃蒙古高原，盘踞于大漠南北，实力尚存，很大程度上威胁着明朝中央在北部边疆的统治。为此，明朝历代帝王都把北疆的边防建设视为头等大事，倾力加固长城。这样的形势对明朝的治藏政策影响尤甚。

名称："如来大宝法王之印"玉印

年代：明永乐五年（1407）

规格：通高8.3厘米，边长12.8厘米，厚3.5厘米

收藏单位：西藏博物馆

Name: The Jade Seal of "Great Treasure Dharma King"

Historical Period: The 5th year of Emperor Yongle of the Ming Dynasty (1407)

Total Height: 8.3 cm, Side Length: 12.8 cm, Thickness: 3.5 cm

Housed in: Tibet Museum

在西藏治理中，因为蒙藏僧俗各方的关系纷繁复杂，明朝充分考虑藏传佛教在西藏地区的广泛影响，特别重视藏传佛教在凝聚民心、强基固本方面的良好作用。总的来看，明朝主要采取了招附、赏赐、“众建多封、贡市羁縻”的特色治藏策略，充分尊重西藏自治权，不派驻大臣督管，也不驻兵，而是通过经济补贴和扶持、物资贸易等措施，促进西藏经济不断繁荣，使得西藏民众对中央政府始终保持着一定的向心力。

首先，明朝对待西藏各教派采取了一视同仁，扶持各教派平衡发展，不单独支持任何一派的政策，改变了以往元朝尤其重视萨迦派的做法。自1406 年后的六七年间，明朝中央将西藏地区五个地方政权的首领册封为王；又分别于 1407 年、1413年、1434 年，分别封噶玛噶举派却贝桑布、萨迦派贡噶扎西、格鲁派释迦也失为大宝法王、大乘法王和大慈法王。三大法王虽互有高低，但互相并不统辖。

虽然互不统属，但“大宝法王”却是明朝时期藏传佛教领袖的最高封号。获得这一封号的噶玛噶举派，是藏传佛教噶举派的一大支派，也是藏传佛教中第一个采取活佛转世制度的宗派。噶玛噶举派活佛的标识，是佩戴元宪宗蒙哥汗赠予的一顶金边黑色僧帽，又称“黑法冠”，所以噶玛噶举活佛又被称为“黑帽系活佛”。早期的黑帽系活佛广求佛法，潜心修证，获得了极高的成就和威望，创立了日后对西藏社会产生巨大影响的活佛转世制。而噶玛噶举五世活佛却贝桑布与明朝中央的良好互动，则有效地加强了中央与西藏地方的密切关系。

其次，在行政上，明朝主要通过两个系统来实现对西藏的管理：在上层，中央王朝通过册封各地方政权首领，实现统一管辖；在基层，主要通过推行都指挥使司和卫所制度，使西藏地方与明朝整个边疆的行政管理体制相一致。都司和卫所的官员，均由朝廷任命藏族贵族首领担任，实行军政一体统治；在地方事务的管理中，明朝中央皆以指导为主，基本不做具体安排，但卫所建制却保障了中央政令能够及时传达到西藏。

吉祥和睦的汉藏关系

为进一步强调册封所包含的政治隶属关系，明朝又建立了与册封相配套的朝贡制度，规定西藏各地僧俗首领向中央朝贡，中央回赐三倍于贡物的财物。与此同时，明朝中央还制定各种政策，有效地维护了藏汉之间茶马互市的繁荣兴旺。

历史地看，明朝中央政府对西藏的管理策略是明智而理性的，有效地延续了元朝对西藏地方的主权统辖。在明朝存世的250多年间，西藏地区一直倾心内附，各个政教首领均积极争取中央的封赐，作为号令地方的权力依据，没有发生过对抗中央的现象。汉藏关系吉祥和睦，藏族地方与祖国内地的交往和联系进一步密切。

In 1407, Zhu Di, Emperor Chengzu of Ming, bestowed the seal of "Great Treasure Dharma King" to the 5th Karmapa Lama of Karma Kagyu Sect, Dezhin Shekpa. The seal attested to the history in which the Ming emperors achieved effective jurisdiction over Tibet by conferring honorary titles on the leaders of Tibetan Buddhism sects and implementing the policies of tribute-trade and halter-bridle.

Forasmuch as the complex relationship between Mongolian and Tibetan monks and seculars, the Ming court highlighted the widespread influence of Tibetan Buddhism in uniting Tibetan people and consolidating national unity. The Ming emperors fully respected the autonomy of Tibet, neither dispatching Han officials nor sending troops. Rather, they provided economic aid to Tibet and encouraged mutual trade, which boosted the prosperity of Tibet and won the support of the Tibetans.

Religiously, the Ming court equally treated all sects in Tibet and balanced the forces of them, in contrast to Yuan that favored the Sakya Sect. At the central level, the Ming government bestowed various titles on Tibetan religious-political leaders to rule their citizens. At the local level, the Ming government appointed Tibetan nobles as officers of Regional Military Commissions and Military Settlements. The administrative management system ensured the military and political jurisdiction over Tibet.

As the case stood, the Ming court successfully continued the sovereignty over Tibet since the Yuan Dynasty. In more than 250 years, Tibetan leaders received the bestowal from the Ming emperors and swore their loyalty to Ming. This established a harmonious relationship between the Ming court and the Tibetan region, and deepened the exchanges among the Han and Tibetan peoples.

茶与马缘何成为游牧民族和农耕民族交往的纽带？

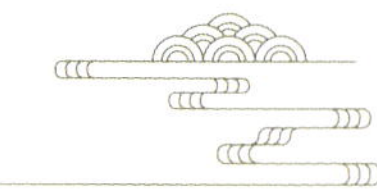

相互依存的共同体

《茶马互市布告》

The Announcement on Tea-Horse Trading

82

文物简读

这则发布于明万历二十八年的《茶马互市布告》，用最明白晓畅的白话文向藏民昭示了政府的茶马互市政策。它见证了茶和马作为农耕民族与游牧民族之间最重要的交流媒介，如何扭结成一种坚韧的经济联系，构筑出多民族牢不可破的互补依存关系，进而推动了中华民族内在的凝聚。

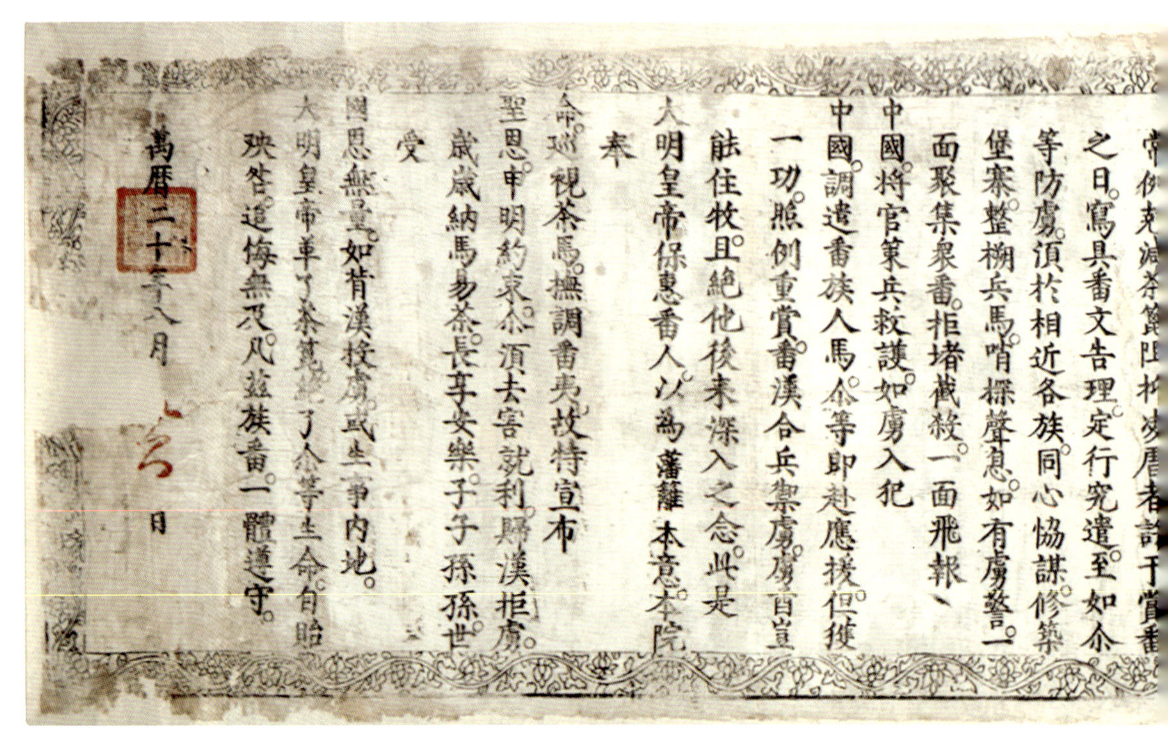

之日寫具番文告理定行究遣至如尒
等防虜須於相近各族同心協謀修築
堡寨整搠兵馬哨探聲息如有虜警一
面聚集衆番拒堵截殺一面飛報
中國將官策兵救護如虜入犯
中國調遣番族人馬尒等即赴應援但獲
一功照例重賞番漢合兵禦虜虜豈
能住牧且絶他後來深入之念此是
大明皇帝保恵番人以為藩籬本意本院
奉
命巡視茶馬撫調番夷故特宣布
聖恩申明約束尒須去害就利歸漢拒虜
歲歲納馬易茶長享安樂子子孫孫世世
受
國恩無量如背漢投虜或生事內地
大明皇帝革了茶篦絶了尒等生命自貽
殃咎追悔無及凡茲族番一體遵守
萬曆二十八年八月　日

名称：《茶马互市布告》
年代：明万历二十八年（1600）
规格：全文共 665 字
收藏单位：青海省博物馆

Name: *The Announcement on Tea-Horse Trading*
Historical Period: The 28th year of Emperor Wanli of the Ming Dynasty (1600)
665 Words
Housed in: Qinghai Provincial Museum

一则能轻易读懂的布告

即便是对粗通文墨的游牧民而言，这则发布于明万历二十八年（1600）的《茶马互市布告》，也是能够轻易读懂的。它用最明白晓畅的白话文，把明朝的茶马互市政策昭告给青海一带的藏民："夫今番人即是吾人，西番的疆土，都是大明皇帝的疆土；西番的人，都是大明皇帝的人。西番以茶为命，得生失死。大明皇帝以夷御夷，纳尔内附，藉为外藩，许尔以茶易马，以全生命……"

布告首先强调了藏民"以茶为命"，因此大明皇帝"以茶易马"，是全其生命之举。

在中华历史上，农耕文明和游牧文明之间的互补依存关系，如果用两种物品来喻示，那么茶和马无疑是最准确的。如同游牧民"以茶为命"一般，马匹在很长一段历史时期里是系于国家命运的刚性需求。所以，茶与马成为中原农耕民族与周边游牧民族之间交往交流的最重要媒介，两者扭结成一种坚韧的经济联系，在多民族的融合过程中发挥了深层次的连接作用，进而推动了中华民族共同体的凝聚。

欽差巡按陝西監察御史徐　諭番文
夫尒番人即是吾人西番的疆土都是
大明皇帝的疆土西番的人都是
大明皇帝的人尒番以茶為命得生失死
大明皇帝以夷禦夷納尒内附藉為外藩
許尒以茶易馬以全生命尒番每年合
當差發依期納馬即給尒茶篦又加尒
賞勞要尒感恩圖報併力拒虜近年虜
數為患荼毒番漢今歲又以劉哼逆賊
勾虜為援虜益乘機跳梁閙尒番不得
寧居故中馬稍遲我
大明皇帝看那劉哼就如釜中遊魚一般
遣將調兵何難剿滅便是虜數入搶掠
亦數被斬殺堂堂
天朝威德廣遠豈因此少損尒番無知或
被虜哄誘送他添巳扙他部落虜性豺
狼貪縱無厭奪尒人口邀尒頭畜燬尒
居室從虜的其害如此
中國以茶篦活尒立國師禪師及衆番僧
以統領尒又能保護尒從
中國的其利如此是向背利害較若黑白
今後各族頭目傳諭番人務要一心頂
戴
大明皇帝日下速將牧養好馬遵照額例
来納本院已申諭將官凡遇番人馬到
相驗毛齒肥瘦時值估價給茶不拘故
常致令虧損又有遠番族名未入冊籍
新願中馬者不必借名熟番但有蓄養
壯大馬匹各具番狀投遞驗中查中多
寡與熟番一體給賞仍立為族分永遠
納馬將官所委員役如有向尒等需索

“茶马，国之要政”

中原王朝和西北游牧民族之间大规模、有组织的茶马贸易起始于唐朝，在宋代趋于成熟，到明朝时臻于繁盛。茶马互市的产生，缘于内地和周边游牧区在生产生活方面的结构性差异。

中原种植茶和饮茶的习俗由来已久。而茶之于游牧民族，因为能够“攻肉食之膻腻，涤通宵之昏寐”，所以，游牧民将茶叶视作日常生活的必需品。到宋代，已出现“夷人不可一日无茶以生”的说法。《明史》则载：“番人嗜乳酪，不得茶，则困以病。”

另一方面，马匹则是中原王朝需求量很大，但却无法依靠自身大量生产的商品。在冷兵器时代，马匹堪称国之重器。尤其是明朝立国后，蒙古残余势力退处漠朔，“屡谋兴复”，实力依旧不容小觑。为了对抗以骑兵为主的蒙古军队的长期侵扰，明朝廷必须拥有一支能与之抗衡的轻骑部队，所以马匹成为明朝十分渴求的军需商品。

因此，明朝政府积极运用制度性手段——通过建立严密的茶马互市制度，从茶法和马政两个方面，明文规定并强制规范茶马互市，最终形成了“东有马市、西有茶市”的繁荣局面。

洪武五年（1372），明政府在陕西秦州设立了第一个茶马司。到万历年间，朝廷更是严格执行“巡视茶马”制度，增强对官营茶马贸易的管理，在庄浪、岷州增设茶马司。这则由陕西监察御史刊布的《茶马互市布告》，正是万历年间朝廷加强对茶马贸易集中管理的文物见证。

明朝的茶马互市一方面繁荣了中原经济，促使中原的茶叶种植业迅猛发展，大量荒地用于茶叶种植，为此雇佣大量的劳动力，茶叶种植逐渐走向专业化和普遍化，促进了资本主义萌芽；另一方面也促进了民族地区的经济发展，游牧区的畜牧业得到了空前的发展，以马匹为代表的畜产品有了更广阔的销售渠道，同时也带动了牛、羊等牲畜的畜养和销售。

茶与马喻示的互补依存关系

事实上，对于中原王朝而言，茶马互市显然具有一定的政治功能，常常演变为中央政府对边疆地区的一种羁縻手段。但是，茶马互市在本质上仍是一种基于农牧双方各取所需、互通有无的产品交换模式。在茶马互市的带动下，各民族人口的流动频率开始增强，以游牧业为主的边疆民族开始在一些适宜地区拓展农业，而农耕区的畜牧业也得到了发展。所以，茶马互市的影响远远超出了茶和马的交换本身。

茶马互市在明朝达到鼎盛后，在清朝来到一个转折点。随着清朝中央政府完成了全国的统一，清廷在西北设立了大规模的牧场，军马的获得不再依赖于以茶易马，国家也随之取消了茶禁，以茶易马的官营体系渐渐失去了存在的基础，民间的茶马贸易开始繁盛。乾隆年间，各地茶马司也逐渐退出了历史舞台。与此同时，民间的茶马古道却空前繁忙起来，川藏之间的茶商星罗棋布，一队队马帮日夜兼程，在为雪域高原送去茶叶的同时，也将大量的畜牧产品带往内地。

所以，茶与马始终都扮演着一个重要的纽带和连接角色，喻示着中原与边疆、农耕与游牧之间不可分离的依存和互补关系，推动各民族凝聚成为一个休戚与共、命运与共的共同体。

The Announcement on Tea-Horse Trading was issued in the 28th year of Emperor Wanli of the Ming Dynasty. With simple language, it introduced the Ming government's policy on tea-horse trading to Tibetans. Tea and horse connected agriculture and nomadism, forged a resilient economic tie among multiple ethnic groups, and enhanced the inherent cohesion of the Chinese nation.

The large-scale tea-horse trading among the Central Plains and the northwestern nomads emerged in the Tang Dynasty, matured in the Song Dynasty, and flourished in the Ming Dynasty. Tea-horse trading arose from the structural differences in the production and life between the Han people and nomadic tribespeople.

After the founding of the Ming Dynasty, the remaining forces of Mongolia retreated to the Northern Desert and "always plotted to restore Yuan". Their military strength pressured the Ming court into building a light cavalry force, in a bid to counteract the Mongolia troops. Against such backdrop, the Ming court was starved of horses. The Ming government institutionalized tea-horse trading and enacted laws on tea-horse management to regulate the tea-horse market, ultimately forming a landscape of horse market in the east and tea market in the west.

In the 5th year of Emperor Hongwu (1372), the Ming government established the first Tea-Horse Department in Qinzhou, Shaanxi. In the reign of Emperor Wanli, the Ming court strictly implemented the "tea-horse inspection system", strengthened the management of state-run tea-horse trading, and added Tea-Horse Department in Zhuanglang and Minzhou.

In the Ming Dynasty, tea-horse trading kindled economic prosperity and accelerated the development of the tea planting industry in the Central Plains. Lots of wasteland was reclaimed for tea planting, and many workers were employed. As tea planting was professionalized and popularized, the seeds of capitalism appeared. Besides, tea-horse trading fostered the economic development of ethnic groups. The stockbreeding developed by leaps and bounds, with horses sold in wider market. The raising and selling of livestock like cattle and sheep also thrived.

作为世界上最大的皇家园林，承德避暑山庄为什么成为乾隆整合民族关系的重要政治舞台？

多民族国家的空前统一

郎世宁等绘《万树园赐宴图》

83

The Imperial Banquet at Ten-Thousand Tree Garden by Giuseppe Castiglione and Others

文物简读

公元1754年，乾隆皇帝在承德避暑山庄连续五天宴请蒙古杜尔伯特部的三位首领，这一幕因郎世宁等宫廷画家绘制的《万树园赐宴图》而永远地留存了下来。它见证了清朝统治者以避暑山庄为舞台，以园林、寺庙、楼台、蒙古包为道具，所上演的维护多民族国家团结统一的历史大剧。

避暑山庄

乾隆生于公元1711年，正是康熙皇帝为避暑山庄命名的那一年。这就像一个奇妙的缘分，避暑山庄后来成为乾隆皇帝整合民族关系的重要政治舞台，甚至可以说，避暑山庄因为乾隆而成为统一多民族国家走向巩固的重要政治中心。

在康熙帝决定建造避暑山庄之前，那里只是一个生活着二三十户游牧民的小村落。康熙四十一年（1702），康熙在木兰围场狩猎时偶然发现了它，于是一个庞大的建园工程开始了。当然，康熙一定没有料到，这座皇家园林的全部工程竣工，需要整整89年。最后，避暑山庄成为世界上最大的皇家园林，宫墙长十公里，面积为564万平方米。此外，避暑山庄外围还建有辉煌富丽的“外八庙”，专供西藏、蒙古、新疆地区少数民族政教首领朝觐皇帝时礼拜之用。

离避暑山庄不远的木兰围场，是康熙当年进行“秋狝”的地方。木兰秋狝是清朝皇帝为了延续游牧传统，加强与北方民族的关系，有效团结各民族上层人物，巩固国家统一而采取的重大政治举措。

康熙年间，前来参加围场行猎的少数民族首领，有青海蒙古、喀尔喀蒙古、内蒙六盟四十九旗的王公贵族，以及察哈尔八旗的蒙古官兵；到乾隆年间，前来木兰围场从猎的首领，已经扩大到西北地区的维吾尔、哈萨克、柯尔克孜等民族。所以，乾隆皇帝扩建避暑山庄的过程，正反映出统一多民族国家进一步增强其向心力和凝聚力的过程。

乾隆十九年（1754），避暑山庄正门落成，乾隆用《易经》中的“日月丽于天”为之取名“丽正门”，并亲自用汉、满、蒙、维、藏五种文字题写了匾额。就在这一年的五月，乾隆皇帝在避暑山庄的万树园，连续五天宴请蒙古杜尔伯特部的三位台吉（首领），这三位台吉因不满准噶尔部达瓦齐的欺凌，率领所属的三千多户部众，离开游牧多年的额尔齐斯河流域，历经艰辛，投奔清朝，回到内地。他们在万树园受到了乾隆皇帝的隆重接见，并受到册封，晚上万树园还举行了野宴、燃放烟火、马技表演等活动。几个月后，乾隆专门派郎世宁等三位宫廷画家来到避暑山庄，用绘画复原了当时的情景，这就是我们眼前的这幅《万树园赐宴图》。在这幅画中，乾隆皇帝乘坐由16名太监抬着的肩舆，进入宴会场地，被接见的蒙古族首领则跪迎皇帝的到来。观赏这幅画，我们需要特别注意万树园的独特景观——它不施土木，没有华丽的宫殿，搭建的是蒙古包式的帐殿。蒙古首领从北方草原风尘仆仆地来到这里觐见皇帝时，便宛如置身于自己的家乡。

也是在这一年的冬天，为了迎接西蒙古准噶尔汗策妄阿拉布坦的外孙阿睦尔撒纳的到来，乾隆冒着呼啸的北风，在两天内骑马急驰350公里，从北京城赶到避暑山庄。后来阿睦尔撒纳叛逃沙俄，辜负了乾隆的期望，但却没有改变乾隆善待西蒙古的决心。乾隆还在避暑山庄隆重接待过三世、四世哲丹尊布巴和六世班禅；作为国师的三世章嘉活佛则经常随同乾隆来往于北京和承德之间。

从万里长城到避暑山庄

以避暑山庄取代万里长城，以欢迎代替防御，这体现了清朝处理民族关系的新思维。统治者在深入总结和深刻反思历史经验教训的基础上，摒弃了消极被动的防御机制，抛弃了“长城式”的民族隔离和军事屏蔽战略，转而采取“以儒治国，以教治心”的理念，贯彻“满汉一家”“中外一体”“因俗而治”等民族事务治理思维，把避暑山庄变成了解决民族问题的重要舞台。康熙说：“我朝施恩于喀尔喀，使之防备朔方，较长城更为坚固也。”他曾直言不讳地宣称：在蒙古地方“建一庙，胜养十万兵”。乾隆继承了这一政治智慧，他以对少数民族宗教信仰和衣冠制度的尊重和维护，“合内外之心，成巩固之业”，有效处理了清前期民族分裂的潜在危机。

从万里长城到避暑山庄，标志着游牧民族与农耕民族重新走向了统一，这是民族关系的一个重要转折点。在处理与边疆民族的关系时，清朝统治者创造了一套独特的制度。如清朝皇室与蒙古王公的世代联姻制度，这一制度最大限度地团结蒙古草原部落，使满蒙之间形成了和谐亲密的关系，甚至能够做到同仇敌忾，如叛离朝廷的蒙古准噶尔部噶尔丹，就成为广大蒙古民众与大清共同的敌人。

从康熙到乾隆，中华民族多元一体的发展进程得到了极大推进，中国作为统一多民族国家的格局得到了历史性的巩固和最终确立，国家得到空前统一。

名称：郎世宁等绘《万树园赐宴图》
年代：清乾隆
规格：纵221.2厘米，横419.6厘米
收藏单位：故宫博物院

Name: *The Imperial Banquet at Ten-Thousand Tree Garden* by Giuseppe Castiglione and Others
Historical Period: In the reign of Emperor Qianlong of the Qing Dynasty
The Vertical: 221.2 cm, The Horizontal: 419.6 cm
Housed in: The Palace Museum

Chengde Mountain Resort was started to be built in the 42nd year of Emperor Kangxi (1703), and completed in the 57th year of Emperor Qianlong (1792), lasting 89 years. It boasts the largest royal garden in the world, with a wall length of ten kilometers and an area of 5,640,000 square meters. Besides, eight temples for Tibetan Buddhism were constructed in the outskirts of the resort, where the Qing emperors met Tibetan and Mongolian political-religious leaders.

In 1754, the 19th year of Emperor Qianlong, the main gate of Chengde Mountain Resort was constructed. Emperor Qianlong named it Lizheng Gate from the line in *Book of Changes*, "The sun and the moon attach themselves to the heaven". He personally inscribed the plaque in five languages, Han, Manchu, Mongolian, Uyghur and Tibetan. In May of the same year, Emperor Qianlong hosted banquets for three *Taiji* (台吉, leaders) of Mongolian Durbat tribe for five consecutive days at Ten-Thousand Tree Garden, Chengde Mountain Resort. Dissatisfied with the bullying of Dawaqi of the Dzungar tribe, the three *Taiji* led over 3,000-household subjects and

left the Irtysh River Basin, where they roved for many years. Going through untold hardships, they travelled to the Central Plains and defected to the Qing Dynasty. They received a grand reception from Emperor Qianlong at Ten-Thousand Tree Garden, who bestowed honorary titles on them. A few months later, commissioned by Emperor Qianlong, three court painters, including Giuseppe Castiglione (*aka* Lang Shining), came to Chengde Mountain Resort and painted *The Imperial Banquet at Ten-Thousand Tree Garden*. In the painting, Emperor Qianlong, seated in a palanquin carried on the shoulders of 16 eunuchs, was entering the banquet venue. The Mongolian leaders knelt to welcome the emperor. Noteworthily, in Ten-Thousand Tree Garden, a Mongolian yurt-style tent took the place of magnificent palaces. This made Mongolian leaders feel at home, when they had an audience with the Qing emperor.

The Qing emperors abandoned traditional strategy of military isolation (as materialized by the Great Wall), and upheld the idea of "ruling with Confucianism and respecting religious customs", in which the resort played an important role in promoting ethnic relations.

"中国"一词从什么时候开始，作为主权国家的名称出现在世界历史舞台？

近代主权国家意识的萌生

"神威无敌大将军"铜炮

"Martial Prowess Invincible Grand General" Bronze Artillery

84

文物简读

这门在雅克萨自卫反击战中立下赫赫战功的"神威无敌大将军"铜炮，是清朝抗击外来侵略取得胜利，使统一多民族国家疆域得以巩固的重要历史见证；同时，它还间接地反映了清朝在与外部侵略势力打交道时，逐步萌生近代主权国家意识的重要历程。

雅克萨之战

沙俄原为欧洲国家，不与中国接壤。从16世纪沙皇伊凡四世开始，沙俄向西伯利亚扩张殖民，渐次抵达白令海峡，完成了向太平洋推进的探险；又进抵贝加尔湖，修筑雅库茨克城，侵入清朝管辖的黑龙江流域，从而引发了中国边境民族的反抗。

1643年冬，一支一百余人的沙俄远征队以雅库茨克城为据点，翻过外兴安岭，进入中国领土，抢掠达斡尔村庄，遭到达斡尔人奋勇反击。1651年春，沙俄远征军卷土重来，侵占了雅克萨城，对达斡尔聚居的村落进行屠杀。以达斡尔为代表的东北少数民族奋勇反击外来侵略者，自觉地参与保家卫国的斗争。而清朝政府在顺治九年（1652）至顺治十七年（1660）间，曾三次派遣驻守在宁古塔的清朝军队，一度将侵入黑龙江流域的沙俄军队予以肃清。

1674年，正当清廷致力于平定南方的"三藩"之乱时，沙俄趁机派兵再次侵占了雅克萨地区。为了反抗沙俄的侵略行径，康熙帝决心一战。

为保证反击作战胜利，康熙帝做了周密的安排和充分的准备——建立相当数量的驿站和粮站，开辟水陆交通线，造船铸炮，组织了一支由多地、多民族组成的自卫军：既有东北地方军，也有山东、

名称："神威无敌大将军"铜炮

年代：清康熙

规格：长248厘米，口径11厘米，重1137千克

收藏单位：黑龙江省博物馆

Name: "Martial Prowess Invincible Grand General" Bronze Artillery

Historical Period: In the reign of Emperor Kangxi of the Qing Dynasty

Length: 248 cm, Mouth Diameter: 11 cm, Weight: 1,137 kg

Housed in: Heilongjiang Provincial Museum

山西、河南、甘肃、福建的水师，还包括台湾的藤牌兵；既有内地的汉族，也有世居黑龙江地区的满、蒙古、达斡尔、赫哲、鄂伦春等少数民族。

1685年4月，三千多名清军乘战舰，携火炮，兵分水陆两路，从瑷珲出发，直抵雅克萨城下，致书俄军，劝其退出清朝领土，但遭到侵略军头目托尔布津的拒绝。清军于是将陆师布于城南，集战船于城东南，列炮于城北，向沙俄军发起攻击，使其伤亡惨重，托尔布津乞降，遣使要求撤离雅克萨，退至尼布楚。清军赶走侵略军后，平毁雅克萨城，即行回师。

但沙俄军贼心不死，在得到莫斯科派来的六百名援兵后，马上卷土重来。俄军这一背信弃义的行为引起清政府极大愤慨。第二年初，康熙帝下令反击。

1686年7月，两千多名清军进抵雅克萨，将其团团围住，打死了托尔布津。但俄军仍旧负隅顽抗。清军在雅克萨的南、北、东三面掘壕围困，切断敌人外援，826名侵略军最后只剩下66人。就在这时，沙皇急忙向清政府"乞撤雅克萨之围"。康熙帝传令前线撤围，任沙俄兵撤回尼布楚。

取得雅克萨反击战的胜利后，清朝政府与沙俄于1689年7月缔结了《中俄尼布楚条约》，规定以外兴安岭、格尔必齐河和额尔古纳河为中俄东段边界；外兴安岭以南、黑龙江和乌苏里江流域、包括库页岛在内的广大地区，都是中国的领土。

首次萌生的近代主权国家意识

《中俄尼布楚条约》是我国历史上第一个以"中国"作为主权国家签订的国际条约。这份条约使用了满、俄和拉丁文三种文字，以拉丁文本作为双方共同签署的正式文本。值得注意的是，条约文本里满篇都是"中国"一词，也就是说，清朝政府在签订条约时，用"中国"作为清朝的代称。

显然，这是一个非常值得注意的细节。在历史上，先秦时期的"中国"，特指"天子所居之地"或"天下之中心"，特指由周天子直接统治的范围，与王城周围的诸侯国相对。后来，"中国"泛指由夏、商、周融合而成的"华夏"所居住的区域。随着中华民族多元一体历史进程的推进，"中国"的概念逐渐扩展。清朝定鼎北京后，历经康熙、雍正、乾隆三代，通过东收台湾、北拒沙俄、西据蒙古、南下青藏，确立了明确的国家疆域和边界，"中国"一词开始明确地指向清朝政府所管辖的所有地域。

早在顺治十三年（1656），清朝与厄鲁特蒙古的往来公文中，就已经出现了明确的"中国"一词。而当《中俄尼布楚条约》签定时，"中国"更加明确地成为国家的名称，这显示出清政府在与一个非古代中国天下体系里的西方国家打交道时，所萌生出来的近代主权国家意识。显然，这在中国历史上还是第一次。

事实上，正是在17世纪西方殖民扩张渐渐显露出的威胁之下，清政府逐渐建立起了近代主权国家的意识。这是一个巨大的历史演进，而它清晰地体现在《中俄尼布楚条约》中。这个条约并非古代历史上粗略的国家势力范围划分，而是受到国际法和国际公约保护的主权保护协定，它体现了清朝统治者对自我的"中国"身份的认同，同时也是清朝逐步脱离古代王朝国家身份、以"中国"为名称向近代主权国家转变的第一步。

“神威无敌大将军”

正是出于这样的“中国”观，清朝对边疆领土的控制和捍卫达到了历史上前所未有的力度。从这样一个角度，我们可以更加深刻地理解雅克萨之战的意义。

现在，能够把我们带回那一场遥远的边疆保卫战的见证物，就是这门“神威无敌大将军”铜炮。据历史记载，在雅克萨之战中，八门“神威无敌大将军”铜炮和12门“神威将军”炮参战，为攻克沙俄军队起到了决定性作用。

“神威无敌大将军”铜炮是一种大型的长管火炮，于康熙十五年（1676）在北京铸造，其名号也由康熙帝钦定，并将其铸在炮身之上。而“神威将军”炮可谓前者的袖珍版，为轻型长管火炮，铸造于康熙二十年（1681）。依靠这两种火炮，清军炸毁了雅克萨的木质城墙和塔楼，获得了雅克萨之战的大胜。

雅克萨之战是中国清朝抗击外来侵略、维护祖国版图的一次战争，彰显了各民族共同抵御外侮的伟大胜利。它可以说是中华民族第一次面对西方殖民扩张而进行的自卫战争，也是中华民族因为面对外来侵略而逐渐从自在实体走向自觉实体的前奏。

Tsarist Russia was originally a European country. In the 16th century, Tsar Ivan IV of Russia expanded Russian colonies to Siberia and the Bering Strait. Russian explorers arrived at the Lake Baikal and built the city of Yakutsk, invading the Heilongjiang River Basin under the jurisdiction of the Qing Dynasty and sparking the resistance from various ethnic groups at the Qing border.

As a long-barrel heavy artillery, “Martial Prowess Invincible Grand General” was cast in Beijing in the 15th year of Emperor Kangxi (1676) and named by Kangxi. “Martial Prowess General” was a long-barrel light artillery and cast in the 20th year of Emperor Kangxi (1681). With the aid of the two types of artillery, the Qing army blew up the wooden city walls and towers at Jaxa, and achieved a great victory in the Battle of Jaxa. Subsequently, the Qing government and Tsarist Russia signed *Treaty of Nerchinsk* in July 1689. In the Battle of Jaxa, the Qing government counter-attacked foreign aggression and safeguarded the territory of China, demonstrating the great victory of all ethnic groups in China that rallied to resisting foreign invaders. The Battle of Jaxa signaled the first self-defense war of the Chinese nation in the face of Western colonialist expansion, and prepared the prelude for the transformation of the Chinese nation from the self-being entity into the self-making entity, triggered by the foreign aggression.

Treaty of Nerchinsk was the first international treaty that China signed as a sovereign state. The authoritative Latin texts were co-signed by the signatories, with translations into Russian and Manchu. As the history proved, in the 17th century, Western colonialist expansion menaced the territorial integrity of China. Under such circumstance, the Qing government honed its consciousness of modern sovereignty, as seen in the appellation of “China” in *Treaty of Nerchinsk*.

清朝为什么不惜付出巨大代价，历经康雍乾三代，与准噶尔分裂势力进行了一场近七十年的斗争？

西北边疆的稳定与巩固

钱维城《平定准噶尔图卷》

Quelling the Junggar Revolt by Qian Weicheng

85

文物简读

这幅描绘乾隆年间清廷平定准噶尔部叛乱的历史画卷，定格了清朝为维护西北边疆安定统一而持续投入的一场近七十年的反分裂斗争并最终取得决定性胜利的场景，承载着统一多民族中国的疆域在清代获得确立和巩固的历史。

一场延续近七十年的反分裂斗争

在群星闪耀的乾隆朝宫廷画师中，钱维城是很特殊的一位。钱维城26岁就高中状元，官至刑部侍郎，但他却热衷于绘画，终成画苑领袖。有一次，他跟随乾隆在木兰围场狩猎，乾隆一枪毙中一虎，便马上命他将这一幕描绘下来，并刻于石上。

钱维城留下了众多画作，但显然，这幅《平定准噶尔图卷》是最具历史意义的作品。图卷长达8米，呈现了“战争场面”“献俘仪式”“凯旋庆功”三个主题，俨然一部大型战争纪录片，而它所反映的那场延续近七十年的反分裂斗争，则更加荡气回肠。

康熙三次御驾亲征

清朝初建时，蒙古分为漠西、漠南和漠北三部分。漠南蒙古诸部皆直隶于清廷；漠北喀尔喀蒙古各部与清结好；漠西蒙古又分为准噶尔、和硕特、杜尔伯特、土尔扈特四部，均向清朝呈奉表贡，确立了与清朝的主从关系。但此后，准噶尔部在噶尔丹取得统治权后，开始向外扩张，先后击败和硕特

名称：钱维城《平定准噶尔图卷》
年代：清乾隆
规格：纵41厘米，横808厘米
收藏单位：中国国家博物院

Name: *Quelling the Junggar Revolt* by Qian Weicheng
Historical Period: In the reign of Emperor Qianlong of the Qing Dynasty
The Vertical: 41 cm, The Horizontal: 808 cm
Housed in: National Museum of China

部、征服哈萨克，称雄西域；又与日益东扩的俄罗斯建立密切关系，求借援兵，购置军火，向东进犯漠北喀尔喀和漠南诸部，甚至提出了由康熙“君南方”、由他“长北方”的要求。

康熙二十九年（1690），噶尔丹再度进犯喀尔喀蒙古。此时，清朝国内政局已经稳固，康熙召集群臣，决定御驾亲征。在此役中，康熙不计“万乘之尊”，与士兵们同甘共苦，“日惟一餐，恒饮浊水，甘受劳苦”，令军队士气大振，最终在乌兰布通大败噶尔丹。噶尔丹逃回漠北，表面臣服清朝，却在暗中招兵买马，在沙俄支持下，于康熙三十四年（1695）再率骑兵三万向东进犯。康熙帝再次御驾亲征，经昭莫多一战，歼敌万余，几令其全军覆没，噶尔丹“引数骑逃去”。为彻底剿灭残存的噶尔丹势力，康熙决定第三次亲征。此役中，噶尔丹残部听说康熙再度亲征，纷纷投降，甚至主动领路追捕噶尔丹。众叛亲离的噶尔丹选择服毒自杀。

雍正四次发动西征

噶尔丹败亡后，其侄策妄阿拉布坦继任准噶尔部台吉。康熙五十四年（1715），策妄阿拉布坦在沙俄支持下，率兵两千人窜入哈密北境，此后又窜扰西藏。清政府即令出兵围剿。

康熙驾崩后，雍正继续坚持对准噶尔分裂势力的斗争。雍正五年（1727）冬，策妄阿拉布坦死，

其子噶尔丹策凌继位后，在沙俄支持下继续叛乱活动。为平定噶尔丹策凌之乱，雍正曾发动四次西征，历经科舍图之战、和通泊之战、鄂登楚勒之战和光显寺之战，付出了巨大代价。其中雍正九年（1731）的和通泊战役，清军曾陷入不利之境，西路军几乎被准噶尔部全歼，损失惨重。但在雍正不折不挠的反分裂斗争下，清军最终大败准噶尔部，迫使噶尔丹策凌罢兵请和。

乾隆两次远征大捷

乾隆十年（1745），噶尔丹策凌去世，准噶尔内部陷入激烈的权力之争。其间，沙俄屡屡介入其中，欲物色人选建立傀儡政权。就在此时，乾隆帝认为统一西北地区的条件已经成熟，决定把握时机，一举消灭准噶尔分裂势力。

乾隆二十年（1755），清军兵分两路，直捣准噶尔阿瓦齐部。此时的准噶尔贵族分裂势力已是强弩之末，清军如摧枯拉朽一般扫荡了其残存力量。

其间，策妄阿拉布坦的外孙阿睦尔撒纳争夺汗位失利后，曾于乾隆十九年（1754）秋前往承德避暑山庄，觐见乾隆，归附清廷，被封为亲王。但他后来却辜负了乾隆的期待和信任，转而投奔沙俄，率兵再叛。乾隆二十二年（1757），乾隆再度出兵西征，两路大军抵达喀什噶尔，连战连捷，平定了

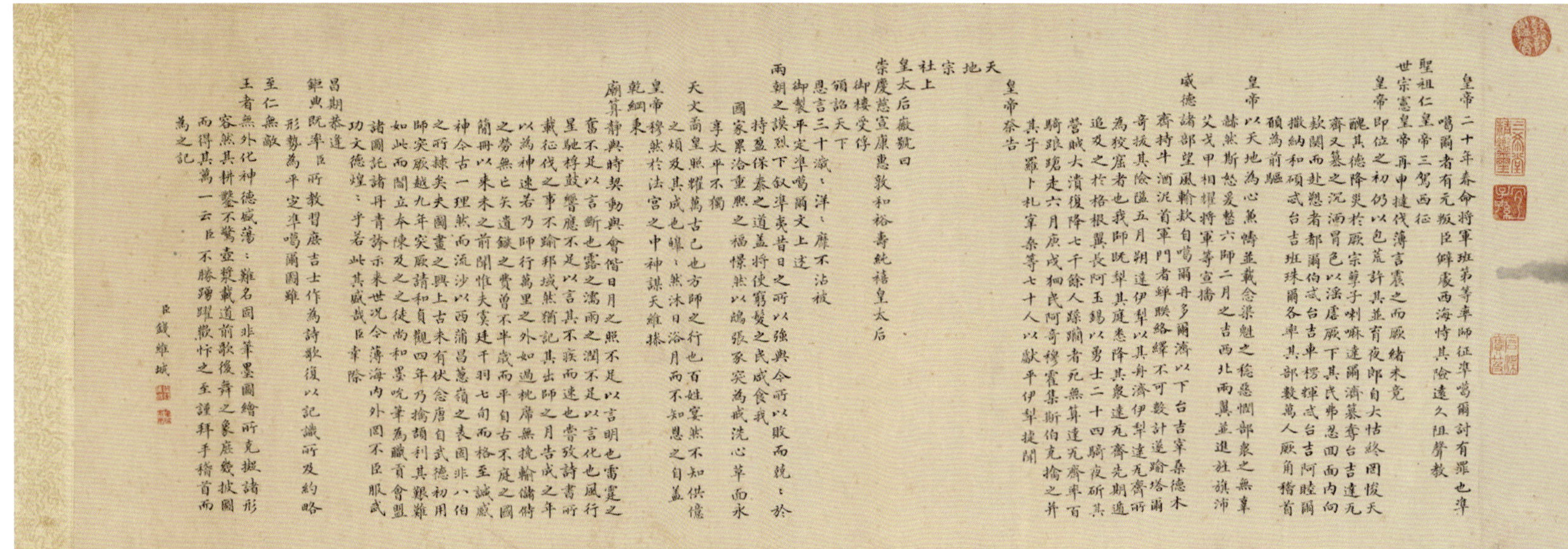

支持阿睦尔撒纳作乱的大小和卓叛乱。阿睦尔撒纳兵败逃往沙俄，不久染病而亡。

清朝对准噶尔部分裂势力进行的持之以恒的斗争，最终取得了决定性胜利，彻底结束了西北地区的长期分裂局面。乾隆帝把这片失而复得的疆域命名为“新疆”，意为“故土新归”之意。

这场斗争的胜利，对于统一多民族国家的进一步巩固具有重大意义。首先，它使与准噶尔部关系密切的西藏、青海问题的迎刃而解；其次，它在一个时期内有效遏制了17世纪以来不断东扩的沙俄对蒙古牧地及西北地区的侵吞与蚕食。此外，原来隶属于准噶尔部的蒙古乌梁海亦随之纳入清朝版图，这更加稳定和巩固了统一多民族国家的疆域。

Quelling the Junggar Revolt was painted by Qian Weicheng, a Qing court painter, in the 20th year of Emperor Qianlong (1755). With a length of eight meters, it covers three parts, i.e. “The Hard-Fought Battle”, “The Defeat of Dawaqi’s Troops” and “The Celebration of Victory”. Like a large-scale war documentary, it represented the nearly-70-year anti-separatist struggle in the reigns of Kangxi, Yongzheng and Qianlong.

In the early Qing Dynasty, Mongolia was divided into three forces in the west, south and north of the desert, or the Moxi Mongolia, the Monan Mongolia and the Mobei Mongolia. The Monan Mongolia acknowledged allegiance to the Qing court, and the Mobei Mongolia forged friendly relations with the Qing court. The Moxi Mongolia comprised four tribes, i.e. Junggar,

Khoshut, Dorbet and Torgut, all of which paid tribute to the Qing court. Later, Galdan seized the power of Junggar. Having conquered Khoshut and Qazaq, Junggar dominated the Western Regions. In alliance with Tsarist Russia, Galdan expanded eastward and encroached on Khalkha of the Mobei Mongolia and the tribes of the Monan Mongolia.

In the 29th year of Emperor Kangxi (1690), Galdan invaded Khalkha. Kangxi decided to go on a personal expedition and ultimately defeated Galdan in the Battle of Ulan Butung. In the 34th year of Emperor Kangxi (1695), Galdan led 30,000 cavalrymen and moved eastward. Kangxi personally directed the Battle of Jao Modo, and the Qing troops routed Galdan's army, who "just fled with several cavalrymen". In the third-time personal expedition of Kangxi, Galdan, deserted by all followers, laid hands on himself. In the winter of the 5th year of Emperor Yongzheng, in order to quell the rebellion of Galdan Tseren, Yongzheng launched four expeditions to the west.

In the 9th year of Emperor Yongzheng (1731), the Qing troops wiped out the Junggar opponents in the Battle of Khoton-nor. In the 10th year of Emperor Qianlong (1745), Galdan Tseren died, causing an internal strife in Junggar. Tsarist Russia seized the chance to establish a puppet regime. In the 20th year of Emperor Qianlong (1755), the Qing troops in two columns pulverized Dawaqi's troops. The quelling of the Junggar revolts further stabilized and consolidated the territory of Qing, a unified multi-ethnic country.

名称："金瓶掣签"苯巴瓶
年代：清乾隆
规格：金瓶高34厘米
收藏单位：西藏博物馆

Name: The Golden Urn (*gser-bum*) & The System of "Drawing Lots from the Golden Urn"
Historical Period: In the reign of Emperor Qianlong of the Qing Dynasty
Height: 34 cm (The Golden Urn)
Housed in: Tibet Museum

用于甄选藏传佛教活佛转世灵童的"金瓶掣签"制度，是怎样产生的？

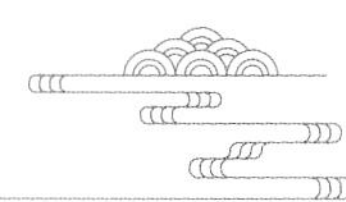

清朝加强对西藏的管理

"金瓶掣签"苯巴瓶

86

The Golden Urn (*gser-bum*) & The System of "Drawing Lots from the Golden Urn"

文物简读

用于甄选活佛转世灵童的金苯巴瓶，是清朝政府实行"金瓶掣签"制度以维护西藏稳定、巩固国家统一的历史见证。"金瓶掣签"既增强了活佛转世制度的透明性和公正性，被佛教界、上层贵族世家和信教群众广泛接受，又加强了西藏的稳定，意义深远。

《钦定藏内善后章程二十九条》

清朝建立后，中央政府对西藏的管理一步步稳固和加强——

1652年，五世达赖正式接受清朝册封的"达赖喇嘛"封号，此后历代达赖都经清朝册封。

1713年，清朝派使者进藏，封第五世班禅罗桑意希为"班禅额尔德尼"，从此"班禅额尔德尼"的封号被确定。

1717年，清朝直接派遣官员驻扎西藏，是为驻藏大臣的开端。

1720年，清军击败窜扰西藏的准噶尔军队，于次年设置噶伦数人，集体管理西藏政务。此外，将康区划入四川省。

1727年，清政府正式留正副大臣驻扎西藏，领川陕兵两千名驻西藏，是为元朝之后中央政府首次在西藏驻扎军队。

1750年，清朝平定西藏叛乱，翌年颁布《西藏善后章程十三条》，废除西藏郡王制，设立噶厦，长官为噶伦，秉承驻藏大臣、达赖喇嘛旨意办事。

1788年和1791年，清军驱逐并反攻入侵西藏的廓尔喀（今尼泊尔），后颁布《钦定藏内善后章程二十九条》，标志着清朝在西藏建立起一套完善的管理体系。

在这一系列重大历史节点中，《钦定藏内善后章程二十九条》至为重要，被视为清朝治藏的“基本法”。它对西藏的宗教事务、外事、军事、行政和司法做出了详细的规定，并在第一条就明确了“活佛转世需实行金瓶掣签制度”。

“金瓶掣签”制度的由来

藏传佛教在实施活佛转世制度初期，曾采用“预示法”“天断法”“指定法”确定转世灵童。由于转世灵童不仅要继承重要的宗教地位，而且享有极大的政治权利，所以转世灵童的选择往往被世俗阶层或者是宗教上层力量控制，他们常常假借神谕，弄假作弊。

康熙时期，五世达赖指定的第巴（总理西藏事务官员）桑杰嘉措，在五世达赖圆寂后秘而不宣，私自册定了转世灵童。1719年，清朝派大军进藏平定侵扰西藏的准噶尔部时，桑杰嘉措才承认了此事。这使清廷清晰地认识到西藏活佛转世制度存在的弊端。

乾隆五十三年（1788），噶玛噶举派活佛确朱嘉措外逃到廓尔喀国，并挑唆廓尔喀国王出兵西藏，引来廓尔喀人第一次侵藏。乾隆五十六年（1791），廓尔喀再次侵藏，将扎什伦布寺洗掠一空，又攻打日喀则宗城堡。乾隆皇帝果断派遣久经沙场的两广总督福康安作为大将军，率兵入藏，从日喀则一路南下，将廓尔喀兵逐出西藏，又挟军威，一路扫荡，最后兵临廓尔喀首都加德满都。廓尔喀国王投降，表示永不敢再犯边界，还许诺向大清国五年一朝贡。

抗击廓尔喀，清廷付出了极其高昂的代价，支付军费高达1052万两白银，占当时全国税收总额的四分之一。战后，乾隆进行了认真的反思，决定趁战争善后的机会彻底整顿西藏事务。他挥笔写下了《喇嘛说》，总结了清政府的藏传佛教政策以及宗教治理经验，比较了清朝与元明两朝藏传佛教政策的不同之处，说明了自己进行藏传佛教相关制度改革的原因以及举措。

正是因此，福康安班师拉萨后，按照乾隆皇帝旨意对西藏事务进行整饬，在与达赖、班禅等僧俗要员商议的基础上，制订了《钦定藏内善后章程二十九条》，内容涉及西藏政制、经济贸易、外交边防、军事、吏治、寺庙管理等方方面面，其中“实行金瓶掣签制度”列居第一条：

> 关于寻找活佛及呼图克图灵童的问题。依照藏人旧例，确认灵童必问卜于四大护法，如此难免发生弊端。大皇帝为求黄教得到兴隆，特赐一金瓶，今后遇到寻认灵童时，邀集四大护法将灵童的名字及出生年月，用满、汉、藏三种文字写于签牌上，放进瓶内，选派真正有学问之活佛，祈祷七日，然后由各呼图克图和驻藏大臣在大昭寺释迦牟尼佛像前正式认定。假若找到的灵童仅只一名，亦须将一个有灵童的名字的签牌，和一个没有名字的签牌，共同放置瓶内，假若抽出没有名字的签牌，就不能认定已寻得的儿童，而要另外寻找。达赖和班禅像父子一样，认定他们的灵童时，亦须将他们的名字用满、汉、藏三种文字写在签牌上，同样进行。这些都是大皇帝为了黄教的兴隆，和不使护法弄假作弊。这个金瓶常放在宗喀巴佛像前，需要保护净洁，并进行供养。

金瓶掣签增加了活佛转世制度的透明性和公正性，体现了清朝中央政府对西藏宗教治理的原则性和灵活性，保障了其对西藏宗教事务管理的有效性，加强了西藏的稳定，意义深远。与此同时，"金瓶掣签"制度的实施完全按照藏传佛教仪轨来进行，在宗教上符合藏传佛教的基本教义，顺利地解决和保障了宗教首领的传承和延续，因此被佛教界、上层贵族世家和信教群众广泛接受。

金苯巴瓶

金瓶又被称为"金苯巴"或"金奔巴"（"苯巴"或"奔巴"，在藏语中意为"瓶"）。"金瓶掣签"制度特别设立了两个金瓶，一个放置在北京雍和宫，专供蒙古地区大活佛转世灵童掣签之用；另一个放置在拉萨大昭寺，专供西藏、青海等地大活佛转世灵童掣签之用。凡蒙藏大活佛如章嘉、哲布尊丹巴、达赖、班禅等转世时，均须经金瓶掣签认定。

In the reign of Emperor Kangxi, Sanggye Gyatso, the fifth regent (*desi*) of the 5th Dalai Lama, hid the death of the Dalai Lama and covertly decided the "reincarnated soul boy". This came to light until 1719, when the Qing troops arrived in Tibet to put down the riot of Junggar. To the Qing court, the long-standing practice of Tibetan reincarnation system proved imperfect.

In the 56th year of Emperor Qianlong (1791), the Gurkha army invaded Tibet, and the Qing court sent troops to expel the Gurkha. The Gurkha army sacked the Tashi Lhunpo Monastery and attacked the Shigatse Castle. Emperor Qianlong wisely appointed the famous general Fu Kang'an, Viceroy of Liangguang, as Grand General, who led the Qing troops to Shigatse. The Qing army marched southward and drove out the Gurkha army, arriving at Kathmandu, capital of Gurkha. The king of Gurkha surrendered to Qing, on condition that Gurkha would never invade Tibet and pay tribute to Qing every five years.

Emperor Qianlong took the opportunity to thoroughly rectify Tibetan affairs. After returning to Lhasa, Fu Kang'an negotiated with Dalai Lama and Panchen Lama and mapped out *Twenty-Nine Regulations for Resolving Tibetan Matters*, under the order of Emperor Qianlong, covering various aspects of the political system, economy & trade, diplomatic relations & border defense, military affairs, official governance, temple management, etc., and prioritizing the system of "drawing lots from the golden urn".

The system of "drawing lots from the golden urn" totally accorded with the rituals and doctrines of Tibetan Buddhism and successfully guaranteed the continuation of religious leaders, thus being widely accepted by Tibetan aristocrats and Buddhists.

清朝在台湾建省时，为何台湾的全称被确定为 “福建台湾省”？

清朝收复台湾

“福建台湾巡抚关防”官印

The Official Seal of “Governor of Fujian-Taiwan Province”

87

文物简读

“福建台湾巡抚关防”官印是清朝收复台湾，采用“福建台湾制”在台湾建省，通过特别强调台湾与福建的紧密关系，着意强化台湾与大陆无法割裂的血脉联系的文物见证。

清朝收复台湾

郑成功驱逐荷兰殖民主义者、收复台湾，这一辉煌功绩闪耀在中华民族的史册上，他为台湾地区的经济开发做出了极大努力并且取得了显著成就。郑成功于康熙元年（1662）五月猝然病逝，其子郑经继位，借助父亲在台湾民众中的威望和开发台湾取得的成就，郑经孤守一隅，不愿顺应清朝的大一统步伐。

康熙继位后的二十多年间，清廷曾派遣官员与郑经进行了十多次和谈。但由于清政府的海上作战能力不够强大，谈判均告失败。在此期间，清政府曾经采用经济封锁手段，促其归附，也未能如愿。康熙帝认识到，要实现台湾的和平统一，没有强大的政治、军事实力作为后盾是无法达成的。

随着三藩之乱的平定，康熙帝治理下的国家政治稳定、经济发展，收复台湾的时机日益成熟。此时，福建水师提督施琅向康熙提出了“因剿寓抚”的战略主张，即以战逼和，用军事手段促成台湾问题的和平解决。

康熙二十年（1681），郑经在台湾承天府去世，其子郑克塽嗣立。两年后，康熙命施琅进军澎湖。此时正值六月，台风频繁，不利海战，郑军守将认为施琅只是虚张声势，因此并无防备；而当清军水师突然出现在澎湖海域时，台湾守军仓促迎战，很快被击溃。澎湖被攻克后，郑氏王朝自知无力抵抗清军，决定接受招抚。台湾因此成为清朝的领土。

康熙二十三年（1684），清廷在福建省之下设立台湾府，辖三县，总兵官一员，使台湾成为福建的第九个府。此外，清廷在台湾驻兵八千；在澎湖设副将一员，兵两千。从此，台湾的行政建制与大陆划一。

台湾收复后，迁离故土的沿海百姓返回了家园，恢复了正常的农业、渔业生产和海上贸易活动，台湾地方官员也注意招徕大陆流民前去开荒，出现了“流民归者如市”“内地入籍者众”的现象，海上贸易空前活跃。

“福建台湾省”

在此后的两百年时间里，台湾都隶属于福建省管辖，被称作“福建台湾府”。然而，鸦片战争期间英国兵船屡次侵犯台湾；1874年日本侵略者以“牡丹社事件”为借口大举进攻台湾岛；1884年台湾又成为法国在东南战场的侵占目标。这一系列事件都让清政府清晰地认识到台湾战略地位的重要性，因此决定在台湾建省。

光绪十一年（1885），清政府参照“甘肃新疆”之制，下诏宣布在台湾建省，但明令规定：“台湾虽设行省，必须与福建联成一气……庶可内外相维。”并将台湾省的全称确定为“福建台湾省”；台湾省最高行政长官的全称为“福建台湾巡抚”；台湾巡抚的关防名为“福建台湾巡抚关防”；台湾布政使司的关防名为“福建台湾布政使司关防”；台湾各县的印信也在县名前冠以“福建台湾”的全称。

台湾建省前隶属福建，归福建巡抚管辖；台湾建省后由“福建台湾巡抚”管辖。至于福建，则在台湾建省后“裁福建巡抚”，由闽浙总督“兼管福建巡抚事，并兼管台湾”。

虽然台湾单独建省，但清政府仍然特别强调台湾与福建的特殊关系，以“福建台湾制”的制度设计，着意强化台湾与大陆无法割舍的联系。

1888年3月，福建台湾巡抚关防正式启用，这标志着在澎湖巡检司设立550年之后，台湾正式成为中央政府的行省。

这枚“福建台湾巡抚关防”官印就是这段历史尘埃落定的见证。第一个使用这枚印章的就是大名鼎鼎的台湾首任巡抚刘铭传。据载，刘铭传上任后，福建省五年内协济台湾省饷银220万两。刘铭传在台湾推行新政，在筹建炮台、购买炮械、修建铁路时，使用的都是福建协济的银两。此后，沈葆桢、丁日昌等晚清著名政治家，都曾被清政府任命为福建台湾巡抚，他们为开发台湾立下了汗马功劳。

清廷收复台湾，并在台湾建省，推动了成千上万的大陆移民到台湾披荆斩棘、辛勤劳动，把一个曾经是麋鹿出没、瘴气弥漫的海岛耕耘成“糖谷之利甲天下”的美丽富饶宝岛，使大陆与台湾血脉相连的关系更加深刻。

Having pacified the Revolt of the Three Feudatories, Emperor Kangxi achieved political stability and economic prosperity. The opportunity to reoccupy Taiwan arrived. Shi Lang, commander-in-chief of Fujian Navy, proposed the strategy of "peace after conquest", which focused on solving the Taiwan issues with military operations. In the 20th year of Emperor Kangxi (1681), Zheng Jing died, and his son Zheng Keshuang succeeded. Two years later, Kangxi ordered Shi Lang to bombard Penghu. After the Qing troops captured Penghu, the force of Zheng surrendered to Qing, with Taiwan incorporated into the territory of Qing.

In the 23rd year of Emperor Kangxi (1684), the Qing court established Taiwan Prefecture, the 9th prefecture in Fujian Province, which administered three counties. 8,000 troops were stationed in Taiwan, led by a commanding officer; 2,000 troops were stationed in Penghu, led by a vice general. For more than 100 years, Taiwan Prefecture had been under the jurisdiction of Fujian Province.

During the Opium War, British warships repeatedly invaded Taiwan. In 1874, Japanese invaders launched a large-scale attack on the Taiwan Island on the pretext of the Mudanshe Incident. In 1884, French cast greedy eyes on Taiwan in the Sino-French War. Faced with domestic trouble and foreign invasion, the Qing court realized the strategic significance of Taiwan and decided to promote Taiwan as a province.

In the 11th year of Emperor Guangxu (1885), the Qing government declared the establishment of Taiwan Province (officially known as Fujian-Taiwan Province). The Governor and Provincial Administrative Commissioner of Fujian-Taiwan Province used their official seals respectively. And all counties in Taiwan inscribed "Fujian-Taiwan Province" in their official seals. In March 1888, the seal of Governor of Fujian-Taiwan Province formally took effect. Liu Mingchuan, an important figure in modern China, was appointed as the first governor of Taiwan. He initiated the reform in Taiwan, including constructing fort barbette, purchasing artillery and building railway. Famous politicians, such as Shen Baozhen and Ding Richang, successors to Liu, made great contributions to the development of Taiwan.

名称：渥巴锡腰刀

年代：清乾隆

规格：通长85厘米，宽约3.5厘米

收藏单位：故宫博物院

Name: The Broadsword of Wobaxi

Historical Period: In the reign of Emperor Qianlong of the Qing Dynasty

Total Length: 85 cm, Width: *c.* 3.5 cm

Housed in: The Palace Museum

一把残破的腰刀，为何成为进献乾隆皇帝的贡礼？

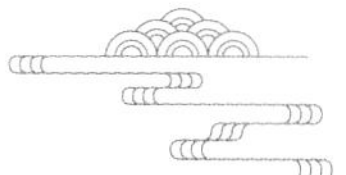

少数民族日益增强的“祖国意识”

渥巴锡腰刀

The Broadsword of Wobaxi

88

文物简读

这把由年轻的土尔扈特汗王渥巴锡进献给乾隆皇帝的祖传腰刀，见证了土尔扈特部从伏尔加河畔万里东归的悲壮史实，承载着清朝时期少数民族对统一多民族国家的深刻认同和强烈归属感，显示出中华民族日益强大的内部凝聚力。

土尔扈特的抉择

1203年，蒙古乞颜部在其首领铁木真的带领下，击败了蒙古高原南部的克烈部，但克烈部的英勇善战却给铁木真留下了深刻印象，他广泛选用克烈部战士作为自己的亲卫军。因为“亲卫”一词在克烈方言中的发音为“土尔扈特”，这个词后来成为克烈部的新名字。此后，骁勇善战的土尔扈特人作为历代蒙古大汗的亲卫，足迹曾踏遍欧亚大陆。

土尔扈特部后来成为卫拉特蒙古的一支。13世纪后的四百余年里，土尔扈特部逐水草而居，逐渐从叶尼塞河上游一带迁徙至天山、阿尔泰山。17世纪初，卫拉特蒙古因为人口增多，牧场紧缺，土尔扈特部在首领和鄂尔勒克率领下，逐步向西游牧，途经哈萨克大草原，越过乌拉尔河，于1630年左右到达人烟稀少、水草丰美且尚未被俄国控制的伏尔加河下游地区，在此驻牧，建立了土尔扈特汗国。

虽然远离故土，但当喀尔喀和卫拉特各部王公决定于1640年召开一次联合会议时，和鄂尔勒克却义不容辞地带领两个儿子，准时返回塔尔巴哈台参加了这次会议。这是一次不同寻常的蒙古王公会议，会议颁布了《蒙古卫拉特法典》，作为蒙古各部共同遵守的典章制度；会议确立藏传佛教为蒙古各部共同信仰的宗教，并明确蒙古各部对清朝的归顺关系。

17世纪，沙俄向东方扩张，土尔扈特逐渐受到沙俄的侵袭和威胁。就在蒙古王公会议召开后的第三年，土尔扈特部集中所有军事力量与俄罗斯进行了一场大战，却惨遭重创。此后，沙俄对土尔扈特的挤压和侵蚀一步步加强——不断移民以侵占土尔扈特牧场，并向土尔扈特强征兵役，尤其是强迫土尔扈特人改信东正教，这严重地伤害了土尔扈特对藏传佛教的神圣感情……

1768年，沙俄与土耳其爆发第五次战争。两年间，土尔扈特部就为俄罗斯军队提供了八万青壮年兵源。此后，俄国女皇又命令汗王渥巴锡把自己的儿子和五位土尔扈特贵族之子送到彼得堡做人质，还要从土尔扈特中选出一万名新兵加入俄国军队。面对渥巴锡的不满，掌管土尔扈特事务的俄国上校基申斯科夫曾轻蔑地对渥巴锡汗说："你必须明白，你只是一头用链子拴着的熊，赶你到哪里就到哪里，而不能想到哪里就到哪里。"渥巴锡清醒地认识到：土尔扈特部面临着生死存亡的威胁。在经过郑重思考和周密准备后，他做出了重大决定——带领部众回到祖国。

万里东归

东归之路异常悲壮。土尔扈特的战士们经历了三场重要战役，击退了沙俄数万军队的围追堵截，浴血奋战，虽然成功突围，但伤亡惨重。他们扶老携幼，穿过了荒无人烟的戈壁荒滩，战胜了饥饿和严寒，行程近万里，终于在1771年7月初，前锋部队突击到伊犁河流域的察林河畔，与前来相迎的清军成功相遇。随后，东归主力部队及家眷也终于抵达伊犁河畔。此时，出发时的16.8万名土尔扈特人仅剩近七万。

土尔扈特部抵达新疆后，乾隆皇帝立即诏令大臣舒赫德火速赶往新疆，协助伊犁将军办理土尔扈特部安置事宜。在了解东归土尔扈特人的生活困境后，清政府迅速调动国家力量，对历尽艰险归来的土尔扈特进行了全力赈济和妥善安置。短短几个月，清廷从全国各地调集来支援土尔扈特的物资有：马牛羊二十余万头，米麦四万余石，茶两万余封，羊裘五万余件，棉布六万余匹，棉花近六万斤，以及大量毡庐等。

休整未及一月，渥巴锡等首领就在舒赫德陪同下，前往承德避暑山庄朝觐乾隆皇帝。此行历经两月有余，于10月15日抵达热河木兰围场伊绵峪。乾隆皇帝在伊绵峪的行帷里接见了他们，并用蒙古语亲切询问了渥巴锡回归祖国的情况和土尔扈特的历史。到达避暑山庄后，乾隆又分别在万树园和溥仁寺赐宴，此后又多次宴请土尔扈特首领们，每次宴请必对土尔扈特首领们进行赏赐，赏赐名目繁多，对渥巴锡的赏赐尤其隆重。而渥巴锡也向乾隆皇帝进献了礼物："撒袋一副，弓一张，十样景一个，腰刀一把。"其中，腰刀为渥巴锡祖传之物，已经残破，显示出东归之路的艰难。但乾隆皇帝十分欣喜，不仅赋诗一首称赞这件珍贵礼物，还命人修补，后珍藏于乾清宫。

乾隆皇帝十分看重土尔扈特东归的意义，亲自书写《土尔扈特全部归顺记》和《优恤土尔扈特部众记》两文，并刻碑纪念。此后，乾隆皇帝将新疆天山南北的巴音布鲁克、乌苏、科布多等地赐予土尔扈特部，供其生活。

土尔扈特人的东归壮举，显示出他们对统一多民族国家的深刻认同，以及各民族日益强化的“祖国意识”。回归祖国后，土尔扈特部和当地各族人民一起内勤耕牧、外御强敌，为开发和稳定我国西北边疆、维护和巩固国家统一、促进民族团结做出了重大贡献。

Torgut originated from one of the four tribes of the Oirats. In the early 17th century, the population boom aggravated the shortage of pasture, and the Torgut tribe had to roam westward. During the 1630s, the tribe moved to the lower reaches of the Volga River via the Kazakh steppe and the Ural River, which had less population and lusher pasture. In the 17th century, while expanding eastward, Tsarist Russia intensified the enslavement and control over the Torgut people, decreased their field, and conscripted them for military service. More seriously, the Torgut people were forced to convert to Eastern Orthodoxy. Wobaxi, who could not bear the rule of Tsarist Russia, decided to lead his armies back to the east and return to their motherland.

The Torgut people broke away from the chase and attack of the Russian cavalry and crossed the Gobi Desert. Having trudged over a long distance, they finally arrived at the Ili River on July 1771. Emperor Qianlong immediately ordered General of Ili to welcome Wobaxi and his people and settle them near Ili. In just a few months, the Qing court quickly mobilized more than 200,000 heads of horses, cattle and sheep, over 40,000 *Dan* (a unit of dry measure for grain) of rice and wheat, over 20,000 bags of tea, over 50,000 pieces of sheep fur coat, over 60,000 pieces of cotton cloth and nearly 30,000 kilograms of cotton, as well as a large amount of daily necessities like yurt, to economically aid Torgut.

On October 15, Emperor Qianlong met Wobaxi and other Torgut leaders at Chengde Mountain Resort. In order to praise and honor Wobaxi for his return, Emperor Qianlong held banquets for him and conferred the title of Zhuoliketu Khan on him. Wobaxi presented tributes to Emperor Qianlong: one bag for containing bows and arrows, one bow, one peep show and one broadsword. The broadsword was handed down from Wobaxi's ancestors. The incompleteness told the difficult journey of its master.

Emperor Qianlong spoke highly of Wobaxi's return. He wrote and inscribed *Records of the Return of the Torgut Tribe* and *Records of the Relief to the Torgut Tribe*. After returning to the motherland, the Torgut people made outstanding contributions in developing northwestern border, consolidating national unity and promoting national solidarity.

乾隆皇帝为什么要组织一支全国性的编绘队伍，历时十年画成《皇清职贡图》？

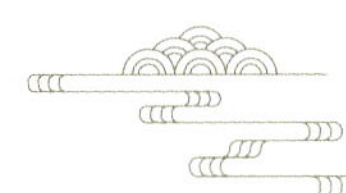

边疆与内地一体性的空前强化

白描本《皇清职贡图》 89

Royal Tribute Pictures of the Qing Dynasty (Line Drawing)

文物简读

由乾隆皇帝亲自主持编绘的《皇清职贡图》，是中国历史上图幅最多、规模最大、涵盖面最广的职贡图，堪称历代官修职贡图的集大成者。它通过展示不同地域的人集合为一个共同体的生动图景，构建出边疆与内地同为一家的大一统中华观，表达出“我们都是中国人”的意识。

历史上规模最大的职贡图

乾隆十六年（1751），乾隆皇帝指示军机处组织编绘《皇清职贡图》。所谓“职贡”，是指我国古代藩属地区或外国对于中央王朝的贡纳制度；职贡图，是为描绘和记录这种贡纳关系而绘制的大型图画。现存最早的职贡图，传说是由南朝梁元帝萧绎所作的《职贡图》。此后历代都有绘制，如唐代有阎立本的《职贡图》、周昉的《蛮夷执贡图》、赵伯驹的《诸夷职贡图》；宋代有李公麟的《万方职贡图》、苏汉臣的《万国朝宗图》、钱选的《西旅贡獒图》；元代有任伯温的《职贡图》；明代有仇英的《职贡图》、陈洪绶的《诸夷职贡图》；等等。但显然，乾隆皇帝着手编绘的职贡图，与历朝历代的都不一样。以往的职贡图都是由某一位著名画家独立完成的，乾隆帝却认为大清的职贡图绝非某一个人能单独承担和完成；他需要组织一支全国性的编绘队伍，有组织、有步骤地来完成这项国家工程。

首先，乾隆谕令各地的总督、巡抚组织当地画家，采集并描绘各地的族群形象，每族男女各一幅；然后由地方官员书写图说，简述族群的分布情况及风俗民情；之后，统一呈送朝廷，由乾隆指派大臣重新修订文字，再由宫廷画师进行统一绘制。

由于规模浩大，这项编绘工程历时十年才得以完成。此后又经四次增绘，至嘉庆时期仍有增补。修撰时间跨度之长，人力物力投入之巨，都令历朝历代的职贡图难望项背。《皇清职贡图》也就成为

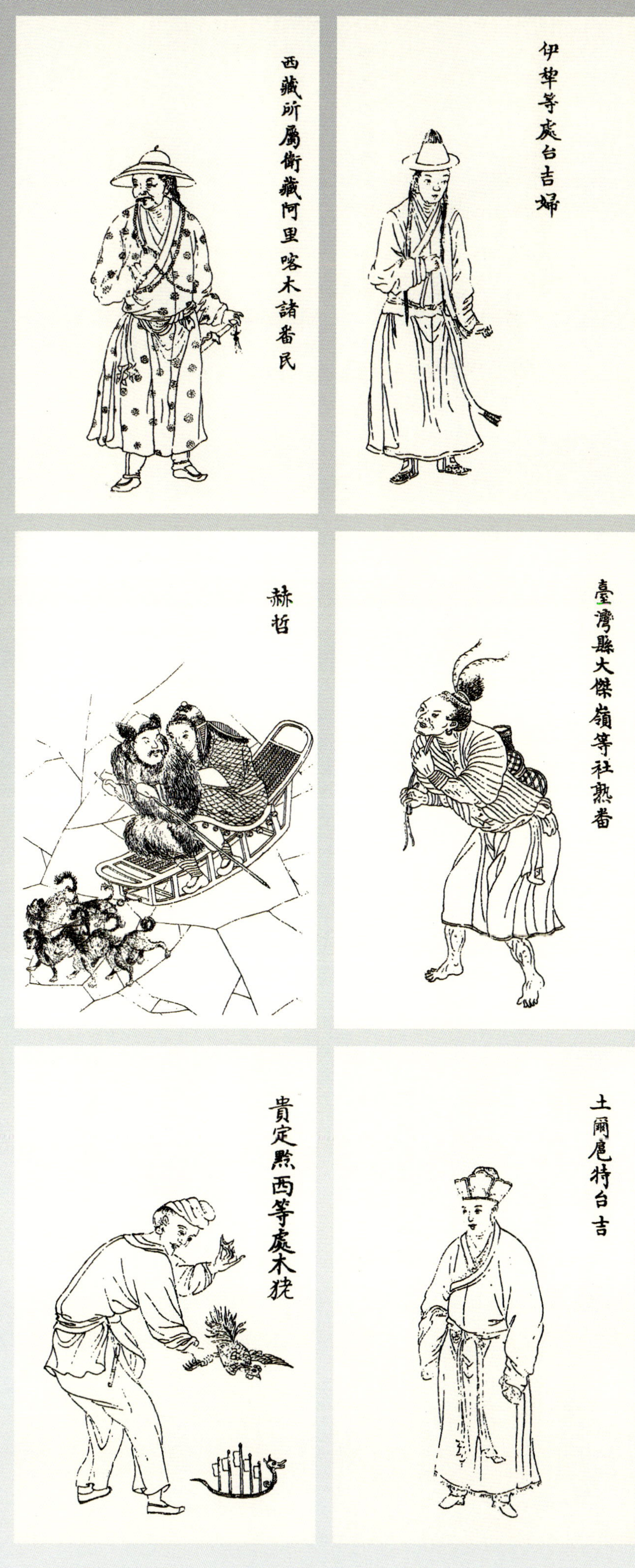

名称：白描本《皇清职贡图》

年代：清乾隆

规格：版框高20.6厘米，宽14.9厘米

收藏单位：故宫博物院

Name: *Royal Tribute Pictures of the Qing Dynasty* (Line Drawing)

Historical Period: In the reign of Emperor Qianlong of the Qing Dynasty

Frame Height: 20.6 cm, Width: 14.9 cm

Housed in: The Palace Museum

中国历史上绘制图幅最多、规模最大、涵盖面最广、影响最为深远的职贡图，堪称历代官修职贡图的集大成者，成为古代大一统的多民族国家走向极盛的历史见证。

边疆与内地同为一体的中华观

《皇清职贡图》版本主要分为正本和副本两类。正本为彩绘本，副本既有彩绘本，又有白描本。彩绘本一般都以满汉合璧的画卷形式绘制，而白描本则以汉文的书籍形式绘制。

《皇清职贡图》绘录了清代中国境内的主要少数族群三百余种。彩绘本图像上方是满汉合璧的文字题记，记述了该族群与中央王朝的关系及其风土民情；从文字题记看，清王朝对边疆族群的了解更为深入，名称较少使用歧视性的字眼；所绘族群图像绝大部分人物相貌端庄稳重，服饰得体，表明了《皇清职贡图》所承载的极力构建“中华一家”的共同体的意识。

乾隆还在一些具有特殊意义的族群图画上，亲自题诗作序、书写卷额。例如对历经千辛万苦东归的土尔扈特人，他不仅做出了须详细绘制其台吉、宰桑、民人，男女共六幅图像的特别指示，而且亲自题写了土尔扈特东归的说明。

乾隆曾为《皇清职贡图》御题一诗：

累洽重熙四海春，皇清职贡万方均。书文车轨谁能外，方趾圆颅莫不亲。
那许防风仍后至，早闻干吕已成宾。涂山玉帛千秋述，商室共球百禄臻。
讵是索疆恢此日，亦惟谟烈赖前人。唐家右相堪依例，画院名流命写真。
西鲽东鹣觐王会，南蛮北狄秉元辰。丹青非为夸声教，保泰承庥慎拊循。

这首诗清晰地表明了《皇清职贡图》的编纂目的，那就是要彰显清朝开疆拓土所实现的前无古人的“大一统”盛世。事实上，清朝对中华“大一统”的贡献尤为突出，因为它奠定了近代中国的疆域，正如雍正皇帝所说：“中国之一统始于秦，塞外之一统始于元，而极盛于我朝，自古中外一家，幅员极广，未有如我朝者也。”对于“大一统”在清朝所达至的极盛，清朝统治者有着清晰的认识与强烈的自信。《皇清职贡图》显然就是这种自信的表现。

《皇清职贡图》还承载着一个更重要的编纂动机和指导思想，那就是要通过这样一次浩大的族群图像集结，来集中展示不同地域的人集合为一个共同体的生动图景，从而构建出边疆与内地互为一家的大一统中华观，表达内地与边疆政治的一体性，即“我们都是中国人”的意识。

对中华道统的秉承

《皇清职贡图》的编纂体例还显示出清朝所持有的大一统天下秩序观以及越来越清晰的“中国意识”。

《皇清职贡图》第一卷为域外诸国，主要有朝鲜、琉球、安南（即越南，1803年由嘉庆帝赐名“越南”）、英吉利、法兰西等；第二卷为西藏、新疆地区；第三、四卷分别为关东、闽台、两湖和两广；第五卷至第八卷为甘、川、黔、滇四地；卷九为续图，收录该书编纂完毕后的新归附者。这一体例清楚地显示出乾隆皇帝的“中国意识”：朝鲜、琉球、安南为域外藩邦朝贡国，可与法兰西、英吉利相提并论，并将之称为“域外”，而新疆、西藏则是中国领土不可分割的一部分，与清王朝的核心统治区域在地位上并驾齐驱。书中每当提及藩属国或欧洲诸国时，均以“中国”自称清朝，如提及意大利：“万历中，西洋人利玛窦航海来中国，自称意大里亚国人，本朝康熙六年通朝贡。”而提及传统藩属国安南：“安南，古交趾地，唐以前皆隶属中国。”

此外，《皇清职贡图》在涉及中国境内的少数族群时，皆用“本朝”“国朝”“我朝”自称，这又表明了清朝对于历代王朝政权的承继关系。满族统治者以边疆民族入主中原，但他们自认秉承中国道统，以此来彰显自己所建立王朝的合法性，这一观念也清晰地体现在《皇清职贡图》中。

In the 16th year of his reign (1751), Emperor Qianlong instructed the Grand Council of State to organize the compilation of *Royal Tribute Pictures of the Qing Dynasty*. *Zhi Gong Tu* (《职贡图》), or *Royal Tribute Pictures*, presented or recorded the tribute system in ancient China, in which vassal states and foreign countries paid tributes to the feudal courts. The earliest *Royal Tribute Pictures* was said to be created by Xiao Yi, Emperor Yuandi of the Liang Dynasty in the Southern Dynasties. Many famous painters, such as Yan Liben, Zhou Fang, Li Gonglin and Qiu Ying, were ordered to independently paint *Royal Tribute Pictures*. *Royal Tribute Pictures of the Qing Dynasty* was out of the common run. To Emperor Qianlong, however, as *Royal Tribute Pictures of the Qing Dynasty* was above a painter's bend, a national editing & drawing team would be organized to advance the imperial project in steps.

Royal Tribute Pictures of the Qing Dynasty meant an Olympian task and took more than ten years to complete or supplement, until the reign of Emperor Jiaqing, with the most pictures, the largest scale and the greatest impact in Chinese history. As the most complete imperial *Royal Tribute Pictures*, it saw the zenith of a unified multi-ethnic country. *Royal Tribute Pictures of the Qing Dynasty* collected and depicted more than 300 ethnic groups in the Qing Dynasty. With Manchu-Han inscriptions, it detailed the local customs of various ethnic groups and their relations with the central government. Evidently, the Qing court deepened the understanding of border minorities and avoided the use of discriminatory expressions. Most of the figures were decorously painted and decently dressed, which spotlighted the consciousness of the Chinese nation as a community.

多达180多种，持续创作150年之久的《百苗图》由谁绘制？为何与改土归流有关？

改土归流与边疆生活

《百苗图》

The Pictures of Bai Miao

90

文物简读

《百苗图》展现了清朝实行改土归流后西南民族地区的民俗风情，呈现出中华民族多元一体历史格局进一步巩固时期的地方人文图景。

《百苗图》

如果说《皇清职贡图》是清朝中央政府为彰显“大一统”盛景而组织的国家级编绘工程，那么《百苗图》就是西南边疆的地方官员在辖区内纷纷自主完成的地方性编绘项目。

乾隆皇帝倡导绘制职贡图，在这一风气带动下，西南边疆地区的官吏都争先延请画师绘制辖区内的风物图景，一时间便出现了众多绘本，如《苗疆人物风俗全图》《全苗图》《苗民图》《全黔苗图》等，包含着贵州及其周边地区的苗、彝、布依、壮、侗、仡佬等支系繁多的群体，这些人群被统称为“百苗”，因此这些图录被后世统称为《百苗图》。《百苗图》描绘的边疆族群生活生动、清晰而真切：它将人物放置在一定的自然场景之中，呈现出众多人物共同参与一项生产活动或文化习俗的情景，流露出浓厚的乡土气息。

《百苗图》中的代表作当数由嘉庆初年担任八寨理苗同知的陈浩绘制的《八十二种苗图并说》，它再现了苗、侗、彝、白、仡佬、布依及其众多支系的耕作渔猎、织染服饰、婚丧嫁娶、歌舞饮食、宗教信仰等景观，设色淡雅而又笔力劲健，还在画面空白处以行草字体对所绘人物进行了简练的介绍。

作为手绘本，《百苗图》的数量极其可观，现存《百苗图》有180多种，大多保存于我国、欧洲与美国的一些图书馆与博物馆中，此外还有一些为私人收藏。

名称：《百苗图》

年代：清

Name: *The Pictures of Bai Miao*

Historical Period: The Qing Dynasty

《百苗图》不仅数量众多，绘制时间跨度也很大。《百苗图》最早绘制于雍正末年至乾隆初年，其创作期至少持续了150年之久。而《百苗图》大规模绘制的一个多世纪，正是“改土归流”打破土司制度的地方割据，让边疆民众的生活被外界清晰“看见”的历史时期。

从这个角度看，《百苗图》显示出与“改土归流”这一重大历史事件紧密相关的意义：它既有可能是那些被中央任命的官员们履新时，执于手中，细细观览、揣摩、品味，用以了解辖地民众的“工作手册”；也有可能是在因“改土归流”而更为开放与融通的社会环境里，那些风尘仆仆的官员比以往更深地走进边土之中，更清晰地看见了边风民俗，并将这一切真切地描画出来的结果。

“改土归流”

“改土归流”是指将土司制改为流官制的一项重大制度变革。土司制在明朝达到高峰后，逐渐暴露出若干弊端，如一些土司专横不法，既对境内人民进行经济压迫，又常在土司间争权夺利挑起械斗，更有对朝廷叛服无常的情况发生。正是因此，改土归流的端倪在明初已经出现，清朝雍正年间大规模推行，最终完成于清末。如果从洪武二年（1369）广西太平府改流算起，这一制度变革前后延续长达五百余年。雍正四年（1726），云南巡抚兼云贵总督鄂尔泰上奏建议在西南地区逐步“改土归流”，雍正皇帝肯定了这一提议，先将云南、贵州、广西、四川、湖南、湖北等地的土司管辖地逐步收归中央直接管制，然后在更多地区实施。

“改土归流”政策主要包括：废除土司制度，改设府、厅、州、县，选派有一定任期的流官直接管理政务，对当地民族编立保甲，建立户籍，清查户口，丈量土地，核实赋税。值得注意的是，改土归流仍旧包含着“因俗而治”的治理观念，清朝政府并未在边疆地区实施强制同化政策，如并未强求边远地区少数民族剃发易服等。

作为一场由中央王朝主导的政治变革，“改土归流”实现了中央政府对边疆地方事务的直接管理，促进了边疆与内地的一体化，增强了改流地区民众对统一多民族国家的认同，极大地加强了中央集权，遏制了地方割据势力，是统一多民族国家进一步走向巩固的重要政策。“改土归流”后，土民按地亩向国家纳税，所受剥削比以往有所减轻，从而促进了地方生产力的解放。“改土归流”还通过中央政府直接对边疆地区的治理，破除了民族交往交流交融的制度性障碍，促使大量汉族向西南地区迁移——从康熙末年到嘉庆末年的一百年间，广西人口由一百余万增加到七百余万，云南人口由九十余万增至四百余万，客观上推动了西南地区的民族交融和社会发展进步。

Emperor Qianlong sponsored the drawing of *Royal Tribute Pictures*. Under such social background, officials in the southwestern regions enthusiastically invited painters to picture local customs, and a great quantity of picture books appeared, such as *The Complete Pictures of the Miao People and Their Customs*, *The Complete Pictures of the Miao People*, *The Pictures of the Miao People* and *The Complete Pictures of the Miao People in Guizhou*. These works focused on a wide range of ethnic groups, e.g. Miao, Yi, Buyi, Zhuang, Dong and Gelao, collectively referred to as *Bai Miao*. Accordingly, these pictures books were called *Pictures of Bai Miao*.

Among more than 180 types of *Pictures of Bai Miao*, the representative work was *82 Pictures of the Miao and Other Nationalities with Textual Comments*, drawn by Chen Hao, who served as vice prefectural administrator of Bazhai (present-day Danzhai, Guizhou), in charge of ethnic affairs, in the early reign of Emperor Jiaqing. It provided a panoramic view of Miao, Dong, Yi, Bai, Gelao, Buyi and many other ethnic groups, in terms of their modes of production (farming, fishing or hunting), dressing styles, wedding & funeral customs, songs & dances, dietary habits, religions, etc., with elegant colors and robust strokes. The figures were also briefly introduced in running script in the blank space of the pictures.

The Pictures of Bai Miao testified to the historical trend of "Bureaucratization of Native *Tusi* Officers", a significant institutional reform that transformed the *Tusi* system to the circulating-official system. In the 4th year of Emperor Yongzheng (1726), E'ertai, Governor of Yunnan and Viceroy of Yunnan and Guizhou, proposed to implement "Bureaucratization of Native *Tusi* Officers" in the southwestern region. Emperor Yongzheng approved the proposal, directly appointing officials to govern the *Tusi* possessions in Yunnan, Guizhou, Guangxi, Sichuan, Hunan and Hubei. Specifically, the Qing court abolished the *Tusi* system, established administrative authorities at the prefecture, sub-prefecture and county levels, appointed circulating officials, institutionalized the *Bao-Jia* system (10 families formed into a *jia* and 10 *jias* formed into a *bao*), launched census of population, measured land and checked taxes. Noticeably, the Qing court rejected the Manchu-centered policies and respected ethnic hairstyles and clothes. As a centrally-initiated political reform, "Bureaucratization of Native *Tusi* Officers" augmented centralization of authority, contained separatist regimes and solidified the unified multi-ethnic country.

为什么说编纂《四库全书》体现了清朝统治者对中华文化的深刻认同和自觉传承？

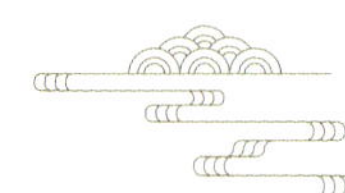

千古巨制，文化渊薮

文津阁《钦定四库全书》

Complete Library of the Four Treasuries at Wenjin Pavilion

91

文物简读

《四库全书》堪称中国古代最大的文化工程，其对中华传统文化进行了一次最系统和最全面的总结，呈现出中国古典文化的完整知识体系；其编纂集中体现了清朝统治者对中华文化的深刻认同和自觉传承。

全世界最大的丛书

盛世修典，这一情景两度出现于康乾盛世。

康熙四十年（1701），康熙帝命皇三子胤祉编纂一部古今文献汇编。胤祉与其侍读陈梦雷花费了28年，广采博集，最终完成了正文一万卷、分为5020册、总计1.6亿字的《古今图书集成》。这部集大成之作涉及天文地理、人伦规范、文史哲学、自然艺术、教育科举、农桑渔牧、医药良方、百家考工等，图文并茂，成为中国历史上规模最大、保存最完整的类书，被称为“类书之最”，同时它也是中国铜活字印刷史上卷帙最浩繁、印制最精美的一部旷世奇作。

《古今图书集成》完成后仅四十多年，乾隆皇帝便决定开启另一项更为宏伟的经典集结工程。乾隆三十七年（1772），以纪晓岚为首的360多名全国学术界精英汇集于京，开始了中国历史上最浩大的文化典籍丛书的编纂工作。

近二十年后，共收录3462种图书，总计79337卷，装订为36315册、230万页，合计9.97亿字的《四库全书》，终于编纂和缮写完成。它分为经、史、子、集四部，故名“四库”，各部总共44类；内容涵盖文、史、哲、理、工、农、医，现代社会的所有人文学科都能从中找到源头。《四库全书》堪称中国古代最大的文化工程，其对中华传统文化进行了一次最系统、最全面的总结，呈现出了中国古典文化的完整知识体系。

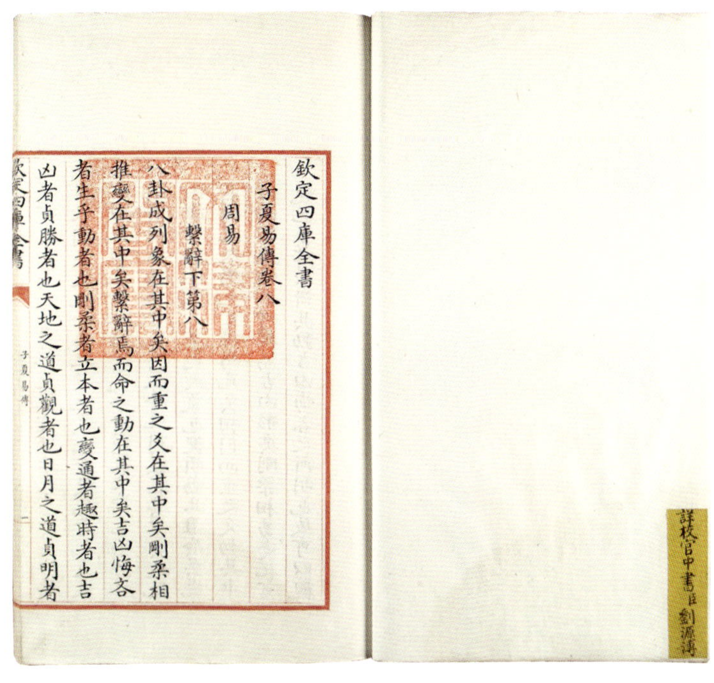

欽定四庫全書

子夏易傳卷八

周易

繫辭下第八

八卦成列象在其中矣因而重之爻在其中矣剛柔相推變在其中矣繫辭焉而命之動在其中矣吉凶悔吝者生乎動者也剛柔者立本者也變通者趣時者也吉凶者貞勝者也天地之道貞觀者也日月之道貞明者

欽定四庫全書

子夏易傳

一

詳校官中書臣劉源溥

名称：文津阁《钦定四库全书》

年代：清乾隆

规格：单册高31.5厘米，宽20厘米

收藏单位：中国国家图书馆

Name: *Complete Library of the Four Treasuries* at Wenjin Pavilion

Historical Period: In the reign of Emperor Qianlong of the Qing Dynasty

Height: 31.5 cm, Width: 20 cm (Each Volume)

Housed in: National Library of China

征书、抄写、装潢、存放

这样一项浩大的文化工程是怎样完成的？

乾隆皇帝成立了《四库全书》馆（简称“四库馆”）。开馆后，第一项工作是征集图书。征书工作历时七年之久，朝廷采取了多种措施以鼓励和表彰进书者，如规定凡进书百种以上者，可择一精醇之本，由乾隆皇帝题咏简端，以示恩宠；凡进书五百种以上者，奖励《古今图书集成》一部。

为了保证《四库全书》的抄写需要，由皇帝“御批监制”，四库馆在全国征集了3800多位文人，担任抄写员。他们用工整的正楷抄书，每天有六百人同时从事抄写工作，每日保证抄写六十余万字。虽然由数千人抄写，但字体风格端庄规范，笔笔不苟，如出一人。

乾隆四十六年（1781）十二月，第一套《四库全书》抄写完毕。在进行装潢时，四库馆的总裁们提出分色装潢的建议，各依春、夏、秋、冬四季，按“经部”绿色、“史部”红色、“子部”月白色、“集部”灰黑色装潢，以便检阅。

首部《四库全书》完成后，抄写员又用了八年时间，抄写了六套。乾隆皇帝仿效著名的藏书楼“天一阁”，在全国各地建造了“南北七阁”，以存放这七套《四库全书》，即紫禁城的文渊阁、沈阳的文溯阁、圆明园的文源阁、承德的文津阁，此之谓“北四阁”；扬州的文汇阁、镇江的文宗阁、杭州的文澜阁，此之谓“南三阁”。

此后，由于战乱烽火，《四库全书》只存三套半，其中文渊阁本现藏于台北故宫博物院；文溯阁本现藏于甘肃省图书馆；文津阁本现藏于中国国家图书馆，这是唯一原架原函原书保存的版本；文澜阁本在太平天国时期一度散失，后经收集和补抄，现藏于浙江省图书馆。

传承中华文脉

被誉为“千古巨制，文化渊薮”的《四库全书》是中国古籍的大总汇，囊括了从先秦到清代乾隆以前中国历史上的主要典籍，它是中华传统文化最丰富、最完备的集大成之作，是举世罕见的文化瑰宝，至今仍保有“世界丛书之最”的桂冠。

《四库全书》的编纂体现了清朝统治者对中华文化的深刻认同和自觉传承，反映了清朝统治者将自身建立的王朝融入中华统序的深层意识。此后，《四库全书》成为中华文明五千多年一脉相承、连绵不断的重要符号象征之一。

值得注意的是，《四库全书》在使中华文脉得以总结性传承的同时，也秉承了“华夷一统”的思想宗旨，因为它致力于保存古代少数民族的语言文化典籍，如《西域同文志》就包含了满文、汉文、蒙古文、藏文、维吾尔文、托忒蒙古文等六种文字的人名、地名对译辞书。在编纂过程中，乾隆谕令规范少数民族语言翻译，下旨取缔诸多歧视性名称，如乾隆要求更正前代史书，特别是辽、金、元三代中有关少数民族人名、地名“沿用鄙字”“颠舛支离”的现象，并将改正后的音译编成《辽金元三史国语解》，作为范本。这也体现了清朝在思想文化上对多元一体的中华民族历史格局的推动与巩固。

In the 37th year of Emperor Qianlong (1772), 361 eminent scholars, with Ji Yun and Lu Xixiong as chief editors, formed the editorial board of *Complete Library of the Four Treasuries*, or *Si Ku Quan Shu* (《四库全书》), the largest collection of books and the most ambitious editorial enterprise in Chinese history. *Complete Library of the Four Treasuries* was divided into four treasuries, 44 categories, in reference to the imperial library divisions, i.e. *Jing* (经, Classics), Chinese classic texts; *Shi* (史, Histories), histories and geographies from Chinese history; *Zi* (子, Masters), philosophy, arts, sciences from Chinese philosophy; and *Ji* (集, Collections), anthologies from Chinese literature, covering all domains of academia. It boasted the largest cultural project in ancient China, providing the most systematic survey of traditional Chinese culture and presenting the complete knowledge system of classical Chinese culture. In December of the 46th year of Emperor Qianlong (1781), scribes completed the first copy of *Complete Library of the Four Treasuries*. As head examiners proposed, the four season-based colors were used to design the four treasuries, green for *Jing*, red for *Shi*, bluish white for *Zi* and grayish black for *Ji*.

Later, scribes spent eight years copying six *Complete Library of the Four Treasuries*. Following the example of the famous library Tianyi Pavilion, Emperor Qianlong constructed seven pavilions across the country to preserve the seven copies of *Complete Library of the Four Treasuries*, i.e. Wenyuan Pavilion in the Forbidden City, Wensu Pavilion in Shenyang, Wenyuan Pavilion in Yuanmingyuan Garden and Wenjin Pavilion in Chengde in the north, and Wenhui Pavilion in Yangzhou, Wenzong Pavilion in Zhenjiang and Wenlan Pavilion in Hangzhou in the south. The copies kept in Zhenjiang and Yangzhou were destroyed during the Taiping Rebellion. During the Second Opium War, an Anglo-French force burned most of the copies kept at Yuanmingyuan Garden. Today, the four remaining copies are kept at National Library of China in Beijing (Wenjin Pavilion Edition), Taipei Palace Museum (Wenyuan Pavilion Edition), Gansu Library in Lanzhou (Wensu Pavilion Edition) and Zhejiang Library in Hangzhou (Wenlan Pavilion Edition).

The compilation of *Complete Library of the Four Treasuries* reflected the Qing emperor's spontaneous recognition and inheritance of traditional culture in the Central Plains and the enthusiasm for legitimizing the Manchu rule.

名称：浅蓝缂丝玉兰蝶纹女衬衣
年代：清
规格：两袖通长154厘米，衣长149厘米，下摆宽116厘米
收藏单位：中国民族博物馆

Name: Light Blue Chemise with Magnolia-Butterfly Pattern Made by *Kesi* Technique
Historical Period: The Qing Dynasty
Total Length (Sleeves): 154 cm, Length (Chemise): 149 cm, Width (Lapel): 116 cm
Housed in: Chinese National Museum of Ethnology

满族“旗女之袍”何以成为中华国粹和中国人的身份标识？

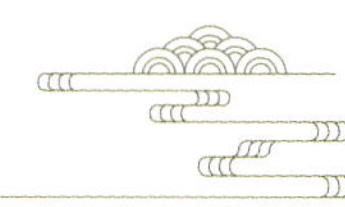

各民族共同创造的中华文化符号

浅蓝缂丝玉兰蝶纹女衬衣

92

Light Blue Chemise with Magnolia-Butterfly Pattern Made by *Kesi* Technique

文物简读

源于满族女性传统服饰的旗袍，逐步发展成为中华国粹和中国人的身份标识，并走向世界，成为代表东方古典美的文化元素，这是各民族共同创造灿烂的中华文化的一个典型代表。

中华国粹

旗袍因能衬托东方女性的身材和气质，彰显温婉、含蓄的体态和曲线，所以成为东方古典美的典型形象。

旗袍来源于何处？

许多研究者认为，旗袍来自满族旗女的袍服。

这件浅蓝缂丝玉兰蝶纹女衬衣，正是清代满族女性袍服的典型形制。它采用了江南珍贵的缂丝工艺，并以最具代表性的中华传统纹饰——玉兰、蝴蝶图案缂绘全身，同时融合了刺绣、镶边、一字疙瘩扣等多种传统工艺，明艳而灵动，婀娜而斑斓，精致而华贵，是民国改良旗袍前的典型代表。

努尔哈赤统一女真各部落并建立后金政权后，推行八旗制度，满族人均在旗，所以他们穿的袍服便被称为“旗装”“旗服”“旗袍”。满族旗袍的形制是圆领、“马蹄袖”（窄袖）、长衣衩、呈宽大状的前后襟、四片裁制。清朝建立后，旗袍被广泛应用于朝堂、祭祀、婚庆等各种场合，成为汉、满、蒙等官民均可穿着的服饰。旗袍便于上下马和射箭活动，体现了满族人早期的生活习惯。满族人逐渐脱离骑射生涯后，还保留了放下马蹄袖的动作。

清朝建立的“大一统”王朝，彻底废弃了长城这道横亘在农牧之间的军事防线，将草原文明与农业文明整合进同一国家秩序之中，开启了民族交往交融更加广阔的地理空间，促使统一多民族国家内部的各民族之间进行更加深入的交流和融合。“满蒙汉一体”的政治实践也成为清朝统治中国三百多年间的政治基石，各民族的交往交流波澜壮阔，高潮迭起。游牧民族的圆领袍服的流行就是这一时期民族文化交融的典型体现。

实际上，清代旗袍本就是数百年来民族融合的产物，其圆领、箭袖等形制与金、元时期一脉相承，其竖领形制又受到明中期立领中衣褙子的影响。历史上，中华服饰有着宽袍大袖、拖裙盛冠、潇洒富丽、纤细柔弱的风格特点，而满族服饰秉承游牧游猎文化特点，形成的衣身修长、衣袖短窄的风格与之形成鲜明对比。清朝建立后，旗装以用料节省、制作简便和穿着方便，影响了中原地区汉人的服饰传统，几千年来飘逸、繁复的衣裙风格为之一变，中华服制迎来了继“胡服骑射”“开放唐装”之后的又一次变革。

此后，随着时代发展，满族传统旗袍再度变革。20世纪30年代，北平、上海等地的汉族女性开展了一场针对女子旗袍的改良运动，缩短衣长，缩小袖口，两边开高衩，腰身紧绷，恰到好处地显示出女性的曲线美，塑造出一个时代的中华女性新形象。40年代，旗袍式样进一步趋向于缩短衣长，降低领口，甚至取消袖子，外形愈发凸显修长秀丽的曲线。此后，随着外来文化的影响，现代旗袍又加入了许多现代设计元素，与西式女装的廓形相吻合，成为代表时尚与潮流的服饰。此时的旗袍已经完全跳出了“旗女之袍”的旧制，成为中西合璧的新服式。

如今的旗袍虽然与清朝时期的“旗女之袍”迥然相异，但它却是在满族旗袍基础之上发展演变而来的，可以说没有满式旗袍就没有现代旗袍。

旗袍演变所蕴含的历史真理

20世纪30年代是旗袍的黄金时代。民国十八年（1929）颁布的《服制条例》，将传统袄裙与旗袍定为女子礼服，旗袍一举成为国服。当著名的女性政治人物、电影明星将旗袍的形象带向国际舞台，旗袍成为极具象征意义的中华文化符号。

21世纪，旗袍的黄金时代已经过去，但中华女性仍对旗袍怀有一种浓厚的情结。当全球化时代来临，旗袍成为中华民族在当今世界强化自我身份形象的一个重要文化符号。此外，旗袍又化作一种独特的设计元素，为世界时尚服饰设计带来源源不断的灵感。旗袍之美不仅属于东方，也属于全世界。

从“旗女之袍”到中华共同文化符号，旗袍的发展轨迹显示出各民族文化互鉴融通的活力机制，显示出中华文化美美与共的发展逻辑，深刻地揭示了“辉煌灿烂的中华文化是各民族共同创造的”这一历史真理。

Cheongsam epitomizes the classic beauty of Chinese women. Many scholars believe that cheongsam sprang from the robes of the Manchu women in the Eight Banners. As a typical form of the clothing of the Manchu women in the Qing Dynasty, the light blue chemise was made by *Kesi* technique (缂丝, Chinese silk tapestry woven in a pictorial design) in Jiangnan, decorated with traditional Chinese patterns magnolia and butterfly. Besides, it integrated various traditional techniques such as embroidery, edge piping and single-thread knot. With bright color and exquisite design, the light blue chemise bred cheongsam in the Republic of China.

After Nurhachi unified the Jurchen tribes and established the Later Jin Regime, he introduced the Eight Banners (*Ba Qi*, 八旗) system, which covered all the Manchu people. Their clothes were called *Qi* attire, *Qi* dress or *Qi* robe, with round neck, narrow sleeves (horseshoe-shaped sleeves), long slit, wide front & back lapels and four-side tailoring. Convenient for equitation and archery, *Qi Pao* tallied with the habits of the Manchu people. In the Qing Dynasty, the Manchu people wore *Qi Pao* on various occasions such as court, sacrifice and wedding. Gradually, Han and Mongolian officials or civilians also wore *Qi Pao*.

In fact, *Qi Pao* was the product of ethnic integration for hundreds of years. Its round neck and arrow-shaped sleeves inherited the Jin and Yuan styles, and its stand collar absorbed sleeved over-dress in the middle Ming Dynasty. Historically, the Han-style dress featured wide robe & large sleeves and *Ru* skirt & high crown, looking gorgeous and delicate. In contrast, the Manchu-style dress embodied the nomadic color, with short and narrow sleeves. In the Qing Dynasty, *Qi Pao* had an impact on the Han-style dress. The elegant and complex Han dress became simple and easy to wear. This meant a dressing reform after the Hu dress and the Tang dress.

Chapter Three

The Chinese Nation: From Self-Being to Self-Making

In the mid and late 19th century, the Chinese people took upon themselves the historic mission of national salvation, jointly resisting imperialist invasion and safeguarding national unity and territorial integrity. The Chinese nation evolved from the self-being stage to the self-making stage.

After the Opium War of 1840, Western powers came to act with impunity on Chinese lands. Gradually, China was reduced to a semi-colonial and semi-feudal society. With the country humiliated, the Chinese people were subjected to great pain, and Chinese civilization was plunged into darkness. The Chinese people and nation suffered greater ravages than ever before. This aroused the sense of the Chinese nation among all ethnic groups. In the struggle against foreign aggression, all ethnic groups shared weal and woe and honor and disgrace, and strengthened the recognition and consciousness of the Chinese nation as a community with a shared future.

In modern Chinese history, as imperialists became the common enemy of the Chinese nation, the idea of motherland penetrated deeply into the hearts of various ethnic groups, and the scope of patriotism extended from the Han people to the whole Chinese nation. The sense of the Chinese nation was augmented, with the entity of Chinese nation evolving from the self-being stage to the self-making stage.

第三章

中华民族自觉实体的形成

历史进入近代。在共同抵御帝国主义发动的侵略战争时，在共同维护国家统一与领土完整的伟大救亡运动中，中华民族走向了从自发到自觉联合的历史阶段。

1840年鸦片战争爆发后，英、法、俄、美、日等外国列强不断发动侵华战争，掠夺和凌辱中国人民，中华民族遭受了前所未有的劫难。在国家蒙辱、人民蒙难、文明蒙尘的空前危机中，中华各民族的共同民族意识不断觉醒；在休戚与共、兴亡一体的反外来侵略斗争中，各民族不断强化着对中华民族命运共同体的体认和自觉。

此一时期，帝国主义成为中华民族的共同敌人，边疆各民族的祖国观念越来越清晰和明确，中华民族从自在的古典爱国主义向着具有高度自觉精神的爱国主义发展。中华民族的整体意识日益坚固和强化，中华民族由自在的民族实体逐渐走向自觉的民族实体。

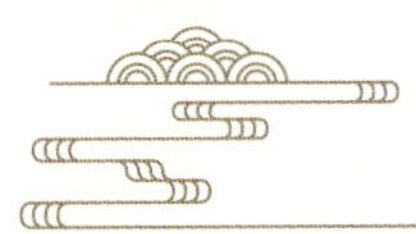

中华民族共同意识的觉醒

The Consciousness of the Chinese Nation as a Community with a Shared Future

从鸦片战争到辛亥革命前，中华各民族共同粉碎了帝国主义的侵略与分裂图谋，共同保卫了国家的统一与疆域的完整，在最艰难的条件下孕育和激发了中华民族自觉意识。

这一时期，民主革命的先驱和各民族的仁人志士在努力探索古代中国转化为现代中国的道路时，受到了西方民族主义思潮和民族国家创建经验的影响，经过反复摸索，逐渐确立了具有现代意义的“中华民族”概念，使中华民族自觉意识上升到了理性高度。

梁启超是第一个提出“中华民族”概念的人。他认为，如果中国要在列强侵夺中不亡而自主，“势不得不取帝国政略，合汉、合满、合蒙、合回、合苗、合藏组成一大民族”。他指出：“现今之中华民族自始本非一族，实由多数民族混合而成。”孙中山在创立中华民国的过程中，最终确立了汉、满、蒙、回、藏“五族共和”的建国理念，这使梁启超的理论构想变成了现实的政治实践。

辛亥革命后不久，沙皇俄国策动外蒙古宣布“独立”。此时，哲里木盟10旗王公举行东蒙古王公会议，商讨赞成“五族共和”，拥护民国，反对外蒙古“独立”；而西蒙古王公会议则以西部22部34旗蒙古王公的名义，向全国发出联合通电，庄严声明：“数百年来，汉蒙久成一家”，“我蒙同系中华民族，自宜一体出力，维持民国”。在近代政治文告中，这是第一次由少数民族代表人物共同决议，庄严宣示自身对中华民族的身份认同。

此时，中国共产主义运动先驱李大钊也提出了“新中华民族主义”概念。在1917年发表的《新中华民族主义》一文中，他指出：“吾国历史相沿最久，积亚洲由来之多数民族冶融而成此中华民族。”面对民族存亡之危，他提出要高揭“新中华民族主义之赤帜”，以追求中华民族之复兴。当其时，李大钊以深邃的识见、青春的激情而揭示的“中华民族”概念，正是中华民族由自在实体转变为自觉实体的鲜明标志。

From the Opium War to the Xinhai Revolution, various ethnic groups in China made joint efforts to smash imperialist aggression and separatist scheme, and protect national unity and territorial integrity. Internal turmoil and external threat ignited the consciousness of the Chinese nation.

During this period, the pioneers of the democratic revolution and the people with lofty ideals of all ethnic groups absorbed the thoughts of Western nationalists on the founding of modern nation-state, when they groped for solutions to save the country and the people. By trial and error, they theorized the idea of the Chinese nation in modern sense and honed the consciousness of the Chinese nation in a scientific way.

Liang Qichao firstly proposed the idea of the Chinese nation. In his view, China should adopt Western political system and form one nation of Han, Manchu, Mongolian, Hui, Miao and Tibetan, in order to remain independent in the face of foreign powers. As he observed, the Chinese nation *per se* originally comprises multiple ethnic groups rather than one. After the founding of the Republic of China, Sun Yat-sen implemented the idea of "Five Races under One Union" (e.g. Han, Manchu, Mongolian, Hui and Tibetan), turning Liang Qichao's theoretical idea into political reality.

Shortly after the Xinhai Revolution, Tsarist Russia instigated Outer Mongolia to declare "independence". Under such circumstance, the dukes of ten banners, including the Jirem League, held the Meeting of the Dukes of the Eastern Mongolia, in which they proclaimed their support of "Five Races under One Union" and the Republic of China and opposition to the "independence" of Outer Mongolia. Meanwhile, at the Meeting of the Dukes of the Western Mongolia, Mongolian dukes of 22 tribes and 34 banners issued a joint telegram to the whole country, solemnly declaring that "For hundreds of years, the Han and Mongolia have long been a family" and that "The Mongolian belongs to the Chinese nation, and all ethnic groups should unite in a concerted effort to protect the Republic of China". In modern China, the political proclamation was firstly drafted by the representatives of ethnic minorities, officially declaring their identity of the Chinese nation.

Li Dazhao, the pioneer of the communist movement in China, proposed the idea of "New Chinese Nationalism". In the article "New Chinese Nationalism" published in 1917, he stated that: "Our country has the longest history, in which the Chinese nation took shape via the fusion of the majority of ethnic groups in Asia." At the critical juncture of life and death, he called on to highly raise the "red flag of New Chinese Nationalism" and tenaciously pursue the rejuvenation of the Chinese nation. With profound insight and ebullient mood, Li Dazhao expounded the idea of the Chinese nation, which tallied with the turn of the self-being entity to the self-making entity.

鸦片战争作为中国近代屈辱史的开端，是怎样唤醒中华民族的自觉意识的？

中华民族自觉意识的萌发

虎门铁炮

Iron Cannon at Humen

文物简读

这门饱经沧桑的虎门大炮，见证了1840年英国对中国发动鸦片战争，各民族为救亡图存自觉联合起来，中华民族从自在发展阶段进入自觉实体阶段的历史节点。

西方殖民者敲开中国的大门

19世纪二三十年代，已率先完成工业革命的英国，以大机器工业替代手工工场，生产力迅猛增长。为了给急剧增加的工业产品寻找销路，资产阶级奔走于世界各地，资本主义走上了全球扩张之路。就在英国拓展海外殖民地的路途中，它遭遇了古老的中华文明，这个庞大的东方国家直到康乾时期经济总量仍位居世界第一，并依靠传统的茶叶、瓷器、丝绸等贸易，使自己对英国保持着巨大的贸易顺差。

显然，这是英国资产阶级极不愿看到的局面。为了改变自身在对中国贸易中的不利地位，英国首先采取外交方式，向清政府强力交涉，但未能达到目的。此后，英国采取了卑劣手段，向中国大量走私鸦片，从中获取了惊人的暴利。而中国二百多年来的贸易顺差被逆转，每年白银外流达到六百万两，引发了严重银荒，以至于财政枯竭、国库空虚，中国人遭受着精神与肉体的双重戕害。

清政府曾屡次颁布禁止鸦片令，但效果甚微。1838年12月，道光皇帝任命林则徐为钦差大臣，前往广东禁烟。林则徐抵达广州后，勒令外国烟贩交出所有鸦片，并承诺“嗣后来船永不敢夹带鸦片，如有带来，一经查出，货尽没官，人即正法，情甘服罪”。1839年6月，林则徐在虎门海滩当众销毁了收缴来的全部鸦片。

“虎门销烟”触动了英国的利益。1840年4月，英国国会以271票对262票通过了对中国发动军事行动的议案。6月，英国舰船从印度出发到达中国广东珠江口，第一次鸦片战争爆发。

名称：虎门铁炮
年代：清道光十五年
规格：通长276厘米，内膛径16厘米，外膛径50厘米
收藏单位：鸦片战争博物馆

Name: Iron Cannon at Humen
Historical Period: The 15th year of Emperor Daoguang of the Qing Dynasty
Total Length: 276 cm, Inner Bore Diameter: 16 cm, Outer Bore Diameter: 50 cm
Housed in: The Opium War Museum

从“神威无敌大将军”铜炮到虎门铁炮

此时，距离康熙时期对沙俄进行的雅克萨自卫还击战已过去一个半世纪。清军在雅克萨战争中，曾凭借“神威无敌大将军”铜炮取得战场优势，但现在，优势早已丧失。清军的虎门铁炮重达六千斤，射程仅过千米；而英军使用的重型加农炮，最大射程可达4500米。在射速上，清军发射一发炮弹需要六分钟，而英军火炮可在两分钟内发射三发炮弹；在弹体上，清军发射的是偏小型的实心铁弹，而英军则大量使用爆炸弹和燃烧弹。

清朝军事力量的落后，缘于此时的清朝已经和世界脱轨。当清朝周边的国家相继沦为西方殖民地的时候，清朝统治者还未意识到西方殖民者来自海上的威胁，仍以天朝上国自居。清朝前期在虎门修造了数量众多的炮台，但长期以来的防卫对象是沿海海盗；受当时炮台修造理念与技术的限制，当鸦片战争爆发时，清朝的统治者无论如何也想象不到，从康熙一直到嘉庆时期所修造的炮台，在西方殖民者的坚船利炮面前是如此不堪一击。

虎门炮台位于广东省东莞市虎门镇，是鸦片战争中爱国将领关天培坚持抗击英军的地点。在虎门战斗中，清军铁炮有的哑火，有的炮膛炸裂，清军只能用肉身抵挡英军的利炮。年过六旬的广东水师提督关天培身先士卒，多次击退英军，终因武器落后，只能眼看着英军登陆炮台，与敌人进行惨烈肉搏。关老将军直到牺牲，双目不闭，双手拄刀，怒视敌人，巍然屹立。这悲壮的一幕永远烙印在中国近代史的开端之处。

中华民族自觉意识的觉醒

鸦片战争带来了中华历史上“三千年未有之巨变”。清朝与英国签订了中国近代史上第一个不平等条约——《南京条约》。

而这只是一个开始。此后，在短短六十年间，中国经历了第二次鸦片战争、中法战争、中日甲午战争、八国联军侵华战争等，遭受了一次又一次的挫败，签订了《天津条约》《北京条约》《马关条约》《辛丑条约》等一系列丧权辱国的条约、契

约、协约、合约共一千多件，不断地向帝国主义割地、赔款，中国一步步沦为半殖民地半封建社会，陷入深重的苦难。

鸦片战争终结了中国的古代历史，标志着中国近代史的开端。在历史的另一面，鸦片战争是中华民族的巨大不幸，也是中华历史的一个重要转折点，这就是中华民族自觉意识的猛醒，它开启了中华民族从自在的民族实体向自觉的民族共同体转变的伟大历程。

鸦片战争的失败深深地震撼了中国人的心灵，它激发了民族危机意识，揭开了近代中国反抗外来侵略的历史篇章，中华民族面临着争取独立与解放的曲折斗争。正是在共同反抗外来侵略的斗争中，各族人民逐渐凝聚成休戚与共、荣辱与共、生死与共、命运与共的共同体，走向了自觉的联合。

Located at Humen Town, Dongguan City, Guangdong Province, the Humen Battery saw how Guan Tianpei, a patriotic general, unremittingly resisted the British army during the Opium War. In the Battle of Humen, the Qing army's iron cannons misfired or had their bores broken. Therefore, the Qing troops had to withstand the British powerful weaponry with their bodies. Guan Tianpei, the 60-year-old commander of Guangdong Navy, led from the front and repelled the British attacks. Nonetheless, as the Qing troops used outdated weapons, the British army finally occupied the battery. Guan Tianpei stood firmly when he died, with glaring eyes at enemies and hands leaning on swords. This tragic scene was forever imprinted on the memory of the Chinese nation.

The Opium War brought about "radical changes that never occurred in three thousand years". The Qing government was forced to sign with the UK *The Treaty of Nanking*, the first unequal treaty in modern Chinese history. Since then, in just 60 years, China underwent the Second Opium War, the Sino-French War, the Sino-Japanese War of 1894-1895 and the Eight-Power Allied Forces Invasion, and admitted defeat in these wars. As a consequence, the Qing government was compelled to sign a series of treaties that humiliated the country and forfeited the sovereignty, such as *The Treaty of Tientsin*, *The Treaty of Beijing*, *The Treaty of Shimonoseki* and *The Boxer Protocol*. As the Qing government constantly ceded lands and paid reparations to imperialist powers, China was eventually reduced to a semi-colonial, semi-feudal state where the Chinese people were enslaved and suffered immeasurably.

The Opium War marked the beginning of a historical chapter for China. It meant a catastrophe to the Chinese nation and represented a milestone in Chinese history. China's military defeat in the Opium War led to the weakening of the Chinese dynastic system and paved the way for uprisings, ushering in the new era of over-100-year struggle for national independence and liberation. More importantly, people of all ethnic groups were bound together in a common cause. They spontaneously united and forged a community in the struggle against foreign aggression.

三元里抗英斗争后，中国民间为什么开始流传“百姓怕官，官怕洋人，洋人怕百姓”的谚语？

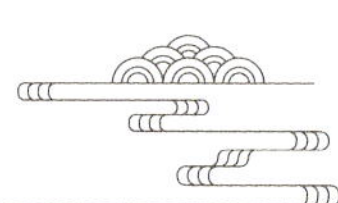

中国人民自发反抗外来侵略的斗争

三元里讨英三星令旗

Three-Star Command Flag in the Sanyuanli People's Anti-British Struggle

文物简读

这面已经破损的三元里讨英三星令旗，见证了近代以来中国人民第一次自发自觉地抵抗帝国主义侵略的斗争，承载着中华民族面对帝国主义时展现的不畏强暴、英勇抗争的民族精神和民族自觉意识。

三元里抗英

鸦片战争前夕，林则徐到达广东后就颁发告示：“本大臣等兹通谕沿海乡村父老绅商居民知悉，仰即遵示会商，购置兵器枪炮，招集村民之身强力壮者，以备自卫。”虎门防线全线失守后，英军溯珠江而上直逼广州，炮击广州城。1.8万多名清军尽退城内，秩序大乱，竖起白旗向英军求和。此后，广州知府与英国代表签订了休战协议，即《广州和约》，约定：外省军队从广州城后撤六十英里（约96公里）；七天内向英军缴纳“赎城费”六百万元；赔偿英国商馆和西班牙帆船“米巴音奴”号；等等。

但《广州和约》墨迹未干，英军就不断窜扰西北郊三元里及泥城、西村、萧冈等村庄，抢掠烧杀，奸淫妇女。广大民众义愤填膺，各地团练共图抵抗。

1841年5月29日，盘踞广州城北四方炮台的小股英军窜到三元里抢掠并调戏妇女，杀人放火，盗坟掘墓，搜劫陪葬品，激起乡民们的奋起反抗，打死了英军数名。为防英军报复，地方士绅开始组织乡民齐心御敌。举人何玉成邀请附近乡代表会聚三元里村东的牛栏岗，议定诱敌围歼之策，以三星旗为令旗，“旗进人进，旗退人退，打死无怨”。三元里附近群众闻讯后“义愤同赴”，组成一支反侵略的武装力量，拉开了民间武力反抗侵略者的序幕。

名称：三元里讨英三星令旗
年代：1841年
收藏单位：中国国家博物馆

Name: Three-Star Command Flag in the Sanyuanli People's Anti-British Struggle
Historical Period: 1841
Housed in: National Museum of China

5月30日晨，四方炮台的英军司令卧乌古带着一千余名官兵下山追捕诱敌的乡民队伍，遭到了埋伏在牛栏岗的上万群众的猛烈攻击。此时恰逢大雨倾盆，英军枪炮皆哑，虽然民众们手持的是鸟枪、刀、矛、锄头，但大家乘势猛攻，人数越聚越多。经一天激战，打死、打伤英军两百多人。英军增援部队到达后，才解救了被围困的英军，狼狈逃回四方炮台。

31日，番禺、南海等县数万人又与三元里乡民一起包围四方炮台，英军不得不通过外交手段向靖逆将军奕山施加压力。广州知府下令乡绅领袖要遵守《广州和约》的停战协定，强迫群众解散队伍，英军才得以解围。

洋人为何怕百姓?

三元里抗英是鸦片战争期间广州民众抗击英国侵略者的重大事件，是一次各阶层爱国群众的联合斗争。这是近代中国人民自发反抗外来侵略的第一枪，表现出中华民族不甘屈服于帝国主义欺凌和压迫的顽强抗争精神。三元里抗英的结果虽然无法改变英军继续肆虐中国沿海、国家落败的结局，但它拉开了全民族反侵略斗争的序幕。

一些历史研究者认为，英军向清朝开战之初，广州民众多是持观望态度的，但是随着英军攻城以来，民众由冷漠、恐惧到反抗，由保卫家园的本能抗争到反侵略自觉意识的觉醒和发扬，斗争水平渐次提高。这表明长期蕴含于中华民族自在实体发展历程中的家国观念，在面对外来侵略时开始逐渐上升为中华民族的整体自觉意识。三元里抗英斗争期间，乡绅们发布了一张对英国侵略者的“晓谕”，其中宣称：“我虽乡愚小民，乃亦天朝赤子。惜身家亦惜土地，终怀父母之邦……”抗英组织者何玉成在他的一首诗中写道：“下以保家室，上以纾国忧。”无论是“天朝赤子”“父母之邦”的深情表达，还是“纾国忧”的忧患意识，都是民众已初具民族主义观念的体现，反映了鸦片战争后一系列的外来侵略与民族危亡境遇，深化了民众的国家认同与团结意识。

三元里斗争后，中国民间开始流传“百姓怕官，官怕洋人，洋人怕百姓”的谚语。这正是鸦片战争激发中国人民自觉形成凝聚力的表现，正因为一荣俱荣、一损俱损的命运共同体情感意识，将民众凝聚起来，才形成了“洋人怕百姓”的局面。三元里抗英所生发的精神对中国近代历史具有深远影响：它树立起了中华民族抵御西方列强侵略的一面旗帜；它是中国人民反帝斗争的光辉前导，激励着中华民族在民族危难时刻坚决反对帝国主义的坚强意志和胜利信心；它显示出中华民族开始凝聚为一个自觉的命运共同体，走上一条不屈不挠的反抗帝国主义的斗争之路，一直到迎来中华民族的独立与解放。

After capturing Humen, the British fleet arrived at the Pearl River and then attacked Guangzhou. More than 18,000 Qing troops withdrew from the city, causing chaos and raising white flags to seek peace with the British army. The Governor of Guangzhou was forced to sign a ceasefire agreement with the British representative, known as *Guangzhou Peace Treaty*. Shortly afterwards, however, the British troops continuously harassed Sanyuanli, Nicheng, Xicun and Xiaogang in northwest suburbs of Guangzhou.

On May 29, 1841, a handful of British troops stationed at the Sifang Battery in the north of Guangzhou fled to Sanyuanli. They raped and looted and committed murder and arson. This sparked resistance from the villagers who killed several British soldiers. To guard against the British retaliation, local gentry organized villagers to unite and combat enemies. He Yucheng, a man with the title of *Juren* (举人), invited representatives from nearby townships to gather at Niulangang in the east of Sanyuanli Village, to discuss the strategy of enticing the enemies to encircle and annihilate them. They agreed to use the three-star command flag. Upon hearing the news, the people near Sanyuanli shared bitter hatred against the enemy and formed an armed force.

On the morning of May 30, Hugh Gough, British commander at the Sifang Battery, led more than 1,000 soldiers to chase after Chinese forces. They were fiercely attacked by tens of thousands of civilians lying in ambush at Niulangang. The heavy rain resulted in dumb fire of British guns and cannons. Using shotguns, broadswords, spears and hoes, Sanyuanli people launched onslaught on the enemies, killing or injuring more than 200 British soldiers. With the help of British reinforcements, Hugh Gough fled helter-skelter to the Sifang Battery. On May 31, tens of thousands of people from Panyu and Nanhai, along with the villagers of Sanyuanli, besieged the Sifang Battery. The British army exerted pressure on Yishan, General of Jingni, by diplomatic means. The governor of Guangzhou ordered local gentry leaders to abide by the ceasefire agreement of *Guangzhou Peace Treaty*, forcing them to disband the armed groups.

The Sanyuanli People's Anti-British Struggle was a major event in the Opium War. The masses jointly resisted foreign aggression, demonstrating the tenacious spirit of the Chinese nation in revolting against imperialist bullying and oppression.

英国两次侵藏战争取得胜利，为什么没能将西藏变成殖民地？

西藏人民捍卫国家领土完整的英勇壮举

西藏地方政府为抗英有功人员请功名单

95

The List of Meritorious Individuals Who Contributed to the Resistance Against the British Aggression Submitted by Tibetan Local Government

文物简读

这是一件19世纪末西藏军民英勇团结抗击英军侵略的珍贵见证物。它见证了西藏人民捍卫统一多民族国家领土完整的民族自觉；见证了在外来侵略者面前，各民族休戚与共的命运共同体意识被唤醒的历史时刻；见证了坚守统一的中华民族开始由数千年的自在实体向自觉实体转变的历史进程。

雪域高原的悲壮历史

1888年3月，英国发动第一次侵藏战争。英军派遣五百人进攻隆吐山，遭到两百名驻守藏军的抵抗，藏军凭借居高临下的地理优势反击，用火绳枪、弓箭、大刀和石块等武器给英军以重创。英国调集两千名援军和四门重炮支援，迫使藏军退守纳汤。6月，藏军三千人发起对英军的反攻，但惨遭失败；10月，为收复失地，清朝驻藏大臣文硕第三次组织一万藏军，用土枪、弓箭、刀、矛对拥有先进武器的英军发动反攻，再遭溃败。

1903年10月，英国发动第二次侵藏战争，于次年1月占领堆纳。西藏地方政府调集各部藏军及大批民兵分赴前线。英军不敢贸然进攻，提出要进行谈判。3月31日，藏军指挥官拉丁色、朗赛林怀着诚意，前往指定地点与英军代表荣赫鹏等谈判，却不料卑劣的英军已偷偷从三面包围了藏军。荣赫鹏等人与拉丁色、朗赛林见面后声称："既然要议和，为表示诚意，我们先将子弹退出枪膛，你们也必须下令

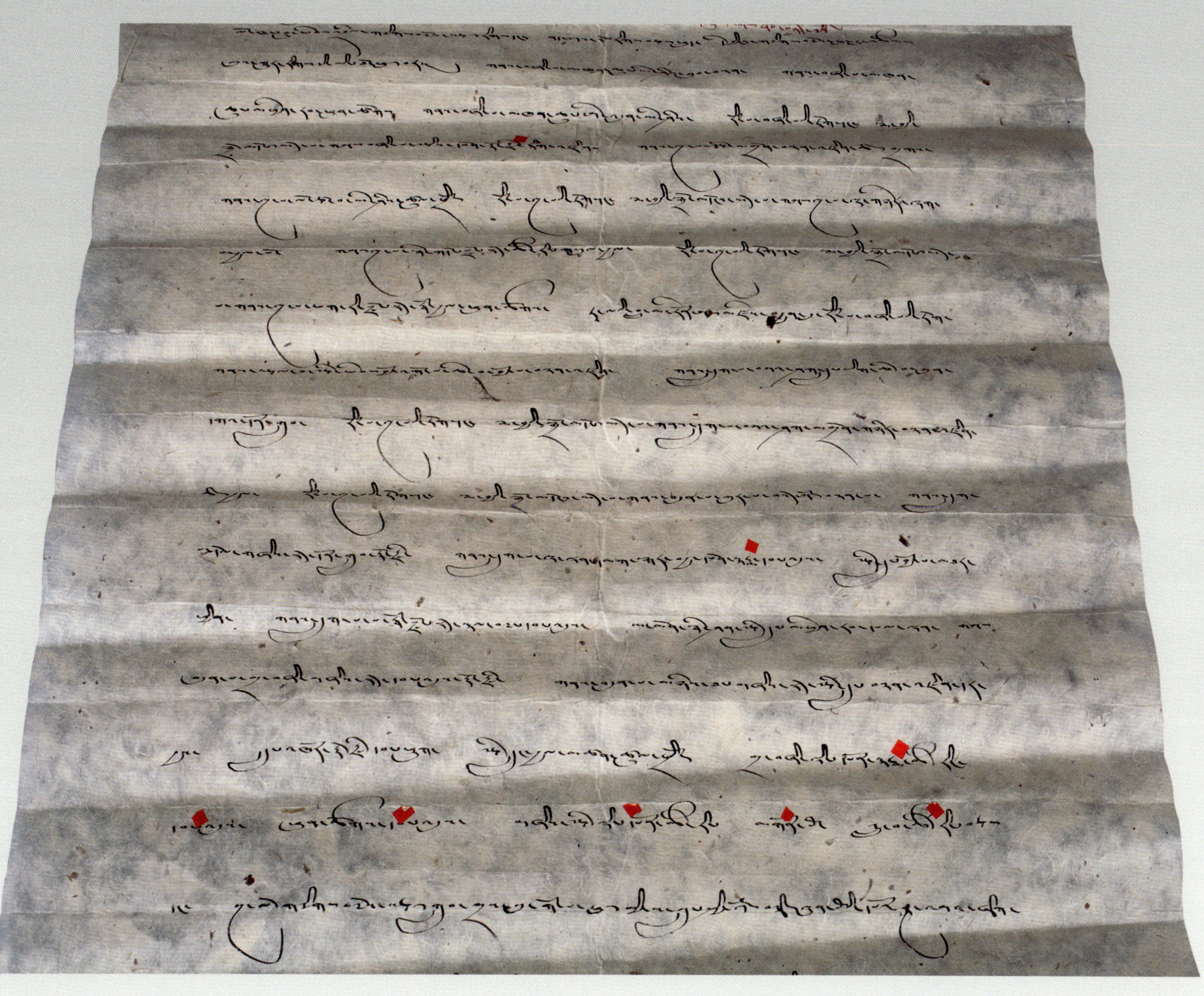

名称：西藏地方政府为抗英有功人员请功名单

年代：清末

收藏单位：西藏博物馆

Name: The List of Meritorious Individuals Who Contributed to the Resistance Against the British Aggression Submitted by Tibetan Local Government

Historical Period: The Late Qing Dynasty

Housed in: Tibet Museum

将火枪的点火绳熄灭！”只见荣赫鹏命令英军士兵把步枪子弹退出一发，但士兵们旋即悄悄推动枪栓，将另一发子弹顶入枪膛。当时藏军不了解步枪的构造，误认为英军的枪膛内已无子弹，便按照议定下令将土枪的点火绳全数熄灭。就在这时，英军指挥官却下令开火，炮火瞬间覆盖了藏军的头顶，但待命的藏军却无法打响火绳枪。在机枪和大炮的密集扫射和轰击中，猝不及防的藏军惨遭残酷的大屠杀，数分钟内即被射杀五百多人，西藏谈判代表数人也被杀害。英军又乘机攻占古鲁，追杀藏军数百人。此役中，一千多名藏军牺牲，仅逃出380余人。藏胞的鲜血一时将曲米香果的泉水浸染成红色。

4月11日，英军进逼江孜。藏军聚集一万多人，准备展开江孜保卫战；西藏噶厦也陆续调集藏军、僧兵、民兵共约1.6万人，增兵江孜方向。6月，英军从南、北方面夹击藏军驻守的乃宁寺，用炮火轰破寺院围墙冲入寺内，藏军与英军展开肉搏。工布地区民兵首领阿达尼玛扎巴兄弟在用刀劈死了英国军官则娜·色赫后，英勇阵亡。英军洗劫了寺内文物，纵火焚毁乃宁寺。

荣赫鹏限令藏军在7月5日撤出江孜，但遭到断然拒绝。7月5日，英军发动对江孜的总攻。这是一场惨烈的保卫战，超过一万军民一起作战，用骑兵肉身面对英军机枪扫射，用土火枪、大刀、弓箭、抛石器与英军作战。在英军密集的炮火之下，古堡之中被炮弹轰炸的藏军像树叶一样纷纷飘落，城内尸体遍布。但即便是这样，藏军仍然坚守了古堡三天，打退了英军的七次进攻。7月7日，英军占领江孜宗山，西藏军民与英军展开肉搏，最后的守军毅然从宗山北侧悬崖纵身跳下，全部身亡。英军此役仅20人阵亡，23人受伤。

后来，荣赫鹏在日记中留下了这样一段关于江孜之战的记录：“不能想象还有什么可以比得上他们个人的勇敢！例如，15名骑黑骡子的战士和四十名步兵，冒着我们暴风雨般的火力，从江孜宗政府猛冲而出，想去救援他们认为是遭遇到强烈压迫的在帕拉的战友们，结果这支援军全部中弹死亡，无一生还。”正是因为这种顽强不息的抗争精神，英国将西藏变为英国殖民地的阴谋未能得逞，最终承认西藏是中国不可分割的一部分。

回看西藏军民抗英史实，有什么可为这场悲壮的战争作证？“西藏地方政府为抗英有功人员请功名单”也许是最珍贵的见证物。它是西藏地方政府致函清政府驻藏大臣，为抗英有功人员请功的珍贵档案，承载着西藏军民用鲜血和生命实践“誓死抵御，绝无二心”之誓言的决心。

中华民族从自在实体向自觉实体的伟大转变

为了分裂和瓦解中国，西方殖民者从边疆地区入手，制造了重重边疆危机——

在广西，法国于1883—1885年发动中法战争，最终胁迫清朝政府签订了丧权辱国的《中法会订越南条约》……

在云南，英国多次武力侵扰片马地区，于1901年12月侵占片马……

在东北，沙俄图谋霸占东三省，将蒙古和华北划为俄国势力范围……

在蒙古，沙俄长期策划外蒙古“独立”，军事强占1400平方公里的土地……

在新疆，沙俄派兵占据伊犁宁远城，又出兵侵入阿尔泰地区，胁迫阿尔泰长官帕勒塔宣布阿尔泰“独立”……

“大一统”的中国沦入山河破碎的境地，但中华历史上贯穿始终的“大一统”信念促使各族人民做出了“维护中华之一体”的历史选择，以共御外侮、共护国土的英勇牺牲，维护了国家统一和领土完整——

在西藏，六世班禅拒绝英人无理要求，明确告知“一切听大皇帝圣旨”；十三世达赖最终立志“不亲英人，不背中央”。

在广西，名将冯子材1885年率领由汉、壮、彝等各族人民组成的边防军，英勇抗击法国侵略军，取得了镇南关大捷。此战是中国近代史上反对外来侵略的战役中难能可贵的一次胜利。

在云南片马地区，傈僳族、景颇族群众对英国侵略军进行了英勇抗争……

在内蒙古，针对沙俄策动外蒙古“独立”，西蒙古王公会议于1913年初在归绥（今呼和浩特）召开，内蒙古西部22部34旗王公一致做出决议：“联合东蒙反对库伦”，反对外蒙古“独立”，反对外蒙古分裂分子分裂蒙古民族。这次会议发出了一份面向全国的通电，声明：“数百年来，汉蒙久成一家”，“我蒙同系中华民族，自宜一体出力，维持民国”。

在外来入侵的共同敌人面前，各民族休戚与共的命运共同体意识被唤醒，维护国家统一的意识促使中华民族步入从自在实体向自觉实体的伟大转变。

The list was a precious document that recorded the report of Tibetan local government to Grand Minister Resident in Tibet on behalf of the Qing court. It tells how the Tibetan soldiers and civilians pledged to fight to the death in defending the Tibetan land.

In March 1888, the British army launched the first-time aggressive war against Tibet, sending 500 troops to attack the Longtu Mountain. 200 Tibetan soldiers garrisoned there counteracted the British enemies bravely. On the strength of geographical advantage, the Tibetan soldiers inflicted heavy casualties on the British army by using firearms, bows, swords and stones.

In October 1903, the British army waged the second-time aggressive war, and occupied Duina in January 1904. Tibetan local government mobilized Tibetan soldiers and militias from various regions, which were dispatched to the front line. The British side proposed to negotiate. On March 31, 1904, Tibetan commanders Ladingse and Langsailin went to the appointed place to negotiate with British representative Francis Younghusband. Unexpectedly, the despicable British army had secretly besieged the Tibetan delegation. Over 1,000 Tibetan soldiers sacrificed their lives in the battle.

On July 5, the British army intensively attacked Gyangzê. The Tibetan soldiers held fast to the old castle for three days and repelled seven times of British attacks. On July 7, the British army occupied the Zongshan Mountain. The Tibetan soldiers and civilians fought at close quarters against the British enemies. The last defenders resolutely jumped off the cliff on the north side of the Zongshan Mountain, and all of them died. It was precisely because of the indomitable spirit that the Tibetans thwarted the British conspiracy to colonize Tibet, compelling the British invaders to ultimately recognize Tibet as an inseparable part of China.

In order to disrupt China, Western colonizers invaded the border areas of China and provoke incidents frequently. Confronted with the grave crisis, China fell apart into pieces. Yet, inspired by the idea of grand unification, people of all ethnic groups died a glorious death, repulsed foreign aggression and safeguarded national unity and territorial integrity.

名称：“五族共和”旗

年代：民国

收藏单位：中国国家博物馆

Name: The Flag of “Five Races under One Union”

Historical Period: The Republic of China

Housed in: National Museum of China

"五族共和"如何保持了中国统一多民族国家的历史延续性?

探求近代多民族国家建构之路

"五族共和"旗

The Flag of "Five Races under One Union"

96

文物简读

这面"五族共和"旗，是中华民国建国之初的法定国旗。旗面五色横条象征着"五族共和"理念，承载着中国近代资产阶级革命家在探求多民族国家建构之路上所做出的政治抉择。

立宪派的思考

近代中国步履蹒跚地迎接着众多严峻挑战，神情仓皇地面对着诸多艰难的社会转型课题。其中，如何选择一条道路，去完成由古代大一统帝制国家向近代多民族国家的转型，是最严峻、最紧迫的一道题目。这是因为，这个题目关系着中华文明是否还能在近代延续其悠久辉煌的传统，关系着中华民族将以怎样的形象和姿态，站在一个正快速完成现代性演变的世界面前。

1902年，梁启超在《论中国学术思想变迁之大势》一书中，首次使用了"中华民族"一词。三年后，他又发表《历史上中国民族之观察》一文，从历史的演变角度专门探讨了中华民族的多元性和混合性："中华民族自始本非一族，实由多数民族混合而成。""中华民族"概念完成了从形式到内容的革命性创造。梁启超提出这个概念具有深刻的内在动因，那就是古老中国的现代转型需要因应西方近代民族国家的"国族"建构说，具体到中国而言，统一国家内部的多民族需要构筑出一个共同身份。

1907年，"中华民族"概念在另一位立宪派代表性政论家杨度的撰述中，得到了呼应性的使用。他在1907年发表的雄文《金铁主义说》中，进一步提出了"五族立宪""五族合一""五族一家"的主张。他认为，从王朝到现代民族国家的转型之路有一个重要问题，即"国民之汉、满、蒙、回、藏五族，但可合五为一，而不可分一为五"。其后，又一位立宪派理论家蒋智由发表《变法后中国立国之大政策论》，进一步推进"五族立宪"思想："于立宪之下，合汉满蒙诸民族皆有政治之权，建设东方一大民族之国家，以谋竞存于全地球列强之间是也。"

从提出“中华民族”概念，到主张“合五族为一”——“五族立宪”思想为此后革命派的“五族共和”纲领准备了阶梯。

革命派的主张

1903年，孙中山提出了“驱除鞑虏，恢复中华，创立民国，平均地权”的政治口号。这个口号把资产阶级革命的矛头直接指向建立清王朝的满族，意在通过当时日益高涨的排满情绪，集聚起民族主义的动员力量，以尽快推翻古老的君主专制，从而完成资产阶级革命的建国任务。但很快，孙中山就意识到了“驱除鞑虏，恢复中华”口号的局限性，认识到以民族主义反对帝制的理论缺陷，以及对维持多民族国家统一性所可能带来的潜在风险等一系列现实问题。就在1906年，孙中山明确指出：“曾听见人说，民族革命，是要尽灭满洲民族，这话大错。”这表明资产阶级革命派已经逐渐转变了简单的驱满、排满情绪。

1912年1月1日，在武昌起义的胜利号角中，中华民国正式成立。孙中山发表《临时大总统宣言书》，提出：“国家之本，在于人民。合汉、满、蒙、回、藏诸地为一国，即合汉、满、蒙、回、藏诸族为一人——是曰民族之统一。”这是关于“五族共和”的正式宣言。1912年9月1日，在北京蒙藏统一政治改良会欢迎会上，孙中山强调说：“今我共和成立，凡属蒙、藏、青海、回疆同胞在昔之受压制于一部者，今皆得为国家主体，皆得为共和国之主人翁，即皆能取得国家参政权……了解共和之真理，与吾内地同胞一致进行，以共享共和之幸福。”

这是一个重大的历史选择。它表明，中国近代资产阶级革命家在探求多民族建国的道路上，终于做出了政治抉择，那就是以“五族共和”来保障中华民国对清朝疆域遗产的完整继承，保持中国统一多民族国家的历史延续性。

历史的选择

1912年2月12日，清帝宣布退位。很快，北京城里遍悬五色旗，这是中华民国的法定国旗，它正式启用于1912年1月10日。旗面上，红、黄、蓝、白、黑的五色横条是对“五族共和”的宣示。中华民国的五色旗升，清政府的黄龙旗落，一个新的历史时代就在易帜之间开启变换。民间很快接受并广泛地使用五色旗，当时的广告、海报上纷纷出现了五色旗。

“五族共和”成为新生的中华民国的标志性政治口号，贯穿于新生政权的各种政治标识之中。现在看来，“五族共和”的提法虽然显得有些简单甚至粗糙，但事实上它却在一个重大的历史关头，对中华民族的整体团结、历史统一起到了重要作用。回头看，当时没有任何一个政治口号像“五族共和”那样被各民族、各阶层普遍接受，它受到了各种政治力量的共同认同。

1912年2月，清帝退位，隆裕太后颁布《退位诏书》，明确宣布：“仍合满、蒙、回、藏、汉五族完全领土为一大中华民国。”这表明在法律上将清朝全部领土交由新成立的中华民国。

1912年4月22日，袁世凯发布就任临时大总统令，宣称：“……蒙、藏、回疆各民族即同为我中华民国国民，自不能如帝政时代，再有藩属名称。”

在充满边疆危机的时代背景中，“五族共和”对濒临分裂的国家局面起到力挽狂澜的作用，稳定了边疆局势：新疆都督杨增新于1912年6月9日电呈大总统议和条件，其中第一款即承诺新疆实行共和；西藏的十三世达赖及九世班禅在经过一段时间后，也先后接纳了“五族共和”……

“五族共和”成为19世纪末至20世纪初中国社会政治领域的核心话语，它表明在从古代帝制大一统国家向近代统一多民族国家转型的关键历史问题上，中华大地上的各种政治力量做出了一个符合中华民族整体利益的政治抉择。这一历史选择深刻地承载着中华文明自身的发展逻辑，体现着中华历史自身发展规律的强大惯性力。

It was the legal national flag of the Republic of China. The five colored stripes symbolized the idea of "Five Races under One Union", which encapsulated the political choice made by bourgeoisie revolutionists in modern China in the cause of building the unified multi-ethnic country.

In 1902, Liang Qichao firstly proposed the term "Chinese nation" in *On the General Trends of the Changes in Chinese Academic Thoughts*. Three years later, he published an article titled "My Views on the Chinese Nation in History", which delved into the diversity and hybridity of the Chinese nation in its historical evolution. In "On Gold and Iron Doctrine", a powerful article published in 1907, Yang Du advanced the constitutionalism, unity and harmony among the five races. Jiang Zhiyou published "On Major Policies of China's Nationhood after the Reform", which further promoted the idea of the constitutionalism among the five races.

On January 1, 1912, the Republic of China was officially founded after the victory of the Wuchang Uprising. In *Inaugural Address of the Provisional President*, Sun Yat-sen said that: "At this I profess to the citizens that the root of the nation lies with the people. The land of the Han, Manchus, Mongols, Hui and Tibetans are one country; and thus, the Han, Manchu, Mongolian, Hui and Tibetan nations are one people." "Since the uprising in Wuhan, ten provinces have declared independence one after another. This so-called independence is, to the Qing court, a separation, but for the provinces, a unification, and this is just as much the case for Mongolia and Tibet. Their actions speak together, and there is certainly no difference of opinion of this matter. The crux of the matter is a triumph over the central government, and its principles are to preserve our boarders. This is a united territory." (Translated by Christopher C. Heselton). This clarified the central tenet of "Five Races under One Union".

On February 12, 1912, Empress Dowager Longyu issued *The Imperial Edict of the Abdication of the Qing Emperor* on behalf of the six-year-old Xuantong Emperor. Soon, the five-colored flag, the legal national flag of the Republic of China, was hung all over Beijing. It was officially used on January 10, 1912. On the flag, the five colored stripes of red, yellow, blue, white and black proclaimed the idea of "Five Races under One Union".

The idea of "Five Races under One Union" played an important role in maintaining national unity in the republican China. It was recognized and accepted by all ethnic groups, social classes and political forces.

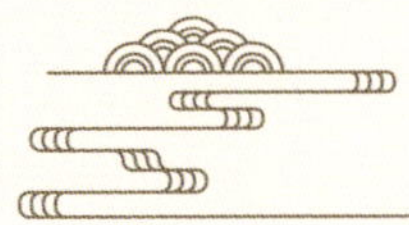

中华民族共同意识的升华

The Sublimation of the Consciousness of the Chinese Nation as a Community with a Shared Future

1937年，抗日战争全面爆发。中华民族到了生死存亡的关键时刻，前所未有的民族危机迫使中华民族的自觉意识空前升华。在外敌面前，中华各民族求同存异，各党派、各阶层、各族群空前地团结起来，结成了更高层次和更大范围的命运共同体。

在中国共产党的倡议和推动下，抗日民族统一战线建立。毛泽东主席指出在此一时期的中国，“帝国主义和中华民族的矛盾，乃是各种矛盾中的最主要的矛盾”。毛泽东主席提出了中国共产党解决中国民族问题的总纲领：“对外求中华民族的彻底解放，对内求中国各民族之间的平等。”此时，在东北、内蒙古、宁夏、甘肃、青海、新疆、云贵、湘西等边疆地区，满、蒙古、朝鲜、鄂伦春、达斡尔、回、维吾尔、苗、佤等民族，奋起加入抗日队伍，涌现出回民支队等抗日组织，一大批英勇顽强的抗日民族英雄血洒战场。

经过14年悲壮的、付出重大牺牲的持久战，中国人民终于取得了抗日战争的伟大胜利，这是近代以来中华民族第一次在反外国侵略斗争中取得完全的胜利，是中华民族获得独立解放的伟大转折。它使中华民族的凝聚力和向心力得到空前增强，并使中华民族成为一个休戚与共、荣辱与共、生死与共、命运与共的共同体。

In 1937, Nationwide War of Resistance Against Japanese Aggression started. The Chinese nation reached a point where its very existence was at stake. The grave national crisis deepened the consciousness of the Chinese nation in an unprecedented way. Confronted with powerful Japanese invaders, all ethnic groups in China sought common ground while reserving differences. All parties, classes and ethnic groups united firmly, forming a community with a shared future at a higher level and in a broader sense.

Proposed and promoted by the Communist Party of China, National United Front Against Japanese Aggression was established. Chairman Mao Zedong went straight to the heart of the matter: "The contradiction between imperialism and the Chinese nation constitutes the most important contradiction among all kinds of contradictions." He designed the general program of the CPC in handling ethnic affairs: "The Communist Party of China pursues the complete liberation of the Chinese nation internationally, and realizes equality among all ethnic groups domestically." In border areas, such as northeastern China, Inner Mongolia, Ningxia, Gansu, Qinghai, Xinjiang, Yunnan, Guizhou and western Hunan, Manchu, Mongolian, Korean, Oroqen, Daur, Hui, Uygur, Miao, Wa and other ethnic groups determinedly joined the war against Japanese aggression. Armed forces were organized, such as Hui People's Detachment. A large number of national heroes laid down their life on the battlefield.

After 14 years of bloody battles, the Chinese people finally defeated the Japanese invaders and obtained the great victory of the War of Resistance Against Japanese Aggression. This signals the first time since the 1840s that the Chinese nation has won a complete victory in the struggle against foreign aggression, and means a significant turn for the Chinese nation to gain independence and liberation, enhancing the unity and cohesion of the Chinese nation, and building it into a community in which the Chinese people share weal and woe, honor and disgrace, and life and death.

抗日民族统一战线如何促成了中华民族从自在实体到自觉实体的真正转变？

中华民族从自在实体到自觉实体的伟大转变

97 毛泽东手迹“巩固统一战线”

Mao Zedong's Original Handwriting of "Consolidating the United Front"

文物简读

这件毛泽东手迹，是中国共产党代表中华民族的根本利益，推动建立抗日民族统一战线的珍贵历史见证；也是抗日战争深刻唤醒中华民族的整体意识，熔铸出一个休戚与共、荣辱与共、生死与共、命运与共的民族共同体的历史见证。

抗日民族统一战线是如何形成的？

1931年9月18日夜，日军策动“九一八事变”，进攻沈阳北大营，进而迅速占领东北；

1932年1月28日，日军策动“一·二八事变”，分三路突袭上海闸北，中日军队第一次全面对抗和较量；

1933年1月1日，日军进犯山海关，把侵略矛头指向了华北；

1935年夏，日军制造“华北事变”，欲策划“华北五省（察哈尔、绥远、河北、山西、山东）自治”，妄图把华北变为第二个伪满洲国……

在日本侵略者步步进逼的威势中，中华民族面临着前所未有的存亡危机。

1935年8月，以挽救民族危亡为己任的中国共产党，向全国公开发表了《为抗日救国告全体同胞书》，呼吁全国各党派、各军队、各界同胞，应有“兄弟阋于墙，外御其侮”的真诚觉悟，不论过去和现在有任何政见和利害不同，都应当集中一切国力去为抗日而奋斗。

名称：毛泽东手迹“巩固统一战线”

年代：1938年

收藏单位：中国人民抗日战争纪念馆

Name: Mao Zedong's Original Handwriting of “Consolidating the United Front”

Historical Period:1938

Housed in: Museum of the War of Chinese People's Resistance Against Japanese Aggression

1936年12月12日，张学良、杨虎城对蒋介石实行“兵谏”，发动“西安事变”。在中共中央和周恩来等人的努力下，“西安事变”和平解决，为抗日民族统一战线的建立准备了必要前提。

1937年2月10日，国民党五届三中全会基本确定了停止内战，实行国共合作的原则，标志着抗日民族统一战线初步形成。

1937年7月7日，“卢沟桥事变”爆发，日本发动了全面侵华战争。就在第二天，中共中央迅即通电全国：“全中国的同胞们！平津危急！华北危急！中华民族危急！只有全民族实行抗战，才是我们的出路！”“全中国同胞、政府与军队，团结起来，筑成民族统一战线的坚固长城，抵抗日寇的侵略！国共两党亲密合作抵抗日寇的新进攻！”

1937年9月22日，国民党中央通讯社发表《中国共产党为公布国共合作宣言》；第二天，蒋介石发表了实际上承认中国共产党合法地位的谈话，宣告中国共产党倡导建立的以国共合作为基础的抗日民族统一战线正式形成。

抗日民族统一战线把抗日战争变成了一场全民族的对外抗争，促成了广泛、彻底的民族意识觉醒。如果说，全面抗战爆发前主要还是青年学生、爱国知识分子和爱国民主人士的民族觉醒，那么到全民族抗战阶段，以抗日民族统一战线建立为标志，中华民族所有成员都被紧紧地联系在了一起，中国人用鲜血和生命表达了这种整体民族意识的觉醒。

全民族抗战与中华民族的空前觉醒

中国国内曾同室操戈的各种政治力量、矛盾对立的各阶级、利益冲突的各阶层、主张差异的各派别，此时前所未有地凝聚在一起。虽然自近代以来中国人民曾频繁面对帝国主义侵略，但却没有哪一个事件像抗日战争那样深刻地唤醒中华民族的整体意识，铸就一个休戚与共、荣辱与共、生死与共、命运与共的民族共同体。在艰苦卓绝的浴血抗争中，“各族人民血流到了一起、心聚在了一起，共同体意识空前增强，中华民族实现了从自在到自觉的伟大转变”。

通过全面抗战，边疆民族更加深刻地熔铸成中华民族不可分割的一部分。1938年4月，藏、蒙古、回等民族组成“联合慰劳抗战将士代表团”，通电全国，宣言：“国内诸民族绝对不可分，惟有团结一致，牺牲奋斗，方可达到保国卫民之目的。”康藏同胞则成立“康藏旅京同乡抗日救国会”，发表《告全国同胞书》，宣言愿“与全国同胞同立一条战线，赴汤蹈火，在所不辞”。日本发动太平洋战争后，云南怒江西岸沦陷，滇西南各民族土司头人以“守土有责”为誓言，纷纷组织抗日武装，英勇抗敌。

费孝通说：“中华民族作为一个自觉的民族实体，是在近百年来中国和西方列强对抗过程中出现的。”抗日战争是近代以来中国历史上最具全民性和最彻底的民族革命战争；抗日战争的长期、艰苦、惨烈、悲壮和前所未有的牺牲，凝聚了全中国各族人民，唤醒了中华民族的整体民族意识，实现了中华民族从自在实体向自觉实体的伟大转变。

The handwriting saw how the Communist Party of China, which represented the fundamental interests of the Chinese nation, promoted the establishment of National United Front Against Japanese Aggression.

Japanese army contrived the September 18th Incident on the night of September 18, 1931 and the January 28 Incident on January 28, 1932. On January 1, 1933, the Japanese army invaded the Shanhaiguan Pass and coveted the northern China. In the summer of 1935, Japan instigated the North China Incidents. The whole country faced the challenge of Japan's aggression and a grave national crisis.

In August 1935, the Communist Party of China took upon itself the historic mission of national salvation, and drafted *An Appeal to All Fellow Countrymen for Resistance Against Japan and for National Salvation*. This document was later publicly promulgated and became commonly known as *The August 1st Declaration*. It called upon all Chinese people to unite and stop the civil war, resist the Japanese, save the nation, establish a national defense government, and organize a united army to fight the Japanese.

After the Xi'an Incident in December 1936, the Communist Party of China quickly agreed to seek a peaceful settlement of the incident and dispatched Zhou Enlai and others to join the negotiations in Xi'an. The peaceful settlement created the conditions for the second KMT-CPC cooperation.

In February 10, 1937, the CPC Central Committee sent a telegram to the Third Plenary Session of the Fifth KMT Central Executive Committee, making five proposals and four pledges as an expression of good faith in removing antagonism between the two parties and building solidarity against Japanese aggression. In September 22, the KMT Central News Agency broadcast *The CPC's Announcement on Kuomintang-Communist Cooperation*, and Chiang Kai-shek's public speech that followed represented *de facto* recognition of the legality of the CPC, marking the formal establishment of an anti-Japanese national united front based on the second KMT-CPC cooperation.

The War of Chinese People's Resistance Against Japanese Aggression was the most nationwide and thorough national revolutionary war in modern Chinese history. The long, arduous, tragic, heroic and unprecedented sacrifices of the war united the people of all ethnic groups in China, awakened national consciousness of the Chinese nation, and achieved the great transformation of the Chinese nation from the self-being entity into the self-making entity.

抗日战争是怎样把中华大地上的不同民族凝聚成一个命运共同体的？

各民族凝聚成一个命运共同体

马本斋指挥刀

The Commanding Sword of Ma Benzhai

98

文物简读

抗日战争时期回民支队司令员马本斋的指挥刀是一件极其珍贵的文物，它见证了被毛泽东赞誉为“百战百胜的回民支队”所进行过的870余次大小战斗和歼敌3.6万余人的赫赫战功，见证了在国家生死存亡的危机之中，中华民族整体意识勃发，凝聚成一个牢固的命运共同体的历史过程。

回民支队

日本帝国主义策动的民族分裂活动，从反面刺激了中华民族的命运共同体意识，促使各民族深刻认识到中华民族的团结统一与救亡图存息息相关，从而使中华民族共同体意识在全民族抗战中实现了升华。

对此，被毛泽东誉为“百战百胜的回民支队”就是一个典型。

回民支队司令员马本斋出身于河北献县的一个回族贫苦农民家庭，17岁就与父亲走西口，曾辗转于内蒙古替人放马，艰辛求生。19岁时，马本斋投身奉军，因为作战勇敢，被选入东北讲武堂学习，凭借过人的胆识和战功，被提拔为团长。其间，他曾受到中共地下党的影响。1932年秋，当部队开往南方“剿共”时，马本斋毅然弃官离职，回归故乡。

全面抗战爆发后，日军侵入河北，烧杀淫掠，无恶不作。马本斋果断地在家乡组织回民抗日义勇队，后改编为回民支队，他担任司令员。在抗日战争中，马本斋体会到了中国共产党的伟大和无私，加入了中国共产党。此后，他率领回民支队驰骋在冀中平原，英勇善战，威名远扬，显示出卓越高超的军事才能。他曾指挥滑营突围、焦花园制敌、大宋庄伏击战、“以饭诱敌”行动、八公桥

名称：马本斋指挥刀
年代：民国
规格：长65.7厘米
收藏单位：河北博物院

Name: The Commanding Sword of Ma Benzhai
Historical Period: The Republic of China
Length: 65.7 cm
Housed in: Hebei Museum

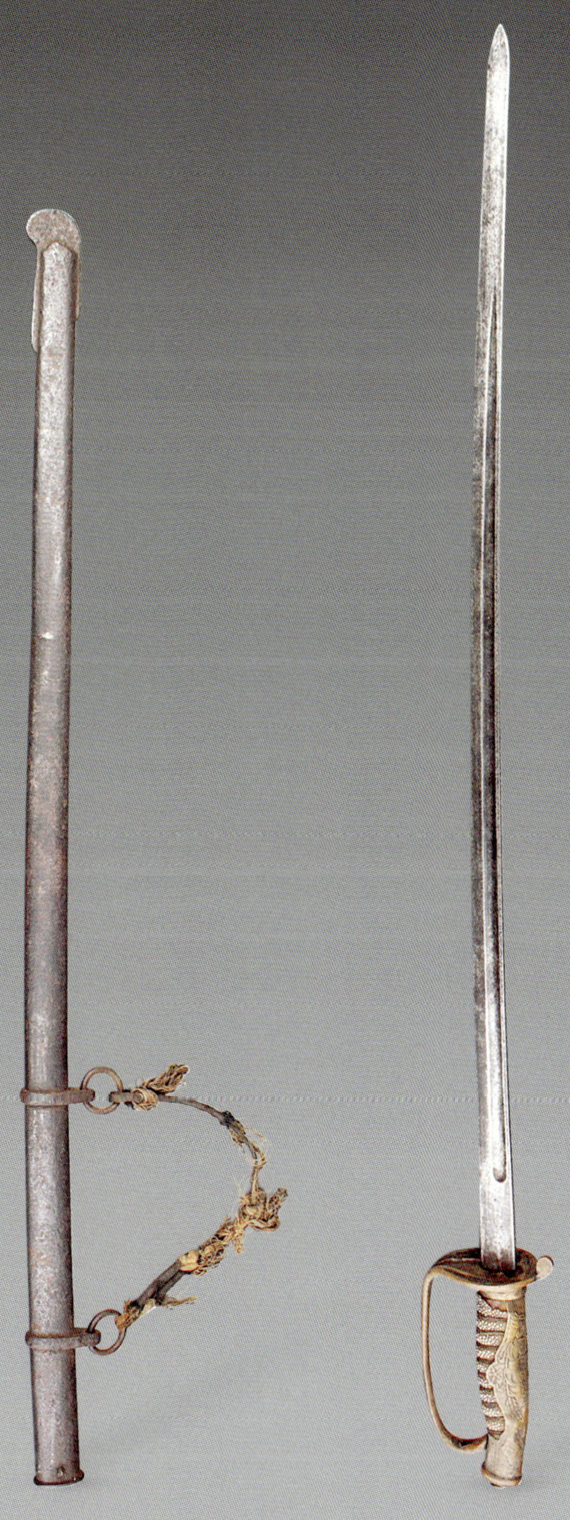

战斗等，战无不胜。仅1943年，回民支队就在朝城、莘县地区攻克敌人据点30多处，烧毁碉堡40多个，对鲁西北抗日根据地的巩固和发展起了重要的作用。从1937年至1944年，马本斋率领回民支队，经历大小战斗870余次，歼灭日伪军3.6万余人，被冀中军区称为“攻无不克，无坚不摧，打不垮，拖不烂的铁军”。

回民支队的接连胜利引起了敌人的极大仇视。日军抓走了马本斋的母亲白文冠，威逼利诱，让她劝马本斋投降，说只要他的儿子“归顺日军”，便会有享不尽的荣华富贵。但白文冠宁死不屈，为了不拖累马本斋，她选择绝食。这位伟大的母亲在绝食七天后，英勇殉国。消息传到回民支队后，马本斋含泪疾书：“伟大母亲，虽死犹生，儿承母志，继续斗争！”

劝降不成，日本人又企图从内部瓦解回民支队。他们四处散布谣言，挑拨离间，制造回汉之间的纠纷。对此，马本斋给战士们上思想课，教育大家回族和汉族都是一家人，应当团结起来共同抗日。在他的教育下，部队里回汉同志之间的友谊更加深厚，大大提高了凝聚力和战斗力。

在长期艰苦卓绝的战斗生活中，马本斋积劳成疾，因为缺医少药，未能及时治疗，病情恶化。1944年1月，在回民支队奉命开赴延安前，他抱病为部队做了最后一次动员报告。2月7日，马本斋病逝于冀鲁豫军区后方医院，终年42岁。

1944年3月17日，延安各界隆重举行马本斋追悼大会。毛泽东赠挽：“马本斋同志不死！”周恩来赠挽：“民族英雄，吾党战士！”

中华民族走向自觉实体的转变

抗战期间，各民族在抵御日本帝国主义侵略的斗争中，同生死，共命运，凝聚成一个不可分割的命运共同体。据不完全统计，在抗日战争中，直接参加武装斗争的有四十个少数民族，数百万少数民族青年应征入伍，奔赴前线——

由回、东乡、撒拉、保安、藏等民族组成的青海骑兵部队，以及由彝、白、汉、哈尼、纳西、壮、苗、瑶、回、傣等民族组成的滇军，出省对日寇作战。

桂、川等省的壮、苗、瑶、京、藏、白、哈尼、傣等民族的青年纷纷应征入伍，奔赴抗日前线。

在东北抗日联军中，有众多的朝鲜、满、赫哲、达斡尔、鄂温克、鄂伦春、锡伯等民族的指战员，包括周保中（白族）、杨靖宇（回族）、赵尚志（满族）、陈瀚章（满族）、李红光（朝鲜族）等著名的抗联领导人。

在远离战火的西藏，僧俗民众一次就捐赠国币五百万元，青海的藏族同胞一次就捐献羊皮衣十万件。

在新疆，各族同胞也纷纷捐钱捐物，仅1937年9月至1940年5月，新疆各族人民共捐款折合现大洋322万余元，捐款购买了十架战斗机，还开展了募集寒衣等活动。尤为感人的是，新疆一位名叫艾沙的维吾尔族贫民因无钱无物可捐，执意要送子上前线，称“倘不忠实抗战，宁可不见子面”。

在贵州，从1938年到1942年，全省征兵45.7万多人，其中很多是少数民族。

在甘肃，有许多少数民族青年自愿从军。如1944年冬，在甘肃拉卜楞地区，一周内就有110多名藏族和蒙古族青年自愿报名参加抗日队伍。

当东部沿海被日军完全占领后，云南成为我国打破日军军事和经济封锁、获得国际援助的咽喉通道。为此，云南少数民族，与汉族人民一道，用鲜血和生命在崇山峻岭中铺就了一条抗战大动脉，二十万各族民工自带干粮和工具，风餐露宿、挖土劈石，仅用九个月时间就筑成了滇缅公路，创造了中国抗战史上的奇迹，而为此献出生命的各族民工有两千多人。在四川，修建川滇公路的民工一半是彝族，他们不计报酬，自带干粮……

在这场伟大的全民族抗战中，血肉相依的战斗使中华民族共同体意识得到巩固和升华。近代以来中国人民第一次取得反抗外来侵略完全胜利的抗日战争，使中华民族凝聚成为一个牢固的命运共同体。

The sword belongs to Ma Benzhai, the commander of Hui People's Detachment, in the War of Resistance Against Japanese Aggression. It bears witness to the illustrious military exploits of Hui People's Detachment, and tells us how the Chinese nation was honed as a community with a shared future in the face of grave crisis.

Ma Benzhai was born in a poor Hui peasant family in Xianxian County, Hebei Province. At the age of 19, Ma Benzhai joined the Fengtian Army. He was cited for bravery in battle and sent to study in Northeast Ground Force Academy. Later, Ma Benzhai was promoted to regimental commander. Simultaneously, he was influenced by underground CPC organizations. In the autumn of 1932, when the troops were heading south to "suppress the CPC army", Ma Benzhai resolutely abandoned his position and returned to his hometown.

After Nationwide War of Resistance Against Japanese Aggression, the Japanese army invaded Hebei Province. Ma Benzhai promptly organized Hui People's Resistance Against Japanese Aggression Volunteer Team in his hometown (later reconstructed into Hui People's Detachment), and served as the commander. In the war, Ma Benzhai realized the contribution and commitment of the Communist Party of China, and joined the CPC. Afterwards, he led Hui People's Detachment to fearlessly fight against Japanese aggression in the Central Hebei Plain, and demonstrated outstanding military talents. In 1943 alone, Hui People's Detachment captured more than 30 enemy's strongholds in the Chaocheng and Shenxian areas and burned down more than 40 bunkers, playing an important role in consolidating and developing the resistance base in northwestern Shandong. From 1937 to 1944, under the leadership of Ma Benzhai, Hui People's Detachment engaged in more than 870 battles and wiped out more than 36,000 Japanese and puppet troops, extolled as "an ever-victorious army" by Mao Zedong.

In January 1944, Hui People's Detachment marched to the front at Yan'an. Ma Benzhai made his final mobilization report for the army in spite of ill health. On February 7, Ma Benzhai passed away at the Rear Hospital of the Hebei-Shandong-Henan Military Region at the age of 42.

In the War of Resistance Against Japanese Aggression, all ethnic groups in China forged a solid community with a shared future. According to incomplete statistics, 40 ethnic minorities directly participated in the armed struggle, and millions of ethnic minority youths were conscripted and sent to the front line.

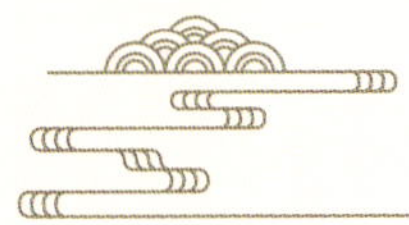

中华民族历史发展新纪元的开启

The New Era for the Chinese Nation

中国共产党自诞生之日起，一直站在争取中华民族独立解放和谋求中华民族复兴的最前列，从纲领、道路、政策、实践上，对推进中华民族共同体建设进行了长期的理论探索和具体实践。

在延安，中国共产党聚集了一批历史学家和研究民族问题的学者，这些专家学者在参与《中国革命与中国共产党》一书的撰述时，特设置“中华民族”章节，专述“中国是一个多数民族结合而成的拥有广大人口的国家”。在实践方面，中国共产党探索在统一多民族国家实行民族区域自治，废除民族压迫，禁止民族歧视，加强民族团结的一系列民族政策。1947年，在中国共产党领导下，内蒙古自治区成立，成为我国第一个省级少数民族自治区，开启了平等联合各民族，推动中华民族独立解放伟大理想的政治实践。

1949年10月，中华人民共和国成立，中华民族以崭新的面貌屹立于世界民族之林。在这个实现了民族平等团结的国家，各民族建立起新型互补依存关系，在新的历史条件下更加紧密地团结起来，走上了团结互助、共同繁荣的道路。在中国共产党的领导下，中华民族踏上了伟大的复兴之路。

Since its birth, the Communist Party of China has been in the forefront of striving for the independence, liberation and rejuvenation of the Chinese nation, and has carried out long-term theoretical and practical explorations of the unity of the Chinese nation from the perspectives of program, path and policy.

In Yan'an, the Communist Party of China invited a group of historians and scholars to compile *Chinese Revolution and the Communist Party of China*. In the chapter of "On the Chinese Nation", they emphasized that "China is a country with a large population, formed by various ethnic groups". In practice, the Communist Party of China upheld and improved the System of Regional Ethnic Autonomy, abolished ethnic oppression, prohibited ethnic discrimination, and strengthened national unity. In 1947, Inner Mongolia Autonomous Region was established, becoming the first provincial-level region of ethnic autonomous in China. It actualized the equality of various ethnic groups and advanced the great ideal of the independence and liberation of the Chinese nation.

In October 1, 1949, the People's Republic of China was founded. Since then, the Chinese nation have stood tall and proud among the nations of the world with a new look. China has realized ethnic equality and unity, and various ethnic groups have forged a new relationship of interdependence. Under new historical conditions, they unite more closely and embark on the path of unity, mutual assistance and common prosperity. Under the leadership of the Communist Party of China, the great rejuvenation of the Chinese nation begins.

中华人民共和国第一面国旗为什么由人民政协交给人民参与设计？五星红旗的象征意义是什么？

中华民族开启历史新纪元

中华人民共和国第一面五星红旗

99

The First National Flag of the People's Republic of China

文物简读

毛泽东主席在天安门城楼升起的第一面国旗，见证了中华人民共和国成立的神圣时刻——这是中华文明五千年发展史上划时代的伟大事件，也是20世纪人类最伟大的事件之一。它从根本上改变了中国历史的发展方向，也改变了世界历史的发展格局。

中华人民共和国第一面国旗

1949年7月，一则面向社会公开征集国旗设计稿的启事，出现在《人民日报》《光明日报》上。这则启事的刊登者为新政治协商会议筹备会，不仅征求国旗、国徽图案，而且还征求国歌词谱。其中，针对国旗图案的设计，启事提出了如下要求：

（甲）中国特征（如地理、民族、历史、文化等）；（乙）政权特征（工人阶级领导的以工农联盟为基础的人民民主专政）；（丙）形式为长方形，长阔三与二之比，以庄严简洁为主；（丁）色彩以红色为主，可用其他配色。

这种把国旗交给人民设计的做法，可谓史无前例，体现着新中国由人民当家作主的理念。

启事刊出后，国旗设计应征稿一时间如雪片般飞来，筹备会收到了来自国内外的各种应征稿1920件，图案2992幅。经过多次讨论、层层筛选，来自上海的普通职员曾联松设计的五星图案脱颖而出。

名称：中华人民共和国第一面五星红旗
年代：1949年
规格：长460厘米，宽338厘米
收藏单位：中国国家博物馆

Name: The First National Flag of the People's Republic of China
Historical Period: 1949
Length: 460 cm, Width: 338 cm
Housed in: National Museum of China

1949年9月27日，中国人民政治协商会议第一届全体会议在北京举行，这是一场意义非凡的会议，它是由全国各党派、各团体、各民族派遣代表，就建国方略达成共识的盛会。会议通过了《关于中华人民共和国国都、纪年、国歌、国旗的决议》，并对国旗图案和制作办法做出以下规定：

中华人民共和国国旗为五星红旗，长方形，红色象征革命，其长与高为三与二之比，旗面左上方缀黄色五角星五颗，象征共产党领导下的革命大团结，星用黄色，象征红色大地上呈现光明。一星较大，其外接圆直径为旗高十分之三，居左；四星较小，其外接圆直径为旗高十分之一，环拱于大星之右，并各有一个角尖正对大星的中心点，表达亿万人民心向伟大的中国共产党，如似众星拱北辰。旗杆套为白色，以与旗面的红色相区别。

毛泽东主席曾说："这个图案表现我们革命人民大团结，现在要大团结，将来也要大团结。"

"中国人从此站立起来了！"

在中国人民政治协商会议第一届全体会议上，毛泽东主席在开幕词中豪迈地说："我们的工作将写在人类的历史上，它将表明：占人类总数四分之一的中国人从此站立起来了。"

人民政协第一届全会代行全国人民代表大会职权，通过了具有临时宪法性质的《中国人民政治协商会议共同纲领》和《中国人民政治协商会议组织法》《中华人民共和国中央人民政府组织法》，选举产生了中央人民政府委员会，庄严宣告中华人民共和国成立，人民成为国家的主人。这标志着自鸦片战争一百多年来，中国人民争取民族独立和人民解放运动取得了历史性的伟大成就，中华民族饱受西方列强欺凌的时代一去不复返了！

五星红旗是中华民族大团结的象征

1949年10月1日下午3时，毛泽东主席在天安门城楼上向全世界庄严宣告："中华人民共和国中央人民政府今天成立了！"

随着天安门广场上激昂的《义勇军进行曲》响起，毛泽东主席按动电钮，升起了新中国第一面五星红旗。当乐曲奏完时，五星红旗升到了22.5米高的旗杆顶端，随风高高飘扬。

中华人民共和国的成立，彻底结束了旧中国一盘散沙的局面，实现了中华民族大团结，实现了近代以来无数仁人志士为之奋斗的民族独立和解放的历史任务，从根本上改变了一百多年来中华民族遭受帝国主义侵略压迫的历史，是中华民族由近代衰落走向强大兴盛的历史转折点；中华民族从此把命运牢牢掌握在自己手中，实现了站起来的伟大历史飞跃，从此开启了发展进步的新纪元。从更宏大的历史视野看，中华人民共和国的成立也是中华民族五千年文明史上划时代的伟大历史事件，是近代以来实现中华民族伟大复兴的里程碑，也是20世纪人类最伟大的事件之一。它不仅从根本上改变了中国历史的发展方向，也开启了世界历史的一个新格局。

开国大典后，这面国旗又在天安门前飘扬了一年多时间。1951年，北京市人民政府决定将它交拨给中国历史博物馆（现中国国家博物馆）永久收藏。

In July 1949, the Preparatory Committee for the Chinese People's Political Consultative Conference published a notice on collecting the designs of national flag among the public in *The People's Daily* and *Guangming Daily*, raising the requirements on the design of national flag and emblem as well as the lyric and music of national anthem. The Preparatory Committee received 1,920 applications from both domestic and international sources, with 2,992 design works. The five-star pattern designed by Zeng Liansong, an ordinary employee from Shanghai, stood out.

On September 27, 1949, the First Plenary Session of the National Committee of the Chinese People's Political Consultative Conference was held in Beijing, and *The Resolutions on the Capital, Chronicles, Anthem and National Flag of the People's Republic of China* was adopted. The following provisions were made for the design and production methods of national flag.

The national flag of the People's Republic of China is the five-star red flag, rectangular in shape. The red symbolizes the Chinese revolution. The length-height ratio is three to two. Five yellow pentagrams are designed on the top left of the flag, symbolizing national solidarity in the Chinese revolution under the leadership of the Communist Party of China. The stars are yellow, symbolizing the brightness over the red earth. One star is larger, with a circumcircle diameter of 3/10 of the flag height, located on the left; the other four stars are smaller, with a circumcircle diameter of 1/10 of the flag height, surrounding on the right side of the larger star, each with its corner point facing the center point of the larger star. This expresses the support of millions of people for the great Communist Party of China, like many stars surrounding the Pole Star. The flagpole cover is white to distinguish it from the red color on the flag surface.

On October 1, 1949, the founding of the People's Republic of China was proclaimed after 28 years of bitter and courageous struggle carried out by the people under the leadership of the Communist Party of China and with the active support of other political parties and democrats without party affiliation, thus realizing the independence of the Chinese nation and the liberation of the Chinese people. This put an end to China's history as a semi-colonial, semi-feudal society, to the rule of a handful of exploiters over the working people, to the state of total disunity that plagued the old China, and to all the unequal treaties imposed on our country by foreign powers and all the privileges that imperialist powers enjoyed on our land, marking the country's great transformation from a millennia-old feudal autocracy to a people's democracy. This also reshaped the world political landscape and offered enormous inspiration for oppressed nations and peoples struggling for liberation around the world.

为什么说“民族团结誓词碑”是中国共产党代表中华民族做出独立自主的解决民族问题道路选择的历史见证？

中国特色解决民族问题正确道路的形成

民族团结誓词碑

Ethnic Unity Oath Stele

100

文物简读

被誉为“新中国民族团结第一碑”的民族团结誓词碑，是中国共产党建立平等团结互助和谐的社会主义民族关系的见证，是中国共产党探索中国特色解决民族问题正确道路，扫除历史遗留的民族压迫，完成有史以来最广泛和深刻的社会变革，开创和实现各族人民大团结局面的见证。

一次民族团结的盟誓

1950年国庆节前夕，一道以政务院总理周恩来名义发出的邀请，飞抵边疆地区——中央人民政府邀请边疆少数民族兄弟到首都参加第一次国庆盛典。

此时，在刚刚解放的云南边疆，受到邀请的少数民族代表却怀有种种顾虑，有的竟认为这是圈套，有被杀头的危险，便以各种理由推辞。其中，佤族头人拉勐还提出了赴京观礼的三个条件：汉族干部要陪同一起去；澜沧县竹塘区区长的儿子作为人质抵押；为山寨提供一千斤盐巴、一百件土布。可见，旧中国留下的民族隔阂十分深重。普洱地委经过耐心动员，最终组成了包括43名土司、头人和代表的云南少数民族观礼团。

1950年10月1日，辗转来到北京的云南少数民族观礼团，在天安门广场投身一片欢乐的海洋，他们观看了盛大而激动人心的国庆阅兵和浩大的群众游行。此后，周恩来总理出现在大家面前，他对每一个少数民族代表都深怀尊重，观礼团成员从来没见过这样亲切的“大官”。10月3日，在中南海怀仁堂，云南少数民族代表终于见到了毛泽东主席，他们纷纷捧出礼物敬献给毛主席，拉勐也敬献了三代祖传的梭镖。毛主席握住拉勐的手说：“听说你们民族有砍人头祭谷的习俗，可不可以不砍人头，用猴头来代替？”拉勐回答说：“用猴头不行，用虎头倒可以，但老虎不好捉哩！”毛主席

名称：民族团结誓词碑

年代：1951年

规格：碑高142厘米，宽65厘米，厚12厘米

现存地点：云南省宁洱哈尼族彝族自治县普洱民族团结园

Name: Ethnic Unity Oath Stele

Historical Period: 1951

Length: 142 cm, Width: 65 cm, Thickness: 12 cm

Housed in: Pu'er Ethnic Unity Park, Ning'er Hani and Yi Autonomous County, Yunnan Province

说："这事由你们民族自己商量着办吧！"毛主席的慈祥和善让拉勐刻骨铭心，他感觉自己已经是这个国家的主人。

国庆观礼后，少数民族代表又参观了天津、南京、上海、武汉等城市，他们受到各地民众的热情欢迎，深切感受到作为新中国一分子的温暖和自豪。

12月，观礼团回到普洱，参加普洱专区第一届兄弟民族代表会议。就在这次会议上，拉勐与傈僳族头人李保提出：为了各民族永远团结不变心，永远跟着共产党，我们应该按照传统习俗，搞一次盟誓！这个提议立即得到各民族代表的热烈赞同，大家当即决定举办"民族团结剽牛盟誓"。

12月26日，盟誓大会在普洱红场举行。来自15个县的各民族支系代表，按照云南少数民族古老的盟誓传统，剽牛、歃血、喝"咒水"。傣族代表召存信、佤族代表拉勐、傈僳族代表李保等48人，共同写成了誓词："我们廿六种民族的代表，代表全普洱区各族同胞，慎重地于此举行了剽牛，喝了咒水，从此我们一心一德，团结到底，在中国共产党的领导下，誓为建设平等自由幸福的大家庭而奋斗。此誓。"

一条符合中华民族自身发展规律的道路

平等团结互助和谐，是新中国确立的新型民族关系，它使中国各民族之间的关系发生了根本性变化。"民族团结誓词碑"的出现，说明中国共产党所开创的中国特色解决民族问题道路，赢得了少数民族的极大信赖和支持。

中国共产党自诞生起，就开始探寻解决民族问题的道路。中共一大、二大召开时，中国共产党提出的民族政策尚带有共产国际指导的色彩。但此后，工农红军长征371天，在民族地区穿行132天，途经十多个省，与许多少数民族相遇，得到了少数民族群众的真诚帮助甚至慷慨牺牲，在完成漫漫征途的同时，也建立起了对多民族国情的深刻认识。全面抗战爆发后，严酷的现实让中国共产党真正站在中华大地上思考解决民族问题的道路，有了不囿于共产国际和苏联经验的思想突破。1947年5月1日，内蒙古自治政府成立（中华人民共和国成立后，内蒙古自治政府改名为内蒙古自治区人民政府）。这标志着中国特色解决民族问题的道路开启了重要一步。

虽然已对民族区域自治之路有了初步探索，但在中华人民共和国成立前夕，党中央还是再度把这个重大抉择摆上案头：中国是走苏联式的民族共和国和联邦制之路，还是走民族区域自治之路？毛泽东主席就这个问题郑重征求拥有丰富民族工作经验的李维汉同志的意见。在将中国和苏联的国情一一比较后，李维汉向党中央提出了"在统一的（单一制的）国家内实行民族区域自治"的建议。此后，中共中央将"实行民族区域自治"作为一大建国纲领，正式提交中国人民政治协商会议讨论。

这是一个关系着未来国家将采取什么样的结构形式的重大问题。第一届政协委员进行了严肃认真的商讨，最终确定建立单一制的人民共和国——在"各少数民族聚居的地区，应实行民族的区域自治，按照民族聚居人口多少和区域大小，分别建立各种民族自治机关"。

由此，一条既不同于苏联模式，也不同于西方民族国家模式，而是符合中华民族自身发展规律的国家治理道路，终于形成。周恩来总理对此总结道："我们的民族区域自治政策，利于合，利于团结，利于各民族的共同发展。""我们主张把全国各民族都联合起来组成一个民族大家庭。"

历史上，中华各民族将国家统一视作最高的政治理想和价值追求，而新中国重新寻回了这一历史价值。此后，半个多世纪的国际政治风云表明：正是中国共产党听从了中华文明发出的历史呼唤，代表中华民族做出了独立自主的道路选择，带领中华民族日益走向团结和壮大，最终踏上了伟大复兴的美好征程。

On October 1, 1950, Yunnan Ethnic Groups Tour Team arrived in Beijing after a long journey. The Tiananmen Square was turned into a sea of happiness. At the Tiananmen Square, the team members watched the exciting moments of National Day military parade and mass pageant. Afterwards, Premier Zhou Enlai met them, showing deep respect for them. On October 3, at Huairen Hall, Zhongnanhai Leadership Compound, representatives of ethnic minorities in Yunnan saw Chairman Mao Zedong. They presented gifts to Chairman Mao one after another. La Meng, leader of Wa, presented the dart that was handed down from his grandfather. After the National Day, the Tour Team visited Tianjin, Nanjing, Shanghai, Wuhan and other cities. Warmly welcomed by people from all over the country, the team members took great pride in being citizens of the People's Republic of China.

In December, the Tour Team returned to Pu'er and participated in the First Brotherhood Ethnic Representative Conference of the Pu'er Special Region. La Meng and Li Bao, leader of Lisu, initiated an oath of alliance according to traditional customs, in order to cement ethnic unity and express fealty to the Communist Party of China. This proposal was immediately accepted by representatives of various ethnic groups.

On December 26, the oath of alliance was staged at Pu'er Red Square. Representatives of 26 ethnic branches from 15 counties acted with ancient oath traditions of Yunnan ethnic minorities, such as slicing cattle, smearing the blood of a sacrifice on the mouth, and drinking the magic water. 48 representatives, including Zhao Cunxin of Dai, La Meng of Wa and Li Bao of Lisu, took oaths.

After the founding of the People's Republic of China, the new ethnic relations feature equality, solidarity, mutual assistance and harmony, which fundamentally reshapes the relationships between various ethnic groups in China and means an epoch-making event in the history of the Chinese nation. "Ethnic Unity Oath Stele" fully proves that the Communist Party of China takes the correct approaches with Chinese characteristics to handling ethnic affairs, which wins deep trust and wide support of ethnic minorities.

参考文献

参考书目

1. 王钟翰：《中国民族史》，武汉大学出版社，2012年。
2. 费孝通：《中华民族多元一体格局》，中央民族大学出版社，2018年。
3. 苏秉琦：《中国文明起源新探》，生活·读书·新知三联书店，2019年。
4. 葛剑雄：《中国人口发展史》，四川人民出版社，2020年。
5. 司马迁：《史记》，中华书局，1982年。
6. 杜预集解：《春秋左传》，中华书局，2015年。
7. 蒋廷瑜：《蒋廷瑜集——岭南铜鼓论集》，线装书局，2011 年。
8. 高洪雷：《另一半中国史》，文化艺术出版社，2012年。
9. 曾庆江、周泉根、陈圣燕：《海南历代贬官研究》，南方出版社，2008年。
10. 王柯：《从“天下”国家到民族国家：历史中国的认知与实践》，上海人民出版社，2020年。
11. 罗贤佑：《中国民族史纲要》，中国社会科学出版社，2009年。

参考论文

1. 高星：《“元谋人”的年龄及相关的年代问题讨论》，《人类学学报》，2015年第4期。
2. 周国兴、胡承志：《元谋人牙齿化石的再研究》，《古脊椎动物与古人类》，1979年第2期。
3. 郑云飞：《中国考古改变稻作起源和中华文明认知》，《中国稻米》，2021年第4期。
4. 苏秉琦、殷玮璋：《关于考古学文化的区系类型问题》，《文物》，1981年第5 期。
5. 徐璐：《华山花图腾研究》，陕西师范大学硕士学位论文，2010年。
6. 尚民杰：《中国古代龙形探源》，《文博》，1995年第4期。
7. 张敬国：《安徽含山县凌家滩遗址第五次发掘的新发现》，《考古》，2008年第3期。
8. 邢文：《数的图式：凌家滩玉版与河图、洛书》，《民族艺术》，2011年第2期。
9. 侯哲安：《伏羲女娲与我国南方诸民族》，《求索》，1983年第4期。

10. 杨建芳：《略论仰韶文化和马家窑文化的分期》，《考古学报》，1962年第1期。
11. 费晓华：《马家窑文化与黄河上游农业文明》，西北民族大学硕士学位论文，2012年。
12. 史卫红：《从我国拔牙风俗看文化传播》，《广西民族研究》，1988年第3期。
13. 张振标：《古代的凿齿民——中国新石器时代居民的拔牙风俗》，《江汉考古》，1981年第S1期。
14. 蒋廷瑜、彭书琳：《桂南大石铲研究》，《南方文物》，1992年第1期。
15. 郑超雄、郑海宁：《大石铲文化与骆越文明的发生——骆越文化研究系列之三》，《广西社会主义学院学报》，2019年第3期。
16. 格勒：《略论藏族古代文化与中华民族文化的历史渊源关系》，《中国藏学》，2002年第4期。
17. 霍巍：《论卡若遗址经济文化类型的发展演变》，《中国藏学》，1993年第3期。
18. 李先登：《试论中国文字之起源》，《天津师大学报》，1985年第4期。
19. 朱乃诚：《三星堆文明形成的年代和机制》，《中原文化研究》，2021年第4期。
20. 丁柏峰：《从考古学材料分析青海游牧社会起源》，《农业考古》，2012年第6期。
21. 乔红：《青海地区古羌人鸟崇拜》，《中国土族》，2013年第2期。
22. 秦小丽：《中国初期国家形成过程中的牙璋及意义》，《中原文化研究》，2017年第4期。
23. 朱乃诚：《从牙璋看夏文化向南方地区的扩散》，《江汉考古》，2021年第6期。
24. 田青刚：《商代民族融合与华夏民族的形成》，《寻根》，2005年第5期。
25. 牛世山：《周族起源与先周文化研究的回顾与思考》，《三代考古》，2017年。
26. 沈长云：《华夏族、周族起源与石峁遗址的发现和探究》，《历史研究》，2018年第2期。
27. 武家璧：《周初“宅兹中国”考》，《考古学研究》，2011年。
28. 马芳芳：《马家塬墓地西戎文化研究》，西北大学硕士学位论文，2018年。
29. 马世之：《关于楚族的族源及其发祥地》，《江汉论坛》，1983年第11期。
30. 彭丰文：《从蛮夷到华夏：先秦楚人的族源记忆与民族认同》，《中国边疆民族研究》，2014年。
31. 徐良高：《周之南土：巴国与巴文化刍议》，《四川文物》，2018年第4期。
32. 李诚、张以品：《古蜀文化与三星堆“神鸟扶桑”新证——兼评〈古代巴蜀与南亚的文化互动和融合〉》，《四川师范大学学报（社会科学版）》，2022年第3期。
33. 周相卿：《古夜郎国地域、民族及法律控制问题探索》，《地域文化研究》，2020年第1期。
34. 张合荣：《赫章可乐“套头葬”再探讨》，《考古与文物》，2012年第5 期。
35. 白兴发：《古滇国主体民族及与周边民族关系考述》，《楚雄师范学院学报》，2019年第2期。
36. 葛季芳：《云南出土铜葫芦笙探讨》，《考古》，1987年第9期。
37. 史为乐：《中山国简说》，《河北师范大学学报》，1981年第2期。

38. 莫阳：《战国中山王墓研究——一种艺术史的视角》，中央美术学院博士学位论文，2015年。

39. 董田、余卫华：《简析“胡服骑射”对中国北方服饰的影响》，《黄石理工学院学报（人文社会科学版）》，2009年第5期。

40. 马执斌：《赵武灵王“胡服骑射”在中华文化史上的价值》，《邯郸学院学报》，2016年第1期。

41. 朱筱新：《对秦统一度量衡制的再认识》，《北京教育学院学报》，2000年6月。

42. 范云松：《“秦王扫六合”与统一度量衡》，《文史杂志》，2003年第5期。

43. 王伟：《文物见证——秦统一文字、货币、度量衡》，《收藏》，2010年第6期。

44. 史明立：《西汉南越王墓“文帝行玺”龙钮金印考辨》，《文物天地》，2019年1月。

45. 何少伟：《方寸天地——广州南越王墓出土金印赏析》，《文物鉴定与鉴赏》，2020年6月。

46. 苗祥瑞：《马踏匈奴的象征内涵》，《西北美术》，2017年第4期。

47. 幸华银：《多元文化背景中的霍去病墓石刻艺术研究——中原农耕文化与草原游牧文化交融的丰碑》，《美术大观》，2020年第8期。

48. 于志勇：《新疆尼雅出土“五星出东方利中国”彩锦织文初析》，《西域研究》，1996年第3期。

49. 王瑟：《“五星出东方利中国”的解说》，《光明日报》，2012年1月6日。

50. 吴朴：《我对“滇王之印”的看法》，《文物》，1959年第7期。

51. 李东红、陈丽媛：《从“滇国三印”看西汉时期的西南边疆治理》，《中国边疆史地研究》，2021年第3期。

52. 孙慰祖：《“朱庐执封”银印的赐主与受主——兼议“朱庐”、“珠崖”之辩》，《上海博物馆集刊》，2012年第0期。

53. 黄展岳：《“朱庐执封”印和“劳邑执封”印——兼论南越国自镌官印》，《考古》，1993年第11期。

54. 顾涛：《论中国最早的石刻教科书——〈熹平石经〉》，《兰台世界》，2013年5月。

55. 王继祥：《汉熹平石经的镌刻及其意义》，《图书馆学研究》，1991年第2期。

56. 单继刚：《证据与推理：铜奔马若干重要问题再思考》，《哈尔滨工业大学学报（社会科学版）》，2021年11月。

57. 郭平梁：《武威雷台墓墓主、铜奔马命名释义及墓葬断代》，《考古与文物》，2008年第5期。

58. 何志国：《甘肃武威市雷台出土铜奔马年代考辨》，《考古》，2008年第4期。

59. 蒋廷瑜：《铜鼓研究一世纪》，《民族研究》，2000年第1期。

60. 萧明华：《青铜时代滇人的青铜扣饰》，《考古学报》，1999年第4期。

61. 邢琳：《云南青铜扣饰研究》，云南大学硕士学位论文，2014年5月。

62. 赵心愚：《藏彝走廊古代通道的几个基本特点》，《中南民族大学学报（人文社会科学版）》，2004年5月。

63. 曹建强、伍晴晴：《汉代陶灶面面观》，《农村·农业·农民》，2020年11月。
64. 丁诗瑶、顾平：《人机工程学与河套地区青铜灶造型研究》，《装饰》，2015年04期。
65. 李圳：《试论羯胡之族源、迁徙及分布》，《新疆大学学报（哲学·人文社会科学版）》，2016年11月。
66. 沈骞：《河西小月氏、卢水胡与河东羯胡关系探源》，《敦煌学辑刊》，2015年第4期。
67. 林幹：《两汉时期“护乌桓校尉”略考》，《内蒙古社会科学》，1987年第1期。
68. 田余庆：《代北地区拓跋与乌桓的共生关系——〈魏书·序纪〉有关史实解析》，《中国史研究》，2000年第3期。
69. 程尼娜：《护乌桓校尉府探析》，《黑龙江民族丛刊》，2004年第5期。
70. 吴松岩：《十六国早期拓跋部与慕容部联姻考——从内蒙古达茂旗出土金步摇冠饰谈起》，《边疆考古研究（第29辑）》，2021年第1期。
71. 赵丹：《慕容鲜卑金步摇冠饰初探》，内蒙古大学硕士学位论文，2013年12月。
72. 江楠：《中国东北地区金步摇饰品的发现与研究》， 吉林大学硕士学位论文，2007年4月。
73. 周伟洲：《吐谷浑晖华公主墓志与北朝北方民族关系》，《民族研究》，2020年第2期。
74. 罗新：《西魏晖华公主墓志所见的吐谷浑与柔然名号》，《中山大学学报（社会科学版）》，2020年第5期。
75. 刘呆运：《陕西西安西魏吐谷浑公主与茹茹大将军合葬墓发掘简报》，《考古与文物》，2019年第4期。
76. 竺小恩：《从北魏服饰改革看胡汉文化关系》，《河西学院学报》，2006年第4期。
77. 冯健、李莎：《温婉之美 馥郁之风——洛阳北魏杨机墓女立俑赏析》，《中原文物》，2014年第1期。
78. 谷敏：《北魏时期的云冈石窟》，山西大学硕士学位论文，2013年6月。
79. 郭静娜：《北魏平城时期佛教发展探讨——以沙门昙曜生平为主线》，《史志学刊》，2018年第4期。
80. 徐宝余：《晋室南迁与江南都市文化品格的塑造》，《江西社会科学》，2010年10月。
81. 高彦：《晋室南迁后建康的经济与文化发展状况》，《齐齐哈尔师范高等专科学校学报》，2010年第6期。
82. 齐东方：《中国早期马镫的有关问题》，《文物》，1993年第4期。
83. 杨泓：《冯素弗墓马镫和中国马具装铠的发展》，《辽宁省博物馆馆刊》， 2010年。
84. 龙真、檀志慧：《徐显秀墓——北齐贵族生活的生动写照》，《中国文化遗产》，2008年第1期。
85. 杨连锁：《北齐徐显秀墓壁画艺术考析》，《文物世界》，2014年第4期。
86. 王博：《民族融合语境下的北齐徐显秀墓室壁画风格浅析》，《艺术科技》，2016年第4期。

87. 周利君：《北朝隋唐独孤氏家族研究》，湖南师范大学硕士学位论文，2020年。
88. 张沛：《旬阳出土的独孤信多面体煤精组印》，《文博》，1985年第2期。
89. 杨易雨：《浅析虞弘墓浮雕壁画》，《东方藏品》，2016年第11期。
90. 师艳明：《隋虞弘墓石椁图像的多元文化因素分析》，山东大学硕士学位论文，2019年。
91. 唐宇：《图写记忆：昭陵六骏的图像纪功传统》，《美术学报》，2020年第6期。
92. 冯思绪：《昭陵六骏述论》，《文物鉴定与鉴赏》，2021年第4期。
93. 赵维平：《丝绸之路上的胡旋舞、胡腾舞》，《音乐文化研究》，2021年第1期。
94. 葛承雍：《甘肃山丹收藏的"胡腾舞俑"辨析》，《文物》，2021年第6期。
95. 高启安：《"来通"传入与唐人"罚觥"——以〈纂异记·张生〉为线索》，《西南民族大学学报（人文社会科学版）》，2018年第12期。
96. 项坤鹏：《何家村窖藏出土兽首玛瑙杯考略》，《文物天地》，2021年第3期。
97. 孙机：《论西安何家村出土的玛瑙兽首杯》，《文物》，1991年第6期。
98. 许永华：《论唐代至琼贬官对海南文化发展的重要贡献》，《长江丛刊》，2019年第13期。
99. 刘建昌、俞保华、刘景云：《我国唐代人口治理的历史考察》，《山西警察学院学报》，2021年第4期。
100. 余辉：《陈及之〈便桥会盟图〉卷考辨——兼探民族学在鉴析古画中的作用》，《故宫博物院院刊》，1997年第1期。
101. 牛致功：《关于唐与突厥在渭水便桥议和罢兵的问题——读〈执失善光墓志铭〉》，《中国史研究》，2001年第3期。
102. 蒋其祥：《蒲类州之印小考》，《新疆社会科学》，1982年第1期。
103. 薛宗正：《庭州、北庭建置新考》，《中国边疆史地研究》，1994年第1期。
104. 管彦波：《试论唐朝在边疆民族地区推行的羁縻府州制度》，《青海民族研究》，2010年4月。
105. 严圣钦：《论渤海国与唐朝的关系》，《北方文物》，1982年第1期。
106. 马洪：《渤海"天门军之印"谫识》，《东北史地》，2012年第2期。
107. 孟凡人：《隋唐时期于阗王统考》，《西域研究》，1994年第2期。
108. 陈粟裕：《五代宋初时期于阗王族的汉化研究——以敦煌石窟中的于阗王族供养像为中心》，《美术研究》，2014年第3期。
109. 李婵玲、丁科：《〈南诏德化碑〉的民族融合思想及其影响》，《大理大学学报》，2015年第1期。
110. 朱飞镝、谢建辉：《德化碑考略兼论南诏对唐蕃战争的影响》，《贵州民族研究》，2015年第12期。
111. 宁宇：《〈步辇图〉绘画中的唐蕃和亲史》，《国家人文历史》，2017年第4期。

112. 谢继胜、朱姝纯：《关于〈步辇图〉研究的几个问题》，《故宫博物院院刊》，2018年第4期。
113. 曹云珍：《湮没的辉煌——辽陈国公主与驸马合葬墓》，《东北之窗》，2022年第7期。
114. 张佳琦：《辽代金属面具考》，《赤峰学院学报（汉文哲学社会科学版）》，2019年第4期。
115. 孙立梅：《10—13世纪的草原丝绸之路与欧洲人的契丹印象》，《白城师范学院学报》，2023年第1期。
116. 赵婉煜：《契丹辽三彩的艺术特征与价值探析》，沈阳师范大学硕士学位论文，2021年5月。
117. 张敏：《捺钵与辽代政治研究》，吉林大学博士学位论文，2022年12月。
118. 邱靖嘉：《“超越北南”：从中枢体制看辽代官制的特性》，《历史研究》，2022年第3期。
119. 陈雷：《试论金代铜坐龙的雕塑造型及饰纹特色》，《中华文化论坛》，2003年第1期。
120. 杨海鹏：《金代铜坐龙的发现与研究》，《北方文物》，2009年第1期。
121. 杨轶婷、陈小锦：《党项拓跋氏族源问题综述》，《文化创新比较研究》，2022年第6期。
122. 孔祥辉：《族群称谓所见西夏与多民族语言和文化的交融》，《西南民族大学学报（人文社会科学版）》，2023年第1期。
123. 照耀：《吉祥遍至口和本续》，《环球人文地理》，2021第23期。
124. 张兆琪：《元代天字拾二号夜巡铜牌》，《兴安日报》，2021年8月16日第4版。
125. 李治安：《元代行省制起源与演化述论》，《南开学报》，1997第2期。
126. 赵军英：《论元朝行省制在专制主义中央集权制中的地位和作用》，《邵阳师范高等专科学校学报》，2002年第4期。
127. 咸成海：《“大一统”国家治理视阈下的元朝土司制度》，《青海民族研究》，2022年第4期。
128. 黄兆宏、李姗山：《“凉州会谈”研究综述及其认识》，《丝绸之路》，2022年第2期。
129. 孙潇祥：《元明两代纸币发行权研究》，武汉大学硕士学位论文，2020年5月。
130. 李俊义：《〈元皇姊鲁国大长公主文庙金博山罏碑跋〉考释》，《元史及民族与边疆研究集刊》，2021年第2期。
131. 云峰：《论元代鲁国大长公主祥哥剌吉及其与汉文化之关系》，《中央民族大学学报》，2006年第1期。
132. 杨潇雅：《元朝鲁国大长公主祥哥剌吉书画收藏探析》，内蒙古师范大学硕士学位论文，2021年。
133. 温睿：《苏麻离青考辨》，《故宫博物院院刊》，2017年第1期。
134. 刘洛君、张春梅：《中古时期西方想象中的中国形象——解码〈马可·波罗游记〉与〈利玛窦中国札记〉》，《汉字文化》，2021年第6期。
135. 杨洁、周润年：《明代治理西藏的特点及其作用》，《西藏研究》，2021年第4期。
136. 林再会、加央：《白玉龙纽“如来大宝法王”印》，《紫禁城》，2010年第12期。

137. 郭佳丽、先巴：《明清时期西北茶马贸易的发展》，《边疆经济与文化》，2022年第1期。
138. 李天顺、李俊清：《茶马互市与民族交往交流交融述论》，《北方民族大学学报》，2022年第1期。
139. 隋晓霖：《〈万树园赐宴图〉相关问题研究》，《故宫博物院院刊》，2020第6期。
140. 齐齐哈尔建华机械厂沙俄侵华史研究小组、黑龙江省博物馆历史部：《康熙十五年“神威无敌大将军”铜炮和雅克萨自卫反击战》，《文物》，1975年第12期。
141. 杨鸿英：《乾隆朝两次平定准噶尔始末》，《故宫博物院院刊》，1988年第4期。
142. 陈庆英、玉珠措姆：《清代金瓶掣签制度的制定及其在西藏的实施（续）（英文）》，*China Tibetology*，2022年第1期。
143. 李蓉：《从〈西藏善后章程十三条〉到〈二十九条〉看清朝对西藏治理的加强与完善》，《西藏民族大学学报（哲学社会科学版）》，2016年第5期。
144. 徐富超：《〈喇嘛说〉中的清朝蒙藏地区治理方略》，山东大学硕士学位论文，2021年。
145. 赵书刚、林志军：《清末台湾建省成功的海权因素》，《江苏师范大学学报（哲学社会科学版）》，2019第6期。
146. 高娃、刘壮：《土尔扈特部东归与构建中华民族共同体意识关系探析》，《新闻论坛》，2022第4期。
147. 王志伟：《从木兰围场到避暑山庄——乾隆帝接见渥巴锡史事述往》，《文史知识》，2022年第7期。
148. 苍铭、张薇：《〈皇清职贡图〉的“大一统”与“中外一家”思想》，《云南师范大学学报（哲学社会科学版）》，2019年第3期。
149. 何罗娜、汤芸：《〈百苗图〉：近代中国早期民族志》，《民族学刊》，2010年第1期。
150. 郭金树：《〈四库全书〉的形成和主要内容及其历史地位》，《社会科学论坛》，2004年第12期。
151. 孙海静：《清末民初满族旗袍文化的嬗变及其历史隐喻》，《地域文化研究》，2021年第6期。
152. 郑大华：《论五四后梁启超的“汉族”含义上的“中华民族”研究》，《广东社会科学》，2023第1期。
153. 何一民、刘杨：《从“恢复中华”到“中华民族命运共同体”——百年来“中华民族”概念内涵演变的历史审视》，《民族学刊》，2019年第4期。
154. 吴敏文：《鸦片战争背后的东印度公司》，《书屋》，2022年第8期。
155. 黎剑珊：《浅谈三元里抗英斗争》，《科教导刊（中旬刊）》，2011第12期。
156. 朱昭华：《藏锡边界纠纷与英国两次侵藏战争》，《历史档案》，2013年第1期。
157. 范新尚：《英国第二次侵藏战争背景探析》，《淮海工学院学报（人文社会科学版）》，2014年第3期。

158. 王江成：《国家认同建构：从“五族共和”到铸牢中华民族共同体意识》，《学术界》，2022年第9期。
159. 张彩云：《从三个“历史决议”看中国共产党坚持统一战线的百年奋斗历史经验》，《湖南省社会主义学院学报》，2022年第6期。
160. 王星、秦娟：《中华民族共同体建设和统一战线的关联逻辑：理论、历史和现实》，《传承》，2022年第4期。
161. 邢帅：《从旧军人到共产党人再到民族英雄——马本斋思想嬗变过程研究》，《石家庄学院学报》，2022年第5期。
162. 侯善才：《新中国第一面国旗的由来》，《史学月刊》，1981第6期。
163. 徐畅：《见证人民政协民主协商的〈共同纲领〉》，《档案记忆》，2022第3期。
164. 左永平：《普洱学院人文学院西南边疆民族的文化认同与国家认同实证研究——以普洱民族团结誓词碑为研究案例》，《普洱学院学报》，2014年第5期。

译后记

我最早接触文物翻译，是在2008年，为一位考古学学者翻译题为《虢国的归宿》的学术论文。不久，我承担元上都遗址世界文化遗产申请材料的英文翻译。彼时，我还在南京大学英文系读书。15年来，在图书出版，尤其是引进、翻译、出版国外学术著作之外，我做了大量古代文献、文物的英文翻译工作；近三年来，翻译中亚史译著一部、佛教考古与文物保护项目一项。“乃至童子戏，聚沙为佛塔。”大抵如此。

长期的翻译经历使我明白，文物翻译超出普通翻译的范畴，是一门专门的学问，是译者与沉寂千年的文物本体之间的对话，也是基于译者创造力的文化再创造。文物翻译要求译者必须准确理解文物领域的术语，通过古色古香的译文，传播文物背后的故事，再现中国古代物质文明的魅力。这对译者的学问功底和语言修为要求颇高，更需要对文物有敬畏之心，对历史有敬畏之心，对读者有敬畏之心。

本书英译，我遵循如下原则：政治性话语的英文表述，为了保持其严肃性和权威性，遵从官方译法；出现的古诗，若有为读者所接受的英文译本，我不再布鼓雷门；学术术语的理解，参考相关领域学者的观点；涉及中国古代器物、工艺、典籍之处，按照“汉文拼音—汉文原词—英文翻译”的模式译出，以体现中国学者的本土视角。

翻译过程中，引用或参考的部分文献如下：

1. 文物“骨制口簧”，《诗经·鹿鸣》选文，引用许渊冲译本。

2. 文物“骨笛”，王之涣《凉州词》最后两句诗的译文，引用许渊冲译本。

3. 文物 “鲜卑山嘎仙洞摩崖石刻祝文（拓片）”，《敕勒歌》的译文，引用许渊冲译本。

4. 文物“虞弘墓石椁雕刻”，“萨宝”一词的英文阐释，参考芮传明的学术贡献。参见：芮传明：《“萨宝”的再认识》，《史林》2000年第3期。

5. 文物“勐往甸军民官印”，土司制度的英文介绍，引用联合国教科文组织网站中“Tusi Sites”的介绍。参见：Tusi Sites-UNESCO World Heritage Centre。

6. 文物“‘五族共和’旗”，《临时大总统宣言书》引文的英译，引用Christopher C. Heselton（史峥）译本。

7. 文物“毛泽东手迹‘巩固统一战线’”，相关术语和文件的译法，参考“中国关键词”网站“中国共产党成立100周年特辑”中“第二次国共合作”“抗日民族统一战线”部分。参见：第二次国共合作 (china.org.cn)，The National United Front Against the Japanese Occupation (china.org.cn)。

8. 文物“中华人民共和国第一面五星红旗”，中华人民共和国成立的意义的英文表述，引用《中共中央关于党的百年奋斗重大成就和历史经验的决议》英文版。参见求是网：Full Text: Resolution of the CPC Central Committee on the Major Achievements and Historical Experience of the Party over the Past Century (qstheory.cn)。

感谢四川民族出版社副社长、副总编辑唐怡对我的巨大信任，邀请我翻译本书、担任本书特约编辑，并在翻译进度上给予充分理解。感谢四川民族出版社编辑赵正梅，她很好地配合出版流程，做了非常细致的基础工作。感谢雯女士和多多在我翻译过程中的陪伴，使我鞅掌有乐。

迟剑锋

2023年7月17日

于山东小城五莲